COOPERATIVE STRATEGY

Cooperative Strategy

Economic, Business,
and
Organizational Issues

Edited by

DAVID O. FAULKNER AND MARK DE ROND

OXFORD
UNIVERSITY PRESS

OXFORD

UNIVERSITY PRESS

Great Clarendon Street, Oxford OX2 6DP

Oxford University Press is a department of the University of Oxford.
It furthers the University's objective of excellence in research, scholarship,
and education by publishing worldwide in

Oxford New York

Athens Auckland Bangkok Bogotá Buenos Aires Cape Town
Chennai Dar es Salaam Delhi Florence Hong Kong Istanbul Karachi
Kolkata Kuala Lumpur Madrid Melbourne Mexico City Mumbai Nairobi
Paris São Paulo Singapore Taipei Tokyo Toronto Warsaw

with associated companies in Berlin Ibadan

Oxford is a registered trade mark of Oxford University Press
in the UK and in certain other countries

Published in the United States
by Oxford University Press Inc., New York

British Library Cataloguing in Publication Data

Data available

Library of Congress Cataloging in Publication Data
Cooperative strategy: economic, business and organizational issues / edited by David O.
Faulkner and Mark de Rond.
p. cm.
Includes bibliographical references.
1. Strategic alliances (Business) 2. Cooperation. 3. International business
enterprises–Management. 4. Business networks. I. Faulkner, David, 1938–
II. De Rond, Mark.
HD69.S8 C666 2000   338.8–dc21   99–086561

ISBN 0–19–829689–4
ISBN 0–19–924853–2 (pbk.)

1 3 5 7 9 10 8 6 4 2

Typeset by Kolam Information Services Pvt Ltd, Pondicherry, India
Printed in Great Britain by
T. J. International Ltd
Padstow, Cornwall

Foreword

Few, if any, phenomena in public or private management and organization have raised so much scholarly attention in such a short period of time as cooperation, alliances, and partnerships between organizations. The pace, diversity, and quality of the research on collaboration, as reflected in this book, are truly astounding.

Perhaps, this intense attention derives from both an intellectual and a social concern. Cooperation between organizations can be fruitfully examined from a wide range of theoretical starting points. They include strategic management, both in its positioning and resource-based complementary perspectives, economic and industry analyses, transaction cost economics and agency theory, network theory, the sociology of collective action theories, organization theory, psychology of trust and commitment theories, evolutionary theories, game theory, and institutional theories to name only the most obvious. Models of bilateral (e.g. marriage) and multilateral (e.g. multi-state coalitions) relationships can also be applied and adapted to the study of interorganizational collaboration. More interestingly, the collaboration phenomenon allows, and challenges, researchers to extend these theories by providing a complex phenomenon to understand. This makes collaboration research intellectually challenging.

From the social side, among academics—who for the most part live in organizations where cooperation is not the rule, but who would like to see cooperation prevail—cooperation is a fascinating topic for inquiry and research. There is a tantalizing dichotomy between academic researchers who, in fields relevant to the study of collaboration, work essentially alone—and value individual achievement—and their field of inquiry. Most researchers would agree, both intellectually and emotionally, that cooperation is a good thing and so the widespread interest in cooperation among management scholars is driven by their own frustration with the rules and the sociology of their academic world.

This book is a testimony to these two concerns. It is delightfully eclectic theoretically, and yet remarkably convergent in the contributions made to our understanding of the collaboration phenomenon. The fascination of the researchers with the topic, and their empathy with the phenomenon they study, shine through most contributions as well.

The problem of achieving cooperation among human beings is hardly new. Indeed, Plato and Caesar are perhaps as good analysts of cooperation as today's management scholars. Corporate cooperation is hardly new either; cooperation, alliances, and joint ventures were already widespread at the turn of the twentieth century in many industries, chemicals in particular.

So why today's resurgence of interest? Perhaps, the theories we har-boured—neoclassical economics in particular—and the leading context in which they flourished—the USA at a time when antitrust issues featured high on the public policy agenda—made researchers oblivious to the possibility, or the reality, of inter-institutional cooperation. A culture of individualism and freedom in the USA also contributed to a lesser interest in cooperation. It is only with the rise of game theory and with the systematic exploration of transaction cost economics beyond the 'market versus hierarchy' dichotomy, nourished by the growing interest in the Japanese challenge in the 1980s and combined with the development of management research in Europe and Japan, that the collaboration phenomenon started to receive the scholarly attention it deserved.

Indeed, cooperation and alliances between firms, and more generally between institutions, public or private, is a rewarding area for research. Not only does it provide a high-level application for various theories of coopera-tion, but it also offers an opportunity to extend these theories. Simple game-theoretic models and static transaction cost analyses can be transcended to study the dynamics of strategic alliance evolution. Theories and conceptual frameworks can be analysed at multiple levels: inter-personal, inter-group, inter-institutional, and at the level of networks and populations of organiza-tions. 'Trust', a much-researched area, provides an example of the value of a multilevel approach. Similarly, the more traditional economic and strategy concepts—based primarily on a competition hypothesis—can be challenged and complemented by models of symbiotic relationships, the ecology of economic systems, co-evolution, and complementarity.

Cooperation is also nice to study; somehow it is a 'good' thing, giving a warm feeling to researchers. How to achieve cooperation without altruism or emotional empathy, or how to turn narrow-minded competition into enlight-ened cooperative self-interest, constitute practical issues for the applicability of research on cooperation.

This book balances theoretical and applied concerns and provides a wonderful integration of multiple theoretical perspectives.

Yves Doz
Fontainebleau
December 1999

Contents

Notes on Contributors   ix

Part I. Perspectives on Cooperative Strategy

1. Perspectives on Cooperative Strategy   3
   David O. Faulkner and Mark de Rond

2. Characteristics of UK International Joint Ventures with Triad
   and Non-Triad Partners   40
   Keith W. Glaister, Rumy Husan, and Peter J. Buckley

Part II. The Rationale for Cooperation

3. The Theory of the Flagship Firm   57
   Alan Rugman and Joseph D'Cruz

4. Transaction (In)Efficiency, Value (In)Efficiency, and Inter-firm
   Collaboration   74
   Anoop Madhok

5. Forming and Managing Shared Organization Ventures:
   Resources and Transaction Costs   96
   Stephen Tallman

6. Differential Learning in Alliances   119
   Kofi O. Nti and Rajesh Kumar

7. The Firm as Differentiator and Integrator of Networks:
   Layered Communities of Practice and Discourse   135
   Ray Loveridge

Part III. The Process of Cooperating

8. From Competition to Collaboration: The Emergence and
   Evolution of R&D Cooperatives   173
   Yves L. Doz and Oğüz Baburoglu

9. Implementing Cooperative Strategy: A Model from the Private
   Sector   193
   David Boddy, Douglas Macbeth, and Beverly Wagner

10. Cooperative Relationship Strategy in Global Information
    Technology Out-sourcing: The Case of Xerox Corporation   211
    Thomas Kern and Leslie P. Willcocks

11. Assessing Inter-Organizational Collaboration: Multiple
    Conceptions and Multiple Methods   243
    Barbara Gray

12. International Joint Venture Instability and Corporate Strategy   261
    Jeffrey J. Reuer and Mitchell P. Koza

Part IV. Cooperative Behaviour

13. National Differences in Acquisition Integration   283
    Robert Pitkethly, David O. Faulkner, and John Child

14. Interpersonal Relationships in International Strategic Alliances:
    Cross-Cultural Exchanges and Contextual Factors   307
    Paul Olk and P. Christopher Earley

15. Joint Venture Trust: Interpersonal, Inter-Group, and Inter-Firm
    Levels   324
    Steven C. Currall and Andrew C. Inkpen

16. Trust and Control: Opposing or Complementary Functions?   341
    David O. Faulkner

V. Cooperative Strategy: The Future

17. Reflections on the Study of Strategic Alliances   365
    Ranjay Gulati and Edward J. Zajac

18. Concluding Thoughts and Future Directions   375
    David O. Faulkner and Mark de Rond

Index   379

Notes on Contributors

Ogüz Baburoglu is on the core faculty in the Graduate School of Management at Bilkent University, Turkey. Prior to this he was on the faculties of the Work Research Institute (Norway), INSEAD (France), Clarkson University (US), and West Chester University (USA). He earned a PhD at the Wharton School of the University of Pennsylvania, and holds degrees from the University of Lancaster and the University of Sussex. His research interests include participative methodologies, developing emergent collaborative strategies, self-managing teams, and the dynamics of stalemated organizations, and his work has been published in refereed journals.

David Boddy is on the faculty of the Department of Management Studies at the University of Glasgow. Most of his teaching is with experienced managers, especially those attending the Executive MBA programme where he coordinates the core courses in Organizational Behaviour. His research interests are in the human and organizational aspects of information technology, the implementation of organizational change, and supply-chain partnering. He is the author or co-author of several articles and books. Email: d.boddy@mgt.gla.ac.uk

Peter Buckley is Professor of International Business and Director of the Centre of International Business at the University of Leeds. He is Visiting Professor at the Universities of Paris I (Pantheon-Sorbonne), Rennes I, Groningen, and Reading. He has published 19 books, many of which have been translated into other languages, and was elected a Fellow of the Academy of International Business in 1985 for 'outstanding achievements in international business'. He is also a Fellow of the British Academy of Management and the Royal Society of Arts, and was awarded an Honorary Professorship at the University of International Business and Economics in Beijing, China. Email: pjb@lubs.leeds.ac.uk

John Child holds the Chair of Commerce at Birmingham Business School, University of Birmingham, and is Visiting Professor at the School of Business, University of Hong Kong. He holds an MA and PhD from Cambridge University, which in 1984 also awarded him an Sc.D. for outstanding work. He has been on the faculties of the London Business School, Aston University, Cambridge University, and the China–Europe Management Centre in Beijing. In January 1992 he became the Editor-in-Chief of *Organization Studies*. He is the author or co-author of fifteen books and over eighty articles in refereed journals, and his works are widely cited. His most recent book is entitled *The Management of International Acquisitions*, co-authored with David Faulkner and Robert Pitkethly (Oxford University Press, 2001). Email: J.Child@bham.ac.uk

Steven C. Currall is Associate Professor of Management and Psychology in the Jones Graduate School of Management at Rice University. He is also Director of the Rice Alliance for Technology and Entrepreneurship. His research focuses on (1) interpersonal and interorganizational trust, (2) conflict and power within corporate boards of directors, and (3) research designs for integrating qualitative and quantitative research methods. He has published in *Organizational Behavior and Human Decision Processes*, *Organizational Research Methods*, *Industrial and Labor Relations Review*, *Journal of Applied Behavioral Science*, *International Journal of Conflict Management*, and *Public Productivity and Management Review*. Currall earned a PhD from Cornell University and a MSc from the London School of Economics.

Joseph D'Cruz is Professor of Strategic Management at the Rotman School of Management of the University of Toronto. He holds a DBA from the Harvard Business School, and consults widely with such corporations as ICI, Exxon, PricewaterhouseCoopers, and DSM. His interests include the globalization of the telecommunications industry, the bench-marking of international competitiveness, and strategies for flagship firms. His work has been published in books, as articles and book chapters, and he was awarded the Touche Ross Award for the best article in *Business Quarterly*.

Mark de Rond is Assistant Professor in Strategy at ESSEC Business School, Paris, and a Research Fellow at the Sol C. Snider Entrepreneurial Research Center at the Wharton School, University of Pennsylvania. He received his DPhil in Strategy and Organization from the Saïd Business School, University of Oxford (Christ Church). His research interests include alliance process, dynamics and evolution, the epistemology of organizations research, and the history of ideas. His most recent paper was nominated for the 2001 William H. Newman Award by the Academy of Management. His new book, provisionally entitled *Alliances as Social Facts: Strategy, Structure and Structuration in Biotechnology Collaborations*, will be published by Cambridge University Press in 2002. Email: derond@essec.fr or rond@wharton.upenn.edu

Yves Doz is the Associate Dean for Executive Education and the Timken Chaired Professor of Global Technology and Innovation at INSEAD. He has been on the faculty of the Harvard Business School and held visiting appointments at Stanford University and at Aoyama Gakuin University in Japan. He received his doctorate from Harvard University and is a graduate of the Ecole des Hautes Etudes Commerciales (Jouy-en-Josas, France). His research on the strategy and organization of multinational companies, examining high-technology industries, has been published widely in such journals as *Strategic Management Journal* and *Harvard Business Review*, in book chapters, and as books. Email: yves.doz@insead.fr

P. Christopher Earley is the Randall L. Tobias Chair of Global Leadership at the Kelley School of Business, Indiana University. His research interests include cross-cultural and international aspects of organizational behaviour, the role of face and social structure in organizations, and motivation across cultures. He is the author of seven books and numerous refereed articles and book chapters. He received his PhD in industrial and organizational psychology from the University of Illinois, Urbana-Champaign, and has taught on the faculties of the London Business School, University of Arizona, University of Minnesota, and University of California Irvine, and his consulting assignments have taken him to England, Hong Kong, Israel, China, Singapore, South Korea, and Thailand. Email: pearley@indiana.edu

David O. Faulkner is University Lecturer in Strategic Management, Saïd Business School, and a Tutorial Fellow of Christ Church, University of Oxford. He was formerly Deputy Director of the Saïd Business School and Director of the MBA Programme. He spent much of his career as a strategic management consultant with McKinsey and Arthur D. Little, prior to earning a DPhil at Oxford University and moving into academic life in 1989. He teaches strategy on the MBA and BA degree programmes and carries out management consulting and lecturing activities with a wide range of companies in both the public and private sectors. He has written a number of books and articles on the subject of cooperative strategy. Email: david.faulkner@christ-church.oxford.ac.uk

Keith Glaister is Professor of International Strategic Management at Leeds University Business School, having earned a PhD and MBA from the University of Bradford Management Centre. His current interests centre around the empirical analysis of the formation, partner selection, management, and performance dimensions of international joint venture activity, and the cognitive aspects of strategic decision-making, and he has published several book chapters and journal articles on these topics. His work has appeared in *Organization Studies, Journal of Management Studies, International Business Review, Management International Review, Long Range Planning,* and *British Journal of Management.* Email: kwg@lubs.leeds.ac.uk

Barbara Gray is a Professor in the Department of Management and Organization at Pennsylvania State University, and Director of the Center for Research in Conflict and Negotiation. Her research focuses on conflict management and collaboration, the design of structures and processes to create collaborative settings for the resolution of complex inter-organizational problems, and on the formation and management of joint ventures. Her work has been published in *Administrative Science Quarterly, Academy of Management Journal, Journal of Applied Behavioral Science, Human Relations, Academy of Management Review, Journal of Management, Review of Higher Education,* among other refereed journals, and she is the author of two books. Email: B9G@psu.edu

Ranjay Gulati is the Michael L. Nemmers Distinguished Professor of Technology and E-commerce and the Research Director of the Center for Technology, Innovation, and E-commerce at the KGSM, Northwestern University. He received his PhD from Harvard University and his Masters from the Massachusetts Institute of Technology. His research interests focus on the creation, evolution, and performance of strategic alliances, interfirm networks, and vertical partnerships, and have been published in *Administrative Sciences Quarterly*, *Harvard Business Review*, *Academy of Management Journal*, *Strategic Management Journal*, *American Journal of Sociology*, *European Management Journal*, and *Sloan Management Review*. Ranjay is on the editorial boards of *ASQ*, *SMJ*, and *OS*, and recently guest-edited a special issue of *SMJ* on strategic networks.

Rumy Husan is a Lecturer in Emerging Markets with special reference to the former Soviet Union and Eastern Europe at Leeds University Business School, and has published in the areas of transitional economics and international business in the *Review of Policy Studies* and *British Journal of Management*. Email: rh@lubs.leeds.ac.uk

Andrew Inkpen is an Associate Professor of Management at Thunderbird. He has been on the faculties of Temple University and the National University of Singapore. His research deals with the management of multinational firms, with a particular focus on strategic alliances, the management of knowledge, and organizational learning. He is the author or co-author of several books and book chapters, and more than 30 articles in journals such as the *Academy of Management Review*, *California Management Review*, *Strategic Management Journal*, *Journal of International Business Studies*, *Organizational Dynamics*, *Journal of Management Studies*, and *Organization Science*. Email: inkpena@t-bird.edu

Thomas Kern is Assistant Professor for Information Management at the Rotterdam School of Management. His areas of expertise are IT outsourcing, application service provision, IT strategy, and relationship management. He received his DPhil in Management Information Systems from the Saïd Business School, University of Oxford. He is also a research affiliate with the Oxford Institute of Information Management at Templeton College and is currently the European Editor of the *Journal of Information Technology*. He was the 1996–8 Lloyds of London Tercentenary Foundation Business Scholar. His research has been published at the European, Hawaiian and International Conference on Information Systems and in the *European Journal of Information Systems*, *Journal of Information Systems*, *Journal of Global Information Management*, and *Journal of Information Technology*. He is co-author of two books: *The Relationship Advantage: Sourcing, Technologies, and Management* (Oxford University Press, 2001) and *Strategic Application Service Provision* (Prentice Hall, USA, 2001). Email: tkern@fbk.eur.nl

Mitchell P. Koza is Professor of International Strategic Management and Director of the Centre for International Business at Cranfield School of Management. He also holds a post as Research Professor (Visiting) at the Fuqua School of Business, Duke University. He has written extensively on partnerships and strategic alliances, and his work has been published in *Organization Science*, *Strategic Management Journal*, *Administrative Science Quarterly*, *Journal of Economic Behaviour and Organization*, *Revue Française de Gestion*, *Research in the Sociology of Organizations, American Journal of Sociology, European Management Journal*, and *L'Impresa*. He has served as guest editor for the *Organization Science* Special Issue on Managing Partnerships and Strategic Alliances. Email: mitchell.koza@cranfield.ac.uk

Rajesh Kumar is an Associate Professor at the Aarhus School of Business in Denmark. He received his PhD from New York University and has taught at the Pennsylvania State University and at universities in France, Finland, and the Netherlands. His interests are in international business and cross-cultural negotiations, and his work has been published in *Organization Science, Journal of Applied Behavioural Science*, and *Columbia Journal of World Business*. Email: rku@hha.dk

Ray Loveridge is a Research Fellow at the Saïd Business School, Oxford University. He previously held positions at Royal Holloway College, University of London, the London School of Economics, London Business School, and Aston University where he holds an Emeritus Chair. He holds degrees from Oxford, Cambridge, and the LSE, and has published ten books and numerous articles and book chapters on the political economy of the firm and comparative management. Email: ray.loveridge@said-business-school.oxford.ac.uk

Douglas K. Macbeth is CIPS/SCMG Ltd. Professor of Supply Chain Management and Head of the Department of Management Studies at the University of Glasgow. After an industrial career, he entered the academic world where he worked at three universities, and developed a research interest in cooperative strategy and practice. As director of the spin-off company SCMG Ltd. he has acted as a consultant to many international client organizations.

Anoop Madhok is an Associate Professor of Management at the David Eccles School of Business at the University of Utah, and a Visiting Professor of Management at the Rotterdam School of Management, Erasmus University, Rotterdam. He holds an MBA from the University of Cincinnati, an MA from Johns Hopkins University, and a PhD from McGill University. His research interests include multinational firm strategy, foreign market entry, inter-firm collaboration, and the theory and boundaries of the firm. His work has been published in the *Strategic Management Journal, Journal of International Business Studies, Organization Science, International Business Review*, and as a number of other articles and books. Email: mgtam@business.utah.edu

Kofi Nti is an Associate Professor at the Smeal College of Business Administration, Pennsylvania State University. He received his PhD from Yale University, and recently spent a sabbatical year at the London School of Economics. His research interests include strategic alliances, auctions, and market entry, and his work has appeared in journals such as *Management Science, Organization Science, Journal of Economic Theory, Economic Theory, International Economic Review, Journal of Economics, Public Choice, European Journal of Political Economy*, and *Mathematical Social Sciences*. Email: kon@psu.edu

Paul Olk is an Associate Professor at the Daniels College of Business of the University of Denver. His research interests address the strategic use of alliances, examining such topics as alliance formation processes, control, performance evaluation, and termination, as well as friendship ties within and across organizational boundaries, organizational legitimacy, and international management. His work has appeared in such journals as *Strategic Management Journal, European Management Journal, Journal of High Technology Management Research*, and *International Journal of Technology Management*, as well as book chapters. He received his PhD and MA in Organization and Strategy from the Wharton School of the University of Pennsylvania, and previously taught at the University of California-Irvine. Email: pmolk@du.edu

Robert Pitkethly is a Lecturer in Management Studies at the Saïd Business School, and a Senior Research Fellow at St Peter's College, University of Oxford. He has been a Visiting Fellow at the Institute of Intellectual Property and the National Institute of Science and Technology in Tokyo, and a Research Fellow at the Judge Institute, University of Cambridge. He holds an MA in Chemistry and a DPhil in Management from the University of Oxford, an MBA from INSEAD, and an MSc in Japanese Studies from Stirling University. He has also worked as a patent attorney and management consultant. He is a co-author with John Child and David Faulkner of *The Management of International Acquisitions* (Oxford University Press, 2001). Email: robert.pitkethly@sbs.ox.ac.uk

Jeffrey J. Reuer is an Assistant Professor of Strategy and Management at INSEAD in Fontainebleau, France. He received his PhD in strategic management from Purdue University. Prior to his doctoral studies he worked in the Office of Strategic Alliances at the Mayo Foundation, and as a systems engineer with EDS. His research examines issues surrounding international joint ventures, the dynamics of strategic alliances, corporate flexibility, and economics exposure, and his work has appeared in the *Strategic Management Journal, Academy of Management Journal, Journal of International Business Studies, Harvard Business Review*, and European Management Journal. He currently serves on the boards of the *Strategic Management Journal*, and the *European Management Journal*. Email: jeffrey.reuer@insead.fr

Alan M. Rugman is L. Leslie Waters Chair of International Business and a professor at the Kelley School of Business, Indiana University, Bloomington, USA. He is also a fellow of Templeton College, University of Oxford. He has published numerous books and articles dealing with the strategic management of multinational enterprises and trade and investment policy. He is co-editor of the *Oxford Handbook of International Business* (Oxford University Press, 2001), *Multinationals as Flagship Firms* (Oxford University Press, 2000), and *Environmental Regulations and Corporate Strategy* (Oxford University Press, 1999). Previously he was a professor at the University of Toronto in Canada.

Stephen Tallman is Professor of Management at the David Eccles School of Business, University of Utah, and a Visiting Professor at the Cranfield School of Management, UK. He is the Chairman of the Management and Marketing departments at Utah and David Eccles Faculty Professor. He graduated from the US Military Academy (West Point) in 1972 and received his PhD in 1988 from UCLA. He served as an officer in the US Army and as a project manager and mechanical engineer with Mobil Chemical Company prior to his academic career. His research on global strategy, international joint ventures, and resource-based strategy has appeared in *Academy of Management Journal, Strategic Management Journal, Organization Science, Journal of Management, Journal of International Business Studies, Management International Review*, and *Advances in Strategic Management*. He is on the editorial review boards of *Journal of International Business Studies, Organization Science, Management International Review*, and *Strategic Management Journal*.

Beverly A. Wagner is a Research Associate at the Centre for Supply Chain Management, and is currently completing her PhD at the University of Glasgow. Her research interests include customer–supplier relationships, the management of cross- functional teams, and knowledge management.

Leslie P. Willcocks is a Fellow in Management Studies at Templeton College, Oxford University, Professor in Information Management at Erasmus University, Rotterdam, and Editor-in-Chief of the *Journal of Information Technology*. He is also Professorial Associate at the University of Melbourne and Freehill, Hollingdale and Page Distinguished Visitor at the Australian Graduate School of Management. He is co-author of fourteen books on information systems and management, and his 120-plus articles have appeared in journals such as *Harvard Business Review, Sloan Management Review, Journal of Management Studies, MIS Quarterly*, and *Long Range Planning*. He is retained advisor to several major corporations and government institutions, and in 1997 was expert witness to the US Congressional Commission on Restructuring the US Internal Revenue Service. Email: leslie.willcocks@templeton.oxford.ac.uk

Edward J. Zajac is James F. Beré Professor of Organization Behavior at the Kellogg Graduate School of Management of Northwestern University. He joined the faculty in 1986, upon completion of his PhD in organization and strategy at the Wharton School, University of Pennsylvania. His research on strategic alliances, corporate governance, and strategic adaptation has been published widely in major academic journals, such as the *Strategic Management Journal, Administrative Science Quarterly, Organization Science, Academy of Management Journal, Academy of Management Review*, and *Management Science*. He is an associate editor of the *Strategic Management Journal*, and an editorial board member at *Administrative Science Quarterly, Organization Science*, and the *Asia Pacific Management Journal*. He is currently Chair of the Business Policy and Strategy Division of the Academy of Management. Email: e-zajac@nwu.edu

PART I

Perspectives on Cooperative Strategy

This opening part sets the scene for the rest of the book. It reviews cooperative strategy through many of the major lenses that commentators on the subject have used to help clarify reasons for cooperation and methods for going about achieving it. These include the economic perspective in all its key aspects from the market power view to real options theory; the organization theory viewpoint including resource dependency theory and organizational learning; and an analysis of aspects of successful cooperative behaviour including trust and commitment. The second part of the section provides some data on the frequency of international joint ventures between the UK and Triad and non-Triad partners, in order to help in the assessment of the current importance of cooperative activity in the developed world at the start of the third millennium.

1

Perspectives on Cooperative Strategy

DAVID O. FAULKNER AND MARK DE ROND

Cooperative strategy became a very fashionable area of intellectual debate in the 1990s, rather as competitive strategy was in the 1980s following the publication of works by Porter (1980, 1985). The reasons for this have been far more profound than mere fashion. Markets have become increasingly global during this period, tastes have converged, technologies have shown a disturbing tendency not to endure for long before being replaced by others, and product life cycles have become ever shorter in a society driven by the restless energy of the advertiser. All this has meant the need for greater capital investment than one firm, however big, can regularly cope with, and the need for allies who span the major markets of the globe and have between them the necessary competencies to meet the demands of the global market (cf. Murray and Mahon, 1993; Ohmae, 1989). Attesting to this proliferation of cooperative activity, Keith Glaister, Rumy Husan, and Peter Buckley (Chapter 2) provide an inventory of joint ventures between UK firms and firms located in the Triad (USA, Western Europe, and Japan) and in non-Triad countries over the 1990 to 1996 period.

The academic and popular business literature has followed suit, with a vast increase in publications on cooperative activity. Though the term 'alliances' may at some point have referred strictly to a particular type of relationship, it now serves as an 'umbrella' label for a host of cooperative relationships. Published studies have emphasized the varied facets of this phenomenon, including antecedent conditions (e.g. Forrest and Martin, 1992; Ingham, 1990; Lorange, Roos, and Bronn, 1992), formation patterns (e.g. Glaister, Husan, and Buckley, chap. 2, below; Gulati, 1995*a*), success factors (e.g. Mohr and Spekman, 1994), critical issues (Doz and Shuen, 1995; Killing, 1988), symmetry and dependency (e.g. Harrigan, 1988; Singh and Mitchell, 1996); outcomes (e.g. Bleeke and Ernst, 1995; Hamel, Doz, and Prahalad, 1989), and alliance functioning (e.g. Faulkner, 1995; Lorange and Roos, 1992; Kanter, 1994; Lynch, 1993; Roehl and Truitt, 1987). Indeed, academics from divergent disciplines have come forward to tender explanations of, and prescriptions for, alliance formation, functioning, singular processes, and evolution, a

---

The authors are listed in order of seniority; each has made an equal contribution to this chapter.

good few of which are treated in this volume. Surveying the terrain from a wide-ranging perspective, this introductory chapter reviews the principal theories of cooperative strategy, and illustrates where and how the various contributions contained in this volume fit within the fast-growing literature.

The Rationale for Cooperation

Empirical studies of cooperative behaviour are ordinarily framed within distinct theoretical perspectives, albeit not always explicitly, the most popular of which appear to be market power theory, transaction cost theory, agency theory, the resource-based view, and resource dependence theory, although game theory, real options theory, and social network theory appear to be growing in popularity. Each makes a singular contribution to our understanding of cooperative behaviour, though a generally accepted and unifying theory is still largely absent (cf. Parkhe, 1993; Child and Faulkner, 1998; Koza and Lewin, 1998). Specific contributions include the identification of antecedent conditions that provide a strategic rationale for entering alliances, the anticipation of specific returns, and the selection of a governance structure (Gulati, 1998). Given particular affinities with either economics or organization theory, they exhibit distinct features. Indeed, a review and comparison of the most common theoretical frameworks may illustrate this.

The Economic Viewpoint

There is little doubt that economics has served as a fertile breeding ground for theories of organization and of collaboration. The more salient of these are: (1) strategic management theory, especially market power theory, (2) transaction cost theory, (3) the resource-based view, (4) agency theory, (5) game theory, and (6) real options theory.

Market Power Theory

The strategic management literature was dominated in the 1980s by market power theory, associated principally with the name of Michael Porter and his book *Competitive Strategy* (1980). In it he suggests that the competitive intensity of industries is determined by five fundamental forces: the degree of rivalry between competing firms dividing up the market, the power of suppliers and buyers, the threat from new entrants, and that posed by potential substitute products or services. Consequently, a company's strategy should be to position itself to take advantage of those forces as best it can. Indeed, argues Porter, profitability is largely a function of positioning, and a strategy of cooperation may enable alliance partners to achieve a stronger positioning together than they would in isolation. 'Coalitions arise when performing an activity with a partner is superior to performing the activity internally on the one hand, and to reliance on arm's-length transactions or merger with another firm on the other' (Porter and Fuller, 1986: 322).

Hymer (1972) was one of the first to apply market power theory to the study of cooperative strategy when distinguishing offensive from defensive coalitions. Offensive coalitions are intended to develop firms' competitive advantages and strengthen their position by diminishing other competitors' market share or by raising their production and/or distribution costs. Porter and Fuller (1986) qualified Hymer's argument by demonstrating that offensive coalitions can have a negative effect by reducing the partners' adaptability in the long run. Defensive coalitions, on the other hand, are formed by firms to construct entry barriers intended to secure their position and stabilize the industry so as to increase their profitability. These may also be sought by firms that have a relatively weak position in the market in order to defend themselves against a dominant player, although, suggest Bleeke and Ernst (1995), such alliances rarely lead to success. Moreover, cooperation can emerge between partners with differing intentions. Such was the case with Rover and Honda in the 1980s, when Rover entered into a collaboration with Honda to secure new model designs and engineering capabilities without which it could no longer survive (defensive), and Honda, in turn, used Rover as a means to enter into the European market (offensive).

Market power theory thus provides several insights into cooperative strategy, one of which is that greater market power, with consequentially enhanced returns, can be attained through collaborating. Cooperation may be a faster and cheaper way to gain market power than mergers, acquisitions, or organic growth. All-out competition is not the only option. However, this theory is a fairly deterministic one, which does not readily lead to an understanding of the strategic visions held by senior managers. For instance, Porter's (1980) framework assumes that the structure of the industry and national environment in which a firm is located dictates its most appropriate generic strategy—cost leadership, differentiation, or focus. The process of forming cooperative alliances is in this way subsumed within an analysis of industrial and national structural determinants and leaves little room for genuine strategic choice (Child, 1972).

The perspective on cooperative strategy offered in the strategic management literature is, however, wider than Porter's market power approach. Essentially, it draws attention to the need for prospective partners to achieve a fit between their respective strategies, so that an alliance between them makes a positive contribution to the attainment of each party's objectives. The strategy literature contains a number of key overlapping themes that are relevant to cooperative strategy. These concern:

1. the motives for forming alliances;
2. the selection of partners so as to achieve compatibility between their goals, and
3. the need to achieve integration between partner cultures and systems.

Much of the strategic management work on alliances has concentrated on why and how alliances are formed (description) rather than on how best to run them (prescription). Consequently, analyses of reasons for setting up alliances, objectives for those alliances, and areas of possible conflict are common themes in the literature (Harrigan, 1988). Tallman and Shenkar (1994) and Bowman and Faulkner (1997), for example, suggest ways in which multinational enterprises might approach the issue of alliance formation as an alternative approach to acquisition or internal development. From a slightly different angle Contractor and Lorange (1988) identify a number of, by no means mutually exclusive, reasons for alliance formation ranging from risk reduction to attempting to achieve scale economies to co-opting or blocking the competition. Faulkner (1995) classifies the motives for alliance formation into internal and external ones of which the key internal ones are currently, he claims:

(a) the need for specific assets or capabilities not currently possessed (the resource-dependency perspective);
(b) those arising from the need to minimize costs;
(c) the need for speed to market not achievable by other means; and
(d) those concerned with the spreading of financial risk.

The key external motives currently most often cited are:

(a) those surrounding the issues of globalization or regionalization;
(b) those concerned with the turbulence and uncertainty of international markets; and
(c) those centered around the need for vast financial resources to cope with fast technological change and the shortening of product life cycles.

Strategic management theory draws attention to these external and internal factors and, in so doing, develops a contingency view on the merits of a cooperative as opposed to a competitive strategy, as well as on partner selection criteria. This contingency view may be more realistic than the universalistic rationales contained in the transaction cost perspective. It also emphasizes the matching of partners, rather than looking at cooperation simply from a single partner's point of view. A further contrast with these two major economic perspectives lies in the way that strategic management theory brings the actors into play. Rather than suggesting that situational contingencies determine which cooperative strategies will be successful, strategic management theory allows for the exercise of strategic choice by the actors who are deciding on organizational policies (Child, 1972).

Alan Rugman and Joseph D'Cruz relate their contribution in The Theory of the Flagship Firm (Chapter 3) to something of a rebuttal of the atomistic view of competitive strategy, proposed by Porter (1980), in which firms largely fight alone. They are far more inclined towards the 'keiretsu' approach to the development of market power, through the medium of networks and close relationships led by a strong flagship leader. In opposition to the neoclassical economists' view of all economic actors as fundamentally independent and narrowly self-regarding and self-motivated within a market inexorably regulated by the laws of supply and demand, they conceptualize the situation as more akin to that described by Richardson (1972) as finding 'islands of planned co-ordination in a sea of market relations'.

Transaction Cost Theory

The perspective on cooperative behaviour offered by transaction cost theory views such arrangements as potentially cost-reducing methods of organizing business transactions. Buckley and Casson have applied the transaction cost perspective to explain how the internalization of production through foreign direct investment, including alliances, enables multinational enterprises 'to replace the market or alternatively augment it' (1985: 9).

Transaction costs are those costs incurred in arranging, managing, and monitoring transactions across markets, such as the costs of negotiation, drawing up contracts, managing the necessary logistics, and monitoring accounts receivable. Transaction cost theory regards the basic choice in organizing economic transactions as being between effecting these through market exchanges and internalizing them within a single firm, where they are governed by hierarchical relationships embedded in organization structures.

Williamson (1975) identifies six factors that are relevant for the choice between internalizing the governance of transactions within firms as opposed to effecting them through market exchanges. These are opportunism, bounded rationality, the numbers of exchanges, and degrees of uncertainty, complexity, and information impactedness. Opportunism refers to behaviour that is self-interested and involves guile and deception. Bounded rationality recognizes that there are informational and cognitive limits to the exercise of rationality. Williamson regards these features as the two human factors that pose a problem for the governance of transactions, because they respectively identify a major source of risk and limitations on the means for dealing with it. Williamson argues that, when two or more parties transact recurrently under conditions where (1) on the one side there are limited numbers of partners to choose between (small numbers), (2) market conditions are uncertain and/or complex, and (3) accurate and adequate information relevant to the transaction is known to one or more parties but not to others without their incurring considerable costs (information impactedness), then the more vulnerable partner is likely to benefit from internalizing the transaction or activity within its own more immediate managerial control if it is not to lose out in the transaction.

According to Williamson, the attributes of a transaction, especially the degree of asset specificity, should play a key role in the choice of an appropriate governance structure. When transactions are one-off, of relatively short-term duration, and where the assets involved are non-specific, market-based transactions are deemed to be suitable. For under such conditions, the market itself, perhaps backed by a formal contract, should provide effective safeguards to the transacting parties. By contrast, when transactions are recurrent, have highly uncertain outcomes which may take a long time to mature, and require unique or transaction-specific investments, they may be conducted more effectively within organizations ('hierarchies').

In his later work, Williamson (1985) gives more attention to asset specificity as a point of reference for choosing between governance structures. Asset specificity refers to durable investments that cannot readily be redeployed to other uses, and which are made in support of particular transactions. The commitment of such assets locks the partners concerned into a given type of transaction. Contractual and/or organizational safeguards are therefore called for to protect the investor in specific-use assets against the risks arising from opportunism, bounded rationality, and uncertainty.

Williamson (1985) also recognizes that two possibilities lie between these two extremes, both of which involve assets of mixed specificity. Transactions, he argues, can either be occasional or recurrent. In the former, market-driven contracting backed by third-party assistance, such as arbitration and litigation, is an appropriate mode of governance. In the second case, he suggests that relational contracting and bilateral governance should prevail instead. Relational contracting involves the long-term investment in building relationships between the parties typical of cooperative activity. Bilateral governance, however, can be implemented by the parties making mutual investments of specific assets that generate mutual dependence and serve as hostages against opportunism.

Relational contracting and bilateral governance frequently lead to hybrid governance structures, intermediate between markets and hierarchies. Hybrids, such as joint ventures, are characterized by bilateral dependency between the partners in that they mutually commit equity and assets and agree on how costs and profits are to be divided between them. In contrast to hierarchies, in which one set of owners and/or managers have unilateral authority, the partners share rights to control and monitor activities, thus potentially weakening the degree of control the other can exercise.

To overcome this problem, partners have to rely on features such as long-term contracts, the offering of mutual hostages such as assets specific to the collaboration, and the development of mutual trust. Although hybrids offer advantages, namely the avoidance of the high uncertainty caused by market failure and the high overhead costs of establishing hierarchies (Kogut, 1988a; Williamson, 1993), their uneasy position with regard to control may make them unstable (Buckley and Casson, 1988; Kogut, 1988a).

Subsequent to Williamson (1985), transaction cost theory has been used to inform a wide range of topics related to cooperative strategy and strategic alliances. These include modes of entry into foreign markets (Anderson and Gatignon, 1986), the selection and structuring of alliance forms (Hennart, 1988; 1991; Parkhe, 1993), and the formation of new ventures (Oviatt and McDougall, 1994). Much of the empirical research conducted within a transaction cost framework has pointed out that equity joint ventures (EJVs) are used to bypass the inefficiencies of intermediate markets with respect to providing raw materials and components, tacit knowledge, loan capital, and distribution systems (Simard, 1996: 19).

Transaction cost analysis contributes important insights into the governance forms that alliances may assume in view of the circumstances under which they are formed. This perspective on cooperative relationships casts new light on the relevance of the partners' possible motives, the nature of the investments they commit to the collaboration, and the specific character of their transactions. Whereas market power theory emphasizes motives for cooperative strategy that relate to market power and profit-attainment, the transaction cost approach stresses the efficiency and cost-minimizing rationales for cooperation. Williamson has been criticized for ignoring the role of power in the choice between market and hierarchy (Francis, Turk, and Willman, 1983) and it must be noted that the transaction cost perspective appears to ignore many factors important to the business decision-maker, including those of risk, potential synergies, and 'effectiveness' which normally joins 'efficiency' as an objective to be sought after. Moreover, whilst it provides a sound framework for exploring the choice between market and hierarchy as governance modes, it does not take into account how the relational aspects of cooperation evolve over time and which, as Parkhe (1993) suggests, affect the nature of the transactions themselves. Rather, it emphasizes the rational aspects of transacting from a static, non- evolutionary perspective, largely ignoring the influence of trust and bonding between partner firms on reducing the risk of opportunism and, conceivably, curbing the boundedness of rationality through a growing willingness to share information. The theory appears concerned mostly with efficiency, and has little to say about questions of fairness or trust in the management of transactions, which any business historian will be sure to emphasize.

This suggests another limitation of transaction cost theory in that it ignores those modes of economic organization which are not highly codified (as both markets and hierarchies are in their own ways), and where transactions are governed by more implicit understandings. As Boisot and Child (1988) point out, the hierarchy–market dichotomy, even when it allows for intermediate positions such as relational contracting, fails to account for how transactions are governed in societies such as those of East Asia on the basis of tacit trust-based cooperative relationships. Such modes of governance, which are certainly not unknown in Western societies, offer important insights for the management of alliances, which are intended to evolve and strengthen over the long term.

The Resource-Based View

The traditional neoclassical, microeconomic view of the behaviour of companies in industries is of a company having a 'business idea', in the form of a product or service, which earns it an economic rent (supernormal profits) for a period of time. However, it suggests, the inexorable forces of the market drive company profits down to those which only earn a normal return on capital, as new firms enter the market, put pressure on prices, and move the market towards an equilibrium. At this point all companies in the market are supplying substantially the same product or service using similar factors of production, and there is little difference between the companies. Clearly in such circumstances, there is little need for management beyond the role of coordination, and unique sustainable competitive advantage is rarely found. Such an approach is perhaps less simplistically and deterministically reflected in the market power approach underlying Porter's frameworks, but its essence remains there nonetheless.

The resource-based view takes quite a different approach. It does not accept the inevitability of forces driving a market towards equilibrium, nor of the necessary competing away of monopolistic rents. Instead, it holds that a company can achieve and sustain a competitive advantage, realizing Ricardian rents, by configuring its tangible and intangible assets in a way that is difficult or indeed impossible to imitate perfectly, or by having resources, skills, or capabilities that are durable, and not appropriable, perfectly transferable, or replicable (Barney, 1991; Grant, 1991; Peteraf, 1993; Rumelt, 1984; 1991; Wernerfelt, 1984). As Rumelt puts it: 'In essence, the concept is that a firm's competitive position is defined by a bundle of unique resources and relationships, and that the task of general management is to adjust and renew these resources and relationships as time, competition, and change erode their value' (Rumelt, 1984: 557–8).

Rumelt (1991) takes issue with Porter by demonstrating that the latter's proposition on industry positioning and firm profitability fails to find support in the empirical data. Rather, his research finds that less than 10 per cent of business unit profitability is explained by industry characteristics, leaving at least 90 per cent of variances in returns not explained by choice of industry. Indeed, 46 per cent appears to be related to choice of strategy. McGahan and Porter (1997), in an aptly entitled rebuttal 'How much does industry matter, really?', qualify Rumelt's findings, arguing that, although these appear supported within the manufacturing sector, they are less relevant to other, non-manufacturing industries.

Heralded by some as a new 'theory of the firm', the resource-based view contrasts with those theories in Industrial Organization (IO) that have aimed for a similar explanation of the existence and scope of 'the firm' These include the *neoclassical* school, according to which firms exist to join the inputs of labour and capital; *Bain-type IO*, in which firms exist to constrain output so as to drive up market prices; the *Schumpeterian* school, where firms exist to create or adopt and exploit innovations; the *Chicago* school, according to which firms serve the purpose of enhancing efficiency in production and distribution; and *transaction cost theory* (Coase, 1937; Williamson, 1975), which suggests that firms exist primarily to minimize transaction costs (Conner, 1991).

Although the concept is credited with having surfaced in the economics literature as early as the 1950s (Penrose, 1959), its roots can be traced back to the far earlier works of David Ricardo (1891) and Joseph Schumpeter (1934). It has, however, only fairly recently been widely adopted within the strategy and organization literature. Interestingly, Porter's more recent contributions (e.g. 1996) reflect an evolution in his thinking, in which organizational activities, and the uniqueness with which these are performed, have become more prominent, thus gradually introducing that theory of the firm which remained of less importance in his earlier works.

To achieve sustainable competitive advantage (SCA), by trading in imperfectly imitable and imperfectly mobile firm resources through a strategy of cooperation, is possible in some circumstances but not in others. An alliance can legitimately provide access to 'the gold mine' or to certain codifiable capabilities, specific assets, or systems, without necessitating an outright acquisition in which one firm is required to relinquish all proprietary skills and resources. It is more difficult, however, to 'absorb' the causally ambiguous, tacit types of competencies enjoyed by a potential partner. Acquiring such competencies requires that a firm develops high receptivity and a strong learning intent. It requires also that the partner has some degree of transparency in knowledge communication, and that the nature of this knowledge itself is sufficiently transferable. Indeed, to transfer the skills of a concert pianist to an untalented musician may prove impossible. Moreover, trading in strategic resources can be subject to high transaction costs, particularly those of adverse selection, moral hazard (shirking), cheating, and hold-up, as imperfect imitability (a requisite for the resource-based view) and transaction costs are thought to be positively correlated (Chi, 1994).

Anoop Madhok (Chapter 4) employs transaction cost theory as a basis for understanding cooperation, but adds to it a discussion of resource-based theory in order to achieve movement from the efficiency viewpoint to that of value creation. He claims that little work has been done on fusing the two theories, and that such a combination is necessary, if competitive advantage is to be gained and a value-creating mission achieved.

Steve Tallman (Chapter 5) attempts a similar fusion in relation to the potential symbiosis of transaction cost and resource-based theories, since understanding the success and failure of collaborations can be significantly furthered by combining the rent-seeking perspective of resource-based theory with the cost efficiency perspective of transaction cost theory. He applies this theory to what he terms 'shared organization ventures' (SOVs). He emphasizes that, whilst value can be achieved through the development of such forms, instability is almost inevitable, and management must be prepared for a life-long process of creation and re-creation of SOVs if they are to appropriate the rents from these vehicles successfully.

Agency Theory

Agency theory is concerned with the ability of 'principals' (generally shareholders) to ensure that their 'agents' (management) are fulfilling the objectives of the principals. Much of the work within this perspective has focused on the special case of the principal–agent relationship between the owners and managers of large public corporations (Berle and Means, 1932). Other writers have, however, extended the principal–agent framework to other relationships such as that of employer to employee, client to lawyer, and buyer to supplier (Child and Faulkner, 1998).

Agency theory is concerned with the governance mechanisms that limit the agent's self-serving behaviour, including various control and incentive mechanisms (Arrow, 1985, Barney and Ouchi, 1986; Eisenhardt, 1989; Jensen and Meckling, 1976). Eisenhardt (1989), in her review, identifies the contract between principal and agent as the central unit of analysis for agency theory. She points out that agency theory contains a number of assumptions about the nature of human behaviour, organizations, and information. It assumes that human behaviour is self-interested, subject to bounded rationality and risk aversion, and is consistent with the assumptions adopted by transaction costs theorists. It assumes also that organizations contain a degree of potential conflict between the goals of their owners and their employees, that there is an asymmetry of information between principals and agents (with agents possessing specific information about what they are doing and relevant contextual conditions), and that efficiency is the key basis of effectiveness. It also assumes that information is a purchasable commodity, so that principals can choose to spend more, in order to secure better information about the conduct of their agents.

Given these assumptions, the focus of agency theory has been on determining the most efficient contract governing the relationship between principal and agent. More precisely, the question has been one of whether a behaviour-oriented contract is more efficient than an outcome-oriented contract. Behaviour-oriented contracts include those which offer a salary in return for being available to work during stated hours, or in given circumstances, and under the authority of a hierarchical superordinate (i.e. hierarchical governance). Outcome-oriented contracts include commissions, stock options, and having rewards or returns subject to performance within a marketplace. The latter appear currently the more in vogue in the less bureaucratic private enterprise companies.

Within the range of structures through which a cooperative strategy may be pursued, a principal–agent relationship is most clearly established when joint ventures are formed whose managers are accountable to their partner-owners. Agency theory would regard the relationship between the partner-owners and joint venture managers as a potentially problematic one. The situation may become more complicated when the partner companies themselves have different risk and time preferences. For instance, one partner may be more risk-averse and have a shorter time preference than the other, in which case they are likely to disagree over the scale of their shared investment and on whether to distribute or reinvest returns on it. Such disagreement could result in a failure to establish mutual trust between them. If situations like these give rise to mixed signals being sent to joint venture managers (the agents), there is a danger of agency costs rising (Buckley and Chapman, 1993). The problem becomes even more complex when there are more than two principals and possibly multiple agents running the joint venture.

The implications of agency theory extend to forms of cooperative strategy other than joint ventures. Indeed, any collaborative relationship is one in which each partner becomes an agent for, and principal of, the other. There is a risk that one partner will engage in self-seeking, opportunistic behaviour at the expense of the other, thus raising the issue of what governance and control systems are most appropriate within a partnership. Part III of this volume treats some aspects of this issue in greater depth.

The practical implication of agency theory is therefore that, just as a principal is advised to put in place a combination of incentives and monitoring mechanisms to ensure that an agent's behaviour remains consistent with the principal's objectives, so the partners to a cooperative venture would be advised to make clear to each other the basis on which each will share the returns from effective cooperation, and to put into place the systems for information to be shared between them. These provisions should reduce suspicion among partners, and so provide a basis for mutual trust to develop through their working relationship. As and when partners do gain each other's trust, the monitoring mechanisms emphasized by agency theory can become less prominent.

Game Theory

Game theory is concerned with the prediction of outcomes from 'games'—social situations involving two or more players whose interests are interconnected or interdependent (Zagare, 1984). The nature of a game might be sporting (as with poker), financial (as with bargaining over pay and other contracts), military (as with threatening air strikes to force compliance to the demands of an alliance), or business strategy. Pioneered by Princeton mathematician Von Neumann, and extended in collaboration with economist Morgenstern in their book *The Theory of Games and Economic Behavior* (1944), game theory initially focused on situations of pure conflict (zero-sum games), where incentives for collaboration are virtually non-existent, making self-interested behaviour optimal. However, recent research on non-zero-sum games, especially the repeated prisoner's dilemma, demonstrates first, that self-interested behaviour does not always lead to the optimum overall outcome and, second, that cooperation can emerge in a world of self-interested agents without a central authority, provided there exists a possibility that they might meet again.

Two-person games such as these are the most elementary, and serve to highlight the dilemma which may attend the choice between a competitive and a cooperative strategy. While game theory supposes that players are self-interested, it does not also assume that competitive behaviour will necessarily follow, as is implicit in Adam Smith's (1776) classic 'invisible hand' theory. Rather, paradoxically, whilst cooperation may maximize joint interest, it does not maximize self-interest, at least not in repeated games. Further, if one player cooperates while another defects, the latter will gain at the expense of the former in the short run. If neither party cooperates, both will lose, though not in one-shot games to the extent of the loss incurred by the non-defecting party when the other reneges.

Although the short-term dominant strategy appears to be defection in one-shot prisoner's dilemma games, the same does not hold for repeated games with an indeterminate end. Nor does it apply if the penalty for defection is made very high or when the game is related to scenarios in which partners value working together, and care about their reputation in the wider business community. Indeed, a strategic alliance partner who is seen to defect might find it very difficult to attract future partners (cf. Gulati 1995a, 1995b).

Iterated versions of the prisoner's dilemma game have been used to analyse how cooperation evolves when the players have a possibility of meeting again and therefore have a stake in their future interaction. Axelrod (1984) refers to this as the 'future casting a shadow over the present'. When this is the case, he argues that cooperation as a social process can develop, even in a context where unconditional defection is the norm, with small clusters of individuals, who base their cooperation on reciprocity and repeatedly engage in interactions. Further, a strategy based on reciprocity can thrive alongside other strategies. However, whilst this approach proves robust in computer simulations, it is rarely found in real life, where a single act of defection generally leads to the break-up of the collaboration as trust dissipates rapidly.

Iterated games also suggest that the probability of cooperation may be improved initially by providing mutual hostages, and then progressively reinforced by the benefits it is seen to provide. This is an important insight, which directly parallels the conclusion that may be drawn from theories about the ways in which trust between partners can develop over time through continued interaction between them. Indeed, Gulati, Khanna, and Nohria (1994) stress the significance of partners making unilateral commitments.

They conclude from research on 17 firms engaged in alliances that one shortcoming of the prisoner's dilemma framework lies in the way it underestimates the importance of partners acting unilaterally to make commitments that enhance the possibility that all the partners will cooperate. They conclude that, such unilateral commitments can be vital to the success of alliances. Parkhe summarizes this as follows:

Experimental evidence suggests that although non-cooperation emerges as the dominant strategy in single-play situations, under iterated conditions the incidence of cooperation rises substantially. Similarly, in strategic alliances, cooperation is maintained as each firm compares the immediate gain from cheating with the possible sacrifice of future gains that may result from violating an agreement... The assumption here seems intuitively reasonable: broken promises in the present will decrease the likelihood of cooperation in the future. By the same token, cooperation in the current move can be matched by cooperation in the next move, and a defection can be met with a retaliatory defection. Thus, iteration improves the prospects for cooperation by encouraging strategies of reciprocity (1993: 799).

Nalebuff and Brandenburger (1996) draw from game theory the view that companies need to weigh up the consequences of cooperative and competitive behaviour. They warn against aggressive strategies that can backfire, citing the example of the US airline industry, which lost more money in its price wars of 1990–3 than it had previously made in all the years since the Wright brothers. They argue that game theory is a way of thinking—an analytical tool—that is well suited to assessing the likely consequences of competitive and cooperative behaviours in conditions where the benefits to one player depend on the actions of others, and where, in a complex world, there are multiple interdependencies such that no decision can be made in isolation from a host of other commitments. The central tenet of their book is that business has to recognize the duality between cooperation and competition—a way of thinking that may be more novel for Western managers than for their counterparts in regions such as East Asia.

Nalebuff and Brandenburger (1996) proceed to develop a variant on game theory, namely a theory of 'coopetition'. This particular phenomenon differs from cooperation in the following way. Coopetition is the scenario in which one's fate depends to a substantial extent on that of a 'complementor' company. Issues of affection, trust, forgiveness, and commitment are no longer particularly relevant, as cooperation is necessary if one is to prosper. The dependence of IBM on the success of Microsoft, and vice versa, serves as a good illustration of a coopetitive relationship. IBM might be quite happy for Microsoft to fail and vice versa, but despite their undoubted rivalry, their coopetitive relationship ensures their cooperation, at least in those matters that stand to benefit both.

Kay (1993) distinguishes between two categories of strategic alliance: the 'common objective' alliance and the 'mutually beneficial exchange' alliance. The former is typically one in which partners possess distinctive capabilities that complement each other. Classic examples of this phenomenon exist in the automotive and computer industries. General Motors' cooperation with Toyota, for instance, centred on introducing lean production manufacturing in the former's operations. This benefited Toyota by allowing them access to the US market. Applying the logic of game theory, Kay concludes that in such a common objective alliance, cooperation is a dominant strategy for both partners, as it pays both partners to put the maximum effort into attaining this shared vision. In the case of a mutually beneficial exchange alliance, however, the dominant strategy for both partners is to act in a predatory fashion, and 'hold back' (i.e. to extract as much as possible from the relationship while giving as little as possible in return). This appears akin to the prisoner's dilemma scenario, in which in the short term self interest is not maximized by cooperation even though joint interest may be. The longer the alliance holds, the more likely it is that a recognition of the mutual benefit from cooperation will prevail, but paradoxically the initial pursuit of self-interest is likely to bring an alliance to a premature end.

Game theory, then, makes valuable contributions to the analysis of co-operative strategy by drawing our attention to situations in which this strategy may be rewarding and those conditions under which cooperation may be undermined. Axelrod's (1984) findings allude to the importance of forgive-ness, simplicity, and predictability. In its present forms, game theory relies on a number of simplifying assumptions which distance it from reality, though without necessarily undermining its essential and valuable insights. Among the features of reality which cannot readily be encompassed by the theory are the personalities of the players, their social ties, verbal communication between the players, the emotional and norm-building consequences of such communication, uncertainty about what the other player actually did previously in the game, and the social conventions and institutional rules in which the players and their interactions are embedded. Game theory also reduces firms to single actors, and has difficulty in coping with the differentia-tion of roles, perceptions, and interests within them. Nevertheless, it con-tinues to have tremendous potential for advancing our understanding of the intrinsic nature of business cooperation.

Kofi Nti and Rajesh Kumar (Chapter 6) provide a novel application of a game theory framework in their treatment of the problem of competition and differential learning in strategic alliances. They demonstrate the risks of appropriation taken by a firm with low knowledge absorptive capacity once it enters an alliance with a higher absorptive capacity firm with the aim of learning and creating value. They apply this conclusion to two case studies for illustration. They question the rationale for an alliance from the viewpoint of the low absorptive capacity firm, but confirm it for the firm that is equal or higher in such a capacity. It follows that if one doubts one's own ability to absorb new knowledge easily, one should be wary of entering into new learning alliances with more quick-witted and flexible partners.

Real Options Theory

Real options theory has only recently been adopted in the literature to tender rationales for cooperative behaviour. An application from the field of finance, it is based on the philosophy that no resource commitments should be made before absolutely necessary, since almost inevitably the future will be different from that expected. Not only does keeping one's options open as long as possible accord a higher chance of success, but multiple investments in a portfolio of options can help diversify risk, leaving the exercise of these options (by increasing resource commitments) at the leisure of a (usually dominant) partner firm. As Copeland and Keenan (1998) put it: 'Real options are especially valuable for projects that involve both a high level of uncertainty and opportunities to dispel it as new information becomes available.'

They divide options into 'compound options' and 'learning options', although these are not mutually exclusive categories. Compound options are those that, when exercised, open up further options, which, in turn, render even more options, and so on. This scenario is most common in staged and sequential investments. Learning options are those where the holder makes small investments primarily to learn about specific technologies or to explore opportunities for future investments. Within the context of a real options strategy, cooperation serves to generate a portfolio of relatively low-risk options, enabling small and incremental 'wagers' to be made that can simultaneously achieve new learning and open up further options for the future. The pharmaceutical industry is an example of one in which such a portfolio approach is frequently adopted through multiple bilateral alliances between major pharmaceutical firms and a number of small biotech companies. Even if just one biotechnology collaboration bears fruit, the potential rewards of this will frequently render the portfolio expenditure worthwhile. Indeed, new capabilities can best be developed *inter alia*, through networks, licences, and access-conveying as well as capability complementing special relationships, including strategic alliances (Baghai, Coley, and White, 1996). Real options theory in relation to cooperative strategy therefore stands in stark attitudinal contrast to more traditional cooperative theory, which holds that success depends heavily on a high level of mutual commitment between the partners. Real options theory is more cynical in this regard, being based on an underlying philosophy of 'playing the field' and delaying commitment as the best means to achieve a successful future.

The Organization Theory Viewpoint

Beyond those explanations informed by economics there exist at least five theoretical treatments of cooperative strategy within the organization theory literature, including (1) resource dependence theory, (2) organizational learning, (3) social network theory, (4) the ecosystems view and (5) structurationist perspectives.

Resource Dependence Theory

Developed most elaborately by Pfeffer and Salancik (1978), resource dependence theory focuses on the context within which organizations operate, and on which they rely for resources. As Pfeffer explains:

because organizations are not internally self-sufficient, they require resources from the environment and, thus, become interdependent with those elements of the environment with which they transact . . . Thus, resource dependence theory suggests that organizational behaviour becomes externally influenced because the focal organization must attend to the demands of those in its environment that provide resources necessary and important for its continued survival (1982: 192–3).

Organizational behaviour is thus accounted for, and justified by the context in which an organization finds itself. Consequently, cooperation may exist primarily to provide organizations with access to financial resources (a typical motive for biotech start-ups), expertise, skills, or processes (a typical motive for pharmaceuticals), or markets (more typical of financial institutions and automotive manufacturers). Alternatively, firms may seek to reduce uncertainty in their environment by cooperating with key parts of it (e.g. Faulkner, 1995), though that may merely replace one source of risk with another (e.g. opportunism, free-riding).

Resource dependence theory is consistent with its counterpart, the resource-based view (Barney, 1991; Hamel and Prahalad, 1994; Grant, 1991; Penrose, 1959; Wernerfelt, 1984), which emphasizes the importance of unique, internal capabilities (or core competencies) that, when leveraged, can provide firms with a sustainable competitive advantage over their rivals. In fact, access to exclusive capabilities held by other firms, such as patents, knowledge, technologies, brands, or processes, may provide a compelling strategic raison d'être for entering into an alliance. The theory is less well suited to informing process research and largely normative in its orientation on rational choice and deliberate efforts to align the organization to its environment (Pfeffer, 1982). Its emphasis on external financial and socio-political forces sensitizes managers to the dependence of their organization on outside stakeholder influences, leading some (e.g. Donaldson, 1995) to criticize it for rendering too much importance to political forces, though this is surely one of its very contributions. Critical also of what he perceives to be an internal inconsistency, Donaldson comments: 'The merger and other interorganizational co-ordination devices studied by Pfeffer and Salancik must reduce the autonomy of the focal organization. Hence it is self-contradictory to argue that organizations seeking to gain greater autonomy will do this by taking steps to reduce their autonomy' (1995: 162).

However, there exists empirical support for Pfeffer and Salancik's (1978) argument. For instance, a driving force behind the long-standing collaboration between The Royal Bank of Scotland and Banco Santander appears to have been the threat of takeovers, in an industry where merger activity is becoming increasingly common. By forging an alliance and exchanging a relatively small equity stake, the banks were able to preserve their autonomy by surrendering some of it through collaborating (de Rond and Faulkner, 1997).

Organizational Learning

The correlation between unique capabilities and sustained competitive advantage provided in the resource-based view, and the recognition that corporate performance depends in some measure on the external environment on which the firm relies for those resources it does not already possess, suggest opportunities for organizational learning by way of cooperating. Organizational learning refers to the capability of organizations to acquire, disseminate, and retain new knowledge so as to improve future performance (Child and Faulkner, 1998), and is of particular interest if each partner possesses a different set of capabilities and experiences. Indeed, it can provide a powerful rationale for entering cooperative arrangements.

Despite having surfaced in the literature as early as the 1970s, it has only fairly recently been applied to the study of inter-organizational alliances (e.g. Child and Rodrigues, 1996; Ciborra, 1991; Doz, 1996; Hamel, 1991; Inkpen, 1995; Inkpen and Crossan, 1995). Much of the extant literature has focused on cognitive and behavioural dimensions of learning, and includes discussions on the acquisition, dissemination, and codification of knowledge, knowledge transfers, and the barriers to organizational learning posed by organizational structures, cultures, and vested interests. Indeed, 'paradoxically, although cooperative strategies are usually intended to enhance the learning of partner organizations, the fact that the strategic and cultural match between them may be less than complete can seriously impede the process' (Child and Faulkner, 1998: 284).

The literature distinguishes between various levels of learning. 'Routine' learning—describing incremental improvements within existing organizational systems to improve performance, such as new skills or techniques to improve productivity—constitutes the lowest level of learning. 'Reframing' learning addresses more fundamental changes to these systems aimed, for instance, at achieving a better integration. 'Deutero' learning refers more specifically to the development and nurture of learning mindsets within the organization (Argyris and Schon, 1978), and is considered the most complex of the three. Child and Faulkner (1998) define the three levels more pragmatically as (1) technical, (2) systemic, and (3) strategic learning. These processes can surface at all three levels, even simultaneously. The literature makes a further distinction between 'collaborative' learning and 'competitive' learning (e.g. Hamel, 1991). Collaborative learning constitutes access to, and transfer of, knowledge and skills held by partner firms, as well as the process of learning more about the intricacies of operationalizing and managing cooperative ventures. The latter can be useful particularly as more and more activities are organized through alliances. Competitive learning, on the other hand, concerns the exploitation by one partner of the knowledge and expertise provided by another, and is of a predatory rather than mutual nature. The extent to which each level and type of learning can be achieved depends on an organization's 'intention' and ability to learn (Hamel, 1991), its 'absorptive capacity' (Cohen and Levinthal, 1990), and its competence in 'codifying' new knowledge and 'converting' it into a collective property (Nonaka and Takeuchi, 1995). It is facilitated by reducing organizational, cognitive, and emotional barriers to learning (e.g. the 'Not-Invented-Here' syndrome), and encouraging openness of communication and circulation of information (Child and Faulkner, 1998). Indeed, the process of cooperation may well be more important than its governance structure in determining learning outcomes (Hamel, 1991).

Social Network Theory

The study of social networks has become rather fashionable, though there appears to be some confusion about quite what a network perspective entails. Ambiguity tends to prevail, which can result in rhetorical whim and *ad hoc* judgement. Jones, Hesterly, and Borgatti (1997) tacitly endorse this observation by providing no less than nine contemporary definitions of network governance and by proceeding to add their own. Often, networks are referenced at a metaphorical level, void of specific characteristics and strategies to form, activate, and maximize network resources (Ibarra, 1992; Aldrich and Whetten, 1981). Wellman (1983) attributes such misconceptions to researchers mistaking parts for the whole which has often served either to 'harden network analysis into a method or soften it into a metaphor' (1983: 156). Networks are often shown as a hybrid form on the spectrum between markets and hierarchies (Powell, 1990; Thorelli, 1986), and as a theory of cooperation it exhibits properties of the resource dependence perspective (Pfeffer and Salancik, 1978) as well as the earlier social exchange theory (Blau, 1967) on which it builds. Indeed, network theory, a structuralist view extended significantly at Harvard in the 1960s by White (1963) and his students Wellman (1980, 1983) and Berkowitz (1982), appears to have surfaced as a competing theoretical explanation to inform cooperative behaviour in business (e.g. Gulati, 1993, 1998, 1999).

Social networks can broadly be defined as persistent and structured sets of autonomous players (persons or organizations) who cooperate on the basis of implicit and open-ended contracts. Such contracts are socially rather than legally binding. Essentially, it is argued that all organizations can be viewed as social networks. The actions and behaviour of individuals and organizations can be explained in the context of their position in a network, that is itself constantly being reproduced by the actions of these individuals and organizations (Nohria, 1992). This reproductive feature of networks, as social structures, is not inconsistent with Giddens's (1984) intellectual tradition in sociology, though one could argue that network analysis, by its very nature, emphasizes structure at the expense of action (cf. Sydow and Windeler, 1998), hence rendering a one-sided account of cooperation.

As Gulati (1998) rightly suggests, research into cooperative strategy has been concerned primarily with dyadic alliances and, therefore, has failed to examine their formation, governance structures, dynamics, evolution, performance, and performance consequences as a function of the larger social networks in which the relationship is embedded, to which it contributes, and which render it 'social capital' (cf. Burt, 1992). Hence, a social network perspective not only transcends the customarily dyadic-oriented agenda, but responds to an 'undersocialized' account of cooperation, whilst providing a process-friendly theory to inform empirical studies, particularly those concerned with the dynamics and evolution of collaborations.

Ecosystems

A close relative of the social network perspective is a view of organizations as members of 'business ecosystems': communities of suppliers, lead producers, competitors, and other stakeholders that evolve under the leadership of one or several central companies as they seek mutual support, align investments, and jointly progress towards a shared vision (Moore, 1996: 26). The incentive for cooperating is embedded in the perceived potential value of core capabilities, an ensuing ability to generate economies of scale and scope based on these capabilities, and a reinvestment of returns into this ecosystem to produce a breeding ground for future generations of product or service offerings. Indeed, given what Moore (1996) views as the collapse of traditional industries, the only sensible way to compete is to be better at building and sustaining ecosystems, the boundaries of which are only loosely defined in a determinedly hands-on fashion, rather than merely providing products or services. A firm's profitability is contingent on its ability to manage relationships within the ecosystem (or network), its centrality within this network, and the ability of this community of firms to compete effectively with similar constellations. As explained by Moore: 'This new approach to strategy makes so much sense today because of a certain truism: the strength that a company derives from its ecosystem can be as much as, or more important than, the competitiveness it derives from its own virtues' (1996: 56).

The 'flagship firm' theory of Alan Rugman and Joseph D'Cruz (Chapter 3), discussed earlier, is a prime example of an ecosystem under the leadership of a single organization. Managing relationships, fostering trust with key suppliers, key customers, certain competitors, and the non-business infrastructure, treated here as mechanisms for achieving strategic purpose and providing strategic leadership, are clearly as crucial to firm profitability as is rivalry. Not dissimilar is the viewpoint taken by Ray Loveridge (Chapter 7), who conceptionalizes the firm as a differentiator and integrator of networks. Superior performance, argues Loveridge, is a function of the firm's ability to manage key relationships and to create a reputation for creditworthiness, design know-how, reliability, and predictability. His chapter provides theoretical support for a network analysis of the functional role of the firm, particularly one that emphasizes flows of information.

The 'collective competition' perspective proposed by Gomes-Casseres (1996) is similar to Moore's (1996) ecosystems view in many respects. Citing the RISC industry experience, Gomes-Casseres argues that competition increasingly takes place among constellations (e.g. Mips, Sun, HP, and IBM) rather than single firms. Hence, here also firm profitability is viewed as a function of collective action (the 'network effect'), though firm strategy remains essentially narcissistic.

Even for firms heavily involved in such competition, what counts to their owners are the profits of the firm, not those of the group. Although the game has changed, we still keep score the old way. In the long run, each group member must benefit from the collective effort. Without private gains, or at least the expectation of such gains, the group will fall apart (Gomes-Casseres, 1996: 109).

Paradoxically, the impact of cooperative behaviour on industry structure and dynamics appears to have enhanced rather than curbed competitive rivalry. Addressing this apparent incongruity, Gomes-Casseres suggests that firms, in combining their capabilities, mimicking one another, and forming groups of like-minded firms to catch up with industry leaders, help intensify competition by creating stronger competitors, narrower competitive gaps, and less differentiation among competing firms (1996: 175). Examples of consolidation prevail and are not limited to a single sector. For instance, in the PC market, Apple, IBM, and Motorola jointly developed the PowerPC chip in an effort to challenge Intel's dominance. In the pharmaceutical sector, SmithKline Beecham announced controversial plans to merge with American Home Products and, later, GlaxoWellcome partly to reduce excess capacity, though both plans were abandoned. In the airline industry, United Airlines joined forces with SAS, Thai Airways, International, Lufthansa, Varig, Aeromar, Air New Zealand, Ansett Australia, Mexicana, and Air Canada to create the 'Star Alliance', and helped transform a fragmented industry into a handful of dominant and fiercely competitive networks. Clearly, cooperative activity influences not just the structure of competition but also its pace of change, by enabling access to new technologies and capabilities, providing the opportunity to reduce excess capacity and, in the process, moving entry and exit barriers.

Structurationist Perspectives

A newcomer to the playing field of cooperative strategy emerges out of the intellectual tradition of Anthony Giddens who, reflecting on the 'phoney war' between determinist views and action theorists, suggests that structure and action are mutually implicated in the process of reproducing social praxis (Giddens, 1984; Sydow and Windeler, 1998). In contrast to traditional economic treatments, structurationists employ a distinctly sociological approach to the study of alliances which is neither focused solely on structure nor occupied merely with strategic choice (e.g. Child, 1972). Indeed, Giddens's 'duality of structure' thesis implies that one cannot speak of structure without referring to action also, and vice versa. Action emerges out of existing social structures, and at the same time reproduces or transforms these structures. Recent examples of applications of a structurationist perspective to cooperative strategy are Sydow and Windeler (1998) and Bouchikhi, de Rond, and Leroux (1998). As a theoretical perspective, it highlights the essentially sociological character of alliances in which individuals, not just organizations, cooperate and make repeated commitments to continue cooperating. It appears particularly well suited to explaining process without negating structure and design, given that both are mutually implicated, and to exploring issues of effectiveness and collaborative success.

In sum, each of the principal 'cooperative theories' reviewed above contributes in some way to explaining and justifying strategies of cooperation in fiercely competitive environments. The strategic management literature, influenced greatly by Porter's work (1980, 1985) draws attention to power relationships within industries and their implications for generic firm strategies for positioning and profit potential. The assumptions underlying transaction cost theory (opportunism, bounded rationality, and asset specificity) emphasize the importance of cost minimization and efficiency rather than issues related to quality and risk in decision-making. The resource-based view highlights the significance of unique resources to sustaining a competitive advantage, and, given their imperfect imitability, the incentive this provides for cooperative behaviour. Game theory draws attention to tit-for-tat games played out in real-life alliances, whilst agency theory provides treatments of the nature of the contractual relationships between them. Real options theory treats cooperative strategy as a means to developing a portfolio of 'real' options that, in due course, may or may not be exercised, and is of an inherently more predatory nature.

Within the organization theory literature, resource dependence theory emphasizes the dependence of partner firms on external resources and socio-political forces. The organizational learning school views cooperation as purposive learning processes, intended to internalize and codify skills needed to improve firm performance. Social network theory suggests that collaborations are embedded in social networks, consisting of individuals and organizations, that are continuously reproduced as a result of their strategic decisions and the unintended outcomes of their actions. The ecosystems view is not dissimilar from the network school in that competition takes place not only between individual firms, but between constellations of cooperating organizations. Firm profitability becomes contingent on the ability to cooperate with others in the larger ecosystem. Structurationist perspectives, finally, view cooperative activity as both empowered and constrained by existing social structures and, in turn, either reinforcing or transforming these same structures.

Some of these theories, like social network and structurationist theories, are process friendly. Others, like transaction cost economics and resource dependence theory are less so. Organization theories claim to provide socialized accounts of collusive behaviour, though may do so at the expense of distinct economic rationales that encourage such behaviour in the first place. As Gulati reminds us: 'Firms don't form alliances as symbolic social affirmations . . . but, rather, base alliances on concrete strategic complementarities that they have to offer each other' (1998: 301). Hence, each has a unique place in our discourse on the alliance phenomenon, although none is sufficiently comprehensive to produce a unified and broadly accepted theory of alliance formation, process, and performance. We agree with Sydow and Windeler:

Although we believe that economic and organization and network theories contribute to a better understanding of creating and organizing interfirm networks, none of these focuses on structure as well as on process, takes the production of structure via action as much into account as the flow of action from structure, and deals simultaneously with power, cognition, and legitimacy issues as interrelated aspects of the process through which economic effectiveness is constituted (Sydow and Windeler, 1998: 270).

The Process of Cooperating

Process studies are less common in the literature than those that focus on rationales for cooperating, partner selection, and performance. 'Scholars . . . have ignored process', note Ring and Van de Ven (1994: 91). Doz likewise argues that the 'growing literature on the strategic alliance phenomenon suffers from imbalance' (1996: 55) with relatively little emphasis on evolution. Koza and Lewin (1998) lament the absence of studies on alliance evolution, particularly with respect to the changing strategies of partner firms and a co-evolving industry and institutional environment, as do Arino and de la Torre (1998).

Process and Evolution

Empirical studies of inter-organizational relationships suggest that these can proceed along very different evolutionary paths. Some alliances exhibit only limited potential for evolution (e.g. ICI–Pharma), others are thought to be more latent for eventual evolution—i.e. their potential is curbed by at least one constraining factor (e.g. Dowty-Sema)—whilst yet others appear truly dynamic (e.g. ICL and Fujitsu), having developed well beyond incipient objectives and/or expectations (Faulkner, 1995).

Van de Ven (1992) differentiates between four process paradigms: evolution, dialectics, teleology, and life-cycle processes. Of these, the life-cycle and teleology views are predictive, in contrast to the dialectics and evolutionary theories that are largely non-deterministic and merely explanatory. Life-cycle processes are inherently linear and predictive in conceptualizing process as a sequence of phases, one following another in a regular pattern from conception or formation to maturity and termination. Teleology explains phenomena by the purpose they serve rather than by postulated causes. It is design and goal oriented and, hence, inherently deterministic, even predictive. A dialectic view conceives of process as an interplay of opposing forces resulting in iterations of convergence and divergence and by implication would appear rather less deterministic and nonlinear. Evolution—a term applied quite liberally in the management literature to explain a quite diverse set of processes—can be either Darwinian or Lamarckian in nature, and refers to a gradual process of change, generally from the more simple to the more complex. Darwinian evolution seeks to explain the gradual adaptation of organisms (or organizations) to a particular environment. The Lamarckian variant is similar except that it posits that acquired characteristics can be passed on to future generations. Either type is non-predictive (i.e. we cannot now predict what the next generation of species will look like) and, generally, non-linear (there are as many diversions creating variety as suit the different environments). More recently, suggestions have been made that the evolution of cooperation is more akin to a punctuated equilibrium view, according to which periods of relative stability are interrupted by shorter periods of instability and change, fusing the evolution and dialectics views into an alternative but inviting process perspective (cf. Gulati, 1998; Gray and Yan, 1997).

Van de Ven's (1992) distinctions appear reflected in the process literature, in which one finds linear and deterministic models alongside more complex and non-linear frameworks that, though still informed by a similar agenda, have relinquished predictability in favour of description. These are the findings of Bouchikhi, de Rond, and Leroux (1998) who, based on a recent critique of alliance process studies, suggest that most attempts to model alliance evolution have been driven by a 'managerial' agenda, interested in identifying life-cycle phases along with corresponding managerial tasks. The earlier process models are typically linear and sequential, and include D'Aunno and Zuckerman (1987), Shortell and Zajac (1988), Achrol, Scheer, and Stern (1990), Forrest and Martin (1992), and Murray and Mahon (1993). Grounded implicitly in a 'closed systems' perspective, each conceptualizes evolution as progressing through a fixed and predictable sequence of stages, in which success and performance are implicitly the product of managerial control. In fact, their rhetoric is singularly 'managerial' and task oriented.

Recognizing the vast complexity of alliance life, other scholars have proposed iterative process models, most notably Ring and Van de Ven (1994) and Doz (1996). Yet, despite their non-linearity and an 'open systems' view of collaborative relationships, these still fail to abandon the sequential orientation typical of the earlier linear frameworks. Furthermore, any 'a priori' assumptions on the 'manageability' of alliances remain intact, though the role of management is now thought to be one of adaptation rather than mere control. Hence, future research agendas into process could include treatments of alliances as social structures, embedded in a wider firm, network, and social context, and informed by social network or structurationist traditions, and the development of descriptive and more inclusive theories of alliance formation and evolution. This need has been legitimately recognized in the organization literature for some time (e.g. Leavitt's (1965) four-dimensional framework; Cohen, March, and Olsen's (1972) 'garbage can model'; Pettigrew's (1987) contextualism; and Kimberly and Bouchikhi's (1995) 'organizational biography'), but this trend has yet to transfer to the study of cooperative relationships (Bouchikhi, de Rond, and Leroux, 1998).

Part III of this volume contains three chapters on process and evolution. Their contributions range from outlining a non-linear, sequential process framework to thick empirical descriptions of alliance evolution. Yves Doz and Oğüz Baburoglu (Chapter 8) extend Doz's prior research (e.g. 1988, 1996), into the evolution of strategic alliances by providing a conceptual framework to inform the emergence and evolution of R&D collaborations. Contrasting their work with both 'thick' descriptive case studies and more quantitative studies, the authors use publicly available data to define their general characteristics. Their framework includes a sequence of phases, and places learning and adjustment processes squarely at the centre of alliance life and evolution.

David Boddy, Douglas Macbeth, and Beverly Wagner (Chapter 9) draw on research into seven partnering organizations in two supply chains, and highlight the scale of changes that can occur as collaborative relationships evolve. Their empirical base consists of a longitudinal three-year research effort into the implementation and management of these cooperative ventures, and one 'thick' case description of an alliance between Sun Microsystems and Birkbys Plastics. When combined with the existing literature on organizational change, this empirical basis serves to develop a five-point managerial agenda, including content, process, control, learning, and integration of cooperative relationships.

Thomas Kern and Leslie Willcocks (Chapter 10) provide an even more elaborate case study to explore IT out-sourcing relationships. Firms increasingly seek to out-source the development, maintenance, and management of their information systems to specialist providers such as Electronic Data

Systems (EDS), IBM, Computer Science Corporation (CSC), and even traditional management consulting firms such as Andersen Consulting and
Gemini. In an effort to refocus on value-adding competencies by leaving
support and maintenance to third parties, to minimize the costs associated
with IT, to gain flexibility, to better control and enforce performance measures, to more aggressively use low-cost labour pools, and to gain access to
new ideas, new ways of thinking, and innovative practices (Lacity, Willcocks,
and Feeny, 1997; McFarlan and Nolan, 1995), out-sourcing has gained in
popularity as a cooperative strategy, though, as the authors point out, it
retains many of the characteristics of buyer–supplier relationships. Kern
and Willcocks's chapter provides a conceptual framework for exploring and
understanding out-sourcing relationships. In addition they provide a number
of insights into global out-sourcing relationship management, exemplified
through Xerox Corporation's experiences.

Performance Assessments

An important contribution from Ring and Van de Ven (1994) and Doz (1996)
is their emphasis on ongoing processes of assessment, of fairness, and of
performance. In the wider alliance literature efforts to isolate and articulate
factors that contribute to alliance process are more common than process
studies themselves. Subsequent findings have not always agreed, however.
Some scholars suggest that the best cooperative relationships are frequently
'messy and emotional' (Kanter, 1994), generating the occasional conflict
(Hamel, Doz, and Prahalad, 1989), though the 'stormy open marriages'
advocated by Roehl and Truitt (1987) do not necessarily ensure partnership
success in the longer term (Faulkner, 1995). Faulkner (1995) suggests that the
most effective alliances tend to be those that show a positive evolution over
time, rather than a mere pursuit of initial objectives. This view is consistent
with that of Lorange and Roos (1992), who emphasize the importance of
evolutionary dynamics and the potentially destructive consequences of ob-
sessive control.

   Lynch (1993) submits that success is determined by architecture and good
architecture characterized by longevity. Some, however, take issue with the
suggestion that longevity is necessarily a good measure of success. Hamel
(1991) suggests that terminating an alliance can be evidence of successful
learning rather than failed collaboration, particularly when learning was a
primary objective. Hamel, Doz, and Prahalad, finally, propose that success
has been achieved when a partner emerges from an alliance 'stronger and
more competitive than when it entered' (1989: 138).

   In response to such a plurality of viewpoints, Barbara Gray (Chapter 11)
provides a summary overview of five typical approaches to the assessment of
collaborative relationships. Each has a different conceptual orientation and
thus provides a singular focus on performance outcomes, including: problem

resolution and goal achievement, the generation of social capital, the creation of shared meaning, changes in the network structure in which the partner organizations are embedded, and, finally, shifts in the distribution of power.

Jeff Reuer and Mitchell Koza (Chapter 12) likewise focus on assessment issues. Given that international joint venture (IJV) longevity and stability are frequently used as indicators of collaborative success, their chapter synthesizes the theoretical and methodological rationales for this approach and the implications for theory development. A corporate strategy perspective on IJVs is provided, which proposes that the effects of IJV dynamics are meaningfully considered at the parent-firm level, and the impact of IJV longevity versus instability depends upon the firm's collaborative objectives, *ex post* exchange conditions, and the IJV's specific governance trajectory. The analysis aids in interpreting prior research and points to the value of more integrative, contingency perspectives on IJVs and their evolution.

Cooperating Behaviour

A third dimension of cooperative theory relevant to this volume is that of issues related to collaborative behaviour. It has been claimed that these, and not transaction cost advantages or resource-based synergies, provide the ingredient for a successful alliance. Faulkner, for instance, suggests that: 'positive attitudes in managing the alliance, and actions to stimulate bonding and organizational learning during the evolution of the alliance, were strongly associated with its effectiveness' (1995: 186). Indeed high levels of trust and commitment were revealed as the attitudinal and behavioural characteristics most strongly associated in his research with alliance success.

The behavioural aspects of cooperative arrangements are to be seen in three key areas (1) differing cultures and the management behaviour they give rise to, (2) the quality of trust which is so important for all joint endeavour and (3) the nature of commitment to the alliance made by the partners.

Culture

The literature on culture is vast and diverse, though marked by a handful of influential publications. Schein's (1985) seminal work on organizational culture and leadership is still one of the most cited references in a field of research much in vogue following Peters and Waterman's (1982) popular volume. It sits comfortably alongside Hofstede's (1980; 1991) work on national cultures in the workplace. Those engaged in international strategic collaborations will have to take into account both types in setting realistic expectations and putting into place appropriate operating rules, including those governing communication and performance measurement, rather than using their own organizational routines at the interface between partners (cf. Doz, 1996).

Within the organizational culture literature, Schein's (1985) proposed distinction between artefacts, values, and basic assumptions appears well accepted. Though some prefer to use a different terminology or add levels to his proposed hierarchy (e.g. Kilmann, Saxton, and Serpa, 1985), his linkages between the three levels of culture (here ranked from the most superficial to the deepest) have not been questioned (Genefke, 1998). This literature also agrees on culture as a deep-seated, sense-making medium, allowing for the allocation of authority, power, status, and the selection of organization members, providing norms for handling interpersonal relationships and intimacy, and criteria for dispensing rewards and punishments, as well as ways to cope with unmanageable, unpredictable, and stressful events (Denison and Mishra, 1995; Schein, 1985).

Although the demarcations between corporate culture and national culture conceptions appear somewhat vague, national culture is thought by some to reside mostly in values (e.g. Hofstede, 1991), whereas corporate culture is lodged primarily in practices. Hofstede (1991) views homogeneity as a measure of strength and heterogeneity as a potential source of weakness. Others think that only companies from different cultures have much to gain from each other in a learning sense. Indeed both opinions would appear as intuitively convincing in relation to the respective cultures of the partners. First, only companies with similar cultures are likely to relate well enough to achieve successful strategic alliances, as companies from very different cultures are likely to spend so much time trying to understand each other or engaging in misunderstandings that they are unlikely to achieve added value. Yet only companies from different cultures have much to gain from each other in a learning sense, appreciating their differences and viewing them as learning opportunities. Hence both conjectures may have some validity depending upon specific circumstances.

Clearly, an understanding of both corporate and national types of culture is important for strategy development, particularly for strategies of cooperation. Not only can they limit the range of strategic options and possible partner organizations sensibly available to a firm, but cooperative strategies cannot be implemented if they run against powerful cultural beliefs (Schein, 1985). However, though most alliances are established because of perceived strategic fit (complementary assets and perceived potential synergies, for instance), the alliances that fail appear to do so frequently because of poor cultural fit (Faulkner, 1995). The ICI–Pharma collaboration is a choice example, illustrating how a too strong corporate culture like ICI's can inhibit collaboration. The cultural aspects of cooperative strategy are therefore crucial, yet often neglected by would-be partners in the selection and negotiation stages of their relationship. Indeed, a cultural fit between collaborating firms can serve to provide a basis on which mutual confidence and trust can develop (Bleeke and Ernst, 1993; Faulkner, 1995).

Although this theme is receiving more attention within both the strategic management literature and alliance practice, it is still under-developed and under-recognized. For instance, it raises the important question of how much autonomy a cooperative unit, such as a joint venture, should enjoy from its parent-partners in order to have the freedom to develop a good cultural fit in terms of its own identity and way of operating (cf. Lyles and Reger, 1993).

Robert Pitkethly, David Faulkner, and John Child (Chapter 13), using examples from the extreme of interdependence of cooperative arrangements (Lorange and Roos, 1992), the international merger or acquisition, examine the effects of the differing management cultures on acquisitions of UK companies by four foreign nationals—American, Japanese, French, and German. They conclude that the national culture of the acquirer does make a difference, and that each of the five researched national cultures had recognizable characteristics, but that there is no clear best way to integrate an acquisition.

Trust

Management is critically about attitudes and interpersonal relationships. Indeed, trust and goodwill have been found to be vital in alliances of all kinds (Killing, 1983; Buckley and Casson, 1988; Lynch, 1993).

Goodwill and trust were found to have a stabilizing effect on the relationship at all development stages. They increased the partners' tolerance for each other's behaviour and helped avoid conflicts. Goodwill and trust also raised the general level of communication between the partners, and thereby increased the chances for uncovering and dealing with operating misfit (Niederkofler, 1991).

Lynch (1993) emphasizes the need for partner rapport, and consequently advises that two-year secondments are too short to build this rapport and commitment. Kanter (1989) stresses that running alliances requires very different attitudes and behaviour from running hierarchies. Consensus building replaces decision taking, and respect in alliances comes not with rank but with knowledge and the ability to get things done.

Historically, however, the trust literature appears to have suffered from concept stretching, as is evident in, for instance, the assumed equivalence of trust and cooperation, or indeed the supposed requisite of trust for cooperative behaviour to unfold (e.g. Deutsch, 1962). When observing cooperative behaviour, it was assumed to be based on trust (Kee and Knox, 1970). As Currall and Inkpen (chap. 15, below) demonstrate, much of the early trust literature based on Deutsch's work can be faulted for stretching the definition of trust, having not maintained a clear distinction between trust and cooperative action. Indeed, not until Kee and Knox (1970) and Kimmel (1974) argued that cooperative behaviour could legitimately result from alternative psychological states, did the literature more carefully distinguish between the two.

Child and Faulkner (1998) break trust down into (1) 'calculative' trust, which sees synergies between firms and takes the risk that the new partner will behave appropriately, (2) 'predictive' trust that is built over time through both firms keeping their promises and meeting their deadlines, and (3) 'affective' trust which comes about as friendship develops between the partners. Sako (1998), similarly, has a threefold categorization of trust. There is, first, contractual trust, which means the expectation that the partner will carry out its contractual agreements; secondly, competence trust, that is, that the partner is capable of doing what it says it will do; and, thirdly, goodwill trust, in which the partner makes a commitment to take initiatives for mutual benefit while refraining from taking unfair advantage of the other partner. In Sako's view, 'Trust is a social norm which lessens the need to use hierarchy to attenuate opportunism...Whatever the formal governance structure, the higher the level of mutual trust, the better the performance is likely to be.'

Barney and Hansen (1994) identify trust as a source of competitive advantage. They also see three types: 'weak form', which arises when there are only limited possibilities for opportunism; 'semi-strong form' is similar to contractual trust and depends on agreements which create a governance structure; and 'strong-form' trust which emerges in response to a set of norms that guide partners' behaviour. They argue that only strong-form trust leads to competitive advantage.

Trust gives rise not only to lower transaction costs and higher investment returns, but also to more rapid innovation and learning according to Sabel (1994), as a consequence of a joint problem-solving attitude by the partners, free of the constraints that follow from anticipated defection.

Commitment

Commitment differs from trust. It is possible to be very committed, even dependent on a partner, but not to trust it. Although perhaps an uncomfortable situation to be in, it is not uncommon in alliances (Bleeke and Ernst, 1995). It is equally possible to trust one's partner, but at the same time be committed only to a limited degree, preserving viable alternative courses of action.

Commitment can be signalled in a number of ways. It may be shown by committing large capital investments to a project (Gulati, Khanna, and Nohria, 1994), or by demonstrating a determination to stick with the deal even when 'the going gets rough', and profits are hard to come by. Sako (1998) suggests that one mechanism for creating commitment is for one partner to provide free technical assistance to another, thus incurring costs by binding the partner to it. The disclosure of proprietary information to a partner may have the same effect, although it does, of course, increase risk.

Evidence shows, however, that the partners at both top management and at lower levels must demonstrate commitment if the alliance is to endure (Faulkner, 1995). It is not sufficient that it be only at top management level, since its absence lower down the partner company may nullify the beneficial effect of the commitment at the top.

Paul Olk and Christopher Early (Chapter 14) examine the importance of interpersonal relationships including trust in international strategic alliances. They regard this aspect of alliances as a much-neglected one, and set out to remedy this neglect. Steven Currall and Andrew Inkpen (Chapter 15) pursue the theme of trust in joint ventures but do not limit it to interpersonal relationships, nor conceive of it as synonymous with cooperative behaviour. They view trust relationships as able to develop at three distinct levels: the interpersonal, the intergroup, and the inter-firm levels, each level requiring different forms of measurement and of analysis. Still pursuing the trust theme David Faulkner (Chapter 16) suggests that the need for control in alliances is in many situations the reciprocal of the existence of trust. If you really trust your partner the need for stringent monitoring and control systems disappears and transaction costs are correspondingly reduced. He illustrates this by reference to a number of case studies. Finally, in addition to the various agendas embedded in each of the chapters, Ranjay Gulati and Edward Zajac (Chapter 17), and Faulkner and de Rond (Chapter 18) propose a number of exciting new opportunities for theory development and the empirical study of cooperative strategy.

Conclusion

This chapter has attempted to provide a synoptic view of the major themes and theories found within the strategy and organization theory literature, particularly in relation to the rationale for the creation of cooperative relationships, their evolution, and behavioural characteristics. It has also indicated where, in the belief of the editors, the individual contributions that compose this book fit, in relation to these theories and themes. The remainder of the book is composed of those contributions.

References

ACHROL, R. S., SCHEER, L. K., and STERN, L. W. (1990), *Designing Successful Transorganizational Marketing Alliances*, (Cambridge, Mass.: Marketing Science Institute).

ALDRICH, H. and WHETTEN, D. A. (1981), 'Organization-Sets, Action-Sets, and Networks: Making the Most of Simplicity', in P. C. Nystrom and W. H. Starbuck Nystrom (eds.), *Handbook of Organizational Design*, (New York: Oxford University Press).

ANDERSON, E. and GATIGNON, H. (1986), 'Modes of Foreign Entry: A Transaction Cost Analysis and Propositions', *Journal of International Business Studies*, 17: 1–26.

ARGYRIS, C. and SCHON, D. (1978), *Organizational Learning: A Theory of Action Perspective* (Reading, Mass.: Addison-Wesley).

ARINO, A. and DE LA TORRE, J. (1998), 'Learning from Failure: Towards an Evolutionary Model of Collaborative Ventures', *Organization Science*, 9: 306–25.

ARROW, K. J. (1985), 'The Economics of Agency', in J. W. Pratt and R. J. Zechauser (eds.), *Principals and Agents* (Boston: Harvard University Press).

AXELROD, R. (1984), *The Evolution of Cooperation* (London: Harper Collins).

BAGHAI, M., COLEY, S. C., and WHITE, D. (1996), 'Staircases to Growth', *McKinsey Quarterly*, 4: 38–61.

BARNEY, J. (1991), 'Firm Resources and Sustainable Competitive Advantage', *Journal of Management*, 17: 99–120.

——and HANSEN, M. H. (1994), 'Trustworthiness as a Source of Competitive Advantage', *Strategic Management Journal*, 7: 175–90.

——and OUCHI, W. (1986), *Organizational Economics* (San Francisco, Calif.: Jossey-Bass).

BERKOWITZ, S. D. (1982), *An Introduction to Structural Analysis* (Toronto: Butterworths).

BERLE, A. A. and MEANS, G. C., JR. (1932), *The Modern Corporation and Private Property* (New York: Harcourt, Brace, and World).

BLAU, P. M. (1967), *Exchange and Power in Social Life* (New York: Wiley).

BLEEKE, J. and ERNST, D. (1993), *Collaborating to Compete: Using Strategic Alliances and Acquisitions in the Global Marketplace* (New York: Wiley).

——(1995), 'Is your strategic alliance really a sale?', *Harvard Business Review*, 97–105.

BOISOT, M. and CHILD, J. (1988), 'The Iron Law of Fiefs: Bureaucratic Failure and the Problem of Governance in the Chinese Economic Reforms', *Administrative Science Quarterly*, 33: 507–27.

BOUCHIKHI, H., DE ROND, M., and LEROUX, V. (1998), 'Alliances as Social Facts: A Constructivist Theory of Interorganizational Collaboration', *ESSEC Working Paper* (École Supérieure des Sciences Économiques et Commerciales), DR98037.

BOWMAN, C. and FAULKNER, D. O. (1997), *Competitive and Corporate Strategy* (London: Irwin).

BUCKLEY, P. and CASSON, M. (1985), *The Economic Theory of the Multinational Enterprise* (London: Macmillan).

——'A Theory of Cooperation in International Business', in F. Contractor and P. Lorange (eds.), *Cooperative Strategies in International Business* (Lexington, Mass.: Lexington Books).

——and CHAPMAN, M. (1993), 'The Management of Cooperative Strategies', *Working Paper* (Bradford: University of Bradford Management Centre).

BURT, R. S. (1992), 'The Social Structure of Competition', in N. Eccles and R. G. Nohria (eds.), *Networks and Organizations: Structure, Form, and Action* (Boston: Harvard Business School Press), 57–91.

CHI, T. (1994), 'Trading in Strategic Resources: Necessary Conditions, Transaction Cost Problems, and Choice of Exchange Structure', *Strategic Management Journal*, 15: 271–90.

CHILD, J. (1972), 'Organizational Structure, Environment and Performance: The Role of Strategic Choice', *Sociology*, 6: 1–22.

—— and FAULKNER, D. O. (1998), *Strategies of Cooperation: Managing Alliances, Networks, and Joint Ventures* (Oxford: Oxford University Press).

—— and RODRIGUES, S. (1996), 'The Role of Social Identity in the International Transfer of Knowledge through Joint Ventures', in S. Clegg and G. Palmer (eds.), *Producing Management Knowledge* (London: Sage), 46–68.

CIBORRA, C. (1991), 'Alliances as Learning Experiments: Cooperation, Competition and Change in Hightech Industries', in L. K. Mytelka (ed.), *Strategic Partnerships: States, Firms and International Competition* (London: Pinter), 51–77.

COASE, R. H. (1937), 'The Nature of the Firm', *Economica N. S.*, 4: 386–405.

COHEN, M. D., MARCH, J. G., and OLSEN, J. P. (1972), 'A Garbage Can Model of Organizational Choice', *Administrative Science Quarterly*, 17: 1–25.

COHEN, W. M. and LEVINTHAL, D. A. (1990), 'Absorptive Capacity: A New Perspective on Learning and Innovation', *Administrative Science Quarterly*, 35: 128–52.

CONNER, K. R. (1991), 'A Historical Comparison of Resource Based Theory and Five Schools of Thought within Industrial Organization Economics: Do we Have a New Theory of the Firm?', *Journal of Management*, 17: 121–54.

CONTRACTOR, F. J. and LORANGE, P. (1988), *Cooperative Strategies in International Business* (New York: Lexington Books).

COPELAND, T. E. and KEENAN, P. T. (1998), 'Making Real Options Real', *McKinsey Quarterly*, 3: 128–41.

D'AUNNO, T. A. and ZUCKERMAN, H. S. (1987), 'A Life Cycle Model of Organizational Federations: The Case of Hospitals', *Academy of Management Review*, 12: 534–45.

DENISON, R. D. and MISHRA, A. K. (1995), 'Toward a Theory of Organizational Culture and Effectiveness', *Organization Science*, 6: 204–23.

DE ROND, M. and FAULKNER, D. O. (1997), 'The Evolution of Non-Joint Venture Alliances: The Case of The Royal Bank of Scotland and Banco Santander', paper presented at the 4th International Conference on Partnerships and Co-operative Strategies (Balliol College, Oxford, July).

DEUTSCH, M. (1962), 'Cooperation and Trust: Some Theoretical Notes', in M. R. Jones (ed.), *Nebraska Symposium on Motivation* (Lincoln, Nebr.: University of Nebraska Press).

DONALDSON, L. (1995), *American Anti-Management Theories of Organization: A Critique of Paradigm Proliferation* (Cambridge: Cambridge University Press).

DOZ, Y. L. (1988), 'Technology Partnerships between Larger and Smaller Firms: Some Critical Issues', *International Studies of Management and Organization*, 17: 31–57.

—— (1996), 'The Evolution of Cooperation in Strategic Alliances: Initial Conditions or Learning Processes?', *Strategic Management Journal*, 17: 55–83.

—— and SHUEN, A. (1995), 'From Intent to Outcome: The Evolution and Governance of Interfirm Partnerships', in INSEAD Working Papers (INSEAD).

EISENHARDT, K. M. (1989), 'Agency Theory: An Assessment and Review', *Academy of Management Review*, 14: 57–74.

FAULKNER, D. O. (1995), *International Strategic Alliances: Co-operating to Compete* (Maidenhead: McGraw-Hill).

FORREST, J. E. and MARTIN, M. J. C. (1992), 'Strategic Alliances between Large and Small Research Intensive Organizations: Experiences in the Biotechnology Industry', *R&D Management*, 22: 41–54.

FRANCIS, A., TURK, J., and WILLMAN, P. (1983), *Power, Efficiency and Institutions: A Critical Appraisal of the Markets and Hierarchies' Paradigm* (London: Heinemann).

GENEFKE, J. (1998), 'Joining Two Organizational Units: Managing Cultural Threats and Possibilities', Paper presented at the 5th International Conference on Multi-Organizational Partnerships and Cooperative Strategy (Oxford, July).

GIDDENS, A. (1984) [1997], *The Constitution of Society* (Cambridge: Polity Press).

GOMES-CASSERES, B. (1996), *The Alliance Revolution: The New Shape of Business Rivalry* (Cambridge, Mass.: Harvard University Press).

GRANT, R. M. (1991), 'The Resource-Based Theory of Competitive Advantage: Implications for Strategy Formulation', *California Management Review*, 33: 114–35.

GRAY, B. and YAN, A. (1997), 'Formation and Evolution of International Joint Ventures: Examples from U.S.–Chinese Partnerships', in P. Beamish and J. P. Killing (eds.), *Cooperative Strategies: Asian Pacific Perspectives* (San Francisco, Calif: New Lexington Press), 57–88.

GULATI, R. (1993), 'The Dynamics of Alliance Formation', PhD thesis (Harvard).

—— (1995a), 'Social Structure and Alliance Formation Patterns: A Longitudinal Analysis', *Administrative Science Quarterly*, 40: 619–52.

—— (1995b), 'Does Familiarity Breed Trust? The Implications of Repeated Ties for Contractual Choice in Alliances', *Academy of Management Journal*, 38: 85–112.

—— (1998), 'Alliances and Networks', *Strategic Management Journal*, 19: 293–317.

—— (1999), 'Network Location and Learning: The Influence of Network Resources and Firm Capabilities on Alliance Formation', *Strategic Management Journal*, 20: 397–420.

—— KHANNA, T., and NOHRIA, N. (1994), 'Unilateral Commitments and the Importance of Process in Alliances', *Sloan Management Review*, 61–9.

HAMEL, G. (1991), 'Competition for Competence and Interpartner Learning within International Strategic Alliances', *Strategic Management Journal*, 12: 83–103.

—— and PRAHALAD, C. K. (1994), *Competing for the Future*, (Boston: Harvard Business School Press).

—— DOZ, Y. L., and PRAHALAD, C. K. (1989), 'Collaborate with your Competitors—And Win', *Harvard Business Review*, 67: 133–9.

HARRIGAN, K. R. (1988), 'Strategic Alliances and Partner Asymmetries', in F. J. Contractor and P. Lorange (eds.), *Cooperative Strategies in International Business* (New York: Lexington Books), 205–26.

HENNERT, J. F. (1988), 'A Transaction Cost Theory of Equity Joint Ventures', *Strategic Management Journal*, 9: 361–74.

—— (1991), 'The Transaction Cost Theory of Joint Ventures', *Management Science* 37: 483–97.

HOFSTEDE, G. (1980), *Culture's Consequences: International Differences in Work-Related Values* (Beverly Hills, Calif.: Sage).

—— (1991), *Cultures and Organizations: Software of the Mind* (Maidenhead: McGraw-Hill).

HYMER, S. H. (1972), 'The Internationalization of Capital', *The Journal of Economic Issues*, 6: 91–105.

IBARRA, H. (1992), 'Structural Alignments, Individual Strategies, and Managerial Action: Elements Toward a Network Theory of Getting Things Done', in

N. Eccles and R. G. Nohria (eds.), *Networks and Organizations: Structure, Form, and Action* (Boston, Mass.: Harvard Business School Press), 165–88.

INKPEN, A. (1995), *The Management of International Joint Ventures: An Organizational Learning Perspective* (London: Routledge).

——and CROSSAN, M. M. (1995), 'Believing is Seeing: Joint Ventures and Organizational Learning', *Journal of Management Studies*, 32: 595–618.

JENSEN, M. and MECKLING, W. (1976), 'Theory of the Firm: Managerial Behaviour, Agency Costs, and Ownership Structure', *Journal of Financial Economics*, 3: 305–60.

JONES, C., HESTERLY, W. S., and BORGATTI, S. P. (1997), 'A General Theory of Network Governance: Exchange Conditions and Social Mechanisms', *Academy of Management Review*, 22: 911–45.

KANTER, R. M. (1989), *When Giants Learn to Dance* (London: Simon & Schuster).

——(1994), 'Collaborative Advantage: The Art of Alliances', *Harvard Business Review*, July–Aug., 96–108.

KAY, J. A. (1993), *Foundations of Corporate Success* (New York: Oxford University Press).

KEE, H. and KNOX, R. (1970), 'Conceptual and Metholodogical Considerations in the Study of Trust', *Journal of Conflict Resolution*, 14: 357–66.

KILLING, J. P. (1983), *Strategy for Joint Venture Success* (London: Croom Helm).

——(1988), 'Understanding Alliances: The Role of Task and Organizational Complexity', in F. J. Contractor and P. Lorange (eds.), *Cooperative Strategies in International Business* (New York: Lexington Books), 55–67.

KILMANN, SAXTON, SERPA & Associates (1985), *Gaining Control of the Corporate Culture* (London: Jossey-Bass Publishers).

KIMBERLY, J. R. and BOUCHIKHI, H. (1995), 'The Dynamics of Organizational Development and Change: How the Past Shapes the Present and Constrains the Future', *Organization Science*, 6: 9–18.

KIMMEL, M. (1974), *On Distinguishing Interpersonal Trust from Cooperative Responding in the Prisoner's Dilemma Game* (Detroit: Wayne State University Press).

KOGUT, B. (1988), 'Joint Ventures: Theoretical and Emperical Perspectives', *Strategic Management Journal*, 9: 319–32.

KOZA, M. P. and LEWIN, A. Y. (1998), 'The Co-evolution of Strategic Alliances', *Organization Science*, 9: 255–64.

LACITY, M. C., WILLCOCKS, L., and FEENY, D. F. (1997), 'The Value of Selective IT Sourcing', in L. Willcocks, D. Feeny, and G. Islei (eds.), *Managing Information Technology as a Strategic Resource*, (London: McGraw-Hill), 277–305.

LEAVITT, H. J. (1965), 'Applied Organizational Change in Industry: Structural, Technological and Humanistic Approaches', in J. G. March (ed.), *Handbook of Organizations* (Chicago: Rand McNally), 1144–70.

LORANGE, P. and ROOS, J. (1992), *Strategic Alliances: Formation, Implementation and Evolution* (Oxford: Blackwell).

————and BRONN, P. S. (1992), 'Building Successful Strategic Alliances', *Long Range Planning*, 25: 10–17.

LYLES, M. A. and REGER, R. K. (1993), 'Managing for Autonomy in Joint Ventures: A Longitudinal Study of Upward Influence', *Journal of Management Studies*, 30: 383–404.

LYNCH, R. P. (1993), *Business Alliances Guide: The Hidden Competitive Weapon* (New York: Wiley).

McFARLAN, W. and NOLAN, R. (1995), 'How to Manage an IT Outsourcing Alliance', *Sloan Management Review*, 36: 9–24.

McGAHAN, A. M. and PORTER, M. E. (1997), 'How Much does Industry Matter, Really?', *Strategic Management Journal*, 18: 15–30.

MOHR, J. and SPEKMAN, R. (1994), 'Characteristics of Partnership Success: Partnership Attributes, Communication Behaviour, and Conflict Resolution Techniques', *Strategic Management Journal*, 15: 135–52.

MOORE, J. F. (1996), *The Death of Competition: Leadership and Strategy in the Age of Business Ecosystems* (Chichester: Wiley).

MURRAY, E. A., JR. and MAHON, J. F. (1993), 'Strategic Alliances: Gateway to the New Europe?', *Long Range Planning*, 26: 102–11.

NALEBUFF, B. and BRANDENBURGER, A. (1996), *Co-opetition* (New York: Doubleday).

NIEDERKOFLER, M. (1991), The Evolution of Strategic Alliances: Opportunities for Managerial Influence, *Journal of Business Venturing* 237–257.

NOHRIA, N. (1992), 'Is a Network Perspective a Useful Way of Studying Organizations?', in N. Eccles and R. G. Nohria (eds.), *Networks and Organizations: Structure, Form, and Action* (Boston: Harvard Business School Press), 1–22.

NONAKA, I. and TAKEUCHI, H. (1995), *The Knowledge-Creating Company* (New York: Oxford University Press).

OHMAE, K. (1989), 'The Global Logic of Strategic Alliances', *Harvard Business Review*, Mar.–Apr., 143–54.

OVIATT, B. M. and McDOUGALL, P. P. (1994), 'Towards a Theory of International Ventures', *Journal of International Business Studies*, 69: 45–64.

PARKHE, A. (1993), 'Messy Research, Methodological Predispositions, and Theory Development in International Joint Ventures', *Academy of Management Review*, 18: 227–68.

PENROSE, E. (1959), *The Theory of the Growth of the Firm* (Oxford: Blackwell).

PETERAF, M. (1993), 'The Cornerstones of Competitive Advantage: A Resource-Based View', *Strategic Management Journal*, 14: 179–91.

PETERS, T. J. and WATERMAN, R. H., JR. (1982), *In Search of Excellence: Lessons from America's Best-Run Companies* (New York: Harper & Row).

PETTIGREW, A. M. (1987), 'Context and Action in the Transformation of the Firm', *Journal of Management Studies*, 24: 649–70.

PFEFFER, J. (1982), *Organizations and Organization Theory* (London: Pitman).

—— and SALANCIK, G. (1978), *The External Control of Organizations* (New York: Harper).

PORTER, M. E. (1980), *Competitive Strategy* (New York: The Free Press).

—— (1985), *Competitive Advantage* (New York: The Free Press).

—— (1996), 'What is Strategy?' *Harvard Business Review*, 61–78.

—— and FULLER, M. B. (1986), 'Coalitions and Global Strategy', in M. E. Porter (ed.), *Competition in Global Industries* (Boston; Harvard Business School Press), 315–44.

POWELL, W. W. (1990), 'Neither Market nor Hierarchy: Network Forms of Organization', *Research in Organizational Behaviour*, 12: 295–336.

RICARDO, D. (1891), *Principles of Political Economy and Taxation* (London: G. Bell).

RICHARDSON, G. B. (1972), 'The Organization of Industry', *Economic Journal*, 82: 883–96.

RING, P. S. and VAN DE VEN, A. H. (1994), 'Developmental Processes of Cooperative Interorganisational Relationships', *Academy of Management Review*, 19: 90–118.

ROEHL, T. W. and TRUITT, J. F. (1987), 'Stormy Open Marriages are Better', *Columbia Journal of World Business*, Summer, 87–95.

RUMELT, R. P. (1984), 'Towards a Strategic Theory of the Firm', in B. Lamb (ed.), *Competitive Strategic Management* (Englewood Cliffs, NJ: Prentice Hall), 556–70.

—— (1991), 'How Much does Industry Matter?', *Strategic Management Journal*, 12: 167–85.

SABEL, C. F. (1994), 'Learning by Monitoring: The Institutions of Economic Development', in N. J. Smelser and R. Swedberg (eds.), *The Handbook of Economic Sociology* (Princeton, NJ: Princeton University Press).

SAKO, M. (1998), 'Does Trust Improve Business Performance?', in C. Lane and R. Backmann (eds.), *Trust In And Between Organizations* (Oxford: Oxford University Press).

SCHEIN, E. H. (1985), *Organizational Culture and Leadership* (San Francisco: Jossey-Bass).

SCHUMPETER, J. (1934), *The Economic Theory of Development* (Cambridge, Mass.: Harvard University Press).

SHORTELL, S. M. and ZAJAC, E. J. (1988), 'Internal Corporate Joint Ventures: Development Processes and Performance Outcomes', *Strategic Management Journal*, 9: 527–42.

SINGH, K. and MITCHELL, W. (1996), 'Precarious Collaborations: Business Survival after Partners Shut Down or Form New Partnerships', *Strategic Management Journal* 17: 99–116.

SIMARD, P. (1996), 'The Structuring of Cooperative Relationships: A Multiple-Case Study of Quebec's Aerospace Sector', *Unpublished First Year Report* (University of Cambridge: Judge Institute of Management Studies), 144.

SMITH, A. (1776) [1937], *The Wealth of Nations* (New York: Modern Library).

SYDOW, J. and WINDELER, A. (1998), 'Organizing and Evaluating Interfirm Networks: A Structurationist Perspective on Network Processes and Effectiveness', *Organization Science*, 9: 265–84.

TALLMAN, S. B. and SHENKAR, O. (1994), 'A Managerial Decision Model of International Cooperative Venture Formation', *Journal of International Business Studies*, 25: 91–113.

THORELLI, H. B. (1986), 'Networks: Between Markets and Hierarchies', *Strategic Management Journal*, 7: 37–51.

VAN DE VEN, A. H. (1992), 'Suggestions for Studying Strategy Process: A Research Note', *Strategic Management Journal*, 13: 169–88.

VON NEUMANN, J. and MORGENSTERN, O. (1944), *Theory of Games and Economic Behavior* (Princeton, NJ: Princeton University Press).

WELLMAN, B. (1980), 'Network Analysis: From Metaphor and Method to Theory and Substance', *Working Paper* (University of Toronto: Structural Analysis Program).

—— (1983), 'Network Analysis: Some Basic Principles', in R. Collins (ed.), *Sociological Theory* (San Francisco: Jossey-Bass), 155–200.

WERNERFELT, B. (1984), 'A Resource-Based View of the Firm', *Strategic Management Journal*, 5: 171–80.

WHITE, H. C. (1963), *An Anatomy of Kinship* (Englewood Cliffs, NJ: Prentice Hall).

WILLIAMSON, O. E. (1975), *Markets and Hierarchies: Analysis and Antitrust Implications* (New York: The Free Press).

—— (1985), *The Economic Institutions of Capitalism: Firms, Markets and Relational Contracting* (New York: The Free Press).

—— (1993), 'Comparative Economic Organization', in S. Lindenberg and H. Schieuder (eds.), *Interdisciplinary Perspectives on Organization Studies* (Oxford: Pergamon).

ZAGARE, F. C. (1984), *Game Theory* (London: Sage).

2

Characteristics of UK International Joint Ventures with Triad and Non-Triad Partners

KEITH GLAISTER, RUMY HUSAN, AND PETER J. BUCKLEY

In the current highly competitive global environment, the international joint venture (IJV) has emerged as an important strategic alternative for many firms. IJVs enable partner firms to combine complementary capabilities and resources in order to enhance their competencies and so more effectively compete across world markets (Contractor and Lorange, 1988; Hamel, 1991; Glaister, 1996). IJVs have attracted a good deal of attention from both practising managers and a variety of academic researchers who have examined the core dimensions of IJV activity in terms of motives for IJV formation, partner selection criteria, issues in IJV management, and control and IJV performance (Parkhe, 1993).

Despite the apparent growth in the incidence of IJVs and the popularity of this organizational form, there is a paucity of systematic information regarding the formation of IJVs by UK firms. In an attempt to rectify this lack of information, this chapter identifies and analyses some basic trends and patterns in international joint venture formation between UK firms and partners in the Triad (North America, Western Europe, and Japan) and non-Triad countries over the 1990–6 period. The principal goal of the chapter is to provide an accurate factual picture of UK international joint venture activity and to examine variation across characteristics of the sample, including partner country groups, industries, and purpose. The salience of IJV activity, in terms of the apparent frequency with which firms are prepared to adopt this organizational form, and the impact on the competitive position of firms engaging in this activity, warrants detailed consideration of this important corporate strategy.

A number of studies have reported on the trend in IJV formation since the late 1970s (Hladik, 1985; Beamish, 1988; Hergert and Morris, 1988; Hagedoorn and Schakenraad, 1993; Hagedoorn, 1996). Recently, Beamish and Delios (1997) have used three large data sources to measure the number of international alliances formed across the Triad. While previous studies have

This article is reprinted with permission from the *Journal of General Management* where it was first published in vol. 24 no. 2 (Winter 1998).

provided information on inter-firm cooperation among the Triad (Hergert and Morris, 1988; Hagedoorn and Schakenraad, 1993; Hagedoorn, 1996; Beamish and Delios, 1997), they report aggregate data for Europe and do not identify IJV formation at the UK level. The detailed activity of UK firms in IJV formation with Triad partners over a significant period of time has been considered in only one prior study (Glaister and Buckley, 1994), which covered the period of the 1980s. There have been no systematic studies recently reported of UK IJV formation with firms from either the Triad or non-Triad countries.

Research Method

The database for this chapter comprises all the IJVs formed between January 1990 and December 1996 that were recorded in the FT M&A File. This is an on-line database providing comprehensive details on international bid activity including mergers, acquisitions, share swaps, buy-outs and buy-ins, as well as joint ventures. The information is researched and collated on a daily basis from an array of major international newspapers and magazines, as well as press releases and corporate and stock-market sources. Examples include the *Financial Times*, the *Wall Street Journal Europe*, *Les Echos*, *Frankfurter Allgemeine Zeitung*, *Il Sole 24 Ore*, *Australian Financial Review*, and *Investors Chronicle*. This wide coverage enables the avoidance of potential 'oversight' and the minimization of 'non-coverage' inherent in previous studies which tended to confine data collection to only one or two newspapers. A further advantage of this database for identifying UK IJV activity is that it uses consistent sample selection criteria.

The focus is, therefore, on the addition to the stock of IJVs over this period. For each of the IJVs in the sample, information was recorded on the following variables:

- the date the IJV was cited in the database—as an approximation for the year in which it was formed;
- the names of the parent firms and the IJV (where applicable);
- the countries in which the foreign parents' head offices were located;
- the principal industry both of the parents and of the IJV itself;
- the purpose of the IJV in terms of its operating function;
- the UK parents' equity share in the IJV.

This method of deriving an IJV database from press announcements follows a well established precedent, with the publications used varying with the geographical area of interest. Hergert and Morris (1988), for example, used the *Financial Times* and the *Economist*; Ghemawat, Porter, and Rawlinson (1986) made use of the *Wall Street Journal*, Osborn and Baugh (1987) the *Japanese Economic Journal* and the *Asian Wall Street Journal*, and Glaister and Buckley (1994) the *Financial Times*.

As with all studies which draw data from newspapers and magazines, it is necessary to recognize the limitations of the data source. The press is more likely to report IJV formation between large and relatively well-known firms than between medium and small-sized partner firms. The sample may therefore be biased towards larger-sized firms. More fundamentally, IJV formation may occur and go unreported even though the press is informed of the activity. Unfortunately, it is not possible to estimate the extent of the unreported activity. Second, the published articles may have used publicity statements by the partner firms as primary sources of information, in which case these statements may represent biased accounts of the characteristics of the IJV (Hergert and Morris, 1998). Partner firms may deliberately misrepresent themselves to the press in order to mislead competitors over their motives and activities. Moreover, some partners may wish to maintain such strict confidentiality that the press is not informed of the activity, so IJV formation may take place but go unreported.

Findings and Discussion

Some illustrative examples of UK IJVs from the sample are shown in Table 2.1.

TABLE 2.1 *Illustrative examples of UK IJVs with Triad and non-Triad partners*

IJVs with Triad partners
1. UK–Western Europe
   In 1995 Cable & Wireless formed two IJVs with the German company Veba to develop their respective telecommunications businesses. The first IJV, named 'Vebacom', is based in Germany and is owned 55% by Veba and 45% by Cable & Wireless, with Veba having management control. The second is 'Cable & Wireless Europe', a 50–50 IJV, formed for the purpose of new business development and management of existing operations in the EU and Switzerland (excluding the UK and Germany), and is under Cable & Wireless's management control.

2. UK–North America
   Scottish Power formed an IJV with Utilicorp of the USA in 1992 for the supply of gas to customers in Scotland. The IJV, called 'Caledonian Gas' (but trading as Scottish Power) is owned 75% by Scottish Power and 25% by Utilicorp.

3. UK–Japan.
   In 1991 BP formed an IJV with Mitsubishi Rayon for the manufacture and distribution of specialist chemicals in Europe. The UK-based IJV, 'Newton Chemicals', is owned 60% by BP, 39% by Mitsubishi Rayon, with Osaka Organic Chemical Industry holding 1%.

IJVs with non-Triad Partners
1. UK–Eastern Europe
   The engineering group Brown and Root set up an IJV with Skoda Koncern Plzen of the Czech Republic in May 1993 for engineering and modernization projects in

Central and Eastern Europe. The IJV, named 'BaR Skoda' is 66% owned by Brown and Root and 34% owned by Skoda Koncern Plzen.

2. UK–China

The brewing and distilling conglomerate Bass plc formed an IJV in July 1995 with Ginsber Beer Group of China (part of the Hong Zui Corp.), for a brewing plant with a 200,000 tonne capacity. The IJV, named 'Bass Ginsber Beer Co.' is 55% owned by Bass and 45% owned by Ginsber.

3. UK–India

In August 1996 Whyte and Mackay announced an IJV with Radico Khaitan of India for the production and marketing of whisky in India. The IJV, named 'Whyte and Mackay (India)' will be 51% owned by Whyte and Mackay and 49% owned by Khaitan.

4. UK–Pacific Rim

Lucas Industries established an IJV with Pindad and Metinca Dirgantara of Indonesia in March 1996 for the manufacturing of precision components for the Indonesian and international aerospace industry. The IJV, named 'Lucas Pindad Aerospace Indonesia' is 51% owned by Lucas, 34% by Pindad, and 15% by Metinca Dirgantara. Metinca will provide sales and marketing support for the IJV.

Trends in UK IJV Formation over Time

Figure 2.1 traces UK IJV formation over the 1990–6 period. For the first four years of the period there was relatively slow growth in UK IJV formation, with the number of ventures formed with partners from the Triad clearly exceeding the numbers formed with partners from the non-Triad countries. From 1993, however, there was an acceleration in IJV formation, particularly with partners from the non-Triad, with new venture formation with partners from the latter exceeding IJV formation with partners from the Triad in the final two years of the period. While there appears to have been a plateau reached in IJV formation with Triad partners, IJV formation with non-Triad partners appears to have peaked in 1995. This is reflected in the total IJV formations which also peaked in 1995 and declined somewhat in the following year. The commonly held view that IJV formation is on a rising trend is supported by the data for most of the period. However, the final year of the data indicates that a peak in IJV formation may have been reached. Whether the bubble has burst on UK IJV formation remains to be seen, but the indications from this study would imply that the popularity of this organizational form may have suffered a setback as far as UK firms are concerned, though this may be a temporary phenomenon.

The geographical distribution of UK IJV formation by major partner groupings in the Triad is shown in Table 2.2. Almost 60 per cent of the IJVs were formed with partners from the Triad, particularly with partners located in Western Europe. The leading partner firms in the non-Triad group are located in China and the Pacific Rim, although none of the individual

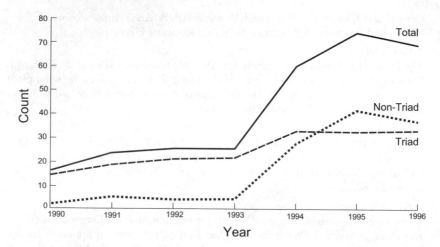

Fig. 2.1 UK International Joint Venture formation with Triad and non-Triad partners, 1990–1996

TABLE 2.2 *UK international Joint Venture formation, 1990–1996, by nationality of foreign partner*

Region	N.	%
North America	58	20.1
Japan	19	6.6
Western Europe	93	32.2
Triad	170	58.8
Pacific Rim	31	10.7
India	24	8.3
China	33	11.4
Transition Economies	19	6.6
Others	12	4.2
Non-Triad	119	41.2
Total	289	100.0

Notes: Pacific Rim includes Australia; Transition Economies include Russia, the former states of the Soviet Union, and the countries of Central and Eastern Europe; Others refers to Algeria, Brazil, Cuba, countries of the Middle East, and South Africa.

Excludes 12 IJVs where nationality of foreign partner is not known.

groupings of the non-Triad partners exceed the frequency with which IJV partnerships are formed with firms in either Western Europe or North America.

To test formally the view that the incidence of IJV formation had changed over the period covered by this study, the number of IJVs established in the first four years of the period (1990–3) was compared with the number formed in the final three years of the period (1994–6), according to the region of the foreign partner (see the summary in Table 2.8, below). The chi-square test shows that the time period of IJV formation and the region of the foreign partner are not independent (chi-square statistic = 31.41; d.f. = 1; p < 0.000). It is clear that there has been a significant increase in UK IJV formation with partners from the two regions of the world over the period of the study, as indicated in Figure 2.1.

Industry Characteristics of UK IJVs

The distribution of UK IJV formation across industry groupings for each year of the time period for both Triad and non-Triad partners is shown in Table 2.3. The proportion of IJVs formed in the manufacturing sector (51.4 per cent) was only marginally greater than the proportion formed in the tertiary sector (48.5 per cent), with very few IJVs formed in agriculture (0.7 per cent). In the tertiary sector IJV formation occurred most frequently in 'other services' and in financial services, while in manufacturing, IJV formation occurred most frequently in 'other manufacturing'. For most of the industries, the incidence of IJV formation is greater over the last three years of the time period. The main exception is in construction, which witnessed marginally more IJVs formed in the first four years of the time period.

TABLE 2.3   *UK IJV formation by industry, 1990–1996*

Industry	Year							Total	
	1990	1991	1992	1993	1994	1995	1996	N.	%
Agriculture	—	—	—	—	—	1	1	2	0.7
Food and drink	—	1	—	1	5	8	7	22	7.3
Metals and minerals	—	—	—	—	6	6	2	14	4.7
Energy	1	1	4	2	3	1	5	17	5.6
Construction	—	3	1	1	—	—	2	7	2.3
Chemicals	—	1	1	—	2	4	4	12	4.0
Pharmaceuticals	—	—	1	1	1	4	1	8	2.7
Telecommunications	—	—	1	1	2	—	—	4	1.3
Other electrical	—	2	1	1	2	1	2	9	3.0
Automobiles	—	—	1	—	2	6	8	17	5.6
Aerospace	1	—	—	1	1	—	4	7	2.3
Other manufacturing	7	2	2	3	7	7	8	36	12.0
Transport	1	3	—	—	1	—	3	8	2.7
Distribution	1	2	4	4	8	6	1	26	8.6
Financial services	2	4	4	—	8	16	6	40	13.3
Other services	3	6	6	10	12	15	20	72	23.9
Total	16	25	26	25	60	75	74	301	100.0

In order to test for changes in IJV formation in particular industries over time, the data was reclassified into the following three broad industry groupings:

Group 1 Manufacturing: Agriculture; food and drink; metals and minerals; energy; construction; chemicals.
Group 2 Manufacturing: pharmaceuticals, telecommunications; other electrical; automobiles; aerospace; other manufacturing.
Tertiary: Transport; distribution; financial services; other services.

The distinction between Group 1 Manufacturing and Group 2 Manufacturing was made because of the generally more sophisticated technology assumed to be embodied in the products and processes of Group 2 Manufacturing compared to Group 1 Manufacturing. IJV formation by these industry groupings and by time period is shown in summary Table 2.8, below. A chi-square test shows that the industry groupings and time period of IJV formation are independent (chi-square statistic = 2.945; d.f. = 2; p = 0.229), i.e. at the level of the industry groupings there is no relationship between industry and time period of IJV formation.

Table 2.4 shows UK IJV formation by industry and regional location of the partner. With the Triad partners, IJV formations occurred most frequently in 'other services', financial services, and 'other manufacturing'. With the non-

TABLE 2.4 *UK IJV formation by industry and region, 1990–1996*

| Industry | Region | | | | | |
| | Triad | | Non-Triad | | Total | |
	N.	%	N.	%	N.	%
Agriculture	2	1.2	0	0.0	2	0.7
Food and drink	3	1.8	19	16.0	22	7.6
Metals and minerals	4	2.4	10	8.4	14	4.8
Energy	14	8.2	2	1.7	16	5.5
Construction	6	3.5	1	0.8	7	2.4
Chemicals	4	2.4	7	5.9	11	3.8
Pharmaceuticals	5	2.9	3	2.5	8	2.8
Telecommunications	2	1.2	2	1.7	4	1.4
Other electrical	7	4.1	2	1.7	9	3.1
Automobiles	7	4.1	9	7.6	16	5.5
Aerospace	4	2.4	3	2.5	7	2.4
Other manufacturing	20	11.8	14	11.8	34	11.8
Transport	3	1.8	2	1.7	5	1.7
Distribution	16	9.4	10	8.4	26	9.0
Financial services	21	12.4	18	15.1	39	13.5
Other services	52	30.6	17	14.3	69	23.9
Total	170	58.8	119	41.2	289	100.0

Triad partners, IJV formation occurred most frequently in the food and drink sector, financial services, and 'other services'. A clear majority of the IJVs with Triad partners were formed in the tertiary sector (about 54 per cent); in comparison just under 40 per cent of IJVs with non-Triad partners were formed in the tertiary sector.

IJV formation by industry groupings and partner nations is shown in summary Table 2.9, below. The extent to which particular industries and partner nations are linked was formally tested in terms of the broad industry groupings. The chi-square test of independence shows that there is a relationship between joint venture industry groupings and the region of the foreign partner (chi-square statistic $= 8.169$; d.f. $= 2$; $p < 0.05$).

IJV Purpose

The purpose underlying IJV formation is shown in Table 2.5. The purpose is the operating function of the IJV and is not an indication of partner motives for establishing the venture. It is apparent from Table 2.5 that the purpose of IJV formation falls into two main categories: service provision was the purpose in about 55 per cent of the cases and production was the purpose in about one-third of the cases. Service provision means that the IJV was formed in order to carry out a service activity, for example, provision of insurance services or banking services.

Table 2.5 shows that for all of the purpose categories more IJVs were formed in the final three years of the time period under consideration than in the first four years of the time period. In order to test whether there is an association between the purpose of the IJV and the time period during which it was formed, the following three classifications were derived, based on whether or not the purpose included marketing:

TABLE 2.5 *UK IJV formation by purpose, 1990–1996*

Purpose	Year							Total	
	1990	1991	1992	1993	1994	1995	1996	N.	%
R&D	2	—	—	—	5	2	1	10	3.3
Production	3	5	6	7	23	26	29	99	32.9
Marketing	—	1	—	—	—	—	—	1	0.3
Development and production	2	—	1	1	2	2	4	12	4.0
Production and marketing	1	2	—	—	—	4	2	9	3.0
Development, production, and marketing	—	—	—	1	—	1	1	3	1.0
Service provision	8	17	19	16	30	39	37	166	55.1
Not known	—	—	—	—	—	1	—	1	0.3
Total	16	25	26	25	60	75	74	301	100.0

- Non-marketing related, i.e. the purpose categories of R&D, production, and development and production.
- Marketing related, i.e. the purpose categories of marketing, development and marketing, production and marketing, and development, production and marketing.
- Service provision, the original purpose category. IJVs here may or may not include marketing activities, but it is not possible to determine from the datafile which IJVs contain significant marketing activity and which do not.

The rationale for categorizing the purpose of the IJV according to whether or not it included marketing is based on the argument that cooperative behaviour begins to occur early in the product development cycle. This is partly explained by the difficulties in managing the IJV as the project becomes closer to its eventual market. The incentive to renege on the cooperative relationship tends to increase as the IJV approaches the marketing phase (Hergert and Morris, 1988; Buckley and Casson, 1988). It may be argued, therefore, that the incidence of non-marketing IJVs would exceed that of marketing-related IJVs. This view is supported by this sample as is shown in summary Table 2.8, below, which sets out the broad purpose categories of the IJVs and the time period of formation. A chi-square test of independence shows that there is an association between the broad purpose of the IJV and the time period of formation (chi-square statistic = 6.685; d.f. = 2; p < 0.05).

IJV purpose by region of partner is shown in Table 2.6. Almost two-thirds of the IJVs with Triad partners were formed for the purpose of service provision, compared with just over 40 per cent for IJVs with non-Triad partners. While almost half the IJVs with non-Triad partners were formed for the purpose of production, this compares with about 23 per cent for IJVs formed with Triad partners.

TABLE 2.6 *UK IJV formation by purpose and region, 1990–1996*

Purpose	Region				Total	
	Triad		Non-Triad			
	N.	%	N.	%	N.	%
R&D	5	2.9	5	4.2	10	3.5
Production	39	22.9	56	47.1	95	32.9
Marketing	1	0.6	0	0.0	1	0.3
Development and production	6	3.5	6	5.0	12	4.2
Production and marketing	7	4.1	2	1.7	9	3.1
Development, production, and marketing	2	1.2	1	0.8	3	1.0
Service provision	109	64.1	49	41.2	158	54.7
Not known	1	0.6	0	0.0	1	0.3
Total	170	58.8	119	41.2	289	100.0

The broad purpose classifications by region of foreign partner are shown in summary Table 2.9, below, which clearly indicates that proportionately more IJVs were formed with non-Triad partners for non-marketing-related purposes than with Triad partners, while proportionately more marketing related and service provision IJVs were formed with Triad partners than with non-Triad partners. A chi-square test of independence shows that there is a relationship between the purpose of the IJV and the region of the foreign partner (chi-square statistic 20.976; d.f. = 2; p < 0.000).

Table 2.7 shows the purpose of the IJV in terms of the industry groupings. IJVs formed for the purpose of production are found in all of the industries in the manufacturing sector. IJVs formed for the purpose of service provision occur mainly in the service sector, but are also found in six of the 11 industries in the manufacturing sector. An example of the latter is an architectural design consultancy offered by firms in the construction industry.

In order to test for the independence of the industry of the IJV and its purpose, the three broad industry groupings were cross-tabulated with the three broad purpose categories. A chi-square test of independence shows that as far as the sample in this study is concerned, there is an association between the broad industry of the IJV and the broad purpose of the IJV (chi-square statistic = 205.621; d.f. = 4; p < 0.000).

Number of Partners

In the majority of cases (about 86 per cent) there is one foreign partner in the IJV, with slightly more of the non-Triad IJVs (about 90 per cent) having one foreign partner compared to the Triad IJVs (about 82 per cent). The incidence of two foreign partners occurs in about 13 per cent of cases (about 16 per cent of Triad IJVs and about 9 per cent of non-Triad IJVs). In relatively few cases (1.4 per cent of the total) are there more than two foreign partners in the IJVs. There are no IJVs in the sample with more than four foreign partners. The finding that a clear majority of the IJVs have only one foreign partner may be rationalized in terms of the increasing difficulties of coordination and management as the number of IJV partners grows.

Equity Shareholding

This section discusses the extent of the UK partners' equity shareholding in the IJVs. The UK equity shareholding was only reported for 88 IJVs (around 30 per cent of the total cases) so caution is required in interpreting the findings. Of the IJVs where the UK equity shareholding is known, a 50–50 equity split is found in about 28 per cent of the cases, with the UK partner having more than a half share in the IJV in about 40 per cent of the cases. The distribution of UK equity shareholder by region of the main foreign partner is shown in Table 2.10. This shows that UK firms have attained a majority

TABLE 2.7 *UK IJV formation by industry and purpose, 1990–1996*

Industry	R and D		Production		Marketing		Development and production		Production and marketing		Devpt., Prodn., and Marketing		Service provision		Not known		Total	
	N.	%	N.	%	N.	%	N.	%	N.	%	N.	%	N.	%	N.	%	N.	%
Agriculture	—	—	—	—	—	—	1	8.3	—	—	—	—	—	—	1	100.0	2	0.7
Food and drink	—	—	16	16.2	—	—	2	16.7	3	33.3	1	33.3	—	—	—	—	22	7.3
Metals and minerals	5	50.0	6	6.1	—	—	1	8.3	—	—	—	—	2	1.2	—	—	14	4.7
Energy	1	10.0	2	2.0	—	—	—	—	—	—	—	—	14	8.4	—	—	17	5.6
Construction	—	—	2	2.0	—	—	—	—	1	11.1	—	—	4	2.4	—	—	7	2.3
Chemicals	1	10.0	11	11.1	—	—	—	—	—	—	—	—	—	—	—	—	12	4.0
Pharmaceuticals	1	10.0	1	1.0	—	—	3	25.0	2	22.2	1	33.3	—	—	—	—	8	2.7
Telecommunications	—	—	4	4.0	—	—	—	—	—	—	—	—	—	—	—	—	4	1.3
Other electrical	—	—	7	7.1	—	—	—	—	1	11.1	—	—	1	0.6	—	—	9	3.0
Automobiles	—	—	17	17.2	—	—	—	—	—	—	—	—	—	—	—	—	17	5.6
Aerospace	—	—	6	6.1	—	—	—	—	—	—	—	—	1	0.6	—	—	7	2.3
Other manufacturing	2	20.0	26	26.3	—	—	4	33.3	—	—	1	33.3	3	1.8	—	—	36	12.0
Transport	—	—	—	—	—	—	—	—	—	—	—	—	8	4.8	—	—	8	2.7
Distribution	—	—	—	—	1	100.0	—	—	1	11.1	—	—	24	14.5	—	—	26	8.6
Financial services	—	—	—	—	—	—	—	—	—	—	—	—	40	24.1	—	—	40	13.3
Other services	—	—	1	1.0	—	—	1	8.3	1	11.1	—	—	69	41.6	—	—	72	23.9
Total	10	3.3	99	32.9	1	0.3	12	4.0	9	3.0	3	1.0	166	55.1	1	0.3	301	100.0

TABLE 2.8 *Summary table: time period of IJV formation*

	1990–3		1994–6	
	N.	%	N.	%
Region				
Triad	74	83.1	96	48.0
Non-Triad	15	16.9	104	52.0
Industry				
Group 1 manufacturing	17	18.5	57	27.2
Group 2 manufacturing	25	27.1	56	26.8
Tertiary	50	54.4	96	45.9
Purpose				
Non-marketing related	27	29.4	94	45.2
Marketing related	5	5.4	8	3.9
Service provision	60	65.2	106	50.9

TABLE 2.9 *Summary table: region of formation*

	Triad		Non-Triad	
	N.	%	N.	%
Industry				
Group 1 manufacturing	33	19.4	39	32.8
Group 2 manufacturing	45	26.5	33	27.7
Tertiary	92	54.1	47	39.5
Purpose				
Non-marketing related	50	29.6	67	56.3
Marketing related	10	5.9	3	2.5
Service provision	109	64.5	49	41.2

TABLE 2.10 *Equity share of UK partner by region of foreign partner*

Equity share of UK partner	Triad		Non-Triad		Total	
	N.	%	N.	%	N.	%
< 50%	16	30.8	11	30.6	27	30.7
50%	21	40.4	4	11.1	25	28.4
> 50%	15	28.8	21	58.3	36	40.9
Total	52	59.1	36	40.9	88	100.0

shareholding in about 58 per cent of the non-Triad IJVs, but have a majority shareholding in only about 29 per cent of Triad IJVs. However, in about 69 per cent of both Triad and non-Triad IJVs, the UK equity shareholding is at least 50 per cent.

The mean UK equity shareholding, for the firms where the shareholding is known, is 49.9 per cent, with a mean of 47.2 per cent for IJVs with Triad partners and a mean of 54 per cent for IJVs with non-Triad partners. A t-test for equality of means shows that the UK mean equity shareholding is significantly different between the two foreign partner groups (t value = −1.72; p < 0.1).

Summary and Conclusions

A major difficulty facing IJV researchers, particularly those concerned with the examination of UK firms' activity in IJVs, is the lack of an official database. This means researchers must have recourse to other methods of identifying IJV trends and patterns of distribution. Typically, this has been through systematically recording IJV announcements in the press. To date only one previous study, that of Glaister and Buckley (1994), has provided a detailed account of UK IJV activity with partners from the Triad, which covered the decade of the 1980s. The purpose of this study has been to update and extend the earlier record of IJV activity of UK firms by considering the patterns and distribution of IJV formation with partners from both Triad and non-Triad countries since the beginning of the present decade. The main characteristics of this activity can be summarized as follows:

1. The flow of new UK IJVs rises slowly in the early part of the 1990s before growing more strongly to reach a peak in 1995.
2. The majority of IJVs were formed with partners from the Triad of advanced economies, particularly partners from Western Europe and North America.
3. Just over half of the IJVs were formed in the tertiary sector, with the leading industry categories of IJV formation being 'other services', financial services, and 'other manufacturing', which together accounted for about half of the IJVs.
4. By far the greatest proportion of IJVs were formed for the purpose of service provision.
5. In the majority of cases there is only one foreign partner in the IJV, with no IJV having more than four foreign partners.
6. Where the UK partners' equity shareholding is known, in about 28 per cent of cases there is an equal division of equity between partners, with the UK partner having at least a half share in about 70 per cent of cases.

A number of exploratory chi-square tests of independence were conducted in an attempt to identify association between the main characteristics of the sample. There was evidence of association across a number of characteristics, in particular between the time period of IJV formation and the region of the foreign partner, the industry of the IJV and the region of the foreign partner, the purpose of the IJV and the time period of formation, the purpose of the IJV and the region of the foreign partner, and the industry of the IJV and the purpose of the IJV.

These findings cast further light on the nature and pattern of UK IJV formation in an area where there is a paucity of systematic information. It should be noted that the data reported here are not a complete record of UK IJV activity over the 1990s. It is likely that the press announcements from which this study is derived under-report the actual number of IJVs. Unfortunately, it is not possible to assess the degree of this under-reporting. The absolute figures for IJVs reported in this chapter are, therefore, likely to be a conservative estimate of actual IJV formation over the period. If there is a consistent under-reporting across all foreign partner groups, then the relative proportion of IJVs formed between UK firms and different national groups of foreign partners may be considered a reasonable approximation to the actual pattern of UK IJV activity.

This chapter has reported on the formation of IJVs by UK firms over the 1990–6 period. In future research we will examine the core dimensions of IJV activity by UK firms with partners from Western Europe. There is a paucity of information and study specifically relating to UK IJV activity in the context of ventures formed with partners from the major trading nations. A differentiating element of the proposed study is that it examines IJVs in a competitive context—between firms from developed nations within a regionalized market framework. It is anticipated that the findings of the study will directly inform practising managers and enable them to understand and intervene in the IJV management process. The study will thus provide the potential to manage more successfully all of the key dimensions of IJV activity and hence it will help to develop the competitive position of the parent firms.

References

BEAMISH, P. W. (1988), *Multinational Joint Ventures in Developing Countries* (London: Routledge).

——and DELIOS A. (1997), 'Incidence and Propensity of Alliance Formation', in P. W. Beamish and J. P. Killing (eds.), *Co-operative Strategies: Asian Pacific Perspectives*, (San Francisco: New Lexington Press), 91–114.

BUCKLEY, P. J. and CASSON, M. (1988), 'A Theory of Co-operation in International Business', in F. J. Contractor and P. Lorange (eds.), *Co-operative Strategies in International Business* (Lexington, Mass.: Lexington Books), 91–114.

CONTRACTOR, F. J. and LORANGE, P. (1988), 'Why Should Firms Co-operate? The Strategy and Economics Basis for Co-operative Ventures', in F. J. Contractor and P. Lorange (eds.), *Co-operative Strategies in International Business: Joint Ventures and Technology Partnerships Between Firms*. (Lexington, Mass.: Lexington Books), 3–30.

GHEMAWAT, P., PORTER, M. E., and RAWLINSON, R. A. (1986), 'Patterns of International Coalition Activity', in M. E. Porter (ed.), *Competition in Global Industries*. (Boston: Harvard Business School).

GLAISTER, K. W. (1996), 'Theoretical Perspectives on Strategic Alliance Formation', in P. E. Earl (ed.), *Management, Marketing, and the Competitive Process*, (Cheltenham: Edward Elgar), 78–111.

—— and BUCKLEY, P. J. (1994), 'UK International Joint Ventures: An Analysis of Patterns of Activity and Distribution', *British Journal of Management*, 5/1: 33–51.

HAGEDOORN, J. (1996), 'Trends and Patterns in Strategic Technology Partnering Since the early Seventies', *Review of Industrial Organization*, 11: 601–16.

—— and SCHAKENRAAD, J. (1993) 'Strategic Technology Partnering and International Corporate Strategies', in K. S. Hughes (ed.), *European Competitiveness* (Cambridge: Cambridge University Press).

HAMEL, G. (1991), 'Competition for Competence and Interpartner Learning within International Strategic Alliances', *Strategic Management Journal*, 12/1: 83–103.

HERGERT, M. and MORRIS, D. (1988), 'Trends in International Collaborative Agreements', in F. J. Contractor and P. Lorange (eds.), *Co-operative Strategies in International Business* (Lexington, Mass.: Lexington Books), 99–110.

HLADIK, K. J. (1985), *International Joint Ventures* (San Francisco: New Lexington Press).

OSBORN, R. N. and BAUGHN, C. C. (1987), 'New Patterns in the Formation of US/Japanese Co-operative Ventures: The Role of Technology', *Columbia Journal of World Business*, Summer: 57–65.

PARKHE, A. (1993) ' "Messy" Research, Methodological Predispositions, and Theory Development in International Joint Ventures', *Academy of Management Review*, 18/2: 227–68.

Part II

The Rationale for Cooperation

Part II of the book deals with the fundamental question of why firms cooperate with each other, sometimes even with their direct competitors. It deals with the question of costs, especially transaction costs, of added value, especially in the resource-based view of firm strategy, and with the critical importance of organizational learning as an incentive for cooperation.

3

The Theory of the Flagship Firm

ALAN M. RUGMAN AND JOSEPH R. D'CRUZ

Today the competitive strategies of MNEs are determined by a complex web of factors at regional, country, industry, firm, business unit, and organizational task level. To cut through this dense jungle of potential cognitive and motivational factors affecting managerial decision-making in MNEs it will be useful to build upon a recent synthesis of work on the theory of the MNE and its interactions with key partners. This is the 'five partners' or 'flagship' model of business networks, as developed by D'Cruz and Rugman (1992, 1993). The five partners model has been applied to analysis of the Canadian telecommunications industry by D'Cruz and Rugman (1994a) and to the European telecommunications industry by D'Cruz and Rugman (1994b). It has been applied to the Canadian chemicals industry by D'Cruz, Gestrin, and Rugman (1995). The five partners model emphasizes cooperative behaviour in network relationships and it can be contrasted with the five forces model of Porter (1980), which emphasizes rivalry and entry barriers as mechanisms to exercise market power and achieve competitive advantage.

The linkage of the D'Cruz and Rugman (1992, 1993) five partners model to earlier work on the theory of the MNE comes through the role of the MNE as a 'flagship firm' at the hub of the five partners model. The MNE is competing globally and it provides strategic leadership to partners such as key suppliers, key customers, and the non-business infrastructure. The rationale for the MNE is explained by transaction cost economics and internalization theory, as first developed by Buckley and Casson (1976). They demonstrated that economic activity by MNEs takes place when the benefits of internalization outweigh its costs and that this usually occurs under conditions when there are market imperfections in the pricing of intangible knowledge. This work was further refined by Casson (1979) and in essays collected in Buckley and Casson (1985). It was expanded into the 'eclectic paradigm' of international business by Dunning (1979). Internalization theory has been extended and applied in a North American context by Rugman (1980, 1981, 1986).

The relationship between the modern theory of the MNE and the flagship model, with its implication for some de-internalization (when successful

This article is reprinted with permission from *European Management Journal* where it was first published in vol. 15 no. 4 (1997).

network relationships are developed) has been discussed by Rugman, D'Cruz, and Verbeke (1995). They argue that the internalization decision for an MNE takes into account concepts of business policy and competitive strategy and that proprietary firm-specific advantages yield potential economic profits when exploited on a world-wide basis. Yet the MNE finds these potential profits dissipated by the internal governance costs of its organizational structure and the difficulty of timing and sustaining its FDI activities. This leads to de-internalization when the benefits of internalization are out-weighed by its costs. De-internalization usually occurs within a business network when successful partnerships are found, as in the flagship model. The movement from internalization to business network requires analysis of parent–subsidiary relationships and the governance costs of running an MNE versus managing relationships in a business network.

Recently internalization theory has been linked to the resource-based theory of the firm by Kogut and Zander (1992, 1993), and others, who argue that issues of organizational learning complicate, and may even undermine, the argument for internalization. To help reconcile the basic thrust of inter-nalization theory with the need for explicit consideration of organizational relationships, it is useful to consider the network relationships captured within the flagship model.

The Flagship Model

Business networks are becoming increasingly common in industries where internationalization and globalization are advanced. In a business network a set of companies interact and cooperate with each other from the manufac-ture of basic raw materials to final consumption. Conventional business relationships are characterized by arm's-length competition between firms as they buy and sell. Such relationships, which are the basis of Michael Porter's (1980) five forces model of competitive advantage, are based, to a large extent, on the development and exercise of market power. They tend to foster a short-term orientation among participants, with each participant being concerned primarily with its own profitability.

The D'Cruz and Rugman flagship model is based on the development of collaborative relationships among major players in a business system. Its focus is on strategies that are mutually reinforcing. By their very nature, such relationships tend to foster and depend upon a collective long-term orientation among the parties concerned. Hence, they form an important facilitating mechanism for the development of long-term competitiveness.

There are two key features of such a system: first, the presence of a flagship firm that pulls the network together and provides leadership for the strategic management of the network as a whole; and secondly, the existence of firms that have established key relationships with that flagship. These relationships are illustrated in Figure 3.1 by black arrows that cross organizational bound-

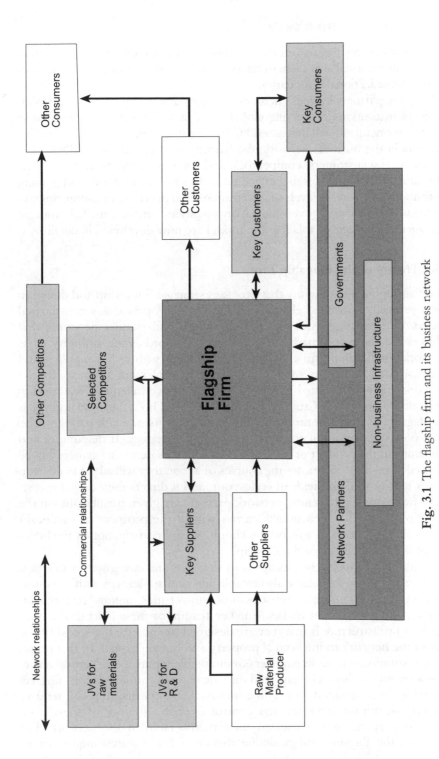

Fig. 3.1 The flagship firm and its business network

aries, symbolizing the nature of inter-firm collaboration that characterizes them. Conventional arm's length relationships are shown as grey arrows that stop at organizational boundaries.

The five partners business network consists of a group of firms and non-business institutions competing globally and linked together through close inter-firm organizational linkages (D'Cruz and Rugman, 1992). There are five partners in the business network: the flagship firm (which is an MNE), key suppliers, key customers, competitors, and the non-business infrastructure. The latter partner includes the service-related sectors, educational and training institutions, the various levels of government, and other organizations such as trade associations, non-governmental organizations, and unions. The strategic management aspects of this flagship model are now developed in detail.

The Theory of the Flagship Firm

The flagship firm is an entity that provides strategic leadership and direction for a vertically integrated chain of businesses that operate as a coordinated system or network, frequently in competition with similar networks that address the same end markets. As the central coordinating authority in its network, the flagship firm establishes relationships with its key suppliers and key customers and ensures that they operate to implement a strategy for the network that is formulated by the flagship. We have called this relationship strategic asymmetry (D'Cruz and Rugman, 1994a). This is meant to imply that the flagship exercises control over the strategy of its network partners who have no reciprocal influence over the flagship's strategy. It determines and sets limits to the product or the markets in which its network partners will be allowed to operate, it chooses the courses of action they will adopt to develop competencies in these fields of endeavour, and it directs their capital investment programmes. In return, network partners are given membership in the flagship's network which usually carries with it the prospect of significant sales volumes, access to advanced technology, and participation in the benefits of the brand image of the flagship.

In addition to such relationships with suppliers and customers in a vertical chain, modern flagships have also established similar alliances with organizations in the non-business infrastructure—universities, unions, research institutes, and government bodies. The key feature of these links to the non-business infrastructure is that they are designed to enhance the access of the rest of the network to intellectual property and human capital. In that sense, these institutions are really suppliers of intangible inputs to the vertical chain. Consequently, it should be expected that the nature of these relationships will resemble those devoted to tangible inputs. Thus, the flagship will tend to exercise significant influence and control over the strategy of these non-business partners as it relates to their membership in the network. For example, the flagship will prescribe the areas for research inquiry of its university partners, set the terms of reference for human-capital development projects with unions, and provide leadership for business–government initiatives aimed at enhancing the competitiveness of the networks.

Finally, some flagship firms have established limited alliances with direct competitors. These include joint ventures for the development of raw material projects or the manufacture of specialized inputs; in both cases, the minimum economic scale of the undertaking is usually larger than would be justified by the requirements of either partner on its own. Other forms of collaboration with competitors are joint efforts for research and development of a pre-competitive nature, membership in consortia to bid for large projects, and agreements on technical standards for the industry. While the flagship's relations with its competitors do not share the strategic asymmetry feature of its links with other network partners, they have another characteristic in common.

A fundamental feature of these relationships is their focus on collaborative rather than competitive behaviour. Thus, in transactions based on a network alliance relationship, the parties are motivated to work closely with each other to further the aims of the network which they regard as compatible with their own welfare. This can be contrasted with the competitive behaviour described in the five forces model by Porter (1980). The latter model encourages firms to behave in competition with their suppliers and customers for a share of the profits in transactions with each other. It focuses on the development and exercise of a market power in business systems, with managerial attention devoted to optimizing results on a transaction-by-transaction basis—a short-run orientation. On the other hand, the network mode of collaboration requires that both parties to a relationship apply the calculus of the benefits they hope to obtain and the costs they will incur across an indefinite stream of transactions rather than on one transaction at a time. It encourages the sharing of market intelligence and intellectual property without recourse to formal contracting to protect the self-interest of either party. In sum, these relationships are collaborative and long term in orientation.

The large car-makers are often cited as examples of firms that have adopted the flagship mode of operations. Thus Chrysler, for example, has developed close collaborative relationships with its key suppliers who are often encouraged to establish their own plants close to its assembly plants. These relationships are of a collaborative nature, with both sides operating on the assumption that they will continue indefinitely. This facilitates the making of highly specialized capital investments by both parties to optimize their joint operations. Similarly, Chrysler develops close long-term relationships with its dealers who operate as an integral part of the overall system which is directed by the car-maker. The entire chain—suppliers, car-maker, and dealers—is managed as a single system whose strategic direction comes almost exclusively from the car-maker who functions as its flagship. The amount and nature of coordination necessary for effective functioning of this system can best be appreciated by considering what occurs when a new platform is created. Decisions about positioning and timing, for example, are the exclusive preserve of the car-maker. The introduction of a new platform also involves adoption of new process technology. On the other hand, there are a myriad operational issues that are the responsibility of the network partners, who are frequently required to make considerable investments in new equipment and training.

As a second example, let us examine the role of France Telecom as the flagship of that country's principal telecommunications system (D'Cruz and Rugman, 1994*b*). Its strategic role is to provide the vision and direction for the technological choices and associated commercial initiatives made by the system. Thus, France Telecom determined to develop a system that was at the leading edge in such technologies as fibre optics and digitalization. It required its suppliers and distributors to devote resources to developing their own capabilities in these areas. Equally important, it provided strategic leadership to a network of government-funded research centres on telecommunications to coordinate the development of technology in these areas. It also directed the country's training institutions in telecommunications to make appropriate changes to their curricula to ensure the availability of a workforce skilled in these technologies. What has emerged is an advanced telecommunications system with a highly centralized process for strategic decision-making coupled with decentralized operational capability. The key features of a flagship network—strategic asymmetry and collaborative relationships—are abundantly evident.

Some of the better known flagship networks are those that have been created by the Japanese. Known as vertical *keiretsu*, these networks have succeeded in building formidable global competitive positions in such diverse fields as consumer electronics (Sony, Matsushita), automobiles (Toyota, Nissan) and computers (NEC, Toshiba). It should be mentioned that the strategies and structures of a vertical *keiretsu* are significantly different from the traditional Japanese *keiretsu*, which is a family of broadly diversified companies with a bank or trading company at its centre. For an account of the dimensions of Japanese business networks see Fruin (1992), Gerlach (1992), and Westney (1995).

The Structure of the Flagship Firm

Having described the flagship firm and provided some examples, let us now turn to the central questions of this chapter—the theoretical rationale for its existence. To do so, we need to establish certain assumptions about the management structure of the typical flagship firm. Treating it as a single, unitary actor is unsatisfactory. First, this assumption inhibits the development of theory about the behaviour of the flagship firm towards its network partners, because it requires a constellation of follow-on assumptions about:

its objective function regarding profit maximization or shareholder value maximization; the unity of purpose at various levels of the firm; the dominance of economic or financial rationality in decision-making.

Second, it introduces a subtle bias in the nature of hypotheses that will be developed for empirical research about business systems led by flagship firms. Hypotheses about a unitary actor naturally tend to be based on expected regularities in its behaviour towards its network partners, given certain conditions. Take the probability of opportunistic behaviour in post-contract transactions. A unitary actor will be hypothesized to have either a non-zero probability or one that is not significantly different from zero, but not both. Researchers in the transactions-cost tradition are likely to be biased towards the former while those with a resource-based view may not, since they regard the firm's reputation as a key resource that managers value and protect. Chandler (1962) initiated a scholarly tradition of inquiry that firmly established the multiple actor assumption, while Mintzberg (1979) legitimated the assumption that even a single actor may work with multiple conflicting objectives.

The structure we propose involves desegregating the flagship firm into three components. These components are based on the function that is being performed by the component, and will generally match specific individuals and organizational positions.

The first component includes strategy functions. These involve articulation of the goals and objectives of the network as a whole as well as the flagship firm itself, the formulation or ratification of the principal courses of action to be undertaken to achieve those goals, and the allocation of resources for their implementation. Readers familiar with the strategy literature will quickly recognize the similarity of this definition with those used to define strategy itself (Chandler, 1962). However, it should be recognized that a flagship firm exercises domain over its entire network and not just over its own organization. This posits that it has a substantial or almost complete measure of control over the strategy of its network partners who, in turn, have given up their strategic autonomy in exchange for the putative benefits of belonging to the network.

The second is a group of management functions, involving guiding and directing the work of others in the flagship firm and its network partners to achieve the objectives established by the strategy function. The commonly held view in the organizational behaviour and strategy literatures is that this includes activities such as planning, decision-making (Gluech, 1976), organizing, staffing, leading, and controlling (Koontz and O'Donnell, 1972), but not the strategy functions described above. Here too it is useful to focus on the distinctive aspects of management in a flagship firm—the domain of its management function extends beyond the boundaries of its own organization and includes a substantial measure of control over the work of its network partners.

Finally, we have the operational functions: these include all the other work performed by employees of the flagship firm, but they do not include any work that is done by employees of the network partners.

The Preference for Vertical Integration

There is a substantial body of theoretical work devoted to vertical integration in chains of production processes where the output of one process becomes a significant input into the next process. In the discussion that follows, we will generalize the propositions of this work beyond the supply of raw materials and the distribution of final consumption goods to include also vertical relationships involving the production of service inputs (engineering services, transportation, systems integration, etc.) and ancillary products and services associated with final consumption (warehousing, after sales service, etc.).

Three schools of thought have had major influence in this area. The central concern of these theorists has been the choice of mode between vertical integration, spot market transactions, or long-term contracts. Under what conditions is one mode likely to be preferred over the others? Which mode is more likely to remain stable as conditions change? And which is likely to induce firms to make investments which will contribute to the overall capacity and efficiency of the system as a whole and its various components? Each school provides a different perspective on the conditions and reasons why markets fail to operate satisfactorily and firms are driven to choose vertical integration.

Traditional industrial organization theory was primarily concerned with the behaviour of firms in oligopolistic and near monopolistic markets—the so-called small numbers condition—and the related ability of incumbents to extract rents. Vertical integration (backwards) is preferred when a firm anticipates that its suppliers have or can develop the potential to monopolize the market for an important input; similarly, forward vertical integration is a defence against foreclosure of markets for the firm's outputs or a pre-emptive attempt to gain the benefits of foreclosure for the firm itself.

The literature on transactions costs (internalization theory) shifted the focus of attention to the nature of assets involved in vertical integration and on difficulties associated with long-term contracts. It argues that when investments are required in assets that are specific to the vertical relationship, the problem of *ex post* opportunistic behaviour by the partner is difficult to deal with and causes firms to prefer vertical integration to dealing on the spot market or through long-term contracts. The latter option has the additional problem of the costs and difficulties related to writing, monitoring, and enforcing contingent contracts. These 'contracting hazards' discourage firms from dependence on long-term contracts when it is feared that adjustment of contract terms to changes in market conditions will be difficult to make or hard to enforce.

Extending this concept to MNEs, internalization theory explains their preference for the FDI mode for international expansion as a function of their need to protect property rights, particularly those of a less tangible nature. Similarly, the theory suggests that MNEs will undertake vertical integration abroad whenever there is a need to protect firm-specific assets such as know-how or a brand name.

Resource-based theory encourages us to regard the firm as a bundle of hard-to-replicate sticky resources, with particular attention paid to managerial capability or similar less tangible resources. This theory suggests that firms will prefer vertical integration when it has surplus managerial and other resources that it anticipates being able to deploy more effectively in the vertical chain than would independent suppliers or customers. These arguments are particularly powerful when transactions in the vertical system involve a significant quantity of intangible factors that are hard to price and monitor.

Failures of Vertical Integration

Given such powerful arguments favouring the vertical integration mode when conditions which frequently lead to market failure exist or are anticipated, why then have so many large firms chosen to move away from this solution and adopt the flagship form? There are two classes of explanations, which we will deal with separately below. First are explanations based on the capture of rent in vertically integrated firms; this involves the appropriation by individuals and groups in the firm of some of the rents that accrue to the firm by virtue of its ownership of resources that are scarce or difficult to replicate. The second set of difficulties relate to failures of the management systems that have been developed within large firms.

Rent Capture.   A major motivation for avoiding vertical integration is to circumvent rent capture by employees in an upstream or downstream unit who are members of the union, particularly but not exclusively when the same union represents employees of the focal unit. Should this union attempt to negotiate wages and employment terms that capture a portion of the rents, management may respond by establishing network relationships with upstream or downstream firms that are not unionized or have less onerous union contracts. It is common for suppliers in the automotive industry to experience lower wage costs than their customers, partly because they are regarded as having fewer opportunities to earn rents. Sometimes this is achieved by establishing operations in low-wage locations. Similarly, firms engaged in the distribution of computer products pay lower wages than their flagship suppliers. In both cases, flagship firms are able to circumvent rent capture by employees in the upstream and downstream parts of their business system when they use network partners for these functions. The alternative of paying lower wages in vertically integrated divisions is usually not available because of a form of conscious parallelism practised by many unions whereby they resist such differentiation.

Note that inflexibilities in personnel practices in large firms can lead to similar outcomes in the absence of unions. For example, many large firms adopt highly structured systems for pay and grade levels and operate a form of seniority system where the employee's length of service is a determinant of wages. The tendency of these firms to apply such schemes uniformly across all vertically integrated divisions can impose a high wage structure on up-stream and downstream divisions.

Rent capture by employees in management positions can also raise costs in a vertically integrated firm. In addition to salaries and benefits, rent capture may take the form of management perquisites that are costly. For example, managers in upstream and downstream units may be entitled to similar office space and administrative staff support as their colleagues in the focal division, thus raising the costs of their units above those in firms in the upstream or downstream industry. A common response to these problems has been for large firms to spin off upstream and downstream activities into separate companies with whom they then establish a network relationship.

Management Failure.   It is our contention that the second major set of reasons have to do with managerial failures in the vertically integrated mode. To explain the causes of such failure of vertical integration, we need to establish the characteristics of the organizational structure and processes used by large, vertically integrated firms. The fundamental organizational form that under-lies most structures for the management of vertically integrated firms is the multi-divisional or M-form arrangement, Williamson (1985). The basic char-acteristics of this form of interest here are: multi-tier levels of management, the profit centre concept, and divisional autonomy.

Management roles and functions are specialized by level in this form. Corporate management has stewardship of the overall direction of the firm, including the appointment of divisional managers and the establishment of the rules of engagement between divisions. Divisional general management is responsible for planning and implementing strategies for the division. Func-tional management in the division reports to the divisional manager and holds responsibility for running a particular function. The profit centre concept is that each division is treated as a quasi firm within the firm; it is given responsibility for managing the affairs of the division to achieve profit performance targets that are negotiated with corporate management. Divi-sional autonomy defines the scope of authority of divisional management and their responsibility for producing results. Despite prescriptions by organiza-tional theorists about the need to make areas of responsibility co-extensive with the scope of divisional authority, in practice corporate management may choose to ignore this principle for pragmatic reasons. Why do vertically integrated firms sometimes fail to perform as effectively as rivals who are less integrated?

The first reason results from internal rivalry among general managers. Corporate systems for the management of divisions in the M-form firm have a built-in bias towards enhancing rivalry among division general managers. Three systems in particular tend to create internal rivalry. First, financial performance measurement systems based on the profit-centre principle of treating the division as a quasi firm place emphasis on overall results calculated by measures such as Return on Net Assets (RONA) and contribution to shareholder value. The message to the divisional general manager is: 'Run your division as if it were an independent firm whose shareholder is the corporation'. Since overall financial results of divisions are easily compared with each other, the incentives for rivalrous behaviour between upstream and downstream divisions are strong, and the incentives for cooperative behaviour almost non-existent. In effect, financial systems of this nature internalize the competitive aspects of the Porter five forces model described above.

Second, the reward and punishment system for divisional managers is similarly biased towards enhancing rivalry. Since they have overall responsibility for running their divisions, both the formal and informal reward systems are focused on outcomes measured by the financial performance measurement systems mentioned above. Good performance is rewarded through bonuses, management perquisites, and formal recognition. Poor performance is punished ultimately by removal of the divisional general manager from that position. A close and frequently reinforced linkage between divisional financial performance and the self-interest of the general manager encourages rivalry between managers of divisions; many corporate managers believe that such rivalry is healthy because it provides incentives for divisional managers to strive to improve the financial performance. However, when applied to divisions in a vertical system, such rivalry also provides disincentives for cooperative behaviour.

Promotion is a special form of reward in large firms. Divisional general managers compete with each other for opportunities for promotion to positions in the corporate office. Since the number of positions available is usually smaller towards the top of the hierarchy, there is a natural tendency for division managers to regard each other as rivals for promotion. Performance in their current job is frequently a major criterion for promotion; hence the incentive for rivalrous behaviour with a view to enhancing one's promotion prospects.

A second cause of ineffectiveness in vertically integrated firms is caused by the asymmetry of power among divisional managers. Corporate directives regarding terms and conditions for interdivisional transactions can have a significant impact on a division's ability to achieve its performance targets. For example, transfer pricing policies, accounting conventions, and even such relatively trivial matters as the scheduling of maintenance shutdowns can all be subject to corporate directives that impact on divisional performance. The formal and informal power of divisional managers to influence such directives can vary considerably because of a number of factors.

The most important is the historical position of the division itself. Divisions that formed the main base from which the vertically integrated firm grew are likely to wield considerable power. Senior corporate managers may have worked their way up through the division, personal relations between division and corporate managers may be deep and of long duration, and the belief may persist that the prosperity of the firm as a whole is intimately connected to the prosperity of the division. This can be particularly true when the acquisitions or internal development of the other components of the vertical system were originally sponsored by the division with a view to enhancing its own profitability.

The power of a division general manager can also be enhanced by the capital intensity of the division, particular when this is driven by economies of scale in its technology. When the division's assets account for a large proportion of the firm's total assets, its general manager tends to acquire special status in the minds of corporate managers. The divisional imperative of operating capital-intensive assets at high capacity utilization rates can easily be reinterpreted as corporate policy. Corporate directives may then be issued to other divisions to support efforts to achieve these high capacity utilization rates, even when they may not be in the interest of these divisions. For example, upstream divisions may be discouraged from seeking new customers when its outputs are needed by the downstream division.

Similarly, managers of a division that is seen as the custodian or repository of the technology base of the firm can wield considerable influence with a corporate office which regards the firm's technology as a core asset. Divisions which hold proprietary technology or which contain research facilities used for generating new technology can come to have a preferential status in corporate offices leading to influence that goes beyond matters strictly related to technology.

Failures of Transfer Pricing.   Policies about setting prices for transfers between vertically integrated divisions are essential for the functioning of performance measurement in a decentralized firm. The preferred theoretical solution is to use some form of market price because that provides the most accurate signals about the performance of both upstream and downstream operations. However, market prices, even when they are readily available, may fail to capture a number of additional considerations that must be addressed. First, market prices may need to be modified to take account of location benefits, product modifications which improve operations in either the upstream or downstream division, investments in learning that are specific to the relationship, or capacity that has been dedicated to the vertical relationship and would otherwise lie idle. Readers familiar with Williamson's (1985) classification of asset specificity will recognize that these characteristics have been derived from his scheme. In the absence of market price data that closely reflect such conditions, corporate management may have to establish rules for transfer pricing that depart from strict reliance on data from the market. Three classes of such departures need to be recognized. Each is prone to a particular type of failure.

First, corporate management may apply the best alternative rule—specifying that the selling division be allowed to charge the best price it could obtain outside the firm for similar transactions or that the buying division should only pay the same price as it can negotiate with an outside supplier, or both. In any case, such policies are vulnerable to opportunistic behaviour from one side or the other. Either division may seek offers from third parties that comply with corporate rules but which are based on tacit understandings which are kept secret from others in the firm. For example, the upstream division may make tacit commitments to outside customers about the level of technical support that will be offered in the future or indicate a willingness to take back unused product at full price. Conversely, the downstream division may entice an outside supplier with forecasts of future requirements that are substantially in excess of its plans. In general, tacit aspects of supply contracts with third parties may be particularly difficult for the internal partner to detect. Should the corporate office be called upon to arbitrate, it is likely to experience even greater difficulty in making judgements about whether or not there are tacit aspects to the offer from the outside party, and may be forced to make its determination on the basis of the explicit features of the arrangement.

An alternative arrangement is some sort of cost-plus pricing formula which sets transfer prices at the costs of the upstream division plus some agreed-upon formula for profit. Apart from vitiating the firm's performance control system with respect to the upstream division, cost-plus formulae create incentives for several kinds of dysfunctional behaviour in both divisions. An upstream division that is treated as a cost centre by the corporate office may seek ways of keeping its costs below budget targets by underspending on maintenance or process development. Downstream divisions may under-invest in market opportunities that are made inaccessible by a high-cost upstream supplier to which it is tied by corporate edict.

The third class of solution is to use corporate staff to analyse the transfer pricing issue and recommend a price or pricing formula which corporate management then imposes by edict. This approach suffers from disadvantages associated with inadequate expertise in corporate staff (lack of deep knowledge about the industry, inadequate market contacts, scarcity of tacit knowledge). Assuming that these problems can be overcome by, for example, promoting an expert from one of the divisions to the corporate staff, there remains the problem of acceptance by divisional management of solutions which they have not played a part in developing. Variations of this approach which involve corporate officials or staff serving as facilitators for negotiations between divisions about transfer prices merely arrive at the same outcome through a different mechanism and do not deal with its fundamental weaknesses.

A Case Study of the Flagship Model

The flagship model has been applied to analysis of the Canadian chemicals industry and its adjustment to regionalization under the NAFTA (see D'Cruz, Gestrin, and Rugman, 1995). Two broad findings emerged from this case study. First is the significance for competitiveness of key supplier relationships for subsidiaries of MNEs in the face of the rapid regional integration of the Canadian industry. Second is the significance for competitiveness of key customer relationships of SMEs with flagship suppliers.

Many of the larger MNEs in Canada are now doing very well as key suppliers. For example, in the paints industry key suppliers such as PPG and DuPont Canada have profitable businesses as key suppliers to the US and Japanese car-makers (OEMs) in Canada. The strategic direction for these businesses is partly determined in the United States, but the production mandate to implement these contracts can result in a successful Canadian business, with many jobs, profits for the company, and a net positive contribution to Canada's social and economic well being. Therefore, managers of MNEs need to continue to adopt a North American 'regional' strategic vision. Especially important within the context of MNEs will be the ability of Canadian managers to articulate in the appropriate strategic forums of the parent the Canadian subsidiary's potential contribution as a key supplier.

Within the institutional format of NAFTA the Canadian MNEs are adopting new and relevant regional strategies and any new MAI-based rules for FDI should be NAFTA consistent to minimize further adjustment costs. An MAI will need not only to enshrine national treatment and right of establishment but to go well beyond these principles. To secure truly contestable conditions on a North American regional basis, or a global basis, additional domestic discriminatory practices must be ended and replaced by new trade, investment, and competition rules.

Somewhat in contrast to the dramatic retrenchment affecting the larger MNEs there is a more subtle change affecting SMEs. These are often niche players driven by entrepreneurs who have a sense of the market. The SMEs are close to their customers; they can build and maintain long-term successful businesses through their marketing skills and flexibility. The SMEs act as intermediaries between the larger MNE suppliers and the wholesale or national distributors. Their flexibility and marketing know-how are vital firm-specific advantages. They can use their labs to customize products and/or respond very quickly to customer demands. They can manage these service functions better than larger MNE suppliers. As key customers of the MNEs, they can actually expand the total market for the MNEs, while not acting as a threat to them. In this sense, the SMEs have to manage the key supplier role with skill and foresight. They can develop close working relationships with a variety of MNEs provided they preserve secrecy and develop a reputation for discretion and non-disclosure to rival MNEs.

SMEs therefore promise to be a source of considerable growth and dynamism in the Canadian chemicals industry as MNEs seek to rationalize the productive structure of their global (or regional) operations while at the same time accessing as many markets as they can. SMEs are, in effect, the keys to new markets insofar as they are able to penetrate markets that are simply too small for MNEs to cater to given the scale of operations to which most MNEs are committed; and they allow for more rapid roll-out of technological advances by making smaller, more specialized product development economically viable. Once again, the lesson from the Canadian chemicals industry is that even SMEs can adjust to a new institutional framework, such as NAFTA.

Conclusions

The flagship model is characterized by the flagship firm's asymmetric strategic leadership over the network partners in common areas of interest. The MNE sets the priorities of the partners with regard to their participation in this flagship firm's business system. Only the flagship firm has the global perspective and resources to lead a business network and to establish the global benchmarks necessary to lead the development of the network. The network's key (flagship) relationships are the organization's mechanisms for achieving the strategic purposes of the network.

Another distinguishing feature of the flagship model is the deintegration of business system activities from the flagship firm—a de facto re-engineering of the value chain. This feature is a reflection of the complexity of competition in the global markets of today. Rather than internalizing ownership of core competencies and firm-specific advantages (Rugman, 1981), firms are deintegrating selectively those aspects of their value chains which they feel, for cost or strategic reasons, can better be performed elsewhere (Rugman, D'Cruz, and Verbeke, 1995).

As a result of deintegration, key suppliers can expect to experience increased volumes through the flagship firm's out-sourcing of activities. There is a reduction in the total number of suppliers serving the flagship, thereby creating value added to key suppliers outside the MNE; and a reduced business risk of more long-term contracts. The key supplier benefits through this partnership by having to benchmark its operations to the global standards of the flagship firm, for example, in adopting quality standards. The technologies, processes, and systems of the supplier will reflect global standards of competitiveness.

Key customers in the five partners business network, by virtue of ceding strategic control to the flagship, fulfil a valuable role beyond being a market for the flagship. These customers are the testing grounds for product and service development. Specifically, by having thick and tight relationships with network members, the customer provides market feedback and, in return, receives products which respond to their needs. Often the key customers will be intermediaries between the flagship firm and the end consumer, such as with car dealers.

For the non-business infrastructure (NBI), the flagship firm provides leadership and vision in terms of resource allocation, competency exploration, and mobilizing financial resources (as they apply to the NBI organization's participation in the flagship's business system). Such organizations contribute human resources, facilities, equipment, and institutional arrangements as their role in business network activities.

Relationships with key competitors include joint ventures in new markets, market-sharing arrangements, technology transfers, supplier development, etc. Unlike static contractual arrangements of the past, flagship model relations depend more on joint working teams and managerial interaction to elaborate and operationalize strategic purpose. This more fluid approach recognizes the adaptability required to change with the market but does not hinder the accrual of benefits through interaction. As with the other flagship relationships, key competitors share in a mutually beneficial cooperative relationship, thereby increasing the amount of trust present in the flagship model.

References

BUCKLEY, P. J. and CASSON, M. (1976), *The Future of the Multinational Enterprise* (London: Macmillan).
———— (1985), *The Economic Theory of the Multinational Enterprise*, (Basingstoke: Macmillan).
CASSON, M. (1979), *Alternatives to the Multinational Enterprise* (London: Macmillan).
CHANDLER, A. D., JR. (1962), *Strategy and Structure: Chapters in the History of American Industrial Enterprise* (Cambridge, Mass.: The M.I.T. Press).
D'CRUZ, J. R. and RUGMAN, A. M. (1992), 'New Compacts for Canadian Competitiveness', *Kodak Canada Inc.* (Toronto: Kodak Canada).
———— (1993), 'Developing International Competitiveness: The Five Partners Model', *Business Quarterly*, 58/2: 60–72.
———— (1994a), 'Business Network Theory and the Canadian Telecommunications Industry', *International Business Review*, 3/3: 275–288.
———— (1994b) 'The Five Partners Model: France Telecom, Alcatel, and the Global Telecommunications Industry', *European Management Journal*, 12/1: 59–66.
—— GESTRIN, M., and RUGMAN, A. M. (1995), *Is the Canadian Manager an Endangered Species?* (Toronto: Faculty of Management, University of Toronto,

mimeo of study prepared for Ontario's Ministerial Advisory Committee on Chemicals).

DUNNING, J. H. (1979), 'Explaining Changing Patterns of International Production: In Defence of the Eclectic Theory', *Oxford Bulletin of Economics and Statistics*, 41: 269–296.

FRUIN, M. (1992), *The Japanese Enterprise System: Competitive Strategies and Cooperative Structure* (Oxford: Clarendon Press).

GERLACH, M. L. (1992), *Alliance Capitalism: The Social Organization of Japanese Business* (Berkeley: University of California Press).

GLUECK, W. (1976), *Business Policy, Strategy Formation and Management Action* (New York: McGraw-Hill).

KOGUT, B. and ZANDER, U. (1992), 'Knowledge of the Firm, Combinative Capabilities and the Replication of Technology', *Organization Science*, 3/3: 383–397.

——— (1993), 'Knowledge of the Firm and the Evolutionary Theory of the Multinational Corporation', *Journal of International Business Studies*, 24/4: 625–645.

KOONTZ, H. and O'DONNELL, C. (1972) *Principles of Management* (New York: McGraw-Hill).

MINTZBERG, H. (1979), *The Structuring of Organizations* (Englewood Cliffs, NJ: Prentice-Hall).

PORTER, M. E. (1980), *Competitive Strategy: Techniques for Analyzing Industries and Competitors* (New York: Free Press).

RUGMAN, A. M., (1980), 'Internalization as a General Theory of Foreign Direct Investment: A Re-appraisal of the Literature', *Weltwirtschaftliches Archiv*, 116: 365–379.

—— (1981), *Inside the Multinationals: The Economics of Internal Markets* (New York: Columbia University Press).

—— (1986), 'New Theories of the Multinational Enterprises: An Assessment of Internalization Theory', *Bulletin of Economic Research*, 38: 101–118.

—— D'CRUZ, J. R., and VERBEKE, A. (1995), 'Internalization and De-internalization: Will Business Networks Replace Multinationals?', in G. Boyd (ed.), *Competitive and Cooperative Macromanagement: The Challenge of Structural Interdependences* (Aldershot: Edward Elgar), 107–128.

WESTNEY, E. (1985), 'The Japanese "Keiretsu" in Perspective', *Perspectives*, 3/2 (Toronto: Centre for International Business, University of Toronto).

WILLIAMSON, O. (1985), *The Economic Institutions of Capitalism* (New York: Free Press).

4

Transaction (In)Efficiency, Value (In)Efficiency, and Inter-Firm Collaboration

ANOOP MADHOK

In military affairs the strength of an army is the product of its mass and some
unknown x ... That unknown quantity is the spirit of the army ... The spirit of
an army is the factor which multiplied by the mass gives the resulting force.
(Leo Tolstoy, *War and Peace*, abridged).

The past decade or so has witnessed the distinct emergence of collaboration
in all its various forms as a critical element of firms' strategies. It has even
been suggested that collaborative organizational forms (the C-form?) are a
'new and dramatic organizational innovation' (Teece, 1992: 24) of potentially
far-reaching significance. Collaborations are especially pervasive in fast-
changing and knowledge-intensive sectors (Hagedoorn, 1993; Mowery,
Oxley, and Silverman, 1997) where, due to difficulties in contracting and in
measurement and evaluation, the cost of transacting tends to be high. This
suggests a different dynamic underlying collaboration formation, one that
goes beyond mainly economizing on transaction costs (Williamson, 1985).
Paradoxically however, in spite of their popularity, there appears to be a
noticeable disparity in outcomes relative to expectations, resulting in a substantial level of dissatisfaction on the part of firms with their collaborations
(Parkhe, 1991; Pearce, 1997; Madhok, 2000*a*; Madhok and Tallman, 1998;
Tallman, chap. 5, below). This seeming paradox underscores the distinction
between form and process, and suggests that although firms recognize the
need for and potential usefulness of collaborations, they find it difficult to
realize the underlying potential. This chapter aims to address this disparity.

Drawing upon some of the key aspects of transaction costs and resource-
based theory, this chapter provides insight into the organization and governance of economic activity through collaborations from a value perspective.
Value is conceptualized as the net rent-earning capacity of an asset or
resource, tangible or intangible. Rather than efficiency through economizing
on (transaction) costs, the value perspective approaches boundary-related
phenomena in terms of cost-effectiveness with respect to rent-earning capacity over the longer term. Such cost-effectiveness can be viewed as the
benefit–cost ratio associated with a particular activity or decision, be it
increased revenues at a certain cost level or lower costs for a certain revenue

level. Specifically in the context of inter-firm relationships, such value can be conceptualized in terms of the ability of the partners to earn rents over and above what could have been achieved in the absence of the partnership, i.e. in alternative organizational arrangements, as a result of synergies. By synergies, I mean both higher revenues and/or lower costs (in the sense of production cost savings, e.g. through better utilization of assets),[1] through resource combinations, the critical issue being the cost-effectiveness of a particular course of action.

From the standpoint of this discussion, the essence of firm behaviour is the pursuit of value in the conduct of its business (also see Madhok, 1997, 2000*a*, 2000*b*). The manner of organizing an activity, both form and process, greatly influences the amount of value created and realized. Even though I do address the former, my primary interest is in the latter process. The crux of my argument is that production and exchange relations are inextricably intertwined. In this regard, the relationship is not just a governance structure of a hybrid nature, as postulated by transaction costs (TC) theory (Williamson, 1991), but also behaves in and of itself as an endogenous factor of production, albeit a 'soft' one (Madhok and Tallman, 1998). Recognition of the relationship as a potential asset, one which needs to be actively managed in order to more fully derive value from it, enables an appreciation of relationship-specific expenditures not just as a cost but as an investment in future value. Not recognizing it as such is detrimental to the pursuit of value. In this regard, I emphasize in the discussion that it is not just the magnitude but also the composition of transaction specific expenditures that becomes a variable of crucial importance. The quote from Tolstoy at the start of the chapter can be adapted in the inter-firm collaborative context as follows:

In economic affairs the strength of a collaboration is the product of the complementary and synergistic resources (the mass) and some unknown x . . . That unknown quantity is the spirit of the relationship . . . The spirit of the relationship is the factor which multiplied by the mass gives the resulting force (the outcome).[2]

My argument goes a step beyond TC-based logic to argue that the 'tone and tempo' (i.e. spirit) of the collaborative relationship influences what kinds of occasions become available to firms to derive value from the collaboration and the extent to which they are actually able to exploit such potential. Since they depend on the manner in which the relationship unfolds, many of these occasions are not foreseeable in advance and therefore cannot be contracted for *ex ante*. Basically, transactions are not just subject to *ex post* opportunism

---

[1] I acknowledge other cost reductions, such as the simple division of project costs between two partners. However, for the purpose of this chapter, I concentrate on the costs associated with realizing the synergistic potential.

[2] Since collaborations are formed for a variety of purposes, the particular outcome (e.g. financial performance) is not so important as the actual relative to anticipated outcome, whatever this might be.

but simultaneously to *ex post* opportunities, the generation and exploitation of which depends on the 'spirit' of the relationship. With respect to opportunism, the chapter contributes by providing a more nuanced approach, one which unpacks and disaggregates the potential for opportunism into its ability and willingness components. Accordingly, the focal lens shifts from mainly protecting against the threat of opportunism towards managerial and process issues to do with a firm's 'collaborating technology', where it is not just the level of transaction-specific expenditures but also their nature which becomes a critical consideration.[3]

The discussion proposes that, rather than a minimizer of transactional (T)-inefficiency (see below),[4] the firm can be better represented as a minimizer of value (V)-inefficiency; this V-inefficiency (outlined in the next section) represents the inability to operate at the value frontier. The following section elucidates the conceptual argument made in the preceding sections through an illustrative example. I then further discuss some of the key points and their theoretical implications for the management of inter-firm relationships. The final section makes some concluding remarks. First, however, I discuss in the following section some essential arguments pertaining to opportunism in the context of inter-firm collaboration.

The Transactions Costs and Resource-Based Views and Opportunism

The discourse on the formation and governance of inter-firm collaborative relationships has been profoundly influenced in recent years by transaction costs theory (Williamson, 1985, 1991). TC theory assumes potential opportunism on the part of economic actors and is concerned with the organization of a transaction through the most efficient governance structure, this being the one which minimizes the (transaction) costs associated with safeguarding against opportunistic behaviour. From the theory, then, if a firm chooses to conduct an activity through some form of collaboration, such choice reflects the fact that the collaborative form is the transactionally efficient mode of organizing that particular activity.

In recent years, an alternative approach towards explaining economic organization and governance has emerged under the loose rubric of the resource-based (RB) view[5] (e.g. Conner, 1991). The RB view is predominantly concerned with the intelligent management of firms' resources,

---

[3] In general, the position I take on opportunism is that the assumption of potential opportunism is necessary but certainly not sufficient for the fuller attainment of value.

[4] Since TC arguments are well known, the discussion is kept very brief, sticking mainly to those aspects which provide a platform for the more substantive arguments made in the subsequent sections.

[5] A more dynamic approach emphasizes firm capabilities or competencies, these referring to the ability to manage the more static resources. For convenience, I refer to the resource-based view more generally to include the latter.

tangible and intangible, in the pursuit of competitive advantage (Peteraf, 1993). From the RB view, collaborations are especially valuable when they provide firms with an avenue for the sustained earning of rents in situations where competitive advantage requires the synergistic combination of resources which a firm is unable to purchase through a market transaction or to develop internally in a timely and cost-effective manner (Madhok and Tallman, 1998; Loasby, 1994; Madhok, 2000*b*). In fact, even though TC may be a necessary consideration, the essential reason, one which can be taken as an underlying assumption (Powell, 1990), why two firms enter into a collaborative relationship is because they anticipate the generation of value through synergistic and interdependent complementarities (Dietrich, 1994; Zajac and Olsen, 1993; Jarillo, 1988). The realization of this value, however, requires greater attention to the collaboration process (Parkhe, 1993) above and beyond the contractual considerations emphasized by TC theory.

Opportunism is central to TC theory but not to RB theory. TC logic does not claim that all economic actors are opportunistic. Rather, the possibility for opportunism is always present and it is too costly to determine who is going to be opportunistic and when (Williamson, 1985). Therefore, it becomes incumbent upon a firm to protect against the potential for such an eventuality at all times. In contrast, RB theorists (Conner, 1991; Kogut and Zander, 1992) do not deny the potential for opportunism but argue that it is not necessary for firms to assume it in their interactions with other firms.

Yet, the undeniable fact of the matter is that firms must confront the potential for opportunism as an inescapable reality. A more realistic middle ground is that opportunism is a variable that can be managed (Ghoshal and Moran, 1996; Noorderhaven, 1996). Treating it as such, rather than approaching it as a given due to the potential for its occurrence, provides greater degrees of freedom to managers and enables them to approach the transaction in a more entrepreneurial manner, instead of being 'shackled' by the purported tension between opportunism and bounded rationality (Williamson, 1985). For instance, in a situation where the bounded rationality of economic actors results in information asymmetries, instead of the solution to possible opportunism being greater protection through more careful contracting and other forms of safeguards, an alternative solution would be to reduce the extent of information asymmetries through a more mutual stance characterized by a greater sharing of information. As I will explain, this has two effects. It can potentially both lower the scope for opportunism, since information asymmetries are reduced, as well as facilitate the attainment of synergistic value.

Moreover, on closer examination, one can disaggregate the probability of opportunism into two components: the ability to be opportunistic and the willingness to be opportunistic. The contractual safeguards emphasized by TC theory are directed mostly towards the former aspect. More careful contracting reduces the ability of an actor to be opportunistic. Even though one could argue that, for example, a 'hostage' situation reduces the willingness of an actor to be opportunistic, this is essentially an issue of ability since the penalty for doing so would be too high. In such a situation of forbearance, even if a firm was faced with a situation where the possibility for opportunism existed, it would refrain from such behaviour.[6] On the other hand, what I mean by willingness is that a firm would refrain from opportunistic behaviour when faced with such a possibility even in the absence of penalties. Other than this, such a situation would also be characterized in all likelihood by a more mutual orientation, by which I mean that the actors, to a reasonable extent, would be willing to make voluntary and unilateral commitments above and beyond the terms of the contract in the interest of the partnership, should the need arise.

The attainment of the synergistic potential, which occasions most inter-firm activity, to its fullest extent rests on two underlying requirements: first, that each actor will not renege on his commitments (i.e., at best mutual forbearance from opportunistic behaviour); and secondly, that each actor will contribute in a positive and mutually oriented manner towards the relationship (i.e., will engage in value-creating behaviour). These requirements address both the safeguarding and the value-creation aspects of exchange. In this regard, I disagree with Buckley and Casson (1988: 35) that 'mutual forbearance . . . is the essence of cooperation'. When firms enter into a relationship of interdependence in order to combine complementary resources, mutual forbearance is clearly not sufficient (Madhok, 1995*a*). In other words, the essence of cooperation goes beyond mutual forbearance to include mutual orientation, of which forbearance is just one component, necessary but not sufficient for value creation.

In making my argument, I explicitly assume that a synergistic potential underlies inter-firm relationships. Were this not so, then perhaps safeguards against opportunism would suffice to attain the intended outcome and a value orientation would result in unnecessary expenditure of money, time, and energy without proportionate returns. However, given such potential, my argument is that firms which approach the relationship through the lens of opportunism as a variable to be managed rather than opportunism as a given constraint, due to the assumed potential for its occurrence, have greater potential to generate and realize greater value through such synergistic exchange.

Transaction(T)-Inefficiency

As mentioned, TC logic is predominantly concerned with organizing and governing exchange in a manner which economizes on the associated TC,[7] under the primary assumption of opportunism. TC occur due to friction in

---

[6] This assumes of course that the behaviour is detectable.

[7] It is worth noting that Williamson (1985: 61) does state that the choice of governance mechanisms (in a comparative static analysis) depends on the sum of production and transac-

economic exchange and involve the costs—search, selection, bargaining, monitoring, and enforcement costs—incurred in order to safeguard against opportunism. In addition, they also include any costs stemming from opportunistic behaviour in spite of safeguards (Williamson, 1975; Hennart, 1993). Perfect protection against opportunism is likely to be too difficult and costly in most circumstances since, after a certain (optimal) level, the reduction in opportunism becomes increasingly marginal relative to the incremental costs incurred in protecting against it. That is, the marginal TC exceeds the marginal returns in terms of reduction in opportunism (Hennart, 1993).

One of the main criticisms of TC logic is that its 'blinding' concern with the potential for opportunism results in undue neglect of the relationship between the partners and its effects (e.g. Granovetter, 1985; Jarillo, 1988; Ring and Van de Ven, 1992; Powell, 1990; Barney and Hansen, 1994; Bradach and Eccles, 1989; Zajac and Olsen, 1993). In a relationship dominated by protection against opportunism, firms tend to perceive a greater need to take costly and elaborate safeguards (Parkhe, 1993; Ring and Van de Ven, 1992; Lado, Boyd, and Hanlon, 1997; Faulkner, chap. 16, below) which increases the TC incurred. In contrast, the same level of safeguards may not be deemed so necessary under a more mutual orientation. First, a partner would be perceived as more prone to forbearance if the opportunity for opportunism arose (Ouchi, 1980) than would be the case otherwise. Second, greater and more willing sharing of information under a cooperative regime lowers information asymmetries between the partners which reduces the scope for opportunistic behaviour and hence the costs of protecting against it (Ring and Van de Ven, 1992; Kumar and Nti, 1998; Dyer, 1997; Ring, 1997a, 1997b). Both of these influences would lower the associated TC.

Transaction(T)-inefficiency can then be defined as the sum of two aspects: the extent of loss from opportunism, in spite of the TC incurred; and the extent of TC incurred in excess of that which would be sufficient in order to attain a similar outcome, that of protecting against opportunistic behaviour.

Value and Value(V)-Inefficiency

In the introduction, I suggested that the representation of the firm as a manager of value in the search for competitive advantage may be a more appropriate basis to understand the behaviour of firms than that of the firm as

tion costs, and recognizes that trade-offs are possible. At the same time, however, he explicitly acknowledges (Williamson, 1985, 1988) that his concentration on TC in explaining the choice of organizational form has been at the expense of under-emphasizing production costs, differences in which mainly occur in the form of economies of scale that distinguish suppliers from in-house production. Effectively, as he subsequently asserts a few pages later, the choice definitively rests on a TC assessment (Williamson, 1985: 71). Accordingly, as Ring (1997a) points out, most of those who work in the TC framework in the management field have tended to focus narrowly on TC.

a cost minimizer. In this section, I elaborate on this notion. For example, concern with comparative costs alone ignores quality. Ability to offer greater quality at the same cost or same quality at lower cost *vis-à-vis* other firms enables the firm to deliver superior value, which then translates into competitive advantage and greater rents. One can expand this concept into n-dimensional space, each dimension representing one of the components of value (e.g. speed, flexibility, reliability, and so on), each of which can be decomposed into further sub-elements (e.g. speed of delivery, speed of new product development, manufacturing lead time, etc).

Value can therefore be conceptualized as a dynamic composite comprising an array of characteristics, where the importance or relative weight of the various components or subcomponents in the mix is context-dependent and shifts around depending on the particular situation in the relevant environment. For example, time to market may be very valuable in the computer industry but less so in the steel industry. The point is that various activities, or combinations of activities, enjoy differing levels of premium in different environments or during different periods in the same environment.

In this light, the economic worth of a firm's offering, product, or service lies not so much in the intrinsic properties of the resources in its possession but, rather, in the firm's ability to participate competitively in a dynamic marketplace where costs and prices are determined by the best performers (Eliasson, 1992). Kim and Mauborgne (1997) provide examples of how Groupe Accor of France staked out a new (and superior) value position in the budget hotel industry through a novel combination of existing value attributes, and how Compaq remained at the forefront of the server industry by continually reconfiguring its offering in terms of new value attributes.

Given that value is a complex and dynamic composite in a state of constant flux, it would be infeasible for a firm to possess or develop all the attributes necessary to operate at the value frontier. At the same time, however, the needed attributes (i.e. value components) cannot always be readily purchased through market exchange (Teece and Pisano, 1994). This is because they may have a high tacit component and therefore require closer and more qualitative coordination to create and realize value (Richardson, 1972; Ghoshal and Moran, 1996), whereas markets are especially appropriate for quantitative coordination through prices. In such situations, the successful conduct of an activity may compel a firm to enter into a synergistic collaboration with a partner as an avenue for the sustained earning of rents. Such collaborations can be viewed as integral elements of the value management proces (Madhok, 2000*b*).

From the discussion of T-inefficiency, it is evident that TC theory is principally concerned with the transactional aspects of inter-firm exchange. Here, the ethos of safeguarding an investment can at best occasion a forbearance from opportunistic behaviour, which would serve to prevent the potential value from synergistic complementarities from being (mis) appropriated. On the other hand, a positive mutual orientation goes one step beyond forbearance and is characterized by the ethos of proactively creating and realizing the underlying potential value. Such an ethos departs from just the transactional aspects to also address the production aspects, above and beyond static scale economies, involved in the pursuit of value through inter-firm exchange.

V-Inefficiency

The discussion of value brings us to the notions of V-efficiency and V-inefficiency. Three decades ago, Leibenstein (1966) elaborated upon the notion of X-efficiency and X-inefficiency. From the viewpoint of a firm, X-inefficiency represented the difference between its theoretically optimal output and the level at which it was currently functioning. The extent of X-inefficiency depends on the intensity of competition that the firm is confronted with. The V-inefficiency argument is similar in principle. The difference between the hypothetically maximal value attainable though an inter-firm collaborative relationship, were the underlying synergistic potential to be fully realized, and the actual level of realization of such value can be conceptualized as value- or (V)-inefficiency. In its essence, V-inefficiency represents the inability to operate at the joint value frontier. On the one hand, V-inefficiency in inter-firm cooperative relationships is the counterpart of X-inefficiency in firms, both being in relation to a hypothetical ideal. On the other, it differs in an important way in that where X-inefficiency takes the production function as an exogenous given, and is determined by the inability to be at this position for various reasons such as shirking (Leibenstein, 1966), V-inefficiency departs from the notion of a given frontier, which can essentially be pushed outward by the behaviour of the partners as events unfold and novel opportunities arise. An inefficient or ineffective dyadic relationship would clearly manifest a higher level of V-inefficiency, demonstrated through a failure by the partners to create and exploit the underlying value potential more fully.

The previous section emphasized that firms can potentially reduce the level of T-inefficiency by approaching the exchange relationship in a more positive manner than TC theory suggests. Likewise, firms can reduce the level of V-inefficiency through a similar approach, as explained further below. This is because production and exchange relations are intertwined. The argument requires greater attention to social relations since these shape and define the nature of interaction, and have even been argued to be the source of efficiency and effectiveness rather than the structural institutional properties emphasized by TC theory (Granovetter, 1985; Powell, 1990; Madhok, 1995b).

The basis of the argument is that there is a premium attached to the quality of the relationship within which the transaction is embedded. This relationship must therefore be actively managed in order to benefit from it. Putting it differently, especially in knowledge-intensive and highly dynamic industries, the joint production function is not fully known and cannot be fully specified *ex ante* but is partially and continually created by the transacting partners through their actions and behaviour in the course of the relationship. The extent to which new opportunity sets are created and/or perceived, be it by accident or by design, and the extent and manner by which the partners are able to capitalize on such opportunities, is a function of the quality and pattern of interaction between them. In this way, the relationship in and of itself behaves as an endogenous factor of production, albeit a 'soft' one, which has a decided impact on the production function and on the value creation and exchange process.

To appreciate the argument more fully, the essential distinction between the true synergistic potential of a relationship and the ability to realize this potential needs to be emphasized (Madhok, 2000*a*; Madhok and Tallman, 1998). While the former depends on the substantive complementarities underlying the relationship which provide the structural capital, the latter depends more on the underlying social capital. Both of these are a potential source of value. While some synergistic rents may be attained through an arm's length relationship, there is greater scope to tap the underlying potential of an inter-firm relationship more fully, above and beyond what could be earned through a safeguarding perspective, when the relationship is characterized by a positive and mutual orientation than just by the avoidance of opportunism (Ring and Van de Ven, 1992; Madhok, 1995*a*). In the latter case, not only are there higher safeguarding costs but, due to poor quality interaction, the value added from cooperation is lower, thus reducing the overall value attained (Hill, 1990; Pearce, 1997). The development of a mutual orientation not only restrains the tendency towards opportunistic behaviour, and thus lessens the perceived need to institute costly and elaborate safeguards, as mentioned earlier, but also provides an opportunity to combine resources more productively due to more voluntary and unilateral commitments outside the terms of the contract.

In general, more committed behaviour and a greater exchange of information under a cooperative orientation results in higher value added as a result of more complete synergy through a more productive blending of capabilities. This difference between the value attained under a predominantly safeguarding orientation and a more mutual one contributes to V-efficiency, or conversely lowers V-inefficiency, and is directly linked to the quality of the relationship itself. In a sense, then, expenditure directed towards improving the quality of the relationship acts as investment in social capital which yields a payoff in future returns through occasioning a fuller attainment of the underlying synergistic potential.[8]

---

[8] Of course, resources dedicated towards improving the relationship entail expenditures which need to be factored into the equation. However, to the extent that these expenditures are offset by correspondingly greater returns, they can be regarded as investments in future value.

To the extent that similar outcomes (i.e. no opportunism in spite of the opportunity for it due to fewer safeguards) can be attained at a lower level of TC, this is T-efficient and itself adds to value, as defined. Similarly, to the extent that superior outcomes can be attained at similar levels of TC, this is V-efficient. Therefore, investment in social capital has the potential to reduce both T-inefficiency and V-inefficiency. Moreover, besides the fact that a predominant orientation of safeguarding against opportunistic behaviour endangers the level and quality of cooperation, which can adversely affect the level of value attained through the collaboration, this value may be difficult to replace internally by a firm with inadequate capabilities. The effect of endangering V-inefficiency would then behave as a form of 'natural protection' against opportunistic behaviour, which in itself may lead to lower T-inefficiency where the perceived need for safeguards becomes lower. There is thus an interdependence between the two.

An Illustrative Example

Let us examine the argument in the preceding section more carefully through an illustrative example. What if a cooperative firm is confronted with a situation where a partner (say in a buyer–supplier relationship entailing joint design and development), in whose competencies it may have a critical (even if limited) interest, misuses an asset or fails to meet contractual specifications, i.e. seemingly opportunistic behaviour? On the one hand, to protect against this eventuality, firms would need to incur TC, say through on-site personnel for monitoring purposes, in order to safeguard against the abuse of the asset due to opportunism. Note, however, that non-performance in the form of behaviour by a partner who diverges from his commitments may not in fact be due to any opportunistic intent but could be simply due to honest misunderstanding, misinterpretation of environmental signals, or inadequate capabilities on his part. The distinction is important since, in such a case, apparently 'defecting' action, being actually unintentional, was really not so. Given that mutual synergies still exist, i.e. there are potential joint gains from cooperation, such a situation may require transaction-specific expenditures of a different kind to correct it, in the form of teaching, training, etc. A knee-jerk 'eye for an eye and tooth for a tooth' reaction may potentially be short-sighted in the context of long-term value.[9]

Instead, in order to generate and realize value, a firm may need to closely monitor how the asset or technology is being used, since this enables the firm to supervise, teach, and guide its application and use and, in general, to

---

[9] Needless to say, continuing cooperation in the face of repeated violations would raise questions about the partner's intent. There comes a point where a firm finally needs to recognize that 'it's being had', otherwise it would be tantamount to sheer naivety. Nevertheless, the essential point being made still holds. This does require the firm to make some trade-offs. This is touched upon in the next section.

facilitate or even ensure that the requisite activities have been understood and are being performed in line with value creation. Moreover, it also enables the firm to learn and better understand what is hindering the appropriate use of the technology or asset as anticipated. Perhaps the firm itself did not adequately communicate its competencies and needs to the supplier. In other words, other than a policing device, monitoring also plays an educational role in terms of providing an occasion for mutual teaching and learning. Such teaching and learning enables greater cognitive convergence and thus, though a more mutual orientation, facilitates value creation. At the same time, to the extent that this is a joint and interdependent outcome, it not only decreases the willingness to be opportunistic but, also, by lowering information asymmetries through greater sharing of information, the ability for opportunism is also reduced.

Monitoring therefore plays a dual function in guarding against dissipation of the rent stream, both through curbing the ability and willingness to engage in opportunistic behaviour as well as through facilitating the creation and realization of value. Now, if placing a team on-site is primarily for purposes associated with value creation, then monitoring costs associated with safeguarding are basically incremental. This does not negate the opportunism-protecting monitoring element but suggests that the balance, in terms of resource allocation—financial, temporal, and managerial—between the two, will tilt towards actions more consonant with cognitive alignment through a mutual orientation. Similarly, where the monitoring is of a safeguarding nature, the costs associated with creating this cognitive alignment are only incremental. In effect, the allocation of transaction-specific expenditures between these two kinds of purposes is an indicator of the quality of the relationship. While safeguarding costs may dominate in the earlier stages of the relationship, the composite has the potential to shift towards a mutual orientation as the relationship progresses (Parkhe, 1993; Dyer, 1997; Ring, 1997a; Ring and Van de Ven, 1994).

The difficulty in assessing a partner's behaviour and reacting appropriately can also be examined in a different light. For an opportunism-protecting regime to work effectively, it is necessary for firms to have unhindered ability to observe the partner's behaviour. If instead, as Kreps (1990) points out, one only observes the outcome, which is found to be wanting, and the outcome is the result of a probabilistic instead of a deterministic (production) function, then one has to decide whether to impute deliberate defection or chance (or both) as the reason for the poor result. As can be imagined, with complex and multidimensional products or services, and especially those that involve innovative aspects, such as product design and development, the outcome is inevitably probabilistic to some extent and thus 'judgement' comes into the evaluation of the delivered product or service and subsequent reaction.

Now consider the inherent trade-off involved when committing to a specialized investment. On the one hand, transaction-specific investment, a notion particularly central to TC (Williamson, 1985, 1991), results in a small numbers bargaining situation, since the salvage value of the asset is lower in alternate uses. This escalates the risks of opportunism and the costs of protecting against it. On the other hand, however, the attraction of a transaction-specific investment is that, by tying together respective assets to a specialized application, it potentially improves the efficiency of the particular transaction. Basically then, efficiency gains from specialization and interdependence are accompanied by increased threats from opportunism and reduced flexibility due to switching costs. These are two sides of the same coin.

In approaching this trade-off, TC theory tends to focus mainly on the loss that a firm could potentially incur as a result of opportunistic behaviour by a partner. However, under a more mutual orientation between the participants, the fundamental transformation to a small numbers situation due to transaction-specific investments can, instead of a negative to be avoided, create an incentive to harness the consequent interdependence for the creation and realization of synergistic value (Johanson and Mattsson, 1987; Zajac and Olsen, 1993; Dyer, 1997). Such interdependence facilitates the willingness to mutually adapt towards one another and make unilateral and voluntary commitments, beyond the minimal contractual level, in the pursuit of value. Not only does a mutual orientation facilitate forbearance, it also enables more efficient coordination and operational and behavioural flexibility in the conduct of the relationship (Ouchi, 1980; Ring and Van de Ven, 1994). This translates into lower T- and V-inefficiency.

Discussion

To recapitulate a key aspect of the argument so far, value, on closer examination, can be unpacked and disaggregated into two aspects: that which can be anticipated and that which cannot. In the former case, the desired outcome can be considered as a given and the predominant concern is the most economical means of attaining this outcome. In the latter case, value cannot be fully contemplated in advance since it is partially occasioned through the dynamic process of interaction among economic actors, both within and across firms. As a result, the benefits are variable, are only partially specifiable upfront, and are partially generated through the behaviour and conduct of the parties concerned. Essentially, the future is continually being created on the basis of current and real time actions. This argument has important implications and emphasizes the need for entrepreneurial behaviour, especially in situations where there are no meaningful output criteria or behavioural rules (e.g. product design and development).

The illustrative example in the previous section suggests that, in the pursuit of value, it may well be more prudent for a firm to invest in the relationship than to simply assume opportunism and protect itself accordingly. The implicit assumption here is that while the potential for opportunism is ever present, the actual act of opportunism is a variable. In a sense, the firm behaves as a 'relationship engineer', devising the appropriate mechanisms and behaviour to narrow the gap between the maximum value that is hypothetically feasible and the challenging reality of effectuating transactions both effectively and efficiently. Achieving this requires the firms to carefully identify and analyse the ties between their relational activities and the value created and attained through the collaboration. To the extent that the characteristics of the transaction themselves remain invariant, TC theory remains indifferent as to the identity of the other party. In the V-efficiency argument, not only does identity matter but, more importantly, identification with that identity matters in the pursuit of value. This is because more opportunities become available to the partners for deriving value from a collaboration, depending upon the 'tone and tempo' (spirit) of the relationship. This argument is in line with opportunism being a variable as a result of 'relationship engineering'.

In essence, the representation of the firm as a rent and value seeker rather than as a seeker of contractual efficiency implies a much more proactive view of the management of a firm's boundaries than cost minimization. Through the lens of value, the focal actors become participants in value creation and realization rather than transactors in exchange, the former being a more integrative process. The argument suggests a different perspective towards transacting through collaborations and emphasizes the importance of the social relations characterizing a relationship, far more than TC theory does. As Jarillo (1990: 498) aptly states, the social dimension 'is not a "soft" ' issue, for it goes to the heart of the question of what are the real causes of transaction costs'. In this regard, Powell (1990) asserts that 'an exclusive focus on the transaction—rather than the relationship—as the primary unit of analysis is misplaced' (p. 323). In this argument, the transaction may not be the appropriate level of analysis in and of itself, since it is embedded in a dynamic relationship and not independent of it. This interdependence between the transaction and the relationship is critical to the attainment of value from it (Madhok, 2000a; Madhok and Tallman, 1998).

While the conventional TC argument addresses the cost of protecting against opportunism plus the cost of opportunism, I would add to this the V-efficiency forgone as a result of excessive reliance on overly and overtly protective measures which tend to hamper development of a closer and more mutual relationship and therefore end up sacrificing the additional opportunities available to tap the value potential. Reinforcing this argument, Pearce (1997) points out that excessive contractual specifications *ex ante*, before commencement, may handcuff the collaboration in its pursuit of value by limiting its flexibility in the face of changed circumstances. As mentioned earlier, a major factor driving inter-firm collaborations is that they potentially enable firms to attain an intended end which would be difficult for them to attain in as productive a manner otherwise within an acceptable time frame or cost level, at least not as cost effectively. Taking this into account, the internalization of a transaction into the hierarchy in order to circumvent the TC associated with collaborating involves a trade-off between production costs and transaction costs. If one momentarily considers only the production side of the equation, in situations where there is an inefficiency in production, in terms of the difference in efficiency between in-house production and that through an inter-firm collaboration, firms can invest until they reach the limit of this differential in developing the quality of the relationship without incurring a 'penalty' in a comparative institutional sense. Moreover, to the extent that such relationally oriented investment has the capacity to lower the level of V-inefficiency or even the level of T-inefficiency, as discussed, such lower V-inefficiency, T-inefficiency, or both potentially provides firms with an additional set of resources of an internally generated nature to further invest in the relationship as and when needed. So long as such expenditures are correspondingly compensated by greater value through the collaboration, whether in terms of greater output for the same level of costs or lower costs for the same level of output, the firm is better off and the investment becomes both worthwhile and economically sensible and can be seen as an investment in future value. In fact, the level of total relationship-specific expenditures could even be greater than the TC-minimizing one (Ring, 1997a). The reason for this is that, in the ultimate analysis, it is not just the size of these expenditures but also their composition, in terms of the allocation between protective and teaching or learning purposes, which affects the level of value attained.

In light of the above, where a firm's capabilities are limited, and the joint production function is potentially superior to the hierarchical one, expending resources on in-house production for reasons to do with safeguards against opportunism instead of investing in the relationship in the pursuit of value is V-inefficient behaviour. Conceptually here, the incremental capital–output ratio of (mistakenly) investing one unit of capital in in-house production would be lower than investing it to reduce V-inefficiency. This is tantamount to a misallocation of resources.

Similar to the X-inefficiency argument, V-inefficiency can be expected to decrease in competitive environments. In fact, an efficient and effective management of relationships from a management of value perspective can enable firms to attain a competitive advantage over those which remain stuck in the TC-minimizing mould (Barney and Hansen, 1994; Lado, Boyd, and Hanlon, 1997). In such a case, the V-inefficient firm would be rendered uncompetitive. This would explain the recent spate of articles in the business press about a radical change in organizing economic activity, e.g. fewer and closer buyer–supplier relationships with more intimate and value-adding interaction among them (Fortune, 1994a). In a recent study of the car industry, Dyer (1997) found that fewer but more intimate and long-term relationships with suppliers not only reduced TC in the long run, in spite of a higher level of asset specificity, but also resulted in superior performance on the part of Japanese firms *vis-a-vis* US firms. This translates into both lower T-inefficiency and lower V-inefficiency. One could then argue that a high level of T- and V-inefficiency on the part of US firms would compel them to move away from a safeguarding and TC-minimizing orientation to a value-maximization one, failing which they would suffer a decline in competitiveness. This change in orientation, both strategic and relational, with US firms (especially Chrysler and Ford but increasingly GM) resorting to fewer but higher quality and value-adding relationships, seems to have occurred in recent years (e.g. Fortune, 1994*b*). The recent re-emergence of the US auto industry as a global powerhouse is testimony to the effectiveness of the V-efficiency strategy.

A true understanding of the relationship between economic organization and performance requires a closer appreciation of the value-creating aspects of different organizational modes (Lazonick, 1991; Madhok, 2000*b*). The rationale proposed in this discussion underlines a more proactive and flexible approach towards collaborations, beyond just TC minimization, which then makes an additional set of tools available to management to generate and realize value from a transaction. As Dodgson states:

The cooperative rather than the universally competitive model of interfirm relationships . . . has implications for those theories that reduce all firm transactions to cost and price considerations without regard to the mutually valuable synergies achievable through the sharing of competencies and knowledge (1995: 291).

In this regard, the V-inefficiency argument shifts the singular attention away from opportunism in an important way. From the standpoint of value, the value-managing firm is undoubtedly a seeker of self-interest but of a different and decidedly more 'intelligent', i.e. V-efficient, kind. Such an 'intelligent' self-interest occurs within the framework of dynamic value-maximization rather than opportunism-minimization, which accordingly shifts the relative emphasis away from safeguards to more entrepreneurial opportunity-seeking within a relationship and consequent V-efficiency.

The above argument does not mean to suggest that firms should not invest in protection mechanisms. Clearly, the risk of opportunistic behaviour is always present, especially when specialized investments are greater, and firms must have recourse to safeguards, even more so since being protected also facilitates the relationship. The more important point is that, while investing in protective mechanisms may be necessary, it is certainly not sufficient in and of itself to fully realize the synergies that inter-firm collaborations potentially engender, and may even hinder the pursuit of value. Moreover, given the potential value of collaborations, concerns about opportunism may need to be traded off against the benefits (Mody, 1993). In this light, a mutual orientation should not be seen as a substitute for opportunism but rather as a complement in the pursuit of value.

In effect, the V-efficiency argument revisits the cost–benefit calculus of opportunism, and the associated payoffs from such behaviour. Though Williamson's TC theory also approaches opportunism through a cost–benefit calculus, the V-efficiency approach differs in two important ways. First, through various examples, such as the merchant banker–shipper transaction which he elaborated on at length, Williamson (1993) examines the cost of opportunism in terms of a particular transaction, while I address it (in the next few paragraphs) in terms of the collectivity of transactions that a firm is engaged in. Second, and more central to the discussion, rather than a superior outcome being one where the available value is not (mis)appropriated, as posited by TC theory, in the V-efficiency argument a superior outcome is one that goes beyond this to extend the value frontier further outward and more fully create and tap into the synergistic opportunities made available through the collaborative relationship.

While I am in full agreement with the assertion made in TC theory that the potential for opportunism exists universally and that it is difficult as well as costly to discover who is going to be opportunistic when, where the V-inefficiency approach differs is in the way in which it deals with such a scenario. That is, opportunism is a variable to be managed rather than a structural constraint. I would contend that behaviour by firms along the lines postulated by TC theory, namely that it is safer to assume potential opportunism by all at all times and approach transactions accordingly, is overly restrictive and conservative and would be contrary to the very ecological principles on which transaction cost theory rests. The notion of V-inefficiency calls for a bolder and more entrepreneurial approach which, while being potentially more risky, is also characterized by the potential for greater returns and could ultimately be a superior strategy in terms of value. Of course, a firm runs the risk of opportunism and, as mentioned, needs to take precautions. The difference is that it is not 'blinded' by it. As I demonstrate next, by not investing in as high levels of protection against the potential opportunist in all its interactions, a firm would lose occasionally in its interactions with the occasional opportunist but, overall across all its transactions, due to the gains from cooperation through a reduction in T- and V-inefficiency, it could well be better off.

Basically, if the gains from greater synergy and lower transaction costs in its interactions are greater than the costs arising both from encounters with the chance opportunist and a higher level of safeguarding costs, then a mutual orientation pays off. The following example serves to illustrate the point. Suppose 20 per cent, say, of actors are opportunistic 30 per cent of the time,[10]

---

[10] Since only some people are opportunistic some of the time, and not most people most of the time, this justifies the use of percentages lower than 50%. The actual percentages used, of course, are arbitrary and merely illustrative of the wider point.

then the probability of opportunistic behaviour is (.2)(.3) or 6 per cent.[11] Also suppose that (*a*) the TC associated with safeguards, assuming opportunism, is $100, (*b*) the value generated through the transaction is $120 and (*c*) the loss as a result of opportunistic behaviour is $0 (due to adequate safeguards). Further, for the reasons provided earlier to do with T- and V-inefficiency, let us suppose that (*a*) the TC is 10 per cent[12] lower, (*b*) the value generated is 10 per cent higher under a cooperative orientation than under an opportunistic one, and (*c*) the loss through opportunistic behaviour as a result of inadequate safeguards is $80. Under such a scenario, the expected value from cooperation will be

$$(1.1)120 - (.9)100 - (.06)80 = 37.2,$$

an amount greater than the net value assuming opportunism which would be

$$120 - 100 = 20.$$

In essence, then, generalizing the above equation and assuming that organizations are interested in survival over the longer term, my argument is that even though a firm may render itself more vulnerable to opportunistic behaviour in its various transactions, on average, across the totality of its transactions, investing in relationships for the attainment of value could well be the superior and more intelligent strategy.

The above argument is important in that, to the extent that from the TC view the firm can be seen as a collectivity of transactions (Ulrich and Barney 1984), there is no particular compulsion to organize each one optimally in the TC sense. Knudsen (1995), in interpreting Winter's (1988) argument, essentially makes a similar case for viewing the firm as a collectivity of transactions:

Since a complex network of interdependent transactions occurs within the firm, the totality of transactions, and not the individual transactions, are subject to a 'market test' of efficiency. We must thus assume that if a firm is characterized by such a bundle of interdependent transactions, some of the transactions will prove to be inefficient (p. 204).

In terms of the above argument, what this suggests is that, at the level of the totality, T-inefficient transactions will be subsidized by V-efficient ones.[13]

---

[11] Even this can be considered to be somewhat conservative in that it assumes independence across different transactions. Yet, it is fairly commonplace for firms to have repeat ties with the same partner, in which case, as Gulati (1995) has shown, the proclivity to be opportunistic decreases.

[12] Again, the percentages are arbitrary but serve to reflect the broader argument that firms would still incur TC, just not to the same extent.

[13] Along somewhat similar lines, though with a different twist, Ring (1997*a*) argues that transaction costs are but one of many elements comprising a firm's overall cost structure. Therefore, superior performance on other cost dimensions can subsidize inefficiencies of a TC nature.

It is worth re-emphasizing that theories which rest on opportunism-dependent arguments, such as transaction costs and agency theory, do not claim that all actors always behave opportunistically, but that some of them do some of the time. It is a probabilistic argument. Yet the difficulty of identifying and filtering out such behaviour makes it less costly (more convenient?) to assume potential opportunism. This can result in such theories becoming 'overdetermined' (Kogut and Zander, 1992). In this respect, Ghoshal and Moran (1996) emphasize that fuller creation and attainment of value requires economic actors to behave entrepreneurially and resourcefully and accordingly to take novel and innovative actions as unanticipated opportunities unfold. In criticizing TC theory, they further contend that 'because opportunism is difficult to distinguish ex ante from partnership, in an effort to control the former, they will destroy the latter' (1996: 38). This point is reflected in the illustrative example above. What the argument amounts to is that not only is TC theory poorly equipped to distinguish between value (mis)appropriation and (potentially) value-creating behaviour but, being 'shackled' by its assumption of opportunism, it tends to be overly conservative. Here, opportunism concerns drive out entrepreneurial ones, possibly because they are of a 'harder' and more clearly defined nature.

Moreover, to continue along the main thrust of the arguments above, if greater gains from cooperation on average induce firms to be cooperative, this can result in a self-reinforcing momentum in a dynamic sense. First, where both partners have a reputation for forbearance, this results in mutually lower costs of safeguards against opportunism. Additionally, besides providing a signal regarding partner selection, reputation also impacts the extent and willingness of resource commitment (Loveridge, chap. 7, below). Second, the probability of interacting with cooperative actors increases over time, which then increases the overall performance gap between cooperative and non-cooperative actors. This is so since, within a framework where economic exchange is embedded in a structure of social relations and where reputation mechanisms are reasonably efficient, the population would evolve into a greater density of non-opportunistic actors, since external mechanisms would convert a part of the opportunistic population or eventually select them out of the market (Axelrod, 1984). The ultimate outcome is both higher T-efficiency and V-efficiency.

In sum, instead of opportunism behaving as a structural constraint, with the key decision variable being the alignment of governance structures to transaction characteristics, the emphasis shifts towards opportunism as a managerial constraint, with the key decision variable being a behavioural and processual one in terms of the level of opportunism and how it is to be managed. Here, it is not just the magnitude but also the composition of transaction-specific expenditures that becomes a variable of crucial importance. This places the focal lens on the firm's 'collaborating technology', which directly translates into the ability of the firm to create and extract value through its collaborations more fully, and ultimately results in differences between firms in terms of competitive advantage.

Concluding Remarks

The shift in orientation proposed in this chapter, away from opportunism and from cost to value, is an important one with significant implications for how firms approach and structure their interactions with other firms in their collaborative relationships. Approaching inter-firm collaboration in terms of T-efficiency and V-inefficiency may not only potentially provide a superior insight into the popularity of collaborations but may also unlock the explanation as to why firms face difficulties in attaining the promise offered by collaboration.

Could it be that the cause of this failure to attain the anticipated value is rooted in firms' behaviour being shaped by the anticipation of opportunism? This discussion suggests that in order to better benefit from collaboration, where it is a potentially superior alternative, greater attention needs to be paid towards the relationship process itself (Madhok, 1995a; Madhok and Tallman, 1998; Tallman, chap. 5, below), going beyond economizing on (transaction) costs in the context of safeguarding against opportunism to reflect the underlying motivation of minimizing V-inefficiency. This demands skill and foresight in the administering of interactions with key partners in a firm's network (Rugman and D'Cruz, chap. 3, above), which in turn requires envisaging the relationship intrinsically as a potential value-bearing asset and governing it more entrepreneurially to increase its 'yield'.

Theorists need to explicitly adopt value as their focus of analysis in the formation and governance of collaborations, and in the analysis of firm boundaries in general. Attention to value also invites and even demands greater attention to issues such as innovation and learning, activities which are increasingly important to competitive advantage in the modern economy but which are admittedly not of central importance to TC theory (Williamson, 1985, 1988, 1998). The discussion in this chapter raises some interesting research questions. Inter-firm collaboration is clearly a mixed motive game (Nti and Kumar, chap, 6, below), where the relationship is characterized by a spirit of collaboration (for creation of the pie) and competition (for distribution of the pie). It is therefore important to know when to collaborate and when to compete. How the tensions associated with such mixed motives, and the associated trade-offs, are fruitfully managed would be an important area of research.

References

AXELROD, R. (1984), *The Evolution of Cooperation* (New York: Basic Books).

BARNEY, J. and HANSEN, M. H. (1994), 'Trustworthiness as a Source of Competitive Advantage', *Strategic Management Journal*, 15 (special winter issue): 175–90.

BRADACH, J. L. and ECCLES, R. G. (1989), 'Price, Authority and Trust: From Ideal Types to Plural Forms', *Annual Review of Sociology*, 15: 97–118.

BUCKLEY, P. J. and CASSON, M. H. (1988), 'A Theory of Cooperation in International Business', in F. J. Contractor and P. Lorange (eds.), *Cooperative Strategies in International Business* (Lexington, Mass.: Lexington Books), 31–54.

CONNER, K. R. (1991), 'A Historical Comparison of Resource-Based Theory and Five Schools of Thought within Industrial Organization Economics: Do we have a New Theory of the Firm?' *Journal of Management*, 17: 121–54.

DIETRICH, M. (1994), *Transaction Cost Economics and Beyond: Towards a New Economics of the Firm* (London: Routledge).

DODGSON, M. (1995), 'Technological Collaboration and Innovation', in M. Dodgson and R. Rothwell (eds.), *The Handbook of Industrial Innovation* (Brookfield, Vt.: Edward Elgar), 285–92.

DYER, J. H. (1997), 'Effective Interfirm Collaboration: How Transactors Minimize Transaction Costs and Maximize Transaction Value', *Strategic Management Journal*, 18/7: 535–56.

ELIASSON, G. (1992), 'The Dynamics of Supply and Economic Growth', in B. Carlsson (ed.), *Industrial Dynamics: Technological, Organizational and Structural Changes in Industries and Firms* (Boston: Kluwer), 21–54.

FORTUNE (1994a), 'The New Golden Rules of Business', 21 Feb.

—— (1994b), 'The Auto Industry Meets the New Economy', 5 Sept.

GHOSHAL, S. and MORAN P. (1996), 'Bad for Practice: A Critique of Transaction Cost Theory', *Academy of Management Review*, 21/1: 13–47.

GRANOVETTER, M. (1985), 'Economic Action and Social Structure: The Problem of Embeddedness', *American Journal of Sociology*, 91/3 481–510.

HAGEDOORN, J. (1993), 'Understanding the Rationale of Strategic Technology Partnering: Interorganizational Modes of Cooperation and Sectoral Differences', *Strategic Management Journal*, 14: 371–86.

HENNART, J. F. (1993), 'Explaining the Swollen Middle: Why Most Transactions Are a Mix of "Market" and "Hierarchy"', *Organization Science*, 4: 529–47.

HILL, C. W. L. (1990), 'Cooperation, Opportunism, and the Invisible Hand: Implications for Transaction Cost Theory', *Academy of Management Review*, 15/3: 500–13.

JARILLO, J. C. (1988), 'On Strategic Networks', *Strategic Management Journal*, 9: 31–41.

—— (1990), 'Comments on "Transaction Costs and Networks"', *Strategic Management Journal*, 11: 497–9.

JOHANSON, J. and MATTSSON, L. G. (1987), 'Interorganizational Relations in Industrial Systems: A Network Approach Compared with the Transaction Cost Approach', *International Studies of Management and Organization*, 17/1: 34–48.

KIM, W. C. and MAUBORGNE, R. (1997), 'Value Innovation: The Strategic Logic of High Growth', *Harvard Business Review*, 75: 102–15.

KNUDSEN, C. (1995), 'Theories of the Firm, Strategic Management, and Leadership', in C. Montgomery (ed.), *Resource-Based and Evolutionary Theories of the Firm: Towards a Synthesis* (Boston: Kluwer), 179–217.

KOGUT, B. and ZANDER, U. (1992), 'Knowledge of the Firm, Combinative Capabilities, and the Replication of Technology', *Organizational Science*, 3/3: 383–97.

KREPS, D. (1990), 'Corporate Culture and Economic Theory', in J. Alt and K. Shepsle (eds.), *Perspectives on Positive Political Economy* (New York: Cambridge University Press), 90–143.

KUMAR, R. and NTI, K. O. (1998), 'Differential Learning and Interaction in Alliance Dynamics: A Process and Outcome Discrepancy Model', *Organization Science*, 9: 356–67.

LADO, A. A., BOYD, N. G., and HANLON, S. C. (1997), 'Competition, Cooperation, and the Search for Economic Rents: A Syncretic Model', *Academy of Management Review*, 22/1: 110–41.

LAZONICK, W. (1991), *Business Organization and the Myth of the Market Economy* (Cambridge: Cambridge University Press).

LEIBENSTEIN, H. (1966), 'Allocative Efficiency vs. "X-efficiency"', *American Economic Review*, 56: 392–415.

LOASBY, B. (1994), 'Organizational Capabilities and Interfirm Relations', *Metroeconomica*, 248–65.

MADHOK, A. (1995a), 'Revisiting Multinational Firms' tolerance for Joint Ventures: A Trust-Based Approach', *Journal of International Business Studies*, 26: 117–37.

—— (1995b), 'Opportunism and Trust in Joint Venture Relationships: An Exploratory Study and a Model', *Scandinavian Journal of Management*, 11/1: 57–74.

—— (1997), 'Cost, Value and Foreign Market Entry Mode: The Transaction and the Firm', *Strategic Management Journal*, 18: 39–61.

—— (2000a), 'Interfirm Collaborations: Contractual and Competence-Based Perspectives', in N. Foss and V. Mahnke (eds.), *Competence, Governance, and Enterpreneurship* (Oxford: Oxford University Press, forthcoming).

—— (2000b), 'Strategic Alliances and Organizational Boundaries: A Knowledge-Based Perspective', in R. Sanchez (ed.), *Beyond the Boundaries: Integrating Theories of the Firm and Theories of Markets* (Oxford: Elsevier Pergamon Press).

—— and TALLMAN, S. B. (1998), 'Resources, Transactions and Rents: Managing Value through Interfirm Collaborative Relationships', *Organization Science*, 9/3: 326–39.

MODY, A. (1993), 'Learning through Alliances', *Journal of Economic Behavior and Organization*, 20: 151–70.

MOWERY, D. C., OXLEY, J. E., and SILVERMAN, B. S. (1997), 'Strategic Alliances and Interfirm Knowledge Transfer', *Strategic Management Journal*, 17 (winter special issue): 77–92.

NOORDERHAVEN, N. G. (1996), 'Opportunism and Trust in Transaction Cost Economics', in J. Groenewegen (ed.), *Transaction Cost Economics and Beyond* (Boston: Kluwer), 105–28.

OUCHI, W. G. (1980), 'Markets, Bureaucracies, and Clans', *Administrative Science Quarterly*, 25: 129–41.

PARKHE, A. (1991), 'Interfirm Diversity, Organizational Learning, and Longevity in Global Strategic Alliances', *Journal of International Business Studies*, 22/4: 579–602.

—— (1993), Strategic Alliance Structuring: A Game Theoretic and Transaction Cost Examination of Interfirm Cooperation', *Academy of Management Journal*, 36/4: 794–829.

PEARCE, R. J. (1997), 'Toward Understanding Joint Venture Performance and Survival: A Bargaining and Influence Approach to Transaction Cost Theory', *Academy of Management Review*, 22/1: 203–25.

PETERAF, M. (1993), 'The Cornerstones of Competitive Advantage: A Resource-Based View', *Strategic Management Journal*, 14/3: 179–92.

POWELL, W. W. (1990), 'Neither Market nor Hierarchy: Network Forms of Organization', *Research in Organizational Behavior*, 12: 295–336.

RICHARDSON, G. B. (1972), 'The Organization of Industry', *The Economic Journal*, 82: 883–96.

RING, P. S. (1997*a*), 'Costs of Network Organization', in A. Grandori (ed.), *The Game of Networks* (London: Routledge).

—— (1997*b*), 'Transacting in the State of Union: A Case Study of Exchange Governed by Convergent Interests', *Journal of Management Studies*, 34: 1–25.

—— and VAN DE VEN, A. H. (1992), 'Structuring Cooperative Relationships Between Organizations', *Strategic Management Journal*, 13: 483–98.

—— —— (1994), 'Development Processes of Cooperative Interorganizational Relationships', *Academy of Management Journal*, 19: 90–118.

TEECE, D. J. (1992), 'Competition, Cooperation and Innovation', *Journal of Economic Behavior and Organization*, 18: 1–25.

—— and PISANO, G. (1994), 'The Dynamic Capabilities of Firms: An Introduction', *Journal of Economic Behavior and Organization*, 3: 537–56.

TOLSTOY, L. (1942), *War and Peace* (New York: Simon and Schuster).

ULRICH, D., and BARNEY, J. (1984), 'Perspectives in Organizations: Resource Dependence, Efficiency and Population', *Academy of Management Review*, 9/3: 471–81.

WILLIAMSON, O. E. (1975), *Markets and Hierarchies: Analysis and Antitrust Implications* (New York: Free Press).

—— (1985), *The Economic Institutions of Capitalism* (New York: Free Press).

—— (1988), 'Technology and Transaction Cost Economics', *Journal of Economic Behavior and Organization*, 10: 355–63.

—— (1991), 'Comparative Economic Organization: The Analysis of Discrete Structural Alternatives', *Administrative Science Quarterly*, 36: 269–96.

—— (1993), 'Calculativeness, Trust, and Economic Organization', *Journal of Law and Economics*, 36: 453–86.

—— (1998), 'Strategy Research: Governance and Competence Perspectives', paper presented at the DRUID Conference on Competence and Entrepreneurship (Bornholm, Denmark, June).

WINTER, S. (1988), 'On Coase, Competence and the Corporation', *Journal of Law, Economics, and Organization*, 4: 163–80.

ZAJAC E. J. and OLSEN, C. P. (1993), 'From Transaction Cost to Transaction Value Analysis: Implications for the Study of Interorganizational Strategies', *Journal of Management Studies*, 30: 131–45.

5

Forming and Managing Shared Organization Ventures
Resources and Transaction Costs

STEPHEN TALLMAN

Firms are turning in increasing numbers to strategic alliances as a means for entering and operating in domestic and international markets. The strategic value of inter-firm cooperative relationships is apparent in the modern context of rapidly growing and changing markets, globalizing competition, network organizations, and dynamic, complex, and expensive technologies. Alliances permit firms to create new joint competencies by rapidly and inexpensively combining sets of resources and capabilities that are not available to them individually, but which are in some way complementary (Geringer, 1988). This possibility would seem to provide considerable competitive advantage. Yet, the rate of failure of cooperative forms of venture is generally found to be very high (Gomes-Casseres, 1987; Parkhe, 1991; Gulati and Nohria, 1992; Cartwright and Cooper, 1993). Managers may well ask why, if cooperative organizations are so effective, do they so often fail? Or, alternatively, if alliances fail so often, why do companies continue to invest their time, effort, and capital in these high-risk ventures? Are there identifiable sources of potential benefit which outweigh the likely costs of organizational failure and encourage continued alliance efforts? If so, why do these benefits so often fail to materialize or at least to surpass the costs of these intermediate forms of organizing? It seems that the costs of managing alliances must be higher than typically anticipated, the benefits less than expected, or both. This chapter combines two theoretical perspectives to create a model of alliance formation, management, and termination in order to address the questions posed above.

This chapter focuses on one specific alliance context, that of Shared Organization Ventures (SOVs), defined as those combinations of organizations in which the partner organizational structures, people, and systems are commingled, but both (or all) parent identities, cultures, and capabilities are retained within the alliance—what Milgrom and Roberts (1990) have called 'preservative/pluralistic' forms. To a large extent, SOVs encompass equity joint ventures and partial acquisitions, as defined by Hennart (1991). While much of our discussion addresses combined ownership forms of organization, legal ownership is not the major issue here. The strategic intent to integrate the complex organizational capabilities and resources of two or more parents into sustained rent-generating joint competencies is.[1]

The two theoretical perspectives on organizational strategy and structure are the resource-based or organizational capabilities view of the firm, and the transaction cost perspective of organizational governance. Both of these theories are built around the concept of economic rent-yielding assets while emphasizing alternative perspectives on this phenomenon. Resource-Based Theory (RBT) views the firm as a bundle of resources, capabilities, and competencies intended to generate maximum benefits. It is primarily concerned with increasing the value of rents that can be obtained from firms' resources (Peteraf, 1993)—the primary benefit is sustainable competitive advantage. In the RBT view, each bundle of strategic and complementary resources has a particular rent-generating potential that changes with resource variations and is highly dependent on management capabilities. Collaboration provides the firm with access to complementary capabilities which provide a potential for synergy in building competencies. Transaction Cost Economics (TCE), on the other hand, treats the organization as a 'nexus of contracts' binding assets more or less tightly together for maximum cost efficiency. TCE analysis is oriented specifically towards the minimization of the costs of the transactions among various assets through structural analysis (Zajac and Olsen, 1993). The primary benefit of concern is that of the reduction in transactional costs. In the TCE view, any governance mechanism is formed because it is the most efficient and least expensive means of governing the particular exchange. An alliance is attractive when it economizes on governance costs in a particular transaction.

Alone, each perspective has limitations. Together, the two theories provide a more balanced and comprehensive understanding of the potential advantages and risks of strategic alliances, and particularly of SOVs. As both address the rent-earning potential of firm-specific resources and capabilities and their relationships, but with differing emphases and focal concerns, they have an inherent complementarity that is exploited in this model. In order to integrate these conceptual models, I first discuss the critical issues raised about SOVs from each theoretical perspective in a static model, and then bring the two sets of concerns together in a dynamic model of the life cycle of the SOV. The chapter ends with a short discussion of the meanings of SOV success, failure and termination without failure, and derives some thoughts for managers to consider.

---

[1] For instance, Salk (1995) describes preservation/pluralistic type full mergers and acquisitions in which organizational characteristics are retained and which face many of the same issues discussed here. Milgrom and Roberts (1990) also describe a complete takeover in which the preservation of the character of the target firm was a key strategic objective, and its loss a major source of failure.

Synergy—The Resource-Based Theory View of SOVs

Resource-based theory tells managers to create core competencies—bundles of resources and capabilities with rent-yielding potential. Collaboration is attractive when it provides desirable resources that a firm cannot develop within an acceptable time frame and cost structure by relying solely on its own capabilities. In forming alliances, this suggests that managers should look for firm-specific, durable, and scarce Strategic Assets[2] within the firm and com- plementary resources in potential partners (Amit and Schoemaker, 1993). Strategic assets are of two kinds: 'hard' and 'soft'. In introducing the notion of invisible assets, Itami (1987) has criticized the tendency to define strategic assets too narrowly, addressing only the 'harder' measurable assets (such as plant and equipment) and ignoring 'soft' assets (such as managerial capabil- ities, knowledge, systems, etc). Both hard and soft assets have a potential for generating value. Frequently, the two are complementary or co-specialized in that they are characterized by interdependence in the generation of value through bundling into complex capabilities (Conner, 1991; Amit and Schoe- maker, 1993). The dynamic capabilities perspective on RB theory suggests that 'soft' managerial assets are the primary source of sustained competitive advantage (Penrose, 1959; Teece, Pisano, and Shuen 1990), as they coordin- ate the application of 'hard' physical and human resources and provide the learning capacity which sustains competitive advantage.

Contractor and Lorange (1988) describe a number of strategic purposes behind the use of cooperative venture forms in international business, gen- erally relating them to the potential value that can be added by combining firm-specific resources. RBT proposes that the most sustainable rents derive from tacit, organizationally embedded, socially complex capabilities which are transmissible only by sharing a part of the organization itself in the SOV, and not transmissible via market transaction (Kogut, 1988). These capabilities are difficult to identify and exchange because they are distributed throughout and embedded in the organization itself. However, they have the character of public goods in that they are not used up, and indeed may be enhanced, by use. Therefore, such strategic capabilities can be applied broadly without additional investment to increase the value of a variety of transactions with- out losing their own inherent value. The hope of synergies, that is, more than simple additive benefits of scale and scope, from combining such resources into complex new competencies makes shared organization ventures appear to be the organizational form of choice when such organizational capabilities are to be combined.

---

[2] Strategic Assets include what Barney (1991) describes as organizational resources, Teece *et al.* (1990) call dynamic capabilities, Prahalad and Hamel (1990) call core competencies, and Itami (1987) calls invisible resources. For the purposes of this chapter, these terms are essentially interchangeable.

The difficulties inherent in learning the organizational skills represented by embedded competencies make structural forms that combine organizational systems, structures, and cultures likely for such transactions. The decision to form an SOV implies three considerations, outlined in the following paragraphs (Madhok and Tallman, 1998).

First, the firm does not possess the entire bundle of resources and capabilities needed to create the desired rent-earning competency and cannot develop the missing resources internally in an acceptable time at an acceptable cost. Dierickx and Cool (1989) show that such idiosyncratic resources are path-dependent, specialized to the history of a given firm, and may not be within the reach of other firms. Even if a firm could develop such capabilities, this effort is subject to diseconomies of scale, scope, and time as compared with the firm that already possesses them. If the firm cannot develop, in a timely and cost-effective manner, the same or equivalent skills as a potential partner (Cantwell, 1991), then it must look beyond its boundaries for them.

Secondly, markets do not adequately bundle embedded resources into rent-yielding capabilities. Markets cannot transmit such knowledge effectively, even if the value of the competency can be established. Markets are effective only in transmitting knowledge that can be fully described in an explicit manner, as in licensing a patent. Kogut (1988) has established the need for extended, intimate relationships to transmit tacit knowledge. The requisite degree of organizational integration to permit organizational learning of embedded knowledge is not available in simple market deals. The same can be said for the extended, but specified and limited, relationships of contractual joint ventures. Contractual joint ventures generally seem to involve sharing explicit resources rather than deeply embedded, 'invisible' capabilities (Osborn and Baughn, 1990). Such alliances, as compared with SOVs, do extend in time, but provide only additive benefits to explicit resources, not synergies from the combination of embedded capabilities. Synergies from an integrated bundle of shared strategic assets, by which new value unique to the SOV can be created, require a deeper and more flexible relationship (Madhok, chap. 4, above).

Finally, if internal development and market acquisition of specific resources and capabilities are not feasible in the search for strategic assets, why should the firm not acquire and fully integrate another firm that does possess the requisite skills? The identification of complementary resources makes acquisition appear rational. However, fully internalizing resources is an expensive and uncertain process that may degrade or destroy the very organizationally embedded competencies most desired for the alliance (Chi, 1994).[3] Complete takeover of another firm may bring in all the physical assets

---

[3] Takeovers or buyouts, which sacrifice managers, change routines for management, and drive out creative talent, seem to result in the target firm changing to become more like the

of the acquired firm, but the synergistic potential of its human and organizational resources are likely to disappear under a new identity. Even in complete acquisitions or mergers, preservation strategies, by which organizational forms, assets, skills, staff, etc. of the target firm are preserved, may provide the maximum potential gain (Salk, 1995), but still face the same organizational difficulties as other SOVs.

Shared organizational ventures permit commingling of embedded strategic assets with a partner by formally affiliating the managerial resources of the partners. They also permit combined control of resource deployment in a flexible manner by the managers of such formal alliances. Therefore, in cases where rents may be expected from bundling organizationally embedded capabilities, managers might logically expect that returns will peak in an SOV. Yet, these expectations are often disappointed. Partnerships dissolve. Joint ventures come apart. Acquisitions are spun off. So what is the problem? At this point, transaction cost arguments, albeit in modified form, offer valuable insights.

Intermediate Levels of Asset Specificity—The Transaction Cost Economics View of SOVs

Asset Specificity: The Traditional View

As was mentioned earlier, in the TCE view a collaborative venture is formed because it is the most efficient and least costly means of governing the particular exchange. Williamson (1975) argues that a fundamental transformation from market to hierarchy occurs through investment in transaction-specific assets, since this results in small numbers bargaining conditions and raises the costs of potential opportunism.[4] As such investment grows, the risks of opportunism associated with market-mediated transactions become more expensive, to the point where the expected cost of moving to a hierarchical structure becomes lower than the expected cost of a market transaction. This results in a preference for hierarchical governance.

More recently, Williamson extended his earlier work to address 'hybrid organizations', which Borys and Jemison define as 'organisational arrangements that use resources and/or governance structures from more than one existing organisation' (1989: 235). Williamson characterizes long-term or equilibrium hybrids (as opposed to intendedly short-lived ones) as intermedi-

---

acquiring firm in most cases—thereby losing the very attributes which made the target attractive in the first place.

[4] Transaction-specific assets or resources are resources acquired or developed by a firm to increase the efficiency of organizing strategic assets for a specific transaction. As such, transaction-specific assets function as complementary resources by increasing the rent-earning potential of the firm's strategic assets in that particular application.

ate in adaptability, incentive intensity, and administrative control between markets and hierarchies. Borys and Jemison's depiction of hybrids as forms that are characterized by stronger pressures for efficiency, a larger scale of operations, and lower risks than unitary hierarchies, but at a lower cost in uncertainty than markets, manifests a similar logic. Basically, in Williamson's (1991) view, long-term hybrid organizational forms (including what we call SOVs) will tend to prevail at intermediate levels of asset specificity, since their governance characteristics tend to be more optimally in alignment with the transaction characteristics.

However, the high failure rate of SOVs (Cartwright and Cooper, 1993; Gomes-Casseres, 1987) and the high risks associated with intensive organizational co-operation (Hamel, 1991) suggest that the costs of SOV transactions may not be optimally balanced by intermediate levels of transaction-specific investment. A modified conception of the transaction costs of hybrid organizations provides a new lens for examining the costs associated with SOVs, and suggests a crucial insight into their instability despite their potential for resource synergies, and into the popularity of SOVs despite their riskiness. Crucial to this modification is a reappraisal of transactional costs as transaction-specific investments (TSI) in strategic assets, particularly relevant to flagship networks (Rugman and D'Cruz, chap. 3, above) and to the sorts of 'network dyads' discussed by Loveridge (chap. 7, below). The next section develops such an approach.

Transaction-Specific Investments: A Modified View

Strategic assets were previously defined as rent-yielding resources and capabilities specific to the firm, which generate or have the potential to generate future value. Such value may be intrinsic to an asset itself (e.g. cash accounts) but, more typically, an asset must be 'managed' in order to realize its potential as a strategic asset in the future. The extent to which the underlying potential for rents is realized depends upon the efficiency with which the firm's strategic assets are managed in individual transactions. The efficiency of bundling assets depends on investment in transaction-specific assets which properly complement the rent-yielding resources applied to the transaction (Chi, 1994). Hill, Hwang, and Kim (1990: 118) refer to committed resources as 'dedicated assets that cannot be redeployed to alternative uses without costs'. That is, specialized assets are those assets which have less value in an alternative use. In the extreme case, the value in an alternative use would be zero. Given loss of value in alternative uses, a firm would make investments in more specialized assets largely because it expects to generate higher rents by such investment. As with strategic assets, transaction-specific assets may also be described as hard (a plant customized to a partner's needs) or soft (cross-organizational development teams).

As described previously, the respective resources and capabilities of two firms are brought together in SOVs essentially because of a hope for synergistic value in rent generation. While there may be some synergy to be attained even in the absence of a healthy relationship, there is greater scope to tap this underlying potential in a more effective manner when the relationship is healthy (Ring and Van de Ven, 1992; Madhok 1995a; 1995b). Such relationships are characterized by greater efficiency and flexibility due to the lower perceived need to take elaborate safeguards and the willingness to make unilateral commitments beyond the terms of the contract. In the conventional TCE view, relational, or soft, transaction costs are incurred as safeguards to minimize losses from opportunism. However, in our model, these soft transaction-specific assets and capabilities represent investments in building the rent-earning potential of the relationship, providing opportunities to earn greater rents through more effective blending of capabilities than is possible in a venture dominated by fear of opportunism. While firms within a community of interest may perceive each other as less likely to expropriate skills, the specifics of the relationship still hold.

Given that the investment in the relationship itself has no use in the absence of that particular relationship, and being that it is of a perishable nature, as it consists primarily of soft resources such as managerial time or bargaining costs, it can be argued that such investments in the SOV are more transaction-specific than the hard assets on which Williamson (1985) focuses. This perspective differs with the conventional TCE view in two respects. First, the conventional TCE view focuses only on the costs of the governance structure rather than on the investment aspects of asset building; consequently the response to high transactional costs should be internalization. In this framework, a high level of expenses upfront— managerial, financial, or temporal—is viewed as an initial investment in future value rather than as a pure cost, and the governance form should be that which maximizes the rents from this investment. If embedded strategic assets and time constraints are involved, this form may well be an SOV, despite high transaction specificity of the investments. Second, because the transaction investment is comprised of both a 'hard' and a 'soft' component, the latter being the relational investment, TSI in total should be higher in SOVs than in other forms of organization, particularly when the SOV is a single transaction (Loveridge, chap. 7, below). The conventional assertion that transaction-specific costs are monotonically (if not linearly) increasing along a market-to- hierarchy axis, with SOVs being characterized by an intermediate level of these costs, may be true for hard assets. However, I argue in the next sections that the costs of investment in 'softer' relationship-building assets, both to create and to maintain the rent-yielding relationship, will be higher for SOVs than for markets or for simple hierarchical structural forms. Thus, I argue that the overall costs of a transaction, in terms of search, bargaining, monitoring, and enforcement, will peak for SOVs.

Selection and Bargaining Costs of Shared Organizations

Milgrom and Roberts (1990) argue that key to the choice of governance structure is not asset specificity but bargaining and influence costs in the transaction. They think of these costs, together with search and control costs, as 'soft' TSI— investment in building the relationship which makes possible the shared strategic assets and synergistic rents of the SOV. Not only will heavy outlays be incurred upfront whenever sharing organizational systems is contemplated, but these outlays will be of a transaction-specific nature. There are two aspects of transaction costs that potentially relate to selection and bargaining between partners in SOVs. First is the problem of choosing the wrong partner. A partner without the anticipated strategic resources and capabilities will not provide the synergies required to generate rents through the SOV. Yet, since resources that are highly valuable tend to be of an embedded and causally ambiguous nature (Barney, 1991; Reed and De-Fillippi, 1990), proper identification of their existence and availability is difficult and will involve extensive search costs.

Second is the problem of the partner behaving in an opportunistic manner before or after the commencement of the venture—the issue of moral hazard. The partner may misrepresent capabilities before the transaction closes or may not provide the expected and promised resources once the venture is in place. After consummation, partners may engage in 'hold-up' of one another, demanding an excessive share of the income stream in exchange for not sabotaging the transaction and its concomitant investment. Therefore, selection of a partner for an alliance, especially one involving shared organizational systems, is a long, involved, considered commitment (Tallman and Shenkar, 1994), and is critically important. One means of reducing these risks in a transaction is careful search for a partner with compatible interests (Ring and Van de Ven, 1994) and similar absorptive capacity (Nti and Kumar, chap. 6, below). Search for partners may involve careful research into the reputations of potential partners, careful evaluation of their strategic and other assets, trial market relationships, go-betweens, and so forth. Again, the more embedded the relevant resources, the higher the investment in search activity.

Before the SOV deal is consummated, managerial recognition of these complications also results in intensive bargaining over the terms of SOV creation. Bargaining difficulties are enhanced in SOVs because such alliances require careful building of commitment to a partner before serious bargaining over terms of the venture can take place, moving the relationship to a small numbers situation very early in an extended transaction. While all merger and acquisition activity entails narrowing the field of possibilities to one before a contract is made, SOVs must involve much longer and more intensive bargaining over terms such as ownership share, board representation, control in general, control over specific activities, and other such concerns than do contractual collaborations or full acquisitions if they are to provide the hoped-for synergies (Gray and Yan, 1992).

In contractual types of venture, selection of the wrong partner or partner violation of the trust or reciprocal norms governing such relationships can be addressed (though sometimes with difficulty) by terminating the contract, and bargaining primarily consists of agreeing on a fair market price for the transaction. On the other hand, organizing through hierarchical governance also involves lower costs than the case of SOVs. Market value can be established through due diligence on the part of the principals or their advisors. The adverse selection problem may be present, but when hard assets are desired, their actuality is simpler to establish. Though there is a moral hazard problem, for instance a project manager may behave opportunistically, opportunism (or agency costs) would tend to be an individual problem, as the target firm ceases to exist in a complete acquisition. Moreover, a firm has superior monitoring and enforcement tools at its disposal. For example, in the case of an acquisition, it can fire the top management team of the acquired company.

These options are not available in an SOV. SOVs, like the marriages to which they are often compared, are not easily terminated. Residual rights, invisible resources such as goodwill or trade names, property owned by the venture, etc., must be divided. Unless a 'prenuptial agreement' has been negotiated, this is a difficult and expensive process. Nor can partners be coerced—an 'unfriendly joint venture' is a recipe for failure. At other times, non-performance may result from accident (Madhok, chap. 4, above) or recognition of a bad bargain due to unequal appropriation of benefits (Nti and Kumar, chap. 6, below). In addition, pricing intangible assets when not incorporating the entire cash-flow stream is difficult if not impossible. Therefore, as described above, we can anticipate a comparably large *ex ante* investment in analysis of the opportunity, search for the partner, and negotiation of the venture agreement (including perhaps a 'prenup').

Internal Governance Costs of Alliances

The previous section argues that search and bargaining costs are higher in SOVs than in markets, contractual ventures, or hierarchical organizations. This section argues that the *ex post* internal governance costs of SOVs are also higher than those of pure markets, contractual alliances, and internal expansion, due in part to potential influence costs. Milgrom and Roberts (1990) suggest that the costs of political activity by individuals or of the monitoring measures installed by the organization to avoid such activity are critical to the survival of an organization. In SOVs, these costs are likely to be high initially and to stay high, as the inherent co-survival of two unlike organizational systems in one venture reduces the possibility of final resolution of any conflict. We might expect to find such concerns in unequal ventures, such as international ones, due to differences in absorptive capacity (Nti and Kumar, chap. 6, below) or flagship relationships, given very different strategic roles (Rugman and D'Cruz, chap. 3, above).

Pure market transactions involve a minimum of bureaucratic governance costs as they are governed almost exclusively by market forces. Contractual ventures involve a higher degree of active intervention on the part of the partners, as those portions of the partner firms which are directly involved in the transaction can be expected to make more substantive adjustments as the venture unfolds. At the same time, the degree of commitment to the venture, and the associated managerial involvement and costs, would be relatively low compared to SOVs, since contractual ventures retain market controls, in that the venture can be directly terminated by non-renewal or termination of the contract.

A pure single hierarchy system will have higher bureaucratic costs than pure or majority market systems (Williamson, 1975; Hill and Kim, 1988). The hierarchy is designed to replace opportunism costs (real or potential) of the market with the internal governance costs of active management. These costs tend to increase as the size and complexity of the hierarchy increase (Williamson, 1975), eventually reaching a point at which the hierarchy becomes only marginally efficient and ceases to grow further. This is a basic transaction cost argument and need not be further developed here. The issue at hand, however, is that of the relative bureaucratic costs of SOVs in which organizational forms—culture, structures, and systems—are shared.

In markets or contractual collaborative ventures, managers are expected to retain loyalty to their parent firm. In SOVs, however, managers must transfer some loyalty to the alliance in order to realize its underlying purpose of effectively transferring, absorbing, and combining complementary capabilities at the heart of the venture, yet they must also retain ties to their parent companies in order to co-ordinate and manage this process (and to protect their own interests). In other words, managerial loyalty in SOVs is necessarily divided. Seconded managers who are over-committed to the alliance are likely to expose parental core competencies in an effort to improve performance, even when this is not desirable from the perspective of the parent. Other managers are reluctant to commit fully to a venture if this entails an attenuation of relationships with the parent. These situations reflect Nti and Kumar's (chap. 6, below) argument that different absorptive capacities exist for new knowledge. As a result, the marriage of organizational systems is likely to remain partial and unsettled unless managed intensively. Governing the activities of a mixed group of managers of varying loyalties and objectives requires considerable ongoing effort, both on the part of the parents and within the SOV. This translates into especially high governance costs.

Furthermore, maintenance of different organizational cultures makes even willing participants likely to face difficulties in blending together and likely to engage in political activity. Good relations are essential to operating joint ventures without intense conflict (Hill and Hellriegel, 1994). Yet, research into organization cultural effects indicates that organizational forms that require the integration of two organizations are difficult to maintain and to manage. Sherman discusses sources of failure in equity joint ventures. He finds that most joint ventures dissolve not because of economic factors or strategic misdirection, but due to strains resulting from 'fuzzy' issues such as the personal relationships of managers (1992: 78). Parkhe (1991) makes a distinction between the sort of resource diversity that leads firms to cooperate for economic purposes and cultural diversity which tends to disrupt and destroy alliances. Others (Madhok, chap. 4, above; Tallman and Shenkar, 1994; Cartwright and Cooper, 1993; Jemison and Sitkin, 1986) have also pointed out the critical nature of the cultural and process dimensions in the success or failure of organizational combinations.

The risks of *ex post* opportunism through organizational learning are also high in SOVs because these alliances are based on combining tacit organizational systems. Just as shared systems are needed to provide the alliance with the opportunity to exploit routines and other complex knowledge, so they expose such organizational resources and core competencies to transmission through the alliance to the partner firm (Nti and Kumar, chap. 6, below; Hamel, 1991). Essentially, the supposed role of equity sharing in providing a profit stream as hostage to cooperative behaviour may be outweighed by the opportunity to acquire organizational competencies for a parent firm, which can then extract all the rents from the combined resources. If the SOV is embedded in a rich network of relationships (Loveridge, chap. 7, below), the likelihood of opportunism may be lower, but costs of defection remain high.

In complete takeovers, individual dissident managers can be dismissed or coerced to modify their attitudes and behaviour and organizational learning is desirable, not a threat. In SOVs, however, the fact that such managers may be representing the interests of their parent, and that these managers probably embody the needed capabilities of that parent, makes forced solutions on an individual basis quite difficult. Influence costs to the SOV may be seen as essential to the parent and its representative managers—they are institutional, not individual. In other words, while TCE theory suggests that the degree of internalization alone determines bureaucratic governance cost, the difficulties of managing mixed organizational structures, systems, and routines for increased rents make SOVs uniquely costly to manage. Milgrom and Roberts (1990: 84–5) demonstrate the high cost of not managing internal governance in the failure of an attempted 'preservative/pluralistic' takeover by Tenneco of Houston Oil to retain the employees or identity of the target firm. Cartwright and Cooper (1993) discuss the difficulty of retaining organizational identities in partial mergers, while Hamel (1991) details the hazards of failing to manage learning opportunities in equity joint ventures.

Given that successful SOVs involve a high level of specialized investment—especially in terms of 'soft' managerial time, resources, and opportunity costs—and, as a consequence, high transaction-specific expenditures, what incentive do firms have to incur these costs? Essentially, if the costs incurred reduce the problems associated with adverse selection and moral hazard, enhancing the probability of future rents to joint strategic assets, then they can be conceptualized as investments in future returns (Madhok, chap. 4, above). From a long-term and broader view of inter-organizational exchange, transaction-specific investments in *ex ante* search and bargaining and *ex post* relationship maintenance generate potentially high rents to the asset of the SOV, but are costly. The next section describes the dynamics of SOV creation and management to place these static concepts in the framework of the 'developmental processes of co-operative [ventures]' (Ring and Van de Ven, 1994).

Combining the Theoretical Perspectives in a Dynamic Model: A Multi-Stage Model of the SOV Transaction: Investment and Resources

This section presents a dynamic 'stages' model of the formation and management of an SOV to demonstrate the relationship of transaction costs or investment to expected rents over the life cycle of the SOV. The essence of the argument presented in this section is that when managers form alliances that involve integrating the organizational identities and systems of the parent firms, the greater the potential benefits, but the greater the cost of investment in alliances too. However, at each stage of the SOV's creation and operation, the key capabilities and the investments which are most critical change in character and intensity. The risk-averse but profit-oriented manager must be aware of these changes in order to make the best judgement about the value of the venture.

Why do alliances form? Because managers believe that they need to add new or complementary resources to their strategic asset bundles, but seek faster, lower cost, and lower risk means of acquiring them. Shared organization transactions appear, from a financial analysis perspective, to be cheaper and less risky than whole ownership or market dealings, and to permit gradual strategic commitment. Zajac and Olsen propose transactional value analysis—a concept quite similar to value analysis of asset bundles—as useful in explaining 'the wide variety of types of interorganisational strategies' (1993: 143). In their terms, SOV transactional values appear to be particularly high and risks particularly low. When this condition holds throughout the process of creating and managing the SOV, it may survive to the point of strategic independence, as in the cases of Owens–Corning or Royal Dutch–Shell.

Again, though, we must ask why, if alliances provide so much value at low risk, do they so often fail? First, the rewards to synergy seem often to be more speculative than realistic, assuming as they do the existence of complex resources and the ability to combine or absorb them (Nti and Kumar, chap. 6, below). Complementarities that appear promising in prospect do not always prove out once the deal is done. As managers learn more about potential or actual partners, they constantly review the potential value of the SOV option (Chi and Nystrom, 1995), and may discover its expected present value is decreasing. Nti and Kumar (chap. 6, below) suggest that declining confidence in the availability of returns leads to declining commitment to the alliance. Also, as argued at length above, alliance transactions are not necessarily cheap or less risky. Combining systems and cultures requires early commitment to a partner. This effort involves extensive negotiation and bargaining, activities that are costly in soft resources, such as managerial time, that are non-recoverable from the transaction. Sharing systems in alliances means that the internal governance costs of the SOV are often higher than anticipated, continue to accrue throughout the relationship, and still provide only limited protection from the opportunism represented by partner learning, or bad faith.

In the following sections, we examine what happens in the SOV formation and operation process. Three distinct stages of the transaction are identified, each with its own perspective on resource synergies and with its own distinct transaction-specific commitments, as shown in Table 5.1. Before using the

TABLE 5.1 *Rents, costs, and the SOV transaction*

Stages of the Transaction

Analysis and search	Selection and negotiation	Operation and maintenance
Resources: *Investment analysis of markets and products *Definition of need for complementary resources *Identification of potential alternatives	Resources: *Evaluation of resource value in context *Evaluation of complementarities with selected partner *Negotiate rent division *Define learning opportunities	Resources: *Manage for synergies with partner competencies *Maximize rents to resource bundle *Invest in 'hard' assets for operations *Invest in 'soft' systems for cooperation
Transaction costs: *Investment analysis *Capability analysis *Partner search costs *Initial negotiation with prospective partners	Transaction costs: *Adverse selection (wrong partner) *Moral hazard (partner trust, negotiating penalties) *Small numbers and transaction-specific investment prior to final contract *Negotiation of contract(s)	Transaction costs: *Avoid costs of over-commitment *Monitor, negotiate, structure to avoid or punish moral hazard, hold-up, costly learning
Complementarity +, Value +, Costs +	Embeddedness +, Value +, Costs +	Synergy +, Value +, Costs +

conditions developed above to propose a dynamic model of the rewards and costs of SOVs as they are formed and mature, three possible outcomes should be mentioned. Some SOVs may continue with more or less success for an indefinite period. Others fail, in the sense that they become too costly to maintain although the conditions that generated the SOVs in the first place are unchanged. Finally, others terminate after an agreed period of time or the accomplishment of limited objectives. In such cases, the SOV may terminate, but cannot be said to have failed.

1.   Ex ante *analysis and search*

This is the period prior to the selection of a specific intended partner, corresponding generally to the initializing stage in Zajac and Olsen's (1993) model and to the first step of Tallman and Shenkar's (1994) decision-making model. Some portion of the preliminary investment in expansion is general and common to all structural forms, but at some point in this stage, the need for complementary resources shifts investment considerations towards alliances and away from whole ownership. This then requires further evaluation of the need for a particular set of complementary resources and evaluation of the SOV form. Firms then incur substantial additional costs in searching for an appropriate set of partners with the right complementary rent-yielding and supporting resources and capabilities. For SOVs, this stage often involves primarily rational analysis of the economic rent potential of hard assets as the focus of the search for a prospective partner, although the evidence suggests that much more effort should be given to finding compatible soft organizational assets. Transaction costs at this stage are largely general, but as the search for a partner narrows, ever more investment in 'soft' costs is committed to the transaction. Consequently, the pain of walking away from the transaction empty-handed increases, and the likelihood of closing a deal, even a bad one, also increases (Tallman and Shenkar, 1994). The more complex the complementary capabilities and resources desired in a partner, the more detailed, broad, and complex the required search and validation process, and the greater the investment. Costs can be lowered when the firm has experience-based routines for search processes and by previously existing contractual arrangements with potential partners that provide an initial level of confidence. Ongoing network relationships can make search easier, and can specifically reduce the cost or risk of choosing an opportunistic partner, but can also artificially restrict search processes, increasing the risk that the value-adding capabilities of the putative partner are not the best available (Loveridge, chap. 7, below).

Success in this stage consists of identifying a preferred partner, an event milestone that marks the transition to Stage 2. Failure might be seen as the inability to find a partner or further to pursue the desired outcome of forming an SOV due to excessive search costs, despite strategic preference for an

SOV. Termination without failure is difficult to identify when 'nothing has happened yet', but could be characterized as a decision that an SOV is no longer the desired outcome.

2.   Ex ante *selection and negotiation*

The second stage is the period between the selection of a specific partner and the formalization of the relationship—that time frame when the serious bargaining about the terms of the prospective relationship takes place. This stage is characterized by one-on-one negotiation, and involves careful, specific analysis of potential resource combinations with the chosen partner and the selection of a specific form for the alliance. It takes place under minimum small numbers conditions—the partner has been chosen. Partner compatibility, both in terms of general outlook as well as more specific resources and competencies, is the most important criterion for combining firms (Tomlinson, 1970). From the RB view this is critical, since value can only be generated if there are available synergies which arise not only from the mere availability of complementary resources but also from a compatible mindset which influences the way the synergies are realized. Unfortunately, the more complex and organizationally embedded (and thus more valuable) the relevant competencies of the potential partners, the more difficult and costly they are to evaluate *ex ante*. As a result, choice of an SOV form is likely to come out of recognition of the need for combining economic resources for their rents rather than from recognition of the need to have complementary management systems or 'similar operating philosophies' (Hill and Hellriegel, 1994) to minimize Type II complementarities (Parkhe, 1991). Thus, while the greatest rents come from embedded, tacit resources, the negotiation is likely to focus on more observable, if less critical, hard resources.

The focus on a particular partner at this stage raises the potential costs of adverse selection and moral hazard described above. The adverse selection problem is amplified by search for embedded competencies which present an extreme of asymmetric information, and the partner may misrepresent (or even mis-estimate) the value of its resources to the firm, which is unable to secure impartial information. For the latter concern, even if the proper partner is selected, there is the future risk of the partner acting in a self-interested manner, for instance seeking to acquire the partner's competencies rather than exploiting complementarities (Hamel, 1991), or being unable or unwilling to commit the needed soft resources. Plus, absorption of such complex resources is uncertain at best (Nti and Kumar, chap. 6, below). Embedded resources also amplify the moral hazard problem since, by their very nature, there exists ambiguity in specification and measurement of contribution, input, and output and, consequently, difficulties in contracting. Avoidance of moral hazard problems increases negotiation costs before the agreement is formalized.

Essentially, the more specialized and embedded the capabilities involved in an alliance negotiation, the higher the potential rents to a successfully tied bundle of resources, and the more likely it is that transactional values will appear highest for SOV forms. However, these same characteristics raise the level of causal ambiguity and uncertainty about the exact nature of the capabilities and therefore increase the investment costs of negotiating the deal. On the other hand, if the resources are much more easily articulable, the transaction costs relating to measurement and observability are reduced but the long-term sustainable advantage, and thus the rents, to such resources are lower. The majority of these transaction costs are 'soft' investments in the relationship, hard to put on account and completely transaction specific. All of the costs related to finding a partner and arranging the joint ownership must be considered non-recoverable.[5]

In brief, then, both the potential cost and value of combining resources increase with their embeddedness. The higher and more sustainable the potential rents, the more they are embedded and tied to the parent firms, and the greater the investment of putting the transaction together to realize this value. The size of the investment can be reduced by uncertainty-reducing conditions such as experience, which reduces internal uncertainty, and dealing with a partner with previous affiliation, which reduces external uncertainties. Success at this stage must be seen as finalizing the SOV deal, but an unwise decision or hasty bargain can sow the seeds of future difficulty. Failure to make a deal with the best partner despite the ongoing investment has become more costly. However, a bad deal may be even more costly in the long run, so termination of negotiations in the face of unresolvable organizational differences is not necessarily failure, just part of an iterative process which returns to Stage 1.

3.   Ex post *operations and maintenance*

After the relationship is formalized, the good news is that rents finally become available to offset costs, the bad news is that managers in both partners and the SOV must now govern the new organization to maintain its transactional value (Madhok, chap. 4, above). As suggested by Zajac and Olsen (1993), this stage of the alliance relationship involves constant reconfiguration. This statement is particularly true of SOVs, where not only must the economic relationship be managed for synergy, but the socio-cultural relationship and individual commitments must also be maintained and developed for a successful outcome (see Ring and Van de Ven,

---

[5] In a network or embedded relationship (Loveridge, chap. 7, below), costs of relationship building may actually be spread over future or ongoing relationships. This shows the hazard of examining transactions out of context. However, as mentioned above, saving on relationship costs can be expensive in terms of opportunity costs in allying with less than optimal value-adding resources.

1994). These conditions translate into ongoing relational investment in our model.

The nature of investments dedicated towards the operations of the venture is a critical aspect of the SOV relationship. From the RBT point of view, concern for individual components of the asset bundle, rather than the bundle as an entirety, sub-optimizes operations. Yet, as the resource bundle becomes increasingly co-specialized, pursuing value maximization, the independent value of any of the resources in the market becomes lower and rent extraction becomes ever more bound to the SOV as an asset (Chi, 1994). Where the value of the components is greater than the sum of the individual parts, and where the resources are embedded in different parents, these rents cannot be captured and deployed by alternative users without incurring substantial costs and sacrifice in productive value. Therefore, the greater the synergy of the combined capabilities, the greater the potential for harm from any opportunism or inattention, and the higher the governance costs and renegotiation costs to avoid such situations. Investment in maintaining the alliance as learning occurs and rent values shift must be rapid enough to offset the benefits of sudden opportunism.

Once again, TCE concerns are not independent of the rents to resources to be transacted. Cost may not be lower, but rents may be higher in a mutual relationship. The resources which are combined only provide the potential for synergy. This is what motivates the two firms to come together and transact these resources. However, in the attempt to realize this potential, expenditures must be incurred which are directly related to the property of resource embeddedness. As in initial negotiations, the greater the embeddedness of the resources-in-exchange, the more complex the process of combining them to realize the synergies and the greater the need for ever more intensive and intimate ongoing interaction. This increases the associated (soft transaction) costs. In Parkhe's (1991) terms, if rents are highest to organizationally embedded Type I complementary resources, then the expected costs of Type II interference or the relational governance costs of avoiding these costs must increase.

This mutual commitment, if it is to hold up, emphasizes the management of the relationship itself. A good relationship is important, both from the TCE and RBT points of view, in order to have more efficient governance and to realize maximum benefits from the collaboration, but requires constant ongoing investment. Ouchi defines a transaction cost as 'any activity which is engaged in to satisfy each party to an exchange that the value given and received is in accordance with expectations' (Ouchi, 1980: 130). Investments in positive social dynamics and sustenance of the relationship are transaction-specific investments in that they are not transferable freely and have long-term value. In situations where the focus is on flexibility and adaptability, that is, those where shared ownership and managerial control are most useful, constant renegotiation of the relationship can be expected, particularly where managers from opposing parents work directly together in the SOV. If the SOV retains a formal bureaucratic relational form, the rents to the relationship are likely to be reduced as the alliance itself never really forms a single asset, but remains two separate entities under the organizational skin. This condition reduces the likelihood of synergy and raises the chance of opportunism—yet may be a less damaging parting when the relationship ends.

Success is usually seen as the continuation of the SOV, ongoing rent extraction, or other value-added activities, and a supportive relationship. Failure results when rents are lower than expected (or other strategic objectives are not attained) or the cost of ongoing investment is higher than expected, so that the SOV is dissolved against the strategic wishes of at least one partner. It is at this stage that SOVs which have termination dates or specific, well-defined objectives must be particularly noted, as they may face termination without failure during Stage 3.

In Sum, Why Do SOVs Tend to Fail?

A key issue introduced at the beginning of this chapter is the relatively high failure rate of alliances, and of SOV-type relationships in particular. In short, this happens because the benefits to Type I complementarity of assets turn out to be less than expected or to be less persistent than expected, while avoiding Type II complementarities or differential absorptive capacities (Nti and Kumar, chap. 6, below) turns out to be more expensive than originally calculated (Parkhe, 1991). On the rent-seeking side of the joint venture decision, the payoff to synergies may well be lower than anticipated, due either to poor search and identification, pressures to make a deal once a partner is identified, or inability to really combine capabilities of the partners after the SOV is formed. Again, the greater the reliance on co-specialization of deeply embedded capabilities, the more likely that reality will diverge from expectation. Also, careful investment for future rents from such assets raises the cost of the venture at each stage. As costs begin to climb before rents can come on stream, rational assessment of the present value of the SOV may change as the transaction progresses (Chi and Nystrom, 1995). Many opportunities arise to end the relationship. On the other hand, limiting investment in the transaction may make full analysis of the value of embedded complementary resources difficult, resulting in a focus on more apparent Type I complementarities and a mistaken arrangement that fails later at great cost. Caution and care result in high and increasing upfront investment in the alliance. In addition, investment in transaction-specific 'soft' costs does not end at signing time, but continues throughout the lifetime of the alliance. Thus, the model proposed here suggests that overall venture costs peak for equity joint ventures and partial acquisitions—the SOV modes of alliance. Yet, most models predict that costs should be intermediate for such forms. Thus, whereas revenues are likely to be lower than expected, real costs are

likely to be higher than expected, and actual margins are likely to be considerably narrower than expected, if not negative. Finally, on top of initial
mis-estimation and continual modification of synergistic relationships, rents
tend to decay over time as imitation and exogenous change reduce the
competitive advantage of any particular capabilities (Reed and DeFillippi,
1990). The real present value of the ultimate stream of rents seems most likely
to be below expectations.

Our longitudinal view of the SOV relationship provides good insight into
this process. Where the resources are more embedded, the costs incurred in
transacting them—in terms of financial, temporal, and managerial resources—are high, especially in Stages 1 and 2, and continue throughout
Stage 3. The benefits, on the other hand, are variable, uncertain, and occur
later in Stage 3. These difficulties occur due to the greater need for effectively
merging a different though complementary set of routines. This requires
greater interaction and greater adaptability on the part of the participating
firms. Anticipated returns are likely to come only after reconfiguration,
reanalysis, and more investment. In brief, costs and returns are temporally
skewed towards different periods of the relationship, and both show greater
variance and uncertainty the more tacit and embedded are the competencies
in question. Therefore, the real present value of the ultimate stream of rents is
often below expectations, and failure of the SOV is the result.

Of course there are ways that firms can avoid or reduce risk. Zajac and
Olsen (1993) are not unrealistic optimists. Transactional value in SOVs can
be positive. Firms with experience in joint operations have a lower risk of
failure in subsequent attempts. Whether through partner choice, managerial
routine (Nelson and Winter, 1982), or superior risk assessment, experience
effects do have an impact on the success rate of alliances (Sherman, 1992), as
does network membership (Loveridge, chap. 7, below). Selection of partner
by organizational culture type (Cartwright and Cooper, 1993), real efforts to
develop a combined and clan-like culture, superior treatment of individuals
from the subordinate partner, and a variety of other techniques in human
resource management and organizational development techniques can be
used to reduce the impact of incompatible institutions. The firm's expertise
is built up through cumulative experience over time with various forms of
governance, which then guides it in subsequent choices. At the same time,
these efforts enhance the probability of real synergies developing.

A possible strategy is to resort to more complex governance structures to
manage risk (Ring and Van de Ven, 1992) such as nested arrangements where
a core technology is licensed within an SOV. Another strategy is one of
continuous investment in the core capabilities and in the technology being
provided to avoid obsolescence of its contribution. In dynamic environments, this outpaces a partner's ability to be opportunistic, or at least its gains
from doing so. Here, the very embeddedness which occasions an SOV also
behaves as a protective umbrella as the returns to real synergy and partnership

can be clearly seen and contrasted to the gains to opportunistic learning and exit. Another path is that of investment in 'relationship management' in order to lower the TC and increase the benefits. With proper management, collaborations can simulate some of the properties of hierarchy (Jarillo, 1988), such as flexibility and role specificity, while avoiding some of its costs.

Conclusions

The model proposed here has used transaction cost and resource-based economic models to suggest a consistent theory-based model of SOV formation, governance, and instability. RBT and TCE theories suggest dramatic benefits to alliances based on combining embedded capabilities. However, organizational studies suggest an alternative approach to transaction specificity in which, while combining unlike economic resources may increase revenues, combining unlike organizational systems (often the very same complex, embedded, tacit resources) can lead to fundamental disagreements about the management of resources (Madhok and Tallman, 1998; Salk, 1994; Hill and Hellriegel, 1994). Resolving or defusing these disagreements raises SOV 'soft' costs dramatically. At the same time, these costs must be borne if the synergies hoped for at the initiation of the SOV process are to be turned into rents in the final analysis.

Given the pressures on revenue advantages to shared forms of organization over either markets or single hierarchy forms, plus the higher transaction costs for joint structures, instability is predictable. Managers must understand that stable SOVs probably should be the exception, and therefore reliance on actual synergistic revenue effects that exceed the associated transaction cost penalties seems to be as much an act of faith as economic rationality. A full understanding of the costs and risks in alliances and the need for a concerted effort to alleviate their causes would increase the probability of success of SOVs, although it might decrease their incidence. Synergies do not arise automatically from combining unlike organizational routines, but are the ultimate outcome of an extended process of investment in relationships and mutuality. Managers must be prepared for a life-long process of constant creation and re-creation of the SOV in order to appropriate the rents expected from this organization capability which is itself a strategic resource.

This chapter has proposed a necessarily complex answer to the question of why SOVs are so often formed and yet so often fail. In the process of doing this, it has defined the resource conditions necessary to make an SOV appealing, it has redefined the transaction cost structure of SOV formation and management as investment in future rents, and has also demonstrated that transaction costs may be higher for such forms than for other organizational forms, and it has outlined a dynamic framework for understanding the integration of rents and costs in the SOV context. The explicit discussion of relational transaction costs as investments in future value (Madhok, chap. 4, above) makes possible the recognition that structural governance costs may be higher for intermediate levels of internalization if the anticipated rewards are also higher. Failure of SOVs is the natural result when such expected value calculations go awry. The fact that such soft costs are not often given full weight in calculating expected values makes under-estimation of investment and over-estimation of rewards a distinct possibility in our model. This situation sounds a warning to managers considering an SOV investment. It also provides a warning to those modellers who focus on one theoretical perspective in the name of purity at the expense of understanding by demonstrating the value of encompassing two compatible theories of the firm in one framework for analysis of a particular phenomenon.

References

AMIT, R. and SCHOEMAKER, P. J. H. (1993), 'Strategic Assets and Organisational Rent', *Strategic Management Journal*, 14: 33–46.

BARNEY, J. B. (1991), 'Firm Resources and Sustained Competitive Advantage', *Journal of Management*, 17/1: 11–120.

BORYS, B. and JEMISON, D. B. (1989), 'Hybrid Arrangements as Strategic Alliances: Theoretical Issues in Organisational Combinations', *Academy of Management Review*, 14: 234–49.

CANTWELL, J. (1991), 'The Theory of Technological Competence and its Application to International Production', in D. McFetridge (ed.), *Foreign Investment, Technology, and Economic Growth* (Calgary, Alta.: University of Calgary Press), 33–67.

CARTWRIGHT, S. and COOPER, C. L. (1993), 'The Role of Cultural Compatibility in Successful Organisational Marriage', *The Academy of Management Executive*, 7/2: 7–70.

CHI, T. (1994), 'Trading in Strategic Resources: Necessary Conditions, Transaction Cost Problems and Choice of Exchange Structure', *Strategic Management Journal*, 15/4: 271–90.

—— and NYSTROM, P. C. (1995), 'Decision Dilemmas Facing Managers: Recognising the Value of Learning while Making Sequential Decisions', *Omega*, 23/3: 303–12.

CONNER, K. R. (1991), 'A Historical Comparison of Resource-Based Theory and Five Schools of Thought within Industrial Organisation Economics: Do We Have a New Theory of the Firm?', *Journal of Management*, 17: 121–54.

CONTRACTOR, F. J. and LORANGE, P. (1988), 'Why Should Firms Co-operate? The Strategy and Economic Basis for Co-operative Ventures', in F. J. Contractor and P. Lorange (eds.), *Co-operative Strategies in International Business* (Lexington, Mass.: Lexington Books), 3–30.

DIERICKX, I. and COOL, K. (1989), 'Asset Stock Accumulation and Competitive Advantage', *Management Science*, 12: 1504–11.

GERINGER, J. M. (1988), *Joint Venture Partner Selection* (Westport, Conn.: Quorum Books).

GOMES-CASSERES, B. (1987), 'Joint Venture Instability: Is It a Problem?', *Columbia Journal of World Business*, summer: 97–102.

GRAY, B. and YAN, A. (1992), 'A Negotiations Model of Joint Venture Formation, Structure and Performance: Implications for Strategic Management', *Advances in International Comparative Management*, vii, (Greenwich, Conn.: JAI Press), 41–75.

GULATI, R. and NOHRIA, N. (1992), 'Mutually Assured Alliances', *Academy of Management Best Papers Proceedings* (Ada, Ohio: Academy of Management), 17–21.

HAMEL, G. (1991), 'Competition for Competence and Inter-Partner Learning within International Strategic Alliances', *Strategic Management Journal*, 12(SI): 83–103.

HENNART, J.-F. (1991), 'The Transaction Costs Theory of Joint Ventures: An Empirical Study of Japanese Subsidiaries in the United States', *Management Science*, 37/4: 483–97.

HILL, C. W. L. and KIM, W. C. (1988), 'Searching for a Dynamic Theory of the Multinational Enterprise: A Transaction Cost Model', *Strategic Management Journal*, 9: 93–104.

——HWANG, P., and KIM, W. C. (1990), 'An Eclectic Theory of the Choice of International Entry Mode', *Strategic Management Journal*, 11/2: 117–28.

HILL, R. C. and HELLRIEGEL, D. (1994), 'Critical Contingencies in Joint Venture Management: Some Lessons from Managers', *Organisation Science*, 5/4: 594–607.

ITAMI, H. (1987), *Mobilizing Invisible Assets* (Cambridge, Mass.: Harvard University Press).

JARILLO, J.-C. (1988), 'On Strategic Networks', *Strategic Management Journal*, 9: 31–41.

JEMISON, D. B. and SITKIN, S. B. (1986), 'Corporate Acquisitions: A Process Perspective', *Academy of Management Review*, 11/1: 145–63.

KOGUT, B. (1988), 'Joint Ventures: Theoretical and Empirical Perspectives', *Strategic Management Journal*, 9: 319–32.

MADHOK, A. (1995*a*), 'Opportunism and Trust in Joint Venture Relationships: An Exploratory Study and a Model', *Scandinavian Journal of Management*, 11: 57–74.

—— (1995*b*), 'Revisiting Multinational Firms' Tolerance for Joint Ventures: A Trust-Based Approach', *Journal of International Business Studies*, 26: 117–37.

—— and TALLMAN, S. (1998), 'Resources, Transactions and Rents: Managing Value through Interfirm Collaborative Relationships', *Organisation Science*, 9: 326–39.

MILGROM, P. and ROBERTS, J. (1990), 'Bargaining Costs, Influence Costs, and the Organisation of Economic Activity', in J. E. Alt and K. A. Shepsle (eds.), *Perspectives on Positive Political Economy* (Cambridge: Cambridge University Press), 57–89.

NELSON, R. R. and WINTER, S. G. (1982), *An Evolutionary Theory of Economic Change* (Cambridge, Mass.: Belknap Press).

OSBORN, R. N. and BAUGHN, C. C. (1990), 'Forms of Interorganisational Governance for Multinational Alliances', *Academy of Management Journal*, 33/3: 503–19.

OUCHI, W. G. (1980), 'Markets, Bureaucracies, and Clans', *Administrative Science Quarterly*, 25: 129–41.

PARKHE, A. (1991), 'Interfirm Diversity, Organisational Learning, and Longevity in Global Strategic Alliances', *Journal of International Business Studies*, 22/4: 579–602.

PENROSE, E. (1959), *A Theory of the Growth of the Firm* (Oxford: Basil Blackwell).

PETERAF, M. (1993), 'The Cornerstones of Competitive Advantage: A Resource-based View', *Strategic Management Journal*, 14: 179–92.

PRAHALAD, C. K. and HAMEL, G. (1990), 'The Core Competence of the Corporation', *Harvard Business Review*, May-June: 79–91.

REED, R. and DEFILLIPPI, R. J. (1990), 'Causal Ambiguity, Barriers to Imitation, and Sustainable Competitive Advantage', *Academy of Management Review*, 15: 88–102.

RING, P. S. and VAN DE VEN, A. H. (1992), 'Structuring Co-operative Relationships Between Organisations', *Strategic Management Journal*, 13: 483–98.

—————(1994), 'Developmental Processes of Co-operative Interorganisational Relationships', *Academy of Management Review*, 19/1: 90–118.

SALK, J. E. (1994), 'Generic and Type-Specific Challenges in the Strategic Legitimation and Implementation of Mergers and Acquisitions', *International Business Review*, 3/4: 491–512.

SHERMAN, S. (1992), 'Are Strategic Alliances Working?', *Fortune*, 21 Sept., 77–8.

TALLMAN, S. B. and SHENKAR, O. (1994), 'A Managerial Decision Model of International Co-operative Venture Formation', *Journal of International Business Studies*, 25/1: 91–114.

TEECE, D. J., PISANO, G., and SHUEN, A. (1990), 'Firm Capabilities, Resources, and the Concept of Strategy: Four Paradigms of Strategic Management', CCC Working Paper No. 90–8 (Berkeley, Calif.: University of California).

TOMLINSON, J. W. C. (1970), *The Joint Venture Process in International Business: India and Pakistan* (Cambridge, Mass.: MIT Press).

WILLIAMSON, O. E. (1975), *Markets and Hierarchies* (New York: Free Press).

—— (1985), *The Economic Institutions of Capitalism* (New York: Free Press).

—— (1991), 'Comparative Economic Organisation: The Analysis of Discrete Structural Alternatives', *Administrative Science Quarterly*, 36: 269–96.

ZAJAC, E. J. and OLSEN, C. P. (1993), 'From Transaction Cost to Transactional Value Analysis: Implications for the Study of Interorganisational Strategies', *Journal of Management Studies*, 30: 131–45.

6

Differential Learning in Alliances

KOFI O. NTI AND RAJESH KUMAR

Inter-firm collaboration through strategic alliances has become important in the contemporary business environment due to the complex and dynamic environment engendered by rapid technological change and globalization. Alliances enable firms with complementary resources and capabilities to collaborate to develop new technologies, enter new product markets, or employ new organizational methods and systems. Pekar and Allio (1994) estimated that US companies alone formed over 20,000 alliances between 1988 and 1992 and that the rate of alliance formation was growing by more than 25 per cent annually.

Although there are many advantages to cooperating through the framework of a strategic alliance, these linkages may expose the partners to strategic hazards. This is especially so when the alliance involves actual or potential competitors. For example, Ahern (1993) discusses a case where a Canadian firm lost its competitive advantage because its alliance partner appropriated a critical technology and used the know-how to become a direct competitor. Another Canadian firm in Ahern's study lost market share when its partner used the alliance to learn about the market, and subsequently developed a product that undermined the Canadian partner's business. These examples show that a firm risks losing its competitive advantage whenever it enters into an alliance relationship. In this chapter we wish to focus on the situation where the relationship exposes a partner to strategic hazards due to the presence of learning opportunities.

Competition among alliance partners appears to be engendered by the presence of learning opportunities. The learning motive is strong in alliances where the firms desire to discover new opportunities or to acquire new capabilities (Koza and Lewin, 1998). One type of learning redistributes skills and competencies among the partners, and can alter the competitive advantage of the firms (Reich and Mankin, 1986; Hamel, 1991; Tucker, 1991). Hamel (1991) observed that managers were highly aware of this type of learning, characterizing alliances as a 'race to learn' and internalize the skills of a partner. Another type of learning involves using an alliance as a mechanism for gathering information about an unknown characteristic of a partner, especially when evaluating the desirability of acquiring or merging with another firm (Kogut, 1991; Balakrishnan and Koza, 1993; Mody, 1993; Bleeke

119

and Ernst, 1995). Learning about the value of a partner's assets or contributions can adversely change the potential value of an alliance option (Tallman, chap. 5, above).

Both the 'race to learn' and the information gathering perspectives suggest that alliances are transitional organizational forms, and may be terminated once learning is completed. This raises an interesting question about how the coexistence of collaborative and competitive motives among the partners shapes their incentives to contribute effort towards an alliance. We propose to study this problem using a game-theory model of a learning alliance.

In this chapter we formulate a game-theory model to study the effect of differential learning on effort contributions and payoffs in an alliance. Specifically, we consider two competitors in a homogeneous product market who have an opportunity to collaborate on an alliance project to gain additional revenues. We assume Bertrand price competition in the product market and also assume that the firms share alliance project revenues in proportion to effort contributions. Aggregate effort supplied by the partner generates knowledge that may be applied towards cost reduction in the product market competition. Differential learning may occur because the firms have different abilities to appropriate alliance-generated knowledge into cost reduction. By entering into an alliance with a competitor, a firm may gain additional short-term profits from the alliance project but its long-term competitive position in the product market may be undermined if its partner appropriates more knowledge. This set-up enables us to study the incentives and trade-offs that emerge when competitors enter into alliances with learning opportunities.

Our analysis is structured to illuminate the incentive differences between alliances where the partners learn equally and those where they do not. We relate equilibrium efforts of the firms as well as their payoffs to their absorptive capacities, the value of the project, and effort costs. Strategic parity is maintained when firms with equal absorptive capacities collaborate. The short- and long-term interests of the partners are perfectly aligned in this case. In contrast, when the firms have unequal absorptive capacities, the effort and payoff of the better learner increases with the learning differential; the effort and payoff of the poorer learner decrease as the learning differential increases. This means that the incentive for alliance formation decreases when partners with large differences in absorptive capacities are linked. This has implications for partner selection and for the structure and management of learning alliances. We briefly discuss the learning and strategic aspects of two international alliances, namely Dassault–Dornier (Alpha Jet Project) and General Motors–Toyota (NUMMI), where equal and differential learning occurred.

The rest of the chapter is organized as follows. First, we discuss the problem of differential learning. Then we formulate and analyse the model. This is followed by a discussion and a conclusion.

Differential Learning

When actual or potential competitors enter into a strategic alliance, the knowledge and experience gained through the alliance may have applications beyond the scope of the collaboration. As Lei (1993) observes, a firm's 'entire array of skills, technologies and competencies are potentially open to absorption by the partner' whenever firms collaborate through a strategic alliance. However, some firms may appropriate more knowledge from the alliance relationship; that is differential learning may occur. Differential learning may alter the competitive advantage and bargaining power of the partners (Hamel, 1991). Differential learning may create process and outcome discrepancies that can undermine alliance stability and social harmony among the partners (Kumar and Nti, 1998).

We follow Cohen and Levinthal (1990) and relate each firm's learning ability to its absorptive capacity. Absorptive capacity refers to the ability of a firm to understand and exploit knowledge in various knowledge domains, and may be used as a measure of a firm's ability to appropriate knowledge from an alliance relationship. We assume that knowledge appropriated by a firm depends on its absorptive capacity and the volume of alliance knowledge created. The greater the absorptive capacity of a firm, the more knowledge it can appropriate from a given volume of alliance-generated knowledge. Differential learning may also occur because the division of work may expose the firms to different amounts of alliance-generated knowledge. To simplify the modelling, we will assume that the firms are exposed to equal amounts of knowledge and attribute differential learning to differences in their absorptive capacities. Later on, we will note how differential learning may be managed by organizing the division of work so that the partners are exposed to different amounts of alliance-generated knowledge.

Absorptive capacity is a characteristic of the firm that is acquired and shaped over many years and is not likely to change during the course of a particular alliance relationship. Absorptive capacity is a product of the firm's organizational culture, which shapes its motivational orientation, technological competence, and the quality of the human assets it attracts and develops. As Cohen and Levinthal have noted, the process of accumulating absorptive capacity depends on a firm's prior preparation, is history- or path-dependent, and requires continuous and sustained investment (Cohen and Levinthal, 1990, 1994). Thus we will consider the absorptive capacity as a characteristic of the firm that is not subject to manipulation or build-up during the course of an alliance.

An important feature of an alliance involving potential competitors is that differential learning can be a source of significant private benefits. Khanna, Gulati, and Nohria (1998) define private benefits as those that a firm can earn unilaterally by picking up skills from its partner and applying them to activities outside the scope of the alliance. This may be contrasted with the common benefits the partners gain by performing alliance-related activities. Private benefits may be realized because the alliance organization facilitates the transfer of new knowledge to the parent companies. Differentially appropriated knowledge may enable one firm to fill a critical gap in its knowledge or skill base, and emerge from the alliance as a more formidable competitor. When competitors collaborate through an alliance, differential learning may produce private benefits that can profoundly change the competitive positions of the firms. In our model, private benefits are revealed as changes in the cost positions of the firms in the product market competition.

The Model

Consider a situation where two firms compete in a homogeneous product market for two periods. Assume that initially the firms have equal unit production cost c_0 and that the market demand per period is given by $Q = a - p$, where p is price, a is market size, and Q is quantity sold. We will assume, as in the classical Bertrand model, that the firms engage in price competition and that the lowest price firm wins all the demand at that price; demand is split equally between the firms if they set the same price. The Nash equilibrium outcome in each period is $p_1 = p_2 = c_0$, resulting in zero economic profit per firm each period. This will serve as the base case for exploring the impact of a learning alliance opportunity on the firms.

Suppose the two firms can enter into an alliance to implement a project which offers a gross revenue V. We will assume that the alliance will exist during the first period only, but that the firms will remain competitors in the original product market for two periods, just as before. To implement the project, the firms must contribute some effort. Let the effort contributed by firm 1 be x_1 and that of firm 2 be x_2. Given the effort levels, we will assume that the firms share the alliance revenue in proportion to their contributions. Specifically, we let the revenue share of firm 1 be

$$s_1(x_1, x_2) = \frac{x_1}{x_1 + x_2}, \tag{1}$$

and let the share of firm 2 be $s_2 = 1 - s_1$. The sharing rule employed here generates a simple contest where the firms expend irreversible efforts to win a share of project revenues (Monahan, 1987; Nti, 1997).

We consider a demand-sharing alliance where revenues are shared according to a negotiated formula but costs are borne privately. Demand-sharing alliances are common in development and co-production arrangements, such as the Alpha Jet Project and NUMMI, which are discussed later. NUMMI, for example, is an equally owned joint venture between General Motors and Toyota, where each partner markets NUMMI assembled cars under its own brand name. We do not consider cost-sharing alliances where the partners share cost according to a negotiated formula but privately appropriate the outputs; these arrangements are commonly employed in cooperative research arrangements where the final product is intangible or uncertain (see, for example, Sinha and Cusumano, 1991).

Let the cost of effort for firm i be $e_i(x) = kx_i$, where x_i is its effort and k is the cost per unit of effort. Then collaboration will increase each firm's first period profit to its share of the revenue from the alliance project minus the cost of effort. The first period profit for firm i, $i = 1$ and 2, is simply

$$R_i^1(x_1, x_2) = \frac{x_i V}{x_1 + x_2} - kx_i.$$

To introduce the effects of differential learning, we will suppose that the firms may have different abilities to appropriate alliance-generated knowledge. We will suppose that the firms apply the knowledge towards cost reduction, which alters their competitive positions in the second period product-market competition. In the interest of simplicity, we will assume that knowledge created through the alliance equals the aggregate effort supplied by the firms. Specifically, we will assume that firm i appropriates $b_i(x_1 + x_2)$ units of knowledge, where b_i is its absorptive capacity. Naturally b_i is non-negative. We assume that knowledge appropriated by firm i directly reduces its second period unit production cost in the product market to

$$c_i = c_0 - b_i(x_1 + x_2), \tag{2}$$

where c_0 is the initial unit production cost. That is, the reduction in unit production cost of each firm equals the knowledge appropriated. The form of the cost reduction function employed here is familiar from the learning and experience curve literature (Spence, 1981; Hax and Majluf, 1982; Devinney, 1987). Naturally, the parameter values must be selected so that the second period unit production costs are always positive.

Thus, if the strategic alliance is implemented, the second period competition will be a Bertrand duopoly model with asymmetric unit production costs c_1 and c_2. It is well known that the least-cost firm will win all the product market demand by setting its price slightly below the unit production cost of the high-cost firm. It is clear in our simple setting that the high absorptive capacity firm will be the least-cost firm during the second period and will capture positive economic profits; the low absorptive capacity firm will be the high-cost firm and will receive zero economic profits. To be specific, let $b_1 \geq b_2$ so that firm 1 is never the high-cost firm. Then the Nash equilibrium in the second period product market has firm 1 setting a price $p_2 = c_2$, selling a quantity $Q = a - c_2$, and gaining a profit margin $c_2 - c_1$ per unit sold. Hence the second period profit of firm 1 if the alliance is formed is

$$R_1^2 = (c_2 - c_1)(a - c_2).$$

Firm 2 will get zero profit in the second period if the alliance is formed.

Adding up the first and second period profits, the total payoff of the firms when they enter into an alliance and supply efforts x_1 and x_2 are given by

$$\pi_1(x_1, x_2) = \frac{x_1 V}{x_1 + x_2} - kx_1 + (c_2 - c_1)(a - c_2) \qquad (3)$$

and

$$\pi_2(x_1, x_2) = \frac{x_2 V}{x_1 + x_2} - kx_2. \qquad (4)$$

Substituting for c_1 and c_2 in the payoff of firm 1, using equation (2), yields

$$\pi_1(x_1, x_2) = \frac{x_1 V}{x_1 + x_2} - kx_1$$

$$+ (b_1 - b_2)(x_1 + x_2)(a - c_0 + b_2(x_1 + x_2)). \qquad (5)$$

If the firms do not enter into the alliance, they each earn zero economic profits in each period. This implies that the firms should enter into an alliance only when both $(\pi_1(x_1, x_2)$ and $\pi_2(x_1, x_2)$ are positive. We should stress that a firm has no incentive to enter into an alliance if joining the alliance will cause its total profit to fall below what it would have obtained on its own. An alliance that has already formed may break up if a partner expects that its total payoff may fall sufficiently close to the status quo payoff, which we take to be zero in our model. We should also stress that when one firm defects from or decides not to join the alliance both firms will receive zero economic profits from the product market competition only. This is just a reaffirmation of the fact that the fruits of collaboration cannot be obtained unilaterally.

The payoff functions given in equations (4) and (5) illustrate the basic structure and trade-off in a learning alliance between potential competitors. Collaboration enables the firms to gain a portion of alliance revenue V but the interaction may alter the long-term competitive advantage of the firms as critical competencies are developed at different rates. The proportion of alliance revenue that each firm can claim is negotiated according to some sharing rule, which we have assumed to be proportional to effort contributions. The first component of total profits is just the firm's share of alliance revenue less its effort costs. We have captured the long-term effects of differential learning in the alliance as an additional payoff to firm 1, which has the greater absorptive capacity. There is incontrovertible business logic to an alliance if the total profits received by each firm exceed its opportunity cost of going alone. The simple model of an alliance developed here captures the essentials. More importantly, we have explicit expressions for the distribution of total profits and costs among the partners, which can be analysed parametrically to reveal the incentives and trade-offs in learning alliances.

Analysis

In this section we determine the equilibrium efforts supplied by the firms and their corresponding payoffs. Also, we investigate how equilibrium effort and payoffs respond to changes in the parameters of the model in order to explore the incentives for alliance formation.

We shall employ the non-cooperative (subgame perfect) Nash equilibrium concept in our analysis of the payoff functions. This is because the cooperative aspects of the strategic alliance have already been factored into the model—the firms cannot achieve the potential benefits from the alliance without cooperating. The game analysed here is similar to those that arise in the economics literature on cooperative R&D (d'Aspremont and Jacquemin, 1988; DeBondt, 1996) but our payoff structure is quite different and we address different issues. The sharing rule and the knowledge appropriation process used here highlights alliance-specific considerations. We study how differential learning influences collaborative efforts and incentives in alliances whereas the economics literature on cooperative R&D attempts to establish whether more innovation is stimulated by collaborative or independent innovative efforts.

In order to provide maximum insight into the problem of differential learning in strategic alliances, it is useful to proceed in stages. The analysis is organized into two parts. First, we consider the situation where both firms learn equally from the alliance. Then we study the situation involving differential learning. We will solve for the equilibrium outcomes numerically in order to highlight the qualitative properties; a laborious but predominantly algebraic analysis may also be developed using the comparative statics approach in Nti (1997). We focus on how variations in the parameters that define the alliance affect the equilibrium outcomes, and use the results to illustrate the learning dimension of the theory.

Equal Learning Abilities

Here we suppose that both firms are equally effective in transforming alliance-generated knowledge into cost reduction. This corresponds to the situation where the absorptive capacities of the firms assume a common value $b_1 = b_2 = b \geq 0$. Substituting these values of the absorptive capacities into the payoffs, we obtain

$$\pi_1(x_1, x_2) = \frac{x_1 V}{x_1 + x_2} - kx_1 \tag{6}$$

and

$$\pi_2(x_1, x_2) = \frac{x_2 V}{x_1 + x_2} - kx_2. \tag{7}$$

TABLE 6.1 *Equal learning abilities*

Project value V	Effort per firm x	Payoff per firm π
200	5.00	50.00
400	10.00	100.00
600	15.00	150.00
800	20.00	200.00
1000	25.00	250.00
1200	30.00	300.00
1400	35.00	350.00
1600	40.00	400.00

Parameter values: $b_1 = b_2 = 0$, $k = 10$, and $a - c_0 = 12$.

The payoff expressions in equations (6) and (7) are perfectly symmetrical and independent of the common absorptive capacity. The firms will supply equal efforts in equilibrium and maintain strategic parity when they have equal absorptive capacities. It is also interesting to investigate how equilibrium effort and payoff per firm respond to variations in the project value V. The computational results are illustrated in Table 6.1.

The table was constructed for project values ranging from 200 to 1600, fixing unit effort cost $k = 10$. The table and other representative numerical simulations show that equilibrium effort and payoff per firm increase with the project value V. Similar numerical simulations showed that effort and payoff per firm decrease with unit effort cost k when project value is fixed. This discussion yields the following proposition.

Proposition 1.   If the partners in an alliance have equal absorptive capacities then equilibrium effort and payoff per firm increase with the value of the alliance project but decrease with unit effort cost. Effort and payoff per firm are independent of the common absorptive capacity.

Proposition 1 suggests that there are minimal strategic hazards when competitors with equal learning abilities enter into an alliance. The sustainability of such alliances depends largely on the attractiveness of the alliance project relative to effort costs. There will be no incentive to form an alliance if the project value is too low or if effort costs are too high. The partners benefit more when the potential revenues from the alliance are large, and are stimulated to supply greater effort to achieve the goals of the alliance. The short- and long-term interests of the partners are perfectly aligned when firms with equal learning abilities collaborate through an alliance. The partners can maintain parity in their competitive positions even as they supply efforts to grow the alliance.

A good case illustrating the synergistic effects of equal learning is a 1968–75 collaboration between the German firm, Dornier, and the French firm, Dassault, to co-develop and manufacture military aircraft through the Alpha

Jet Project. Tucker (1991) provides a full description of the case. Tucker observes that the two firms were about equal in capabilities and were not likely to create a disparity in competitive positions through the alliance. Collaboration would enable the firms to share development costs, achieve production economies, and moderate market competition. Dassault had substantial experience in project management and in integrating aircraft systems with jet engines. Dornier had valuable manufacturing experience and superior analytical skills.

The learning objectives of Dornier and Dassault were complementary. Dornier desired to gain project management experience; Dassault wanted to gain exposure to Dornier's manufacturing and analytical skills in structures and aerodynamics. However, the problem of differential learning was carefully managed through the division of work, which kept Dornier away from the Dassault's core areas of avionics and instrumentation. Both partners would learn equally, maintaining parity through the acquisition of complementary skills and experience.

Tucker (1991) reports that the alliance worked very well from the perspectives of both of the partners. Dassault gained access to Dornier's material composite manufacturing technology while Dornier, on the other hand, reaped significant profits and acquired project management know-how from Dassault.

Unequal Learning Abilities

We study the situation where the firms differ in their abilities to appropriate knowledge from the alliance by assigning different absorptive capacities to the firms. Here we assume that firm 1 has a greater absorptive capacity than firm 2. That is, $b_1 > b_2 \geq 0$. The solution procedure is to start with specific numerical values for V, k, $a - c_0$, b_1, and b_2 to define the opportunities for the alliance partners as well as their learning abilities. We then compute equilibrium effort and payoffs from the payoffs given in equations (4) and (5). The effect of differential learning is explored by fixing b_2 and increasing b_1.

The structure of equilibrium efforts and payoffs when firm 1 has a greater absorptive capacity than firm 2 is illustrated in Table 6.2. The table was constructed for an alliance with project value $V = 1000$, effort cost parameter $k = 10$, and product market margin $a - c_0 = 12$. The absorptive capacity of firm 2 was fixed at $b_2 = 0$ as we varied b_1 from 0.1 to 0.8. Examining columns 3 and 4 of the table, it is evident that firm 1 supplies more effort than firm 2. In addition, as the difference in absorptive capacities increases, the effort of firm 1 increases while that of firm 2 decreases. The firms' payoffs are shown in columns 4 and 5. The payoff of firm 1 increases but that of firm 2 decreases as the difference in absorptive capacities increases.

The adverse impact of differential learning is manifested by the steep decline in the payoff of firm 2, and also by the increasing difference between

TABLE 6.2 *Different learning abilities*

Absorptive capacity	Efforts		Payoffs	
b_1	x_1	x_2	π_1	π_2
0.10	28.29	24.90	312.81	219.10
0.20	32.28	24.54	381.72	186.47
0.30	37.18	23.80	457.47	152.29
0.40	43.28	22.51	540.86	117.04
0.50	51.02	20.41	632.65	81.63
0.60	61.04	17.09	733.40	47.85
0.70	74.32	11.89	843.04	19.03
0.80	92.46	3.70	960.06	1.48

Parameter values: $b_2 = 0$, $V = 1000$, $k = 10$, and $a - c_0 = 12$.

the payoff of the firms. When the differential is 0.8, firm 2 has a very little incentive to participate in the alliance since it only gains 1.48 while firm 1 gains 960. This shows that large differences in absorptive capacities may reduce the incentive for alliance formation. Similar numerical simulations showed that, for a fixed learning differential, effort and payoff per firm increase with project value and decrease with unit effort cost, as one would expect. The results pertaining to differential learning are summarized in the propositions below.

Proposition 2.   If the partners in an alliance have unequal absorptive capacities then the equilibrium effort of the high absorptive capacity firm exceeds that of the low absorptive capacity firm. Furthermore, as the learning differential between the firms increases, the effort of the high absorptive capacity firm increases but the effort of the low absorptive capacity firm decreases.

Proposition 3.   If the partners in an alliance have unequal absorptive capacities, then as the learning differential between the firms increases, the payoff of the high absorptive capacity firm increases but the payoff of the low absorptive capacity firm decreases. The incentive for alliance formation decreases when partners with large differences in absorptive capacities are linked.

Propositions 2 and 3 provide useful insights into the effect of differential learning on strategic alliances. Proposition 2 suggests that large differences in absorptive capacities may lead to a real time outcome where the better learner supplies most of the effort, carrying the poorer learner. Large disparities in effort contributions can be a barrier to alliance formation and management. When effort supplied is observable but knowledge appropriated is not, it may be difficult for the partners to renegotiate equitable revenue shares as disparities in effort contributions emerge. This can put considerable stress on the social harmony between the partners (Kumar and Nti, 1998).

Proposition 3 also suggests that an alliance between firms with large differences in absorptive capacities is likely to be unstable or unsustainable. Large differences in learning abilities can lead to a real time outcome where the poorer learner incurs substantial economic losses as a result of the deterioration of its competitive position. When revenues gained from the project are observable or verifiable but changes in competitive positions are not, it may be difficult for the poorer learner to convince the better learner to agree to renegotiate terms. One or both parties may exit from the relationship if they continue to hold incompatible perceptions about each other's gains or losses from the relationship. This suggests that additional incentive structures and administrative mechanisms, such as the use of side payments and knowledge sharing, may be required to hold an alliance together if the partners differ significantly in their absorptive capacities. Thus substantial relationship-specific investments may be required to sustain alliances with differential learning (Madhok, chap. 4, above).

New United Motor Manufacturing, Inc. (NUMMI) is a good example of an alliance where differential learning occurred. Equally owned by General Motors (GM) and Toyota, NUMMI assembles a Toyota-designed car, which is marketed by each company under its own brand name. Forbes (1987), Niland (1989), and Badaracco (1991) provide additional details on the alliance. The joint venture would enable GM to market a high quality subcompact it had been unable to develop on its own. Toyota, on the other hand, would be protected against rising American protectionism by initiating a US-based production strategy. Economically, the project would enable both firms to produce Toyota-designed subcompact cars for the US market at a relatively low investment cost. Both firms would also benefit by sharing production costs.

The learning objectives of GM and Toyota appeared to be complementary. GM wanted to learn Toyota's lean production methods in order to become more successful in producing high-quality subcompact cars. Toyota, on the other hand, wanted to learn how to adapt its manufacturing and human relations system to produce high quality cars in the USA using American workers and suppliers, including how to deal with an American labour union.

Most industry experts agree that Toyota achieved its learning objectives but GM was unable to learn from NUMMI (see Keller, 1989; Badaracco, 1991.) Toyota successfully transplanted its human relations and materials management system to the USA and also gained new experience in ocean freight logistics and environmental rules for US-based plants. Subsequently, Toyota established a new $800 million US-based automobile plant in Georgetown, Kentucky. Toyota has integrated NUMMI into its North American operations, transferring seasoned NUMMI managers to other plants and using common suppliers. GM, on the other hand, has been criticized for failing to create an organizational structure that would enable it to learn from NUMMI. Apparently, GM went into NUMMI, 'expecting to find some secret technology, proprietary information' when the key to Toyota's success was the integration of 'the people systems with the technology systems' (*Wall Street Journal*, 20 May, 1986). GM was unable to embody the NUMMI 'system' into its operations and did not develop a learning infrastructure that would enable it to utilize the skills of GM managers who were involved with NUMMI in its other operations. Learning opportunities in NUMMI are now exhausted, and the alliance provides an interesting example of an out-sourcing relationship between two flagship firms in the automobile industry (Rugman and D'Cruz, chap. 3, above).

Discussion

The model and the cases discussed in this chapter have interesting implications for partner selection, design of sharing rules, and the management of learning in strategic alliances. Our main finding is that extreme differences in learning abilities may reduce incentives for alliance formation and also undermine the stability of ongoing alliances. Learning alliances are likely to be successful from a strategic perspective when the absorptive capacities of partners are equal or close together. This suggests that desirable partners for learning alliances will tend to be close in absorptive capacities. Thus similarity of absorptive capacity is also a relevant criterion for partner selection, perhaps just as important as similarity in organizational structure and size (Geringer, 1991). Firms with extremely high or low absorptive capacities may have difficulty finding compatible alliance partners, and they may actually end up in unstable learning alliances because they are likely to link up with firms whose absorptive capacities are very different. Therefore, firms entering into alliance would benefit by directing investment and resources towards the identification of partners with compatible learning abilities (Tallman, chap. 5, above).

Because our model is explicit about the defining characteristics of learning alliances, it can also be used to explore how to select equitable sharing rules to properly value the effort contributions of partners with different absorptive capacities. In order to convey our ideas expeditiously, we assumed alliance revenues were shared in proportion to effort contributions. However, when the partners have different absorptive capacities, it may be in the interest of the firms to value relative efforts differently. In other words, even if the partners have mismatched absorptive capacities, incentive for alliance formation may be improved by modifying the revenue sharing rule. Basically, the better learner should induce the poorer learner to contribute more effort by letting the latter capture more alliance revenues. This trade-off of alliance revenues for long-term strategic advantage may actually harmonize the interests of the partners.

We have stressed the benefits of forming alliances between firms with equal learning abilities, but we employed a model where the firms had equal access to alliance-generated knowledge. If the partners have unequal absorptive capacities, it may still be possible to equalize learning by managing the partners' access to knowledge. Formally, this can be arranged within our model. Suppose that when a volume of knowledge $x_1 + x_2$ is created, firms 1 and 2 are given access to proportions b_2 and b_1, respectively. Then both firms will achieve equal cost reductions, namely $b_1 b_2 (x_1 + x_2)$. In practice, differential access to alliance-generated knowledge is achieved by using the division of work to keep some partners away from certain activities, as was done in the Alpha Jet Project, or by using recognized gatekeepers and gateways to control the type and volume of information that flow to the partners (Hamel, Doz, and Prahalad, 1989).

Even where the partners objectively have equal access to alliance-generated knowledge, the GM–Toyota alliance shows that the learning outcomes can be quite different if some partners focus on the wrong type of learning. GM was looking for some secret technology and proprietary information when it needed to understand and implement a new organizational form. Within our model, focusing on the wrong type of learning may be attributed to a very low absorptive capacity or to insufficient access to alliance-generated knowledge.

Conclusions

This chapter addressed the problem of differential learning in strategic alliances. We focused on how differential abilities to appropriate alliance-generated knowledge may alter the future competitive positions of the firms, and how this may affect incentives facing the partners. We offered a game-theory model to study how the supply of effort by the alliance partners, as well as their payoffs, depends on the characteristics of the alliance. In our model changes in competitive positions occurred as a result of differential abilities to transform knowledge into cost reduction in the product market where the firms compete.

We organized the analysis to highlight the differences between equal and differential learning. When the firms have equal absorptive capacities, we showed that effort and payoffs were independent of absorptive capacities. Thus the firms can maintain strategic parity even as they supply effort to grow the alliance. In contrast, when the firms have different absorptive capacities, we found that the effort and payoff of the better learner increases but that of the poorer learner decreases as the difference in absorptive capacities increases. This causes a divergence in incentives as the competitive position of the poorer learner deteriorates. Our model suggests that an ongoing alliance may collapse if a large enough learning differential emerges. We noted, for both equal and differential learning, that effort and payoffs increase with the value of the project but decrease with effort cost. We briefly discussed the learning objectives and outcomes of the GM–Toyota and the Dassault–Dornier alliances.

Our analysis has implications for the formation, stability, and contractual terms of strategic alliances. In particular our model suggests that as the difference in absorptive capacities increases, the stability of such alliances may be in question. Astute low absorptive capacity firms should demand compensating contractual terms in order to join or remain in such an alliance. But a short-sighted high absorptive firm may refuse, perhaps complaining about the greater effort it must supply or the smaller compensation it must take to maintain the relationship. These are clearly barriers to alliance formation. Alliances are likely to be successful from a strategic perspective when the learning abilities of partners are equal or similar. Learning alliances require supportive relationship-specific investments and resources to enhance and sustain the value-creation process (Madhok, chap. 4, above).

Since absorptive capacity may be influenced by a firm's motivational orientation and organizational culture, our analysis offers some insights into some of the problems that impede the progress of some Western and Japanese strategic alliances. As Hamel (1991) has noted, Japanese firms tend to have explicit learning intent when they enter into alliances with Western firms. They also make a greater effort to learn and have a greater degree of organizational memory due to low labour turnover. They may therefore have greater absorptive capacities compared with some of their Western partners. Our analysis suggests that the heightened learning intent of the Japanese may actually limit the number of suitable Western partners they can successfully collaborate with once the game theoretical considerations are factored in. Alliances with high-absorptive-capacity Japanese firms must be more creatively structured and managed if they are to be sustainable and mutually advantageous to both sides.

Our analysis also suggests ways whereby the problem of differential learning may be controlled. We have identified extreme differences in absorptive capacity as a barrier to alliance formation and stability. It may, therefore, be in the interest of alliance partners to establish formal structures to manage and promote equal learning. Within such a structure emerging learning differentials can be detected, monitored, and neutralized. By confronting the problem of differential learning directly, the partners will be better positioned to identify and adopt the necessary measures to facilitate information exchange and stimulate equal learning within the alliance.

The analysis presented here assumed that the absorptive capacities of the firms were known and unchanging during the course of the alliance. We also assumed a specific form for the revenue-sharing rule. It would be interesting to study how different revenue-sharing rules may affect the incentives for alliance formation between firms with unequal absorptive capacities. It would be useful to extend our model to study the effects of asymmetric information and dynamics. With asymmetric information, some firms may strategically misrepresent their capabilities either to secure better contractual terms or to induce their partners to supply greater effort. The absorptive capacities of some firms may change if collaboration extends over a long period. This may occur either spontaneously or through conscious investment decisions. It would be useful to study how such changes may dynamically affect incentives and contractual terms in learning alliances.

References

AHERN, R. (1993), 'Implications of Strategic Alliances for Small R&D Intensive Firms', *Environment and Planning A, 25: 1511–26.*

BADARACCO, J. L. (1991), *The Knowledge Link: How Firms Compete Through Strategic Alliances* (Boston, Mass.: Harvard Business School Press).

BALAKRISHNAN, S. and KOZA, M. (1993), 'Information Asymmetry, Market Failure and Joint Ventures: Theory and Evidence', *Journal of Economic Behavior and Organization*, 20: 99–117.

BLEEKE, J. and ERNST, D. (1995), 'Is Your Strategic Alliance Really a Sale?', *Harvard Business Review*, 73: 97–105.

COHEN, W. and LEVINTHAL, D. A. (1990), 'Absorptive Capacity: A New Perspective on Learning and Innovation', *Administrative Science Quarterly*, 35: 128–52.

———— (1994), 'Fortune Favors the Prepared Mind', *Management Science*, 40: 227–51.

D'ASPREMONT, C. and JACQUEMIN, A. (1988), 'Cooperative and Noncooperative R&D in Duopoly with Spillovers', *American Economic Review*, 78: 1133–7.

DE BONDT, R. (1996), 'Spillovers and Innovative Activities', *International Journal of Industrial Organization*, 15: 1–28.

DEVINNEY, T. M. (1987), 'Entry and Learning', *Management Science*, 33: 706–24.

FORBES, D. (1987), 'The Lessons of NUMMI', *Business Month*, 129: 34–7.

GERINGER, J. M. (1991), 'Strategic Determinants of Partner Selection Criteria in International Joint Ventures', *Journal of International Business Studies*, 22: 41–62.

HAMEL, G. (1991), 'Competition for Competence and Inter-partner Learning within International Strategic Alliances', *Strategic Management Journal*, 12 (summer special issue): 83–103.

——DOZ, Y. L., and PRAHALAD, C. K. (1989), 'Collaborate with Your Competitors—and Win', *Harvard Business Review*, 65: 133–9.

HAX, A. and MAJLUF, N. (1982), 'Competitive Cost Dynamics: The Experience Curve', *Interfaces*, 12: 50–61.

KELLER, M. (1989), *Rude Awakening: The Rise, Fall and Struggle for Recovery of General Motors* (New York: William Morrow).

KHANNA, T., GULATI, R., and NOHRIA, N. (1998), 'The Dynamics of Learning Alliances: Competition, Cooperation, and Relative Scope', *Strategic Management Journal*, 19: 193–210.

KOGUT, B. (1991), 'Joint Ventures and the Option to Expand and Acquire', *Management Science*, 37: 19–33.

KOZA, M. and LEWIN, A. Y. (1998), 'The Co-evolution of Alliances', *Organization Science*, 9: 255–64.

KUMAR, R. and NTI, K. O. (1998), 'Differential Learning and Interaction in Alliance Dynamics: A Process and Outcome Discrepancy Model', *Organization Science*, 9: 356–67.

LEI, D. (1993), 'Offensive and Defensive Uses of Alliances', *Long Range Planning*, 26: 32–41.

MODY, A. (1993), 'Learning Through Alliances', *Journal of Economic Behavior and Organization*, 20: 151–70.

MONAHAN, G. E. (1987), 'The Structure of Equilibria in Market Share Attraction Models', *Management Science*, 33: 228–43.

NILAND, P. (1989), 'US–Japanese Joint Venture: New United Motor Manufacturing, Inc. (NUMMI)', *Planning Review*, 17: 40–5.

NTI, K. O. (1997), 'Comparative Statics of Contests and Rent-seeking Games', *International Economic Review*, 38: 43–59.

PEKAR, P., JR. and ALLIO, R. (1994), 'Making Alliances Work: Guidelines for Success', *Long Range Planning*, 27: 54–65.

REICH, R. B. and MANKIN, E. D. (1986), 'Joint Ventures with Japan Give Away our Future', *Harvard Business Review*, 86: 78–86.

SINHA, D. K. and CUSUMANO, M. A. (1991), 'Complementary Resources and Cooperative Research: A Model of Research Joint Ventures among Competitors', *Management Science*, 37: 1091–106.

SPENCE, M. (1981), 'The Learning Curve and Competition', *Bell Journal of Economics*, 12: 49–70.

TUCKER, J. B. (1991), 'Partners and Rivals: A Model of International Collaboration in Advanced Technology', *International Organization*, 45: 83–120.

Wall Street Journal (1986), 'Nummi Auto Venture is Termed Success', 20 May.

7

The Firm as Differentiator and Integrator of Networks
Layered Communities of Practice and Discourse

RAY LOVERIDGE

In much recent analysis of strategic management the firm is portrayed as a possessor of a unique capability to create added value or quasi-rent. Usually this is seen as relating to an ability to differentiate its products or to innovate rapidly in either product or process. More generally the firm is seen as providing a least-cost location for knowledge creation and transformation: a managerial ability to bring about this condition, through a fusion of existing competencies with those of other organizations in the value chain, is regarded by some observers as itself providing the capability that creates competitive advantage.

This view is supported by the arguments and case histories presented here. The notion of appropriative learning provides a central explanation for the structural modes and styles of organizational behaviour examined in this chapter. This entails the absorption, adaptation, and application of information along socio-technical networks in a manner that expands the existing capabilities of the firm. However it is proposed that information is exchanged along three distinct clusterings of transactional networks. These are seen as comprising distinctive communities of practice in the creation of the firm's reputation for creditworthiness, for design know-how, and for operational reliability and predictability. Within these communal clusters, stakeholders in the firm's continued survival and success judge its performance against ideational rationales and logics of action that can be disparate, but compatible or incompatible, with the expounded objectives and aims of corporate management.

The distinctive enabling competence of the firm is that of orchestrating and integrating the separate stocks and flows of information in such a way as to produce an optimal reputational mix in its capital and operational environments. This reputation is, however, generally and increasingly dependent upon the firm's ability to appropriate design knowledge from its environmental context. The process of creative appropriation may be facilitated or inhibited by the pursuance of complementary or conflicting aims along capital and operational networks.

This chapter suggests the existence of three distinctive styles of managing innovation concerted, contested, and diffused. These are shaped by the strategist's perceptions of the status and influence of designers along their appropriate networks and their significance for the firm. However, this judgement is itself conditioned by the agency role of corporate management across different national business systems and by the amount and type of uncertainty engendered by the operational context.

Resource Dependency Theories

Over the last twenty years or so the notion that firm 'competitiveness' stems primarily from a monopoly over idiosyncratic assets or, more particularly, of core competences, has come to dominate the business literature (see particularly Porter, 1985). In economic theory this analysis has its origins in the work of Schumpeter (1934), Penrose (1959), and Caves (1971) but is particularly associated with 'the internalisation of the knowledge market' predicated by Buckley and Casson (1976) and Teece (1977). More recently Kogut and Zander (1993) have developed the notion that 'Firms are social communities that specialize in the creation and internal transfer of knowledge' (p. 625). This knowledge is seen to be embodied in human resources by some commentators (Becker, 1964; Kamoche, 1996; Mueller, 1996). Other sociologists see the capabilities of the collective as being contained in a wider 'cultural capital' (Bourdieu, 1977).

The relationship between the possession of clear focus in a company's product portfolio and strong corporate performance revealed by Rumelt (1980) has provided a basis for a widely adopted model of strategy in the 1980s. This has led to the divestment of all but 'core competencies' by most leading corporate groups in the West and the break-up of others such as ICI. However identification of what Hitt and Ireland (1986) describe as the firm's 'distinctive competences' remains elusive in spite of Porter's (1985) programmatic approach to the task. Prahalad and Hamel (1990) evidently associate these competencies with the design of product or process. Amith and Schoemaker (1993) see them as extending to marketing and finance, while Gupta and Govidarajan (1991) suggest that in the multinational corporation (MNC) significant internal flows of knowledge-bearing information concern either capital investment, or the 'professional' design of products and processes, or, lastly, the management of operational processes in relation to local or global demands.

Clearly the identification of 'core' competencies, and of an associated core labour force, is as problematic for practising managers as for scholars (Wood, 1989; Jackson, 1997). Indeed there might seem to be a weakness in any market-based analysis that separates out supply-side characteristics (resource dependence) from expressed demand (present and future market positioning). The unique value of the firms' competencies is that attributed to them by potential users. The long-term development of such competencies is therefore based on an assumed future customer valuation of resources that may or may not emerge or prove to be sustainable. To focus on a competency that offers a limited range of applications remains a high risk strategy, however favourable is the current market position of the corporation, unless future demand is assured and market boundaries are high and impermeable (Bain, 1959; Porter, 1980).

Current writing offers four related solutions to this problem based on the managerial practice of the last decade or so. The first is found in the width, scope, and combinative qualities of the skills and knowledge to be found in the MNC. According to Kim and Kogut (1996) these provide a platform from which the large global organization can enter any one of the new trajectories taken by technological derivatives in sectors that provide a so-called hypercompetitive environment such as telecommunications. This is an extension of the view that the MNC provides a unique vehicle for transferring knowledge between locations put forward earlier by Buckley and Casson (1976), by Teece (1977), and by others. It also gells with the view of Hamel and Prahalad (1993) that the large firm, and not the sector, is to be seen as the source of product innovation in a world in which convergent generic technologies serve to lower costs of entry to many product markets.

A second perspective has been that which emphasizes the 'dynamic capabilities' for learning possessed by successful firms (Teece and Pisano, 1994). This approach suggests that it is in management's ability to mobilize the fractionated contributions of suppliers, customers, and internal providers towards a common 'problem solving' orientation that one finds the key to successful technology innovation. Thus the 'core competence' rests in management's ability to design the administrative systems, provide the leadership, and create an integrating culture and climate rather than in any single source of technological knowledge.

Two other paths have been followed in the literature. The first also focuses on the learning capabilities of the firm, and more particularly on what might be called 'appropriative learning' (Teece, 1986; Loveridge, 1990; Child and Loveridge, 1990; Loveridge, 1997). The second is contained in terms such as 'co-operative capitalism' (Chandler, 1990). It may also be seen in the creation of a new meaning for the term business 'networks' as a stylized analytical category to be contrasted with 'markets' and with 'hierarchies' (Powell, 1990). Essentially both terms extend empirical observation into the 'stylized facts' that underlie the analyses of New Institutional Economics (NIE). Networks are represented as a distinctive mode of collaboration between parties based on long-lasting relationships and a degree of trust not present in the other two typifications (Lane and Bachmann, 1996). In the next two sections the meaning of these concepts will be examined in greater depth.

Appropriative Learning

The association of capitalism with an opportunistic contest for monopoly rents, or 'added value', derived from the novelty of new invention, is hardly a new idea (Schumpeter, 1934). In Williamson's (1975) explanation of the evolution of institutionalized boundaries to such markets, organizational structures became defensive barriers against the costs of opportunism. Subsequently, however, many of Williamson's associates in the extension of NIE analysis have reverted to the more Marxian view of corporate opportunism, in which the firm becomes the initiator and predator in a search for idiosyncratic knowledge belonging to other contestants rather than a defender (e.g. Teece, 1986). In this context appropriative learning becomes, as it once was, in Schumpeter's neo-Marxian analysis, the primary reason for hierarchy. Organizational structures and processes have to be geared to 'capturing added value' rather than allowing such rents either to be lost through inefficiency or ceded to other contestants. The capabilities of the successful innovator are thus geared to the absorption of new knowledge through surveillance, selection, and translation of contextual opportunities in ways designed to enhance or to complement an existing internal fund of knowledge (Cohen and Levinthal, 1990); or as Kogut and Zander (1992) express it, to translate 'know-that' into 'know-how'.

Teece's (1986) original conceptualization of the process of appropriative learning lays greatest emphasis on the context in which it takes place. In particular he sees the innovator's ability to capture the value added deriving from innovation as resting with (*a*) the relative strength or weakness of the 'regime of appropriability' surrounding the innovator and potential imitators, (*b*) the stage of development towards an industrially dominant design, and (*c*) the availability of complementary assets. These latter may be described as those parts of the value-adding process that contribute in a direct sense to the innovation process, most particularly the contributions of production, marketing, and sales. These functions are seen not only to be vital for the successful design and implementation of new products and processes, but also to the acquisition of non-imitable properties unique to the firm. The precise synergies achieved within the internal systems of the firm will, to some extent at least, be based on the experiences of cross-functional activity possessed by its members as well as upon codified procedures. To the extent that this tacit knowledge has led to the creation of effective operational routines it represents a unique asset embodied in prevailing group norms within the organization. Such routines can form the basis for incremental innovations and for a path-dependent development of technologies unique to the firm or 'sectoral set' (Nelson, 1994)

By contrast much of the writing on organizational learning has represented an extension to a long-running OD (organizational development) approach to the cognitive 'un-freezing' of beliefs and attitudes at the personal and primary-group level (Pettigrew, 1985; Huber, 1991). The underlying focus of recent OD discourse has been on the necessity for continuous adaptation to change and to multiple levels of meaning within a 'post-modern' context (Clegg, 1990). In the structuralist literature the focus of discussion has been on relational configurations, both inside the firm and across its boundaries, that enable or stimulate the transfer and appropriation of knowledge. In the case of small or medium-sized enterprises (SME) much of this analysis has focused on the creation and maintenance of organic structures enabling maximum interaction and free exchange of information (Burns and Stalker, 1961; Dodgson, 1992).

In emergent sectors, or hypercompetitive environments, the adoption of relatively small operating units with organically democratic structures has become normal even after growth in numbers of employees follows from early success, as in the case of Texas Instruments and Microsoft (Burgelman and Sayles, 1988). As the firm grows in size the need for formally organized internal diffusion networks increases if advantage is to be taken of both internally generated knowledge of potential value or intelligence gathered from external sources. The process of appropriation is often reduced to distinctive sets of activities, the last of which is the formalization of 'organizational memory' in modes of cumulation and integration.

In the case of the larger bureaucracy contained in multinational corporations (MNCs) there has been much more debate among business strategy writers about the relative significance of the functional roles of different structural elements such as strategic business units (SBUs) and overseas affiliates in the internal creation and diffusion of company-specific knowledge as well as portals through which to gather external information (Prahalad and Hamel, 1990). Some analysts distinguish between the type of information flowing between the centre and the periphery of the MNC. For example Gupta and Govindarajan (1991) have suggested that the role of the SBU can be determined in terms of three discrete flows of information internal to the MNC. These are those relating to capital-allocative decisions, those concerning design know-how, and those relating to operational concerns. The devolution of authority to the SBU can follow a path from operational autonomy through design creation to autonomy in capital allocation.

Networks in Innovation

Of equal importance in the managerial literature of the last fifteen years has been the concept of inter-organizational networking. Networks are represented as a distinctive mode of collaboration between parties based on long-lasting relationships and a degree of trust not present in the other two typifications (Lane and Bachmann, 1996, 1997). All this has been seen to extend managerial responsibilities beyond the immediate corporate hierarchy to long-term obligations towards actors in other organizations with which the firm has strategic alliances often including joint ventures involving mutual capital investment. Again this scholarly interest may be seen as no more than a reflection of a historical phenomenon. For many reasons collaboration between legally autonomous firms has become a familiar response to a turbulent environment. The current source of turbulence that has been seen by many observers to constitute a historic climacteric combining the effects of rapid change in generic technologies such as micro-electronics with the 'globalization' of markets, including supply chains, and the responses of national governments which have tended to favour market solutions rather than protective interventionism (Freeman Sharp, and Walker, 1991).

A distinctive feature of these alliances is their proactive and developmental nature. Unlike corporate responses to previous climacterics, often associated with the economic recessions of the 1880s–90s and 1920s–30s, alliances have generally not taken the form of defensive cartels aimed at controlling supply price mechanisms and erecting barriers to market entry. (At least, not in the directly focused manner of former times.) The example provided by what has been variously described as the 'alliance capitalism' or 'co-operative capitalism' (Chandler, 1990) within Germany and, more significantly, in Japan, has clearly provided a model for this new orientation among corporate decision-makers (Dore, 1986). This has been most evidently true in the attempted adaptation to 'relational' or 'obligational' modes of transacting along vertical supply-chains (Sako, 1992; Lamming, 1993).

But equally horizontal agreements between firms in the same sector have gone beyond the familiar cross-licensing of new technologies, a practice that often reinforced global cartels in growing markets in the past (Grindley and Teece, 1997). Perhaps most significant to the process of so-called globalization has been the exchange of complementary assets, such as market access, for production 'know-how' often to be found in foreign direct investment undertaken as a joint venture (Rugman and Verbecke, 1997). A third important area of inter-organizational collaboration has been in so-called 'pre-competitive' R&D, in which networks often encompass universities and other specialized centres of research and product development (Callon, 1986; Nelson, 1993). Very often a national or regional state agency will sponsor and/or convene such consortia. Membership is usually somewhat larger than market-based, or spontaneous, alliances and often participants represent a national interest in the development (Freeman, Sharp, and Walker, 1991).

Small wonder, then, that scholarly endeavour has been directed at conceptualizing and explaining this phenomenon and that the long-standing notion of networks as both structures and processes of social action has undergone a revival. In particular the idea that monopolies such as hierarchies, clans and networks, might actually provide means to increased efficiency, has caused a distinctive shift in debates around the central economic disciplinary paradigm of market competition (see for example Williamson,

1985). In organizational theories a regulatory continuum ranging from (spot) markets, through contingency contract, to hierarchy, and thence to networks, and then to clans has also gained currency (Powell, 1990).

These stylized conditions often seem poorly supported as discrete taxonomies in real life and under-theorized in scholarly explanations. There is, for example, an uneasy relationship between explanations based on the attribution of rational intent to actors by transaction cost theorists, whether from the position of defender (Williamson) or opportunistic predator (Teece), and that of the institutional sociologist. For the latter, the coincidence of current functional utility with socially embodied patterns of behaviour in pre-existent institutions can create a 'discovered' basis for effective exchange. (For example in the work of Biggart and Hamilton, 1992, or of Whitley, 1992.) There is, indeed, a case for suggesting that sometimes the conceptualization of the term 'inter-organizational network' has offered an assumed basis for distinguishing between actor orientations that may be misleading and obscuring (De Bresson and Amesso, 1991).

Perhaps the distinguishing theoretical characteristic of the network concept is its basis in an assumed trust between the parties (Lane and Bachmann, 1997). This is seen by many economists to derive from knowledge of the other gained in a long-term process of 'gaming' (Casson, 1992). The importance of proven competence to trust-building is encapsulated by Butler and Gill (1997) in the concept 'reliable knowledge'. This is seen to be based on a recipient's confidence in the processes by which the knowledge was produced and, in turn, in its ability to provide a reliable basis for action on the part of the recipient. Sako (1992) suggests a stepped progression in learning about other actors in an alliance that includes an increasingly large affective and ascriptive component. Lowndes and Dkeleher (1997) suggest that inter-organizational relationships can exist at a high level of informal goodwill even though somewhat remote and loose linked up to the point of entering a formal arrangement. The new alliance can then involve introducing individual actors to others at different levels of the organization, resulting in a period of status conflict between employees in the two organizations. If this conflict is resolved resort to formal contractual behaviour of a juridical type might be adopted before the final bedding down of an institutionalized partnership.

Critics point to the utilitarian motives that usually drive corporate actors to collaborate and which remain the basis for survival in conflictual environments. Some point to the underlying imbalances of power and exploitable nature of relations between suppliers to Japanese original equipment manufacturers (OEMs) and their Western imitators (Florida and Kenney, 1990). Nor are outcomes always successful. The majority of joint ventures so far have resulted in either early divorce or takeover, often of one parent by another (Lorange and Roos, 1992).

Doz (1988) and other strategic analysts emphasize the ongoing problems of managing shifting dependencies between members of a strategic alliance.

Exogenous pressures, particularly from changes in stock-market position, can raise serious doubts about any one partner's ability to meet its obligations (Inkpen and Beamish, 1997). This may also be true if they are adjudged to have become over-extended in their commitments to other external alliances and so to have fragmented their competencies. Opportunism in a situation in which each collaborator may be a competitor through another alliance cannot be discounted. This can be particularly true when industrial boundaries are broached by a fusion in technologies, where acquisition of a crucial linking technology or bridging knowledge can assure even relatively small organizations of a flagship role (as can currently be observed in emergent telecommunications technologies). Finally the complexity of coordinating the actions of large numbers of collaborators over such a widely defined agenda may bring a reversion to hierarchical governance. This can be seen in the recent histories of both NASA and Airbus.

It appears to be difficult to create trust within the time span and scope of a single contractual agenda. This can be particularly so when the overriding intention of each partner can be that of the survival as an autonomous entity in a period of great threat and uncertainty. Expropriation rather than appropriation might appear to be the more likely outcome of transactions in an atmosphere of opportunism both in theory and on the strength of empirical evidence.

Communities of Interest as Obstacles or Aids to Collective Learning

By contrast Granovetter (1992, 1995) sees social networks as a preliminary stage in creating institutional 'facticities', whilst at the same time being 'embedded' and therefore shaped by prevailing institutionalized structures. As emergent or nascent structures they face possible problems of legitimization through recognition and sponsorship from prevailing sources of authority (Osborn and Hagedoorn, 1997). In the case of interpersonal linkages this recognition is likely to remain implicit and sponsorship outside the group intermittent or non-existent. But, as Granovetter's earlier work (1974) suggests, institutionalized networks can form the basis of restrictingly strong ties. Indeed as Grabher (1993) demonstrates, strong social ties within a regional network, such as that of the Ruhr steel industry, can block adaptation to the wider needs of the market. 'Unfreezing' of personal beliefs and attitudes in such a case can involve disrupting loyalties to multiple levels of community identity.

Within most large organizations internal boundaries grow up around 'communities of practice' created by daily interaction in specialized tasks. These tend to develop their own localized 'logic of action' (Karpik, 1972) peculiar to their function or department. These can extend to the creation of 'local histories' to substantiate the continuance of present practice (March, Sproull, and Tamuz, 1991) and the construction of departmental thought worlds. These may be expressed in the use of vernacular language to preserve locally situated knowledge to the exclusion of outsiders (Katz and Allen, 1982). In the face of contextual uncertainty such groups can develop power dependencies within the organization which become self-reinforcing in their contribution to the administrative complexity generated by the need to coordinate such fractionated knowledge (Crozier, 1964; Kanter, 1989).

However it is evident that the institutionalization of networks within the firm can be complemented and extended into the external community. Callon (1986) describes the manner in which information exchanged along personal or small-group interconnections becomes translated into specific operational knowledge: he emphasizes the manner in which interests shape the process. 'Solutions' discovered in the codified knowledge are those which match 'problems' in a mutually reinforcive political process of translation. Like Pettigrew's (1972) computer systems designers, networked actors can design 'problems' to match the expertise they have on offer in the market. Conway (1995) also implies that technical gatekeepers play a strong role in inferring the focus of the transmitted information within their own definition of the firm's capability. Their unique position and interpretative expertise provided them with considerable potential power *vis à vis* corporate management through the absorption of uncertainty deriving from both the novelty of the technology and the perceived complexity of analysing it (Pettigrew, 1972; Hickson *et al.*, 1971). This is particularly likely to occur in periods of radical technological change when corporate managers are more likely to take on the role of 'clients' *vis à vis* groups possessing expertise in the new areas of knowledge (Loveridge, 1972).

There is, indeed, a large literature on the development of networks among the burgeoning ranks of design specialists within corporate structures. The importance of such specialists to large firms is evidently increasing but, as suggested earlier, modes of networking between employing organizations can assume a variety of forms across different national institutions, regions, and sectors (Callon, 1986). Historically, professional associations have played an important role in Anglo-Saxon countries (Abbott, 1988). In many areas of expertise the influence of such associations as modes of knowledge transfer now extends far beyond a national or regional level. These institutionalized networks can take on a vital role in the creation and transfer of expertise between firms and can complement the emergence of design consultancies and other knowledge-based service enterprises (Clark, 1987). Equally, their claim to unilateral self-regulation of the training and education of professionals, and, often, to set performance standards in the workplace, has been contested by corporate management and, increasingly over the last two decades, by state agencies. This can be seen both in traditionally professionalized areas of work such as medicine, and in emerging sectors of specialization such as financial trading (Mayer, 1997).

Other analysts see networks across corporate executives as providing a superordinate influence over the innovation process. This can assume different forms in different national contexts—all of them potentially important to the manner in which inter-organizational alliances are formed in those countries (Teubner, 1993; Scott, 1986, 1997; Scher, 1997). Scher emphasizes the social layering of the Japanese corporate elite with the *uchi* (outsider) having to move between successive layers to arrive at the insider status of *soto*. The tests are those of reliability in meeting the insiders' standards over a long period. In this sense the Japanese, and some might say also the German, business elite is not so open as those in Anglo-Saxon societies, even if normal entry is by way of in-company promotion. Membership of the business–government elite in the former countries tends, therefore, to be made up of men whose first loyalty is to their company. At the same time there appears to be a strong ideal of national stewardship which causes them to collaborate with their peers and to recognize the existence of the external economies to be gained through the 'concertation' of their actions *vis à vis* foreign competitors (Lodge and Vogel, 1987).

However, even in the Anglo-American context mergers and acquisitions involving the corporate identities of global organizations can be recalled by their chief executives as having been initiated in 'chance encounter' within settings or events confined to particular corporate elites. The wider institutionalized contexts that shape the emergent outcomes of such meetings include those of securities markets which, in the latter countries, provide a major source of uncertainty and risk for corporate decision-makers (though not, usually, their most significant source of credit). These markets are conjoined by networks of traders, brokers, arbitrageurs, and investment bankers. Their languages are devoted to the translation of the operational performance of corporations (the 'fundamentals') into abstract tradeable assets upon which rents can be earned by financial intermediaries (Adler and Adler, 1984; Kindleberger, 1996). Financial analysts appear to occupy bridging roles along such networks. One was reported as saying of the recent Lucas–Varity merger, seen as a reverse takeover by the US company, 'Lucas was just breakfast' (*Sunday Times*, 6 July 1997). The role of such analysts may well have previously been crucial in shaping information flows to stock markets that helped to define the breakfast menu (and, as it turned out, the luncheon taken by TRW in acquiring Lucas–Varity in April 1999).

It is at the operational level of the firm's activities that predictability in the delivery of the outcomes of its value-adding activities seems often to have proved most problematic. It would not be an exagerration to suggest that most attempts to develop managerial knowledge as an intellectual discipline have hinged around operational control and coordination (Wood, 1989). Over the last two centuries attempts to codify and to reify knowledge within the value-adding activities of the firm have led to an increasingly specialized division of labour within the design of both products and processes and their embodiment within related discourses (Braverman, 1974). This has, in turn, often led to attempts at internal, or intra-firm, appropriation of knowledge by task-related groups, and to occupational, or inter-firm, associations in the manner described above. Such attempts have been particularly present in the development of new sectors in Britain and North America where the conditions defining the 'regime of appropriability' operating within the labour market have been more conducive to the formation of occupational interest associations (OIAs) than those in later developing countries (Webb and Webb, 1897; Loveridge, 1983).

By way of contrast, much has been made in the managerial literature of the last two decades, of the revolution in supply-chain relationships inspired by the work and achievements of Japanese operations management (Lamming, 1993). The revelatory nature of this change in corporate management views in the West might, in itself, be taken as evidence of their former isolation from the value-adding processes in their organizations. There is reason to believe that this isolation continues to exist. The endorsement of 'continuous improvement', 'lean production', and 'just-in-time' techniques in the rhetoric of Anglo-American corporate management is often accompanied by contradictory actions at strategic level and by relatively poor achievement in the creation of reliable trust in supply chain relationships (Sako, 1992; Helper, 1990). It is, perhaps, paradoxical that these relational practices of the pioneering Japanese managers have become translated into the intensely bureaucratic procedures of ISO 2000, and subsequent derivatives, during their propagation by agencies of Western governments, trade associations, professional bodies, and, of course, by the ubiquitous army of management consultants.

Discourse as Appropriation

What is notable in the literature on inter-organizational communication is the relatively discrete manner in which each type of network has been studied and conceptualized by scholars in business schools. In spite of the rhetoric of integration, the basis for these disciplinary perspectives may be seen to continue to be shaped by the need to meet the functional logics represented by the specialized division of labour within bureaucracies (and present in every MBA class). These tend to cluster around those reproduced in Gupta and Govindarajan's (1991) analysis of information flows within the MNC. The discourses of corporate management are likely to be shaped by their imperative need to gain and retain a reputation for creditworthiness within financial and governmental networks. Those of design specialists will be shaped by the paradigmatic legitimacy of their diagnostic tools and the manner in which they display 'know-how' in their application. Operational managers are likely to gain network reputation for their ability to meet the expectations of their peers along the supply chain, in conditions that are likely to vary by sector, but which are generally seen to be increasing in volatility over recent years.

What is suggested here is that disparities in judgement and action can be more, rather than less, likely to occur within the complex bureaucracy that constitutes the large MNE as a result of multiplex networking. Misunderstandings are likely to reflect a growing specialization in the knowledge that provides a currency in any one of the multiple design and operational networks along which inter-corporate relations and reputations are created and sustained. It is, of course, just such fractionation in the operational understandings of diverse groups that collaborative ways of organizing such as team working, concurrent engineering, and devolved structures of responsibility are designed to solve. As suggested earlier, their early success has often been undermined by actions taken at the corporate level according to a strategic logic which has threatened the livelihood of junior employees and transformed ' communities of practice' within the organizational hierarchy into 'communities of interest' within the marketplace. But, probably of equal importance in increasing strategic complexity has been the development of new knowledge disciplines. While often bringing together separately existing *epistemes*, historical climacterics, such as that experienced in the last 20 years, have also tended to provide a new division of intellectual labour and new focal paradigmatic bases for products and processes—often expressed in new sectoral boundaries.

Of course, the capitalist firm has often provided the shell within which such new knowledge has been created. Indeed, it seems evident that the solution of customer or user problems (or technology-pull) has provided a major source of innovation throughout the Industrial Revolution (von Hippel, 1988). It should not be surprising therefore that much of the existing literature reviewed above focuses, explicitly or implicitly, upon the ability of the firm to appropriate and exploit the, so-called, tacit knowledge that exists in the performance of its operational activities (Polanyi, 1964). This process generally requires its explication in a manner that enables its reconstruction and codification by designers in a portable and manipulable form. The Japanese researchers Nonaka and Tacheuchi (1995) draw off their observations in a range of corporations in their country to suggest a staged process of explication and codification of design knowledge within the firm. There is, however, little in their analysis to suggest that the basis for actor commitment to the process of 'socializing' information (to use their term) may be critical to its success, and that this might be a function of actor socialization in the cognitive sense.

In the Western context claims by OIAs for self-regulation have also usually rested on their superior ability to perform this function based on a generalizable corpus of knowledge related to problems experienced by clients within a particular sector or function. As the French sociologists Jamous and Peloille (1970) have observed, the professionalizing strategy normally constitutes two elements. The first is the construction of abstract and elaborated codes based on a systemic and algorithmic explanation of the phenomenon creating a 'problem'. The second is that of preserving, to its accredited members, sole rights to the interpretation of that generalized explanation within the task context. Tacitness becomes a means to the appropriation and retention of knowledge property by the professionalized worker, as it had once been for the craft worker. Initiation requires an apprenticeship in which observation of the application of the canons underlying the discipline is a necessary part of the training and also serves to socialize the individual into a collective identity. (A great deal of recent interpretivist literature on management has been devoted to demonstrating that this process of mystification of client problems has often contributed to the essential ambiguity surrounding the role of managers, rather than clarifying the 'problems' experienced by them. See for example Alvesson, 1995.)

National Innovation Systems

For occupational boundaries to extend beyond the employing organization requires an awareness of shared market and/or social status that leads to a mobilization of claims to recognition and sponsorship in wider society. For would-be professionals these claims can relate to an identity with a body of believed expertise that goes beyond the localized vernacular discourses described by OD analysts. In countries such as Japan and Germany such claims were rebutted by governmental and corporate elites at an early stage of the industrializing process, sometimes violently (McClelland, 1991; Streek, 1992). Both countries followed France in locating research and teaching in vocational knowledge disciplines, especially applied sciences, within universities at an early stage of their industrialization. In both countries centralized industrial laboratories within large corporations contributed to the strategic use of technological innovation in gaining early supremacy in new sectoral markets.

Lazonick (1992*a*) borrows heavily from the Chandlerian (1990) explanation of the effect made by different national modes and styles of corporate governance upon the history of relations between operative and professional design groups. In British 'proprietorial' capitalism professional education was not well sponsored by corporate employers who preferred entry to specialist design roles through apprenticeship or experience 'on the job'. In the USA professional education in general operational management complemented that of engineering and natural science in a university-based professionalism modelled on that of France. Specialists often found careers through promotion into senior corporate teams but operative workers and their supervisors became cut off from long distance upward mobility by their graduate educated managers. In Japan, by contrast, promotion was largely 'in-house' with entry to management careers usually extending to supervisory level. However the operational workforce was dichotomized between 'permanent' workers or 'salarymen' and a majority of 'temporary' workers usually consisting mainly of women and sub-contractors. (A comparison can be made with the effect of 'guest workers' on the internal market structure of post-war West German firms.) In a more specific comparison, Meiksins and Smith (1991) differentiate between 'craft' systems of professionalization in British engineering, 'managerial' modes of professional education adopted in North America, 'estate' forms of sponsorship in the Rhenish model, and the 'corporatist' or 'manorial' system to be found in Japan and South-East Asia.

In their analysis of the recent economic development of Pacific Asian nation-states, institutional theorists such as Whitley (1992) place a great deal of significance on the role of the family, rather than occupation, as a source of commitment and connection with, and between, business organizations. This is seen as, in part, due to underlying ideational factors such as the importance of Confucianism in the pre-industrial society and its continuing influence as an elite-driven ideology during the process of industrialization (Morishima, 1982; Masahiro and Ng, 1996). Family networks can also be important sources of capital because of the lack of institutionalized bases for the establishment of corporate creditworthiness other than through 'relational lending'. As was noted above, the very informality of these relational transactions along affectively underwritten networks became the basis for an alternative ideal type of capitalism within Western management teaching and research. After the panic flight of finance capital from East Asia in 1997 the role of the 'main bank' creditor in supporting such systems, together with that of the 'concerting' government, became the subject of much criticism. The lack of formally standardized financial accounts and the unavailability of audited performance data led to such systems being relabelled as 'crony capitalism' by free-market economists in international financial agencies such as the World Bank and the International Monetary Fund (Delhaise, 1998).

Such nationally concerted economies had previously been presented as ideal types of 'national innovation systems' (Best, 1990; Nelson, 1993). The existence of 'patient capital' provided through banks that were deeply involved in the valorizing activities of their corporate clients was seen to provide the basis for the success of these later developing nations in international competition with market economies. Nor was this success confined to East Asia. The historical template was sometimes traced to the *Hausbank* relations and the mode of cooperative capitalism seen to have contributed to the success of German national development by Chandler (1990) and others. More recently, the research of Colin Mayer (1999) has revealed the extent to which such modes of corporate governance adopted across mainland Europe can be associated with a remarkable concentration of ownership by families and individuals. In other words, if the Chandlerian distinction between the mode of corporate governance adopted within British ' personal capitalism' and that of 'cooperative capitalism' seen to typify large German firms is to be sustained, it can only be on the basis of differently motivated family owners in the two countries.

Rowes (1999) provides one possible answer. This is that families establishing firms in later developing countries avoided the 'agency' problems associated with devolving control to corporate executives by retaining relatively simple personal networks with their peers in banks and in government. At the same time they promoted the formal structures of employee participation, or, as Rowes describes it, of social democracy, to secure the compliance necessary for industrial peace. This proposition matches the thesis put forward earlier by Dore (1973) that 'late developer' *post hoc* learning was consciously undertaken by the industrializing Japanese elite in order to avoid the fractionated and conflictual nature of transactional networks seen to be present in Anglo-American market-based systems. Thus, family owners learned from the mistakes of their Anglo-American predecessors and did hasten to 'harvest' their wealth through sale of stock and dispersal of ownership.

The supposition of strategic intent in the work of Dore and other developmental theorists is based on the further supposition of a coherent national elite which, in the terms of Kerr and colleagues (1960), will 'lead the march to industrialization' (p. 6). As other authors (for example, Evans, 1995) have pointed out, the very process of industrialization is one that challenges legitimacy of prevailing elites. The challenge of retaining their leadership seems most often to be solved by the encouragement of an ideological goal of 'modernization' in terms which retain the institutionalized authority given by traditional institutions including religious faith. But as Kerr and colleagues point out, the cognitive and rhetorical framing of the need for change will take different forms dependent upon the circumstances in which the 'march' is undertaken. Its frequent coincidence with the formation or reinstatement of a nation-state usually provides a patriotic appeal often based on ethnicity (or family), an identity extended to a national differentiation from other states—nowadays normally portrayed as rivals in global economic development (Tajfel, 1982). In recent times this historically pervasive ideal of industrial nationalism has become articulated in an overt strategic attempt by elites in Pacific Asian countries to construct an export-led economy after the manner of Japan (Best, 1990). This movement has been presented by national leaders in the region under the slogan of 'Look East' or, more prosaically, by the World Bank (1987) as 'developmental'.

Over much of the last half of the twentieth century the appeal of industrial nationalism has been reinforced by the effects of the Cold War, especially in Central Europe and East Asia, where the threat, and the occasional actuality, of armed aggression accentuated the role of the military in the industrializing process. The interventionary role played by state agencies in the coordination of industrial development in Pacific Asia was therefore acceptable, not only to other members of emergent corporate networks in these countries, but also to their sponsors in Western financial and developmental agencies—that is up to 1997.

Modes and Styles of Innovation

If one accepts this relatively simplistic distinction between national 'systems' as heuristically useful, then it may, possibly, be extended to an analysis of current trends in inter-corporate alliances and of problems in their governance of the kind discussed earlier. The functional problem of controlling and coordinating the activities of members, and their attendant reputations, along diverse clusters of national and cross-national networks in the way suggested by the resource dependency theorists becomes of central significance to the success of the corporation. In the governance of strategic alliances it can be critical to the presentation of a coherent corporate face to partners in the alliance and for the creation of 'reliable knowledge'. Complementarity in expectations might appear more likely to occur when shaped by similar national institutional and ideational constraints (Park and Ungson, 1997), although as Doz (1988) and others have emphasized, the instrumental nature of the relationship usually makes a complementarity in goals of greater significance to the success of the venture.

The connection made between the ideational orientations held within national and regional business systems and the formal structural configurations adopted by individual firms is one that has a long history in the literature (Child and Francis, 1981; Chandler, 1990). These longitudinal comparisons tend to emphasize the retention of holding group or 'federal' structures among British firms compared with the early adoption of the multi-divisional (M) form of devoluted authority in the USA and the more unitary control structures in Japan and Germany. These modes of formal administrative structures could, possibly, be mapped in terms of Goold and Campbell's (1987) identification of two major emphases in control strategies in pursuance of corporate objectives: either in terms of the desire of corporate management simply to monitor performance outputs against budgets, through the adoption of loose-linked holding structures, or their wish to engage head office in the orchestration of knowledge and resource inputs at operational level. Or, of course, they may attempt to optimize both.

For instance, Loveridge (1982) suggested that the holding-group structure adopted by much of British engineering in the 1970s could be explained by a number of contextual factors, one of the most important being a corporate belief in 'allowing the local manager to be captain of his own team'. Operational knowledge inputs to local businesses were contained in the vernacular discourses of skilled engineers and largely shared only with a few suppliers and customers. The greatest fear expressed by corporate members of the national Engineering Employers Federation was that of reversion to craft unionism and the restoration of long, costly apprenticeships. American corporations with facilities in Britain, most notably Ford and General Motors, remained outside these associational arrangements and pursued policies of tight central (divisional) control.

It is important, however, to note that the large corporations studied by Goold and Campbell had all adopted the formal structures of the ubiquitous M-form and were all drawn from one parent country, Britain. Hence, the stylistic differences in the emphasis given to inputs or outputs of information took place within similar institutional and formal administrative structures. They were attributed by the authors to differences in corporate ideologies. It may be possible to extend this analysis to the manner in which authority is exercised within differing styles adopted in the innovation process. Three are set out in Figure 7.1 as contested, concerted, and diffused. It is proposed that the first of these styles is likely to be present in the firm that adopts a central budgetary control over operational performance, the second in firms in which strong 'staff' authority over outputs and inputs of design knowledge is

Style of innovation / Network cluster	Concerted	Contested	Diffused
Capital	Elite initiates projects within ongoing multiplex dialogues.	Elite judges bids in regular auctions. Often chair s action required between auctions.	Elite sponsors exemplar sites. Often multiple options with more or less central intervention in final standards.
Design	Strong emphasis on and awareness of leading edge theory. Strong involvement with operational problems.	Position depends on strategies/ tactics of research champions. Can be frustrated pioneers or gophers for operations.	Tends to become champion of one or other option. Can be in competition with outside consultants.
Operational	Strong awareness of leading edge design. Strong commitment to corporate values.	Largely short-term in perspective but can bend the budgetary constraints to set up own skunk works. Usually dismissive of central R&D.	Tendency to form up behind one or other option or to disregard because not invented here .

Fig. 7.1 Three styles of innovation

exercised, while the third allows the inputs of knowledge to be devolved in a diffusion process, but monitors outputs, as far as it is possible, against corporate goals.

The differences will be illustrated briefly with examples from a longitudinal study of two producers of electrical and electronic components for motor vehicles and aircraft; Joseph Lucas, founded in Britain and Robert Bosch, founded in Germany (a more detailed account appears in Loveridge, 1992). These are taken from case studies conducted by the author in the 1980s within the ESRC Work Organization Centre at Aston Business School and augmented by subsequent study. At their zenith in the mid-1970s each company employed nearly 100,000 people in 20 or more countries and were included in Fortune's Top 200. The choice of these firms for study had to do with their significance in the twentieth-century development of their sector, a contribution that is largely ignored because vehicle assemblers are credited with the inclusion of innovative equipment in the final product.

As suggested by the strategic literature reviewed earlier, successful appropriative learning styles depend on the internal ability to translate and to integrate information exchanged along three largely discrete socio-political conduits. This, in itself, is an immensely time-consuming activity. For example, when corporate managers have to maintain constant awareness of short-term shifts in their reputation with information brokers, such as financial journalists and analysts, then the nature of their networking activity is heavily biased towards narrowly focused impression management. This will tend to make them give priority to short-term signals, such as interim financial results, and to approach annual budgeting procedures with a rationing logic. This perspective normally translates into project assessment procedures which emphasize debt repayment and short-term profit rather than the long-term benefits derived from current investment. Competing projects from both design and operational interests are solicited on this basis in what amounts to an internal auction in the allocation of funding. Although quantitative assessments of technological feasibility and marketing potentiality usually play a part in detetermining project assessment 'gates', the chief executive's ability to intervene on the basis of an ill-defined strategic consideration can often create a degree of scepticism about the planning process among competing SBUs. In Figure 7.1 this is described as contested innovation.

It is paradoxical that 'product champions', 'entrepreneurs', and 'sponsors' have gained recognition as necessary elements in the innovation process within the internal market of the firm, as have those designers and operational management who build 'skunk-works' with their operational budgets, having lost out in auctions for D&D funding (Schon, 1963; Rothwell et al., 1974; Peters, 1988). What is rarely recognized in case-history reconstructions by Anglo-American business teachers is the effect that 'beating the bean-counters' has on the way the involved operational managers view their employer and their career within that group after their victory over 'bureaucrats' at head office. In many instances it seems likely that such small victories serve to reinforce a deeply held disbelief in the 'mock bureaucracy' of the firm (Gouldner, 1957). Thus, although the central system might give the impression of providing a series of rigorously evaluative stages for project proposals, all driven by overall strategic parameters, in practice such procedures can encourage deception, wasteful window-dressing, and a mis-allocation of resources to time spent in the political process (Hopwood and Miller, 1994).

This might well be a description of Lucas Industries by the beginning of the 1980s. Founded in 1875 as a manufacturer of oil lamps, it began to supply electrical components to the British Daimler Company in 1900. Its founder Joseph Lucas and his son issued public shares for the first time in 1911, but the bulk of the stock was still held by its local Birmingham bank (Lloyds) and other Midlands businessmen who occupied board seats as external directors. The 1914 War brought a demand for magnetos, formerly largely manufac-tured in Germany by Robert Bosch, and, after acquiring a British licensee, Lucas expanded its production and employment fourfold. In the period between the Wars Lucas continued to expand both through internal growth and through acquisition. Family control was diluted through the expansion of equity but the engineer grandson of the founder remained as joint managing director (then CEO) until his premature death in 1948. He was succeeded by a succession of three subsequent CEOs, all of whom were accountants who had acted as his personal assistants early in their careers. The immediate post war period was one of continued growth, to some extent based on a lack of overseas competition in both the automobile and aircraft industries. For most of this period the company was run as a holding group and only adopted an M-form after a Monopolies Commission investigation in 1960 revealed the extent of its holdings. Even then product divisions retained their separate company names, often those of the acquired firm.

By the 1970s the favoured position in world markets held by British assemblers had been eroded and a government orchestrated consolidation of both the motor vehicles and aircraft industries had begun. Lucas was persuaded to play a leading role in the latter exercise. Unlike the bulk of their counterparts in the British West Midlands, and in spite of its holding-group form, the Lucas board had long attempted to exercise central control over budgetary allocations and in the imposition of the so-called Lucas System of production and work-study engineering. (In this endeavour the need to emulate global peers in the sector such as Bosch and their American counter-parts, particularly Bendix, was more important than local West Midlands comparators.) The tensions produced at board level, and onwards down the group, by these attempts to standardize operations across a diversity of conditions were intensified by declining resources, by deteriorating labour relations, by the success of European competition and by the need to agree a coherent strategy on new technologies, the most important of which was, of course, microelectronics. The oldest division (company) in the group, Lucas Electric, had established an early lead in the production of microchips, but it was by no means clear to other companies in the group that they should be dependent on this capability. Indeed, the boards of other subsidiaries like Aerospace and CAV (fuel pumps and injectors) believed their hi-tech customers lacked faith in the reputation of this oldest part of the group to supply the integrated circuits that were central to the design of their new products.

The conflict within the board became articulated in the appointment of candidates from Electric and from CAV as joint-MDs under the Chairmanship of an ex-CAV executive in 1980. In little more than three years the former appointee had left the company, and in 1989, the remaining MD, Anthony Gill, was appointed as Chair and CEO. Under his sponsorship a programme of devolvement of responsibility to SBUs had been initiated in 1983. Unfortunately, this did not end conflict between entrenched interests, even though the group endeavoured to present a corporate brand image across all its product range, marketing itself in the currently fashionable mode of systems designer and supply-chain coordinator. At least two potential 'crown princes' made well reported departures before an outside appointment as Gill's successor was achieved in 1994 in the person of George Simpson from British Aerospace. Within two years he had announced his departure to British GEC and had arranged a merger with the US-based Varity Corporation. In early 1999 a substantially restructured board sold the company to the TRW group with the backing of the US institutional investors brought in by the last CEO, Victor Rice. Both of these latter CEOs enjoyed substantial 'golden parachutes'. In the opinion of journalists Rice appeared to have acted out of pique, having failed to persuade British shareholders to back his plan to remove the merged company to the New York stock exchange. Although criticized in the House of Commons, the sale induced no governmental action to save the firm.

By contrast it is suggested that the style of innovation likely to be adopted in situations in which the institutionalization of networks has created an integrative environment with a 'developmental' ideology is one in which a concerted approach to change the firm is most likely to be pursued. The nature of relationships along capital networks is postulated as being that based on a floor of trust which can derive from a variety of structuring features, among which relational banking has figured prominently in a number of analyses (Best, 1990; Whitley, 1992). In a societal context of conditional trust between interests, combined with an overarching developmental ideology, it seems likely that corporate goals can attract a more normative commitment on the part of the individual organizational members. Equally the language developed in communication between communities of practice is likely to be shaped by these higher-order beliefs and values. This will be especially so when reinforced by an economic nationalism or symbolic association with high-tech and leading edge technology (i.e. 'modernism')

(Loveridge, 1997). It is evident that the 'prototypical knowledge-creating company' described by Nonaka and Takechi (1995) exists within such an institutional and ideological context, in their case modern Japan.

Paradoxically, such unitary ideologies are often based on a 'romantic' linking of an idealized past with aspirations for the future at both national and corporate levels. No better example exists than Robert Bosch GmbH, established in 1886 by a Stuttgart artisanal engineer and prolific inventor (Heuss, 1946). The founder's portrait and reported quotations are still used as the basis for explaining and legitimating most corporate decisions, however trivial. At the same time identification of this icon with both efficient performance and altruistic work in the community conveys what is expected of Boscher citizens; self-regulation therefore derives from the individual's striving to meet this ideal. Until recently strategic control was, at one and the same time, highly concentrated in a four-man executive meeting weekly at the Schiller Heights headquarters outside of Stuttgart. Each executive was, however, highly visible because of the role played by senior management in associational life across the sector, region, and nation.

The company markets itself on the basis of its electrical engineering expertise, even though the bulk of its products are mass produced. (Bosch was one of the first European employers to implement a Taylorian design in production methods; he imposed a six-week lock-out of most of his 4,000 employees over the Christmas of 1913 in order to do so.) The professional image has been reinforced by the output of technical publications from its own publishers established in the 1920s, and by the placing of research papers at significant professional conferences. The fact that almost all corporate net profits go to charitable trusts provides endorsement for its reputation as a trustworthy partner. This status also ensures that the extent to which the trust's enormous financial resources support the strategies pursued by the GmbH is unknown publicly. What is known, is that Bosch acted with Deutsche Bank as intermediary in the 1924 marriage of Daimler and Benz, which was to become its major domestic customer and collaborator in the design of both motor vehicles and aircraft engines. (The latter were abandoned after World War II.) When that company was threatened by a Middle Eastern takeover in 1973, Bosch became a potentially dominant shareholder through a holding group set up with other German industrialists intent on preserving this symbol of national excellence. It may be equally significant that the Mercedes-Benz holding was sold in 1996 (Wenger and Kaserer, 1997).

The third category in the typology presented in Figure 7.1 is that of diffused innovation. This is not always a discrete style, since it can be adopted as a tactical approach to innovation within the context of either concerted or contested strategic orientations. It refers to the sponsorship of an exemplar introduction of new products or processes on a site, or sites, in the belief that it will encourage managers in other SBUs to adopt similar innovations. It can, of course, also be used as an initial stage in choosing one of several optional applications of new ideas. In this case the choice may rest with the head office and/or be the result of concerted dialogue across and up and down the internal hierarchy. The major difficulty with this style of innovation is that it is often attempted where the corporate elite have little comprehension of the implications of the new use of the new technology and where the trial sites are geographically and socially isolated from the core operations of the group. It is easy in these circumstances for other plants to adopt a 'not-invented-here' response to success in the exemplars, and to point to the uniqueness of their own position on regionally based or specialized design or operational networks. It is most likely to be attempted in professional bureaucracies, such as in health care, where evaluation is conducted within design parameters set by a professional community of practice that extends across all operational sites and where the ideology contains a high level of belief in operational autonomy or self-regulation (Loveridge and Starkey, 1992).

This can also be the case in groups such as the former Lucas Industries, where local autonomy has been preserved through the vernacular languages of local 'custom and practice'. In 1983, when the executive of this old established firm resolved to devolve operating responsibility to its 100 or so SBUs, an internal consultancy was set up under a new main board director, Professor John Parnaby, who was a known champion of Japanese modes of production management. The consultant's model that emerged over the next decade resembled what later came to be known as 'business process re-engineering'. Early sites for its introduction were chosen by the executive board as exemplars for the whole group. They included known centres of political extremists among their shop stewards. Its successful adoption by teams of local operational managers on these sites produced important symbolic achievements for its later diffusion across the group. Unfortunately, neither market conditions nor the short-term budgetary controls operated by the group's executive were always conducive to sustained commitment within SBUs, and the publicity given by financial analysts to early performance achievements declined over time (Turnbull, 1986).

Further case-study evidence of diffused innovation can be drawn from a six-nation study of the implementation of communications and information technology (CIT) in services, carried out by an international team of scholars in the 1980s (Child and Loveridge, 1990). The effect of CIT on the delivery of direct services was likely to be more profound than in manufacturing, since the service itself was an immediate source of value to the consumer. The sectors chosen for study were intended to reflect varying levels of value contained in the performance of the service, these being retailing (department stores and supermarkets), high-street banking, and hospitals. In accordance with the hypothesis lying behind the choice of sectors, the case histories seemed to suggest that the greatest participation in the diffusion of the new technology did occur among medical staff, who, as often as not, initiated its introduction (see also Coleman, Katz, and Menzel 1966). The general outcome of the process of diffused change was, however, to afford greater opportunity for the central monitoring of task performance across all three sectors through the automatic recording of both knowledge inputs, in the form of diagnosis and prescription, and of performance outputs. Operator commitment to the management of the new technology was generally solicited by offering responsibility for the allocation of limited budgets (in medicine) or sales activity (banking and retailing). Thus the difusion of new innovation was facilitated by an apparent 'empowerment' of operatives over modes of implementation and a consequent diversity in operational styles of management.

Contradictions or Complementarities in Current Trends?

Although the ideational influences of corporate style, and behind this of national style, are important in shaping innovation strategy, there remain similarities experienced in market and material conditions that lend themselves to common interpretations of 'best practice' across actors within particular sectors (Spender, 1980; Huff, 1990). Some indications of sectoral effects can be seen in the choice of corporate style revealed in Goold and Campbell's sample and in other cross-sectional studies. Perhaps the most influential of these is the research on operations technology carried out by Woodward (1965). Her claims for the superordinate influence of uncertainty in the valorizing process of the firm's operations at that time (late 1950s) were disputed. Yet her rich descriptions of the relationship between R&D departments and the operational activities of her sample of manufacturers in South-East Essex seem to have had an underlying consistency and a robustness which reappears in later, wider cross-sectional studies.

In the author's current research in 20 large (over 25,000 employees) European MNCs, the sectoral shaping of views on the relationship between D&D and their operations in Pacific Asia (the focus of the study) are clearly evident. There are, for instance, a limited number of ways of exploring for and extracting crude oil and natural gas: currently these seem to be represented by no more than three or four specialist sub-contractors within that sector which may represent a stable optimum. The development of operations technology is, however, a longitudinal process that takes place over the life cycle of the sector and is affected by the emergence of a sectoral identity along all three network clusters (Abernathy, Clark, and Kantrow, 1982; Gemser, Leenders, and Wijnberg, 1996). It might well be affected by divergent trajectories in the institutional and/or ideational development of the firm's relations along different network clusters, either those involving capital, or design, or operations. For instance, while most large firms still retain some form of, what might loosely be described as an R&D or D&D establishment, over the last decade such establishments in Anglo-American manufacturing have increasingly been forced to seek financial resources through sub-contracting their services to SBUs within their parent group or to outside clients (Whittington, 1990; Bruce and Morris, 1996). This practice has now spread to mainland Europe. Large chemical and pharmaceutical firms such as Hoechst, which seem on any contingency analysis like that provided by Woodward or Williamson (1985) to have every reason to preserve their proprietary knowledge in-house, are adopting a policy of out-sourcing their R&D.

This could be seen as having greatly reduced the strategic significance of the R&D department within the group or, more usually, to have submitted its potential long-term contribution to the strategic goals of the group to comparisons with the current costs and prices of external knowledge providers. The 'relevance' of R&D can thus be constrained by the length of a short-term contract. This was illustrated for the author by a recent experience in a British avionics manufacturer. After three years of client assessment of a new hi-tech product, an order was finally placed. It was found that the 'black box' product could not be produced on the basis of computer records, the design staff having departed at the end of project carrying with them their tacit knowledge on its implementation! On the other hand, proponents of the dispersal strategy argue that the current emergent state of technological knowledge within many sectors make this the most viable strategy. In such circumstances it may be argued that the matching of operational and design capabilities in the manner suggested by contingency analysis is best achieved through such loose-linked market-based networks rather than those of internal hierarchy.

In earlier sections of this chapter the normative assumptions underlying the analytical dichotomy often made between networks and markets were questioned; the tensions present in the concept of collaborative competition were also examined. For the most part it seems safest to assume that commercial collaboration, even in the Japanese context, takes place within a market, however imperfect, and that trust is instrumentally contingent (Scher, 1997). Furthermore, discrete or short-term contractual alliances between firms have to be distinguished from institutionalized channels of communication within wider society, which often pre-date such alliances, but which form part of the multiplex linkages brought into play in successful partnerships between large firms. The importance attributed to the latter over the last part of this century may be attributed, either directly or indirectly, to the turbulence and discontinuity felt by most corporate management in a period often described in terms of a climacteric in the development of capitalism. Three underlying causes for this supposition have been emphasized in most analyses—changes in generic technologies, globalization, and government responses to both phenomena in the form of privatization or 'marketization'.

It is feasible, then, to see the strategic alliance as often providing a facilitating stage in waves of A&M that seem to be bringing about a growing concentration of capital in most sectors of a global economy (Rybczynski, 1989; Weston, Chung, and Hoag, 1990). But, at the same time the slowing down in the global rate of growth in consumption accompanied by a growth in savings has produced an unusual increase in available credit at relatively low prices. This is seen to have produced two effects on institutionalized national business systems. First, reliance on *Hausbanks* or other forms of relational banking across European countries is eroding rapidly as both credit vendors and vendees prefer to adopt the apparently cheaper Anglo-American modes of securities issues (Jurgens, Naumann, and Rupp, 1999). Similarly, the type of cross-shareholding that protected some European and Japanese firms from hostile takeovers and, in the French case at least, was an important element in governmental control over national development, has diminished radically (Morin, 1999). Thus, family capitalism may well be under threat and, with it, the institutionalized basis of the long-term, or patient, capital essential for a particular form of internal and external concertation of networks in the family-owned firm.

A second effect comes from within the financial agencies themselves. Faced with a vast expansion of 'institutional' funds (mutuals and pensions) with an expressed need for sustained return on investment, these agencies have brought pressure to bear on corporate borrowers to show high performance in terms of current revenue (Lazonick, 1992*b*). (These financial agencies have often converted themselves into public companies and are therefore under a dual pressure to perform.) The currently most popular instrument by which performance is measured is 'economic value added' (EVA—a term copyrighted by US consultant Stern Stewart). This relatively simple mode of comparing residual income with a weighted average of the cost of capital has been adopted, in various forms, by most MNCs in the West (and in all of the European MNCs in the author's current research). The result is to focus all elements of the firm's activities to audit in terms of their short-term financial returns and to provide shareholders with a standard against which to compare operating results across their investments. As a concept it is not new. Bromwich and Walker (1998) trace its origins to the 1920s. Hamel (1997) has pointed to the circulatory nature of the reasoning behind the techniques, which excludes any managerial assessment of long-term synergies present in the use of human capital. Some recently reported comments by Kouji Nishigaki, President of NEC, provide a different perspective on this process: 'I don't want to become too involved in mechanical methods for deciding what business to be in. If we had used discounted cash-flow, we would never have got into the liquid crystal display business' (*Financial Times*, 28 May 1999, p. 29).

Froud *et al.* (1999) describe the use of EVA as symptomatic of the second wave in the restructuring of Western capital. First came the 'productionist' period when corporate strategy was shaped by the attempts by Western operations engineers to codify Japanese modes of team working, now accountants are attempting to restore the link with the corporate network through 'financialization' of the changes. Both operations engineers and accountants can normally be considered as essentially designers of regulatory systems rather than as exploratory enactors of new products. As such they have been seen to be important in the restoration of corporate confidence after periods of rapid transition and ambiguity (Hopwood and Miller, 1994; Nixon, 1995). (As already suggested, it is ironic, but possibly significant, that after nearly a century of advocacy of teamwork by OD specialists, it should be operations engineers who have been largely responsible for its widespread implementation over the last twenty years.) The growing emphasis on short-term financial performance shown by Western corporations has coincided with the devolution and dispersal of tasks in both operations and design. While theoretically confined to 'non-core' activities, these are often difficult to define and the application of financial criteria, such as EVA can appear easier for the board to justify both to redundant staff and to institutional shareholders. In many cases the so-called N-form (networked) firm seems little more than a regression to the financial holding company, albeit a sectorally focused one.

In emerging sectors consisting of a few global flagship firms serviced by multiple small enterprises the role of occupational interest associations may re-emerge as a potential shell for design networking. There are those who would suggest that it has never gone away—particularly as a source of information exchange among consultants and as organizers of sectoral trade fairs (Newall and Clark, 1990). Government departments have, of course, often treated them as sources of experts in policy-making, and when 'the Science' is needed to justify a politically unpopular decision. In recent times the role of professional associations has been extended to include their use as agencies in attempts to elicit collaboration between firms in sectorally targeted campaigns, such as the current Foresight Programme in Britain. In the USA their advisory role on Presidential and Senate Advisory Committees is better established: somehow the Chinese wall between 'learned society' and interest representation appears to be handled in a manner that allows appropriate recognition and sponsorship for the latter. Certainly it might appear that the designer networks that exist in the Anglo-American context have been a rich source of both information and imitative knowledge for enterprises in Japan and in the so-called Tiger Economies (Kim, 1997). A question that provides a focus for current debate on public policy in all of these countries is, what kind of designer networks produce Nobel Prize winners? In other words, the unitary corporation common to the developmental economy of the region does not promote or sponsor fundamental research, without which no country can compete with the USA in the next climacteric.

Conclusion

This chapter has been based on the proposition that one way of analysing the functional role of the corporation is as a node on a complex series of interorganizational networks. Across these networks it is possible to distinguish three significant information flows. These are characterized by Gupta and Govindarajan (1991) as capital flows, knowledge flows, and product flows. The view put forward here is that these bodies of information, both stocks and flows, are shaped by three separate 'logics of action' (Karpik, 1972). That is to say that people engaged in these common functional activities tend to develop a shared frame of reference and, often, an implicit ordering of causal explanation relating to a shared paradigm. Access to this information can be closed through the use of discourse and language, both formal and informal. Such frames and discourses can be shared across corporate boundaries and, increasingly, across national boundaries.

While inter-organizational networks can contribute to the long-term performance of the firm, they can equally be a source of monopolistic closure that can work to the cost or benefit of other parties including the national community in which they are embedded. By the same token appropriative action by members of the firm who owe a stronger loyalty to the mores of the external network to which they belong—whether corporate, professional, or operational—can have the effect of destroying the firm as an independent entity. This might seem to be most possible at the corporate level, for example through the actions of senior executives who engineer the acquisition of their company by another in exchange for new careers in the larger group or for 'golden parachutes' (Chandler, 1990). But, as suggested earlier, the pursuit of vested interests along professional and operational networks can equally, if less directly, be destructive of the firm's autonomy.

While outside threat can help to curb each party's expectations and to reinforce adherence to a central rationing of resources, collaboration between internal communities of interest will be much more easily obtained if the corporate leader can set expansionist goals for the whole organization. On the contrary, it is more likely that defensive and confrontational stances will be adopted along different networks of practice in conditions of competition for scarce resources within participating firms. But much will depend upon the orientation common along different networks of actors. Professional knowledge workers in the USA may well prefer to work in a loosely linked collegiate mode of organization such as that of Microsoft, where their vocational commitment can be more successfully exploited than it would be in a paternalistic hierarchy offering life-long employment such as that of Mitsubishi.

The three logics interact in the daily process of decision-making at all levels of the organization but are particularly present within various sub-sets of employees whose functional roles provide them with a primary significance. The ability of executives to mobilize these potential assets in a focused manner is described by Kogut and Zander (1992) as their 'combinative capability'. However, since the firm exists as a node along three distinctive types of network the act of product or process innovation normally involves concerting flows of external knowledge in a process of what might be described as appropriative learning (Loveridge, 1990). This entails the absorption of knowledge shared along each set of networks, its combining into a knowledge capability unique to the corporation, and its further transformation, internally, into an operationally realized competence.

External reputation provides both a bridge into networks and an important source of leverage. At its most abstract, reputation is an external judgement on past performance that is used by others in making future choices. As such it helps to determine the boundaries of future markets for the reputable service provider. Past achievements can be 'massaged' for a distal audience, but a corporate reputation among its immediately proximal neighbours on a network is likely to be 'sticky'. Reputation, then, provides an important signal when choosing collaborators along networks, along with positional leverage, and the availability and commitment of resources. All of these factors are important assets in the orchestration of action along networks. It has been suggested that the influence exercised by actors along each of the network clusters will shape the style of innovation adopted by corporate decision-makers.

In the past, much of the discussion of wider political and economic issues has been inhibited, on one side by the over-deterministic critique adopted by writers in both Marxian and Weberian traditions, and on the other by the narrowly functionalist focus of most OB analysis. Latterly writers in the new institutional sociology have opened up discussion on sources of national competitive advantage to wider explanation related to societal development within nation-states (Biggart and Hamilton, 1992; Whitley, 1992). However institutionalist explanations tend to place determinant emphasis on the role of pre-industrial structures, particularly that of the family, in shaping national economic development. The independent effect of ideology upon the interpretation of institutionalized practice is likely to be mediated by events and situations in a way that makes individual orientations difficult to predict. Nevertheless it is likely that dominant ideologies within national societies will affect those held at firm level, even though it is evidently feasible for countervailing cultures to be encouraged where contextual conditions serve to reinforce a 'deviant' ideology.

It seems likely that concerted styles of innovation will be attempted by corporate management in situations in which their reputation for creditworthiness is high along capital networks and where internal actors on all three clusters of networks share a developmental collectivistic ideology. By contrast contested styles are likely to be adopted where more reactive individualism is combined with high uncertainty in respect to capital acquisition. Diffused innovatory styles often reflect an internal balance of power towards operational networks and a strongly individualistic ideology. On the basis of the evidence of the effect of national institutions and ideologies on styles of corporate control or governance it is reasonable to believe that the country of origin can be seen to exercise an important influence over the manner in which a firm emerges as an entrepreneurial node on the societal networks of that country. Thus it has been suggested in this chapter that firms having their origins in Anglo-American networks, hitherto, have been shaped by significantly different institutional and ideological contexts to those existing in later developing nations.

References

ABBOTT, A. (1988), *The System of Professions: An Essay on the Division of Labour* (Chicago: University of Chicago).

ABERNATHY, W. J., CLARK, K. B., and KANTROW, A. N. (1982), *Industrial Renaissance* (New York: Basic).

ADLER, P. A. and ADLER, P. (1984), *The Social Dynamics of Financial Markets* (Greenwich, Conn.: JAI Press).

ALVESSON, M. (1995), *The Management of Knowledge Intensive Firms* (Berlin: de Gruyter).

AMITH, R. and SCHOEMAKER, P. J. H. (1993), 'Strategic Assets and Organizational Rent', *Strategic Management Journal*, 14; 35–46.

BAIN, J. S. (1959), *Industrial Organisation* (New York: Wiley).

BECKER, G. (1964), *Human Capital*, (Stanford, Calif.: Stanford University Press).

BEST, M. H. (1990), *The New Competition* (Oxford: Polity Press).

BIGGART, N. W. and HAMILTON, G. G. (1992), 'On the Limits of a Firm-Based Theory to Explain Business Networks', in N. Nohria and R. G. Eccles (eds.), *Networks and Organisations* (Boston: Harvard Business School Press), 471–90.

BOURDIEU, P. (1977), *Outline of a Theory of Practice*, trans. R. Nice 1999 (Cambridge, Mass.: Harvard University Press).

BOWER, J. (1992), 'A Good Return on Investment', *The Times Higher Education Supplement*, 9 Oct. 32.

BRAVERMAN, H. (1974), *Labor and Monopoly Capital* (New York: Monthly Review Press).

BROMWICH, M. and WALKER, M. (1998), 'Residual Income, Past and Future', *Management Accounting Research* 9/4: 391–420.

BRUCE, M. and MORRIS, B. (1996), 'Challenges and Trends Facing the UK Design Profession', *Technology Analysis and Strategic Management*, 8/4: 407–23

BUCKLEY, P. and CASSON, M. (1976), *The Future of the Multinational Enterprise* (London: Macmillan).

BURGELMAN, R. A. and SAYLES, L. R. (1988), *Inside Corporate Innovation: Strategy, Structure and Managerial Skills* (New York: Free Press).

BURNS, T. and STALKER, G. (1961), *The Management of Innovation* (London: Tavistock).

BUTLER, R. and GILL, J. (1997), 'Knowledge and Trust in Partnership Formation', paper presented at the *Fourth International Conference on Multi Organisational Partnerships and Co-operative Strategies*, New College, Oxford, 8–10 July.

CALLON, M. (1986) 'Some Elements of a Sociology Translation', in J. Law (ed.), *Power, Action and Belief* (London: Routledge and Kegan Paul).

CASSON, M. (1992), 'Internalisation Theory and Beyond', in P. Buckley (ed.), *New Directions in International Business* (Cheltenham: Elgar), 994–1027.

CAVES, R. E. (1971), 'International Corporations: The Industrial Economies of Foreign Investment', *Economica*, 38: 1–27.

CHANDLER, A. (1990), *Scale and Scope* (Cambridge, Mass.: Belknap Press).

CHILD, J. and FRANCIS, A. (1981), 'Strategy Formulation as a Structured Process', *International Studies of Management and Organisation*, 7/2: 110–26.

—— and LOVERIDGE, R. (1990), *Information Technology in European Services* (Oxford: Basil Blackwell).

CLARK, P. A. (1987), *Anglo-American Innovation* (New York: de Gruyter).

CLEGG, S. R. (1990), *Modern Organizations* (London: Sage).

COHEN, W. and LEVINTHAL, D. (1990), 'Absorptive Capacity: A New Perspective on Learning and Innovation', *Administrative Science Quarterly*, 35 (March): 128–52.

COLEMAN, J. S., KATZ, E., and MENZEL, H. (1966), *Medical Innovation: A Diffusion Study* (New York: Bobbs Merrill).

CONWAY, S. (1995), 'Link-Pins, Bridges, and Liaisons: Strategic Links in Successful Technological Innovation', in D. Bennett and F. Steward (eds.), *Technological Innovation and Global Challenges, Proceedings of the European Conference on Management of Technology* (Birmingham: Aston University), 11–19.

CROZIER, M. (1964 trans.), *The Bureaucratic Phenomenon* (Chicago: University of Chicago Press).

DE BRESSON, C. and AMESSO, F. (1991), 'Networks of Innovators: A Review and Introduction to the Issue', *Research Policy*, 20/5: 363–79.

DELHAISE, F. (1998), *The Asian Financial Crisis* (Singapore: Macmillan).

DODGSON, M. (1992), 'Strategy and Technological Learning: An Interdisciplinary Micro-Study', in R. Coombs, D. Saviotti, and V. Walsh (eds.), *Technological Change and Company Strategies*, (London: Academic Press) 136–63.

DORE, R. (1986), *Flexible Rigidities* (Stanford: Stanford University Press).

DOZ, Y. L. (1988) 'Technology Partnerships between Larger and Smaller Firms: Some Critical Issues', in F. J. Contractor and P. Lorange (eds.), *Co-operative Strategies in International Business* (New York: DC Heath).

EVANS, P. (1995), *Embedded Autonomy* (Princeton, NJ: Princeton University Press).

FLORIDA, R. and KENNEY, M. (1990), *The Breakthrough Illusion* (New York: Banc Books).

FREEMAN, C., SHARP, M., and WALKER, W. (1991), *Technology and the Future of Europe* (London: Pinter).

FROUD J., HASLAM C., JOHAL, S., and WILLIAMS, K. (1999) 'Consultancy Promises, Management Moves: Shareholder Value and Financialisation', paper presented at a workshop on The Political Economy of Shareholder Value, The Management School, Royal Holloway College, University of London, 16–17 Apr.

GEMSER, G., LEENDERS, M. A. A. M., and WIJNBERG, N. M. (1996), 'The Dynamics of Inter-Firm Networks in the Course of the Industry Life Cycle: The Role of Appropriability', *Technology Analysis and Strategic Management*, 8/4: 439–53.

GOULD, M. and CAMPBELL, A. (1987), *Strategies and Styles: The Role of the Centre in Managing Diversified Corporations* (Oxford: Basil Blackwell).

GOULDNER, A. (1957), 'Cosmopolitan and Locals: Towards an Analysis of Latent Roles', *Administrative Science Quarterly* 2: 281–306.

GRABHER, G. (1993), 'The Weakness of Strong Ties', in G. Grabher (ed.), *The Embedded Firms* (London: Routledge), 255–77.

GRANOVETTER, M. (1974), *Getting A Job* (Cambridge, Mass.: Harvard University Press).

—— (1992), 'Problems of Explanation in Economic Sociology', in N. Nohria, and R. G. Eccles (eds.), *Networks and Organisations: Structure, Form and Action* (Cambridge, Mass.: Harvard Business School Press).

—— (1995), 'Coase Revisited: Business Groups in the Modern Economy', *Industrial and Corporate Change* 4: 93–130.

GRINDLEY P. C. and TEECE, D. J. (1997), 'Managing Intellectual Capital: Licensing and Cross-Licensing in Semi-Conductors and Electronics', *California Management Review* 39/2: 8–41.

GUPTA, A. K. and GOVINDARAJAN, V. (1991), 'Knowledge Flows and the Structure of Control within Multinational Corporations', *Academy of Management Review* 16/4: 768–92.

HAMEL, G. (1997), 'How Killers Count', *Fortune* 23 June, 23–6.

—— and PRAHALAD, C. K. (1993), 'Strategy as Stretch and Leverage', *Harvard Business Review*, Mar./Apr., 75–84.

HEUSS, T. (1946), *Robert Bosch: Leben and Leistung* (Munich: Wilhelm Heyne Verlag).

HICKSON, D. J., HININGS, C. R., LEE, C. A., SNECK, R. H., and PENNINGS, J. M. (1971), 'A Strategic Contingencies Theory of Intraorganisational Power', *Administrative Science Quarterly*, 16: 216–29.

HIPPEL, E. VON (1988), *The Sources of Innovation* (New York: Oxford University Press).

HITT, M. A. and IRELAND, R. D. (1986), 'Relationships among Corporate Level Distinctive Competences, Diversification Strategy, Corporate Structure and Performance', *Journal of Management Studies*, 23: 577–90.

HOPWOOD, A. G. and MILLER, P. (eds.) (1994), *Accounting as Social and Institutional Practice* (Cambridge: Cambridge University Press).

HUBER, G. (1991), 'Organisational Learning: The Contributing Processes and their Literatures', *Organisational Science* 2/1: 88–115.

HUFF, A. (ed.) (1990), *Mapping Strategic Thought* (Chichester: Wiley).

INKPEN, A. C. and BEAMISH, P. W. (1997), 'Knowledge, Bargaining Power, and the Instability of International Joint Ventures', *Academy of Management Review*, 22/1: 77–202.

JACKSON, T. (1997), 'Out of the Corporate Soup', *Financial Times*, 12 May, 10.

JAMOUS, H. and PELOILLE, B. (1970), 'Professions as Self-Perpetuating Systems', in J. A. Jackson, (ed.), *Professions and Professionalisation* (Cambridge: Cambridge University Press).

JURGENS, U., NAUMANN, K., and RUPP, J. (1999) 'The Political Economy of Shareholder the German Case', paper presented at a workshop on The Political Economy of Shareholder Value, Royal Holloway College, University of London, 16–17 Apr.

KAMOCHE, K. (1996), 'Strategic Human Resource Management within a Resource Capability View of the Firm', *Journal of Management Studies*, 33/2: 213–33.

KANTER, R. H. (1989), *When Giants Learn to Dance* (London: Unwin).

KARPIK, L. (1972), 'Les politiques et les logiques d'action de la grande enterprise industrielle', *Sociologie du Travail*, 1: 82–105.

KATZ, R. and ALLEN, T. (1982), 'Investigating the Not Invented Here (NIH) Syndrome: A Look at Performance, Tenure, and Communication Patterns of 50 R&D Projects', *R&D Management*, 12/1: 7–19.

KERR, C., DUNLOP, J. T., HARBISON, F., and MYERS, C. A. (1960), *Industrialism and Industrial Man* (Cambridge, Mass.: Harvard Business School Press).

KIM, D. J. and KOGUT, B. (1996), 'Technological Platforms and Diversification', *Organisation Science*, 7/3 (May–June): 283–301.

KIM, L. (1997), 'The Dynamics of Samsung's Technological Learning in Semi-Conductors', *California Management Review*, 39/3 (spring): 86–100.

KOGUT, B. and ZANDER, U. (1993), 'Knowledge of the Firm, Combinative Capabilities and the Evolutionary Theory of the Multinational Corporation', *Journal of International Business Studies*, 4: 625–45.

———— (1996), 'What do Firms do? Co-ordination, Learning and Identity', *Organisation Science*, 7/5 (Sept.–Oct.): 502–18.

LAMMING, R. (1993), *Beyond Partnership: Strategies for Innovation and Lean Supply* (New York: Prentice Hall).

LANE, C. and BACHMANN, R. (1996), 'Co-operation in Vertical Interfirm Relationships in Britain and Germany: The Role of Social Institutions', *Working Paper No. 21* (ESRC Centre for Business Research University of Cambridge).

———— (eds.) (1997), *Trust Within and Between Organisations* (Oxford: Oxford University Press).

LAZONICK, W. (1992a), *Business Organisation and the Myth of the Market Economy* (Cambridge: Cambridge University Press).

—— (1992b), 'Business Organisation and Competitive Advantage: Capital Transformations in the Twentieth Century', in G. Dosi, R. Giannetti, and P. A. Toinelli (eds.), *Technology and Enterprise in a Historical Perspective* (Oxford: Clarendon Press), 118–63.

LODGE, G. C. and VOGEL, E. F. (1987), *Ideology and National Competitiveness* (Boston: Harvard Business School Press).

LORANGE, P. and ROOS, J. (1992), *Strategic Alliances* (Cambridge, Mass.: Blackwell).

LOVERIDGE, R. (1972), 'Occupational Change and the Development of Interest Groups among White Collar Workers in the UK: a Long Term Model', *British Journal of Industrial Relations*, 10/3: 340–65.

—— (1982), 'Business Strategy and Community Culture', in P. Dunkerley and G. Salamon (eds.), *The International Year Book of Organisation Studies* (London: Routledge & Kegan Paul).

—— (1983), 'Sources of Diversity in Internal Labour Markets', *Sociology*, 17: 44–62.

—— (1990) 'Incremental Learning and Appropriative Learning Styles in Direct Services' in R. Loveridge and M. Pitt, *The Strategic Managment of Technological Innovation* (Chichester: Wiley).

—— (1992), 'Crisis and Continuity: Reviewing the Past to Preview the Future', in S. Srivastva, R. E. Fry, *et al.* (eds.), *Executive and Organizational Continuity* (San Francisco: Jossey-Bass).

—— (1997), 'Putting Nationalism back into National Business Systems', in A. Bugra and B. Usdiken, (eds.), *State Market and Organisational Form* (Berlin: de Gruyter).

—— and STARKEY, R. (1992), *Continuity and Change in the National Health Service* (Milton Keynes: Open University Press).

LOWNDES, V. and DKELEHER, C. (1997), 'Modes of Governance and Multi-Organisational Partnerships: Reflections from the British Urban Regeneration Exercise', paper presented at the Fourth International Conference on Multi Organisational Partnerships and Co-operative Strategies, New College, Oxford, 8–10 July.

MCCLELLAND, C. E. (1991), *The German Experience of Professionalization* (Cambridge: Cambridge University Press).

MARCH, J. G., SPROULL, L. S., and TAMUZ, M. (1991), 'Learning from Samples of One or Fewer', *Organisation Science*, 2/1 (Feb.): 1–13.

MASAHIRO M. and NG, S. K. (1996), 'The Role of the State and Labour's Response to Industrial Development: An Asian "Drama" of Three New Industrial Economies', in I. Nish, S. G. Redding, and S. K. Ng (eds.), *Work and Society: Labour and Human Resources in East Asia* (Hong Kong: Hong Kong University Press), 215–32.

MAYER, C. (1999), 'Firm Control', Inaugural Lecture as Peter Moores Professor of Management Studies, Examination Schools, University of Oxford, 18 Feb.

MAYER, M. (1997), *The Bankers: The Next Generation* (New York: Penguin Putnam).

MEIKSINS, P. and SMITH, C. (1991), 'Why American Engineers Aren't Unionized: A Comparative Perspective', *Working Paper 2*, Centre for the Study of the Professions (Birmingham: Aston University).

MORIN, F. (1999), 'The Transformation of the French Model of Shareholding and Management', paper presented at a workshop on The Political Economy of Shareholder Value, Royal Holloway College, University of London, 16–17 Apr.

MORISHIMA, M. (1982), *Why has Japan Succeeded?* (Cambridge: Cambridge University Press).

MUELLER, F. (1996), 'Human Resources as Strategic Assets: A Resource-Based Evolutionary Theory', *Journal of Management Studies*, 33/6: 15–26.

NELSON, R. R. (1993), *National Innovation Systems: A Comparative Analysis* (New York: Oxford Univeristy Press).

—— (1994), 'Evolutionary Theorizing about Economic Change', in N. J. Smelser and R. Swedberg (eds.), *The Handbook of Economic Sociology* (Princeton, NJ: University of Princeton Press).

NEWALL, S. and CLARK, P. (1990), 'The Importance of Extra-Organisational Networks in the Diffusion and Appropriation of New Technologies', *Knowledge: Creation, Diffusion, Utilization*, 12: 199–212.

NIXON, B. (1995), 'Technology Investment and Management Accounting Practice', *British Journal of Management*, 6: 271–88.

NONAKA, I. and TAKEUCHI, H. (1995), *The Knowledge Creating Company* (Oxford: Oxford University Press).

OSBORN, R. N. and HAGEDOORN, J. (1997), 'The Institutionalisation and Evolutionary Dynamics of Interorganisational Alliances and Networks', *Academy of Management Journal*, 40/2: 261–78.

PARK, S. H. and UNGSON, G. R. (1997), 'The Effect of National Culture, Organisational Complementarity and Economic Motivation on Joint Venture Dissolution', *Academy of Management Journal*, 40/2: 279–307.

PENROSE, E. (1959), *The Theory of the Growth of the Firm* (Oxford: Basil Blackwell).

PETERS, T. (1988), 'The Mythology of Innovation or the Skunkworks Tale: Part II', in M. Tushman and W. L. Moore (eds.), *Readings in the Management of Innovation* (New York: Harper), 138–47.

PETTIGREW, A. M. (1972), 'Information Control as a Power Resource', *Sociology*, 6/2: 187–204.

—— (1985), *The Awakening Giant* (Oxford: Blackwell).

POLANYI, M. (1964), *Personal Knowledge* (New York: Harper).

PORTER, M. (1980), *Competitive Strategy* (New York: Free Press).

—— (1985), *Competitive Advantage* (New York: Free Press).

POWELL, W. W. (1990), 'Neither Market nor Hierarchy: Network Forms of Organisation', *Research in Organisational Behaviour*, 12: 295–335.

PRAHALAD, C. K. and HAMEL, G. (1990), 'The Core Competence of the Corporation', *Harvard Business Review*, 68/3: 79–91.

ROTHWELL, R., FREEMAN, C., HORSELY, C., JARVIS, A., ROBERTSON, A. B., and TOWNSEND, J. (1974), 'SAPPHO Updated—PROJECT SAPPHO Phase 2', *Research Policy*, 3: 258–91.

ROWES M. J. (1999), 'Peace as a Predicate to Production', Clarendon Lectures, Examination Schools, University of Oxford, 10–12 May.

RUGMAN, A. and VERBECKE, A. (1997), 'Global Strategies for Multinational Enterprises' in I. Islam and W. Shepherd (eds.) *Current Issues in International Business* (Cheltenham: Edward Elgar), 132–50.

RUMELT, R. P. (1980), 'The Evaluation of Business Strategy', in W. F. Glueck (ed.), *Business Policy and Strategic Managment* (New York: McGraw-Hill).

RYBCZYNSKI, R. (1989), 'Corporate Restructuring', *National Westminster Bank Quarterly Review*, Aug: 18–28.

SAKO, M. (1992), *Prices, Quality and Trust: Interfirm Relations in Britain and Japan* (Cambridge: Cambridge University Press).

SCHER, M. J. (1997), *Japanese Interfirm Networks and their Main Banks* (New York: Macmillan–St Martins Press).

SCHON, D. (1963), 'Champions for Radical New Innovations', *Harvard Business Review*, Mar./Apr.: 133–60.

SCHUMPETER, J. (1934), *The Theory of Economic Development* (Cambridge, Mass.: Harvard University Press).

SCOTT, J. (1986), *Capitalist Property and Financial Power* (Brighton: Wheatsheaf).

—— (1997), *Corporate Business and Capitalist Classes* (Oxford: Oxford University Press).

SPENDER, J.-C. (1980), 'Strategy-Making in Business' PhD thesis (Manchester Business School).

STREEK, W. (1992), *Social Institutions and Economic Performance* (London: Sage).

TAJFEL, H. (ed.) (1982), *Social Identity and Intergroup Relations* (Cambridge: Cambridge University Press).

TEECE, D. J. (1977), 'Technology Transfer by Multinational Firms: The Resource Costs of Transferring Technological Know-How', *Economic Journal*, 87: 242–61.

—— (1986), 'Profiting from Technological Innovation', in D. J. Teece (ed.), *The Competitive Challenge* (Cambridge, Mass.: Ballinger).

—— and PISANO, G. (1994), 'The Dynamic Capability of Firms', *Industrial and Corporate Change*, 3/3: 557–608.

TEUBNER, G. (1993), 'The Many-Headed Hydra: Networks as Higher-Order Collective Actors', in J. McCarey, S. Picciotto, and C. Scott (eds.), *Corporate Control and Accountability: Changing Structures and the Dynamics of Regulation* (Oxford: Clarendon Press).

TURNBULL, P. (1986), 'The "Japanisation" of Production and Industrial Relations at Lucas Electrical', *Industrial Relations Journal*, 17/3: 193–206.

TUSHMAN, M. and KATZ, R, (1980), 'External Communication and Project Performance: An Investigation into the Role of Gatekeepers', *Management Science*, 26/11: 1071–85.

WEBB, S. and WEBB, B. (1897, 1919 edn.), *Industrial Democracy* (London: Longmans).

WEBER, M. (1914, 1968 trans.), 'The Economy and the Arena of Normative and De Factor Powers', in G. Roth and C. Wittich (eds.), *Economy and Society* (Berkeley, Calif: University of California Press).

WENGER, E. and KASERER, C. (1997), 'The German System of Corporate Governance: A Model Which Should Not be Imitated', *Working Paper* (University of Wuezburg, Dept of Economics).

WESTON, J. F., CHUNG, K. S., and HOAG, B. (1997), *Corporate Merger: Restructuring Control* (London: Prentice Hall).

WHITLEY, R. (1992), *Business Systems in East Asia: Firms Markets and Societies* (London: Sage).

WHITTINGTON, R. (1990), 'The Changing Structures of R&D: From Centralisation to Fragmentation', in R. Loveridge and M. Pitt (eds.), *The Strategic Management of Technological Innovation* (Chichester: John Wiley), 183–203.

WILLIAMSON, O. E. (1975), *Markets and Hierarchies* (New York: Free Press).

—— (1985), *The Economic Institutions of Capitalism* (New York: Free Press).

WOOD, S. (1989 edn.) *The Transformation of Work?* (London: Unwin).

WOODWARD, J. (1965), *Industrial Organisation Theory and Practice* (Oxford: Oxford University Press).

World Bank (1987), *World Development Report* (New York: Oxford University Press).

PART III

The Process of Cooperating

Part III of the book focuses its attention on the process of actually bringing about cooperative behaviour. Central to its concern are the issues of how alliances between firms evolve over time, how to implement the plans that establish partnerships between firms, and how to deal with the inevitable and variable levels of stability and instability in such inter-organizational enterprises. In the study of cooperation the process perspective is the most neglected, and this section of the book makes some effort to redress the balance in its direction.

8

From Competition to Collaboration
The Emergence and Evolution of R&D Cooperatives

YVES L. DOZ AND OĞÜZ BABUROGLU

The potential benefits of collaboration in research and development (R&D) activities between firms are well known, and obvious, and so are the difficulties faced by such collaboration. There are many reasons for R&D collaboration between firms and R&D seems to be an increasingly frequent component of inter-company alliances (Aldrich and Sasaki, 1995; see Tripsas, Schrader, and Sobrero, 1995 for a summary). Economies of scale and scope in R&D, a desire to avoid duplications, to access complementary technologies and scientific and technical capabilities, and to control the spillovers from innovative activities underlie many collaborative projects in R&D.

Despite the clear potential benefits that drive firms into cooperating, the increasingly well recognized difficulties they face in obtaining those benefits makes the choice of form of collaboration, and the relative merits and performance of various forms of collaboration, controversial issues (Hane, 1995). The debate is fuelled partly by the significant commitments of public funds (subject to close political scrutiny) to collaborative R&D in Europe, Japan, and to lesser extent the USA (in the European Union today, for instance, support to the information technology industry, mostly for research, ranks second only to agricultural subsidies, and well ahead of other public resource commitments). Beyond the proper use of public funds, the issue is whether the costs of collaborative research outweigh its advantages, for the partner firms and/or for the governments sponsoring their projects.

Departing from the usual economic policy evaluation approaches used in researching this issue, and aiming to complement them, this chapter draws on concepts and research on the evolution of cooperation in alliance situations (Gulati, 1995; Khanna, Gulati, and Nohria, 1998; Gulati, 1996; Doz, 1988, 1996), and on interaction processes in broader conditions of repeated cooperation over time (Blau, 1964; Axelrod, 1984; Trist, 1983; Whetten, 1981; Van de Ven and Walker, 1984; Gray, 1985, 1989; Ring and Van de Ven, 1994), to develop a process model of the emergence and evolution of R&D cooperatives between competitors. Our basic premise is that effective R&D cooperatives, like other collaborative efforts, share at least some process

characteristics that allow them to start successfully and to evolve construct-
ively over time.

We attempt here to complement the already abundant research on cooperation in R&D by focusing on a comparative analysis of cooperation
processes in various types of collaborative efforts in R&D. Most research
on collaborative R&D so far consists of individual research case studies, only
some of which focus on dynamic processes within alliances (e.g. Browning,
Beyer, and Shelter, 1995; Gibson and Rogers, 1994; Hausler, Hans-Willy, and
Lütz, 1994; Sakakibara N., 1993; Grindley, Mowery, and Silverman, 1994),
and both the 'thickness' of the description they provide and the conceptual
insight to be gained from them are quite uneven. Another line of research,
comprising comparative larger-sample studies, provides valuable insight, but
their typically cross-sectional nature limits somewhat the understanding these
studies offer of dynamic and evolutionary aspects of R&D cooperatives (e.g.
Aldrich and Sasaki, 1995; Fransman, 1990; Evan and Olk, 1990; Sakakibara,
1996). Yet other research takes an explicit policy evaluation standpoint but
often focuses more on the value of the actual consequences of cooperation
than on how and why a different cooperation process could have made them
better (e.g. Peterson, 1993). Moreover, detailed studies of some of the early
and most visible cooperation efforts, such as the microelectronics Very Large
Scale Integration (VLSI) project in Japan, the Microelectronics and Computer
Corporation (MCC), and the ESPRIT programme in Europe, all collaborations based in the information technology and electronics sector, but hardly
comparable in design, ambition and scope, may have had an excessive
influence on thinking in the area of effective cooperation practices (Hane,
1995).

Our starting assumption is that R&D cooperatives need to overcome some
very specific barriers that are likely to make the shift from open market
competition to effective collaboration among their members difficult in the
context of R&D. Although the forms of cooperation vary greatly, we observed that their generative processes shared some similarities based in a
process of developing common ground, both through formal structures and
informal relationships and through engaging in explicit mutual commitments.
In this chapter we begin by summarizing the observed similarities in generative processes and structuring them into a framework, drawing on what is
known about the emergence and evolution of cooperation in other settings,
such as strategic alliances and long-term customer–supplier relationships. We
then use the framework to analyse secondary, publicly available data on
various R&D collaborative efforts.

The Generation of Cooperation: A Framework

Cooperation between competitors in an industry to carry out joint research
does not arise spontaneously. It results from a generative process following a

series of steps, and evolving through several forms of collaboration. In this section we describe the framework we propose, based on an inductive analysis of the inception of cooperation. We proceed in three stages. First, we outline preconditions for the generative process leading to collaboration, then we describe and compare various forms of collaboration, and finally we discuss the sequence and interaction between the steps in the process and the forms of collaboration.

Collaboration: Preconditions to the Process

1. *Identifying Interdependencies.* First, collaboration requires, as a precondition, the recognition by key stakeholders and potential participants in the collaboration process of some interdependence of a type that markets and competition alone are unlikely to address effectively. Collective goods may need to be created. This type of interdependence makes the collaboration justified. Interdependence may arise from a multiplicity of causes. Network externalities are a form of interdependence that markets do not address well—calling for agreements on standardization and market development—and often for technology cooperation to define standards and pioneer compatible technologies. Other forms of externalities, such as pollution, may call for collaboration, as the balance of costs and benefits is unlikely to be settled by market forces, unless public goods, and pollution in particular, are accurately priced. Uncoordinated efforts by diverse participants in an industry may not yield environmentally sound and economically effective outcomes. Interdependence may also arise from the recognition that 'leaky' technologies need to be combined, a situation where the technologies may not be well enough specified for ownership rights to be clearly spelt out, for instance around new manufacturing processes where pooling the experience and the work of several firms would be helpful. To combine ownership-specific ill-specified technologies, and more generally intangible assets, may require cooperation.

Depending on their origins, interdependencies may be more or less clear (and easily understood from the outset) to potential cooperation participants. Dyadic alliances to perform a well-defined task—such as a paint company installing and operating painting tunnels in the plants of its car manufacturing customers—rather than the usually more tentative R&D work, acknowledge a clear complementarity of skills and capabilities, anchored in the willingness to co-specialize assets. The nature of interdependencies around new and emerging technologies, or new knowledge, may be less clear, the need for cooperation less visible, and, thus, commitments to co-specialization much more tentative. The first step in the generative process for R&D collaboration may therefore have to be the discovery of unseen connectedness and interdependence. Such discovery may require constituting a new information network and building common ground around shared interests and an awareness of mutual interdependencies between the network members. Sometimes, a government agency, such as MITI in Japan, can provide the focal point for the identification of unseen interdependencies. Joint sense-making (Ring, 1996) is required among potential participants in the coopera-tion, and is impossible unless they undertake some form of multiplex com-munication, and are thus part of a shared communication and information network. Some industries in some locations have a strong social community, with pre-existing social links (Kreiner and Schultz, 1993; Gulati and Gargiu-lio, 1999; Uzzi, 1997). The awareness of interdependence may also be triggered by an external threat to which the country, region, or group of firms becomes sensitive, and which creates a pressure to collaborate. Many of both the Japanese and US R&D consortia in electronics, for instance, were created in response to an actual or expected competitive challenge from the other country. The broader point here is that cooperation beyond markets is not to be expected unless there is a clear mutual recognition of interdepend-encies—actual or potential—between stakeholders, of a variety that markets alone may find difficult to address successfully. In industries characterized by intense competition and limited contact between competitors, such recogni-tion needs to be triggered and constructed, it cannot be taken for granted. Mutual benefits that could result from cooperation may otherwise be ignored by managers steeped in a tradition of open competition.

2. *Developing Shared Norms of Problem Solving.* Producing collaboration re-quires the existence of norms of problem solving and collaboration. If the various potential participants in the collaboration process do not share similar behavioural norms they will find communication difficult, and if they do not share common ethical standards they may find agreement difficult. Hetero-geneous cultural norms of behaviour may also get in the way of effective collaboration by creating misunderstandings and other forms of 'noise' in the communication between potential cooperators. The same applies to wide differences in organizational processes between organizations, for example in the speed and nature of their decision-making (Doz, 1988). Potential collab-orators need to 'meet' not only intellectually and strategically, but also culturally and ethically. To a large extent, the European Community's ESPRIT programme was designed to foster the emergence of a normative community in the European Information industry, through multiple networked interac-tions between European researchers in European firms, partly to counter-balance the natural US influence on R&D and on other managers whose formative experience had often taken place in companies such as Motorola, Texas Instruments, or Hewlett Packard.

3. *Triggering Cooperation: The Need for a Focal Entity.* Cooperation may re-quire the initiative to be taken, and early leadership to be exercised, by some legitimate triggering entity or individual. The issue of who initiates collabora-

tion between hitherto competitive firms is central. Even in situations where it is clearly potentially beneficial, and seen as such by potential participants in the cooperation effort, collaboration may not arise if no one will take the initiative lest the motives of the initiator of cooperation be suspect, and collaboration may not take off or may turn against its initiators. Potential participants may not expect costs and benefits to be shared in a balanced fashion unless the triggering entity is legitimate, and is seen as a guarantor of 'fairness' between the partners involved in collaboration. The legitimacy, neutrality, and reputation of the collaboration initiator may therefore play a key role in assuring that the relevant potential partners join the collaboration process. Processes of inclusion and exclusion, the definition of key inter-dependencies and collaboration issues, the sequence and mode in which potential participating firms are approached, and the perceived fairness and procedural justice that characterize these processes, are thus quite important. The legitimacy and relevance of the first participants, and the credibility they bring to the effort in the eyes of other potential participants, largely determine the cooption of future participants into the cooperative effort.

4. *Selecting Participants.*   Any area of science or technology, in a country or a region, involves a few firms and public research institutes and/or universities which between them carry out the bulk of the research in the area. Collabora-tion without the inclusion of the primary contributors and stakeholders in the sector would be futile. Stakeholders, though, may not all be seen as equally important at the outset, given likely differences in the definition of the issues and in the assessment of the need to collaborate between various partners. In other words, who to include depends on the definition of the problem, and that may not be fully clear at the outset. A process of joint problem definition and primary stakeholder inclusion is therefore almost unavoidable. Facilitat-ing these intertwined processes may be a key role for the triggering entity, and a serious test of its legitimacy. In Japan facilitation was usually performed by MITI officials and related government agencies. In the USA, key well-respected individuals, such as Robert Noyce for Sematech, Admiral 'Bobby' Inman for MCC, and Charlie Sporck (the Chairman of National Semicon-ductor and a well-regarded Silicon Valley figure) played this role. In Europe, DG XIII of the European Commission played a role somewhat similar to MITI's in Japan. The main difficulty in these roles is to include key con-tributors, and not just a few obvious 'leading' firms, without diluting the focus of the effort to the point where membership becomes akin to that in a club. In such an atmosphere the visibility and impact of contributions and benefits may be so diluted as to become meaningless. In the end, programmes range from very broad umbrellas, or even mere labels for government funding (e.g. the EUREKA framework in Europe) to very focused integrated efforts with a very clear-cut single goal (e.g. the VLSI project in Japan) with many inter-mediate formulas, such as integrated host structures bringing together

multiple complementary but distinct projects (e.g. MCC, or now Sematech in the USA).

5.   *Making the Shadow of the Future Visible.*   Cooperation is facilitated by the recognition of a greater rather than smaller 'shadow of the future', i.e. assumptions of sustained further mutually beneficial cooperation in the future, in which the goodwill, commitment, and mutual forbearance of the partners, and thus the reputation they acquire in early cooperation, are going to be essential. To a large extent, therefore, a history of successful past cooperation (with 'success' assessed on several dimensions, in particular adjustability and trustworthiness in addition to efficiency and effectiveness), is a strong predictor of future cooperation (Doz, 1996). Reputational effects in existing networks also obviously play a role (Gulati, 1995). The more future cooperation is based on reputation acquired in past cooperations—with other partners but by whom future partners may be informed—the more likely it is to succeed. Reputational effects provide a safeguard against opportunism in the cooperation which extends beyond the cooperation itself. Contrary to an ongoing strategic alliance, which often carries a presumption of longevity, R&D cooperations are normally of limited duration and linked to specific projects with a given time horizon, but what matters here is the assumption that the partners may engage in new cooperative programmes in the future, and that a tarnished reputation would jeopardize such undertakings.

6.   *Securing the Participants' Sustained Ability to Contribute.*   Collaboration can be sustained only when the various parties have the ability to contribute to the collaboration. This ability to actually deliver has various aspects. First, the credibility of each member's commitments is essential for collaboration to last over time. The sustained willingness to contribute needs to be there. Continuity of policy and priorities on the part of the various collaborators is thus essential. The very design of the collaboration may be well enough balanced to encourage participants to stay the course, but external destabilizing forces are almost unavoidable.

Second, participants have to contribute part of the value to be created via the collaboration. In some forms of R&D collaboration they may have to keep contributing, over time, knowledge developed outside the cooperative work proper. Put differently, free-riding is a permanent threat to the sustainability of R&D consortia, particularly in Europe where access to public funding is often based on a *juste retour* principle according to which the project has to draw on contributions from (or, more accurately, to provide work to) the firms of various countries in direct proportion to how much their respective governments contribute to the consortium's kitty. These issues have plagued various cooperative undertakings in Europe, such as CERN's new particle accelerator outside Geneva, or some of the European Space Agency's programmes. In most skill combination and learning alliances, where the collaboration is used partly to perform new research, but also partly to exchange existing knowledge, the various partners have to keep contributing new, independently developed skills over time, as the value of further cooperation would erode prematurely should the skill base of the various partners become increasingly homogeneous through the collaboration process itself.

More generally, collaborators may need to be beyond a threshold of strength, where they will recognize each other as effective contributors, and will each have enough self-confidence to participate strongly in the collaboration without being threatened or despised by the other participants. Cooperation between differently positioned but equally credible and capable firms is probably most effective. Conversely, Sematech's beginnings, for instance, were plagued by concerns that some partners were more advanced than others in manufacturing technologies, leading quickly to a reassessment of the consortium's objectives towards supporting the semiconductor manufacturing equipment industry rather than jointly developing leading-edge manufacturing practices among semiconductor producers. Collaboration between excessively unequal partners is unlikely to be effective.

The ability to contribute is also conditioned by the interface put in place between the partners, in particular the way in which different organizations succeed in communicating and building a common, or at least compatible, understanding of the task at hand, of the value to be created by collaboration, and of each other's way of operating, for instance around key commitments, policy decisions, and the like (Doz and Hamel, 1998). Enough mutual understanding also needs to be built to allow effective signalling to take place between the collaborators, for example on difficult issues like the balance of efforts and contributions.

7. *Designing Cooperation.* Collaboration may be facilitated or hampered by its very design. The structure and process put in place to govern and implement collaboration may give rise to more conflicts, or, on the contrary, design out some conflict. In other words, some collaboration designs and processes facilitate further collaboration, while others make it more difficult. For instance, in the VLSI project, MITI officers paid great attention to overcoming barriers to collaboration by the very design of the alliance. To get the firms to really work together, MITI first obtained a joint lab (in a separate wing of an NEC facility) and set up two types of sub-projects: three competitive core technology projects, each under the leadership of one partner, but 'sprinkled' with researchers from the other partners, and three supporting process technology projects, each delegated to a firm, or to MITI, but performed in the joint lab (Sakakibara, 1993). Each company sent neither its top-class researchers nor mediocre ones, but mid-range scientists for whom this effort provided a significant opportunity to learn and build new networks (Bower and Murphy, 1982). Both the structure of the overall

project and the micro-design of how scientists were nominated to the project, how their work was organized, how the intellectual property rights were defined, and how their incentives were structured were conducive to collaborative and joint learning.

8.   *Learning and Adjusting over Time.*   This, in turn, may call for evolution and adjustment over time in expectations, collaboration processes, organizations, commitments, and governing rules and bodies. The ability to make the collaboration process evolve to reflect the learning achieved by the partners about the collaboration itself is essential to successful long-term collaboration (Doz, 1996).

9.   *Expansion of Scope and Deepening of Commitments.*   Finally, successful collaboration feeds on itself, on its effectiveness and legitimacy. The ability to establish more common ground between the partners over time, and the fulfilment of cooperative commitments—explicit contracts or relational commitments—allow the cooperation to grow in scope and duration. Successful cooperation often leads to the discovery of even more successful ways to cooperate and of new objects of cooperation. In that sense, both the design and the process of collaboration should not be seen purely in a static efficiency perspective, but also as part of the generative process of further cooperation.

Forms of Cooperation

Cooperation can take place in several ways. Broadly, one can contrast explicit and specified forms of cooperation with less explicitly structured ones, or formal mutual commitments with common-ground arrangements. Common ground results from parties with a stake in a problem situation actively seeking a mutually determined solution (Gray, 1989). Building common ground starts with accepting each other's views, goals, and interests within a particular problem domain. Stakeholders acknowledge their differences and agree to put their energy into working on the common ground. Examining each other's reality and identifying future aspirations is the key to discovering common ground. Participants in the process may be led into redefining and transcending their initial aspirations and into a reformulation where collaboration creates more value than was visible at the outset (Heifetz, 1994). An example of this process is provided in a study of R&D cooperation around adhesive technologies in Germany (Hausler, Hans-Willy, and Lütz, 1994). In this situation, all participants had to change their initial definition of what the cooperation would be in order to find common ground. The initial situation, for example, was framed by a customer, a car-maker, as a way to select suppliers of adhesives, with their products vetted by research institutes. This locked chemical industry participants into a zero-sum situation where they would separately compete for orders: hardly a way to foster cooperation among them. As the research institutes' tests showed that all available products fell short of meeting the needs of automotive customers, the need for joint pre-competitive research became obvious, and the chemical industry partners discovered they each had something to learn. More slowly, the car-maker also accepted the need to shift from its usual way of handling suppliers—contractually and separately—to investing in a collective R&D effort that would not pitch suppliers one against another. Interestingly, it was the collective resistance of the suppliers towards the selection approach of the customer that led to that redefinition of the relationships, and to the discovery of collective, multilateral common ground, in a process that broke with the customary relationships between customers and suppliers in the German car industry. In many potential R&D cooperation projects the discovery and building of common ground is an important aspect, almost a *sine qua non*, of collaboration, particularly when the technologies or the applications that are the object of cooperation are so new, or sufficiently hybrid in nature, to bring together participants in cooperation that have little knowledge of each other and no experience of working together.

Common ground is not enough, though. Unless supported by actual firm commitment to joint work, common ground may not result in real cooperation with tangible outcomes. In some cases common ground is merely the breeding ground for specific, often bilateral, cooperation, which arises from the joint sense-making achieved in the building of common ground. Existing, ongoing professional networks may provide enough common ground for specific commitments to be made to actual cooperation among subsets of the network members (c.g. in the Danish biotechnology community, as described by Kreiner and Schultz, 1993). How formalized and contractually specified commitments need to be, and can practically be, is a matter of debate. The nature of R&D, with all the uncertainty that affects innovative work, makes the contractual formalization of R&D cooperation difficult. Very detailed and specific contractual arrangements may well turn into straightjackets. Furthermore, the benefits of relational contracting in uncertain alliance situations are increasingly recognized (Van de Ven and Ring, 1992). Cultural differences also influence the need for and, the form of, safeguards and other enforcement mechanisms. The important point here is not the form of commitments but the fact that commitments are regarded as mutual and binding by the involved parties, and that mutually acceptable and understood rules are developed on key aspects of contribution (such as the secondment of engineers to a mutual effort) and of benefits (such as the devolution of intellectual property rights from the effort).

R&D cooperative efforts differ along a second significant dimension: the extent to which they are designed and structured in one stroke, according to some pre-existing concept, or evolve in a self-structuring mode, as the outcome of the early phases of cooperation. In broad terms, an R&D

cooperative can be designed, structurally, *a priori*, and members asked to join a well-specified structure, with clear rules and procedures. Or, alternatively, rather than precede the members' participation, the design of the collaborative effort may emerge over time from their interactions.

Our categorization of cooperation processes, using the two dimensions outlined above, is summarized in Figure 8.1. Various forms of cooperation can be positioned differently along the two dimensions. An equity joint venture, for instance, is a design form that spells out formal mutual commitments. While the joint venture may be capable of adaptation, it nonetheless constitutes a rather stable and usually well-specified design. As such it may be more suited to cooperation for the exploitation of well-defined technical areas between partners who share roughly the same kind of expertise (e.g. pharmaceutical firms cooperating over the screening of new active chemical ingredients) than to the exploration of new areas where partners bring very differentiated expertise (Leveque, Bonazzi, and Quental, 1993).

Yet, as partners gain more experience in working together, and learn to trust and understand one another more fully, and as interpersonal commitments and trust take precedence over inter-institutional ones, they may shed some of the formality in their cooperation and accept an evolving cooperation process, moving to the top right-hand corner on the axes of Figure 8.1 (Ring and Van de Ven, 1994; Doz, 1996). Powell, for instance, identified the existence of many informal alliances in the Californian biotechnology community (Powell, Koput, and Smith-Doerr, 1996). A working group in the context of an industry association, or of a researchers' professional association, can be a design for the development of common ground,

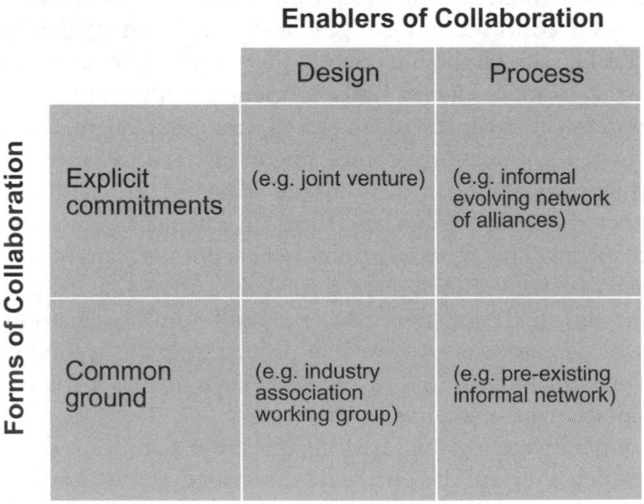

Enablers of Collaboration

		Design	Process
Forms of Collaboration	**Explicit commitments**	(e.g. joint venture)	(e.g. informal evolving network of alliances)
	Common ground	(e.g. industry association working group)	(e.g. pre-existing informal network)

Fig. 8.1 Types of collaboration

by providing a neutral forum for the airing and exchange of issues and information. For instance, in the German cooperative project concerning adhesives, the chemical industry's association provided the critical neutral and collective ground to develop an industry position on the need for pre-competitive research in the area, and a critical step towards moving away from traditional customer–supplier relationships (Hausler, Hans-Willy, and Lütz, 1994). Although common ground requires a design, unless its develop-ment piggybacks an existing network or community, common ground is usually only discovered through a protracted process of interaction leading to joint sense-making. Most of the collaborative efforts from which we obtained information were characterized by a relatively lengthy consultation process which followed the discovery of common ground but preceded the inception of actual cooperation.

A Process Model

Cooperation is likely to evolve through several phases. Common ground is likely to be a precondition for the implementation of flexible incomplete contracts allowing specific commitments. In fact, the stronger the common ground between the collaborators, the more incomplete their contracts can be. Common ground may be the result of prior cooperation, and prior ties between the partners (Gulati, 1995). This may allow the process to bypass the early stages of recognizing the need to collaborate, of developing and sharing common norms of problem solving and collaboration, of includ-ing primary stakeholders, and of reaching a commonly agreed, or at least compatible, definition of the issues to be addressed in the collaboration process. In the absence of strong prior cooperation and ties, or in the case of failed prior cooperation, building common ground may be a precondition for collaboration. While such building may happen informally, particularly in the face of strong external pressures or high collective costs, it may none-theless require an initial design, and a deliberate effort on the part of the triggering entity to develop common ground between the primary stake-holders.

Common ground is unlikely to be fully defined by an act of design. While premises, information, analyses and the like may be provided early on, the common-ground development process is likely to be consultative and inter-active, to slowly reveal the costs of non-cooperation, to identify the primary stakeholders, to tease out the hidden agendas of the various primary stake-holders, and to develop an issue set acceptable to all key stakeholders. The process also allows these stakeholders to learn more about each other and to gain the level of mutual understanding that allows them to enter more formalized agreements.

We would therefore expect successful common-ground definition pro-cesses to yield specific formalized collaborative agreements. By formalized we mean implying visibly identified and publicly stated commitment to goods and allocation of resources. The agreement itself may well be more or less complete as a function of the quality and robustness of the identified common ground. If it is shaky, and soft, collaborators may be driven into seeking more complete contractual arrangements; if it is firm and stable, they may be much more likely to have only very incomplete contracts. In turn, the specific collaborative agreement design may, or may not, foster a deeper collaborative process over time. The quality of the process leads to the adaptation of the collaborative design, to periodic improvements, and to the widening or renewal of its scope over time, and to renewed ties between the collaborators.

The hypothesized evolutionary process of collaboration is sketched out in Figure 8.2. The numbers on Figure 8.2, from 1 to 9, correspond to the steps in the development of the collaborative processes. While some steps correspond clearly to a stage and a form of collaboration, others represent transitions from one form to another, for example 3 (a key role of the triggering entity is to start the process of collaboration) or 7 (a key feature of the contractual design of the collaboration is to foster a collaborative process). The transition from common ground to contractual collaboration is a less straightforward one than shifts from design to process, as the outcome of the common-ground development process may be a series of discrete specific agreements between individual stakeholders, or a broader collective agreement between them, or even a broad agreement serving as an umbrella to facilitate the development of a series of more specific ones.

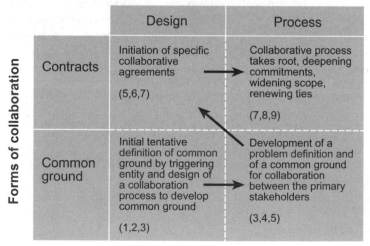

Fig. 8.2 The evolution of cooperation

Evidence from the Semiconductor Industry

The semiconductor industry offers a rich territory for an analysis of R&D cooperation, as it boasts several cooperative ventures in Europe, Japan, and the USA, and as the underlying technologies are both uncertain and 'leaky', thus making cooperation more difficult. For each cooperative venture, we have constructed a chronology of key events and critical steps, based on a thorough search of secondary data sources (the press, case studies, academic articles, etc.). Thus, in terms of empirical research this chapter is somewhat unorthodox, more in line with conceptual development and literature review than with the generation and use of new empirical data. We undertake here a kind of meta-analysis of existing research reports and data sources. For each of the R&D cooperation projects for which we found sufficient evidence, we consolidated our observations into the conceptual framework. Figure 8.3 illustrates our approach with the example of Sematech, the US microchip manufacturing process development cooperative.

Several features make Sematech a particularly revealing cooperative, from the standpoint of how to build collaboration over time. First, several institutions provided a 'borrowed' design for the development of common ground,

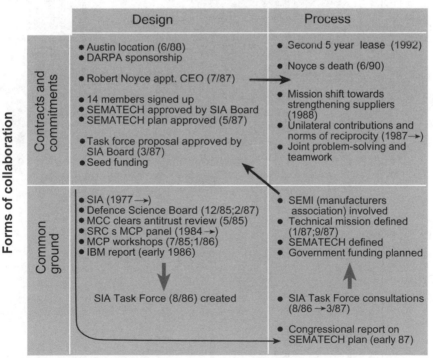

Enablers of collaboration

Design

Process

Contracts and commitments
- Austin location (6/88)
- DARPA sponsorship
- Robert Noyce appt. CEO (7/87)
- 14 members signed up
- SEMATECH approved by SIA Board
- SEMATECH plan approved (5/87)
- Task force proposal approved by SIA Board (3/87)
- Seed funding

- Second 5 year lease (1992)
- Noyce s death (6/90)
- Mission shift towards strengthening suppliers (1988)
- Unilateral contributions and norms of reciprocity (1987→)
- Joint problem-solving and teamwork

Common ground
- SIA (1977→)
- Defence Science Board (12/85;2/87)
- MCC clears antitrust review (5/85)
- SRC s MCP panel (1984→)
- MCP workshops (7/85;1/86)
- IBM report (early 1986)

SIA Task Force (8/86) created

- SEMI (manufacturers association) involved
- Technical mission defined (1/87;9/87)
- SEMATECH defined
- Government funding planned

- SIA Task Force consultations (8/86→3/87)
- Congressional report on SEMATECH plan (early 87)

Forms of collaboration

Fig. 8.3 The formation and evolution of SEMATECH

TABLE 8.1 *A comparative synopsis of selected R&D cooperatives*

Enabling Processes	VLSI—Japan	Eureka	MCC	Sematech
1. Identification of interdependencies that markets are unlikely to solve; need for joint cooperative solutions.	Everyone against IBM's Future Systems (FS). LDP promotes cooperation.	'Near to market'. Technology combinations, networks.	Japanese threat (5th generation discussion). Shortage of engineers, high cost of R&D vs. capital shortage (1982).	Recovery of US semiconductor industry; need to avoid dependence on Japanese equipment suppliers.
2. Opportunity and problem-solving norms recognized.	Common basic technologies in common lab. Group labs to develop applied technologies; comparable partner companies; all key diversified electronic groups.	Need to share technology costs/SME-market orientation; projects to circulate on central EUREKA database for at least 45 days + national government coordinators as relays. Two Levels Programs. Governments, highest level, little change to usual R&D policy.	Loss of consistency over time; mission defined broadly.	Pre-existing industry networks, 'bottom-up' process to test and ascertain common norms.
3. Legitimacy of triggering entity, neutrality, and reputation.	Head of joint lab is MITI scientist—task leader, also an MITI social leader, with experience of managing national projects.	Projects: individual companies using pre-existing contacts of networks (2/3 had collaborated before).	William Norris (Control Data); Admiral Bobby Inman (ex-CIA).	US government quite involved; SIA is new, but successful industry association; C. Sporck and R. Noyce are credible.
4. Inclusion of relevant shareholders and participants.	MITI led; 2 groups (A: Fujitsu, Hitachi, Mitsubishi; B; NEC—Toshiba). (Oki, in financial difficulties, left out).	Having Eureka status makes for easier private financing as well.	16 key companies, committed to (1) equity participation; (2) enhancement of competition for computing; (3) active involvement in MCC governance; (4) appropriate personnel being assigned, and (5) sharing funds for the relevant projects.	14 key makers of semiconductors participate; manufacturers of equipment are involved via their industry association and in specific projects.
5. Recognition of the shadow of the future	Companies had already collaborated in the past, although less closely, and expected to cooperate again in the future. 'Uniqueness' of the project. Path-breaking nature of technology.	LT Projects, 84% may work with same partners again, but 'erosion' of current partners. 2/3 have coop. exp.; 50% include partners who have already worked together, piggy-back on existing linkages.	No clear hypothesis of continued collaboration between MCC partners.	Expectations that the problem won't go away, and that membership is stable and appropriate to the task.

6. Ability: Credibility, continuity; Contribution value; Contribution sustainability; Strength and self-confidence; Acceptance of mutual dependence.	Researchers selected by MITI. Mostly relatively young 'second-tier' researchers. Core group of engineers had been personally acquainted. Mixed teams, but leaders and majority from one company only in each team. Take only leading companies.	Collaborators who work with new partners are more enthusiastic than the others, more committed to future work. SMES perhaps less clear. Fewer legally valid MOUs; less clear understanding of intellectual property rights.	Limited: 65% of shift planned to be secondees from member companies (but not worked, 1983); key people hired from outside. Interface started at CEO level, but sinks down. MCC has to go to each sponsor company for each project. Slow difficult process not commited to MCC.	Key companies involved; mix of secondees and newly-hired personnel.
7. Design.	Common lab (contrary to others), and two sub group labs: series of committees formal process of documentation and management processes to reach a common framework between managers.	'Umbrella' and government 'blessing' concept.	'Collection of (smaller) consortia' project.	Common facility, joint teams, series of formal documentation and interaction processes.
8. Evolution.	One-time project; built networks between companies.	2/3 of projects evolved substantially after/during consultation with the partners.	Portfolio of discrete projects; evolving membership.	Initial management style made evolution relatively easy and feasible: open egalitarian culture, collective problem-solving.
9. Scope expansion and commitment deepening.	Increasing commitment over life of project but set finite time frame.	New collaborative links between firms who would not have chosen to undertake their current R&D projects without support or new partners (about 1/2 survey respondents signalled so). Expand number of participants, cross-border exchanges.	Not on the part of the founding partners.	Renewal after 5 years.

in particular the Semiconductor Industry Association (SIA), and the Semi-conductor Research Corporation (SRC), both of which allowed the development of a collective awareness of the need for action in the semiconductor industry supplier base. Various substantive inputs, such as the Defense Science Board review, an IBM report, and DARPA's (the Defense Advanced Research Agency) work, fed the emerging common ground. An SIA task force, and the CEO of National Semiconductor, took a leading role in a consultation process that built common ground among all industry members, and allowed fourteen of them to commit to the technical mission of Sema-tech, a focused effort to improve 'submicron' process technologies. This process of common-ground building occupied the better part of a year (autumn 1986 to summer 1987), and was made considerably easier by the personal networks which already existed between many participants (many of them came originally from Fairchild and knew each other (Browning, Beyer, and Shelter, 1996; Rappa and Debackere, 1994). In parallel, common ground was built within the US government, allowing consensus on the funding of Sematech. Formal contractual and operational commitments could be made on the basis of both the industry and government common ground that emerged from the process. The early management style of Robert Noyce (a founder of INTEL who had been brought out of retirement to head Sema-tech) allowed flexibility and adaptation to develop in the cooperation process (Browning, Beyer, and Shelter, 1996).

Among the projects we reviewed, Sematech, and the Japanese VLSI project of the 1970s (Bower and Murphy, 1982; Sakakibara, 1993) were the most focused and structured: each corresponded to a clear-cut collaborative priority, not a broad and diffuse agenda. At the other end of the spectrum, some of the European programmes, such as ESPRIT and especially EUREKA, were broad frameworks, designs for the building of common ground, and pro-forma designs for potential specific projects. Beyond its formal aspects, though, ESPRIT, in particular, was seen as a vehicle to foster inter-company networking among European companies. Table 8.1 summarizes the key characteristics of these various projects.

Within the broader European frameworks specific projects more akin to Sematech occasionally flourished, the Joint European Silicon Structures In-itiative (JESSI) for example. JESSI shared many of the same initial conditions as the VLSI project and Sematech: a clear, well-defined mission, a sharp focus on leverage points for the future of the whole semiconductor industry, the inclusion of the key industrial participants, a patient definition of common ground, the progressive extension of the common ground, and a flexible and adaptive design and process of collaboration over time.

Between the integrated projects (VLSI, Sematech, JESSI) and the broad framework umbrellas (ESPRIT and EUREKA in Europe, SRC in the USA) there are a set of hybrid projects which share characteristics of both, such as the Micro Electronic and Computer Corporation (MCC) and Bell

Communications Research (Bellcore) in the USA. They are relatively tightly focused on a set of technologies and research areas, and have a well-defined and quite stable membership, but combine a variety of projects, each sponsored by a subset of the members, often within a set of prescribed areas.

Bellcore, the inheritor of the Bell Labs, thrived on the divestiture of ATandT, as the cooperative R&D centre of the seven Bell Operating Companies. MCC, as a new venture, faced greater difficulty. Contrary to VLSI, Sematech, or JESSI, its charter was too broad to allow the development of a well-defined mission. Some of the key industry participants, IBM in particular, stayed out of MCC, and over time it evolved towards smaller, faster, shorter-term projects for partners. Its establishment as a for-profit company, dependent on research contracts from the members, combined with a less than clear mission, led to fragmentation of efforts and a possible loss of focus (Corey, 1997). MCC lacked the focused response to a clear threat that characterized VLSI, Sematech and JESSI (in particular as it became clear that the Japanese 'fifth generation' computing project was less formidable than it had appeared), but also lacked the flexibility of frameworks designed as vehicles to link projects and sponsoring authorities (ESPRIT, or the SRC for example). This relatively weak focus led MCC to rely on outside hires rather than transfers from its member firms in staffing its projects, and on spin-offs and technology licensing rather than active transfer of its innovations back to member companies. The usefulness and legitimacy of MCC to its partners suffered accordingly.

In summary, focused projects have the potential for a successful collaboration process, and for a collective questioning and reorientation of collaboration when the process runs into difficulties. (Sematech, for instance, was able to redefine its priorities as a provider of assistance to the semiconductor manufacturer equipment industry when it became clear that knowledge asymmetries and free-ridership issues compromised the sharing of process technology directly among semiconductor manufacturers.) Less focused projects, or projects where consensus on common ground could not emerge without making that common ground too broad to grasp, faced greater difficulties. Framework programmes, such as ESPRIT, provided a safe common ground at critical points in time, in particular when the potential participants in specific collaborative efforts did not know each other, or did not trust each other, at the outset. Hybrid projects failed to create a broad enough common ground, and yet were not sufficiently sharply defined to move ahead rapidly. Frameworks also provided safe designs for individual projects, making collaboration easier and less risky for the participants in specific projects. Specific projects and framework projects thus played complementary roles in fostering and sustaining R&D collaboration. Figure 8.4 provides a summary sketch of the respective roles of the two: projects evolve along the 'inverted-Z' trajectory that we have illustrated with Sematech, while

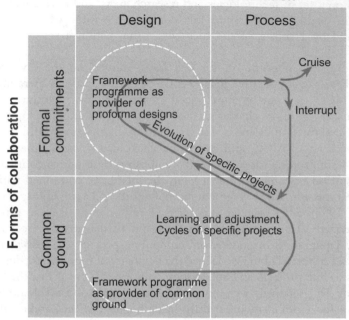

Fig. 8.4 Projects and programmes

programmes provide a context for multiple projects at critical junctures, offering common-ground design early on and models for formal cooperation contracts later. In-between formulae seem to be too ill focused to evolve like a specific project, but too structured, as an independent entity (such as MCC), to just provide a booster to projects at particular stages.

Conclusions

R&D cooperatives between competitors provide an interesting territory to explore transitions between competition and collaboration, and the development of collective goods in situations where concerns for appropriation and private gains tend to predominate. We observed R&D cooperative projects through several phases, from informal common ground to specified commitment and contracts, and alternating between using formal designs, such as collective government-sponsored frameworks, and informal evolving processes. We also observed several successful R&D cooperatives that conformed to a pattern of evolution: from gaining an awareness of common issues that market competition alone is unlikely to solve to specifics of design and process that allow the cooperative to adapt, or not, and even to reassess and redirect its mission as needed.

References

ALDRICH, H. E. and SASAKI, T. (1995), 'R&D Consortia in the United States and Japan', *Research Policy*, 24: (1984), 301–316.

AXELROD, R. M. (1984), *The Evolution of Cooperation* (New York: Basic Books).

BLAU, P. M. (1964), *Exchange and Power in Social Life* (New York: Wiley).

BOWER, J. L. and MURPHY, W. J. (1982), *The Microelectronics and Computer Technology Corporation*, Harvard Business School case no. 386181.

BROWNING, L. D., BEYER, J. M., and SHELTER, J. C. (1995), 'Building Cooperation in Competitive Industry: SEMATECH and the Semiconductor Industry', *The Academy of Management Journal*, 38: 113–51.

COREY, E. R. (1997), *Technology Fountainheads: The Management Challenge of R&D Consortia* (Boston: Harvard Business School Press).

DOZ, Y. (1988), 'Technology Partnerships Between Larger and Smaller Firms: Some Critical Issues', *International Studies of Management and Organization*, 17/4: 31–57.

—— (1996), 'The Evolution of Cooperation in Strategic Alliances: Initial Conditions or Learning Processes?', *Strategic Management Journal*, 17: 55–83.

—— and Hamel, G. (1998), *Alliance Advantage: The Art of Creating Value Through Partnering* (Boston: Harvard Business School Press).

EVAN W. M. and OLK, P. (1990), 'R&D Consortia: A New U. S. Organizational Form', Working Paper (University of Pennsylvania).

FRANSMAN, M. (1990), *The Market and Beyond: Cooperation in Competition in Information Technology Development in the Japanese System* (Cambridge: Cambridge University Press).

GIBSON, D. and ROGERS, E. (1994), *R&D Collaboration on Trial: The Microelectronics and Computer Technology Corporation* (Boston: Harvard Business School Press).

GRAY, B. (1985), 'Conditions Facilitating Interorganizational Collaboration', *Human Relations*, 38/10: 911–36.

—— (1989), *Collaborating: Finding Common Ground for Multiparty Problems* (San Francisco: Jossey-Bass).

GRINDLEY P., MOWERY, D. C., and SILVERMAN, B. (1994), 'SEMATECH and Collaborative Research: Lessons in the Design of High-Technology Consortia', *Journal of Policy Analysis and Management*, 13/4: 723–58.

GULATI, R. (1995), 'Does Familiarity Breed Trust? The Implications of Repeated Ties for Contractual Choice in Alliances', *Academy of Management Journal*, 38/1: 85–112.

—— and GARGIULO, M. (1999), 'Where Do Networks Come From?', *American Journal of Sociology*, 105/4 (1999), 177–231.

HANE, G. J. (1995), 'Clearing the Fog Around R&D Consortia in Japan', *Science and Public Policy*, 22/2: 58–94.

HAUSLER, J., HANS-WILLY, H., and LÜTZ, S. (1994), 'Contingencies of Innovative Networks: A Case Study of Successful Interfirm R&D Collaboration', *Research Policy*, 23: 47–66.

HEIFETZ, R. A. (1994), *Leaderships Without Easy Answers* (Cambridge, Mass.: Belknap Press).

KHANNA, T., GULATI, R., and NOHRIA, N. (1998), 'The Dynamics of Learning Alliances: Competition, Cooperation and Relative Scope', *Strategic Management Journal*, 19/3: 193–210.

KREINER, K. and SCHULTZ, M. (1993), 'Informal Collaboration in R&D: The Formation of Networks Across Organization', *Organization Studies*, 14/2: 189–209.

LEVEQUE, F., BONAZZI, C., and QUENTAL, C. (1993), 'Dynamics of Cooperation and Industrial R&D: First Insights into the Black Box II', paper presented to ASEAT Conference, Manchester, April.

PETERSON, J. (1993), *High Technology and the Competition State* (London: Routledge).

POWELL, W., KOPUT, K., and SMITH-DOERR L., (1996), 'Interorganizational Collaboration and the Locus of Innovation: Networks of Learning in Biotechnology', *Administrative Science Quarterly*, 41: 116–45.

RAPPA, M. A. and DEBACKERE, K. (1994), 'Technological Communities and the Diffusion of Knowledge: A Replication and Validation', *R&D Management*, 22/4: 355–72.

RING, P. S. (1996), *Networked Organizations: A Resource Based Perspective* (Sweden: Uppsala University).

—— and VAN DE VEN, A. H. (1994), 'Developmental Processes of Cooperative Interorganizational Relationships', *Academy of Management Review*, 19/1: 90–118.

SAKAKIBARA, M. (1996) 'Participation in Cooperative Research and Development: An Empirical Study of Motivation, Design of Consortia, and Conduct', paper based on PhD thesis (Harvard).

SAKAKIBARA, N. (1993), 'R&D Cooperation Among Competitors: A Case Study of the VLSI Semiconductor Research Project in Japan', *Journal of Engineering and Technology Management*, 10: 393–407.

TRIPSAS, M., SCHRADER, S., and SOBRERO, M. (1995), 'Discouraging Opportunistic Behavior in Collaborative R&D: A New Role for Government', *Research Policy*, 24: 367–89.

TRIST, E. (1983), 'Referent Organizations and the Development of Inter-Organizational Domains', *Human Relations*, 36/3: 269–84.

UZZI, B. (1997), 'Social Structure in Interfirm Networks: The Paradox of Embeddedness' *Administrative Science Quarterly*, 42/1: 35–67.

VAN DE VEN, A. H. and WALKER, G. (1984), 'The Dynamics of Interorganizational Coordination', *Administrative Science Quarterly*, 29: 598–621.

—— and RING, P. S. (1992), 'Structuring Cooperative Relationships between Organizations', *Strategic Management Journal*, 13: 483–98.

WHETTEN, D. A. (1981), 'Interorganizational Relations: A Review of the Field', *Journal of Higher Education*, 52: 1–2.

—— and ROGERS, D. L. (1982), *Interorganizational Coordination: Theory, Research, and Implementation* (Ames: Iowa State University Press).

9

Implementing Cooperative Strategy
A Model from the Private Sector

DAVID BODDY, DOUGLAS MACBETH, AND BEVERLY WAGNER

There is clear evidence that many attempts at significant organizational change do not achieve what their promoters hoped for. Boddy *et al.* (1998) conducted a questionnaire survey of 100 companies that had attempted to introduce supply-chain partnering. Less than half of the respondents considered that their organization had been successful in implementing the change. Other studies of change tell a similar story. Kearney (1992) and the Economist Intelligence Unit (1992) found a high failure rate when European companies adopted Total Quality Management (TQM) systems. Wastell, White, and Kawalek (1994) concluded that 'Business Process Re-engineering (BPR) initiatives have typically achieved much less than promised' (p. 230). As Burnes observed, 'even well established change initiatives, for which a great deal of information, advice and assistance is available, are no guarantee of success' (Burnes, 1996; 172–3).

Part of the difficulty may lie in the novel and unfamiliar nature of these changes. Management may underestimate the systemic nature of organizations and the scale of what needs to be done to implement an innovation (see McLoughlin and Clark, 1994 or Boddy and Gunson, 1996 on IT changes; and Clark, 1995 on a radical production change). If managers neglect these wider consequences they achieve less than they expect to. Another possibility is that failure comes from the way people manage the change. The processes of change are the problem, rather than the substantive novelty of the change itself. Boddy and Buchanan's (1992) research into project management skills showed that how well people dealt with the processes of change (irrespective of the specific content) had significant effects on the outcomes.

To suggest ways of increasing the success rate of supply-chain partnering, we conducted a three-year study of seven companies in two chains who were implementing partnering relationships. In the next section we outline briefly the models of change that informed the research. In the following sections we describe the distinctive features of partnering from an implementation perspective, present some conclusions from the case, and suggest some implications for practice. The final section offers a wider model which may apply to other forms of cooperative strategy.

Models of Change

Most empirically based analyses of organizational change now emphasize the influence of the historical and contemporary context (Pettigrew, 1987; Clark, 1995). People use their experience of the individuals and companies involved when they decide how to react to proposals. They use information about the external context to support their intentions and work these out through various dimensions of the internal context—structures, politics, and cultures. Structures affect the flow of information and provide the mechanisms which determine whose interests are represented (Pettigrew, 1985; Hinings, Brown, and Greenwood, 1991). Cultures encourage or discourage innovation and commitment to change (Lorsch, 1986). Political models (including Egan, 1994; Kanter, 1983; Markus, 1983; Pfeffer, 1992; Dawson, 1994) emphasize that change affects the interests of stakeholders unevenly. Those who believe they are losing will resist the change despite the rationality of the arguments.

Fairly common ground is that the outcomes of innovation are unpredictable. They reflect both the substantive novelty of the change and how parties promote their interests through the structures, cultures, and political systems of the organization. So to understand how companies turn their strategic intention to cooperate into working reality, we focus in this chapter on two areas of management action. These are the nature of the change itself (content) and how people try to implement it (process).

The Content of Change

At the centre of any change is the substantive content—what is it that is being changed? Any significant change to one part of an organization requires some realignment of others (Leavitt, 1965; Hardy, 1996). If management in two cooperating organizations decide to restructure the product planning process, what issues should they attend to? What headings should they use? Changes to the planning process will affect people's work and areas of responsibility. Can information technology support the process? What further implications could that have for staff? It will help us to understand the full implications of cooperation if we can identify these primary and secondary changes. We suggest a common framework for the content agenda which practitioners can use to highlight areas which need attention when working cooperatively.

The Process of Change

We need to understand how people envision cooperative strategy and how they implement concrete changes. Some writers have focused on the interpersonal or political skills of the individual change agent. Kanter (1983) suggests that the modern change agent needs a portfolio of 'power skills' to overcome resistance and apathy to new ideas. Buchanan and Boddy (1992) explore the competencies the change agent requires. Without some human agency, without someone putting personal effort into the problem, nothing will change. In contrast Pettigrew (1985, 1987) acknowledges the role of the skilled and determined individual, but stresses the role of institutions. Those promoting change can use such institutions to raise legitimate concerns and debate the issues.

If change is difficult to implement in one organization, it is likely to be even more difficult in several. Achieving a cooperative strategy will usually depend on introducing reasonably consistent changes in two or more of the partners. There will be ripple effects to manage in the separate systems, which in turn may have further repercussions. The communication and other methods through which the changes are implemented will be more complex than when they are made in a single enterprise. Models of change will need to be developed to take account of this.

Supply-Chain Partnering

Macbeth (1998) argues that partnering is an approach to inter-firm business relationships in which companies recognize, monitor, and encourage these types of action:

- expect continuing involvement over an extended time;
- develop complementary capabilities;
- share information to permit more coherent planning;
- consider the mutual impact of decisions;
- make joint plans to remove waste (such as inventory) and enhance innovation;
- agree on the principles of interaction;
- accept the need to make a margin and also the need to reduce real cost.

In all of this the business case is the most important, since without a positive impact in the final marketplace neither party has any long term to consider. 'Partnering is therefore a co-destiny situation in which the mutual high dependence requires mutual best efforts to ensure that the commitment is both sensibly targeted and effectively managed' (Macbeth, 1998: 352).

The basic argument is that extreme forms of both hierarchies and markets have disadvantages. Partnering occupies the middle ground between them as a way of organizing economic activity. It is an attempt to build close, long-term links between organizations that are distinct, but which see benefits in working closely together. While proponents claim many advantages (more rapid innovation, reduced time to market, higher quality) companies find this change difficult to implement (Boddy et al., 1998). There is a gap between executive intentions and achievements which may reflect the nature of the change being attempted.

Significant Content

Introducing partnering involves substantial changes in both organizations. There is more to it than a willingness to work together to develop a trusting relationship. If this happens it does so on the foundation of many tangible changes in the way the two organizations work, and in the organizations themselves. As we shall see in the case study there is scope for radical changes in the allocation of responsibilities for doing and coordinating work. We also see how the companies redesigned several business processes and some of their technologies and physical facilities. An adequate model of partnering change needs to capture the shape of the partners at the start of the relationship, and how those dimensions change as the relationship develops.

Complex Process

Partnering is not a free-standing change project that people introduce apart from the day-to-day business. Typically staff on both sides will also be dealing with current operating issues with other customers and suppliers not directly related to the partnering project. The success or otherwise of the enterprise depends on the players making and sustaining their commitment to this new way of working—when there are competing, and more familiar, ways of spending their time. They need to be able to manage both stability and innovation at the same time. Partnering typically involves many players, including managers and operating staff in relevant departments of both organizations. It will affect some at more distant points in the chain who have different interests in the change. This adds to the volatility of the change being managed.

Case Study

To illustrate this we now present a brief account of the development of a close partnering arrangement between Sun Microsystems and one of their suppliers of plastic mouldings—Birkbys Plastics. The account draws on many discussions with those who were creating the link and on documentary and statistical data.

Sun Microsystems

Sun Microsystems is one of the leading players in the world electronics industry. It designs, makes, and sells a range of work-stations, file servers, and related products. The company has deliberately limited its involvement in manufacturing, with the two sites (at Milpitas, California and Linlithgow, Scotland) concentrating on assembly and test operations. Sun buys most components—such as disk drives, memory keyboards, and monitors—

from external suppliers. This out-sourcing strategy allows the company to focus expertise and capital on design, development, and high-value manufacture.

Birkbys Plastics

The company makes plastic mouldings at its headquarters near Leeds and at a plant in Glenrothes in Scotland. It was founded in 1926 to make telephones. After several changes in ownership it was sold in 1990 to the current owners—Marubeni Corporation, a Japanese trading company. The company sells most of its production to the automotive industry, but a significant amount now goes to electronics companies. A range of presses mould plastic resin to designs specified by the customer. They often use Birkbys' design expertise, as the company has pioneered the use of CAD technologies in the plastics industry. It had long-term relationships with several customers in the motor industry, though not of the close partnering-type arrangements which Sun envisaged.

Objectives

For Sun Linlithgow the partnering link with Birkbys was in line with the corporation's wider out-sourcing strategy. Product development is rapid in Sun's market: the average life cycle of a work-station design is less than a year, and the rate of product innovation is increasing. Management believes that a constant flow of new products is essential to the continued rapid growth of the company. The company has always been reluctant to expand its manufacturing base, preferring to invest in product and software development.

When production at the Linlithgow plant began in 1989, existing sources in the USA supplied the plastic enclosures. As production built up, the Supply Management team wanted to shorten supply lines for the bulky enclosures by sourcing more materials from within the UK. The manager whose personal initiative played a large part in building the link recalled that Birkbys was attractive because of their established technical expertise:

They were an old well-established company and they showed the kind of engineering expertise that we were looking for at the time. They had a fine lab, plenty of chemical analysis equipment, plenty of coordinate measurement machines, and a variety of presses. They also had very experienced staff.

For Birkbys, the attraction was the chance to widen the customer base. It depended heavily on sales to the automotive industry and the opportunity to make enclosures for a prestigious customer like Sun was attractive. The relationship with Birkbys began in 1991, when Sun gave the first order: 'We were ecstatic when we got that. It was the first big chunk of the electronic industry—up to that point we'd been mainly automotive'. There appear to have been few formal discussions at the start of the relationship to clarify the shared vision to which the parties were working. The priority of the Sun staff most closely involved at the time was to establish a reliable local supplier of bulky enclosures for their new plant. They wanted to secure their supply base by building up Birkbys' ability; Birkbys welcomed the opportunity to do business in the electronics industry.

Results

As the companies overcame initial difficulties, Sun became more confident of Birkbys' ability, and in March 1993 the opportunity arose to extend the relationship. Linlithgow was to begin manufacturing a new product. The company had previously sourced sheet-metal components themselves, and assembled them into the enclosures. The commodity manager, an influential figure who had worked with Birkbys earlier in his career, questioned this approach. He proposed instead that the company should find a supplier who could manage both activities on behalf of Sun, delivering the enclosure with the sheet-metal already inside. Birkbys agreed to take on this additional work, even though it took them into areas of manufacture of which they had no experience. A later development was that Birkbys began to add power cables to the enclosure, further enhancing its value to Sun. They also began supplying Sun's US factory as well as the one in Scotland. Sun has also benefited from lower inventory as Birkbys has taken more responsibility for managing the inventory.

Birkbys has gained from this emerging extension of the original relationship. Their managers acknowledge that in 1991 they did not foresee the amount and type of business they would eventually be undertaking for Sun:

I think it was something we found out as we went on. By learning that we've been able to pass it on to other customers, the package we've developed. It's something we've learnt by being with Sun—we didn't imagine that at the time. Also at the time we wouldn't have imagined we would be dealing with America the way we do now— it was far beyond our thoughts.

It has allowed them to broaden their customer base and offer higher-value products—which has contributed to improved financial performance.

In summary, the objectives which Sun sought from the link with Birkbys have evolved since 1991. By 1996 clear benefits were being achieved which included:

- securing a local source of supply of a bulky product;
- lower and more predictable costs than from US suppliers, with minimal transport costs;
- adding more value so as to release Sun's assembly capacity for higher value work;
- lower inventory (about one day's supply now held, rather than one week's).

What actions did the parties take to turn their original vision of a closer relationship into what they have now achieved? They had clearly adapted many substantive (content) aspects of their respective businesses as they pursued their cooperative strategy. A significant example was a 'demand-pull' system. This was introduced by Sun as part of a corporate level initiative intended to simplify business processes within the supply chain. It required Birkbys to meet Sun's requirements for enclosures within 4 hours of them being called. This challenging target was only achieved by the introduction of technological and structural changes. Birkbys built a new factory near to the Sun plant, and the two companies changed their storage and transport arrangements. A structural change which also helped the demand-pull system to work was in materials planning. The activity of converting Sun production demands into the materials required from Birkbys passed from Sun to Birkbys. Previously the work had been done by the Sun buyer-planner, but it was now done by the 'Resident Planner'. Birkbys employed the person, who worked in a dedicated area of the Sun plant. She also had access to Sun information systems.

These (and many other) changes in the content agenda altered the inner context within which people in the two companies worked. They took place over several years, through the efforts of staff in the two companies working on the process of implementation. It seems useful here to distinguish between personal initiatives and institutional action.

People Acting Individually

The Sun culture values individual initiative highly, and encourages staff to do whatever is necessary to overcome problems. Several interviews testify to the close working relations that had developed at the operating level—such as between the buyer-planners at Sun and the customer service staff at Birkbys. Each came to appreciate the other's requirements and did their best to make things easier for the other side. The supplier engineers gave many examples of how they acted on their initiative or through informal means to ensure that people kept production moving and the relationship developing.

Staff in the two companies developed closer interpersonal contacts: Sun staff learned about Birkbys, and vice versa. This allowed both sides to 'harmonize their expectations', and to develop closer interpersonal ties:

Schedule changes can be every day, to which we again have to react very quickly. Communication is the main thing. Email and Fax are all very well, but unless you talk to a customer, you're lost—you've got to talk to them. And a bane of my life is the answering machine—because you lose that personal touch, which can be detrimental.

These personal initiatives were supported by a developing array of institutional mechanisms.

People Acting through Institutions

As well as the close personal contacts that developed, the companies gradually created a series of more formal joint institutions to manage the relationship, as outlined below.

Weekly schedule review.   This meeting is between the Sun buyer-planner and the Birkbys sales coordinator to ensure that Birkbys are fully informed about changes in the (volatile) schedule. It also ensures that the Sun staff are comfortable that their supplier will be able to meet the requirements.

Monthly quality meeting.   This is attended by the Sun quality engineer, the Birkbys production manager, and/or the quality engineer. It is an opportunity to review any continuing quality issues that staff have not resolved by themselves.

Monthly commercial review.   This was normally attended by the most senior people involved. It helped to ensure that the companies settled all outstanding commercial issues between them on a regular basis. It was particularly important as it allowed individuals to act with considerable discretion and informality in the mean time. Engineers could decide to authorize changes in tools or materials to keep the line going, without waiting for agreement or paperwork on the commercial issues. This meant they could keep the line going, confident that the next commercial review meeting would deal with any financial aspects. The meeting was also an opportunity to discuss all aspects of the relationship, both current and new projects.

Quarterly product cost reviews.   These were held between the Commodity Manager (Enclosures) from Sun and the Sun account manager from Birkbys. This allowed the parties to agree the price over the next period for both existing and new products.

There are also some significant incidents where the lack of such structures led to difficulties. The regularity of some of these meetings varied, and was sometimes a cause of concern. For example the monthly quality meeting had become intermittent at one point:

It has fallen off, probably through busyness, with a lot of new product introductions just now. I think there's a danger in diverting energies onto new products, away from this one—people are all over the world. There's no doubt that it is difficult to keep your eye on the ball.

There should also be a monthly commercial review meeting, but recently that hasn't happened as regularly as it should— everyone's so busy.

There was no evidence of a regular meeting at the strategic level to review the long-term progress of the relationship.

Institutions also took the form of new documents and procedures, such as:

- creating a common matrix of current and developing products, with likely launch-times;
- the forward production forecast by product, being passed to suppliers and sub-tier suppliers;
- the demand-pull letter, which sets out what Sun expect of Birkbys;
- minutes of meetings, which provide links and continuity;
- establishing and stating clearly Sun corporate policy on an issue.

It was clear that while Sun in particular had a culture that valued personal initiative, they and their partner had developed institutions to support individual work. The significance of these structures to support the relationship had increased as both sides discovered their value.

Conclusions

Several themes relevant to cooperative strategy emerge from this account.

1. The Sun–Birkbys relationship has progressed significantly since the companies decided to work more closely together, and has brought tangible benefits to both. It is an example of how the aims of cooperation evolve between the different kinds of outcome discussed by Gray (chap. 11, below). The partnering began as an exercise in problem resolution and goal achievement (securing a local supplier of a bulky product). As the relationship evolved, the customer in particular began to emphasize the value of a common interpretation of the problem and how the parties should deal with it (developing in suppliers a deeper understanding of the demands in Sun's market).

2. These benefits have been made possible only by a cumulative series of substantial changes in the organization of both companies. Both acknowledge that they have had to resolve wider issues than they appreciated at the outset.

3. These changes were achieved by a combination of people acting as individuals and people acting through institutions. A significant feature of the relationship has been the way that individual initiative was supported by more formal mechanisms to manage the issues. These have been both within and between the companies, and at several levels. These have provided a forum in which to resolve issues of common concern and can help to capture the learning that is taking place.

4. The move towards this closer relationship has raised problems that the parties only discovered as they implemented it. The details of the cooperative strategy were not mapped out in advance, but emerged as the parties learned to work together, and realized the scope for extending the form of their cooperation—what Doz and Baburoglu (chap. 8, above) refer to as the expanding scope and deepening commitment of the relationship.

Implications

This view of the partnering change process has several implications for practitioners managing cross-organizational change.

The Content Agenda and its Consequences

Their primary responsibility is for setting the overall scene within which cooperative strategy works. This includes being clear about the general mission and objectives of the partnering or similar cooperative effort, and how it will support broader strategies. It also includes acknowledging the emergent rather than the planned nature of the process, and that much will be learned along the way. Neither of the parties realized the scale of the changes they would need to make to reach the relationship they now enjoy. Nor did they fully appreciate the ripple effects throughout the organization of the changes introduced to make partnering work. This implies that senior management need to ensure that staff set the content agenda widely rather than narrowly, look for ripple effects, and act on them in good time.

The Process Agenda—People and Institutions

Senior management is also responsible for clarifying the role(s) of those charged with implementing the policy. The role will be unique to each situation, shaped by the factors on the content agenda being redesigned within a particular context. Change agents are unlikely to be able to use simple prescriptions. They do need to develop their diagnostic skills—being able to identify the key variables on the (wide) agenda, and anticipating how one change will lead to another. They need to know when to rely on personal initiative to get things done, and when an institutional approach will be better. The role itself is therefore highly ambiguous and easily misunderstood. Most are not specifically appointed to the role as distinct from their regular duties. Typically they are responsible for some aspects of the partnering project, while continuing with their normal responsibilities. This suggests a willingness to work in ambiguous and uncertain conditions and to cope with the considerable stress that the role involves.

We have shown that change was not implemented by change agents acting alone. They were essential to the process, but were supported by appropriate institutional mechanisms. Many of these, as with the content agenda, emerged as the project developed. These mechanisms provided a forum to bring issues into the open and to resolve them. They required people to meet for specific activities, which in turn led to the development of closer understanding of each other's positions. They prevented the relationship from becoming too reliant on good interpersonal relations.

Senior management is responsible for creating these institutions. In doing so they adjust the balance between individual and institutional activity. This includes ensuring the right membership of project teams, and that teams are properly briefed and supported. It also means ensuring that there are proper reporting mechanisms to link the teams to the wider information and decision-making structures. This gives the project links to and visibility in high places. They also establish how individuals driving change are rewarded and what incentives they have to put effort into a cooperative strategy.

An Integrative Model

To capture these features of the change to partnering we have developed a model that aims to represent the way organizations move towards a partnering relationship. We base it on earlier change models, while its distinct features come from our observations of seven companies in two supply chains who were moving towards a closer supply-chain relationship. The distinct feature of this model is that we identify five connected agendas that need attention if companies are to move towards an effective partnering relationship. These agendas concern:

- Content—the substantive issues being managed in the change,
- Process—the way in which the change is managed and implemented,
- Control—monitoring events in both the content and process agendas,
- Learning—in which project lessons are captured and spread, and
- Integrating—overseeing and managing the other agendas.

The central argument is that how well the companies manage and link these agendas will have a strong influence on the results obtained from their cooperative partnering strategy.

The Content Agenda

We can describe the current state of the relationship between the parties in terms of eight interacting segments within the content agenda. This follows Leavitt (1965) but we have adapted that model in the light of this research. Management in both companies initiating a move to partnering have some objectives in mind. Their actions, both past and present, affect results. The central proposition in the content agenda is that the degree to which the results obtained match the objectives depends on how managers deal with the issues represented by the other six segments, mediated of course by what happens in the wider business context.

This reflects the view of organizations as open systems. The particular subsystems identified vary with the author (Leavitt, 1965; Galbraith, 1977; Peters and Waterman, 1982). We suggest that the elements that affect supply-chain partnering are:

- Business processes—the way the companies have designed the processes for moving materials and information across their respective boundaries;

- Technology—the type and location of physical facilities, machinery, and information systems used by the partners;
- Structure—the way tasks required to deliver goods and services are divided and coordinated, both within and between the two organizations;
- People—the knowledge, skills, attitudes, and goals of the people working for the organizations;
- Culture—the prevailing norms, beliefs, and underlying values which characterize the two organizations; and
- Power—the amount and distribution of identifiable sources of power available to people within the two organizations.

Each segment contains dimensions and elements that delineate that part of the content agenda in increasing operational detail. We propose that, for example, some configurations of business processes, culture, or technology are more likely to support partnering than others. Managers wanting to secure an effective partnering relationship need to work on at least some of these elements to move them towards those forms that are likely to support the results intended.

These segments (and their component dimensions and elements) can describe the position at any level of the organization—corporate, divisional, and operating. Management acts within and across these levels. Actions at one level will influence, and be influenced by, actions at other levels. People implement partnering within this contemporary context.

They also implement it within the historical context of both organizations. This affects both actions and their results. Management acts against a background of previous actions within both organizations. Decisions made in the past shape the segments as they are today and affect how easy or otherwise it is to implement change. Past actions may have created a culture of innovation

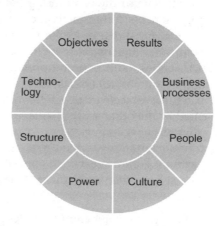

Fig. 9.1 The content agenda

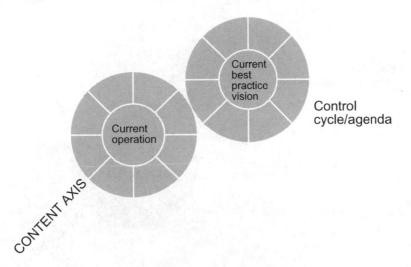

Fig. 9.2 Content and control agendas

and a structure that supports the flow of ideas. They may have created systems in which technologies are outdated and people suspicious and defensive. The past affects both the receptivity of an organization to change and its ability to change (Pettigrew, Ferlie, and McKee, 1992).

Change is triggered by an influential player or group (internal or external) expressing dissatisfaction with current operations. Something motivates them to move from the present way of operating towards some vision of future best practice. The segments in the content agenda are a way of broadly expressing the operational form of that vision. If the idea secures support and takes root, the parties work together to redesign those segments that they believe will help achieve their shared vision of partnering. They aim to do so by reshaping the items in the content agenda into a unique combination that delivers the results expected.

The parties move gradually from an existing state to a desired vision of what they could be together. As they make changes they will more or less diligently monitor results against expectations. They also take account of new developments, and adapt their approach in the light of them. In this they are using the familiar control cycle to help guide an emergent new vision. The activities people undertake to implement these changes constitute the process agenda.

The Process Agenda

Partnering develops in a historical and shifting contemporary context. Some internal or external event triggers sufficient dissatisfaction with current operations for someone to want to change current practice. People see threats or

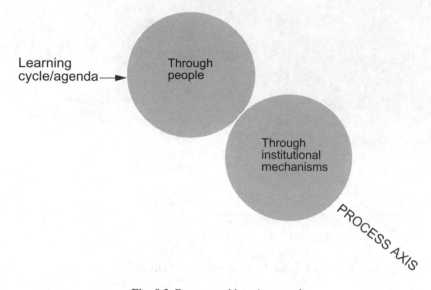

Fig. 9.3 Process and learning agendas

opportunities and muster enough support from other players to initiate a policy decision to move towards a partnering relationship (the current best practice vision). People in both organizations attempt to move from current practice towards the current vision by intervening in the stream of events that make up the lives of the two organizations. The fundamental task for the change agent (or some higher authority) is to construct a change process that ensures those interventions move the parties towards their vision.

Sometimes these interventions will consist of people acting individually and largely on their personal initiative. At other times they get things done by working through and with various institutional mechanisms. In some cases the process is largely in place with clear institutions and procedures to follow. In others someone must create it. Both individual and institutional tracks need to work effectively. Together they constitute the process axis in the model that we show in Figure 9.3.

People Working Individually

Identifiable change agents (though not called that) usually take on the foreground, boundary-spanning roles to drive a partnering initiative forward. They may do so on a part-time or full-time basis, with one or several partners. They include those who are leading or initiating the project, and those who work on operating improvements to processes that span the organizations' boundaries. They may act on their own initiative to make the change happen, or they may progress their ideas through existing institutions, such as gaining approval from the Board, and aim to do so in a way that is acceptable within the prevailing political and cultural landscape.

To handle all this the people taking a leading role in partnering need an unusual combination of expertise. In some respects this consists of being able to apply familiar management practices to the particular circumstances of partnering. Partnering is also likely to require an additional set of skills to cope with some of its distinctive challenges arising from making internal and external change within a volatile environment. These include skills of diagnosis, awareness of different perspectives on project management, and acute political judgement about the use of front-stage and back-stage techniques (Buchanan and Boddy, 1992). The role can be satisfying and rewarding to the individuals, and to the organization that benefits from their commitment.

However there are limitations to what people acting on their own to solve a problem or improve a process can achieve. These include the possibility that:

- they ignore wider considerations in their decisions;
- they have limited means of gathering and integrating a range of ideas from others who could contribute;
- they do not have sufficient power with which to exert influence;
- continuity is lost when individuals change jobs, so that systems decay; and
- learning remains local rather than being spread through the organization(s).

People Acting through Institutions

One way to overcome these limitations is to support individual action with institutional devices. People may create new institutions to support their personal initiatives—such as pulling together a task force of people whom they know support their idea. More broadly support mechanisms can take the form of:

- relatively formal bodies which bring the players into regular face-to-face contact through teams of various kinds;
- documentary or electronic systems to record information about the proposals, decisions, and agreements made in the course of the partnering project.

These are independent of any one individual and can easily move to widely dispersed sites. Others can then act in more informed and mutually consistent ways.

Such institutional devices also have disadvantages. They can take time that is not available; may have the wrong people in membership; may be poorly managed; and may not be sufficiently flexible to cope with varying local circumstances. They may slow the process, blunt initiative, and demotivate creative and energetic staff.

So in constructing a change process there is a tension between those institutions that support and enhance individual action and those that suppress or delay it. Our research has given some insights into the dimensions and elements that may need attention in creating the institutional track of the process agenda. Its purpose is to support individual action in managing the other agendas of partnering (content, control, and learning). Institutional mechanisms can do this by:

- adding corporate perspectives to their diagnosis;
- bringing wider skills and capabilities to bear, through well-selected teams;
- providing institutional sources of power;
- building formal communication systems and methods to record and disseminate information, procedures, and rules consistently; and
- supporting the transfer of learning.

The Control Agenda.   An issue raised but not fully explored in our study is how partnering projects were controlled. Complex, often emerging projects, with change happening in separate organizations, places unusual demands on conventional monitoring and control methods—which were not used by the parties to any extent. The hazards are obvious. The benefit of an emergent, adaptive approach to a partnering strategy is that it allows quick and flexible response to unforeseeable change. That same response, wrongly conceived or badly implemented, could rapidly break the organization. We suggest that these issues can best be captured through what we call the integrating agenda.

The Learning Agenda.   This represents the way in which, and the extent to which, personal and institutional learning occurs. This may take place as a result of deliberate intervention or training strategies, or as people and organizations learn from their direct experience. The central intervention and learning strategy is to help people at the interfaces:

- to implement or accept existing knowledge and procedures;
- to understand and accept existing tacit knowledge; or
- to develop new tacit and codified knowledge about the best way to make a cooperative strategy work in that situation.

Barriers to partnering are the things which prevent that tacit or codified knowledge from being transferred.

The Integrating Agenda.   The way these four agendas are managed cannot be taken for granted, so we conclude with the idea of an integrating agenda. Partnering is a complex change, affecting many interdependent parts of two or more organizations. The agendas to be managed are inevitably complex. They themselves need to be managed and linked together so that all move

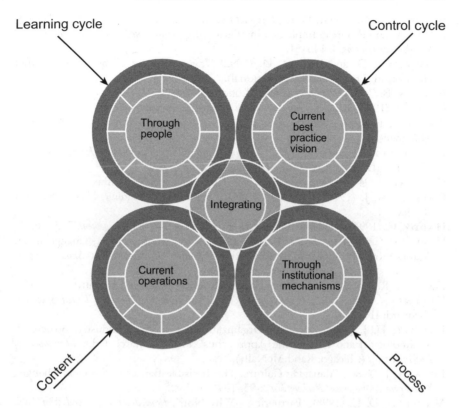

Fig. 9.4 Five agendas in major change

forward with a degree of intelligence about what is happening elsewhere. They also need to fit the strategic direction of the business. Those directly involved cannot work through these issues themselves. There is an additional responsibility to:

- oversee the content agenda and the committing of resources;
- construct a process that supports personal activity with institutional forms and devising controls;
- ensure that learning is captured and transferred.

Figure 9.4 represents the five agendas of the model.

References

BODDY, D. and BUCHANAN, D. (1992), *Take the Lead* (Hemel Hempstead: Prentice Hall International).
—— and GUNSON, N. (1996), *Organizations in the Network Age* (London: Routledge).

BODDY, D., MACBETH, D. K., CHARLES, M., and FRASER-KRAUS, H. (1998), 'Success and Failure in Implementing Partnering', *European Journal of Purchasing and Supply Management*, 4: 143–51.

BUCHANAN, D. and BODDY, D. (1992), *Expertise of the Change Agent* (Hemel Hempstead: Prentice Hall International).

BURNES, B. (1996), *Managing Change* (London: Pitman).

CLARK, J. (1995), *Managing Innovation and Change* (London: Sage).

DAWSON, P. (1994), *Organisational Change: A Processual Approach* (London: Paul Chapman).

Economist Intelligence Unit (1992), *Making Quality Work: Lessons from Europe's Leading Companies* (London: Economist Intelligence Unit).

EGAN, G. (1994), *Working the Shadow Side* (San Francisco: Jossey-Bass).

GALBRAITH, J. (1977), *Designing Complex Organizations* (Reading, Mass.: Addison Wesley).

HARDY, C. (1996), 'Understanding Power', *British Journal of Management*, 7: 3–16.

HININGS, C. R., BROWN, J. L., and GREENWOOD, R. (1991), 'Change in an Autonomous Professional Organization', *Journal of Management Studies*, 28/4: 375–93.

KANTER, R. M. (1983), *The Change Masters* (London: Allen and Unwin).

KEARNEY, A. T. (1992), *Total Quality: Time to Take Off the Rose-Tinted Spectacles* (Bedford: IFS).

LEAVITT, H. J. (1965), 'Applied Organizational Change in Industry: Structural, Technological and Humanistic Approaches', in J. G. March (ed.), *Handbook of Organizations* (Chicago: Rand McNally).

LORSCH, J. (1986), 'Managing Culture: The Invisible Barrier to Strategic Change', *California Management Review*, 28/2: 95–109.

MACBETH, D. K. (1998), 'Partnering—Why Not?', *Proceedings of the 2nd Worldwide Symposium on Purchasing and Supply Chain Management* (Stamford, Lincs.: Chartered Institute of Purchasing and Supply), 351–62.

McLOUGHLIN, I. and CLARK, J. (1994), *Technological Change at Work*, 2nd edn. (Milton Keynes: Open University Press).

MARKUS, M. L. (1983), 'Power, Politics, and MIS Implementation' *Communications of the ACM*, 26/6: 430–44.

PETERS, T. J. and WATERMAN, R. H. (1982), *In Search of Excellence* (New York: Harper & Row).

PETTIGREW, A. M. (1985), *The Awakening Giant: Change and Continuity in ICI* (Oxford: Blackwell).

—— (1987), 'Context and Action in the Transformation of the Firm', *Journal of Management Studies*, 24/6: 649–70.

——FERLIE, E., and McKEE, L. (1992), *Shaping Strategic Change* (London: Sage).

PFEFFER, J. (1992), *Managing with Power* (Boston, Mass.: Harvard Business School Press).

WASTELL, D. G., WHITE, P., and KAWALEK, P. (1994), 'A Methodology for Business Process Redesign: Experience and Issues', *Journal of Strategic Information Systems*, 3/1: 23–40.

10

Cooperative Relationship Strategy in Global Information Technology Out-sourcing

The Case of Xerox Corporation

Thomas Kern and Leslie P. Willcocks

Information technology (IT) out-sourcing is a decision taken by an organization to contract-out or sell the organization's IT assets, people, and/or activities to a third party vendor, who in return provides managed services for an agreed time period and monetary fee (Lacity and Hirschheim, 1993; Loh and Venkatraman, 1992). Out-sourcing as such is not a new concept; it has been around in the form of application development contracts, in facilities management agreements, and time-sharing deals for several decades (Earl, 1991, 1996). More recently, though, it has become increasingly popular with the drive for organizational core competencies (Prahalad and Hamel, 1990). Its rapid growth since Eastman Kodak's watershed total out-sourcing arrangement in 1989—to an estimated 1999 total of global market revenues of over $80 billion with an annual growth rate of 15 per cent (IDC, 1998; Willcocks and Lacity, 1998)—has ensured it receives extensive world-wide business attention (see, for example, Applegate and Montealegre, 1991; Cross, 1995; Huber, 1993).

Within these developments, and despite their widespread recognition in the non-IT literature on business-to-business cooperation, relationship issues in IT out-sourcing have received surprisingly little academic attention. In the search for an understanding we argue, as others have for comparable business-to-business relationships (e.g. Boddy, Macbeth, and Wagner, chap. 9, above; Doz and Hamel, 1998; Gray, chap, 11 below; Ring and Van de Ven, 1992), that the core notion underlying IT out-sourcing client–vendor relationships is that of exchange. Exchange in inter-firm relations, as Dwyer, Schurr, and Oh (1987) and Hagel and Singer (1999) emphasize, has achieved perennial recognition as a conceptual approach to understanding business relations.

While IT out-sourcing research to date generally emphasizes the criticality of the relationship, very few studies (see Kern, 1997; Klepper, 1995; McFarlan and Nolan, 1995; Willcocks and Choi, 1995; Willcocks and Kern, 1998), have attempted, or been in a position to delineate, the out-sourcing relationship in its main constructs as a basis for analysing out-sourcing arrangements,

211

or for making normative management suggestions. Those who have ad-dressed the out-sourcing relationship commonly present a number of nor-mative management pointers (see, for example, McFarlan and Nolan, 1995) without placing them in the context of the out-sourcing relationship taken as a whole. As a consequence researchers have, for example, understated the degree that out-sourcing will intrinsically raise relationship and transaction costs, in terms of allocating resources, implementing a management structure, and developing operating processes with the vendor. Earl (1996) suggests these are responsible for some of the hidden costs of out-sourcing. It is surprising that such costs have been largely disregarded when considering out-sourcing from the value-chain perspective. IT can be shown to permeate many contemporary complex organizations, not only laterally but also vert-ically. Thus when a vendor is contracted to deliver IT services, especially on a large-scale basis, as at Xerox for example, their exchanges and the impacts will inherently pervade most of the organization (Porter, 1985; Porter and Millar, 1985) and thus raise additional control and monitoring costs (Williamson, 1979; Blois, 1996). Such service pervasiveness can be argued to push the supplier towards a close integration with the client's operations. In fact we argue, with Blois (1972), that out-sourcing relationships of the 'total' kind (80 per cent or more of the IT budget under third party management) in general leads to a 'vertical quasi-integration' of the vendor, by which we refer to a relationship that develops to a level of interdependence where a significant proportion of either party's operations depends on the other(s). And indeed such relationships may move beyond vertical integration towards a form of value-adding partnership (Child and Faulkner, 1998; Faulkner, 1995; John-ston and Lawrence, 1988; Willcocks and Lacity, 1998).

In these situations management exchanges and costs are likely to increase even further and thus place great management demands on both the client and supplier. Lacity and Willcocks (forthcoming) in a study of over 250 case histories, found that such management overhead typically ran to between 4 per cent and 8 per cent of IT out-sourcing's total cost, even before the effectiveness of those management arrangements was assessed. Con-sequently, we argue that large-scale out-sourcing ventures can only be under-taken in the light of a cooperative strategy, as investigated here in the case of Xerox Corporation, or else they are likely to be the subject of significant disappointment. Indeed, this is supported by Willcocks and Lacity (1999), who found some 35 per cent of total out-sourcing arrangements ending in failure, and 28 per cent gaining mixed results due to, amongst other factors, significant weaknesses in the area of relationships and cooperative strategy (see also Lacity and Willcocks, 1998). But the questions this raises are: what contingent factors need to be included in a cooperative out-sourcing strategy to ensure the successful 'vertical quasi-integration' of the supplier? Moreover, what management arrangements need to be in place to ensure effective management and success of such ventures?

In this chapter we investigate these questions by first detailing a conceptual framework of the out-sourcing relationship derived from the inter-organizational, relational contract, and transaction cost literatures, and subsequently empirically substantiated by Kern (1999) in in-depth studies of five organizations. We then apply the framework as a heuristic tool to investigate the Xerox–EDS IT out-sourcing relationship and identify those factors emerging as fundamental for the development of a cooperative out-sourcing strategy. The first part of the chapter reviews briefly three founding theoretical perspectives and develops the logic behind the constructs of the analytical framework. The second section describes the Xerox Corporation case study, with an emphasis on understanding the development of the relationship between Xerox and EDS at the operational level. The third section analyses the case study in light of the analytical framework, elucidating those issues that arose during the development of the relationship that demand consideration in the cooperative strategy at the outset, and proposing those indicators arising for effective management.

Theoretical Perspectives and Analytical Framework

From an in-depth review of the literature three theory sets emerged as particularly relevant to the study of the relationship dimensions of large-scale IT out-sourcing arrangements. These we label inter-organizational relationship (IOR), relational contract (RC), and transaction cost (TCT) theories. Inter-organizational relationship theorists include Aiken and Hage, 1968; Levine and White, 1961; Ford, 1980; Hunt and Nevin, 1974; McAmmon and Whittle, 1963; Van de Ven and Ring, 1994; Wilson, 1989; Dwyer, Schurr, and Oh, 1987. Common to the various types of IOR theories are such constructs as the reasons for the relationships which also determine their context (cf. Galaskiewicz, 1985; Oliver, 1990), the exchanges or interactions between the participants, and the working atmosphere that outlines essentially the behavioural dimension of relations (see, for example, Aldrich and Whetten, 1981; Cunningham, 1980; Van de Ven, 1976). These constructs can be assumed to outline a simple macro perspective of inter-organizational relationships, which in respect to our research also defines a starting point for a simple macro framework of out-sourcing relationships. However this is not a complete picture of business-to-business relations.

Relational contract theory can be traced to Macneil's (1974, 1980, 1987) contributions on the nature and future of contract in business relations. The starting point is classical and neoclassical contract theory's narrow definition of business relations as discrete and completely contingent arrangements, in which no relations exist apart from the simple exchange of goods or services (Goetz and Scott, 1981; Macneil, 1980). Yet Macneil found the existing legal arrangements contradictory to current contracting practice in business relations, especially since Macaulay's (1963) seminal study into contracting practice in manufacturing had clearly highlighted that exchange relations are seldom completely planned, but still entail regular interactions. Contract nevertheless remains an integral part of business-to-business exchange relations, commonly outlining the relations and their interactions (see Blois, 1999), yet the existing legal system does not provide adequate representation. Finally transaction cost theory, particularly as represented by Williamson (1975, 1979, 1985) and as elaborated by Gurbaxani and Whang (1991) and critiqued by Lacity and Willcocks (1995) provides a means for analysing transaction determinants in relation to the efficiency of, and outcomes from, alternative contracting forms.

In a critical review Kern (1999) points out that each theory set has inherent limitations for the study and explication of IT out-sourcing arrangements. Thus, for example, IOR theorists often ignore endogenous and explicit contractual factors. Of primary concern in the case of RC theory is the limited empirical research underlying Macneil's arguments, raising concern about its applicability, while Barnett (1992) further argues that Macneil's concepts suffer from being too polarized on either a relational or discrete agenda. In the case of TCT, Lacity and Willcocks (1995) found the theory operating at too high a level, with concepts too uncalibrated, to be easily testable. Faced with these concerns Kern (1999) developed a composite framework that built upon the complementary, and in some cases overlapping, strengths of the three theory sets and that could be utilized for analysing IT out-sourcing relationships over time. The resulting framework, as shown in Figure 10.1, was subsequently utilized and validated in an in-depth longitudinal study of five IT out-sourcing case histories. Here only a brief description of the framework can be presented, but see Kern (1999) for full details and a discussion on the development and utilization of the framework.

The framework begins with the notion of 'out-sourcing intent', derived largely from the IOR theory set and referring to the objectives and scope pursued through contracting with a vendor. *Necessity* to form exchange relations arises commonly from the need for particular resources (Galaskiewicz, 1985), and can have a mandated or voluntary dimension. *Reciprocity* refers to exchange focusing on common or mutually beneficial goals or interests. *Legitimacy* refers to the underlying political motivations that influence the organization to legitimize IT operations by out-sourcing (Lacity and Hirschheim, 1993) while *efficiency* is employed here as an analytical concept because the out-sourcing relationship has most often been formed to enhance the efficiency of the IT resource and reduce costs (DiRomualdo and Gurbaxani, 1998; Lacity and Willcocks, 1998).

The RC theory set offers understanding of the essential differences between contractual relations along a number of contractual and behavioural dimensions. Here 'contract' is taken to be a promise or set of promises that

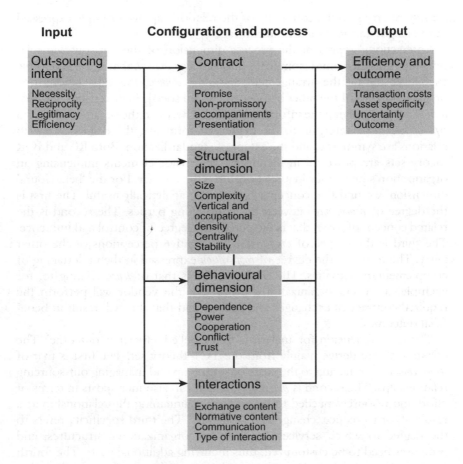

Input

Out-sourcing intent

Necessity
Reciprocity
Legitimacy
Efficiency

Configuration and process

Contract

Promise
Non-promissory
accompaniments
Presentation

Structural dimension

Size
Complexity
Vertical and
occupational
density
Centrality
Stability

Behavioural dimension

Dependence
Power
Cooperation
Conflict
Trust

Interactions

Exchange content
Normative content
Communication
Type of interaction

Output

Efficiency and outcome

Transaction costs
Asset specificity
Uncertainty
Outcome

Fig. 10.1 Conceptual framework for analysing IT out-sourcing relationships

are legally enforceable and binding for the duration of the contractual relationship. The three elements for analysis are *promise*, that is the expected and required exchanges in the relationship, *non-promissory accompaniments* that are non-contractual but help to provide contractual completeness, and *presentiation*, referring to the degree to which future requirements have been brought into, and are covered by, the present contract.

The IOR perspective provides a focus on the 'structure' of an out-sourcing arrangement. The main elements are the *size* of the arrangement and of the parties involved; the *complexity* of services and exchanges, for example some IT out-sourcing arrangements involve multiple suppliers; *vertical and occupational density*, in terms of the number of hierarchical levels, roles, and specialists involved in the relationship; *centrality*, referring to the degree to which information flows are centralized and controlled by the client organization; and *stability*, referring to the continuity of the relationship, for example expressed in the length and renewal of the contract.

'Interactions' represent the process dimension of the out-sourcing relationship. This element decomposes into *exchange content*, that is the economic exchanges during the arrangement; *normative content*, the expectations one organization has of the other because of certain social characteristics; *communication content* involving the information passed between the organizations, and *type of interaction*, referring to the degree of formality, the degree to which relations are symmetric, and the extent of standardization. Both RC and IOR theory sets are powerful in identifying the major elements influencing an organization's behaviour in a relationship with another. For the 'behavioural dimension' we find five concepts as the most analytically useful. The first is the degree of *dependence* between the contracting parties. The second is the related concept of *power*, that is the perceived degree of control and influence. The third is the degree of *conflict* due to negative perceptions of the other party. The fourth is the degree of *cooperation* expressed in the undertaking of complementary activities. The final concept is that of *trust*, relating to, for example, the client organization's belief that the vendor will perform the required contractual exchanges and actions and that this will result in beneficial outcomes.

The final dimension for analysis is that labelled 'efficiency-outcome'. The constructs here derive mainly from the TCT theory set. The first is that of *transaction costs*, referring to the costs of setting up and managing out-sourcing relationships. The second is *uncertainty*, which can also incur costs in terms of effort and resources needed to be put into maintaining the relationship as a result of, or to reduce, change and ambiguity. The third specificity refers to the degree to which services, applications, organizational structures, and processes need to be customized, thus incurring additional costs. The fourth output measure is labelled *outcome*, referring to the degree of expectations that are achieved, including expected benefits, and perceived adequacy of vendor performance.

Operationalization of the out-sourcing deal will depend on cooperation and the development of relationships over time, as Willcocks and Choi (1995) argue. For an understanding of cooperation in out-sourcing we can look to Axelrod's (1984) four strategies for cooperation:

(i) avoid unnecessary conflict by cooperating, as long as the other party does;
(ii) avoid provocation in the face of conflict;
(iii) practise forgiveness after provocation; and
(iv) practise clarity of behaviour so that the other party can adapt to your behaviour.

These are all highly relevant to out-sourcing, but the key for the effectiveness of these strategies is clearly durability of the out-sourcing relationship.

Durability is based on the assumption that if parties can negotiate minimal, congruent expectations for a cooperative inter-organizational relationship, they will make commitments to a course of action for the long term (Van de Ven and Ring, 1994). Thus, punishing non-cooperation in relations at any point in time will create hostility, diminish social solidarity, break down satisfaction and trust; it thus needs to be avoided at all costs (Rogers-Gillmore, 1987). It is the analytical framework and these concepts that guide the construction and study of the Xerox–EDS relationship.

Research Approach

To investigate the out-sourcing relationship and the potential of the framework in a distinctive context we selected the Xerox–EDS out-sourcing case, signed in June 1994. The case was chosen because:

1. it represents one of the largest global IT out-sourcing deals with considerable uncertainties that demand extensive cooperation;
2. it was negotiated with the specific intention to develop a 'strategic relationship' as the contract specifics could not be formulated to include all technology and service requirements; and
3. we could gain access to major participants and stakeholders over a period of six months, which, combined with existing case materials, allowed us to study the relational developments longitudinally.

For the case we interviewed managers in Europe from Xerox and EDS, including senior managers in charge of overseeing numerous IT accounts internationally, an account manager, IT managers, the finance director, and operation managers in charge of local IT strategy, infrastructure, contract, service levels, telecomms, and networks. Some participants were interviewed twice across the six-months research period. Interviews varied from 60 minutes to 120 minutes in length and were conducted using a semi-structured questionnaire with many open-ended questions. All interviewees were assured of anonymity to promote open discussions. Interviews were then transcribed, and verified with the relevant respondents. We then developed a higher level of abstraction and interpretation by applying the precepts of intentional analysis to the transcripts (Sanders, 1982). Additionally we sought supporting documentation in order to construct the case histories. This further corroboration and information was derived from internal documents, annual reviews, reports, presentations by senior managers at Xerox, organizational charts, and secondary literature, including a DBA thesis (Davis, 1996), journal articles, books, existing published case studies, newspapers, and trade press. These sources and procedures allowed us to develop a qualitative, interpretative approach to case-study construction (cf. Walsham, 1995). So constructed, the case history will now be detailed in the next section.

Case Study: Global IT Out-Sourcing at Xerox Corporation

Xerox Corporation contracted EDS for $3.2. billion in 1994 to handle the Corporation's information technology (IT) requirements world-wide. The deal was part of Xerox's strategic restructuring programme to halt its dwindling turnover and to redevelop its global competitiveness. Large investments were required to replace existing legacy and proprietary information systems, and to ensure that Xerox's information infrastructure would support the business processes needed to compete against the strong Asian pressures (Kearns and Nadler, 1995).

This case is of particular interest because, first, it was reputed at the time to be the largest out-sourcing deal ever and the first to be implemented on a global scale. Only a few suppliers could support such a contract. Secondly, the complexity of the undertaking made it necessary to pursue out-sourcing as a cooperative strategy, where the contract would not limit or demarcate the venture in any way. As noted by Jagdish Dalal, head of Xerox's global out-sourcing team, in 1994:

The term outsourcing is inappropriate. This is really more of an integration of two separate businesses. We wanted to take the best parts of each culture and put them together. The same goes for structure, strategy, and people. We will realise substantial economic value if we can achieve commitment to a high degree of integration. It is the spirit of the agreement that creates this commitment; there are no 'mechanisms' that can be put into place as a substitute for the spirit (quoted in Davis and Applegate, 1995.)

However, the intention to cooperate strategically and implement the contract on this basis took a particular twist during post-contract management. Successes are evident in some areas, for example the rapid roll-out of the new information infrastructure was effected in record time, but management of the contract at the local level ran into a number of challenges and difficulties. Reflecting on two and a half years of operating the out-sourcing venture the Head of IT noted:

Generally the reasons that drove us to out-source are still valid. Some of the things we've done over the last couple of years we would not have achieved without an IT partner. But, I think we were naive the way we went into the relationship and we are now having to almost do it again, redefine big areas of the relationship based on the knowledge we now have. Some areas we are probably not getting great value added. *I'm not sure we've achieved anything through out-sourcing.* If we did it again we would probably be more selective, about what we did and what we didn't do. All of that with 20 : 20 hindsight (italics added).

This case presents the story of Xerox's local out-sourcing operations, which is generally representative of the complexities encountered throughout the global venture in 1996.

Company Background

Xerox Corporation is a leading global document processing organization, with revenues in excess of $17.4 billion (Xerox Corporation, 1996). It develops, manufactures, markets, finances, and offers services on a range of products for handling documents around the organization, including photocopiers, digital publishing systems, printers, facsimile machines, scanners, document handling networks, and so on. Xerox's golden years of market dominance in the 1960s and 1970s in this industry declined dramatically in the 1980s, with the loss of its patent protection on Xeroxing, i.e. photocopying. The Japanese onslaught by Canon, Minolta, Ricoh, and Sharp, with improved and cheaper machines, resulted in a decline in market share from an estimated 80 per cent (1970s) of the US copier market to only 13 per cent by 1982 (Kearns and Nadler, 1995). Profits plummeted from $1.15bn in 1980 to $600m in 1982. In comparison to its competitors, 'Xerox's unit manufacturing cost was equal to the Japanese US selling price—and they were making a profit' (Walker, 1992). Xerox's profitability progressively spiralled downwards up to the 1990s. First signs of recovery were apparent in 1993, and since then profitability has steadily improved.

Xerox's turnaround was a result of reinventing the business through extensive restructuring programmes focusing on benchmarking, 'leadership through quality', operational efficiency, and core competencies. Taking into account its inefficiency, restructuring entailed not only a total change of Xerox from a classical command-and-control structure, consisting of discrete hierarchical functions, to a cross-functional participative organization, with a strong team-oriented work ethic, but also entailed a focus on total quality management. Xerox's year 2000 strategy envisaged a completely new organization. Paul Allaire, Xerox CEO, explained: 'each Xerox division [was to have] end-to-end responsibility for a set of products and services, a set of primary market segments, an identifiable set of competitors and an income statement and balance sheet' (Xerox Corporation, 1992: 9).

As part of these efforts Xerox also focused on its core competencies, which eventually resulted in 1993 in the sale of its finance and insurance business. In June 1994, in accordance with its operational efficiency and core competency drive, it globally out-sourced its information technology function to EDS in a 10-year $3.2 billion deal. From 1994 onwards Xerox has experienced a steady recovery, with a growing turnover.

Information Management (IM) Context

Low profitability and the restructuring programmes of the 1980s and early 1990s significantly impacted the IM function at Xerox. Due to insufficient funds, existing systems were unable to supply the required technological support for the envisaged Xerox2000 organization. An internal study sponsored by senior management in mid-1993, found most of the current systems needed renewal since the proprietary technologies and legacy systems were no longer flexible enough to guarantee Xerox's competitiveness. More importantly, they were unable to support the requirements of the new functionally structured organization and systems took up too much management time to keep operational: 'IM managers were probably spending 80 per cent of their time managing legacy systems and 20 per cent of their time worrying about new developments' (Global Head of IT).

Renewal of the current infrastructure was seen as very costly and would undoubtedly necessitate further investments, since the current rate of implementation of new systems and services was not meeting the business requirements. Global out- sourcing was seen as the bridging strategy that would allow IT to support the current business while retiring the outdated infrastructure and applications, and developing the foundation for the future IT strategy to support the business beyond the year 2000. In particular Xerox pursued the following objectives with out-sourcing:

- concentrate resources on future business critical information management (IM) solutions;
- provide a framework where the information management investment becomes a 'variable' cost rather than the current 'fixed' cost;
- reduce or redirect Xerox's spending on information management activities and optimize yield on assets;
- improve IM service levels; and
- gain access to technology to facilitate transition to the new IM environment.

IT Out-Sourcing and Contracting

In August 1993 Xerox began its out-sourcing project. The selection process was initiated in earnest with a 'request for information' (RFI) in September 1993. In a nine-month selection process in which three groups competed for the deal, EDS was eventually selected as the preferred vendor. According to Jagdish Dalal, head of Xerox's Global Out-sourcing team, EDS was chosen because it had a superior global presence, offered a better human-resource programme for transferred employees, and had entered a very competitive bid. In June 1994 Xerox signed the contract with EDS for all of its desktop computing, mid-range, and mainframe systems, which included the worldwide data-centre operations (Mainframe and Midrange), help desks, network operations (both voice and data), legacy applications (maintenance and enhancements—the legacy applications defined 95 per cent of the existing applications), desktop systems support (current and future), and telecommunications services (private networks and use of public networks). EDS also agreed to pay approximately $170 million for transferred IT assets and accepted 1,900 IM employees. According to Johnson (1998), Xerox retained the overall strategic planning role, architecture, and new application development for business process re-engineering.

The eventual 10-year contract signed by senior management at Xerox's US corporate headquarters was a global blanket contract split into two parts: (1) Xerox North and South America and Canada, and (2) Rank Xerox North and Western Europe. Xerox assured adequate legal representation through internal lawyers and third party legal advisors. The contract eventually became a very lengthy document exceeding 1,000 pages. Xerox generally found it very difficult to write a detailed contract for an arrangement of this magnitude.

One of the problems was we wanted to out-source something that we were not doing and particularly in the infrastructure where we were really just at the beginning of a major change in our technical environment; we were moving a whole office infrastructure from Xerox proprietary software and hardware to industry standard PCs and networking. We really weren't doing any of that, we were at the start of that exercise but we out-sourced the management of that new environment to EDS. And it's very difficult to out-source something you don't understand. [Thus,] a number of out-sourcing criteria were completely unpredictable and unspecifiable because we had no experience with the technology we needed (Head of IT).

To ensure EDS would commit sufficient resources, experts, and skilled people, Xerox decided to write a very open contract with financial arrangements that would encourage EDS to perform. Senior management was intent on developing a partnership with EDS rather than establishing a supplier–buyer model. This was to be apparent throughout the contract:

We went into it with the partnership idea in mind. I don't mean a financial or legal partnership, but a cooperative, collaborative approach in mind... And the only way you can make that kind of partnership arrangement work is if you write a contract that encourages that. And then it probably has to be very loose because you are almost into a contract that says EDS will manage our whole IT operation for us, and here are some objectives (Head of IT).

Additionally, a distinct and unique 'evergreen concept' that ensured an adaptive contract was to be contractually integrated. The concern was to have sufficient flexibility to cater for the uncertainty of the changes to be implemented with the roll-out of the new infrastructure and other changes:

We have an IM strategy which is called 'Evergreen Strategy' in that it sits in an electronic document that we both have access to and it defines our infrastructure and IM goals in about an 18-month to 2-year planning horizon. So it's targeted at people like programme managers, departmental managers, who want to make investments in their area. It acts as a guideline for them over their planning period to determine how and where they should make their investments. It also acts at the next level down as our project and programme plan with EDS (IT Strategy Manager).

In line with the 'evergreen' concept, an adaptive pricing strategy was adopted, with an emphasis on decreasing the overall costs. EDS committed to pay cash for assets and expense reductions and to provide year-on-year productivity improvements. To assure pricing remained in line with EDS's proposal, the contract incorporated a benchmark scheme. This guaranteed that EDS's prices remained competitive world-wide. The price benchmarks consisted of forty different price elements rather than an aggregate price. These were then measured annually according to a previously compiled price index. This diminished the possibility of dramatic price swings and avoided renegotiation of the contract to adjust pricing, since every year prices would be automatically renewed.

Post-Contract Management

Transition Period (1994–1995).   As proposed by EDS in its bid, the transition activity took 6 months. Through the creation of a transition alliance team, staff and asset transfers were completed for the 20 countries in a remarkably short time, by December 1994. EDS's integration was well on its way. Having taken ownership and accountability of the out-sourced IT functions, the next steps were migration and closer integration. Actions were taken that supported change in processes, people, structure, strategy, and culture. In particular, initial post-contract management focused on operationalizing the service-level agreements, clarifying the contract for the local level, establishing rapport, and implementing management infrastructure and processes at local levels. In parallel EDS initiated programmes to consolidate, standardize, and change the proprietary and legacy systems.

Central IT was placed in charge of coordinating standardization, and generally controlling the strategic direction. For each part out-sourced a separate strategy framework was established—e.g. infrastructure, computing, applications, and telecommunications—that defined on a two-year basis the local strategic direction. Throughout the lifetime of the contract, the central management group was to be the custodian of the contract. Any clarification needed was negotiated and agreed by central management and then communicated back to the operational level.

IT managers at the local level, in turn, had to rely on EDS initially to take the lead in implementing the particulars of the contract. Local managers were given only limited access and sight of the contract, and basically inherited the contract. Their understanding strongly depended on EDS:

Xerox negotiated and initiated this world-wide contract centrally, corporately with EDS in the States. So we had to then just pick up on the back of that, and that has then been implemented in each country on the back of this blanket contract (Finance Director).

I can't go to EDS and renegotiate the charges, the pricing structures or charging methods, or basic terms and conditions of the relationship. They are set. So when we meet with our local EDS counterpart, we can't do anything about changing the contract structure in the terms and conditions in which we are operating, all we can do is try and work together to make sure that we get the best out of the structure that we are presented with in terms of contract and cooperation (IT Manager).

Continuity of service in the transition phase was guaranteed through the residual group of IT managers and the former employees who had transferred from the IM department to the vendor. However, total reliance on this management infrastructure was however not possible, as some of the former colleagues were geographically relocated early on. Relations quite quickly faded away and new relations had to be built. The local infrastructure generally consisted of retained IM managers. For example, seven key managers were retained and each was placed in charge of a particular area, mainly infrastructure, cost control, service-level management, telecomms strategy and operations, IM strategy, and process area support.

EDS, in turn, dedicated at the outset an entire 'global strategic business unit' (SBU) to the account. In theory service management was to be handled through this business unit, whereas individually created customer-facing groups would interact with the managers and users at the local level. For example, for Xerox at the local level EDS's management infrastructure consisted of an account manager, an operations manager, and a number of managers who had previously been the technical IM staff at Xerox. This structure was to ensure that managers were culturally in touch with Xerox and understood the organizational pressures.

Similar arrangements were made by EDS for the management processes. EDS initially had to work with the existing processes, before they could begin adding new processes. It was a matter of learning and understanding the inheritance before changing processes:

When you take over an operation in out-sourcing you don't understate the processes that you are going to take over. A lot of the customers say 'Oh, we thought you'd bring your own processes'. But you can't just come and break what's there and throw it away and impose processes, you have to work with what's there to some extent. And maybe we could do with some other processes which we could bring into the account. So we are dependent upon the relationship and if the relationship doesn't start off well things tend to deteriorate. People become focused on the letter of the contract rather than the spirit of the contract or the intent. And then they start to focus on it's us and them (EDS Account Manager).

In summary, the transition period for EDS was about taking accountability and ownership, whereas for Xerox it meant an initial payment of a lump sum for the assets transferred. The infrastructure and management processes were laid down. All parties reported the transition as having been handled well.

Post Transition Period: Migration and Operationalization at Xerox (1995–1996). Following the successful transition, Xerox was now expecting EDS to truly overhaul its existing centralized mainframe systems and roll out the new decentralized IT infrastructure. Desktop computing and client-server systems were to replace existing proprietary systems. Local area networks, wide area networks, and telecomms systems were to be changed in accordance with the installation of PCs and the new client-server architecture. In addition, relations were to be fostered and strengthened, and management processes established. This entailed making sense of the contract at the local level and shaping it to local, idiosyncratic operational methods.

EDS's revamping of the infrastructure progressed rapidly in this period, with up to 70,000 new desktop computers expected to be installed and integrated into a corporation-wide network architecture. The undertaking was of enormous size:

The new infrastructure roll out is going very well. We will complete the whole thing in 2.5 years which everybody in the industry told us we are crazy to even attempt. People talked about it taking 3-4-5 years to do that, and we will have done it in 2.5 years and it's working. It's well accepted now by the general population. So in that sense it's been very successful. We could not have done that before the contract, we could not have done that at the time even if we'd wanted to. Equally well we could not have got as far as we have as quickly as we have in building that new infrastructure without an IT partner (Global IT Manager).

At the local level, in early 1995 EDS began implementing a new 'Novell'-based local area network architecture, which would eventually cater for approximately 2000 industry-standard desktop computers running Microsoft Office. This was a considerable step towards phasing out the Xerox XMS-based work-stations. To manage this changeover key dates were agreed and integrated into an electronic 'evergreen strategy' that outlined the dates by when implementations were to be completed, and when new projects were to begin. This document guided management on both sides for a two-year planning horizon and allowed IM managers strategic oversight. It also allowed managers, in the light of specific requirements, to forecast the annual IT budget. In addition there were all the daily routine problem resolutions and request issues to be overseen. In the beginning, IM managers had to rely on EDS to provide them with the information to monitor service performance, which was only conveyed by specific requests. The formalization of management processes was taking time but it was believed to be EDS's account team's responsibility to implement these.

To smooth operations, efforts were made to foster relations. EDS managers required a period of adjustment, and IM managers gave them space to adapt to their idiosyncratic operations. In addition, they helped where possible by coaching and advising on former practices. A number of social activities were instigated. These team-building exercises gave both sides the opportunity to actually meet their counterparts outside the workplace. This was an important part of fostering interpersonal relations, and was in the spirit of developing the Xerox–EDS partnership.

A big part of post-contract management at the operational level focused on localizing the contract. In the cases where contract parts were available both management groups informally agreed a local understanding of the contract. It was a matter of clarifying between the parties how best to implement the agreement. For example, the contract specified a single charge for the installation of software on a PC. So, if a user wanted five programs loaded on his PC, that would be one charge. Xerox UK's interpretation of this for five PCs with software requirements in one room also meant one charge. EDS obviously interpreted that differently, and a local understanding of this type of charging was reached. More complicated matters were referred to the central headquarters, but these high-level interpretations slowly began to subside. However, relations remained tense between EDS's management team and Xerox's IM group. EDS was encountering serious management difficulties, causing service levels to suffer: 'After the transition was the low. In many areas service levels went to hell in a hand basket, [and] there were lots of issues in the business about IT costs' (Head of IT).

The revamping was progressing rapidly, but a number of problems were not being addressed. For example, the high demand for desktop computing resulted in networks being so overloaded that they eventually crashed. EDS found itself fire-fighting to fix problems and not addressing the root cause of the problems:

Over the year we must have installed well over 2000 terminals on to the LAN and during that time nobody has been looking at what's happening with the traffic. Consequently most of the services we have grounded to a halt. Users are complaining that it takes 5 minutes to get a response back on your terminal. Not long ago the network just collapsed. When they came to fix it they found that it was running the traffic levels at 87 per cent. Just to give you an example, I would expect an average network to run at 15 per cent. When it gets to 20 per cent you are talking about it being overloaded and you ought to start looking at ways of reducing the traffic, segmenting it to keep some of the traffic off (Telecomms Manager).

In effect, EDS's managers were running into problems managing the migration and integration, while in parallel handling the day-to-day problems and requests. IM managers realized their difficulties and tried to help as much as they could, but circumstances were generally not improving:

I didn't bother complaining because it's a waste of time. There was a state even in the early days, 6 months into the contract, where the IM team sat down and prioritized what we wanted to talk to EDS about—which problems. And although we'd got major problems in one area we said alright we will just ride that and not say anything; we will just give them these because we don't want to swamp them with too much to do' (Strategy Manager).

Frustrated managers began to micro-manage their former staff, taking control of service delivery management. This was, however, clearly contrary to the idea of freeing managers from routine service management to focus on the strategy and oversight of EDS. In addition, they were in effect, on several points, doing EDS's job:

After a while, though, it was clear that things weren't happening the way we would have liked, so we started creeping back in and just having a look to see what was going on. Then I carried out a coaching and guidance role with other members of my team; if they had a problem they would speak to me about it. And I gradually crept back in carrying out that management role (Telecomms Manager).

The difficulties were reflected by the inadequate management infrastructure EDS had implemented at the local level. One respondent commented: 'they [EDS] promoted their best programmers to managers, so producing a community of poor managers and deficient programmers. So this led to a very weak supervisory capability, which still exists to a certain extent' (Strategy Manager).

EDS had appointed only one operational manager to face off against six IM managers—each with a different and specific set of queries and requests. The operational manager became inundated with demands and requests, and was rarely able to follow them up. Although EDS as an organization had all the specialist managers and technicians in the background, they were not supposed to be interfacing with the customer. For example, when Xerox managers wished to discuss an issue with a technical manager they either had to go through the account team, or the technical manager would be chaperoned by an EDS manager. In addition, the account manager and the IT manager did not get along too well, which further complicated relations. Relations eventually came to a standstill. End user satisfaction was at an all-time low of 52 per cent (Johnson, 1998). The initial high level of confidence following the transition was eroded. Trust was at an all-time low and technology and services were failing. Problems were mounting.

It turned out that neither party at the highest levels had really planned for the actual operationalization of the contract at the local level. The vagueness of the contract complicated matters for the IM managers, as they were dependent on EDS to implement the specifics. Indeed, the visionary perspective of what EDS was to do for Xerox was there, but the detail of the management processes was missing.

The severity of the problems had filtered through to the senior levels at EDS, and senior management had to become more actively involved in developing relations. No blame was to be apportioned. It was recognized amongst Xerox managers that more attention should have been paid initially to clearly defining roles and responsibilities, services, level of service, and pricing (Johnson, 1998). These had been found to complicate effective processes. As a result Xerox decided in 1996 to clarify the individual frameworks. The first one to be addressed was the infrastructure framework. The others were to be renegotiated at a later stage.

Global Contract Renegotiation (1996).   After only one and a half years contract renegotiations were initiated by Xerox for three reasons. First, it became possible following the revamping of the legacy infrastructure to specify in detail the service levels. Secondly, both parties found that the contract in totality should have been more robust on a number of issues, which were to be clarified in the renegotiation. And thirdly, Xerox's IM management had concluded that partnering was not going to work as initially envisaged and relations would have to become more formalized.

The middle of last year (1996), maybe a bit earlier, when the IM management team across Xerox really came to the conclusion that we were going to have to change the way we were trying to manage the relationship and move it to a strict supplier relationship. And that's really when we got into redefinition of the whole infrastructure agreement (Head of IT).

In effect, in the coming years each framework was to be formalized. To begin with, the service requirements and pricing for the 'global desktop management services (GDMS)' were to be addressed. This agreement focused purely on the new infrastructure and included network architecture, computing (PC, mid-frame, and mainframe), software, and new developments. Prior to the GDMS, services were sparsely documented. In some cases, simple rules guided infrastructure services and pricing. In large part these were based upon Xerox's IM2000 infrastructure intentions, but exact service levels could not be formalized. Prices were calculated on a time rate, and a minimum charge was raised for call-outs, including software and PC installations. These unprecedented costs pushed the overall cost up and since the infrastructure after two years had been more or less complete, it became possible to formalize pricing and services. By having an agreement that outlined the charges and services it was hoped the amount of local negotiations and disputes could be diminished: 'with the GDMS we can understand now what each side is talking about. In there you find everything about services. It's down in writing now so we can refer to a page and say it does mean X or Y, because it was agreed with EDS locally. Whereas before there wasn't anything' (Contract Manager).

The importance of the GDMS for Xerox was that services were now working out cheaper to run because the agreement defined certain activities as being for free, for example standard software upgrades on PCs were no longer charged for. Moreover, the service levels stated in the GDMS became better defined and more precise than they had been, giving the residual IM groups at the local level the means for monitoring service performance.

We can measure against service levels and both sides can judge and see whether we are getting the service, and EDS can see what they need to do to get up the service level that they've got to provide. The down side of it is that service levels are only measured at a very high level so we don't have a separate measure . . . So we are trying to push for those same measures more locally. So here we should be measuring how

EDS is doing rather than doing it at the European level. It should be done at a smaller level. That's the only thing I've got against it. It's very detailed; it's all in there. But then it's measured at too high a level to be meaningful and to give us a reassurance that we are having a bad service but it's being acted upon (Contract Manager).

The lack of local consideration comes back to the nature of the contract being global and negotiated centrally. Out-sourcing as well as all other service changes such as the GDMS are imposed on each subsidiary. The logic of this was economies of scale and the avoidance of duplication, but the subsidiaries implementing the out-sourcing terms tended to have difficulties with the obscurity of the details of the contract. In many circumstances, centralized IM management was found to be too detached from the operational level of the subsidiaries. Moreover, input from the operational level was marginalized. At the same time operational managers reported that a globally negotiated agreement might be the only option for large-scale out-sourcing ventures.

Throughout 1996 Xerox's central IM group proceeded with its in-depth evaluations of the other out-sourced functions. In particular they looked into telecomms and their service agreement.

There are some of the services under the telecomms umbrella where it's difficult to see what value EDS have added. All that has happened in that area is that EDS collects the bills from whoever the carrier is and passes them on to us. So we've said what value added is there in this? Are they really incentivized in any way to make sure that we are getting the best deal, which is a serious concern in Europe right now with deregulation and the growing competition. Tariffs are changing so rapidly and vendor offerings are changing so rapidly. And that's an area where we are in discussions with EDS (Head of IT).

Also, the support agreement of the client-server applications environment came under discussion. Xerox expected, through the eventual renegotiations, to be able to manage EDS more in line with other service procurement arrangements they had operated prior to the total out-sourcing venture. Indeed, they hoped that EDS's commitment to the service agreement would help rebuild the confidence in IT services all round and improve overall satisfaction.

Maturing Relations (1997 and Beyond).   Following the difficulties between 1994 and 1996, relations at the local level became more structured. The GDMS allowed both parties to operate more along the lines of the required service levels, and processes could be implemented to ensure these were being achieved. The venture to date has been successful in a number of areas and has provided some real benefits to its end-users. According to Johnson (1998) Xerox end-users now have access to IT capabilities that allow them to:

- develop and share spreadsheets, databases, and correspondence with Xerox, customers, and suppliers;

- use powerful graphics for better communication;
- work virtually anywhere with a laptop computer;
- communicate with other employees, customers, and suppliers from any-where internally and externally;
- access CD-ROM-based information; and
- browse both the Internet and Xerox Intranet, and take advantage of this new communication medium to keep up with competitors and colleagues.

The success of these changes has been in the value added for Xerox. According to senior Xerox managers it has brought Xerox closer to its customers, enhanced their ability to position their products better in the marketplace, generally improved computer literacy in the organization, and enabled the development of new applications on the common infrastructure (Johnson, 1998).

However, operations at the local level, especially in the UK, still remained strained initially following the contract clarification. Dramatic changes had to be undertaken that saw the IM group take control of the account. They called for an exception review in early 1997, as a number of ongoing problems needed urgent attention and EDS was mainly fire-fighting with routine problems. A root cause analysis identified 81 areas requiring urgent action. For example, technology requirement actions included a review of the wide area network, changes for network links between different sites, local area network upgrades, new telecomms technology, and so on. As one respondent noted:

It was very much a two-way thing. We identified the issues and EDS recognized and reacted very positively to them. It could have gone differently. If our relationship with EDS hadn't been particularly good it could have been just a head-to-head stand off... But they worked with us in a quality manner, went through the quality process, brought people in with experience to identify the root cause and came up with recommendations. They went through a process of clearance with us, we agreed them and now they are implementing them (IT Manager).

Of the 81 actions, 41 had been completed by EDS, 29 were in progress, and 11 were on hold by April 1997. An area that demanded particular attention and change was EDS's account structure. Xerox required EDS to mirror their structure, which meant appointing an operational manager in charge of each framework, i.e. application service delivery, infrastructure, telecomms, computing, and contract coordinator.

Establishing a formal structure was an important step. At least now dedicated managers would focus on issues in specific areas. In addition, the IM group formalized the management processes, which they imposed on EDS. This specified the regularity of meetings, i.e. weekly, monthly, quarterly, and yearly, the type of review meeting, i.e. infrastructure, finance, SLA, or account review, and the required documentation and people to attend. The management processes enabled managers to table problems, requests, and specific issues, and new procedures were agreed on how to handle these. For example, all changes requests and EDS quotes were to be authorized by both parties, so disputes could no longer arise about pricing and changes.

EDS was committed to improving relations at the local level, as is evident through the willingness to take the changes on board and enforce the actions that emerged from the exception review. Moreover, EDS's senior management involvement was another sign of their cooperativeness to improve relations. Their endeavours to improve relations had a positive impact on the IM managers. Confidence in EDS was improving and trust in the new account managers' honesty and openness about certain issues was welcomed. IM managers understood the frustration they themselves faced internally at EDS. EDS's account team were customers in their own strategic business unit for certain services. For example, when problems occurred with the telecomms at Xerox the account manager had to contact EDS's telecomms organization, which is another arm's-length organization sub-contracted to deliver these services. This organization is far removed from the actual site, as a result of which the response rate to problems has been low.

What we are doing now is that EDS have come in to conduct a complete audit and operational analysis of our telecomms networks and structures and back-up facilities and contingency plans. Because again we've had back-up facilities and contingency plans, and lo and behold when they've been called upon they haven't worked either (Finance Director).

Cooperating to ensure resolution to problems was of importance in these issues, for not even the account management team could be made responsible for all the problems. Of course this was realized by both parties. Ultimately, their earlier decision about formalizing services in the frameworks would be most likely to improve relations at the local level.

However, the more recent changes and the renegotiation in 1996 were clearly in line with senior management's decision to formalize relations. As pointed out by a manager with reference to Xerox's future strategy:

The route we are going down now is moving more towards a supplier relationship. I think we've pretty much given up any ideas we had that this was going to be a partnership or closer to the partnership end of the scale. What that means to us is we will have to go back and more closely define some of the services, we will have to review the pricing, we will have to be much more formal in the way we deal with EDS in terms of giving them a demand case for what we want, in terms of setting expectations very clearly and in terms of measuring their performance against those service level agreements and project agreements. But that will cost us in resources for sure, because when we out-sourced we didn't plan to manage the relationship as closely as we are actually doing, and will do in the future. So we didn't keep a resource to do that. We will almost certainly have to put some back in place.

Analysis and Discussion

The Xerox case demonstrates some early successes and difficulties with total out-sourcing on a global scale, and also emphasizes the challenges of fostering a relationship at the operational level that is constrained by contractual incompleteness and technological uncertainty. Generally, in terms of forming a relationship it is fairly clear that Xerox and EDS started with high hopes of a 'strategic partnership' based on integration, trust, and close relations. However, the complexity of the global deal lead Xerox's senior managers over time to secure a more traditional client–supplier relationship based on a much more formalized and detailed contractual basis. On one view, this could be interpreted as a straightforward progression of filling out the details of the contract that was not available at the beginning, due to high degrees of uncertainty about what was technically and organizationally required and could be expected. On another view, indeed the retrospective view of many senior Xerox managers, the 'strategic partnering' concept was always a flawed one. It was an over-generalized approach requiring too little attention to contract detail, performance measurement, and the formalization of management processes and arrangements necessary to operationalize and deliver such a large-scale mutual undertaking. The need to renegotiate in 1996 underlines the plausibility of this second interpretation. Indeed, it became clear that a poor contract did not help in securing good relationships, but that the improved (but still developing) post-1996 contractual arrangements were a better basis on which to develop cooperative relationships.

Out-Sourcing Intent

Out-sourcing at Xerox became a necessity because of the financial difficulties and the lack of funds to invest in restructuring the proprietary systems. Throughout the case strong Asian competitive pressure continued to push Xerox towards greater operational efficiency and a focus on its core competence. To cope with such pressures Xerox envisaged a more nimble and responsive company, built around a divisional organization structure spanned by modern information and communication systems that would enhance communications throughout the organization and with its customers. The investment needed to implement such a new systems infrastructure, that would be technologically capable of supporting the operational efficiency drive and Xerox's envisaged IM2000 organization, exceeded the financial liquidity of Xerox. Out-sourcing in turn identified an option that Xerox could not disregard. It offered access to the necessary resources and ensured IT service continuation, while in conjunction giving rise to a one-off cash injection of $170 m, decreasing the head-count, eliminating a number of assets, and securing an annual cost reduction.

However, out-sourcing presented not only a bridging strategy to procure the necessary human, technological, and financial resources, but also enabled the IM department to legitimize both its operations and its radical revamp of Xerox's IT infrastructure globally, in an environment where IM's services were essentially seen as ineffective and costly. For IM managers, out-sourcing provided access to resources that in-house would have required extensive cost–benefit justification and senior management approval. In turn out-sourcing also alleviated the political bureaucracy for the IM group.

Finally, a high degree of reciprocity was envisaged as Xerox pursued out-sourcing with the intention of forming a 'strategic relationship' with EDS. Xerox actually had few alternatives but to enter into an arrangement with ample flexibility and a high degree of cooperation and collaboration. This was essential as Xerox had little experience with the technology they were aiming to implement for their new infrastructure and had to rely on EDS's expertise.

In essence, Xerox planned to out-source a problem and a number of highly uncertain IT functions and operations, but expected through close collaboration to attain technical, business, and financial improvements. Previous research warns of such undertakings, since they give suppliers too much control and the chance to act opportunistically (Lacity and Hirschheim, 1993; Currie and Willcocks, 1997; Willcocks, Fenny, and Islei, 1997). A large proportion of similar cases almost all encountered serious problems (Willcocks and Lacity, 1998). Moreover, in terms of cooperation the resulting asymmetry in the relationship provides an unbalanced basis upon which to develop closer relations.

Contract

Xerox encountered a number of complexities in devising a contract that provided sufficient promissory comprehensiveness in terms of its requirements. The scale of the venture prohibited Xerox from integrating the numerous divisions and subsidiaries in the contract formulation and thus the contract was negotiated centrally. The contract in turn became very general and lacked local, i.e. operational, clarity. Furthermore Xerox's uncertainty as to what its exact technological requirements were for revamping the infrastructure meant that it could not formulate specific promises, but could only provide specific technological objectives. This led to the development of guiding promissory 'evergreen' frameworks or strategies, which were updated and amended as requirements arose.

Xerox's reliance on two key non-promissory accompaniments to ensure it would be able to achieve its out-sourcing intent—the 'evergreen' framework and the strategic relationship—proved insufficient. The 'evergreen' approach was to facilitate promissory flexibility for EDS to develop and implement the infrastructure in a record time. However, EDS focused too much of their attention on achieving the high-level strategic objectives and too little on maintaining Xerox's ongoing day-to-day service requirements. Relying solely on the non-promissory discretion of EDS (i.e. the ideals of a strategic partner) proved insufficient to ensure the successful continuation of the venture and the achievement of Xerox's service expectations, forcing Xerox eventually to renegotiate the individual technology frameworks with the objective of formalizing the promissory requirements.

The case highlighted that by not attempting to provide the service requirements the supplier was given too much control and free reign. It also made the operationalization of the contract at the local level near impossible and led to a relational breakdown and frequent conflicts. Both parties suffered locally from the lack of presentation and ultimately it led to a decrease in confidence in EDS's capabilities at both operational and senior management levels.

Two key factors influenced the shape of the out-sourcing contract: the parties' decision to form a 'strategic partnership, based on closer integration, and the technological uncertainty and hence unspecifiability of Xerox's exact requirements in substantial parts of the contract. The renegotiation led to a detailed redefinition of the infrastructure agreement, much more detailed definitions of service levels, equipment, and pricing, and tightening of EDS's competitiveness throughout. In summary, although the original contractual framework had all the hallmarks for cooperation, the incompleteness proved debilitating and actually hampered relational developments.

Structure

Few suppliers were sufficiently resourced to handle the complexity and size of Xerox's proposed undertaking. Indeed, the bidding process highlighted that such mega-deals have been restricted to only the largest out-sourcing service suppliers, and even for those players it still presents an enormous business venture. The selection of EDS as the sole vendor presented EDS with the largest global out-sourcing deal ever in 1994, and in turn a considerable percentage of their business. The significance of the deal to EDS was apparent in the allocation of a strategic business unit to handle the venture. In addition, EDS agreed to integrate Xerox's business services into their service portfolio, with the objective of benefiting from Xerox's long standing industry excellence for quality and leading-edge technology in handling documents around an organization.

The complexity of Xerox's global infrastructure renewal and general service demand pushed EDS to dedicate an entire strategic business unit to appropriately resource the venture. Yet again in some areas EDS was clearly at its limits and the strain became evident in, for example, the frequent local firefighting situations to deal with problems for the short term, the lack of sufficiently experienced staff to resource account management teams, and the general decrease in service-level satisfaction ratings. The demand of the infrastructure renewal seemed to consume an enormous amount of resources, especially with the goal of revamping it in two and half years, rather than the industry norm of four to five years. The benefit of completing it in such a record time was not apparent, as the contract was set for 10 years, yet in the mean time confidence, service levels, and expectations of EDS decreased to such a degree that senior managers preferred to formalize relations in the future.

The case highlighted that Xerox should have required EDS to mirror the vertical and occupational density arrangements of their management infra-structure at the operational level from the start. Although both parties had formalized a high-level management structure of the proposed X*EDS organization, it provided little detail for operationalization of the deal at the local level. Indeed managers at the operational level were left to develop and implement a management structure that best suited their own individual requirements. The result was that at Xerox UK few overlaps existed between EDS and Xerox's management infrastructure. Clearly EDS's manager was overburdened and his inability to respond to all demands eventually lead IM managers to micro-manage their former staff and circumvent EDS's manage-ment structure. The resolution came through forcing EDS to mirror Xerox's infrastructure in 1997. An improvement in the work situation was soon noted by all managers involved. It is also plausible to assume that the stability of the relationship at Xerox could have been improved if Xerox had indeed determined from the start that EDS should mirror their management infra-structure.

The degree of information centrality contributed to the conflicts and relational problems. Indeed up to 1997 Xerox UK had little influence over the centrality of the information flows, which frequently caused frustrations to IM managers. Their dependence on information from EDS to monitor their performance was only alleviated with the implementation of a manage-ment process that both parties followed. This marked a change in the degree of centrality, which generally proved to have a positive effect on the relation-ship.

Interactions

It is evident that the contract negatively influenced interactions in the rela-tionship at local levels in Xerox. The lack of exchange content detail con-tributed to the operational and relational complexities encountered by managers from both parties. In fact, the uncertainty surrounding the ex-change content and EDS's service delivery responsibilities increased the confusion during the initial turmoil of the transition period. In terms of the relationship this had a negative impact on the operational managers as they had little basis upon which to develop a relationship. In fact the ongoing disputes about the exchange content unsettled relations and disrupted the development of a true working relationship. Xerox's decision to renegotiate and formalize exchange content and its relations in late 1996/7 brought about an improvement in this direction.

The case also illustrated that the interactions in terms of communication between the parties during the initial two years, up to 1997, were characteristically asymmetric in favour of EDS and lacked any degree of formality and standardization. Two corroborative reasons can be identified. First, the deficiency of clear management processes on both sides meant no formal interaction arrangements existed that required EDS to report regularly about performance targets, problems, requests, and new technological developments. Secondly, the lack of detail concerning the exchange content and the technological developments EDS was undertaking to revamp the infrastructure, meant IM managers had to rely on EDS for information to monitor their performance. This information dependence was further complicated by the ineffective management infrastructure and processes, which hindered regular interactions.

Once the management processes were formalized in 1997 by Xerox's managers and imposed on EDS, the communication content was also determined. In intervals of weekly, monthly, quarterly, and yearly meetings particular information was expected to be exchanged concerning technical, organizational, strategic, and financial aspects of the venture. By enforcing these processes Xerox effectively regained control. It ensured consistent information flows about the progress and performance of EDS.

Behavioural Dimension

The case highlights that the principles of cooperation cannot be transferred across the client or vendor organization's management levels in out-sourcing, but need to develop between every client–vendor management team handling a part of the deal. Although integral to both parties' objective of forming a 'strategic relationship', the high degree of cooperation and collaboration fostered during the initial contract negotiations between Xerox (headquarters) and EDS's senior management could not be transferred to Xerox UK's account management team. Indeed, it was planned that the centrally negotiated contract and the 'spirit of strategic partnership initiative' would inform how relationships were to operate globally. But local relations could not conform to this 'ideal', as they encountered too many routine problems, i.e. conflicts. The approach was too distant from operational reality, as noted by a local account executive:

The approach taken of 'let's work together' probably was the correct approach but maybe it was done a little naively; because two people can work together who have built a relationship in the centre, but the assumption that that relationship, which has been built up over a few months, not just like this, can just be delegated to people locally is wrong (EDS Account Manager).

In this case the persistence of conflicts and EDS's inability to resolve these, diminished Xerox UK's managers' willingness to cooperate and eventually led to stalemate. The development towards a relational breakdown became visible in the growing degree of dis-trust and lack of confidence, which eventually peaked with Xerox's IM managers circumventing EDS's account managers and approaching their former IT staff directly. At senior management levels the ongoing operational problems across the numerous Xerox accounts diminished the degree of confidence and openness and led managers to decrease the extent to which EDS managers were strategically involved. Relations became essentially more formalized.

In combination these actions signified a turning point in the relationship and the behaviour of IM managers towards the venture across management levels. Indicative of the changes to come was the balance of power-dependence levels. Xerox entered the venture knowing that it depended on EDS to formalize, define, implement, and then manage its technological requirements for the new infrastructure. Some alleviation of this high degree of dependence was sought through developing a strategic relationship, but the early signs, after one-and-a-half years, suggested this seemed unachievable as planned. Xerox thus had to backtrack speedily and to contractually formalize the relationship to regain greater control, i.e. power over how the venture would continue over the next eight years.

Efficiency-Outcome Dimension

The uncertainty surrounding Xerox's venture disrupted contract implementation and relationship management and substantially increased transaction costs. In particular during the transition period it became evident that the uncertainty of the technological requirements and the contractual incompleteness seriously disrupted local operationalization of the contract, as little guidance was available by which operational managers could maintain service demands and Xerox managers could monitor EDS's performance. The unavailability of specific service terms in the long run presented considerable management difficulties and had to be addressed by formulating local interpretation of the contract and separate informal service agreements. Alleviation was only to come with the renegotiation of the first technology framework in 1996. Others were to be renegotiated in the following years.

Both the high degree of uncertainty and specificity effectively pushed the venture towards a 'strategic partnership'. Two issues in particular emphasized the degree of specificity involved, which equivalently meant that for either party switching would be extremely costly, if not impossible. First, the 'evergreen concept' presented a unique industry and contract innovation that was essential to ensure the ongoing representativeness of Xerox's contract in relation to the technological innovations EDS was implementing with the infrastructure overhaul. Xerox identified this arrangement as a necessity to achieve its objectives and maintain its IT service needs and mandated EDS to implement it. Secondly, the planned integration of Xerox and EDS was to result in the X*EDS organization. The amount of resources Xerox had transferred (1900 people) led EDS to dedicate a complete strategic business unit. This specificity effectively implied a lock-in for both parties.

The transaction costs for Xerox of having to localize the contract, develop over the initial transition year another local service agreement, and to impose a pre-formalized management structure and processes substantially increased the overall costs for Xerox. The problem resulted in part from the uncertainty about what exactly Xerox wanted, which was not evident at a high level and consequently could not be communicated to the people at the operational level who had to make it work. Xerox had to rely on EDS as an IT partner to formalize their technological specifications. However, Xerox's overarching infrastructure-renewal objective quite possibly over-spanned EDS's resource competence at the time. The effect was insufficiently resourced account management teams in terms of skills and experience in the UK, which caused IM managers to take on management responsibilities that normally EDS should have covered. Substantial coordination costs for Xerox UK arose and were only alleviated through the subsequent exception review in late 1996 and the imposition of a formal management structure and processes that EDS had to mirror.

In terms of outcomes at the macro level EDS's achievements were significant. The transition period was handled successfully within six months. EDS's resource competence and experience led to the successful deployment of a new infrastructure within two-and-a-half years. The enormity of the changeover of the centralized structure to a decentralized structure with the roll-out of approximately 70,000 PCs is unusual in out-sourcing cases. EDS was revealed as relatively competent at large-scale changes in the sense that very few suppliers could have handled the magnitude and complexity of Xerox's undertaking. EDS also gave access to technology that would otherwise not have been available so quickly, if at all, to Xerox. However, at the micro level it became clear that out-sourcing did not allow the refocusing of IM managers' attention. In a not untypical finding (Feeny and Willcocks, 1998), in-house staff still found themselves doing a lot of the work, this being partly an indicator of the underestimation by EDS and Xerox of the management time and effort needed to manage long-term mega-deals. The effect of poor operations management led to an all-time low level of end-user service satisfaction.

Links Between the Dimensions

At least nine strong links are evident in the case.

- The reciprocal and efficiency intent was clearly reflected in the contract in terms of forming a strategic partnership and ensuring continuous cost reductions.

- A link can be determined between structure and efficiency-outcome in terms of the size and complexity of the venture and the resulting influence it has on specificity. Another was evident between an effective management infrastructure and the positive effect it can have on the amount of transaction costs.
- A link was found between contract and interactions as it seemed the greater the promissory clarity was, the easier it was for managers to manage the deal at the operational level.
- There is a link between interactions and contract in terms of the uncertain and unspecifiable technical requirements and need for 'evergreen frameworks'.
- Structure affected the contract as the complexity and size of the venture affected the promissory comprehensiveness.
- A link between contract and outcome was evident as the lack of promissory clarity caused problems at the operational level that affected the levels of satisfaction.
- Structure and interactions were linked as vertical and occupational density influenced communication patterns.
- Interactions in terms of communication influenced the degree of control (behaviour).
- Finally, a link was evident between structure and behaviour, as the centrality of information affected the power-dependence balance, since Xerox managers increasingly depended on EDS for information to monitor their performance.

Conclusions

Out-sourcing of any IT function—but even more so in mega-deals like that of Xerox—requires a cooperative strategy to convert the objectives into reality. The case study revealed the complexity of total out-sourcing at a global level, and the complex impacts of business and technical uncertainties and contractual incompleteness. At the same time the impacts of the size and complexity of the undertaking of global IT out-sourcing is revealed as considerably underestimated by both vendor and client—a feature of other such deals. The declaration of a cooperative strategy supported by a contract negotiated at the centre, and with many incomplete aspects—partly arrived at in the spirit of 'partnering' and mutual commitment—led to a contract renegotiation within the first two years. It also led to a rethink about the level of detail needed on service, expectations, and pricing across Xerox activities, and senior managers actively pursued a more formal, traditional type of client–supplier relationship. Amongst some senior managers, with the benefit of hindsight, it was felt that a more selective IT sourcing approach would have been more appropriate right from the beginning. It was also clear that both client and vendor underestimated how much work was needed to secure appropriate management processes and procedures, though these were eventually being revamped and invested in, and were manifestly then helping the cooperative strategy three years into the contract. In all this global IT out-sourcing is revealed as high risk and heavily dependent not just on the will to cooperate but on the many detailed contractual and monitoring arrangements, management procedures, and processes that act as the foundation for the behavioural and informal interactions needed to generate and support effective cooperative strategy.

References

AIKEN, M. and HAGE, J. (1968), 'Organizational Interdependence and Intra-Organizational Structure', *American Sociological Review*, 33/6: 912–30.

ALDRICH, H. and WHETTEN, D. A. (1981), 'Organization-Sets, Action-Sets, and Networks: Making the Most of Simplicity', in P. C. Nystrom and W. H. Starbuck (eds.), *Handbook of Organizational Design* (New York: Oxford University Press) i: 385–408.

APPLEGATE, L. and MONTELEAGRE, R. (1991), *Eastman Kodak Company: Managing Information Systems through Strategic Alliances*, Case 9–192–030 (Harvard Business School, Boston).

AXELROD, R. M. (1984), *The Evolution of Co-operation* (New York: Basic Books).

BARNETT, R. E. (1992), 'Conflicting Visions: A Critique of Ian Macneil's Relational Theory of Contract', *Virginia Law Review*, 78/5: 1175–1206

BLOIS, K. J. (1972), 'Vertical Quasi-Integration', *Journal of Industrial Economics*, 20/3: 253–72.

—— (1996), 'Relationship Marketing in Organizational Markets: When is it Appropriate?', *Journal of Marketing Management*, 12: 161–73.

—— (1999), 'Assessing Business to Business Relationships: Using a Fuzzy Framework', *Working Paper* (Templeton College, University of Oxford).

CHILD, J. and FAULKNER, D. O. (1998), *Strategies of Co-operation: Managing Alliances, Networks, and Joint Ventures* (Oxford: Oxford University Press).

CROSS, J. (1995), 'IT Outsourcing: British Petroleum's Competitive Approach', *Harvard Business Review* 73/3 (May-June): 94–102.

CUNNINGHAM, M. T. (1980), 'International Marketing and Purchasing of Industrial Goods—Features of a European Research Project', *European Journal of Marketing*, 14/5–6: 322–38.

CURRIE, W. and WILLCOCKS, L. (1997), *New Strategies In IT Outsourcing* (London: Business Intelligence).

DAVIS, K. J. (1996), 'IT Outsourcing Relationships: An Exploratory Study of Interorganisational Control Mechanisms', DBA thesis (Harvard).

—— and APPLEGATE, L. (1995), *Xerox: Outsourcing Global Information Technology Resources*, Case 9–195–158 (Harvard Business School, Boston).

DiROMUALDO, A. and GURBAXANI, V. (1998), 'Strategic Intent for IT Outsourcing', *Sloan Management Review*, 39/4: 67–80.

DOZ, Y. L. and HAMEL, G. (1998), *Alliance Advantage: The Art of Creating Value through Partnering* (Boston, Mass.: Harvard Business School Press).

DWYER, F. R., SCHURR, P. H., and OH, S. (1987), 'Developing Buyer-Seller Relationships', *Journal of Marketing*, 51: 11–27.

EARL, M. J. (1991), 'Outsourcing Information Services', *Public Money and Management*, 11/3: 17–21.

—— (1996), 'The Risks of Outsourcing IT', *Sloan Management Review*, 37/3: 26–32.

FAULKNER, D. (1995), *International Strategic Alliances: Co-operating to Compete* (Maidenhead: McGraw-Hill).

FEENY, D. and WILLCOCKS, L. (1998), 'Core IS Capabilities for Exploiting Information Technology', *Sloan Management Review*, 39/3: 9–21.

FORD, D. (1980), 'A Methodology for the Study of Inter-Company Relations in Industrial Market Channels', *Journal of the Market Research Society*, 22/1: 44–59.

GALASKIEWICZ, J. (1985), 'Interorganizational Relations', *Annual Review of Sociology*, 11: 281–304.

GOETZ, C. J. and SCOTT, R. E. (1981), 'Principles of Relational Contracts', *Virginia Law Review*, 67/6: 1089–2054.

GURBAXANI, V. and WHANG, S. (1991), 'The Impact of Information Systems on Organizations and Markets', *Communications of the ACM*, 34/1: 59–73.

HAGEL, M. and SINGER, J. (1999), 'Unbundling of the Corporation', *Harvard Business Review*, 77/2 (Mar.-Apr.), 63–71.

HUBER, R. L. (1993), 'How Continental Bank Outsourced its Crown Jewels', *Harvard Business Review*, 71/1 (Jan.–Feb.), 121–9.

HUNT, S. and NEVIN, J. (1974), 'Power in a Channel of Distribution: Sources and Consequences', *Journal of Marketing Research*, 11: 186–93.

IDC (1998), *European Outsourcing Markets and Trends 1995–2001* (London: International Data Corporation).

JOHNSON, M. (1998), 'Local versus Global—Managing the Local End of the Xerox Global Outsourcing Contract', Proceedings of the First Annual Outsourcing Management Group Conference, London, 28–9 Apr.

JOHNSTON, R. and LAWRENCE, P. R. (1988), 'Beyond Vertical Integration—The Rise of the Value-Adding Partnership', *Harvard Business Review*, 66/4 (July–Aug.), 94–101.

KEARNS, D. T. and NADLER, D. A. (1995), *Prophets in the Dark: How Xerox Reinvented Itself and Beat Back the Japanese* (New York: HarperCollins).

KERN, T. (1997), The Gestalt of an Information Technology Outsourcing Relationship: An Exploratory Analysis', paper presented at the 18th International Conference on Information Systems, Atlanta, Ga. 14–18 Dec.

—— (1999), 'Relationships in IT Outsourcing: An Exploratory Research Study of a Conceptual Framework', DPhil thesis (Oxford).

KLEPPER, R. (1995), 'The Management of Partnering Development in IS Outsourcing', *Journal of Information Technology*, 10/4: 249–58.

LACITY, M. C. and HIRSCHHEIM, R. (1993), *Information Systems Outsourcing: Myths, Metaphors and Realities* (Chichester: Wiley).

—— and WILLCOCKS, L. P. (1995), 'Interpreting Information Technology Outsourcing Decision from a Transaction Cost Perspective: Findings and Critique', *Accounting, Management and Information Technology*, 5/3: 203–44.

—— —— (1998), 'An Empirical Investigation of Information Technology Sourcing Practices: Lessons From Experience', *MIS Quarterly*, 22/3: 363–408.

—— —— (forthcoming) *Global IT Outsourcing: Search for Business Advantage*.

LEVINE, S. and WHITE, P. E. (1961), 'Exchange as a Conceptual Framework for the Study of Interorganizational Relationships', *Administrative Science Quarterly*, 5/4: 583–601.

LOH, L. and VENKATRAMAN, N. (1992), 'Diffusion of Information Technology Outsourcing: Influence Sources and the Kodak Effect', *Information Systems Research*, 4/3: 334–58.

MCAMMON, B. C. and WHITTLE, R. (1963), 'Marketing Channels: Analytical Systems and Approaches', in G. Schwartz, (ed.), *Science in Marketing* (New York: Wiley), 321–85.

MACAULAY, S. (1963), 'Non-Contractual Relations in Business: A Preliminary Study', *American Social Review*, 28/1: 55–67.

MCFARLAN, F. W. and NOLAN, R. L. (1995), 'How to Manage an IT Outsourcing Alliance', *Sloan Management Review*, winter: 9–23.

MACNEIL, I. R. (1974), 'The Many Futures of Contracts', *Southern California Law Review*, 47/3: 691–816.

—— (1980), *The New Social Contract: An Inquiry into Modern Contractual Relations* (New Haven, Conn.: Yale University Press).

—— (1987), 'Relational Contract Theory as Sociology: A Reply to Professors Lindenberg and de Vos', *Journal of Institutional and Theoretical Economics*, 143/2: 272–90.

OLIVER, C. (1990), 'Determinants of Interorganisational Relationships: Integration and Future Directions', *The Academy of Management Review*, 15/2: 241–65.

PORTER, M. E. (1985), *Competitive Advantage: Creating and Sustaining Superior Performance* (New York: Free Press).

—— and MILLAR, V. E. (1985), 'How Information Gives you Competitive Advantage', *Harvard Business Review*, 63/4 (July–Aug.), 149–60.

PRAHALAD, C. K. and HAMEL, G. (1990), 'The Core Competence of the Corporation', *Harvard Business Review*, 69/3 (May–June), 79–91.

RING, P. S. and VAN DE VEN, A. H. (1992), 'Structuring Co-operative Relationships Between Organizations', *Strategic Management Journal*, 13: 483–98.

ROGERS-GILLMORE, M. (1987), 'Implications of General Versus Restricted Exchange', in K. S. Cook (ed.), *Social Exchange Theory* (Newbury Park, Calif.: Sage), 170–89.

SANDERS, P. (1982), 'Phenomenology: A New Way of Viewing Organizational Research', *Academy of Management Review*, 7/3: 353–60.

VAN DE VEN, A. H. (1976), 'On the Nature, Formation, and Maintenance of Relations Among Organizations', *Academy of Management Review*, 1/4: 24–36.

—— and RING, P. S. (1994), 'Developmental Processes of Co-operative Interorganizational Relationships', *Academy of Management Review*, 19/1: 90–118.

WALKER, R. (1992), 'Rank Xerox—Management Revolution', *Long Range Planning*, 25/1: 9–21.

WALSHAM, G. (1995), 'The Emergence of Interpretivism in IS Research', *Information Systems Research*, 6/4: 376–94.

WILLCOCKS, L. and CHOI, C. (1995), 'Co-operative Partnership and "Total" IT Outsourcing: From Contractual Obligation To Strategic Alliance?', *European Management Journal*, 13/1: 67–78.

—— and KERN, T. (1998), 'IT Outsourcing as Strategic Partnering: The Case of the UK Inland Revenue', *European Journal of Information Systems*, 7: 29–45.

WILLCOCKS, L., and LACITY, M. C. (1998), 'Introduction—The Sourcing and Outsourcing of IS: Shock of the New?', in L. P. Willcocks and M. C. Lacity (eds.), *Strategic Sourcing of Information Systems* (Chichester: Wiley), 1–41.

—————— (1999), 'Information Technology Outsourcing: Practices, Lessons and Prospects', *ASX Perspective*, Apr.: 64–8.

——FEENY, D. F., and ISLEI, G. (eds.) (1997), *Managing IT as a Strategic Resource* (Maidenhead: McGraw-Hill).

WILLIAMSON, O. E. (1975), *Markets and Hierarchies: Analysis and Antitrust Implications, A Study in the Economics of Internal Organization* (New York: Free Press).

—— (1979), 'Transaction-Cost Economics: The Governance of Contractual Relations', *Journal of Law and Economics*, 22: 233–61.

—— (1985), *The Economic Institutions of Capitalism: Firms, Markets, Relational Contracting* (New York: Free Press).

WILSON, D. D. (1989), *A Process Model of Strategic Alliance Formation in the Information Technology Industry*, Case no. 89-070:52 (Sloan School of Management, Massachusetts Institute of Technology, Boston, Mass.).

Xerox Corporation (1992), *Annual Review 1992: The Document Company* (Stamford, Conn.: Xerox Corporation).

—— (1996), *Annual Review 1996: The Document Company* (Stamford, Conn.: Xerox Corporation).

11

Assessing Inter-Organizational Collaboration
Multiple Conceptions and Multiple Methods

Arguments extolling the importance of inter-organizational collaboration and its benefits have gained prominence in the management and policy literature in the last decade (Gray, 1989; Wood and Gray, 1991; Huxham and Mc-Donald, 1992; Smith, Carroll, and Ashford, 1995; Evans, 1996*b*; Huxham, 1996*b*). Two distinct streams of research have emerged: one focusing on strategic alliances and joint ventures among business organizations and the other addressing cross-sectoral alliances among business, governments, schools, NGOs, and other stakeholders concerned about a particular problem domain. Particularly in education, social services, planning health care, and environmental arenas, collaboration among cross-sectoral sets of organizations concerned about a particular problem domain is increasingly necessary and often mandated (Trist, 1983; Carpenter and Kennedy, 1988; Gray, 1989; Potapchuk and Polk, 1993).

Among business firms, interest in collaborative strategic alliances has skyrocketed over the last decade (Nohria and Eccles, 1992; Ring and Van de Ven, 1992; Hagedoorn, 1993; Powell, 1995; Gulati, 1995*b*). Linkages between firms and their suppliers, their customers, and even their competitors are becoming the *modus operandi* for remaining competitive. Still, managing such partnerships is not easy; many such alliances are frequently unstable (Franko, 1971; Beamish, 1985; Kogut, 1989) and fail to achieve the ends the partners initially sought (Kern and Willcocks, chap. 10, above).

Cross-sectoral alliances also present management challenges, since stakeholders with an interest in the problem domain can no longer take unilateral action to control the direction of the domain towards their own desired ends. Instead their actions are inextricably linked to those of other stakeholders, and if development, rather than fragmentation or gridlock, is to occur in the domain, some coordinated effort among the stakeholders is required. Considerable effort has been devoted to the documentation of these collaborative efforts, often in the form of detailed case studies (cf. Gray and Hay, 1986; Gray, 1989; Gray and Wood, 1991; Wood and Gray, 1991; Brown and Ashman, 1995; Huxham, 1996*b*; Kern and Willcocks, chap. 10, above), and to consideration of the obstacles to collaboration (Gray, 1994; Sink, 1996;

Kern and Willcocks, chap. 10, above), its integrity (Gray, 1995; Hardy and Phillips, 1998), sustainability, and diffusion (Cropper, 1996; McCaffrey, Faerman, and Hart, 1995).

Despite this flurry of attention, collaboration remains a somewhat elusive concept and few guidelines exist for how to ascertain whether and when it has occurred and to what degree it has been successful. While collaborative efforts are designed to increase the chances of survival for individual organizations, they also produce collective impacts on society as a whole (Trist, 1983; Gray, Westley, and Brown, 1998) that, according to Stern and Barley (1996) have largely been unacknowledged. Collaborative efforts, can, for example, introduce new governance mechanisms for the domain (Kennelly-McGinnis, 1997), reframe values and precipitate power shifts (Schon and Rein, 1994; Hardy and Phillips, 1998) and, effectively, restructure entire organizational fields (Heimer, 1985; Powell, 1993; Powell, Koput, and Smith-Doer, 1996; Gray, Westley, and Brown, 1998).

This chapter proposes several approaches to the assessment of collaborative endeavours. Each approach is based on a different conceptual orientation towards collaboration and offers a different focus for assessing the extent of collaboration and/or its impacts. Several scholars have suggested that no single approach to assessment is sufficient. Gray and Wood (1991), for example, have shown how different theoretical perspectives emphasize different outcomes of collaboration: transaction cost theory focuses on efficiency while resource dependence theory emphasizes shifts in power, and institutional theory concerns itself with the impacts of collaboration on institutional or community norms and values. In his study of collaborative governance mechanisms, Powell (1995) classified collaborative approaches according to the sources of trust that inhere in them (e.g. kinship, professional membership, historical obligations, and mutual dependencies), although he did not expressly consider how such trust should be measured. Gray, Westley, and Brown (1998) have proposed three general outcomes of collaborative efforts: problem solutions, social-capital generation, and changes in the degree of institutionalization within the domain. According to them, reaching the optimal level of collaboration requires striking a balance between social capital formation and domain organization. Finally, Gray (1996) proposed different criteria for judging success for four generic types of collaboration: appreciative planning, collective strategies, policy dialogues, and negotiated settlements. These four types of collaboration differ according to whether they first, are initiated to advance a shared vision or to resolve an existing conflict, and secondly, generate ideas for change or actually implement those changes. For example, appreciative plans produce a shared vision but leave implementation to individual stakeholders. In contrast, negotiated settlements are initiated to resolve a conflict and make provisions to implement whatever agreement is jointly reached. Gray (1995) suggests that the criteria for judging the success or failure of each of these generic types of

Theoretical focus	Key concept	Indicator of collaboration
Problem-focused	Problem resolution or goal achievement	• Extent to which problem is resolved • # of goals achieved
Relational	Trust	Degree of 3 types of trust: • Calculus-based • Knowledge-based • Identity-based
Cognitive	Shared meaning	Degree to which parties have coincident interpretations
Structural	Structure of network	about the domain network density
Political	Power sharing	• Degree of diversity in contributions • Extent of active participation by multiple groups • Redistribution of resources

Fig. 11.1 Criteria for judging the success or failure of types of collaboration

collaboration will differ (see Figure 11.1). Differences between appreciative plans and collective strategies are illustrative. In the former, reaching agreement on a problem definition for the domain may be a sufficient outcome whereas judging the success of a collective strategy would include assessing goal achievement (e.g. market penetration, profitability, or alleviation or amelioration of a community problem).

In this chapter, five conceptual perspectives on assessment are introduced. Each perspective focuses on one key outcome:

1. problem resolution or goal achievement;
2. generation of social capital;
3. creation of shared meaning;
4. changes in network structure, and
5. shifts in the power distribution.

For cross-sectoral collaborations, the first perspective focuses on the extent to which collaborative activities have ameliorated the negative aspects of the domain problem (e.g. reduced illiteracy or limited the spread of illness) or increased positive outcomes (such as the creation of new jobs, increased self-reliance of communities, etc.). For strategic alliances, assessment using the first perspective would focus on whether the partners have achieved their strategic objectives, which may include profitability, market penetration, technology acquisition, and so forth (Yan and Gray, 1995a).

The second perspective focuses on social-capital formation, where social capital refers to the aggregate of actual or potential resources that can be mobilized through social relationships and membership in social networks (Nahapiet and Ghoshal, 1998). From this perspective, evidence that collaboration has generated social capital within the domain would be the presence of, or increase in, trust and norms of reciprocity among the stakeholders (Putnam, 1993; Coleman, 1990). Increasing levels of trust among stakeholders and the construction of shared norms about stakeholder interaction has been used to compare collaborations in different settings (Gray, Westley, and Brown, 1998).

The third perspective derives from social constructionism (Berger and Luckman, 1966). From this view collaboration occurs when the various stakeholders share a common interpretation about the problem domain and what actions should be taken with respect to it. Assessment of the extent of collaboration from this perspective focuses on the degree of shared meaning among stakeholders (Bougon, Weick, and Binhorst, 1977; Weick and Bougon, 1986; Smircich, 1983; Donnellon, Gray, and Bougon, 1986).

The fourth perspective is a structuralist one. In this view, the focus evolves around changes in the network relationships among the stakeholders. One possibility here is that an increasing density within the network of stakeholder interactions represents an increased organization of the domain.

The last perspective focuses on the power dynamics among the stakeholders and considers the extent to which a more equal distribution of power emerges as the domain develops (Gricar and Brown, 1981; Gray, Westley, and Brown, 1998; Hardy and Phillips, 1998). Implicit in this perspective are questions about the extent of institutional change induced by the collaboration and shifts in the governance structure of the domain.

Research illustrating each of the perspectives will be reviewed in detail and consideration will be given to the appropriate indicators or measures of collaboration that are consonant with each theoretical perspective. Those seeking to assess their collaborative efforts will hopefully find guidance in doing so.

Brief consideration is also given to a critical view of assessment. From this perspective, measurement or assessment in itself presupposes an epistemological position, which is that collaboration exists as a uniform, objective phenomenon that can be apprehended by independent, external observers, rather than only as a subjective interpretation in the minds and experiences of the stakeholders. In the latter case, measurement, as such, is inappropriate. Thus, the chapter will problematize the issue of assessment and raise the question, 'Assessment by whom and for what purpose?' (Gray, 1995). Implicit in this discussion is also consideration of the role of the researcher with respect to collaborative processes.

The chapter concludes with a note of caution to researchers engaged in evaluation of collaborative efforts. It recommends that multiple methods be used routinely and that the role and stance of the researcher with respect to the collaboration also be examined.

Assessing Collaborations

A Problem-Centred Assessment of Collaboration

The first approach to assessing the extent to which collaboration has occurred adopts a pragmatic or problem-centred focus. It emphasizes the extent to which collaborative activities have ameliorated the negative aspects of the problem (e.g. reduced illiteracy or limited the spread of illness) or produced positive outcomes (such as the creation of new jobs or the increased self-reliance of communities, in the case of public–private partnerships, or generated new products or increased revenues, in the case of strategic alliances among business entities).

In their study of network effectiveness of community mental health systems, Provan and Milward (1995) gathered data on the quality of life, satisfaction, and psychiatric/medical status of mental health patients from the perspectives of case workers, patients, and their families. They related structural characteristics of the network (such as density) to the effectiveness of the health systems' efforts. Selsky's (1991) study of collaboration among social service agencies assessed their collective capacity to reduce environmental turbulence. Schmitz (1997) used cost–benefit ratios and found that consortia that reported high cost–benefit ratios in their second year 'remained significantly different from their counterparts in year four'. Potachuk and Polk (1993) provided case-study evidence of community improvements in several American cities where grassroots citizen involvement efforts were underway. In these situations, measures such as the number of new jobs created, a decrease in the number of high school drop-outs, or a reduction in teenage pregnancies could be concrete measures of community collaboratives. In a comparative case analysis, Brown and Ashman (1995) clustered 13 community development collaboratives using three criteria to assess their substantive impacts:

1. the scope of their problem-solving impact (e.g. how many people were affected by the initiative);
2. the availability of resources to sustain the projects over time; and
3. the development of local capacity (e.g. grassroots people have acquired skills, participated in problem solving, etc.).

They concluded that the most successful collaborative development projects were those that created strong norms of reciprocity among the stakeholders. This issue is taken up in more detail in the next section under social-capital formation.

In strategic business alliances, outcome measures typically include traditional measures of organizational performance (e.g. ROI, market share, and number of new products developed). These measures, however, are not without their problems (see Yan and Gray (1995*b*) for a detailed review).

Some of these include the inappropriateness of quantitative performance measures during the start-up phases of these alliances, the overemphasis on one partner's [e.g. the MNC's) perspective (Yan and Gray 1995)], and the inability to acquire confidential data when the alliances are not free standing entities. Still other measures of performance are more evolutionary in nature and include the degree of learning of the IJV's parents (Hamel, 1991) as well as its stability or instability (Reuer and Koza, chap. 12, below).

Other recommended measures of performance include achievement of objectives, achievement of specific contract provisions (Kern and Willcocks, chap. 10, above), and more general satisfaction measures (provided they reflect the views of both or all the stakeholders) (Killing, 1982; Hebert, 1994; Hill and Hellriegel, 1994). For example, Yan and Gray (1995) asked joint venture partners to rank their objectives for the venture and then to rate the degree to which each of these was achieved. They then constructed a ratio of the actual achievement level compared with the highest possible one. A composite measure of performance for the joint venture as a whole was also calculated in similar fashion.

Assessing Collaboration in Terms of Social-Capital Formation

The second conceptualization of collaboration builds on the notion of social-capital formation. The concept of social capital has recently gained prominence in social psychology (Coleman, 1990: Fukijama, 1995), sociology (Anheiser, Gerhards, and Romo, 1995; Portes, 1998), and political science (Putnam, 1993). Although differences in operationalization of the concept arise at different levels of analysis, generally it refers to the mobilization of actual or potential resources through social relationships (Nahapiet and Goshal, 1998). Evidence that parties in a network or domain have created social capital through collaboration can be seen in the emergence of trust and norms of reciprocity among members of a community (Putnam, 1993; Coleman, 1990). Coleman (1990) explains that 'social capital inheres in the structure of relations between persons and among persons' (p. 302). Since trust and norms of reciprocity are conceptually distinct, we treat them here as separate outcomes of collaboration.

With the recent renewed interest in trust in organizational science, a host of definitions have emerged (see the special issue of the *Academy of Management Review*, 1998). We draw here on a review article by Lewicki and Bunker (1995) that identifies three general types of trust:

1. calculus-based trust derived from consistency of behaviour that leads to expectations that the other party will behave predictably;
2. knowledge-based trust in which there is a willingness to rely on the other person because of direct knowledge about their behaviour;
3. identification-based trust in which parties develop a social bond with each other based on mutual appreciation of each other's needs.

These three types of trust can be linked sequentially such that the first is a precursor to the second and the second to the third (Lewicki and Bunker, 1995); thus, we can think of them as increasing degrees of trust. In a relationship characterized by identification-based trust, the level of trust would be deeper, and less easily broken by minor infractions of expectations than in either of the previous two. These differences in level or depth of trust suggest that different dimensions are needed to measure the depth of trust in a relationship. Lewicki and Bunker (1995) suggest that calculus-based trust could be determined by the perceived costs and benefits from staying in the relationship vs. the costs and benefits of cheating on the relationship. One consequence of trust advanced by Ring and Van De Ven (1992) is that the presence of trust initially largely frees the parties from the fear that their partner will behave opportunistically (as transaction cost theory predicts (cf. Hamel, 1991; Blodgett, 1991)). Considered from this perspective, Schmitz's (1997) analysis of perceived cost–benefit ratios can really be viewed as a measure of calculus-based trust. Another way to get at calculus-based trust may be to determine how much monitoring of each other's behaviour the parties believe is necessary. This issue is well illustrated in Xerox's inability to effectively monitor the performance of its partner, EDS (Kern and Willcocks, chap. 10, above).

For knowledge-based trust to develop regular communication among the parties is required (Lewicki and Bunker, 1995) as well as courtship behaviour (Shapiro, Sheppard, and Cheraskin, 1992) in which the parties explicitly work on relationship development. To get at this level of trust, therefore, questions might be asked about the frequency of communication among the parties as well as the nature of the relationship itself, in addition to more general questions about the degree of trust experienced. Sabel (1993) notes that monitoring serves to create such regular interaction among the parties. Identification-based trust could be assessed by the parties' association or preference with similar names or descriptors or their willingness to be considered 'like' the other. Since this level of trust requires an understanding of the other's needs, comparisons of how well each party understands the other's needs could be made.

The above framework is primarily operationalized at the individual level of analysis, although occasional extrapolations to institutional level are proposed. Still, the measures of trust described so far reflect relationship dynamics between individuals, although they could be representatives of stakeholder organizations within a domain. Powell (1995) offers a typology of trust-based collaboration at the network level. He suggests that trust may be built on

1. norms of reciprocity and civic engagement à la Putnam (1993);
2. common professional membership;
3. shared historical experiences and group membership; and
4. mutual dependencies.

All four appear to be explanations of why networks form in the first place. However, norms of reciprocity that are crafted where none existed before could also be indicative of successful collaborative efforts.

Norms of reciprocity represent an ingredient of what Putnam (1993) refers to as social capital. According to Brown and Ashman (1995) and Gray, Westley, and Brown (1998), collaboration is effective when it generates social capital within an inter-organizational domain by increasing the levels of trust among stakeholders and constructing shared norms about stakeholder interaction. The development of shared norms suggests that, in a rudimentary way, a unique culture is evolving within the domain such that the stakeholders agree upon appropriate behaviours to take with respect to each other and/or the problem or task of mutual interest. In the most rudimentary way, norms can also guarantee rights or privileges of membership, such as freedom of assembly or the right to express dissent (Evans, 1996b). Therefore, the emergence of constructive norms, where none existed previously, could be an indicator of collaboration.

A constructive way to conceptualize social-capital formation in inter-organizational domains is to think of it as a social tie characterized by a modicum of trust. Thus, when grassroots organizations build links to international NGOs, they are building social capital (Gray, Westley, and Brown, 1998). Evans (1996b) notes that the creation of personal ties between health-care agents and community members in North-East Brazil was pivotal to the success of a health delivery programme. 'Social capital inheres, not just in civil society, but in an enduring set of relationships that spans the public–private divide' (Evans, 1996b: 1122).

In recent literature on international joint ventures and strategic alliances, the concept of trust is also considered a critical ingredient of success (Inkpen, 1992; Hebert, 1994; Yan and Gray, 1995; Gulati, 1995; Madhok, 1995; Sheppard, 1995; Zaheer, McEvily, and Perrone, 1998; Olk and Early, chap. 14, below). In a study of Japanese–American IJVs, Inkpen found a positive relationship between trust and performance. Hebert (1994) found similar results for Canadian IJVs. While Yan and Gray (1995b) did not measure trust directly, they found a positive relationship between the quality of the partners' working relationship and the achievement of their strategic objectives. Trust was also found to be central in repeat alliances (Gulati, 1995a). While these studies all treated trust as an antecedent of other performance indicators, trust could also be used as a separate indicator of collaboration, or preferably used in conjunction with other indicators.

The Social Construction of Collaboration: Assessing collaboration as Shared Meaning

Collaboration has been conceptualized as a socially negotiated order (Gray, 1989; Heimer, 1985) that evolves though a process of joint appreciation about a domain (Vickers, 1965; Trist, 1983). Stakeholders usually begin with different, and often fragmented, conceptions of a shared domain (Nathan and Mitroff, 1991; Vaughan and Siefert, 1992). They often have limited conceptions of how their actions impinge on other stakeholders and incomplete or mistaken perceptions about what other stakeholders want or believe (Vancina and Taillieu, 1997; Gray, 1997). Gaining a broader appreciation of their dependence on each other and creating a joint appreciation of the domain are prerequisites for coordinated action (Trist, 1983; Gray, 1989). The divergence in views, interests, and knowledge becomes a valuable asset, enabling the collaborators to develop a rich, shared picture of the problem situation before they reach agreement on a shared problem definition. Building this joint appreciation means sharing appraisals of the domain and trading individual and collective perceptions of what is and what is not possible. As Boje (1982) notes, if the stakeholders do not develop a sense of positively correlated fate, they will not be able to agree on a collaborative task.

Research on the framing of negotiation provides some insight into the difficulty of reaching agreement about the problem domain (Mather and Yngvesson, 1980–1; Vaughan and Siefert, 1992; Gray, 1997). When stakeholders start from fundamentally different premises, how they frame problems may make it virtually impossible to arrive at a shared problem definition. Difficulty in adopting a coincident interpretation of the critical issues facing the domain is often at the root of intractable environmental disputes (Vaughan and Siefert, 1992; Gray, 1997). For example, in disputes over occupational health hazards, labour advocates prevented joint discussion among the disputants by refusing to consider economic risks and health risks within the same framework (Hilgarten, 1985). Without a common framework for assessing risks, dialogue was restricted and collaboration was impossible.

Viewing collaboration as the evolution of a negotiated order, it is possible to map the extent of shared meaning that has developed among the stakeholders regarding the problem definition as an indicator of collaboration. Here the techniques of cognitive mapping can prove useful. Cognitive mapping offers a graphical representation of the concepts that stakeholders rely on to understand the domain and the relationships among those concepts (Bougon, Weick, and Binkhorst, 1983; Weick and Bougon, 1986; Eden, 1988). Comparisons could be made, for example, of stakeholders' initial interpretations of the problem and the extent to which they have shifted over time as they engage in collaborative activities with each other. Data for these maps are typically acquired through interviews with and/or questionnaires distributed to the stakeholders (see Weick and Bougon, 1986 for details on the techniques). Discourse analytic techniques of interview or negotiation data have also been used to demonstrate the degree and content of coincident interpretations (Donnellon, Gray, and Bougon, 1986; Donnellon and Gray, 1990). These techniques lend themselves to tracking the evolution of interpretations in real time, and to studying the incidences of reframing that occur (cf Putnam, 1990; Gray, Younglove-Webb, and Purdy 1997). Discourse analysis, however, is extremely time consuming to conduct.

Stakeholders can also be queried about the extent to which their interpretations about the problem have changed and the extent to which they have been influenced by other stakeholders' views or arguments. For example, following a study tour in which participants with conflicting views about hazardous waste incineration inspected incineration facilities in several cities and interviewed proponents and opponents of the facilities, participants indicated that their understanding of the issues had changed. Eighty-five per cent changed or broadened their definition and the scope of hazardous waste issues (to reflect an increased interest in social and policy issues), and 76 per cent increased their understanding of the perspectives of other stakeholders although none changed their stance on what actions should be taken (Chess et al., 1990). During a multiparty simulation, Vancina and Thallieu (1997) periodically requested input from participants on the nature of the issues they were addressing, their perceptions about the other parties, and kept track of the breadth of agreements that were reached, contrasting many bilateral agreements with preferable multilateral ones.

Some researchers have fruitfully used group decision support tools to assist stakeholders in identifying areas of agreement and disagreement and moving towards common interpretations (Eden, 1988, 1989; Huxham, 1996a). With the help of decision support tools, they have facilitated a process of consensus-building that leads to actionable decisions (Huxham, 1996a). In this process, of course, the researcher serves as a facilitator playing a very direct role in the elicitation and representation of the maps' contents.

Overemphasis on a single shared interpretation may be too restrictive a conception of what constitutes a collaborative outcome. Instead, the concepts of enhanced diversity (Vancina and Taillieu, 1997), increased voice (Gray, 1989) or multi-voicedness (Bouwen and Steyaert, 1995) may be desirable outcomes. In this view, collaboration is successful to the degree that the voices of those with no previous voice are incorporated (Hirshman, 1970). The appropriate metaphor may be a chorus of voices rather than solos or small groups dominates. More on this perspective is considered under shifts in power below.

The Structure of Collaboration: A Network Perspective on Assessment

The fourth perspective is a structuralist one. In this view, collaboration is considered in terms of the number and type of connections that exist among organizations (Van de Ven and Walker, 1984; Gulati, 1995b; Provan and Milward, 1995). For example, Van de Ven and Walker (1984) measured the level of coordination among social service sector organizations at two points in time. They focused on the number of contacts among the organizations (e.g. for client referrals) at two different points in time. The degree of collaboration (although it is usually called coordination or cooperation in this literature) can be represented by changes in the network relationships among the stakeholders. As the number of interactions among stakeholders becomes more frequent, their inter-organizational networks become more dense—thereby increasing the degree of institutionalization of the domain as a whole (Gray, Westley, and Brown, 1998).

Using similar reasoning, Provan and Milward (1995) developed a theory of network effectiveness (based on a comparative study of mental health networks in four cities) that includes network integration as one critical component. They found that the most effective networks were the most densely connected, although integration could also be achieved through a central entity or directly among network members. This is consistent with Gulati's (1995a) research on strategic alliances that shows that as trust builds among alliance partners, their inter-organizational networks tend to become less formal; their governance systems are based more on personal interactions and less on formal, contractual arrangements. Provan and Milward (1995) also found that networks that had both centralized authority and dense, cohesive decentralized links, were less effective than those with a centralized authority structure only. One explanation for this may be that in centralized networks there is clear agreement about authority and accountability whereas confusion may exist about such authority when high levels of centralization and decentralization exist simultaneously. Roberts (1994), for example, has suggested that successful collaboration depends on delegating sufficient authority to the collaborative task group.

Using a structural perspective, then, one could track the degree of institutionalization within a domain by mapping the density of interactions among the stakeholders. Changes in network characteristics may be useful indicators of increased institutionalization of a domain. We urge caution, however, in equating increased institutionalization with increased collaboration. Although increasing the degree of institutionalization of the domain may indeed be an important step in building collaboration, especially in under-organized domains (Gricar and Brown, 1981), the positive relationship between the degree of organization and collaboration may not hold at higher levels of institutionalization (Gray, Westley, and Brown, 1998). Beyond a certain threshold, increased density within a network may prove constraining and inhibitive of adaptation (Ziller, 1996; Granovetter, 1973, 1985; Cohen and Levinthal, 1990). Therefore, we urge caution in measuring collaboration solely on the bases of increased network density and suggest that such measures be combined with others that have been discussed earlier, such as trust, the extent to which task performance was achieved, and the degree of diversity in the number of perspectives included (see below).

Collaboration or Cooptation: Assessing Collaboration from a Power Perspective

The last perspective focuses on the power dynamics among the stakeholders and considers the extent to which a more equal distribution of power emerges as the domain develops (Gricar and Brown, 1981; Gray, Westley, and Brown, 1998; Hardy and Phillips, 1998). In its ideal form, collaboration involves a sharing of power among the domain's stakeholders. Himmelman (1996) refers to these types of collaboration as transformational because the expectation is that collaboration increases the 'voice' of low power community member as well as their socio-economic status (Gricar and Brown, 1981; Brown and Ashman, 1995). Still, few domains are comprised of equally powerful stakeholders at the outset, so if shared power is to emerge, some allocation of power among the stakeholders may be a necessary component of successful collaboration. 'The power dynamics associated with collaboration generally involve a shift from the kind of unequal distribution of power associated with elitist decision making to more participative, equally shared access to the decision-making arena' (Gray, 1989: 120). This kind of power sharing is referred to as agenda-setting power for the domain (Gray, 1989).

Gray (1989) also identified other types of power that stakeholders could exercise. These included:

1. the power to mobilize in order to gain voice;
2. the power to organize a forum for discussion about the domain (the power of convening);
3. the power to strategize about what domain-level actions to take;
4. process control; and
5. the power to authorize actions by some on behalf of all stakeholders.

Several practical measures of collaboration could be derived from these sources of power. For example, stakeholders could be asked about the extent to which they and their counterparts exercise these sources of power within the domain.

Hardy and Phillips (1998) have noted that distinguishing between true collaboration and manipulation of weaker parties by stronger ones can be tricky. They caution that in addition to resource-dependent relationships among the stakeholders, it is important to consider which stakeholders have formal authority and which have discursive legitimacy. Depending on this mix of power sources, the domain may be characterized by compliance, contention, or contest instead of collaboration (Hardy and Philips, 1998). The first occurs when one party has resources and formal authority and the others have little or no other countervailing sources of power. Such cases clearly represent cooptation of the weaker party by the stronger, and not collaboration. In contention, formal authority is not clearly pre-scribed and stakeholders are vying for discursive legitimacy. In the contest situation, one stakeholder possesses formal authority and some resources while another derives discursive legitimacy (and some resources) from a constituency they represent. The potential for cooptation exists in this situation also.

Assessing collaborative efforts in terms of their power dynamics may be the most difficult of the approaches considered here. Weaker parties are unlikely to admit to cooptation especially if they are dependent on more powerful parties for survival resources. It is also possible that subtle control of how problems in the domain are framed, gives some parties a clear advantage over others by keeping certain issues off the table, limiting participation by certain stakeholders, or in devising ground rules favourable to themselves (Gray and Purdy, 1994). Three criteria for judging the legitimacy of public policy decisions offer some help in assessing the power dimensions of collaborative efforts (Michelman, 1989). The first concerns whether the parties reach a new understanding of the situation. Second, and key, is whether the parties reached this new understanding at the expense of their own self interest. Third, the process must be free from domination by one party. Gray and Purdy (1994) apply these conditions to two environmental collaborations to illustrate how they might be used to distinguish collaboration from cooptation. One limitation of such attempts, of course, is that different stakeholders may hold different interpretations of the degree to which the criteria are met, and researchers themselves may tacitly or overtly be psychologically sympathetic to one view or another. Despite these drawbacks, it is imperative that researchers be willing to take a critical look at the power distribution in the domain and question their own stance with respect to it as part of the assessment process (Gray, 1994).

A Critique of Assessing Collaborative Efforts

Additionally, in this final section of the chapter I want to problematize research efforts to measure collaboration by questioning the researcher's role in this activity. Researchers who are being asked to 'evaluate' a collaborative undertaking need to be cognizant of what role their assessment may play in the project. The key question to ask is 'Whose interests are being served by the assessment effort and by the way in which it is framed?' Answers to these questions may vary depending on whether the researcher takes a critical or a positivist stance towards the research efforts (Burrell and Morgan, 1979; Gray, 1994). Far too often, researchers, in the name of science, unselfconsciously conduct evaluations of social activity that perpetuate existing power dominant relations (Gray, 1994) and fail to challenge institutions to critically question their own practices. This failure to ask the hard questions of ourselves and of the institutions we work for can lead to a false consciousness (Sievers, 1994). As researchers and practitioners of collaborative processes we need to ensure that we do not contribute to or perpetuate the very hegemonic dynamics that the collaboration may be seeking to change.

Conclusion

This chapter has presented a variety of conceptual lenses through which to view the assessment of collaborative efforts. The selection of the most useful and appropriate perspective to adopt will depend on the type of collaboration under consideration, the nature of the problem domain, the audience for whom the assessment is being done (e.g. the stakeholders themselves, the research community, or funding agencies), and the researcher's relationship to the parties. If the collaboration is being carried out for developmental purposes, for example, the researcher will want to include the participants in the design of the inquiry (Reason, 1994). Finally, several approaches could also be used in tandem to gain a richer, more differentiated analysis of the collaborative endeavour.

References

ANHEISER, H., GERHARDS., J, and ROMO, F. P. (1995), 'Forms of Capital and Social Structure in Cultural Fields: Examining Bourdieu's Social Topography', *American Journal of Sociology*, 100/4: 859–903.

BEAMISH, P. W. (1985), 'The Characteristics of Joint Ventures in Developed and Developing Countries', *Colombia Journal of World Business*, 20/3: 13–19.

BERGER, P. L. and LUCKMANN, T. (1966), *The Social Construction of Reality* (New York: Doubleday).

BLODGETT, L. L. (1991), 'Partner Contributions as Predictors of Equity Share in International Joint Ventures', *Journal of International Business Studies*, 22: 63–78.

BOJE, D. (1982), 'Toward A Theory and Praxis of Transorganizational Development: Stakeholder Networks and Their Habitats', *Working Paper* 79–6 (Behavioral and Organizational Science Study Center, Graduate School of Management, University of California at Los Angeles), Feb.

BOUGON, M. G., WEICK, K. E., and BINKHORST, D. (1977), Cognition in Organizations: An Analysis of the Utrecht Jazz Orchestra', *Administrative Science Quarterly*, 22: 606–39.

BOUWEN, R. and STEYAERT, C. (1995), 'From Dominant Frames toward Multi-Voiced Cooperation: Mediating Metaphors for Global Change', paper presented to the Academy of Management Joint Divisional Conference on The Organizational Dimensions of Global Change: No Limits to Cooperation, Case Western Reserve University, 3–5 May.

BROWN, L. D. and ASHMAN, D. (1995), 'Intersectoral Problem-Solving, Participation, and Social Capital Formation: African and Asian Cases', paper presented at the Conference on Global Change: No Limits to Cooperation, Case Western Reserve University, 3–5 May.

BURRELL, G. and MORGAN, G. (1979), *Sociological Paradigms and Organizational Analysis* (Portsmouth, NH: Heinemann).

CARPENTER, S. L. and KENNEDY, W. J. D. (1988), *Managing Public Disputes: A Practical Guide to Handling Conflict and Reaching Agreements* (San Francisco: Jossey-Bass).

CHESS, K., SALOMONE, K. L., GREENBERG, M. R., SANDMAN, P. M., and SAVILLE, A. (1990), *Impact of a European Hazardous Waste Study Tour on Participants' Viewpoints*, Environmental Communications Research Program, Rutgers University, May.

COHEN, W. M. and LEVINTHAL, D. A. (1990), 'Absorptive Capacity: A New Perspective on Learning and Innovation', *Administrative Science Quarterly*, 35: 128–52.

COLEMAN, J. S. (1990), *Foundations of Social Theory* (Cambridge, Mass.: Harvard University Press).

CROPPER, S. (1996), 'Collaborative Working and the Issue of Sustainability', in C. Huxham (ed.), *Creating Collaborative Advantage* (London: Sage), 80–100.

DONNELLON, A. and GRAY, B. (1990), 'An Interactive Theory of Framing in Negotiation', *Working Paper*, Center for Research in Conflict and Negotiation, Pennsylvania State University.

———— BOUGON, M. (1986), 'Communication, Meaning and Organized Action', *Administrative Science Quarterly*, 31/1: 43–55.

EDEN, C. (1988), 'Cognitive Mapping', *European Journal of Operational Research*, 36: 1–13.

—— (1989), 'Using Cognitive Mapping for Strategic Options Development and Analysis (SODA),' in J. Rosenhead (ed.), *Rational Analysis in a Problematic World* (Chichester: Wiley), 21–42.

EVANS, P. (1996a), 'Introduction: Development Strategies across the Public-Private Divide', *World Development*, 24/6: 1033–7.

—— (1996b), 'Government Action, Social Capital and Development: Reviewing the Evidence on Synergy', *World Development*, 24/6: 1119–32.

FRANKO, L. G. (1971), *Joint Venture Survival in Multinational Corporations* (New York: Praeger).

FUKUYAMA, F. (1995), 'Social Capital and the Global Economy', *Foreign Affairs*, 5: 89–103.

GRANOVETTER, M. (1973), 'The Strength of Weak Ties', *American Journal of Sociology*, 78/6: 1360–80.

—— (1985), 'Economic Action and Social Structure: The Problem of Embeddedness', *American Journal of Sociology*, 91/3: 481–510.

GRAY, B. (1989), *Collaborating: Finding Common Ground for Multiparty Problems* (San Francisco: Jossey-Bass).

—— (1994), 'A Feminist Critique of "Collaborating"', *Journal of Management Inquiry*, 3/3: 284–93.

—— (1996), Cross-Sectoral Collaboration among Business, Government and Communities', in C. Huxham (ed.), *Creating Collaborative Advantage* (London: Sage).

—— (1997), 'Framing and Reframing of Intractable Environmental Disputes', in R. Lewicki, B. Sheppard, and R. Bies (eds.), *Research on Negotiation in Organizations*, 6: 163–88.

—— and HAY, T. M. (1986), 'Political Limits to Interorganizational Consensus and Change', *Journal of Applied Behavioral Science*, 22/2: 95–112.

—— and WOOD, D. (1991), Collaborative Alliances: Moving from Practice to Theory, *Journal of Applied Behavioral Science*, 27/1: 3–22.

—— and PURDY, J. (1994), 'Theoretical Issues in the Resolution of Environmental Disputes: Collaboration or Co-optation?', *Working Paper*, Center for Research in Conflict and Negotiation, Pennsylvania State University.

GRAY, B., YOUNGLOVE-WEBB, J., and PURDY, J. M. (1997), 'Conflict Styles, Frame Repertoires and Negotiation Outcomes', paper presented at the International Association of Conflict Management Meeting, Bonn, Germany, 15–19 June.

——, WESTLEY, F., and BROWN, L. D. (1998), 'Where Have All the Rhinos Gone: The Transformation of Volatile Interorganizational Domains', paper under review.

GRICAR, B. and BROWN, L. D. (1981), 'Conflict, Power and Organization in a Changing Community', *Human Relations*, 34/10: 877–93.

GULATI, R. (1995*a*), 'Does Familiarity Breed Trust? The Implications of Repeated Ties for Contractual Choice in Alliances', *Academy of Management Journal*, 38/1: 7–23.

—— (1995*b*), 'Social Structure and Alliance Formation Patterns: A Longitudinal Analysis', *Administrative Science Quarterly*, 40/4: 619–52.

HAGEDOORN, J. (1993), 'Understanding the Rationale of Strategic Technology Partnering: Interorganizational Modes of Cooperation and Sectoral Differences', *Strategic Management Journal*, 14: 371–85.

HAMEL, G. (1991), 'Competition for Competence and Inter-Partner Learning within International Strategic Alliances', *Strategic Management Journal*, 12: 83–103.

HARDY, C. and PHILLIPS, N. (1998), 'Strategies of Engagement in Interorganizational Domains', *Organization Science*, 9/2: 217–30.

HEBERT, L. (1994), 'Division of Control, Relational Dynamics and Joint Venture Performance', PhD thesis (Western Ontario).

HEIMER, C. (1985), 'Allocating Information Costs in a Negotiated Information Order: Interorganizational Constraints on Decision Making in Norwegian Oil Insurance', *Administrative Science Quarterly*, 30: 395–417.

HILGARTEN, S. (1985), 'The Political Language of Risk: Defining Occupational Health', in D. Nelkin (ed.), *The Language of Risk* (Beverly Hills, Calif.: Sage), 25–66.

HILL, C. R. and HELLRIEGEL, D. (1994), 'Critical Contingencies in Joint Venture Management', *Organization Science*, 5/4: 594–607.

HIMMELMAN, A. T. (1996), 'On the Theory and Practice of Transformational Collaboration: From Social Service to Social Justice', in C. Huxham (ed.), *Creating Collaborative Advantage* (London: Sage), 19–43.

HIRSHMAN, A. O. (1970), *Exit, Voice and Loyalty: Responses to Decline in Firms, Organizations and States* (Cambridge, Mass.: Harvard University Press).

HUXHAM, C. (1996*a*), 'Group Decision Support for Collaboration', in C. Huxham (ed.), *Creating Collaborative Advantage* (London: Sage), 141–51.

—— (ed.) (1996*b*), *Creating Collaborative Advantage* (London: Sage).

—— and MACDONALD, D. (1992), 'Introducing Collaborative Advantage: Achieving Interorganizational Effectiveness through Meta-Strategy', *Management Decision*, 30: 50–6.

INKPEN, A. (1992), 'Japanese–American IJV's: The Relationship between Trust and Performance', PhD thesis (Western Ontario).

KENNELLY-McGINNIS, S. (1997), 'An Empirical Test of Social Control by Interorganizational Lobbies in the Health Sector', *Working Paper*, Center for Research in Conflict and Negotiation, Pennsylvania State University.

KILLING, J. P. (1982), 'How to Make a Global Joint Venture Work', *Harvard Business Review*, May-June: 120–7.

KOGUT, B. (1989), 'The Stability of Joint Ventures: Reciprocity and Competitive Rivalry', *The Journal of Industrial Economics*, 38/2: 183–98.

LEWICKI, R. J. and BUNKER, B. B. (1995), 'Trust in Relationships: A Model of Development and Decline', in B. B. Bunker, J. Z. Rubin, and Assoc. (eds.), *Conflict, Cooperation and Justice: Essays Inspired by the work of Morton Deutsch* (San Francisco: Jossey-Bass), 133–74.

McCAFFREY, D. P., FAERMAN, S. R., and HART, D. W. (1995), 'The Appeal and Difficulties of Participative Systems', *Organization Science*, 6: 603–27.

MADHOK, A. (1995), Revisiting Multinational Firms' Tolerance for Joint Ventures: A Trust-Based Approach', *Journal of International Business Studies*, 26/1: 117–37.

MATHER L. and YNGVESSON, B. (1980–1), 'Language, Audience, and the Transformation of Disputes', *Law and Society Review*, 15/3–4: 775–821.

NAHAPIET, J. and GHOSAL, S. (1998), 'Social Capital, Intellectual Capital, and the Organizational Advantage', *Academy of Management Review*, 23/2: 242–66.

NATHAN, M. L. and MITROFF, I. I. (1991), 'The Use of Negotiated Order Theory as a Tool for the Analysis and Development of an Interorganizational Field', *Journal of Applied Behavioral Science*, 27/2: 163–80.

NOHRIA, N. and ECCLES, R. G. (eds.) (1992), *Networks and Organizations: Structure, Form and Action* (Boston: Harvard Business School Press).

PORTES, A. (1998), 'Social Capital: Its Origins and Applications in Modern Sociology', *Annual Review of Sociology*, 24: 1–24.

POTAPCHUK, W. R. and POLK, C. G. (1993), *Building the Collaborative Community* (Washington, DC: National Institute for Dispute Resolution).

POWELL, W. W. (1993), 'The Social Construction of an Organizational Field: The Case of Biotechnology', paper presented at the conference on Strategic Change at Warwick Business School, Warwick, UK.

—— (1995), 'Trust-Based Forms of Governance', in T. Tyler and R. Kramer (eds.), *Trust in Organizations: Frontiers of Theory and Research* (Thousand Oaks, Calif.: Sage), 114–39.

—— KOPUT, K., and SMITH-DOER, L. (1996), 'Interorganizational Collaboration and the Locus of Innovation: Networks of Learning in Biotechnology', *Administrative Science Quarterly*, 41: 116–45.

PROVAN, K. and MILWARD, H. B. (1995), 'A Preliminary Theory of Interorganizational Network Effectiveness: A Comparative Study of Four Community Mental Health Systems', *Administrative Science Quarterly*, 40: 1–33.

PUTNAM, L. (1990), 'Reframing Integrative and Distributive Bargaining: A Process Perspective', in B. H. Sheppard, M. H. Bazerman, and R. J. Lewicki (eds.), *Research on Negotiation in Organizations*, ii (Greenwich, Conn.: JAI Press), 3–30.

—— (1993), *Making Democracy Work: Civic Traditions in Modern Italy* (Princeton, NJ: Princeton University Press).

REASON, P. (1994), 'Three Approaches to Participative Inquiry', in N. K. Denzin and Y. L. Lincoln (eds.), *Handbook of Qualitative Research* (Thousand Oaks, Calif.: Sage), 324–39.

RING, P. S. and VAN DE VEN, A. H. (1992), 'Structuring Cooperative Relationships between Organizations', *Strategic Management Journal*, 13: 483–98.

ROBERTS, V. Z. (1994), 'Conflict and Collaboration: Managing Intergroup Relations', in A. Obholzer and V. Z. Roberts (eds.), *Unconscious at Work* (London: Routledge).

SABEL, C. F. (1993), 'Constitutional Ordering in Historical Context', in F. W. Scharpf (ed.), *Games in Hierarchies and Networks* (Boulder, Colo.: Westview), 65–123.

SCHMITZ, C. (1997), 'Direct and Indirect Approaches to Measuring Collaboration in Intersectoral Coalitions', paper presented at the 1997 Annual American Education Association Meeting, San Diego, Calif., Sept.

SCHON, D. and REIN, M. (1994), *Frame Reflection* (New York: Basic Books).

SELSKY, J. W. (1991), 'Lesson in Community Development: An Activist Approach to Stimulating Interorganizational Collaboration', *Journal of Applied Behavioral Science*, 27/1: 91–115.

SHAPIRO, D., SHEPPARD, B. H., and CHERASKIN, L. (1992), 'Business on a Handshake', *Negotiation Journal*, 8/4: 365–77.

SIEVERS, B. (1994), *Work, Death and Life Itself: Essays on Management and Organization* (Berlin: De Gruyter).

SINK, D. (1996), 'Five Obstacles to Community-Based Collaboration and Some Thoughts on Overcoming Them', in C. Huxham (ed.), *Creating Collaborative Advantage* (London: Sage), 101–9.

SMIRCICH, L. (1983), 'Organizations as Shared Meanings', in L. R. Pondy, P. J. Frost, G. Morgan, and T. C. Dandridge (eds.), *Organizational Symbolism* (Greenwich, Conn.: JAI Press).

SMITH, K. G., CARROLL, S. J., and ASHFORD, S. J. (1995), 'Intra- and Interorganizational Cooperation: Toward a Research Agenda', *Academy of Management Journal*, 38/1: 7–23.

STERN, R. N. and BARLEY, S. R. (1996), 'Organizations and Social Systems: Organization Theory's Neglected Mandate', *Administrative Science Quarterly*, 41: 146–62.

TRIST, E. L. (1983), 'Referent Organizations and the Development of Interorganizational Domains', Human Relations, 36/3: 247–68.

VAN DE VEN, A. H. and WALKER, G. (1984), 'The Dynamics of Interorganizational Coordination', *Administrative Science Quarterly*, 29/4: 598–621.

VANCINA, L. and TAILLIEU, T. (1997), 'Diversity in Collaborative Task-Systems', *European Journal of Work and Organizational Psychology*, 6/2: 183–99.

VAUGHAN, E. and SIEFERT, M. (1992), 'Variability in the Framing of Risk Issues', *Journal of Social Issues*, 48/4: 119–35.

VICKERS, SIR G. (1965), *The Art of Judgment* (London: Chapman and Hall).

WEICK, K. E. and BOUGON, M. G. (1986), 'Organizations as Cognitive Maps: Charting Ways to Success and Failure', in H. P. Sims, Jr., D. A. Gioia *et al.* (eds.), *The Thinking Organization* (San Francisco: Jossey-Bass), 102–35.

WOOD, D. and GRAY, B. (1991), 'Toward a Comprehensive Theory of Collaboration', *Journal of Applied Behavioral Science*, 27/2: 139–62.

YAN, A. and GRAY, B. (1995a), 'Reconceptualizing the Determinants and Measurement of Joint Venture Performance', *Advances in Global High-Technology Management*, 5(B): 87–113.

———— (1995b), 'The Exercise of Management Control in International Joint Ventures', paper presented at the Academy of Management Meeting, Dallas, Tex., Aug.

ZAHEER, A., McEVILY, B., and PERRONE, V. (1998), 'Does Trust Matter? Exploring the Effects of Interorganizational and Interpersonal Trust on Performance', *Organization Science*, 9/2: 141–59.

ZILLER, R. C. (1996), 'Toward a Theory of Open and Closed Groups', *Psychological Bulletin*, 64/3: 164–82.

12

International Joint Venture Instability and Corporate Strategy

JEFFREY J. REUER AND MITCHELL P. KOZA

The practice of adopting international joint venture (IJV) longevity and stability as performance indicators is very well established. Since the literature's inception, this approach has been followed in conceptual work, descriptive studies, and fieldwork, and continues to be employed by scholars studying cross-border collaboration (e.g. Beamish, 1985; Brown, Rugman, and Verbeke, 1989; Dymsza, 1988; Franko, 1971; Killing, 1983; Li and Guisinger, 1991). In part, this tradition reflects the literature's focus on IJV formation issues, theoretical diversity, and continued fragmentation. These factors have impeded the development of an overarching typology to classify heterogeneous alliances, to investigate their evolution and effectiveness, and to link specialized streams of research (Doz, 1996; Oliver, 1990; Osborn and Hagedoorn, 1997; Parkhe, 1993a; Smith, Carroll, and Ashford, 1995).

The more recent popularity of this approach is manifest in the large number of studies building longitudinal models to uncover factors that exacerbate or ameliorate IJV instability (e.g. Barkema, Bell, and Pennings, 1996; Barkema *et al.*, 1997; Blodgett, 1992; Li, 1995; Millington and Bayliss, 1997; Park and Russo, 1996; Park and Ungson, 1997; Pennings, Barkema, and Douma, 1994). An ecological or selection approach to fit underlies this work (Drazin and Van de Ven, 1985), the implicit assumption being that only the fittest IJVs survive and those ill suited to environmental conditions are weeded out by market mechanisms. The supposition that IJV longevity or stability is in parent firms' best interests, while IJV instability reflects failure by parent firms or the venture itself, is also evident in the popular courtship-marriage metaphor for JVs (e.g. Bartlett and Ghoshal, 1995: 377–9; Berg and Friedman, 1980; Harrigan, 1986; Kanter, 1994; Pfeffer and Nowak, 1976).

This chapter contends that these assumptions and practices have important implications, both for how IJV research should be interpreted and for how the literature on collaborative strategy might be advanced. By way of introduction to these issues, the next section begins on the basis that this approach has substantial precedent in IJV research spanning several decades.

This work has yielded important insights into IJVs as hybrid organizational and competitive entities. Thus, this section draws together the theoretical and methodological rationales for using IJV longevity and stability as indicators of collaborative success.

Two subsequent sections bring out the limitations of this approach and advocate the development of contingency perspectives on collaborative dynamics. Based on the observation that IJV longevity or stability relates more directly to an IJV's performance rather than to the venture's impact on a parent firm, the next section takes up level-of-analysis issues that must be considered when assessing the effectiveness of collaboration. The chapter submits that placing focus on the venture as the unit of analysis can be constraining for several reasons: the IJV is often a means to an end rather than an end *per se*; it is common for parent firms to have different IJV objectives as well as payoffs; venture survival or adaptability is not a necessary or sufficient condition for parent firms' desired collaborative outcomes like corporate flexibility; and it is difficult to draw inferences from an individual IJV's behaviour or performance when the venture is embedded in a network or portfolio of alliances. However, even if it is assumed that IJV longevity is positively related to parent firm performance in general, the following questions remain unexplored: Under what conditions is IJV instability more or less detrimental to parent firms? Can venture longevity or stability be unrelated or even inversely related to parent firm performance in some circumstances?

The chapter suggests that a focus on IJV longevity or stability can limit advancement of IJV theory, generate partial or even incorrect normative guidelines for firms, and discount the functions transitional IJVs can serve in a parent firm's evolving corporate strategy. A subsequent section proposes that collaborative effectiveness is meaningfully viewed from a corporate strategy perspective that considers all collaborative phases from venture formation to termination. For instance, the effects of IJV longevity versus instability on a parent firm are contingent upon the parent firm's initial and evolving objectives, in particular the degree to which the firm uses the venture to exploit an existing advantage rather than to acquire knowledge. The attractiveness of IJV continuance and stability also depend upon *ex post* exchange conditions. Stylized examples derived from transaction cost theory illustrate the potential efficiency implications of IJV evolution. Finally, the effects of IJV longevity versus instability hinge upon the venture's specific governance trajectory as it evolves and ultimately ends by one of several means. While the literature treats IJV instability as a residual or miscellaneous category, distinct instability types can be subject to different influences and can lead to different parent firm performance outcomes. A concluding section brings out the chapter's implications for empirical research on IJVs and theory development on collaborative strategy.

IJV Longevity and Stability: Proxies for Collaborative Success

There are several rationales for using longevity and stability as performance proxies for IJVs, including, but not limited to, limitations on available data. Nevertheless, it is not surprising that these justifications, however categorized, are closely connected with IJVs' unique governance features, namely that parent firms have residual claimancy and shared control over a separate business entity (e.g. Chi, 1994; Hennart, 1988, 1993). Just as transaction cost theory emphasizes that the incentives for on-going cooperation are strongest when the venture is subject to performance ambiguity and both firms make transaction-specific investments (Kogut, 1988b), the rationales offered for evaluating IJV effectiveness in terms of longevity or stability also turn on IJV uncertainties and performance measurement difficulties and the impact of IJV longevity or instability on parent firms' resources and transaction costs.

IJV Uncertainties and Performance Ambiguity

When external or internal start-up uncertainties are significant, it can be problematic to appraise IJV effectiveness with standard accounting measures or other indicators used to evaluate the performance of established businesses. For instance, Harrigan (1988) suggests that in uncertain industry environments, IJV longevity provides a better indication that the venture has achieved a source of differentiation. Venture longevity can also reflect parent firms' success in overcoming internal uncertainties, since parent firms may limit the IJV's initial scope to reduce relational risks until a base of trust develops to provide a foundation for more substantive decisions requiring discretion (Buckley and Casson, 1988).

Venture effectiveness can also be difficult to assess due to the complexity of the venture's output and its transformation process (Anderson, 1990; Ouchi, 1979). Parent firms often enter IJVs for intangible purposes (e.g. Hamel, 1991; Harrigan, 1985), and IJV–parent spillovers can be difficult to quantify and track. Anderson (1990: 23) therefore recommends providing alliances with substantial autonomy, especially during early years when alliance outputs and processes tend to be the most ambiguous: '[E]ncouraging the joint venture to find its own way promotes harmony among parents (since sacrificing the venture's stand-alone performance to suit one parent is not likely to suit the others).'

Researchers similarly face constraints when gauging IJV effectiveness. The variety of venture types limits the validity of any single performance proxy when studying a broad cross-section of ventures. Even if performance measures such as IJV profitability are appropriate for a particular sample, data on individual IJV's performance levels are difficult to come by.

The fact that IJV longevity and survival tend to correlate with parent firms' overall perceived satisfaction with IJVs is another justification offered for studying IJVs using survival analyses (e.g. Barkema *et al.*, 1997; Geringer and Hebert, 1991):

It must be clearly noted that longevity is an imperfect proxy for 'alliance success.' Longevity can be associated, for instance, with the presence of high exit barriers. And in some instances, success can be operationalized in terms of other measures such as profitability, market share...Yet, achievement of these latter objectives may be thwarted by premature, unintended dissolution of the GSA [global strategic alliance]. Furthermore, objective performance measures (e.g., GSA survival and duration) are significantly and positively correlated with parent firms' reported (that is, subjective) satisfaction with GSA performance...so that for many research purposes the use of longevity as a surrogate for a favorable GSA outcome is probably not too restrictive (Parkhe, 1991: 582).

It should be emphasized, however, that empirical research also identifies limitations associated with employing IJV longevity or similar performance proxies. For instance, statistical research and fieldwork indicates that the durability of an alliance is not related to the satisfaction of the parent corporation's strategic needs (Hamel, 1991; Parkhe, 1993*b*). Venture age is uncorrelated with parent firms' satisfaction levels (Beamish and Banks, 1987) and specific dimensions of IJV performance such as cost control, quality control, labour productivity, and the need for parental involvement (Geringer and Hebert, 1991). Reuer (forthcoming) shows that the stock market often reacts favourably to both IJV formation and termination, and firms that do well at the formation stage also tend to fare well upon termination.

Parent Firms' Resource Contributions and Transaction Costs

Theoretical research on IJVs points out a number of direct and indirect benefits that parent firms may derive from cultivating long-lived and stable relationships. Authors invoking transaction cost theory, for example, suggest that IJV longevity is desirable to safeguard parent firms' resource contributions *ex post* (e.g. Ring and Van de Ven, 1994). Likewise, the *ex ante* expected duration of an IJV encourages parent firms to make transaction-specific investments that can enhance efficiency (e.g. Parkhe, 1993*b*). Long-lived and stable relationships can facilitate the development of specialized language, can reduce costs through learning-by-doing, and can economize on set-up costs (Williamson, 1979). Over time, deepening trust and inter-dependence encourage information sharing and simpler terms of exchange to coordinate activity (Beamish and Banks, 1987; Ring and Van de Ven, 1992).

The benefits of venture longevity and stability also depend on the robustness of the IJV governance structure to changes in transactional conditions as the relationship evolves. Chi (1994) submits that JVs are advantageous relative to outright acquisitions because residual claimancy and control can be flexibly adjusted. On the other hand, when the collaborative basis of a venture shifts, perhaps due to changes in parent firms' strategies, transaction costs from renegotiations can increase and adversely affect the relationship (Klein, Crawford, and Alchian, 1978). As such, the flexibility of residual claimancy and control is not absolute, and IJV adaptation costs can be non-trivial and can undermine the strategic rationale for the IJV (Beamish and Banks, 1987: 9).

Although the focus of the above discussion is on individual ventures, the benefits of IJV longevity and stability potentially extend across alliances and time. For instance, IJVs have been seen as investments in reputational assets, the value of which affects the firm's transaction costs incurred in engaging in future collaborative relationships. More specifically, firms that are able to develop a reputation for forbearance may be in a position to reduce their search and negotiation costs when they seek out alliances in the future (Buckley and Casson, 1988).

Having synthesized the major rationales for using IJV longevity and stability as indicators of collaborative success, the next two sections critically examine this practice. First, level of analysis issues are examined that must be considered when theorizing about IJV effectiveness. This discussion high-lights the limitations of focusing attention solely on the venture as the unit of analysis. Second, some of the parameters of a corporate strategy view of IJV dynamics are introduced. This perspective suggests that the value of IJV longevity or stability is contingent upon the IJV's role within the firm's evolving strategy.

Level of Analysis Issues

'What if a joint venture "does well", but at the expense of a parent's interests?' (Anderson, 1990: 19). This question highlights that in any joint venture there are at least three parties with their own interests and some discretion in pursuing their own agendas. This question also underscores the fact that the impact of an IJV on a parent firm might be very different from the firm's share in an IJV's performance. The factors that enhance or reduce IJV performance may also have effects of different magnitudes or directions on parent firm performance. It is therefore important to consider several issues that arise when the IJV is adopted as the unit of analysis for studying inter-firm collaboration. From a corporate strategy perspective, four primary concerns become evident:

1. the IJV is viewed independently from the parent firm's corporate strategy;
2. differential payoffs to parent firms are overlooked;
3. corporate flexibility can be confused with IJV adaptability; and
4. the IJV is abstracted from other related alliances.

IJVs as Ends versus Means

When the IJV rather than the parent firm is the unit of analysis for assessing effectiveness, the venture is seen as an end in itself rather than as a means by which the parent firm achieves some objective. A corporate strategy perspective on collaboration would instead view IJVs as specific instruments of the parent firm's overarching strategy for deploying and developing resources and for participating in product and geographical markets. Lorange and Roos develop this line of reasoning:

[I]t is the parent's perspective regarding strategic positioning as well as the input/ output of resources that dictate the form of strategic alliance. This underscores the fact that strategic alliances are a means to an end—not the end per se, and is in contrast to authors who argue for the alliance as a phenomenon on its own, with its own strategic life and value. . . . [W]e discuss how a strategic alliance should be seen as evolving over time, thus certainly taking on a life of its own. However, *we strongly contend that a strategic alliance should always be viewed from the perspective of its parents* (emphasis added; 1993: 12).

When the IJV and parent firm are interdependent, decisions regarding the IJV that are optimal for the parent firm can be sub-optimal when viewed from the perspective of the IJV as a stand-alone entity. For example, if positive IJV–parent spillovers result from a venture's R&D efforts, the parent firm may seek to over-invest in venture R&D from the IJV's point of view. Conversely, any negative IJV–parent spillovers stemming from an IJV activity (e.g. product cannibalization from IJV exports) may encourage the parent firm to under-invest in that activity from the venture's vantage point (Hladik, 1985). In either case, the IJV's impact on a parent firm can differ from what IJV performance may indicate.

Differential Parent Firm Payoffs from IJVs

When collaborative effectiveness is judged at the IJV level, using performance proxies such as longevity and stability, a related problem arises: parent firms' unique payoffs from a venture are not explicitly considered. The assumption is that whatever influences IJV performance has a similar effect on both parent firms. However, what constitutes a good IJV outcome for one parent firm may be less attractive to a partner. This is particularly the case when parent firms maintain different priorities regarding the acquisition of know-how, financial returns, risk-sharing, and so on. Even for a common collaborative objective, however, firms may experience very different IJV payoffs. For instance, Doz (1996) identifies five dimensions along which parent firms may learn at different paces: environmental, task, process, skill, and goal learning. Parent firms may also differ in their abilities to integrate such knowledge obtained from the IJV into other business units (Inkpen and Crossan, 1995).

IJV Adaptability and Corporate Flexibility

The frequent result of asymmetric payoffs, particularly when learning is involved, is that the IJV terminates, often in an unexpected manner for one of the parties (Inkpen and Beamish, 1997). However, when the IJV is taken as the level of analysis, parent firm objectives like corporate flexibility can be incorrectly equated with venture continuance and adaptation. Even if many IJVs are unresponsive to external or internal disturbances (Williamson, 1991), firms can achieve flexibility by using a portfolio approach of forming and ending alliances as capabilities evolve (Garud, 1994). Go-it-alone entries commonly supplant collaborations in uncertain, high-tech industries placing a premium on flexibility (Mitchell and Singh, 1992), and research finds that IJVs are susceptible to shifts in parents' strategies and organizational structures (Franko, 1971; Harrigan, 1985). While the individual IJV may not be adaptable as a governance structure, flexibility can be achieved in terms of parent firms' development and deployment of resources and business portfolios. Reuer and Leiblein (forthcoming) discuss some of the challenges firms must address in using IJVs to enhance flexibility and reduce risk.

IJV Embeddedness

Finally, just as performance assessments at the IJV level can fail to account for a venture's particular role in a parent firm's evolving corporate strategy, important relationships between parent firms' alliances are minimized when effectiveness is judged at the IJV level. When an IJV is related to other alliances with a partner, or the IJV is embedded in a more dispersed network of alliances, drawing inferences from an individual IJV's behaviour or performance is problematic given the interdependences among alliances that can both constrain action and open up new opportunities (e.g. Gulati, 1998). Applications of network analysis demonstrate that the structural and dynamic features of networks influence firms' internalization decisions, innovation, and performance (e.g. Barley, Freeman, and Hybels, 1992; Kogut, Shan, and Walker, 1992; Powell and Brantley, 1992). To the extent that an IJV is embedded in a network of collaborations, the firm's share in the IJV's performance may understate or overstate the actual impact of the collaboration on an individual parent firm.

IJV Dynamics and Corporate Performance

If the effectiveness of an IJV is meaningfully viewed from a parent firm's perspective, then IJV investment decisions and processes need to be evaluated within the context of the parent firm's evolving corporate strategy (Koza and Lewin, 1998). From this vantage point, the value of different phases of collaboration and IJV phenomena—venture formation, longevity, instability, termination, etc.—depends upon the parent firm's objectives for the venture,

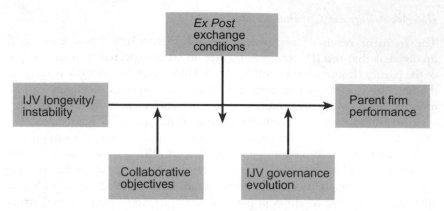

Fig. 12.1 IJV dynamics and parent firm performance

ex post exchange conditions, and the evolution of the IJV's governance structure (see Figure 12.1). In the following discussion of these contingencies, we submit that long-lived IJVs or venture stability can actually be less attractive than transitory IJVs or venture instability in specific contexts. Likewise, gauging the effectiveness of collaboration using indicators such as longevity or stability might be more appropriate in certain circumstances than others. The main conclusion for theoretical and empirical research on IJVs is that longevity or stability *per se* provides little indication of a collaborative strategy's effectiveness. Antecedents to IJV longevity versus instability can provide insights into IJV dynamics, but these influences may or may not be related to parent firm performance.

Collaborative Objectives

While the value of venture longevity versus instability is likely to differ across the numerous types of alliances and the specific motivations firms attach to each, the distinctions are perhaps most pronounced along the dimension of learning. Take, for instance, a parent firm forming an IJV purely to exploit an existing product advantage in a new country in which a local partner provides downstream capacity. Such an IJV might be initiated to overcome local ownership restrictions or to obtain scale economies if a market failure exists in an intermediate product market (Hennart, 1988). Firms often structure such alliances as autonomous businesses designed to penetrate and serve the local market on an ongoing basis.

Koza and Lewin (1998) distinguish such IJVs, or exploitation alliances, from collaborations in which one or more parties has an exploration intent. They emphasize that researchers face the challenge of choosing a suitable level of alliance disaggregation, since heterogeneous alliances should not be pooled yet all alliances cannot reasonably be treated as unique. The exploration–exploitation categorization scheme provides an intermediate solution and has implications for alliance formation and management. For instance, firms may use joint ventures to overcome information asymmetries that would otherwise create valuation problems in acquisitions (Balakrishnan and Koza, 1993; Reuer and Koza, forthcoming). Oxley (1997) observes that firms' exploration objectives make the specification of property rights problematic. As a result, appropriation hazards are higher, such alliances are potentially more sensitive to disturbances, and termination is likely to lead to asymmetric payoffs for parent firms. Khanna, Gulati, and Nohria (1998) apply patent race models to exploration alliances and suggest that racing behaviour reflects the firms' private and common benefits and partners' incentives for investing in learning. Hamel's remarks suggest that parent firm performance and venture longevity can be inversely related for parent firms seeking to learn a partner's skills:

Where internalization [of the partner's skills] is the goal, the longevity and 'stability' of partnerships may not be useful proxies for collaborative success.... A long-lived alliance may evince the failure of one or both parties to learn... [W]here a failure to learn is likely to undermine the competitiveness and independence of the firm, such contentedness should not be taken as a sign of collaborative success (1991: 101).

The conclusion from this work is that longevity and stability are not suitable as performance proxies when one party has or develops a learning objective. Although IJVs might be classified into exploration and exploitation categories, many will involve both objectives to varying degrees. That parties may also differ in their collaborative objectives, and learning ventures often create a winner and a loser, reinforces the importance of viewing collaborative effectiveness at the parent firm level. Although IJV longevity or stability may be more appropriate for IJVs of an exploitation variety, the following discussion considers *ex post* problems confronting these and other IJVs within the more general class of hybrid governance structures.

Ex Post *Exchange Conditions*

Researchers studying IJVs using a transaction cost perspective have discussed the challenges firms confront in keeping collaborative relationships stable in the face of opportunism (e.g. Brown, Rugman, and Verbeke, 1989; Park and Russo, 1996; Park and Ungson, 1997; Teece, 1992). Although IJV instability may often be an outcome of some manifestation of opportunistic behaviour, this instability can also be seen as a specific choice or response to changes in other transactional conditions, as the examples presented below illustrate. Because firms initially select IJVs over alternative governance structures under well-defined conditions, changes in these conditions can affect the ongoing attractiveness of an IJV. The value of IJV longevity, and thus the suitability of using it as a performance proxy, depends upon the magnitude and direction of changes in *ex post* exchange conditions.

In transaction cost analyses, asset specificity is considered to be the most important transactional attribute (e.g. Williamson, 1985), so for illustrative purposes the focus of the discussion will be on this element of the framework. Figure 12.2 depicts the main theoretical result: firms choose market-mediated exchange at low levels of asset specificity, internal organization is preferable beyond some threshold value, and hybrid governance structures blending features of markets and hierarchies are most efficient at intermediate levels (Hennart, 1993; Williamson, 1991).

Figure 12.2 also illustrates that IJV termination rather than IJV continuance can be an efficient response under several circumstances. First, parent firms' perceptions of asset specificity may change during their involvement in a partnership. Transaction cost theory acknowledges that 'failures in alignment' can occur because of managers' cognitive limits, and '[t]he standard transaction cost economics [treatment assumes] that parties to a transaction adopt a relatively farsighted approach (or quickly learn from mistakes, including the mistakes of others)' (Williamson, 1994: 371). Parent firms' perceptions of transactional attributes such as asset specificity may change over time, particularly if parties' resource contributions are organizationally embedded or are to be combined in complex ways. Further, because the context of exchange has both social and economic dimensions (Itaki, 1991; Zaheer and Venkatraman, 1995), perceptions of transactional features are likely to change a good deal during IJV formation and IJV implementation phases as information accumulates and collaboration unfolds. To the extent that the 'learned' level of asset specificity is substantially different from the initial appraisal, a governance misalignment can become apparent.

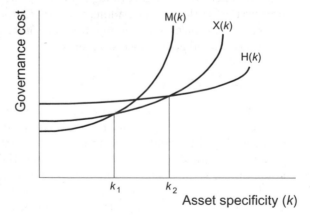

Fig. 12.2 Governance cost curves for market-mediated (M), hybrid (X), and hierarchical (H) exchange
Source: Williamson, 1991

The attractiveness of IJV survival versus IJV termination depends upon changes in asset specificity involving movements along the governance cost curves in Figure 12.2. For example, Honeywell and Ericsson formed a 50–50 IJV to develop software for adapting a telecommunications switch to the US market. Honeywell learned the relevant technologies to link its control and information systems businesses, and it had little incentive to commit resources to the expanding venture. Ericsson, however, was particularly interested in a packet switch to support email and was becoming increasingly dependent on the IJV. As the expanding venture required more investment and coordination, Ericsson acquired Honeywell's equity stake and converted the IJV to an internal unit (Kogut, 1988a). If asset specificity instead diminishes significantly, the firm may prefer to switch to a less hierarchical alliance type or even market-mediated exchange. Such a switch parallels Dunning's contention that the 'shifting of the balance of advantages of hierarchies and external markets ... has led to frequent re-alignments of the functions and boundaries of MNEs', and 'divestment will occur, *providing* that the exit costs (which themselves involve transaction costs) do not outweigh the savings of using the market' (emphasis in original; 1988: 23).

Third, the efficiency of an IJV relative to alternative governance structures also depends on changing exogenous factors that can shift the three governance cost curves in Figure 12.2. Relative shifts in the curves result in new placements for threshold levels k_1 and k_2, and hence altered governance structure policy regions. For instance, changes in political risk are thought to have a greater impact on the governance costs for internal organization than for hybrids, since a local partner can shield the firm from hold-up on the part of the local government (Teece, 1986). As a result, decreases (increases) in political risk can make IJVs less (more) attractive relative to internal organization over time.

Similarly, changes in host country conditions can affect the ongoing attractiveness of an IJV by changing the feasible set of governance structures. For instance, the firm might initially select an IJV in response to investment constraints imposed by the local government (e.g. Blodgett, 1991; Fagre and Wells, 1982; Gomes-Casseres, 1989; Stopford and Wells, 1972; Vernon, 1971). Liberalization expands the firm's feasible set of governance structures such that complete ownership might be attractive for a now second-best IJV. This pattern appears consistent with the recent conversion of IJVs to wholly owned subsidiaries in the former Soviet bloc as legal systems have become more accommodating (Shama, 1995). Use of IJV longevity as a performance proxy is therefore less appropriate when sampled ventures operate in countries with shifting investment policies. The general conclusion of this section is that the parent firm consequences of IJV longevity versus IJV instability are contingent upon endogenous and exogenous changes in *ex post* exchange conditions (see Figure 12.3).

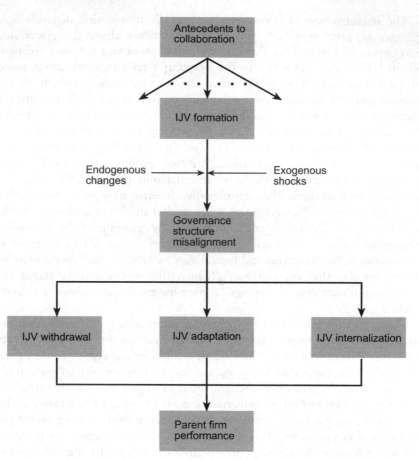

Fig. 12.3 *Ex post* exchange conditions and IJV governance changes

IJV Governance Evolution

The discussion above suggests that the parent firm performance implications of IJV longevity versus IJV instability also depend upon the specific means by which the venture ends. For example, if asset specificity is significant, internalizing the IJV to achieve greater coordination by buying out the partner's equity stake will be more attractive for the parent firm than selling its equity stake or liquidating the venture and losing some of the value of resources committed to the IJV. Conversely, the impact of IJV internalization may well be negative when continuation of the IJV or a simpler governance arrangement would suffice due to low asset specificity.

One result of the literature's use of IJV longevity and stability as performance proxies is that IJV instability has come to represent a miscellaneous, residual category that has been under-theorized. Despite the widespread use of the term, it is often not defined; it is used to mean different things across empirical studies, and many distinct types of instability are aggregated in theoretical and empirical research on IJVs. For example, the term has been applied to incremental ownership changes in ongoing ventures (Blodgett, 1992), transcending the 50–50 ownership boundary (Franko, 1971), venture reorganizations (Killing, 1983), and various kinds of termination (e.g. Barkema, Bell, and Pennings, 1996; Li, 1995), and studies pool multiple types of instability together. To the extent that different types of instability are subject to different influences or have different consequences for parent firms, however, it is necessary to differentiate specific IJV trajectories for a parent firm, since different governance changes are involved.

The importance of differentiating IJV instability types also falls out of the perspective that IJVs should be viewed within the context of a parent firm's evolving corporate strategy. For instance, in many cases IJVs end by one firm acquiring the venture from a partner. The acquiring firm expands its boundary and increases its resource commitment to the venture's business while the selling party incrementally constricts its boundary and applies the financial proceeds to other uses in the organization. As such, the two parent firms in an IJV regularly experience instability in different ways. The parent firm performance implications of these changes depend upon the IJV's transactional features, switching costs, the price at which the buyout occurs, and other factors. For example, the acquiring firm may capture value from internalizing a venture subject to an unexpectedly favourable demand shock (Kogut, 1991). The selling firm potentially benefits through a capital gain, yet this firm cannot rely on a competitive bidding market as in other asset divestitures. The value of IJV continuance versus IJV internalization or sell-off to a partner therefore depends on many factors that make it difficult to assume that IJV instability affects parent firms adversely or equally.

In other cases, parent firms may divest the venture to a third party or liquidate the IJV. Here IJV longevity can be unattractive if firms maintain or escalate their commitment to a relationship in the face of negative signals due to top management biases, managers' emotional attachments, internal political processes, agency problems, and so forth (e.g. Cullen, Johnson, and Sakano, 1995; Tallman and Shenkar, 1994). The fact that firms can use divestitures to create value for shareholders (e.g. Boudreaux, 1975; Hearth and Zaima, 1984; Jain, 1985; Klein, 1986; Rosenfeld, 1984), in particular when exiting an industry with the aim of reconfiguring operations (e.g. Montgomery and Thomas, 1988; Montgomery, Thomas, and Kamath, 1984), suggests that some IJV divestitures can be more attractive than IJV continuance. By contrast, IJV liquidation, especially early in the venture's evolution, may indicate that firms were unable to generate much common value (e.g., Hennart, Kim, and Zeng, 1998). The conclusion is that just as the attractiveness of IJV longevity or stability is contingent upon firms' collaborative objectives and *ex post* exchange conditions, the performance implications of an IJV depend upon the IJV's specific governance changes and the circumstances surrounding these changes.

Implications for IJV Research

This chapter has considered the frequent use of IJV longevity and stability as performance indicators since the literature's inception and has brought together the theoretical and methodological rationales for this tradition. Prior research based upon this approach has yielded important insights into cross-border collaboration, the obstacles firms face when building an international presence via partnerships, and the distinctiveness of IJVs as hybrid competitive and organizational entities. This chapter has also sought to identify the limitations of this approach and the value of building more integrative, contingency perspectives to investigate collaborative effectiveness and the dynamics of IJVs within firms' evolving corporate strategies.

One of the conclusions of the chapter is that care is needed when interpreting or drawing normative implications from survival models of IJVs. The discussion of level of analysis issues, for example, indicates that if variable X_1 is positively related to IJV longevity, it does not follow that 'more of' X_1 is to one or both parent firms' advantage. Implicit in such statements is the view that IJV longevity is in parent firms' best interests, while IJV instability reflects the failure of parent firms or the venture itself, an assumption that we have suggested is questionable in a wide array of situations and that merits testing. Such statements also discount the roles transitional IJVs can play in firms' corporate strategies and the different options available to parent firms in managing IJV evolution. Future studies of IJV survival might therefore avoid or qualify normative conclusions when drawing inferences from IJV instability models.

A related implication of this chapter is that assumptions regarding IJV longevity or stability are neither universally valid nor invalid, but these basic assumptions can be more or less appropriate in different partnering contexts (see also Gray, chap. 11, above). One could envision many research questions for which the IJV is a relevant unit of analysis and IJV instability would be an interesting regressor or outcome. The chapter also emphasized that IJV longevity is more apt to be tightly connected with parent firm performance outcomes in specific circumstances. These issues can be addressed in part through sampling as well as by being sensitive to the generalizability of empirical results. In particular, the chapter suggested that it is worthwhile to distinguish exploitation versus exploration ventures when studying IJV dynamics, that the appropriateness of using IJV longevity as a performance proxy depends upon IJVs' different *ex post* exchange conditions, and that observed effects may well differ across specific types of IJV instability representing different governance changes.

Beyond these specific suggestions for interpreting IJV survival analyses and conducting work in this area, the chapter represents a call for alliance research to develop and test contingency perspectives on alliance dynamics and their effects on parent firms. However, a number of challenges exist for building more integrative alliance models that tie together antecedents to collaboration, firms' governance choices across the IJV life cycle, post-formation events and processes, and parent firms' performance outcomes, as portrayed in Figure 12.3. First, alliance research in these directions requires the development of a theoretical framework or multiple frameworks to build and test contingency perspectives on alliance dynamics. For instance, existing applications of transaction cost theory in the alliance literature tend to be static in nature and do not directly incorporate parent firm performance (Shelanski and Klein, 1995; Silverman, Nickerson, and Freeman, 1997). Research is therefore needed to determine the applicability of transaction cost theory in such dynamic settings to address selection-based assumptions employed in reduced-form analyses of firms' governance choices, to study the changing attributes and governance of transactions and their inter-relationships, and to consider the possible efficiency consequences of different forms of IJV evolution. Other theoretical perspectives such as real options theory, organizational learning, and bargaining models might also be used alone or in combination to improve understanding of IJV dynamics and the performance implications for parent firms.

Second, researchers continue to face the practical constraint of measuring and modelling the parent firm outcomes of alliances. Event-study methods relying on share price reactions can be useful for examining the impact of discrete governance decisions such as IJV formation or different types of IJV termination on parent firms (Reuer and Miller, 1997), but these techniques are not suitable for assessing gradual or anticipated changes in IJV governance. Methodological challenges also arise in building cross-level models from secondary data that incorporate dependent and independent variables at different levels of analysis, including the parent firm, the partner, the venture itself, and the IJV's environment (Klein, Dansereau, and Hall, 1994).

Finally, alliance research would greatly benefit from the development of typologies to study IJVs and their evolution. The chapter noted that this has been a call of many scholars for some time, and some progress has recently been made in this direction. The distinction between exploration and exploitation represents one way to deal with alliance heterogeneity in a manageable fashion. Other recent research into the contractual hazards of alliances suggests that collaborations might be classified into unilateral non-equity, bilateral non-equity, and equity categories (Oxley, 1997). Opportunities also exist in terms of advancing the evolutionary component of an IJV framework. The chapter observed that the term 'IJV instability' is widely used, yet is applied in many different ways, and multiple distinct types of IJV instability are pooled together in theoretical and empirical research. Rather than searching for a uniform or exhaustive definition of IJV instability, the literature would benefit more by distinguishing alternative types of IJV evolution and termination, uncovering underlying mechanisms, and addressing the implications for parent firms. Different parent-specific types of IJV termination involving different governance changes are relatively straightforward to distinguish (e.g. the parent firm internalizes the IJV, sells out to a partner, sells out to a third party, liquidates the venture, etc.), yet more incremental governance changes during IJV evolution may be considerably more difficult to identify and categorize (see Doz and Baburoglu, chap. 8, above). Very little is known, for instance, about the influences and implications of changes in IJV scope, coordination, the functioning of venture boards, rights allocations, and so forth. Future research might address unexplored questions such as the following: What affects such governance changes? Are these changes effective in stabilizing IJVs or do such changes hasten the venture's termination? How do firms choose between alternative types of IJV adaptation and termination and with what effect? As more attention is devoted to the evolution and termination of IJVs, questions such as these will probably take on greater importance in the IJV field. Our chapter helps in interpreting prior research on IJVs and also highlights the importance of assessing IJV dynamics at the parent firm level.

References

ANDERSON, E. (1990), 'Two Firms, One Frontier: On Assessing Joint Venture Performance', *Sloan Management Review*, 31: 19–30.

BALAKRISHNAN, S. and KOZA, M. P. (1993), 'Information Asymmetry, Adverse Selection, and Joint Ventures', *Journal of Economic Behavior and Organization*, 20: 99–117.

BARKEMA, H. G., BELL, J. H. J., and PENNINGS, J. M. (1996), 'Foreign Entry, Cultural Barriers, and Learning', *Strategic Management Journal*, 17: 151–66.

——SHENKAR, O., VERMEULEN, F., and BELL, J. H. J. (1997) 'Working Abroad, Working with Others: How Firms Learn to Operate International Joint Ventures', *Academy of Management Journal*, 40: 426–42.

BARLEY, S. R., FREEMAN, J., and HYBELS, R. C. (1992), 'Strategic Alliances in Commercial Biotechnology', in N. Nohria and R. G. Eccles (eds.), *Networks and Organizations* (Boston: Harvard Business School Press), 311–47.

BARTLETT, C. A. and GHOSHAL, S. (1995), *Transnational Management*, 2nd edn. (Chicago: Irwin).

BEAMISH, P. W. (1985), 'The Characteristics of Joint Ventures in Developed and Developing Countries', *Columbia Journal of World Business*, 20: 13–19.

—— and BANKS, J. C. (1987), 'Equity Joint Ventures and the Theory of the Multinational Enterprise', *Journal of International Business Studies*, 18: 1–16.

BERG, S. V. and FRIEDMAN, P. (1980), 'Corporate Courtship and Successful Joint Ventures', *California Management Review*, 22: 85–91.

BLODGETT, I. L. (1991), 'Partner Contributions as Predictors of Equity Share in International Joint Ventures', *Journal of International Business Studies*, 22: 63–78.

—— (1992), 'Factors in the Instability of International Joint Ventures: An Event History Analysis', *Strategic Management Journal*, 13: 475–91.

BOUDREAUX, K. J. (1975), 'Divestiture and Share Price', *Journal of Financial and Quantitative Analysis*, 10: 619–26.

BROWN, L. T., RUGMAN, A. M., and VERBEKE, A. (1989), 'Japanese Joint Ventures with Western Multinationals: Synthesizing the Economic and Cultural Explanations of Failure', *Asia Pacific Journal of Management*, 6: 225–42.

BUCKLEY, P. J. and CASSON, M. (1988) 'A Theory of Cooperation in International Business', in F. J. Contractor and P. Lorange (eds.), *Cooperative Strategies in International Business* (Lexington, Mass.: D. C. Heath), 31–53.

CHI, T. (1994), 'Trading in Strategic Resources: Necessary Conditions, Transaction Cost Problems, and Choice of Exchange Structure', *Strategic Management Journal*, 15: 271–90.

CULLEN, J. B., JOHNSON, J. L., and SAKANO, T. (1995), 'Japanese and Local Partner Commitment to IJVs: Psychological Consequences as Outcomes and Investments in the IJV Relationship', *Journal of International Business Studies*, 26: 91–115.

DOZ, Y. L. (1996), 'The Evolution of Cooperation in Strategic Alliances: Initial Conditions or Learning Processes?', *Strategic Management Journal*, 17 (summer special issue): 55–84.

DRAZIN, R. and VAN DE VEN, A. H. (1985), 'Alternative Forms of Fit in Contingency Theory', *Administrative Science Quarterly*, 30: 514–39.

DUNNING, J. H. (1988), 'The Eclectic Paradigm of International Production: A Restatement and some Possible Extensions', *Journal of International Business Studies*, 19: 1–31.

DYMSZA, W. A. (1988), 'Successes and Failures of Joint Ventures in Developing Countries: Lessons from Experience', in F. J. Contractor and P. Lorange (eds.), *Cooperative Strategies in International Business* (Lexington, Mass.: D. C. Heath), 403–24.

FAGRE, N. and WELLS, L. T. (1982), 'Bargaining Power of Multinationals and Host Governments', *Journal of International Business Studies*, 11: 9–23.

FRANKO, L. G. (1971), *Joint Venture Survival in Multinational Corporations* (New York: Praeger).

GARUD, R. (1994), 'Cooperative and Competitive Behaviors during the Process of Creative Destruction', *Research Policy*, 23: 385–94.

GERINGER, J. M. and HEBERT, L. (1991), 'Measuring Performance of International Joint Ventures', *Journal of International Business Studies*, 22: 249–63.

GOMES-CASSERES, B. (1989), 'Ownership Structures of Foreign Subsidiaries: Theory and Evidence,' *Journal of Economic Behavior and Organization*, 11: 1–25.

GULATI, R. (1998), 'Alliances and Networks', *Strategic Management Journal*, 19: 293–317.

HAMEL, G. (1991), 'Competition for Competence and Interpartner Learning within International Strategic Alliances', *Strategic Management Journal*, 12: 83–103.

HARRIGAN, K. R. (1985), *Strategies for Joint Ventures* (Lexington, Mass.: Lexington Books).

—— (1986), *Managing for Joint Venture Success* (Lexington, Mass.: Lexington Books).

HARRIGAN, K. R., (1988), 'Joint Ventures and Competitive Strategy', *Strategic Management Journal*, 9: 141–58.

HEARTH, D. and ZAIMA, J. (1984), 'Voluntary Corporate Divestitures and Value', *Financial Management*, 13: 10–16.

HENNART, J.-F. (1988), 'A Transaction Cost Theory of Equity Joint Ventures', *Strategic Management Journal*, 9: 361–74.

—— (1993), 'Explaining the Swollen Middle: Why Most Transactions are a Mix of "Market" and "Hierarchy"', *Organization Science*, 4: 529–47.

—— KIM, D.-J., and ZENG, M. (1998), 'The Impact of Joint Venture Status on the Longevity of Japanese Stakes in US Manufacturing Affiliates', *Organization Science*, 9: 382–95.

HLADIK, K. J. (1985), *International Joint Ventures: An Economic Analysis of U.S.-Foreign Business Partnerships* (Lexington, Mass.: Lexington Books).

INKPEN, A. C. and BEAMISH, P. W. (1997), 'Knowledge, Bargaining Power, and the Instability of International Joint Ventures', *Academy of Management Review*, 22: 177–202.

—— and CROSSAN, M. M. (1995), 'Believing is Seeing: Joint Ventures and Organization Learning', *Journal of Management Studies*, 32: 595–618.

ITAKI, M. (1991), 'A Critical Assessment of the Eclectic Theory of the Multinational Enterprise', *Journal of International Business Studies*, 22: 445–60.

JAIN, P. (1985), 'The Effect of Voluntary Sell-Off Announcements of Shareholder Wealth', *Journal of Finance*, 40: 209–23.

KANTER, R. M. (1994), 'Collaborative Advantage: The Art of Alliances', *Harvard Business Review*, 72: 96–108.

KHANNA, T., GULATI, R., and NOHRIA, N. (1998), 'The Dynamics of Learning Alliances: Competition, Cooperation, and Relative Scope', *Strategic Management Journal*, 19: 193–210.

KILLING, J. (1983), *Strategies for Joint Venture Success* (New York: Praeger).

KLEIN, A. (1986), 'The Timing and Substance of Divestiture Announcements: Individual, Simultaneous, and Cumulative Effects', *Journal of Finance*, 41: 685–96.

KLEIN, B., CRAWFORD, R. A., and ALCHIAN, A. A. (1978), 'Vertical Integration, Appropriable Rents, and the Competitive Contracting Process', *Journal of Law and Economics*, 21: 297–326.

KLEIN, K. J., DANSEREAU, F., and HALL, R. J. (1994), 'Levels Issues in Theory Development, Data Collection, and Analysis', *Academy of Management Review*, 19: 195–229.

KOGUT, B. (1988*a*), 'A Study in the Life Cycles of Joint Ventures', in F. J. Contractor and P. Lorange (eds.), *Cooperative Strategies in International Business* (Lexington, Mass.: D. C. Heath), 169–85.

—— (1988*b*), 'Joint Ventures: Theoretical and Empirical Perspectives', *Strategic Management Journal*, 9: 319–32.

—— (1991), 'Joint Ventures and the Option to Expand and Acquire', *Management Science*, 37: 19–33.

—— Shan, W., and WALKER, G. (1992), 'The Make-or-Cooperate Decision in the Context of an Industry Network', in N. Nohria and R. G. Eccles (eds.), *Networks and Organizations* (Boston: Harvard Business School Press), 348–65.

KOZA, M. and LEWIN, A. (1998), 'The Co-evolution of Strategic Alliances', *Organization Science*, 9: 255–64.

LI, J. (1995), 'Foreign Entry and Survival: Effects of Strategic Choices on Performance in International Markets', *Strategic Management Journal*, 16: 333–51.

—— and GUISINGER, S. (1991), 'Comparative Business Failures of Foreign-Controlled Firms in the United States', *Journal of International Business Studies*, 22: 209–24.

LORANGE, P. and ROOS, J. (1993), *Strategic Alliances: Formation, Implementation, and Evolution* (Cambridge, Mass.: Blackwell).

MILLINGTON, A. I. and BAYLISS, B. T. (1997), 'Instability of Market Penetration Joint Ventures: A Study of U.K. Joint Ventures in the European Union', *International Business Review*, 6: 1–17.

MITCHELL, W. and SINGH, K. (1992), 'Incumbents' Use of Pre-Entry Alliances before Expansion into New Technical Subfields of an Industry', *Journal of Economic Behavior and Organization*, 18: 347–72.

MONTGOMERY, C. A. and THOMAS, A. R. (1988), 'Divestment: Motives and Gains', *Strategic Management Journal*, 9: 93–7.

—— —— and KAMATH, R. (1984), 'Divestiture, Market Valuation, and Strategy', *Academy of Management Journal*, 27: 830–40.

OLIVER, C. (1990), 'Determinants of Interorganizational Relationships: Integration and Future Directions', *Academy of Management Review*, 15: 241–65.

OSBORN, R. and HAGEDOORN, J. (1997), 'The Institutionalization and Evolutionary Dynamics of Interorganizational Alliances and Networks', *Academy of Management Journal*, 40: 261–78.

OUCHI, W. (1979), 'A Conceptual Framework for the Design of Organizational Control Systems', *Management Science*, 25: 833–48.

OXLEY, J. E. (1997), 'Appropriability Hazards and Governance in Strategic Alliances: A Transaction Cost Approach', *Journal of Law, Economics, and Organization*, 13: 387–409.

PARK, S. H. and RUSSO, M. V. (1996), 'When Competition Eclipses Cooperation: An Event History Analysis of Joint Venture Failure', *Management Science*, 42: 875–90.

—— and UNGSON, G. R. (1997), 'The Effect of National Culture, Organizational Complementarity, and Economic Motivation on Joint Venture Dissolution', *Academy of Management Journal*, 40: 279–307.

PARKHE, A. (1991), 'Interfirm Diversity, Organizational Learning, and Longevity in Global Strategic Alliances', *Journal of International Business Studies*, 22: 579–601.

—— (1993a), '"Messy" Research, Methodological Predispositions, and Theory Development in International Joint Ventures', *Academy of Management Review*, 18: 227–68.

—— (1993b), 'Strategic Alliance Structuring: A Game Theoretic and Transaction Costs Examination of Interfirm Cooperation', *Academy of Management Journal*, 36: 794–829.

PENNINGS, J. M., BARKEMA, H., and DOUMA, S. (1994), 'Organization Learning and Diversification', *Academy of Management Journal*, 37: 608–40.

PFEFFER, J. and NOWAK, P. (1976), 'Joint Ventures and Interorganizational Interdependence', *Administrative Science Quarterly*, 21: 398–418.

POWELL, W. W. and BRANTLEY, P. (1992), 'Competitive Cooperation in Biotechnology: Learning through Networks?', in N. Nohria, and R. G. Eccles (eds.), *Networks and Organizations* (Boston, Mass.: Harvard Business School Press), 366–94.

REUER, J. J. (forthcoming), 'Parent Firm Performance across International Joint Venture Life-Cycle Stages', *Journal of International Business Studies*.

REUER, J. J., and KOZA, M. P. (forthcoming), 'Asymmetric Information and Joint Venture Performance: Theory and Evidence for Domestic and International Joint Ventures', *Strategic Management Journal*.

—— and MILLER, K. D. (1997), 'Agency Costs and the Performance Implications of International Joint Venture Internalization', *Strategic Management Journal*, 18: 425–38.

—— and LEIBLEIN, M. J. (forthcoming), 'Downside Risk Implications of Multinationality and International Joint Ventures', *Academy of Management Journal*.

RING, P. S. and VAN DE VEN, A. H. (1992), 'Structuring Cooperative Relationships between Organizations', *Strategic Management Journal*, 13: 483–98.

—— —— (1994), 'Developmental Processes of Cooperative Interorganizational Relationships', *Academy of Management Review*, 19: 90–118.

ROSENFELD, J. D. (1984), 'Additional Evidence on the Relation between Divestiture Announcement and Shareholder Wealth', *Journal of Finance*, 39: 1437–48.

SHAMA, A. (1995), 'Entry Strategies of U.S. Firms to the Newly Independent States, Baltic States, and Eastern European Countries', *California Management Review*, 37: 90–109.

SHELANSKI, H. A. and KLEIN, P. G. (1995), 'Empirical Research in Transaction Cost Economics: A Review and Assessment', *Journal of Law, Economics, and Organization*, 11: 335–61.

SILVERMAN, B. S., NICKERSON, J. A., and FREEMAN, J. (1997), 'Profitability, Transactional Alignment, and Organizational Mortality in the U.S. Trucking Industry', *Strategic Management Journal*, 18 (summer special issue): 31–52.

SMITH, K. G., CARROLL, S. J., and ASHFORD, S. J. (1995), 'Intra- and Interorganizational Cooperation: Toward a Research Agenda', *Academy of Management Journal*, 39: 7–23.

STOPFORD, J. M. and WELLS, L. T. (1972), *Managing the Multinational Enterprise* (New York: Basic Books).

TALLMAN, S. and SHENKAR, O. (1994), 'A Managerial Decision Model of International Cooperative Venture Formation', *Journal of International Business Studies*, 25: 91–113.

TEECE, D. J. (1986), 'Transaction Cost Economics and the Multinational Enterprise: An Assessment', *Journal of Economic Behavior and Organization*, 7: 21–45.

—— (1992), 'Competition, Cooperation, and Innovation: Organizational Arrangements for Regimes of Rapid Technological Progress', *Journal of Economic Behavior and Organization*, 18: 1–25.

VERNON, R. (1971), *Sovereignty at Bay* (New York: Basic Books).

WILLIAMSON, O. E. (1979), 'Transaction-Cost Economics: The Governance of Contractual Relations', *Journal of Law and Economics*, 22: 233–61.

—— (1985), *The Economic Institutions of Capitalism* (New York: Free Press).

—— (1991), 'Comparative Economic Organization: The Analysis of Discrete Structural Alternatives', *Administrative Science Quarterly*, 36: 269–96.

—— (1994), 'Strategizing, Economizing, and Economic Organization,' in R. P. Rumelt, D. E. Schendel, and D. J. Teece (eds.), *Fundamental Issues in Strategy: A Research Agenda* (Boston: Harvard Business School Press), 361–401.

ZAHEER, A. and VENKATRAMAN, N. (1995), 'Relational Governance as an Interorganization Strategy: An Empirical Test of the Role of Trust in Economic Exchange,' *Strategic Management Journal*, 16: 373–92.

PART IV

Cooperative Behaviour

This final part of the book deals with the human part of the cooperative process. Success in alliances depends upon getting many things right, and not too many wrong. The human behavioural issues must be right, at least to an acceptable degree, yet in planning cooperative activity they are often the most neglected. Such issues as trust, cultural compatibility, commitment, and control are vital to success. The four chapters in this section of the book provide some thoughts, theories, and evidence in relation to these vital areas of cooperative behaviour.

13

National Differences in Acquisition Integration

ROBERT PITKETHLY, DAVID O. FAULKNER, AND JOHN CHILD

This chapter deals with the highest level of firm interdependence short of outright total integration of the wholly owned and internally developed subsidiary, namely the merger or acquisition. Appropriate behavioural attitudes of a cooperative nature are as vital in these circumstances as in a partly owned joint venture, if the respective cultures and competences of the two companies are to be married effectively together. The chapter thus concentrates on the key issue of integrating acquisitions, drawing on a study of acquisitions of UK companies by firms from the USA, Japan, Germany, and France. Four major aspects are considered: the overall level of integration; the control mechanisms adopted; the communication methods; and the strategic philosophy pursued by the new parent in relation to its acquisition.

During the past decade there has been significant direct investment into the UK by foreign firms. The scale and nature of this investment is discussed in greater detail by Child, Faulkner, and Pitkethly (forthcoming, 2000). First, between 1986 and 1995 companies from the USA, Japan, Germany, and France were the largest sources of foreign investment with between 70.8 per cent and 80.9 per cent of the total. Secondly, in 1996 foreign acquisitions of UK firms exceeded the total value for all other European Union countries combined and was topped worldwide as a takeover target only by the USA (KPMG, 1997). Thirdly, an extensive search using numerous sources covering the period 1985 to 1994, identified 1422 UK activities comprising new acquisitions, joint venture formations, collaborations or consortia involving foreign investment (but excluding greenfield developments or expansions of existing facilities[1]) and found that 79 per cent of these activities involved acquisition activity.

---

[1] These sources are unlikely to be comprehensive. In particular, smaller deals may go unnoticed by the British press and unrecorded by the DTI and CSO. The actual level of activity will therefore certainly be higher than that captured by the above sources. However, it is believed that the relative size of the number of activities by type, nationality, and industry will reflect the overall picture, and these are the only data readily accessible to researchers.

Categories of Change

Acquisitions weaken the ability of local management to resist the introduction of new practices more than joint ventures or alliances do. Greenfield development might offer even less resistance, but does not offer such a clear comparison of practices prevailing before and after FDI.

Many factors may bear upon changes in management practice in subsidiaries following acquisition. First, there may be 'background changes' which would have occurred anyway even in the absence of an acquisition. These changes in management practice may come from general conditions affecting UK industry during the period of study, be they the influence of new management ideas or the economic cycle of boom and recession. Secondly, however there may be various 'acquisition effects' which only occur following acquisition. Amongst these are changes which would have occurred anyway eventually and which may, following an acquisition, be catalysed by it and proceed faster or more effectively. New investment may be made in plant and information technology, providing opportunities for new practices to be introduced. The rationale for many acquisitions is to exploit perceived opportunities for securing a greater return from assets, and this may bring about a further impetus for change in management practice within the subsidiary. There is also likely to be a general 'new broom sweeps clean' effect and some changes implemented which would never have occurred in the absence of an acquisition. The acquisition effect is, however, characteristic of acquisitions *per se*, rather than reflecting any particular foreign approach to management and organization. It comprises both changes which would have occurred anyway but which are catalysed by the acquisition, as well as changes which occur directly as a result of the acquisition but which do not differ by the nationality of the acquirer. Thirdly, however, there is change which is specific to the nationality of the new owner, and may be called the 'transfer of foreign practice effect'. This comprises the transfer of foreign management practice to domestic companies following foreign acquisition. It can also proceed by emulation within domestic companies, whether acquired or not, as Oliver and Wilkinson (1992) noted in the case of Japanese-type production methods.

These considerations prompt two questions 'What is being transferred from foreign investing companies?' and 'What are we comparing?' (Morris and Wilkinson, 1996: 727). The first concerns the characteristics of management practices that are transferred directly or through emulation. What differences in this respect might one find between companies from each of the 'big four' countries investing in the UK? The second question concerns the difference that FDI, as opposed to acquisition by UK companies, makes to the management practices introduced into UK subsidiaries. This chapter addresses the first of these questions, and in particular the extent to which what is transferred is affected by the overall integration, control, communication, and strategic philosophy exhibited by the new parent company.

Until the 1980s many students of management assumed that there were general principles that might be applied to situations, irrespective of the culture of the companies being studied. The dominant view was that the appropriate approach to management and organization should be determined in the light of prevailing contingencies, particularly those established by the market, technology, and scale of operation. Culture was either thought to be of limited relevance (e.g. Hickson *et al.* 1974) or just one of several contingencies to be considered (cf. Child, 1981).

In the last two decades, however, the pendulum has swung strongly in the opposite direction. Company and national culture are now seen as critically important in selecting management methods, strategies, and structures (cf. Hampden-Turner and Trompenaars, 1993). A growing body of research on national management systems, and relevant national cultural differences, has led to the expectation that companies of different nationalities will introduce distinctive management practices. At the same time, markets and corporations have been globalizing rapidly, and many more companies now face two distinct cultures—their own and that of a foreign partner or parent. Work on acquisitions and their performance (Haspeslagh and Jemison, 1991; Norburn and Schoenberg, 1994) as well as on the effects of differing national management cultures on the performance of acquisitions (Very, Lubatkin, and Calori, 1996; Morosini and Singh, 1994) has also led to interest in the wider implications of national and managerial culture for acquisitions and their performance. Very, Lubatkin, and Calori (1996) study differences in acculturative stress and Calori and De Woot (1994) differences in control mechanisms in acquisitions by US, French or UK companies of French, or British firms. However, the literature which studies post-acquisition integration generally avoids looking at national differences altogether or looks more at national differences between the acquired and the acquiring company rather than between different nationalities of acquiring company. Thus whilst differences in national management are much studied, differences in national approaches to acquisition integration, which this chapter addresses, have been little studied.

Key Issues

This chapter focuses on the respective methods of integration of the four types of national acquirer, and three aspects of it: control, communication, and strategic philosophy.

Overall Integration

There have been a number of writers who have touched on the issue of integration. Norburn and Schoenberg (1994) identify the need for 'relatively specialised integration skills different from those required within an intra-UK context' and identify three needs:

1. integration by facilitating a transfer from owner-management to professional management;
2. integration by proactive transfer of skills to overcome a lack of integration that their research found; and
3. the need to overcome potentially conflicting national cultures.

Morosini and Singh (1994), whilst concentrating on implementing a 'national culture-compatible strategy' as a means to improving the performance of acquisitions, draw attention to the difficulties of integrating resources across both acquiring and acquired companies, something seen as detrimental to the performance of the acquisition. Datta (1991) also highlights the importance of integration and the finding that procedural integration problems are less detrimental to the performance of the acquisition than cultural integration problems associated with some but not all differing management styles. Shrivastava (1985) identifies three types of integration: procedural, physical, and managerial/sociocultural, the last of which is found by Datta to encompass the potentially important cultural differences in management style. Gall (1991) identifies integration as a key organizational issue faced by the management of a new acquisition and emphasizes the role of employee communication in building a positive post-acquisition climate.

A tendency to over- or under-integrate as a result of cultural factors hindering integration or pressuring moves towards it may result in suboptimal solutions. Haspeslagh and Jemison (1991) have proposed a set of 'metaphors' to classify acquisitions into four types depending on whether their needs for organizational autonomy and for strategic interdependence are high or low. Thus in their typology:

1. a 'Holding' acquisition involves a low need for both organizational autonomy and strategic interdependence;
2. 'Absorption' acquisitions involve a low need for organizational autonomy but a high need for strategic interdependence;
3. 'Preservation' acquisitions have a high need for organizational autonomy but a low need for strategic interdependence; and
4. 'Symbiosis' involves a high need for both organizational autonomy and strategic interdependence.

However, whilst this categorizes acquisitions, it is clear, as Haspeslagh and Jemison (1991) point out, that:

The usefulness of choosing an overall metaphor for an acquisition integration does not change the fact that acquisitions bring with them many positions and capabilities, the integration of which, seen in more detailed perspective, might be best served by a different approach.

It is thus possible in considering acquisitions to anticipate both cases where either the overall picture or one detail of it suggests one of the types of acquisition Haspeslagh and Jemison describe (Holding, Preservation, Symbiosis, or Absorption) and yet also to see that in most cases there is a subtlety in the approaches adopted by some managers and a multitude of detail that exists, including the many resources, capabilities, and other factors to be considered. Angwin (1998) focuses on the two categories of acquisition which are not integrated into the acquiring company. He distinguishes between the 'holding' category, where the acquirer tries to effect a turnaround but without any degree of integration, as opposed to the 'preservation' approach, where the acquired company is left unintegrated because this is judged to be the best way for it to continue making good profits.

Whichever way one looks at acquisitions though, there appears to be a potential continuum in the degree of integration, or what might be called a spectrum of integration. This is shown in Figure. 13.1, which illustrates the acquisition by company A of company B with varying degrees of integration. This spectrum of integration ranges from acquisitions with little integration (1–2 on the scale, corresponding to Preservation and Holding) and where the parent and subsidiary remain distinguishable and their functions largely unintegrated, to those where the integration is almost total (6–7 on the scale, corresponding to Absorption) and all functions and departments of B are absorbed into A. Symbiotic acquisitions fall at intermediate points on this continuum corresponding to partial integration, where some but not all functions and departments of B are integrated into A. Whilst this view simplifies integration into one continuum it does of course comprise or summarize a multitude of different components.

Figure 13.1 also suggests the way in which the integration of the new subsidiary may vary. With a low level of integration (1–2) regular financial and other operating figures will be required for the parent to monitor the performance of the subsidiary. Some top level personnel changes may be initiated, and some restrictions are likely to be imposed on capital spending. However, the subsidiary will continue to operate and present itself to the market much as before acquisition.

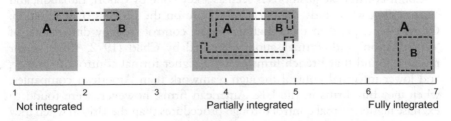

Fig. 13.1 Spectrum of integration

With higher levels of integration (3–5) the new parent is likely to take over and run centrally whole areas of activity. This is likely to cover strategy, and may involve finance, personnel policy and systems, procurement, product development, IT systems, and possibly the whole area of branding and management of the company image. Depending on how strong the new parent regards the reputation of the subsidiary's name and trademarks to be, it may or may not decide to continue using them. At these partial levels of integration the parent is likely to have recognized that it has something to learn from the acquired company. However, it will only centralize functions if it believes this is to the advantage of the corporation as a whole.

The highest integration levels (6–7) correspond to total absorption into the parent's organization. Brand names may be retained if they are strong, but, particularly in service organizations, may be discontinued after a transitional period.

Control

When one company acquires another it needs to exercise some control over the company that is now acting in its name and using its resources. Control is in many ways the antithesis of trust, since the greater the level of trust between the companies the less the perceived need for tight control systems (Faulkner, chap. 16, above). However, control can take many forms.

Control systems may be limited to control over budgets and capital expenditure. They may involve appointing staff to key positions in the subsidiary company, carrying out certain important functions like planning and personnel in the parent company, or imposing 'need for approval' requirements on identified decisions (Geringer and Hebert, 1989). The control system selected illustrates the degree to which the parent is willing to grant a level of autonomy to the newly acquired subsidiary, and may be crucial in terms of influencing the level of motivation of the acquired company personnel. Whilst not discussing national culture, Goold and Campbell (1988) draw attention to three main approaches to managing subsidiaries, depending on the degree of control and planning by the centre that is involved.

Control of new acquisitions is seen as a key issue by Calori, Lubatkin, and Very (1994), who study the effect of culture on the process of integration. Calori et al. depend in their analysis on the control strategy dimensions of 'centralisation' and 'formalisation' identified by Child (1972, 1973). Their research found that French firms exercise higher formal control of strategy, and lower informal control through teamwork than American companies, when they buy firms in the UK. American firms, however, were found to exercise higher formal control through procedures than the British when they buy firms in France. In fact Dunning, writing about an earlier wave of FDI, notes that 'we may perhaps say with some certainty that US managerial and financial control is more likely than not to be fairly rigid for the first five years or so [after investing in a UK firm]' (Dunning, 1958: 112).

Other research has shown that French decision-making is concentrated towards the top of hierarchies (Horowitz, 1978; Hickson and Pugh, 1995). Research by Maurice, Sorg, and Warner (1980), comparing French with West German and UK manufacturing firms, found that in France there are usually more levels in the hierarchy. They claim that French hierarchies tend to be more top-heavy, with between 1.5 and 2 times as many supervisors and managers as in German firms. Calori and De Woot (1994) add to this hierarchical characterization by noting that French companies have a far higher number of organizational levels, and a lower level of participation than German or other northern European countries.

Culturally, the Germans emerge from surveys as tending to have high levels of uncertainty avoidance (Hofstede, 1991). This is associated with attaching a high value to stability, and has been taken by commentators to be a main reason why in German organizations there tends to be a strong orientation towards the use of and adherence to rules, and a heavy stress on control procedures (Hampden-Turner and Trompenaars, 1993). Relationships exhibit a high level of formality and commitment to paper, and attention to detail is painstaking. As Hickson and Pugh (1995: 97) have put it, 'One of the most characteristic aspects of the German culture, which certainly strikes an outsider, is their way of managing uncertainty through an emphasis on planning and orderliness.'

This penchant for order is, according to some writers, shown in their attention to organizational structure rather than to process (e.g. Stewart et al., 1994). Germans also tend to score highly on Hofstede's measure of 'power distance' and this cultural disposition manifests itself in the presence in most German organizations of ordered and status-dominated hierarchies.

Datta and Grant (1990) suggest that autonomy should be proportional to the unrelatedness of the acquisition's business. Abo (1994) describes the Japanese management system as very flexible with few rigid job demarcations. Workers, supervisors, and managers collectively take part in the discussion of managerial and operational functions. Assembly-line workers are responsible for on-line inspection and quality. There is a use of 'implicit control' based on shared corporate norms and understanding. The importance of control of acquisitions and the fact that a wide variety of approaches to it exist are thus widely acknowledged in the literature.

Communication

Communication is partly a matter of systems and style, but also a question of the communicators' skill at getting this message across to colleagues. This is an area where national style and skill with languages is very important, since different cultures have different attitudes towards communication, and language barriers inevitably make communication difficult. Some nationalities have differing communication styles that are indirect, for example the often unspoken style and 'implicit understanding' of Japanese culture, whilst the distant understatement and explicit comprehension of British culture confuses some nations, and contrasts strongly with the highly direct but very jargon-ridden communication style of US culture. Within this variety, French and German communication styles may differ in respect to issues of logical necessity and formality respectively. For example French organizations often have more non-managerial white-collar specialists performing either commercial-cum-administrative or technical functions, which reflects the French tendency to separate technical, planning, administrative, and supervisory tasks from executive and operational ones (Sorge, 1993). In order to make this segmented and complex operation predictable and reliable, French organizations tend to use written rules, instructions, and communications extensively. The formality of German organizations, on the other hand, has already been noted (Stewart *et al.*, 1994) and this formality can be seen to extend to methods of communication too.

The methods and style of communication adopted by a parent company in dealing with a foreign subsidiary are thus likely to play a critical role in the integration of any foreign subsidiary into its parent company's organization by reflecting the differences which exist between the parent's and subsidiary's natural communication styles.

Strategic philosophy

The parent company's strategic philosophy may be crucial to the subsidiary's future well-being. This comprises the parent company's management style and culture as well as whether it adopts a primarily strategic or financial orientation. It also comprises the extent to which autonomy is granted to the subsidiary, the expectation or otherwise of immediate and short-term profits, and will set a framework within which the new subsidiary will have to learn to work.

The short-termism of UK management has frequently been commented upon, both in academic studies (Lane, 1995) and by those working in industry (Marsh, 1995). Acquisitions by French companies, on the other hand, tend to be strategic rather than based on short-term financial considerations. This strategic emphasis is often phrased in a quasi-military language in which the contestants (for France has a large number of contested takeover bids) adopt, by analogy, the stance of the great generals and marshals (Barsoux and Lawrence, 1990). In contrast US management culture places a stronger emphasis on achieving short-term financial results (Jacobs, 1991) and many US companies tend to be managed for the short-term maximization of profits and the maximization of shareholder value (Calori and De Woot, 1994; Lawrence, 1996).

The strategic approach or philosophy adopted by a new parent company in relation to a new foreign subsidiary is thus another critical component involved in the integration of the subsidiary into the parent's organization.

Methodology

The data used in this chapter were obtained primarily through semi-structured interviews with managing directors of acquired companies (as illustrated in Table 13.1). The essential details of the company selection process for the interviews were as follows. A list of potentially relevant examples of FDI was prepared using data from the Central Statistical Office, Reuters, Predicasts, DTI, the journal *Acquisitions Monthly*, and other sources. This covered acquisitions of UK companies by US, French, German, and Japanese companies in the period 1985–1994. Interviews were held with companies selected from among those companies acquired by a US, French, German, or Japanese company. Forty out of 79 companies asked (50.6 per cent) agreed to being interviewed with the companies being divided equally among the four nationalities. Interviewed companies were spread over the whole of the United Kingdom with the exception of Wales and Northern Ireland. Seventy per cent of companies interviewed were in the manufacturing sector and 30 per cent in service industries.

The interview schedule covered a wide range of management practices. Background information on the story behind the acquisition was also

TABLE 13.1 *Interviewees*

No. of Interviewees	French	German	Japanese	US	Total	% of Total
CEO/MD/General Manager	5	8	8	8	29	72.5
Chairman	2	1	0	1	4	10
Other director	1	1	2	1	5	12.5
Non-board level — Manager/Director	2	0	0	0	2	5
Total	10	10	10	10	40	100
Subsidiary board-level directors	8	10	10	10	38	95
Appointed from parent	0	3	0	2	5	13
Appointed from subsidiary	10	7	10	8	35	88
Joined company before acquisition	8	7	8	7	30	75
Average no. of years since acquisition	7.4	5.6	7.2	5.5	6.4	
Average no. of subsidiary employees	983	212	922	1213	833	

gathered. Respondents were asked open ended questions about which changes they felt had been the greatest and had the most impact on the company. The interviews involved questions under the following headings:

1. General background to the acquisition: reasons and consequences.
2. Background to major changes and influences:
    2.1. Discussion of 2–3 major areas of change;
    2.2. Patterns of influence;
    2.3. Integration.
3. Impact of acquisition on performance:
    3.1. What have been the main benefits of the acquisition?
    3.2. What have been the main disadvantages of the acquisition?
    3.3. How has the acquisition contributed to profitability and growth?

In each case the interviews lasted for at least an hour and in all save one case were conducted at the offices of the acquired company.

The interviewees were mostly (73 per cent) CEOs, managing directors, or general managers of the subsidiary company, most of whom had been with the subsidiary company since before the acquisition and almost all of whom (95 per cent) were board-level directors of the subsidiary company. Some (13 per cent) had been appointed by the new parent company from among parent company staff. In order to avoid any bias that might still result from such a mix, the interviews focused on significant events, and minimized more judgemental and qualitative questions. All interviewees were also asked to rate the degree of integration achieved by the acquisition on the scale of 1 to 7 described above. All interviews were tape-recorded.

Results

The 40 companies interviewed had an average integration level of 3.61. However, within this overall figure there were significant national differences. American companies were the most committed to total integration of subsidiaries with an integration level of 4.77, whilst Japanese and German companies tended to be the least inclined to integrate with average integration scores of only 3.05 and 2.95, respectively. French companies interviewed had an average integration level of 3.65. An ANOVA test showed that the overall differences between the average integration scores for each country were significant at the 7 per cent level ($p = 0.072$).

Overall, the interviews showed that the most common form of control imposed was through financial means, i.e. approval and monitoring of subsidiary budgets, and control of capital expenditure. This form of control was generally allied to the provision of a strategic framework within which subsidiary decision-making was to be confined. Differences between national approaches in this area mirrored those found in levels of integration.

TABLE 13.2 *National contrasts in parent–subsidiary relationships*

	Integration	Control	Communication	Strategic philosophy
USA	Fully integrated	Targets/budgets strict financial control	Open but formal	Short-term financial
France	Partially integrated	Strategic and financial control	Need to know/ top down	Long-term 'imperial'
Japan	Not integrated	Budgets/systems 'advisers'	Need to know/ implicit	Long-term strategic
Germany	Not integrated	Varied: budgets/systems informal controls	Upward formality; downward informality	Long-term indistinct

The parents were generally able to reassure their subsidiaries that their investment was for the long term. Communication was an area in which there was a clear differentiation between individual national styles. From the interviews it was apparent that American companies were professional communicators, relishing the use of first names, regular meetings at all levels, notice-boards with mission and vision statements on them, and company newspapers. Communication between Japanese companies and their UK subsidiaries did not seem as easy or open in comparison. German companies, on the other hand, appeared to veer between the stiffly formal and the self-consciously informal, whilst French companies seemed to suffer little self-doubt, communicating well amongst themselves but informing subsidiary staff only on a 'need to know' basis and adopting what one interviewee referred to as a generally 'colonial attitude'. The four countries' attitudes to the four key areas concerned are summarized in Table 13.2. These four areas of overall integration, control, communication, and strategic philosophy will now be reviewed in more detail with respect to each of the four countries.

Integration

American post-acquisition management tended primarily towards total absorption even where this required some time for readjustment. In the case of a diversified US manufacturer's subsidiary USA3[2] the new US manager said: 'The people here seem to hate all things American, even the size of the note pads. Some of the personnel still have to adjust to the fact that they are now part of a very successful American-based multinational, not a little family company.' In this case the company was very much 'absorbed', and other examples of total integration of UK companies by US parents abounded. USA4 progressively absorbed its new UK subsidiary, strengthening both

---

[2] For reasons of confidentiality, all companies are referred to by numbered codes denoting the parent company nationality: USAn for US, Jn for Japanese, Gn for German, and Fn for French parent companies where n = 1 to 10. Former UK parent companies are denoted by UKn.

control systems and financial reporting. The MD said the new subsidiary: 'had been totally integrated. There was about a year of separateness, but for full integration 5 years was needed. We have a well organized account management structure which doesn't tolerate weak performers.' In some cases the nature of the business made integration inevitable. For example, USA5, a US freight company, totally integrated a UK company into its worldwide organization, reorganizing its systems to match USA5's global systems. Of the ten US acquisitions interviewed five had an integration level of 5 or more, three were at the 3–4 level, and only 2 at the unintegrated 1–2 level. With an average score of 4.77 the preference of US parent companies was for a high level of integration.

Japanese companies' attitude to integration contrasted strongly with the American one, with any change achieved incrementally by slow adaptation to the parent company's norms. One Japanese bank had acquired a UK financial services company in order to establish a presence in the City of London, but having done so made very few changes, assuming that the UK management understood the business better. In another case, a UK pharmaceutical company was acquired inadvertently by a Japanese pharmaceutical firm when it acquired a US-owned group in order to preserve a Japanese licensing arrangement. Nevertheless, it provided the UK firm with substantial financial support and technical assistance, despite having little other involvement with the company.

The new Japanese owners of a UK consumer products company J01 which was interviewed, supported them steadily financially, and did not interfere in operational matters, leaving the company essentially unintegrated, a hands-off attitude which surprised the director interviewed. In the case of a UK electronics company (J02) acquired by a major Japanese company, which again remained unintegrated, the MD said: 'Historically most of their sales organizations are totally controlled from Japan...but not with us! We are quite an experiment... the numbers are not crucial, so long as we are going in the right direction...'

In all acquisitions there is a balance between allowing the subsidiary freedom from interference by the parent, and on the other hand seeking the benefits that closer integration could bring. There is thus a balance between independence and intervention along the spectrum of integration. In the case of Japanese acquisitions the balance is often one where supportive independence dominates. Of the ten Japanese acquisitions interviewed none had been integrated at the 5 or higher level, 6 were at the 3–4 level, and 4 were left at the 1–2 unintegrated level, giving a low average of 3.05 overall.

German acquirers, in a similar way to the Japanese, tended to avoid closely integrating their new acquisitions if at all possible. Of the ten companies interviewed none had an integration score above 6; 5 were in the 3–4 range and the other 5 were at the 1–2 unintegrated level, the average German score being 2.95. A major German safety equipment manufacturer acquired a small entrepreneurial firm (G06) in the same line of business. Unusually the entrepreneurial MD has remained with the company with the German parent saying: 'We don't want you to change. Stay the way you are, because you have the ability to move in a market place more than we can.' Another UK company, in this case a very high-tech instrument company (G04) acquired by a German competitor with a larger global presence, was also left alone by its new parent. The MD said: 'They have never sought to change anything. They really have left us alone. I don't think we have learnt much from them, but they may have learnt something about the flexibility of a small company, and what they need to do to become more flexible.' It is worth noting that where little change occurred it was often due to the subsidiary's management gaining the trust and acceptance of the new parent's management and convincing them that it knew its business better than they did.

The *French* acquirers interviewed were in the middle of the integration spectrum at an average level of 3.65. Less determined to integrate acquired companies than American parent companies, but more than Japanese and German companies. Four of the ten companies interviewed were at a 5+ level of integration, a further four at 3–4, and two at an unintegrated 1–2 level. The level of integration varied from total integration of a previously British IT consultancy company to form a French-based transnational, to water companies that have been largely left alone to operate substantially as before, at least in part due to regulatory restrictions. A manager in a French-owned UK public utility company said: 'the general philosophy is "local management". Although they are interested in this high up view they really leave the rest of it to local management.... Because we are a regulated business there's a limit to what they can do'.

Control

For the *Americans* an emphasis on financial control and shorter financial time horizons was typical. In many cases the change in financial controls was sudden and related to a lack of the controls expected in a US financial environment, with quarterly reporting requirements which privately owned UK companies do not face. The MD of a small UK company USA6 acquired by a larger US company said: 'The Americans had to justify their investment. They put in financial reporting systems much quicker and ones which were compatible with their own systems and what they have done has improved the business. It needed a financial controller rather than a part time accountant'.

The need for regular financial returns by US companies facing quarterly reporting constraints was common. According to the UK MD of USA7 this is also linked with a pragmatic style of management depending on trust but with a heavy emphasis on performance: 'The relationship with the US CEO was one of trust. He asked "is this British Management delivering that which we require?"... if it was he didn't interfere... He said to me "you know what style of management we have? It's the management of the Mafia—send us the money and we leave you alone!"... it worked very well.'

A requirement for consistency with the corporate profile often came along with the financial controls. This could be tempered by a realization that there had to be a balance between integration involving instilling big company values and trying to preserve the small company's entrepreneurial spirit and flexibility. However, all ten US acquired companies interviewed reported substantial tightening of control systems especially financial ones.

Japanese companies not only use budgets and financial control systems to monitor their acquisitions but also other methods of keeping informed. Japanese companies uniquely introduced 'advisers' and they generally permitted rather more decision-making autonomy to their new subsidiaries. The 'advisers' were often managers sent abroad for two to four years to gain international experience prior to promotion back in Japan. In one subsidiary it was said that:

there are no formal links, there have been some placements of Japanese personnel but they've been in new staff roles.... The few that have done it have been perceived by J08 to be up and coming managers and have come to learn about management internationally rather than take part in day-to-day management.

However, in many cases these advisers had substantial expertise in some specialist area. J07's MD said that once he realized one Japanese manager was a highly skilled engineer he was able to make very good use of his expertise in production management. The advantages of specialist technical support were also available as the MD of J06 found: 'We ran into a problem on a product. It required technology on adhesives which we hadn't got experience of and they quite easily said we'll send our adhesives man in.... But then they had all these experts—very, very, focused experts.'

In general, where decisions were required from Japanese parent companies, they could prove rather slow in arriving, according to several interviewees. The MD of a UK retailing company J05 said that a problem with their Japanese parent was: 'Getting a clear answer, a clear "yes go ahead". We keep battling away and sometimes they'll never say no. If they said "no, go away" we'd know where we stand but their culture doesn't permit them to say no.' Another MD of a Japanese subsidiary J06 said: 'It was very frustrating, it would sometimes take weeks to get an answer. In reality you actually knew the answer to it. It was very annoying for the guys on the shop floor.'

On the other hand where trust over a particular issue or range of issues had been established, considerable independence could be expected, but the trust and respect had to be earned. The MD of J07 said:

I learned very quickly... that because of the communication problems they are only interested in figures not written words. It makes my life very much easier.... My first presentation in Tokyo was to the effect that we needed 3–4 years to get things going.

Where we stand today is where we predicted we would be [4 years ago] achieving what you promise is very, very important to a Japanese...so it's a very happy relationship.

The ways in which Japanese acquirers stand out compared to the other national groups support some but not all of the normal characterizations of Japanese management practice. Their long-term and strategic orientation and collective orientation were clearly apparent. As the MD of a pharmaceutical company's subsidiary J09 said: 'There is a feeling that we should know what we need to do and that we don't need to go to [our parent] for counsel. But they know what is going on and have been very supportive.' Overall, Japanese companies' attitude to control was to believe in budgets and forecasts and expect them to be met in detail, and to give considerable operational latitude but to take the big decisions in Japan, often agonizingly slowly.

The *German* attitude to control revealed by the interviews is varied, ranging from Board representation and use of management accounts to putting in an MD who then controls very directly. The subsidiary managers interviewed generally felt that their German parent companies exercised relatively little influence over their acquisitions. Compared with the other firms, the German acquisitions were less likely to have parent company managers as CEOs, or as marketing and R&D directors. One successful subsidiary (G04) of a German acquirer comments: 'We report with management accounts on a monthly basis which we send direct to Germany.... Since we have never been wildly off budget, there is no major response to these. Anyway financially we out-perform our parent as a whole.'

Even less successful companies enjoyed a fair degree of freedom. One (G06) manager said: 'We are visited from Hamburg once a quarter. They get involved in the thinking as well as the numbers. But in general their aim is to keep a tight rein on the finances and not worry too much about how we achieve the results.' But there were also more muddled companies. One (G08) director said:

The German company has a combined board of five people all of whom came over in the first few months to see their new acquisition...to be totally honest all of their views were totally different. So we produced a five-year business plan and rang them up and they said "that's good, get on with it"...We did look to them for guidance in the early days...but their ability to make decisions was somewhat strange to say the least.

Another German company (G09) started out very autocratically but showed that personal relationships as well as success could influence the degree of freedom a subsidiary enjoyed. The MD of the subsidiary commented that:

We would use G where we needed them but push them away where we didn't...we were able to wave our results as justification for the UDI that we declared. It was a quirk of the changing times within G and our success that led them to that method of control. It was also personal. I very quickly developed a relationship of 100% trust with the chairman in both directions and he left it to me.

French companies' way of exercising control is nationally distinct. In general they operate very hierarchically and determine major decisions between French managers, regarding acquired company personnel with a 'colonial' attitude—another example of the colonialist attitude to acquisitions noted by Empson (1998). An executive from a French-acquired aerospace company (F01) states: 'Things are decided informally amongst Frenchmen to the exclusion of British middle management. If contacts were plotted, pretty well all the informal links would be between the French.' The British part-time chairman of a French-acquired financial services company (F02) said: 'They have difficulty in understanding the British concept of a Board. So far as they are concerned a Board is a kind of registration. It is like a levée, not a discussion and decision-taking body.' French companies seem to place great emphasis on the distinction between strategic decisions (to be made by French managers at HQ) and operational decisions (to be made by local managers on the spot), though financial controls remain important. As an executive from a French-acquired water company (F10) said: 'They appointed a French Financial Controller... that is one post they try and keep for themselves. On the operational side it's all local.'

Communication

The *American* companies interviewed also tended to pursue informal communications in a relatively formal way. That is not to say that US parent companies are always formal, but as one MD of a US multinational manufacturing company's subsidiary USA8 said:

On the one hand there's a very informal style. I was at the site when the takeover took place and the CEO of USA8 came over and said "Call me Hank", well you wouldn't call the chairman of UK01 [the former parent Co.] "Hank". He wouldn't invite you to.... But on the other hand there's a very high degree of toughness and insistence on conformity... conform—or you're dead. With UK01 ... a signal from on high was a signal for wide-ranging debate—was this meaningful, useful, and were we going to obey it! USA8 cannot cope with a stand-alone subsidiary. They have to integrate everything.

Companies acquired by US parents, reported moves towards shorter planning time horizons and a more short-term employment philosophy, but the toughness mentioned above also extended to employee relations as the MD of USA8 also said: 'I find American business culture pretty difficult. UK01 never talked about caring and valuing people but its actions showed that it did. USA8 talks a huge amount about caring and valuing people but when the going gets tough... it doesn't care at all.'

For the *Japanese,* the area of communication can be a difficult one for both linguistic and cultural reasons. For example, in one interview with a previously family-owned engineering company J01 the MD said:

Because all Japanese companies' managers speak good English, language is not a problem on a day-to-day basis. It does, however, pose a barrier in terms of control and information. Virtually all written communication to and from Japan is in Japanese and I cannot understand it. Nor is it translated for me. I therefore don't know for certain exactly what they are saying.

Language problems can thus lead to communication barriers. However, in another Japanese acquisition (J10) the interviewee said: 'I think language is undoubtedly an issue at times but it's never a significant problem. I think it can be at the more junior level... When it's just straightforward technical reports it's no problem but when they are trying to get over areas of subtlety it can be difficult.' Thus communication barriers due to language could be overcome more easily where technical terminology was involved, perhaps due to the preponderance of imported foreign words or *gairaigo* in technical Japanese.

The *German* analysis emphasized the fact that the issue of personal relationships also concerns communication. On the question of formality, two photographs belonging to the MD of a company (G10) which had been part of a US-led MBO subsequently sold to a German company illustrate the point. One showed the US-led MBO team on a beach at 10 am celebrating the fact that they had just bought the company. The other showed a row of sober, suited people in a wood-panelled hotel reception room the day the contract to sell the company to a German company was signed. This, the UK MD felt, graphically illustrated the difference in formality between the two companies.

However, whilst there may sometimes be a sober, suited formality associated with German management, there is also a sense, as the interviews revealed, in which German management style can be very informal. Various explanations were offered for this apparent paradox. One MD in a German-owned subsidiary (G02) held that it was a generational issue: 'The Germans are quasi-formal and the first management team was very traditional and formal. The new management, however, is much younger and much less formal. We have "casual days", "funny tie days" and "sandals days" and this sort of thing!'

Other managers saw increased informality as a reaction to the recession of the early 1990s, and a learning process, whereby a more informal approach would preserve some of the small company characteristics that large German companies might learn from in a recession. In the latter case this approach was contrasted with an earlier approach which involved management quite literally 'by the book' using a rigid set of procedures. A German manager managing a UK subsidiary (G07) said: 'We Germans are still pretty formal ...I can use first names with the British but use titles with my German colleagues.' Despite such cultural differences German managers were seen to be closer to UK culture than many other nationalities, as a financial services company (G03) manager observed: 'The culture is not that different. A bit more formal, but they are in my opinion far closer to us than any other European lot. You wouldn't have any trouble having dinner with them.'

In *France* communication tends to be very hierarchical and top-down, with little involvement of British managers in the decision-making hierarchy. The head of a financial services company (F03) acquired by a French bank said: 'Communications are largely on a need-to-know basis. I don't get involved in the Paris business at all, although I try to network as much as I can. I don't ferret around with things that don't concern London.' An executive of an engineering company (F04) added :

The French hierarchy is a 'power' hierarchy and it is the power that we find the most difficult to live with. I don't think most of industry in the UK, certainly a TQM-inspired participative modern ethos, has the power element that the French have built in to everything, and they do have an arrogance and a dominance characteristic that one finds very difficult to live with.

Strategic Philosophy

The *American* philosophy of post-acquisition management appears to be very much a hands-on approach. The MD of USA7, which had been German-owned but which was bought by a US company said:

They expect instant returns... There's no "Well, we wait for three years, make sure there's synergies, and then look for a return"—they want it *now* ... The shock is not just financial ... the speed at which change is to be introduced is quite extraordinary. So no doubt about it, a much more interventionist type of policy, much more dynamic, much more forcible, and much more demanding.

Despite a shortening of financial time horizons imposed by USA acquirers, the larger size of many US parent companies relative to their UK subsidiaries meant that very significant investments were still made in the subsidiaries. The MD of a small UK technology-based company USA9 said that the main benefit of the acquisition of his company was that: 'Our company was going down the tubes fast. USA9 has been very successful in turning around the business and putting in huge sums of money. One must give them credit for that which UK2 (our former owners) probably could not have done.' Another MD of the UK service company USA9 said:

Now we are preparing five-year plans... before we never went further forward than 12 months. But at the same time, there is pressure for quarterly results ... You get all kinds of absurd requests to make more profit or collect more debt each quarter... so we've noticed both a lengthening and a shortening of the time horizons.

However, whilst experiencing the financial demands of US ownership the subsidiaries of some US companies have tended to have more autonomy over capital expenditure and changes in strategy. One MD of a US company's subsidiary USA10 said that if one is fairly dynamic in one's approach it may be possible to drive strategy which the parent company might not think of. In the case of the UK company concerned this was mainly apparent through marketing and liaison initiatives which it, not its US parent, had initiated.

The US acquirers tended to install formal, multi-year planning systems, and adopt a global approach to business but demand good short-term financial results. The implication is that if the company does not perform in a relatively short time-scale it or at the very least the MD will be divested.

The *Japanese* companies' strategic philosophy was consistently long term, even if the strategic details could often appear to be rather fuzzy and *ad hoc*. The MD of a UK pharmaceutical company J03 acquired along with its US parent by a Japanese company said:

I think we have benefited from the takeover from being able to address issues which prior to the takeover would have been difficult... through lack of funding or lack of strategic direction... Sometimes the patience for the return amazes even me. They seem quite laid back about it... the return on these things will stretch way out into the future.

Another UK company, J04, which manufactured a specialist consumer product and was bought by a major Japanese firm said that: 'The main benefit has to be the investment that was made. Our subsequent success has stemmed from the fact that it gave us the breathing space to move forward.' The same company is also a good example of the 'slingshot effect', in that the subsidiary was eventually sold due to the parent's financial difficulties in Japan and left having received substantial technical and financial support. This, when put together with their own in-house development, arguably put them ahead of their former Japanese parents.

With the exception of a longer-term employment philosophy, we did not find significant differences between Japanese and other acquirers in personnel policy changes. Virtually every company had introduced some or all of the operational practices associated with Japanese companies. It appears that Japanese acquiring companies adjust their HRM practices to suit the local UK context, while in the operations area most companies have gone a long way towards adopting a Japanese approach, as Oliver and Wilkinson (1992) concluded.

All ten Japanese acquisitions interviewed described new owners whose major merit was their long-term philosophy, and willingness to back their purchase with financial resources. The logical incremental attitude commonly ascribed to Japanese companies meant that, whilst detailed plans were often not in place or apparent, the general objectives behind the acquisitions, such as developing closer customer relations, or becoming more international, were discernible.

German parent companies, as with Japanese companies, had a long-term view of investment decisions. However, even this could have an apparent downside by being almost too good. The MD of a manufacturing subsidiary G10 said: 'I think our financial director...would almost have welcomed being pressed more to be self-sufficient. It was almost a failing of the Germans to be as supportive as they were. Quite frankly I think it would have done us good if they had said "look there's no more money—you've got to sort yourself out".' Looking at several other acquisitions it seems that for long-term financial support to be a success the subsidiary has not only got to have the support but also some idea about how to use that support and about the long-term direction of the company—whether that direction is self-generated or dictated by the parent. Just support or just direction is insufficient. This was reflected by the above MD's sense that the UK company under its German owners suffered from a lack of strategic direction: 'it failed to have a long-term strategic objective. The business objectives were not known by the board so how on earth could they be transmitted to the rest of the troops.'

German management seems definitely influenced by the differing nature of the home financial markets (compared to US financial markets). For example, the manager of a German company's subsidiary (G03) said what might be difficult for a US company manager to say: 'They are long-termist. They do not have making a profit itself as a prime matter. They are not profit-driven. They want to know about quarterly results but they are not dominated by them.' The remarkable aspect of these findings is that whilst they confirm the long-term nature of the German management approach they directly contradict one of the assumptions about German management practice found in the literature. Commentators tend to stress a high level of formality, rule-orientation, orderliness, and formal provisions for participation as salient characteristics of German management. These features did not distinguish the changes brought about by German investors in the UK; in fact quite the contrary. This may reflect, to some extent, the observation made by Stewart *et al.* (1994) that a German penchant for order is manifest in organizational structure rather than in process, since several of the changes which were distinctively less formal among German acquisitions concerned process rather than structure *per se*. Nevertheless, our findings raise questions regarding the validity of the typical German management stereotype, even if it represents an over-simplified view which is in any event subject to change. However, it can be challenged both on grounds of the present contradictory findings and also in view of the fact that confirmation of other elements in the stereotype presented by the literature was absent from our comparative data.

French companies generally have a long-term strategic philosophy in relation to acquisitions. A manager in a major French electronics company's subsidiary (F01) said: 'A strategic rather than a financial orientation exists; it has to, since the company loses money. However, it is thought to be important to stay in the market.' The MD of a high-tech manufacturing firm (F09) acquired by a French company said:

The way in which the business is being approached is interesting—'the centre and several self-sufficient satellites'—but in my opinion it was never going to be a workable philosophy because it weakens the whole thing rather than strengthens it... It's wonderful to manage a subsidiary where one is totally empowered, but on the other hand how is one going to grow the business without the help of the group?

Another interviewee (F05) said: 'Decision-making is collective, but the French are very autocratic, but on big strategic issues only.'

This shows that the attitude may depend on the size of the decision being made. A French financial services company, for example, was said to reserve larger decisions for itself but to allow its British subsidiary (F07) considerable local autonomy. Indeed, one personnel director related an incident that occurred shortly after being acquired when this became quite clear:

The FD spoke about the state of the business—you can imagine the air of gloom... then another (UK) director said 'What do you want us to do?' and there was a pregnant silence and the French director paused, looked straight down the table, and said 'Monsieur, if we have to tell you what to do we have the wrong people'. So I thought this is good news because nobody is going to tell us what has to be done.

In other words the French management considered that it was not for them to influence the UK management so much as for the UK management to run their business. This apparently surprised the UK manager concerned, who said he had always regarded French companies as bureaucratic and centralist. This also shows that to a certain extent it is up to a subsidiary to manage its owners as much as be managed by them.

Conclusion

In general all four nationalities struggled to get the best out of their acquisitions, dealing with problems pragmatically, but often revealing differing national tendencies in management style. The issue of integration was an important differentiator in the way companies from different countries tackled the problem of post-acquisition management. American companies showed a tendency to absorb their acquisitions closely into the group corporate structure, whilst the other three countries tended to keep them more separate, but to selectively integrate where they perceived potential advantages from doing so. Japanese companies were the least integrationist.

All national acquirers used financial, investment, and budgetary control to monitor and control performance. American companies were more likely to impose parent-company personnel on the subsidiary in executive roles. Japanese companies preferred 'advisers' seconded from Japan. French companies tended to separate strategic from operational decisions, and to keep strategic decisions within the French orbit. German companies were less consistent in their methods.

All four countries professed to communicate more openly than the British. However, American companies communicated professionally in a systematic fashion, often trying to impose US culture through this means. Japanese companies had more difficulties with communication for reasons of language and culture. French companies tended to communicate in a top-down manner, and German companies tried to be informal, whilst retaining a German respect for formality in their dealing with fellow Germans.

All except American companies exhibited a long-term strategic philosophy, which was their strongest card in developing newly acquired company loyalty. American companies tended to emphasize short-term profits, sometimes in a somewhat menacing way. The impression was that if the new acquisition did not show adequate profits in short order it, or at least its MD, would be divested.

Management behaviour was, of course, to some extent conditioned by the state in which the acquisition was found. But over and above that, some national management style tendencies were clearly discernible. Furthermore, the differences in styles of overall integration, control, communication, and strategic philosophy illustrated the importance of the concept of integration to successful acquisitions, as well as the way in which it tends to differ by nationality.

References

ABO, T. (ed.) (1994), *Hybrid Factory: The Japanese Production System in the United States* (New York: Oxford University Press).

ANGWIN, D. (1998), 'Post Acquisition Management of Corporate Take-overs in the UK,' PhD thesis (Warwick).

BARSOUX, J.-L. and LAWRENCE, P. (1990), *Management in France* (London: Cassell).

CALORI, R. and DE WOOT, P. (1994), *A European Management Model* (Hemel Hempstead: Prentice-Hall).

CALORI, R., LUBATKIN, M., and VERY, P. (1994), 'Control Mechanisms in Cross-Border Acquisitions: An International Comparison', *Organisation Studies* 15/3: 361–79.

CHILD, J. (1972), 'Organization Structure and Strategies of Control: A Replication of the Aston Study', *Administrative Science Quarterly*, 17: 163–77.

——(1973), 'Strategies of Control and Organizational Behaviour', *Administrative Science Quarterly*, 18: 1–17.

——(1981), 'Culture, Contingency and Capitalism in the Cross-National Study of Organisations', *Research in Organisational Behaviour*, 3: 303–56.

——FAULKNER, D., and PITKETHLY, R. (2000), 'Foreign Direct Investment in the UK 1985–1994: The Impact on Domestic Management Practice,' *Journal of Management Studies*.

DATTA, D. K. (1991), 'Organizational Fit and Acquisition Performance: Effects of Post-Acquisition Integration', *Strategic Management Journal*, 12/4: 281–97.

—— and GRANT, J. H. (1990), 'Relationships between Type of Acquisition, the Autonomy Given to the Acquired Firm, and Acquisition Success: An Empirical Analysis', *Journal of Management* 16/1: 29–44.

DUNNING, J. H. (1958), *American Investment in British Manufacturing Industry* (London: Allen & Unwin).

EMPSON, L. F. (1998), 'Mergers between Professional Services Firms : How the Distinctive Organisational Characteristics Influence the Process of Value Creation', PhD thesis (London Business School).

GALL, E. A. (1991), 'Strategies for Merger Success', *Journal of Business Strategy*, 12/2: 26–9.

GERINGER, J. M. and HEBERT, L. (1989), 'Control and Performance of International Joint-Ventures', *Journal of International Business Studies*, 20 (summer), 235–54.

GOOLD, M. and CAMPBELL, A. (1988), 'Managing the Diversified Corporation: The Tensions Facing the Chief Executive', *Long Range Planning*, 21/4: 12–24.

HAMPDEN-TURNER, C. and TROMPENAARS, F. (1993), *The Seven Cultures of Capitalism* (London: Doubleday).

HASPESLAGH, P. and JEMISON, D. (1991), *Managing Acquisitions* (New York: Free Press).

HICKSON, D. J. and PUGH, D. S. (1995), *Management Worldwide* (London: Penguin).

—— HININGS, C. R., McMILLAN, C. J., and SCHWITTER, J. P. (1974), 'The Culture-Free Context of Organisation Structure: A Tri-National Comparison', *Sociology*, 8: 59–80.

HOFSTEDE, G. (1991), *Cultures and Organisations* (Maidenhead: McGraw-Hill).

HOROWITZ, J. (1978), 'Management Control in France, Great Britain and Germany', *Columbia Journal of World Business*, 13: 16–22.

JACOBS, M.T. (1991), *Short-Term America: The Causes and Cures of our Business Myopia* (Boston: Harvard Business School Press).

KPMG (1997), *Corporate Finance Survey* (London: KPMG).

LANE, C. (1995), *Industry and Society in Europe* (Aldershot: Edward Elgar).

LAWRENCE, P. (1996), *Management in the USA* (London: Sage).

LORANGE, P and ROOS, J. (1992), *Strategic Alliances: Formation, Implementation and Evolution* (Oxford: Blackwell).

MARSH, D. (1995), 'Contact between Cultures: Germany and the UK: Learning from each Other', *Financial Times*, 29 May, p. 15.

MAURICE, M., SORGE, A., and WARNER, M. (1980), 'Societal Differences on Organizing Manufacturing Units: A Comparison of France, West Germany and Great Britain', *Organization Studies*, 1: 59–86.

MORRIS, J. and WILKINSON, B. (1996), 'The Transfer of Japanese Management to Alien Institutional Environments', *Journal of Management Studies*, 32: 719–30.

MOROSINI, P. and SINGH, H. (1994), 'Post Cross-Border Acquisitions: Implementing National Culture Compatible Strategies to Improve Performance', *European Management Journal*, 12: 390–400.

NORBURN, D. and SCHOENBERG, R. (1994), 'European Cross-Border Acquisition: How was it for You?', *Long Range Planning*, 27/4: 25–34.

OLIVER, N. and WILKINSON, B. (1992), *The Japanisation of British Industry: New Developments in the 1990s*, 2nd edn. (Oxford: Blackwell).

SORGE, A. (1993), 'Management in France', in D. J. Hickson, (ed.), *Management in Western Europe* (Berlin: De Gruyter).

STEWART, R., BARSOUX, J.-L., KIESER, A., GANTER, H.-D., and WALGEN-BACH, P. (1994), *Managing in Britain and Germany*, (Basingstoke: Macmillan).

SHRIVASTAVA, P. (1985), 'Post Merger Integration', *Journal of Business Strategy*, 7/1: 65–76.

VERY, P., LUBATKIN, M., and CALORI, R. (1996), 'A Cross-National Assessment of Acculturative Stress in Recent European Mergers', *International Studies of Management and Organisations*, 26/1: 59–86.

14

Interpersonal Relationships in International Strategic Alliances

Cross-Cultural Exchanges and Contextual Factors

PAUL OLK AND P. CHRISTOPHER EARLEY

The proliferation of international strategic alliances has led researchers to develop explanations for the formation and management of these hybrid structures. The proposed accounts for an alliance—two or more organizations pooling resources to create a new, legal entity—have typically centered on the nature of the technology (Williamson, 1991), the strategies of the organizations pursuing the alliance (Harrigan, 1986), or the home countries represented by the partnering organizations (Gomes-Casseras, 1990). Ignored in most of these analyses is the role of interpersonal relationships. Overlooking this dimension of alliances is of note because alliances are considered to be a 'relational contract' (Williamson, 1985), a mixture of formal, legal provisions and interpersonal exchanges (Ring and Van de Ven, 1992). The limited empirical research that exists (Eisenhardt and Schoonhoven, 1996; Dickson and Weaver, 1997) supports the importance of individual-level interactions in the development of strategic alliances.

Towards filling this gap, this chapter extends arguments we have made elsewhere on the nature of interpersonal relationships in international strategic alliances (Olk and Earley, 1996). Our focus here is on the types of interpersonal exchanges and their interactions, with one another and with contextual conditions. We begin with a discussion of basic exchange models, paying particular attention to basic dimensions of exchange in a cross-cultural setting. We then argue that the importance of these exchanges will depend upon contextual conditions, those represented in the more studied aspects of international alliances—the technological, organizational, and institutional dimensions.

Exchange Perspective and Strategic Alliances

An exchange perspective underlies much of the research on interpersonal relationships as well as on strategic alliances. It is central to an exchange-based approach that the parties involved have some alignment in their understanding of what is to be exchanged and of the conditions determining a successful exchange. This understanding has been discussed at the interpersonal level by a number of researchers, labelling the consensus on the nature of the exchange as domain consensus (Gray, 1989), logic of action (Bacharach, Bamberger, and Sonnenstuhl, 1996), sense-making (Weick, 1995), and team mental models (Klimoski and Mohammed, 1994). While there are differences among these concepts, several similarities exist. First, the understanding of the exchange is at the interpersonal level (or higher) and not at the individual level. Individuals may help shape the understanding, but it does not reside in any one individual. In fact, the specific understanding may vary among the individuals, but at the collective level a common understanding exists.

A second, and related, concept is that the understanding does not have to be completely shared by all individuals. The participants' views need only be aligned and not inconsistent with one another (Bacharach, Bamberger, and Sonnenstuhl, 1996). For example, while one participant may engage in an exchange for instrumental reasons (e.g. to achieve a specific task), the exchange partner may enter into the exchange for affiliative reasons (e.g. social recognition or friendship). As long as the interests do not conflict, there is the basis for a possible exchange. Third, the understanding is recursive and dynamic. It is recursive in that it emerges from an interactive process among the social members and represents and influences the belief structure. The process links the actions of individuals and their beliefs, and can begin with either (Weick, 1995). It is dynamic in that the initial understanding leads to an interaction that creates a new relationship. The repeated interactions may create a fairly stable pattern of interactions, one the actors may tend to invoke even when confronting a new situation. If actors recognize that the logic of the exchange is not appropriate for a situation, however, they may modify their approach and develop a new one.

The shared interpersonal understanding has direct relevance for the formation, development, and structure of an alliance (e.g. Dickson and Weaver, 1997; Eisenhardt and Schoonhoven, 1996; Larson, 1992; Olk and Earley, 1996; Ring and Van de Ven, 1994). For example, at the initial point of alliance development, interpersonal relationships have a significant role in identifying the reason for creating the alliance. As described by Gray (1989), collaborative efforts begins with the identification of a problem requiring more than a single organization. The organizing often involves a 'champion'—a person discussing the original motive with those in his or her social network. Individuals contacted tend to be those who share a similar interest in the problem and with whom the champion has already interacted, including prior working relationships (Eisenhardt and Schoonhoven, 1996). As the individuals meet to discuss the issue, the purpose of the relationship often evolves and becomes more specific, leading to the shared understanding. Interpersonal relationships have also been linked to the degree to which the collaboration relies upon formal mechanisms to ensure compliance. A strong interpersonal relationship has been argued to reduce the need for contractual mechanisms (Ring and Van de Ven, 1994). The development of a shared understanding of the alliance as well as trust between liaisons decreases the need to rely upon more formal contractual provisions. Similarly, Larson (1992) documented how alliances, with strong relationships between the respective organizations' managers, became less formal and more tightly coupled than alliances without such relationships.

While the relevance of interpersonal relationships for strategic alliances has been noted, less understanding of the specific nature of interpersonal exchanges exists. This issue is particularly challenging given the international context for many strategic alliances. Alliance research has not examined various types of interpersonal interactions across nations, nor has it examined the dynamics of combining different interpersonal styles of exchange, or the relative advantages of when and how to combine similar or differing styles.

Interpersonal Exchange Types

A recent model, proposed by Fiske (1991) in his book *Structures of Social Life*, examines an interesting perspective on exchange in social interaction. Fiske identified four basic forms of social exchange behaviour and he argued that these are universal aspects of social exchange. The first form is *communal sharing*, and it refers to the behaviour often observed in a family context. Resources in such a circumstance are shared according to need, and people monitor their consumption of community resources themselves. The second form is *authority ranking*, which allocates resources based on status differentials. For example, in traditional Chinese society, the eldest son receives command over the family's resources after the death of a father. In nearly all organizations, the CEO receives more attention and respect than a shop-floor employee. The third form is *equality matching*, which allocates resources based on an equality principle. In other words, each person (by virtue of his or her humanity) equally deserves a comparable share of resources as each other person in a community. In this form of exchange, there is an emphasis on reciprocity and fairness, and it is characteristic of western systems of justice. Finally, the fourth form is *market pricing*, which refers to an equity-based distribution of resources using general market principles. In this case, if someone spends twice as long working in a company, she or he should receive twice as much in terms of reward.

According to Fiske, social behaviour is based on these four universal resource exchange principles, but the specific form generally endorsed varies within and across societies. As a result, a common institution such as marriage occurs universally, but its underlying exchange style and expectations may differ. For example, in certain cultures people may marry for love (e.g. communal sharing), but in other cultures they may marry for position and status (e.g. authority ranking) (Triandis and Bhawuk, 1997). Likewise, individuals across all cultures may form friendships with substantially different expectations of the satisfactory terms of such a relationship. In a highly hierarchical society, friendship across social strata may imply subservience, whereas in an egalitarian society it may dictate equal sharing and mutual obligations.

An important aspect of Fiske's argument is that all four styles of social exchange exist within each society and that they vary in relative magnitude of importance, as well as specific manifestation. So, market pricing may be observed generally in the United States but less frequently in Sweden. Further, in the United States market pricing may manifest itself as individual achievement over others in a business context (e.g. the corporate 'rat race') but as a social achievement in Sweden (e.g. individual achievement in an environmental cause). However, market pricing is present in both countries. The expectations individuals have concerning the type of exchange used in different types of relationships vary within cultures as well. That is, in a relationship such as paid employment people may place a strong emphasis on a market pricing arrangement, whereas they may emphasize an authority ranking arrangement in their family setting. Thus, the type of exchange practised, and its specific manifestation, varies both within and across cultural boundaries.

An argument presented in Fiske's analysis and model is that these four exchange expectations act in a quasi-independent fashion within any given culture. This suggests that social relationships may be governed by tendencies that are, at times, complementary, independent, or even conflicting. We can extend this argument and suggest that within any given social exchange, various exchange mechanisms may be evoked as the exchange unfolds. That is, during the early period of a relationship there may be a strong emphasis on a market pricing arrangement. After some degree of exchange expectations are established then the relationship may shift towards some other form such as authority ranking. Presumably, as a relationship intensifies and matures there will be an increasing tendency for participants to depend on a communal sharing arrangement, although this is not necessarily the case.

To a large extent, we initially expect a market pricing arrangement to be a general default for interactions across most cultures because it reflects a simplified set of expectations for exchange. That is, a market pricing arrangement does not depend on long-term exchange agreements among parties nor does it require a qualitative understanding of each party's social status (Earley, 1997). A market pricing arrangement minimizes potential exploitation through a dependence on simple rules for exchange as well as ample opportunity to flee a given relationship if one partner attempts to exploit the other (Williamson, 1975). In support of this idea are a number of cross-cultural empirical studies (see Leung, 1997 for a review) demonstrating that an equity-based allocation procedure (inherent in a market pricing arrangement) is used across a wide variety of cultures and settings as a primary or secondary distributive justice mechanism. While the literature we cited (e.g. Leung and Bond, 1984) suggests that an equity basis for reward allocation is often observed, this pattern appears to conflict with work by Tajfel and his colleagues (Tajfel, 1982). They proposed two complementary models of group process: social identity theory (Tajfel, 1982) and self-categorization theory (Turner, 1987). A fundamental assumption of these theories is that individuals form group memberships based on a relative similarity to others. Once groups are formed, individuals seek to distinguish their in-group from other groups by emphasizing their differences from outsiders and derogating out-group members. In the instance of reward allocation, this in-group preference is reflected in a general tendency for in-group members to give allocation preference to fellow in-group members. Thus, a general in-group bias reflects a digression from a market pricing arrangement to some extent. This type of in-group bias reflects facets of an authority ranking arrangement in as much as in-group favouritism reflects a clearly defined social hierarchy in which status is tied to social membership. Applying this favouritism principle to arrangements involving multiple cultural groups suggests that a general default arrangement among alliance partners is one of a hybrid market pricing and authority ranking combination.

Our basic argument centres on a matching principle in which the exchange expectations of multiple parties in an alliance are culturally anchored and potentially in conflict. If such discordance exists then it is likely that early interactions may be problematic. This situation is complicated further, since the use of exchange practices is dynamic and a single pattern is likely to give way to a stream of exchanges as relationships develop and mature. Although someone from a low power distance and low individualism culture may have a general orientation towards communal sharing, we argued earlier that such an orientation may only be applied towards others who are viewed as in-group. At the onset of an alliance, the partners may not consider each other as part of an in-group. Thus, in the formation of a new alliance a communal sharing exchange may be preceded by a relative equity distribution focus found in the market pricing context. It is only through the establishment of an alliance partner as an in-group member that a communal sharing orientation is applied. In this sense, there may be a relative emphasis on a universal form of exchange (market pricing) during early phases of an alliance or joint venture that is shifted towards a more culture-specific form over time. Ironically, such a shifting towards a more 'familiar' pattern may create significant difficulties in the relationship among members after the initial interactions go well.

To better understand the importance of exchange expectations for a relationship's evolution we can think about popular concepts such as trust (Faulkner, chap. 16, below; Kramer and Tyler, 1996; Rousseau et al., 1998), covenantal ties (Van Dyne, Graham, and Deinesch, 1994), and psychological contracts (Rousseau, 1995). Market pricing and equality matching practices do not require high degrees of trust or psychological contracts among exchange partners. The reason for this is that the structure of exchange itself tends to be relatively straightforward and relationships are not necessarily long term. This exchange has a relatively lower condition of risk (Currall and Inkpen, chap. 15, below). However, if an exchange partner violates the agreement with another partner then he or she will be abandoned by the partner. Further, the violator's reputation within the marketplace will suffer, making it problematic to establish subsequent partnerships. These pressures help ensure a consistency of word with action. In an authority ranking or a communal sharing exchange relationship there is an inherent long-term emphasis. People belong to well-established in-groups having a significant shared history and implied future with one another. As a result, there is a strong emphasis on interdependence and shared fate. This interdependence also reflects a strong social control within the in-group and violations of group norms are not tolerated (Earley, 1997). Essentially, someone who violates in-group rules is a significant threat to the in-group because he or she is a long-term presence and cannot easily be discarded, unlike the case for a market pricing exchange relationship. A strong emphasis on normative control inherent in the authority ranking and communal sharing exchange patterns regulates (and prevents) exploitation of group members. This suggests that, *ceteris paribus*, calculative trust and psychological contracts are more central to market pricing and equality matching exchanges because there are fewer opportunities to socially regulate an exchange. With that said, however, the increased independence of parties in a market relationship suggests less need for trust, since the level of opportunity to defect from an exploitative relationship is high.

Given our general description of exchange practices as a variation of cultural context, we now turn our attention to capturing the influence other more proximate contextual factors have on alliance dynamics.

Interpersonal Exchanges and Contextual Conditions

So far this chapter has focused on the importance of interpersonal relationships for understanding international strategic alliances. Having elaborated the role of interpersonal relationships in alliances, we now turn to the question of relevance. When do interpersonal exchanges matter in developing alliances? In this section we develop an answer by examining interpersonal exchanges relative to the more studied contextual factors addressed in most alliance research. Specifically, we examine how the nature of the technology of the alliance, the organizing routines, and the institutional context reflect and affect interpersonal relationships in alliances. While research has discussed the importance of each specific contextual factor (e.g. Auster, 1994) and has examined the relationship between specific contextual factors (e.g.

Hagedoorn and Narula, 1996; Osborn and Hagedoorn, 1997; Papanastassiou and Pearce, 1997), we adopt an interactive perspective on interpersonal relationships and each factor.

Technology

Several different research streams have focused on the role of technology in accounting for strategic alliances. Transaction cost theory (e.g. Hennart, 1988; Pisano, 1991) offers an explanation of how alliances emerge when the uncertainty regarding the transaction, due in part to the nature of the technology, requires a hybrid governance structure. Likewise, contingency-based approaches (Hagedoorn, 1993) have argued that alliances exist when the technology is too complex, volatile, or uncertain for a single organization to manage. Compared to other structures, an alliance permits greater control and coordination among the various organizations involved in the task.

Each of these approaches generally assumes that the social structure reflects the nature of technology. Alliances emerge because the technology requires coordination across organizational boundaries. Any interpersonal exchanges that develop come from interactions due to coordinating the technology. Similar to intra-organizational findings that technology changes may alter the power distribution within the organization (Burkhardt and Brass, 1990), the social interactions between members of the organizations stem from the nature of the technology. For example, Powell, Koput, and Smith-Doerr (1996) argued that among organizations sharing a common technology, alliances tend to be emergent forms, developing from the present social interactions.

Other research, not considering strategic alliances, however, has noted that the social interactions affect the nature of the technology—how it is viewed and its importance to the organization. As described by Fulk (1993), technologies are equivocal because they can be interpreted in multiple and conflicting ways. Zack and McKenney (1995) provided evidence of this when they found that groups conducting the same tasks but operating in different social contexts appropriated the communication technology differently, each in a way consistent with and reinforcing to their existing social structure. The specific interpretation depends, in part, upon the social structure's familiarity with the technology. This determines the perceived technological uncertainty (Barley, 1986) and affects the level to which the actors adopt the technology and change their activities to accommodate it. The more uncertain, the less likely they will adopt it. In this view, concepts that have often been considered to be a property of the technology (e.g. complexity and uncertainty) are considered to represent an interaction between the machinery and the social system. Dickson and Weaver (1997) recently extended this argument to strategic alliances. They found a relationship between an informant's perception of uncertainty, including technological uncertainty, and the propensity to use strategic alliances. Also of interest for our framework, they showed that this relationship is moderated by the informants' cultural values of individualism or collectivism and their entrepreneurial orientation.

Recently, an interactive perspective has been argued to explain the relationship between technology and social structure. Labelled the 'duality of technology' (Orlikowski, 1992), technology is considered to affect the social structure which in turns affects the technology. For the social structure, the consideration is the degree of familiarity with the new technology. The more familiar the technology, the less effect it will have on the social system. For technology, the influence will depend upon the degree of specialization. More specialized and fixed technologies will require less 'contextualizing' (Orlikowski et al., 1995). As such, the social structure will have less influence on the technology and will have to adapt to it. With more generic, open-ended technologies, there is more opportunity for the social system to modify the technology. Research into this perspective has differed in terms of whether the relationship is a discontinuous or a co-evolutionary process. In the former, the social structure initially affects the technology. Once accepted there is a limited window of opportunity (Tyre and Orlikowski, 1994) during which users explore and modify the use of the technology. After this initial period when the users develop a stable practice, however, the practices are unlikely to change and the social structure becomes constrained by the technology's use. Only through external interruptions is there a change in the technology. In the latter, the relationship is an ongoing, reflexive process (e.g. Lea, O'Shea, and Fung, 1995). The set of actors considered to be part of the social group is continually modified by social interactions, which in turn are influenced by the technology, and the social group's composition affects the characteristics of the technology.

Because the primary research thrust in studying strategic alliances has assumed that technology affects structure, there has been less research from the interactive view. We argue that there will be an interaction between the social structure and the technology in alliances. Building from the above arguments, we anticipate that the social structure's familiarity with the technology will reduce the influence of technological uncertainty and complexity, increasing the importance of interpersonal exchanges for international strategic alliances.

Organization

Central to most strategy research is the assertion that the structure of the organization reflects its strategy. The connection between strategy and structure occurs through top management's interpretation of the company's identity as well as its image (Gioia and Thomas, 1996). This interpretation can be used to reinforce the status quo or, when changes in identity and image are sought, motivation for altering an organization's activities. This linkage between strategy and structure has been extended to strategic alliance research where, for example, a company's global strategy is reflected in the structure of its alliances (Anand, Anuddin, and Makino, 1997). Extending this beyond a focal alliance, companies have been found to develop consistent structural arrangements across alliances (Olk, 1999). Whether companies have consistent strategies towards using alliances, such as learning (Hamel, 1991), that affect the structure or develop routines on how to manage alliances based on previous experiences (Lyles, 1987; Simonin and Helleloid, 1994), both result in an organizational-level approach to alliances.

Moving from a single organizational view to the dyadic exchange that develops during an alliance, we see that respective partners' strategic objectives and approaches towards alliances are reflected in the alliance structure (Li and Shankar, 1997; Saxton, 1997). The advantages and disadvantages of these differences have been extensively focused on in terms of understanding partner selection (Geringer, 1988), alliance control arrangements (e.g. Geringer and Hebert, 1991; Parkhe, 1993) and performance (Saxton, 1997). Research has also argued for their implications for the development of the alliance's social structure. Companies tend to form alliances with those whom they have previously had alliance relationships. Subsequent alliances tend to be more informally structured than initial efforts (Gulati, 1995). Through repeated exchanges, the organizations jointly develop norms and routines of trust and commitment (e.g. Aulakh, Kotabe, and Sahay, 1997; Browning, Beyer, and Shetler, 1995; Florin, 1997; Heide and John, 1992). These norms extend to subsequent alliances and reduce the need for more formal structures.

The dyadic interactions are argued to affect relationships of managers in the alliance, primarily through the generation of interpersonal trust. Ring and Van de Ven (1994) argued that because the alliance strategy requires boundary spanning activities, the individuals in these roles are likely to develop greater levels of interpersonal trust. Empirical evidence is inconclusive, however, on the importance of interpersonal trust relative to interorganizational trust. While Inkpen and Currall (1997) and Zaheer, McEvily, and Perrone (1998) found a positive relationship between them, Zaheer *et al.* concluded that interpersonal trust plays a decidedly subordinate role to interorganizational trust in determining the costs of negotiations. From our own discussion of exchange relationships, we argue that trust is not an inherently central aspect of an alliance. In fact, trust may likely be an outcome variable, resulting from a particular exchange relationship, rather than a predictor of relationship success as has been argued by others. As Currall and Inkpen (chap. 15, below) noted, the source of this indeterminacy may be due to research confusion over definition, measurement, and level of analysis. As research into trust further develops, and overcomes these issues, the importance of interpersonal trust for alliance development will likely become clearer.

While strategic alliance research has only begun to examine this relationship, research on organization routines provides an understanding of how interpersonal relationships may not just be a product of the organizing routines but may create them. A routine is a set of possible patterns from which actors choose (Pentland and Reuter, 1994; Schank and Abelson, 1977) and requires cognition and effort for enactment. Routines and scripts not only capture specific actions that may be engaged in but they reflect expectations for social exchange and behaviour. For example, a script for an initial encounter with a potential business partner will probably include expectations for signals sent to convey a willingness to deal with a partner in good faith. These cues will be tied to the general cultural orientation of social practices such as deference to superiors (authority ranking) or exchanges in kind (equality matching). Thus, cultural context not only shapes the general norms concerning exchange within a society but it also shapes the specific expectations underlying people's routines and scripts.

Enacting a routine requires effort and some choice by the actor. As such, this provides an opportunity for the actor to modify the routine. Changes in organizational scripts and routines develop in two ways. External shocks— from the institutional environment or from changes in technology—may interrupt or invalidate existing routines (Pentland, 1995). This disruption requires a secondary effort at an interpersonal level to create a new meaning and modify an existing, or create a new, routine to cope with the shock. Such a shock can occur as a result of diverse individuals meeting to form an alliance because each party may bring new types of technology into the partnership. The second source of change comes when there is slippage between the routine and the realities of actual life. While there is a tendency for actors when facing a novel situation to apply existing routines, at some point they may find that the routine no longer applies. In this situation, actors engage in a renewed sense-making process, where they seek to develop new routines. This source of change is inherent in many new alliances, particularly partnerships involving individuals from different cultural backgrounds. Thus, we conclude that in the absence of strong routines on how to proceed in developing an alliance, or the more the situation challenges the appropriateness of existing routines, the greater the impact interpersonal exchanges will have on the alliance.

Institutional Environment

Strategic alliance research examining the institutional context has generally addressed how different contexts relate to strategic alliance activities. Numerous studies equating the institutional environment with national borders have documented differences in the use and structuring of alliances in various countries (e.g., Aldrich and Sasaki, 1995; Beamish and Delios, 1997; Hagedoorn, 1995; Pan and Tse, 1997; Parkhe, 1993), and of the added difficulties in managing an international alliance compared to a domestic alliance (e.g. Gulati, 1995; Yan and Gray, 1994).

Research into the more specific dimensions of the environment can be classified along Scott's (1995) differentiation of the three pillars of the institutional environment: cognitive, normative, and regulatory. The cognitive perspective incorporates cultural differences in social exchange practices as we discussed earlier. Alliance research has linked the formation and management of strategic alliances to cultural differences between the cultures in which the partnering organizations are based (e.g. Kogut and Singh, 1989; Nooteboom, Berger, and Nooderhaven, 1997; Park and Ungson, 1997). Normative considerations examine the accepted practices of using alliances. Gomes-Casseras (1987), for example, documented a bandwagon effect on joint venture formation. The use of joint ventures for entering into countries has gone through cycles of use based on changes in the perceived appropriateness of the structure. At a more micro-level, Pearce and Branyiczki (1997) showed that how different expectations about how to organize led to conflicts in Hungarian–Western European collaborations. Hungarian managers persisted in actions that were in conflict with incentives offered by the foreign partner, because the actions were consistent with their accepted norms of behaviour. Finally, researchers have noted a regulatory aspect in strategic alliances (Nordberg, Campbell, and Verbeke, 1996), including changes in antitrust regulations designed to affect strategic alliance activity. Internationally, the formation and structuring of alliances has been affected by government restrictions on foreign ownership (Hill, Hwang, and Kim, 1990). To enter into a country, foreign companies may need to establish a strategic alliance with a domestic partner. Even within a country, variations in the regulatory environment will affect alliance structure. Gray and Yan (1997) found evidence that US–Sino joint ventures founded in different political circumstances had different equity arrangements and these arrangements persisted for a number of years.

In most strategic alliance research, the specific effect of the institutional environment on interpersonal relationships remains implied. Institutional theory, however, has noted two processes through which institutional context influences interpersonal relationships. The first is by constraining the range of activities or options enacted during an exchange. Roberts and Greenwood (1997) differentiated two types of constraints. The first they labelled 'post-conscious effects', elements that are tangible forces in the environment that affect organizing decisions. Decision-makers cognitively consider these factors (e.g. legal restrictions or formalized practices) in choosing how to organize. Perhaps more important to the organizing efforts are what Roberts and Greenwood (1997) referred to as the 'preconscious effects' of the institutional environment. These factors are the taken for granted aspects—e.g. schemas or routines—that shape what is or is not perceived by the decision-makers. They limit what is considered to be a legitimate organizing approach and reduce the information the actors need to process. Pitkethly, Faulkner, and Child (chap. 13, above) demonstrated this in summarizing national variations towards integrating an acquired UK company. Although the goal of each acquisition was to effectively combine the acquired company, the researchers' document national differences in the approaches taken among companies from the USA, France, Germany, and Japan.

Institutional environments also influence interpersonal exchanges by defining the 'actor'. As Meyer, Boli, and Thomas (1994) noted, the institutional environment defines who is an actor by developing what Scott (1995) labels, a constitutive rule. This rule defines who are considered legitimate actors, the endowment of these actors' rights and their capabilities. In some environments, the actors may be individuals, in others corporations, while in others they may be professions or the state (Jepperson and Meyer, 1991). The importance of interpersonal relationships, for organizing efforts such as strategic alliances, will depend upon the extent to which individuals are considered to be appropriate actors.

While for the most part institutional theory has not considered individuals to be of much significance, leading to the criticism of providing an 'over-socialized' view of individuals (Zucker, 1987), some researchers have argued that individuals have choice in deciding to follow institutionalized practices and are active in producing and reproducing the institutional environment (Borum and Westenholz, 1995). The significance of interpersonal relationships stems, in part, from considering institutionalization as a variable rather than a constant (Scott, 1995). As a variable, environments will differ to the degree to which they explicitly define acceptable practices. The less institutionalized the environment, the more individuals will have discretion in establishing an agreed practice. Discretion is also likely to exist in situations where there are conflicting or ambiguous contexts, where the appropriate practice is not clear (D'Aunno, Sutton, and Price, 1991). In such a setting, individuals will have a choice in deciding which actions to take. Their interpretation of the institutional forces, and the resulting actions taken, has been argued to be a function of the actors' interests and positions within an organization, giving rise to the importance of their cognition and power (Fligstein, 1991). Thus, the more postconscious the influence of the institutional environment and the more individual actors are considered legitimate, the greater the influence of interpersonal relationships on strategic alliances.

Conclusions

The literature on strategic alliances has generally focused on the importance of technology, organizational routines and strategy, and institutional forces at the expense of interpersonal exchanges. The purpose of this chapter was to begin to develop an argument for the importance of interpersonal exchanges for understanding international alliances. We first set out to describe types of exchanges and the nature of their possible interaction. We then examined when these exchanges will have greater influence *vis-à-vis* other dimensions. The next step in this research is to elaborate upon the above discussions by developing formal propositions regarding the nature of interpersonal exchanges in international strategic alliances and the relative importance of these exchanges to the more studied explanations. Continuing with this line of inquiry will help to provide an understanding of the role of individuals in international strategic alliances and a more complete theoretical explanation for the development of alliances.

References

ALDRICH, H. and SASAKI, T. (1995), 'R&D Consortia in the United States and Japan', *Research Policy*, 24: 301–16.

ANAND, J., AINUDDIN, A., and MAKINO, S. (1997), 'An Empirical Analysis of Multinational Strategy and International Joint Venture Characteristics in Japanese MNCs', in P. W. Beamish and J. P. Killing (eds.), *Cooperative Strategies: Asian Perspectives* (San Francisco: The New Lexington Press), 325–40.

AULAKH, P., KOTABE, M., and SAHAY, A. (1997), 'Trust and Performance in Cross-border Marketing Partnerships: A Behavioral Approach', in P. W. Beamish and J. P. Killing (eds.), *Cooperative Strategies: North American Perspectives* (San Francisco: The New Lexington Press), 163–96.

AUSTER, E. (1994), 'Macro and Strategic Perspectives on Interorganizational Linkages: A Comparative Analysis and Review with Suggestions for Reorientation', *Advances in Strategic Management*, 10B: 3–40.

BACHARACH, S., BAMBERGER, P., and SONNENSTUHL, W. (1996), 'The Organizational Transformation Process: The Micropolitics of Dissonance Reduction and the Alignment of Logics of Action', *Administrative Science Quarterly*, 41: 477–506.

BARLEY, S. (1986), 'Technology as an Occasion for Structuring: Evidence from Observations of CT Scanners and the Social Order of Radiology Departments', *Administrative Science Quarterly*, 31: 78–108.

BEAMISH, P. and DELIOS, A. (1997), 'Improving Joint Venture Performance through Congruent Measures of Success', in P. W. Beamish and J. P. Killing (eds.), *Cooperative Strategies: European Perspectives* (San Francisco: The New Lexington Press), 103–27.

BORUM, F. and WESTENHOLZ, A. (1995), 'The Incorporation of Multiple Institutional Models: Organizational Field Multiplicity and the Role of Actors', in W. R. Scott and S. Christensen (eds.), *The Institutional Construction of Organizations: International and Longitudinal Studies* (Thousand Oaks, Calif.: Sage), 113–31.

BROWNING, L., BEYER, J., and SHETLER, J. (1995), 'Building Cooperation in a Competitive Industry: SEMATECH and the Semiconductor Industry', *Academy of Management Journal*, 38: 113–51.

BURKHARDT, M. E. and BRASS, D. J. (1990), 'Changing Patterns or Patterns of Change: The Effects of a Change in Technology on Social Network Structure and Power', *Administrative Science Quarterly*, 35: 104–27.

D'AUNNO, T., SUTTON, R., and PRICE, R. (1991), 'Isomorphism and External Support in Conflicting Institutional Environments: A Study of Drug Abuse Treatment Units', *Academy of Management Journal*, 34: 636–61.

DICKSON, P. and WEAVER, K. (1997), 'Environmental Determinants and Individual-Level Moderators of Alliance Use', *Academy of Management Journal*, 40: 404–25.

EARLEY, P. C. (1997), *Face, Harmony, and Social Structure: An Analysis of Organizational Behavior Across Cultures* (New York: Oxford University Press).

EISENHARDT, K. and SCHOONHOVEN, C. (1996), 'Resource-Based View of Strategic Alliance Formation: Strategic and Social Effects in Entrepreneurial Firms', *Organization Science*, 7: 136–50.

FISKE, A. (1991), *Structures of Social Life: The Four Elementary Forms of Human Relations* (New York: Free Press).

FLIGSTEIN, N. (1991), 'The Structural Transformation of American Industry: An Insitutional Account of the Causes of Diversification in the Largest Firms 1919–1979', in W. Powell and P. DiMaggio (eds.), *The New Institutionalism in Organizational Analysis* (Chicago: The University of Chicago Press), 311–36.

FLORIN, J. (1997), 'Organizing for Efficiency and Innovation: The Case of Nonequity Interfirm Cooperative Arrangements', in P. W. Beamish and J. P. Killing (eds.), *Cooperative Strategies: North American Perspectives* (San Francisco: The New Lexington Press), 3–24.

FULK, J. (1993), 'Social Construction of Communication Technology', *Academy of Management Journal*, 36: 921–50.

GERINGER, J. M. (1988), *Joint Venture Partner Selection: Strategies for Developed Countries* (New York: Quorum Books).

—— and HÉBERT, L. (1991), 'Measuring Performance of International Joint Ventures', *Journal of International Business Studies*, 22: 249–63.

GIOIA, D. and THOMAS, J. (1996), 'Identity, Image, and Issue Interpretation: Sensemaking during Strategic Change in Academia', *Administrative Science Quarterly*, 41: 370–403.

GOMES-CASSERES, B. (1987), 'Joint Venture Instability: Is it a Problem?' *Columbia Journal of World Business*, 22/2 (summer), 71–7.

—— (1990), 'Firm Ownership Preferences and Host Government Restrictions: An Integrated Approach', *Journal of International Business Studies*, 21: 1–22.

GRAY, B. (1989), *Collaborating: Finding Common Ground for Multiparty Problems* (San Francisco: Jossey-Bass).

—— and YAN, A. (1997), 'Formation and Evolution of International Joint Ventures: Examples from U.S./Chinese Partnerships', in P. Beamish and P. Killing (eds.), *Global Perspectives on Cooperative Strategies: Asian Perspectives* (San Francisco: The New Lexington Press), 57–88.

GULATI, R. (1995), 'Does Familiarity Breed Trust? The Implications of Repeated Ties for Contractual Choice in Alliances', *Academy of Management Journal*, 38: 85–112.

HAGEDOORN, J. (1993), 'Understanding the Rationale of Strategic Technology Partnering and Interorganization Modes of Cooperation and Sectional Differences', *Strategic Management Journal*, 14: 371–85.

—— (1995), 'A Note on International Market Leaders and Networks of Strategic Technology Partnering', *Strategic Management Journal*, 16: 241–50.

—— and NARULA, R. (1996), 'Choosing Organizational Modes of Strategic Technology Partnering: International and Sectoral Differences', *Journal of International Business Studies*, 27: 265–84.

HAMEL, G. (1991), 'Competition for Competence and Inter-Partner Learning within International Strategic Alliances', *Strategic Management Journal*, 12: 83–103.

HARRIGAN, K. (1986), *Managing for Joint Venture Success* (Lexington, Mass.: Lexington Books).

HENNART, J.-F. (1988), 'A Transaction Cost Theory of Equity Joint Ventures', *Strategic Management Journal*, 9: 361–74.

HEIDE, J. and JOHN, G. (1992), 'Do Norms Matter in Marketing Relationships?', *Journal of Marketing*, 56: 32–44.

HILL, C., HWANG, P., and KIM, W. (1990), 'An Eclectic Theory of the Choice of International Entry Mode', *Strategic Management Journal*, 11: 117–28.

INKPEN, A. and CURRALL, S. (1997), 'International Joint Venture Trust: An Empirical Examination', in P. W. Beamish and J. P. Killing (eds.), *Cooperative Strategies: North American Perspectives* (San Francisco: The New Lexington Press), 308–34.

JEPPERSON, R. and MEYER, J. (1991), 'The Public Order and the Construction of Formal Organization', in W. Powell and P. DiMaggio (eds.), *The New Institutionalism in Organizational Analysis* (Chicago: University of Chicago Press), 204–31.

KLIMOSKI, R. and MOHAMMED, S. (1994), 'Team Mental Model: Construct or Metaphor?', *Journal of Management*, 20: 403–37.

KOGUT, B. and SINGH, H. (1989), 'The Effect of National Culture on the Choice of Entry Mode', *Journal of International Business Studies*, 19: 411–32.

KRAMER, R. M. and TYLER, T. R. (1996), *Trust in Organizations: Frontiers of Theory and Research* (Thousand Oaks, Calif.: Sage).

LARSON, A. (1992), 'Network Dyads in Entrepreneurial Settings: A Study of the Governance of Exchange Relationships', *Administrative Science Quarterly*, 37: 76–104.

LEA, M., O'SHEA, T., and FUNG, P. (1995), 'Constructing the Networked Organization: Content and Context in the Development of Electronic Communications', *Organization Science*, 6: 462–78.

LEUNG, K. (1997), Negotiations and Reward Allocations Across Cultures, in S. Zedeck (ed.), *Frontiers of Industrial and Organizational Psychology* (San Francisco: Jossey-Bass).

—— and BOND, M. (1984), 'The Impact of Cultural Collectivism on Reward Allocation', *Journal of Personality and Social Psychology*, 47: 793–804.

LI, J. and SHANKAR, O. (1997), 'The Perspectives of Local Partners: Strategic Objectives and Structure Preferences of International Cooperative Ventures in China', in P. W. Beamish and J. P. Killing (eds.), *Cooperative Strategies: Asian Perspectives* (San Francisco: The New Lexington Press), 300–22.

LYLES, M. A. (1987), 'Common Mistakes of Joint Venture Experienced Firms', *Columbia Journal of World Business*, 22: 79–85.

MEYER, J., BOLI, J., and THOMAS, G. (1994), 'Ontology and Rationalization in the Western Cultural Account', in W. R. Scott, J. Meyer and Associates (eds.), *Institutional Environments and Organizations* (Thousand Oaks, Calif.: Sage), 9–27.

NOOTEBOOM, B., BERGER, H., and NOORDERHAVEN, N. (1997), 'Effects of Trust and Governance on Relational Risk', *Academy of Management Journal*, 40: 308–38.

NORDBERG, M., CAMPBELL, A., and VERBEKE, A. (1996), 'Can Market-Based Contracts Substitute for Alliances in High Technology Markets?' *Journal of International Business Studies*, 27: 963–79.

OLK, P. (1999), 'A Multi-Dimensional Approach to Explain a Member's Influence in an R&D Consortium', forthcoming in *Journal of High Technology Management Research*.

—— and EARLEY, P. C. (1996), 'Rediscovering the Individual in the Formation of International Strategic Alliances', *Research in the Sociology of Organizations*, 14: 223–61.

ORLIKOWSKI, W. J. (1992), 'The Duality of Technology: Rethinking the Concept of Technology in Organizations', *Organization Science*, 3: 398–427.

—— YATES, J., OKAMURA, K., and FUJIMOTO, M. (1995), 'Shaping Electronic Communication: The Metastructuring of Technology in the Context of Use', *Organization Science*, 6: 423–44.

OSBORN, R. and HAGEDOORN, J. (1997), 'The Institutionalization and Evolutionary Dynamics of Interorganizational Alliances and Networks', *Academy of Management Journal*, 40: 261–78.

PAN, Y. and TSE, D. (1997), 'Cooperative Strategies between Foreign Firms in an Overseas Country', in P. W. Beamish and J. P. Killing (eds.), *Cooperative Strategies: Asian Perspectives* (San Francisco: The New Lexington Press), 135–56.

PAPANASTASSIOU, M. and PEARCE, R. (1997), 'Cooperative Approaches to Strategic Competitiveness Through MNE Subsidiaries: Insiders and Outsiders in the European Market', in P. W. Beamish and J. P. Killing (eds.), *Cooperative Strategies: European Perspectives* (San Francisco: The New Lexington Press), 267–99.

PARK, S. and UNGSON, G. (1997), 'The Effect of National Culture, Organizational Complementarity, and Economic Motivation on Joint Venture Dissolution', *Academy of Management Journal*, 40: 279–307.

PARKHE, A. (1993), 'Partner Nationality and the Structure-Performance Relationship in Strategic Alliances', *Organization Science*, 4: 301–14.

PEARCE, J. and BRANYICZKI, I. (1997), 'Legitimacy: An Analysis of Three Hungarian-Western European Collaborations', in P. W. Beamish and J. P. Killing (eds.), *Cooperative Strategies: European Perspectives* (San Francisco: The New Lexington Press), 300–22.

PENTLAND, B. (1995), 'Grammatical Models of Organizational Processes', *Organization Science*, 6: 541–56.

—— and RUETER, H. (1994), 'Organizational Routines as Grammars of Action', *Administrative Science Quarterly*, 39: 484–510.

PISANO, G. P. (1991), 'The Governance of Innovation: Vertical Integration and Collaborative Arrangements in the Biotechnology Industry', *Research Policy*, 20: 237–49.

POWELL, W., KOPUT, K., and SMITH-DOERR, L. (1996), 'Interorganizational Collaboration and the Locus of Innovation: Networks of Learning in Biotechnology', *Administrative Science Quarterly*, 41: 116–45.

RING, P. and VAN DE VEN, A. (1992), 'Structuring Cooperative Relationships between Organizations', *Strategic Management Journal*, 13: 483–98.

—— —— (1994), 'Developmental Processes of Cooperative Interorganizational Relationships', *Academy of Management Review*, 19: 90–118.

ROBERTS, P. and GREENWOOD, R. (1997), 'Integrating Transaction Cost and Institutional Theories: Toward a Constrained-Efficiency Framework for Understanding Organizational Design Adoption', *Academy of Management Review*, 22: 346–73.

ROUSSEAU, D. (1995), *Psychological Contracts in Organizations : Understanding Written and Unwritten Agreements* (Thousand Oaks, Calif.: Sage).

—— SITKIN, S., BURT, R., and CAMERER, C. (1998), 'Not so Different after All: A Cross-Discipline View of Trust', *Academy of Management Review*, 23: 393–404.

SAXTON, T. (1997), 'The Effects of Partner and Relationship Characteristics on Alliance Outcomes', *Academy of Management Journal*, 40: 443–61.

SCHANK, R. and ABELSON, R. (1977), *Scripts, Plans, Goals, and Understanding : An Inquiry Into Human Knowledge Structures* (Hillsdale, NJ: L. Erlbaum Associates).

SCOTT, W. R. (1995), *Institutions and Organizations* (Thousand Oaks, Calif.: Sage).

SIMONIN, B. and HELLELOID, D. (1993), 'Do Organizations Learn? An Empirical Test of Organizational Learning in International Strategic Alliances', in D. Moore (ed.), *Best Papers Proceedings, Academy of Management Meetings* (Atlanta, Ga: Academy of Management), 222–6.

TAJFEL, H. (ed.) (1982), *Social Identity and Intergroup Relations* (New York: Cambridge University Press).

TRIANDIS, H. C. and BHAWUK, D. P. S. (1997), 'Culture Theory and the Meaning of Relatedness', in S. Zedeck (ed.), *Frontiers of Industrial and Organizational Psychology* (San Francisco: Jossey-Bass).

TURNER, J. C. (1987), *Rediscovering the Social Group: Self-Categorization Theory* (Oxford: Blackwell).

TYRE, M. J. and ORLIKOWSKI, W. J. (1994), 'Windows of Opportunity: Temporal Patterns of Technological Adaptation in Organizations', *Organization Science*, 5: 98–118.

VAN DYNE, L., GRAHAM, J., and DIENESCH, R. (1994), 'Organizational Citizenship Behavior: Construct Redefinition, Measurement, and Validation', *Academy of Management Journal*, 37: 765–802.

WEICK, K. (1995), *Sensemaking in Organizations* (Thousand Oaks, Calif.: Sage).

WILLIAMSON, O. (1975), *Markets and Hierarchies: Analysis and Antitrust Implications* (New York: Free Press).

—— (1985), *The Economic Institutions of Capitalism: Firms, Markets, Relational Contracting* (New York : Free Press).

—— (1991), 'Comparative Economic Organization: The Analysis of Discrete Structural Alternatives', *Administrative Science Quarterly*, 36: 269–96.

YAN, A. and GRAY, B. (1994), 'Bargaining Power, Management Control, and Performance in United States–China Joint Ventures: A Comparative Case Study', *Academy of Management Journal*, 37: 1478–517.

ZACK, M. and McKENNEY, J. (1995), 'Social Context and Interaction in Ongoing Computer-Supported Management Groups', *Organization Science*, 6: 394–422.

ZAHEER, A., McEVILY, B., and PERRONE, V. (1998), 'Does Trust Matter? Exploring the Effects of Interorganizational and Interpersonal Trust on Performance', *Organization Science*, 9: 141–59.

ZUCKER, L. (1987), 'Institutional Theories of Organizations', *Annual Review of Sociology*, 13: 443–64.

15

Joint Venture Trust

Interpersonal, Inter-Group, and Inter-Firm Levels

STEVEN C. CURRALL AND ANDREW C. INKPEN

Breakdowns in the value creation process in joint ventures (JVs) often stem from problems in managing interdependencies. A lack of trust between partners is one such problem (Borys and Jemison, 1989). Our assessment of the extant literature indicates that, despite substantial conceptual and empirical writings, confusion exists regarding the interpretation of research findings in the area of JV trust. A key reason why this confusion exists is that researchers have devoted little attention to issues of level.

Building on the theoretical foundation of the 'cooperating behaviour' perspective on inter-organizational alliances (Faulkner and de Rond, chap. 1, above), the objective of this chapter is to explicate conceptual, measurement, and analysis issues associated with studying JV trust at the interpersonal, inter-group, and inter-firm levels. We offer two reasons why the JV trust literature has obfuscated issues of level, namely: overdependence on single key informants, and 'concept stretching' (i.e. blurred distinctions between the JV trust concept itself, its antecedents, and its consequences). Next, because risk is a central component of trust, we examine how risk differs at the three levels. Further, we show how researchers can collect data and create indices to analyse the amount of JV trust and the mutuality of JV trust. The conceptual, measurement, and analytical issues we discuss in this chapter deserve careful consideration by theoreticians and, especially, researchers involved in empirical examinations of JV trust.

Scope of the Chapter

Strategic alliances can have a variety of organizational arrangements, such as JVs, licensing agreements, distribution and supply agreements, research and development partnerships, and technical exchanges. The governance structures of the various forms can be differentiated as either equity alliances or non-equity alliances (Hennart, 1988). Equity alliances involve the transfer or creation of equity ownership either through direct investment or the creation of an equity joint venture. Non-equity alliances neither involve transfer of equity nor do they usually entail the creation of a new organization. From a transaction cost economics perspective, quasi-market ties like non-equity alliances are the default mode for organizing alliances (Gulati, 1995). To explain the use of equity versus non-equity forms, researchers have argued that the problems of opportunism and uncertainty can be better handled with equity alliances. The rationale offered is that equity alliances usually result in the creation of new entities that require a hierarchical management structure. This structure can oversee the functioning of the alliance and handle contingencies as they arise (Gulati, 1995). Additionally, equity alliances can 'provide a mechanism for distributing residuals when *ex ante* contractual arrangements cannot be written to specify or enforce a division of returns' (Teece, 1992: 20).

The scope of our discussion focuses on equity JVs, an alliance form that combines resources from more than one organization to create a new organizational entity (the 'child') distinct from its parents. Siecor, an alliance between Siemens and Corning, provides an example. In this JV, the partners brought together their complementary capabilities in telecommunications and glass technology to build an independent organization with its own headquarters, CEO, board of directors, and staff. We focus on equity JVs for several reasons. First, the development of trust associated with equity JVs requires a depth of analysis not necessary for other types of alliances. Second, most of the conceptual and empirical research in the alliance area has dealt with equity JVs. Third, because equity JVs involve independent organizations, the identification of individual alliance managers and reporting relationships associated with inter-firm trust is more apparent (and consequently, more amenable to empirical study) than in non-equity alliances such as licensing agreements. As a boundary condition, our discussion focuses on two partner JVs. Multiple-party JVs are extensions of the two-party case. We restrict our discussion to the two-party case because the complexities of multiple-party JVs are beyond the scope of the chapter.

There is an extensive literature examining the role of trust as a key JV management issue. As a factor critical to successful JVs, many researchers have argued that JVs should be established in a spirit of mutual trust and commitment (Beamish and Banks, 1987; Buckley and Casson, 1988; Faulkner and de Rond, chap. 1, above; Gulati, 1995; Harrigan, 1986; Koenig and van Wijk, 1991; Madhok, 1995; Parkhe, 1993; Yan and Gray, 1994). More generally, similar arguments have been advanced for inter-organizational collaboration (Alter and Hage, 1993; Fichman and Levinthal, 1991; Gambetta, 1988; Granovetter, 1992; Jarillo, 1988; Johnson *et al.*, 1996; Kumar, 1996; Powell, 1996). It has been posited, for example, that trust is advantageous because it strengthens inter-organizational ties (Fichman and Levinthal, 1991), speeds contract negotiations (Reve, 1990), and reduces transaction costs (Bromiley and Cummings, 1993).

Issues of Level: Definitions

Like other organizational constructs, such as climate, participation, and communication (Klein, Dansereau, and Hall, 1994), JV trust may be viewed from multiple organizational levels. Writers on issues of level in organizational research (e.g. Glick, 1985; House, Rousseau, and Thomas-Hunt, 1995; James, Joyce, and Slocum, 1988; Klein *et al.*, 1994; Rousseau, 1985) have identified three fundamental ideas that are necessary to explicate issues of level: (1) *level of theory*, (2) *level of measurement*, and (3) *level of analysis*.

Level of theory describes the unit that the researcher seeks to explain and about which generalizations are made. If, for example, the unit of theory is the extent of interpersonal trust between managers involved in a JV (which we term 'JV managers'), theoretical explanations would focus on the psychological antecedents of JV manager trust (e.g. perceptions of the honesty, integrity, and fairness of the counterpart JV manager) that impact the decision by JV managers to trust each other. *Level of measurement* describes the source of data, such as surveys, interviews, or archival records. Archival records, for example, showing the nature of an inter-firm JV relationship (e.g. equity split or interlocking board membership), typically involve a level of measurement at the firm level. Use of surveys or interviews implies the individual JV manager as the level of measurement. *Level of analysis* describes how the data are treated statistically. If data on the features of JVs (e.g. equity split, type of licensing, or exchange of personnel) are compiled and hypotheses tested about the effect of these features on JV performance, then the level of analysis is the firm. Alternatively, if survey responses by several JV managers within a partner firm are aggregated by using a mean, then the level of analysis typically is the group. By clarifying levels of theory, measurement, and analysis, our aim is to develop internally consistent formulations of JV trust for use in future hypothesis testing.

Dependence on a Single Key Informant and 'Concept Stretching' in the JV Trust Literature

The literature on JV trust shows an excessive dependence on single key informants. Furthermore, a pattern of concept stretching has obfuscated theoretical distinctions among JV trust and related constructs. Both deficiencies in the literature have generated confusion regarding conclusions to be drawn from, and the appropriate level of analysis for, research on JV trust.

Dependence on a Single Key Informant

The most prevalent approach in empirical studies of JV and alliance trust has been to ask a single key informant to describe trust as a property of a JV (i.e. inter-firm) relationship. For example, Aulakh, Kotabe, and Sahay (1996)

studied trust in cross-border marketing partnerships. Using a single informant, trust was measured with questions such as 'our firm and the partner
firm generally trust that each will stay within the terms of the contract'.
Similarly, Inkpen studied international JVs using a single key informant
approach. The trust measure included questions such as 'there is a high
level of trust in the working relationship between the partners' (Inkpen,
1995: 133).

The use of key informants is one viable method of data collection. The
exclusive use of a single key informant, however, has weaknesses that are
rarely discussed or acknowledged in literature on JV trust. Kumar, Stern, and
Anderson (1993) focused on two major problems in the use of key informants: selection and perceptual agreement. A selection problem stems from the
difficulty in finding key informants who are 'competent' (i.e. knowledgeable)
to report on the level of trust in a JV relationship. Researchers heretofore
have done little to empirically verify the competency of informants. Additionally, even if researchers identify multiple informants who are competent, a
perceptual agreement problem can exist because these informants may have
systematically different perceptions based on different roles (e.g. an informant
who has been involved in a JV from the start-up versus an informant who has
been brought in later to run the operations of a JV). Moreover, perceptions of
trust may be heavily influenced by differences in informants' personality traits
and by biases of social construal or attribution. Kumar, Stern, and Anderson
(1993) provided methodologies for examining perceptual convergence of
informants such as the 'consensus' procedure through which informants
resolve perceptual discrepancies. Such methodologies, however, have rarely
been applied by researchers using key informants to assess trust between JV
partners. As a result, measures of JV trust may reflect idiosyncratic perceptions of key informants.

Concept Stretching

Precisely defined concepts pave the way for operationalized measures and
provide a foundation for well-conceived propositions about organizational
phenomena. Imprecisely defined concepts, however, misinform researchers
in the development of propositions and make it difficult to produce cumulative research knowledge. Too often, organizational researchers have been
quick to redefine, reconceptualize, and recreate concepts. This results in what
Osigweh (1989) called concept stretching: 'when concepts are broadened in
order to extend their range of applications, they may be so broadly defined (or
stretched) that they verge on being too all-embracing to be meaningful in the
realm of empirical observation and professional practice' (Osigweh, 1989:
582; emphasis in original). Concept stretching may occur because of the
failure to make distinctions among the concept itself, its antecedents, and
its consequences.

In the JV trust literature, concept stretching has occurred because of failure by researchers to make conceptual and empirical distinctions among JV trust itself, its antecedents, and its consequences.[1] An example of a study that purported to measure trust between alliance partner firms, yet actually measured an antecedent of trust, was Mohr and Spekman (1994). They identified the unit of analysis in their study as the relationship between a computer dealer and one of its suppliers (i.e. an inter-firm relationship). Using questionnaire data from an informant in the computer dealer, three questions were used to measure inter-firm trust, such as 'this relationship is marked by a high degree of harmony' (Mohr and Spekman, 1994: 152). Conceptually and empirically, however, this was not a measure of the inter-firm trust concept itself (i.e. trust by a firm). More accurately, the concept of harmony is an antecedent (or a consequence) of inter-firm trust. Another example of a study that purported to measure JV trust was Parkhe (1993), who concluded: 'Successful interfirm cooperation may rest on two basic building blocks: (1) initiation of a mutually beneficial relationship . . . and (2) fading of the fear of opportunism as the partners build a cooperative history and mutual trust develops between them (Parkhe, 1993: 821). Although Parkhe's (1993) empirical measure used individual-level questionnaire data on perceptions of opportunistic behaviour, trust was attributed to the inter-firm relationship. Thus, we question whether Parkhe's measure of individual perceptions of opportunistic behaviour was the conceptual and empirical equivalent of trust between JV partner firms. In sum, a common theme of these studies was that they measured a variable (e.g. harmony or absence of fear of opportunism) that is either an antecedent or a consequence of the JV trust concept.

Furthermore, both Mohr and Spekman and Parkhe depict 'misspecification' (Rousseau, 1985), which occurs when trust is attributed to one level when it has been measured at another level. Parkhe's statement that 'mutual trust develops between them' (i.e. firms) qualifies as a misspecification because, although the empirical measure was at the individual level of mea-

---

[1] Historically, concept stretching has plagued the general trust literature. One example was the assumed equivalence of trust and cooperative behaviour in Deutsch's seminal research using the Prisoner's Dilemma paradigm (e.g. Deutsch, 1962). Deutsch used the Prisoner's Dilemma paradigm as a social situation where trust was presupposed to be an antecedent of cooperative behaviour. As noted by Kee and Knox (1970), when cooperative behaviour was observed it was assumed to stem from trust. The result was that much of the early trust literature based on Deutsch's work used a stretched trust concept because distinctions between trust and cooperation were not maintained. This situation continued until Kee and Knox (1970) and Kimmel (1974) argued that, to assume that a specific psychological state (e.g. trust) preceded observed cooperative behaviour, failed to preclude the possibility that alternative psychological states could have caused the behaviour (e.g. under certain interaction strategies, a non-trusting motivation can underlie cooperative behaviour). Kimmel (1974) was the first to distinguish empirically between trust and cooperation in the Prisoner's Dilemma game by measuring trust as a personality trait versus cooperative behaviour displayed by players in the game.

surement, trust was attributed to the inter-firm relationship. Stated somewhat differently, misspecification occurred because trust at the individual level was taken to be isomorphic with inter-firm trust. Isomorphism means that constructs mean the same thing across levels (Rousseau, 1985). Trust between individuals and trust between JV partner firms, however, is not isomorphic because the antecedents and consequences of trust by individuals are different from the antecedents and consequences of trust by firms. For example, psychological antecedents (e.g. perceptions of a counterpart's trustworthiness) cannot operate at the firm level.[2] Thus, because the antecedents of trust at the individual level are different from the antecedents of trust at the firm level, it cannot be said that trust at the two levels is isomorphic.

Measuring trust itself or its antecedents or consequences is acceptable as long as clear theoretical and empirical distinctions among them are maintained. Unfortunately, in the JV trust literature, trust and its antecedents have been largely referred to interchangeably.[3] The result has been stretching of the JV trust concept. This makes patterns of research findings in the area of JV trust difficult to discern because studies do not make clear whether they are testing relationships about trust itself, about its antecedents, or about its consequences.

Defining JV Trust

We propose the following definition of JV trust, which can be used as a basis for examining trust at multiple levels. Trust involves two principle concepts: (1) *reliance* (Giffin, 1967; Rotter, 1980) and (2) *risk* (Deutsch, 1962; Gambetta, 1988; Kee and Knox, 1970; Lorenz, 1993; Mayer, Davis, and Schoorman, 1995). Following Inkpen and Currall (1998) (also Inkpen and Currall, 1997; Currall and Judge, 1995), *JV trust is defined as reliance on another JV party (i.e., person, group, or firm) under a condition of risk*. Reliance is volitional action by one party that allows that party's fate to be determined by the other party (Zand, 1972). Risk means that a party would experience potentially negative

---

[2] That is, unless the researcher measures aggregates (e.g. means) of perceptions of JV managers within each partner firm. We will discuss the aggregation of individual-level data later.

[3] Some authors have begun to clarify distinctions among trust and its antecedents. These distinctions are discussed in Gulati's (1995) research on alliances, in which he cautioned against blurring the distinction between trust and its antecedents. Specifically, Gulati (1995: 94) used secondary data on the history of prior ties between alliance partners as an indirect indicator of trust: 'I chose to use a factor that likely produces trust as its proxy...prior alliances between firms. This substitution is based on the intuition that two firms with prior alliances are likely to trust each other more than other firms with whom they have had no alliances.' Gulati acknowledged that his measure of history of prior alliances was not a direct indicator of trust. Rather, his measure was an antecedent of (i.e. it 'produces') inter-organizational trust. He urged future researchers to focus on direct measures of trust obtained from the collection of primary data (e.g. survey measures of trust between JV managers aggregated to the firm level).

outcomes, i.e. 'injury or loss' (Isen, Nygren, and Ashby, 1988; March and Shapira, 1987; Sitkin and Pablo, 1992), from the untrustworthiness of the other party. Thus, under a condition of risk, a party's trust is signified by action that puts its fate in the hand of the other party.

Differences in Risk Across Levels

The risk component of our definition deserves further elaboration. Risk is a precondition for the existence of trust, and the trustor must be cognizant of risk (Mayer, Davis, and Schoorman, 1995; Sitkin and Pablo, 1992). Without risk, trust is irrelevant. The sources of risk differ across the interpersonal, inter-group, and inter-firm levels. At the interpersonal level, the following sources of risk for JV managers may be observed. One type of JV manager, a business development executive, has responsibility for formulating the strategic objectives and developing agreements designed to ensure that the JV accomplishes its strategic objectives. For a development executive, risk stems from possible untrustworthiness by a counterpart executive (trustee) from the partner firm, which could result in failure to formulate and launch a successful JV. As a result, the executive may suffer disciplinary action (e.g. pay cuts or demotions) or fail to receive promotions. Moreover, the possibility of untrustworthiness by a counterpart is heightened because relations are in their nascent stages and executives experience uncertainty about the skills, knowledge, and objectives of their counterparts. Because of this uncertainty, trust at the time of JV formation is often consistent with the notion of 'impersonal' trust (i.e. trust based on reputation or credentials (Shapiro, 1987)). Cross-cultural factors can also exacerbate uncertainty about untrustworthiness. A second type of JV manager, an operations manager, is an individual who has been transferred from a parent to the JV. These managers work inside the JV itself and are focused on day-to-day running of the JV. Untrustworthiness by a trustee operations manager could result in diminished JV performance leading to disciplinary action taken against the trustor manager (e.g. a poor performance appraisal, a pay reduction, omission from consideration for future JV assignments, or loss of employment).

Risks for groups of JV managers involve threats to group coherence or group existence. For example, untrustworthiness by the trustee group is likely to lead to conflict, which may cause fractionalization of the trustor group into coalitions, thereby reducing group coherence. Relatedly, untrustworthiness by a trustee group may precipitate a downward spiral of conflict (Zand, 1972) leading to diminished JV operations or JV failure. In turn, this may result in the dissolution of the trustor group thereby eliminating the group from existence. Furthermore, if the JV's performance diminishes due to untrustworthiness by the trustee group, both parent firms may take disciplinary action against their JV managers in the form of group-level punishments (e.g. omission from consideration for future JV assignments).

The primary risk for JV partner firms is opportunistic action and abuse of trust by a JV partner. When parties in a cooperative relationship refrain from acting opportunistically, they are said to forbear (Buckley and Casson, 1988). The greater the probability of opportunistic action by the trustee partner firm, the greater the risk to the trustor partner firm. Opportunistic action associated with partner resources is probably the largest source of firm risk. A JV will often involve the exposure of key knowledge and technology resources to a partner. In this situation, there is risk that a partner will appropriate the resources as the basis for eliminating partner dependence and making the JV bargain obsolete. From a competitive perspective, a firm may help create a competitor when it shares resources with a partner. Alliances have been described as a 'race to learn', with the partner who learns the fastest dominating the relationship (Hamel, 1991). As a JV partner's commitment to acquire partner knowledge increases, the probability of JV instability increases because of changes in partner dependency (Inkpen and Currall, 1997). A second type of firm-level risk is associated with the resources and efforts devoted to building a cooperative relationship. These resources and efforts will probably have no external value and cannot be recovered if the JV terminates due to the untrustworthiness of the partner firm (Smith and Barclay, 1997). A third type of risk involves the inability of a partner firm to execute its share of the JV bargain. When a JV is formed, the partners must decide how tasks will be jointly performed. Before the partners have worked together, they have little information about each other's skills. If one firm misleads the other into believing it can perform certain tasks when it cannot, it may be impossible to achieve the objectives set out by the JV agreement. As opposed to opportunistic action, the risk in this case stems from partner incompetence.

Conceptualizing JV Trust at the Interpersonal, Inter-Group, and Inter-Firm Levels

At the interpersonal level, trusting action is exhibited in the form of a JV manager's behaviour. For groups of JV managers, trusting action is exhibited by group-level action (i.e. based on group decision-making, such as consensus or majority vote). At the inter-firm level, trusting action is signified by firm-level actions and policies (i.e. based on corporate board votes or top management team decisions).

Figure 15.1 specifies both the trustor and the trustee at the interpersonal level. This depicts JV trust from the perspective of the party (e.g. the JV manager) that does the trusting, namely, the 'trustor' and the target of trust, the 'trustee' (a JV manager). Specification of the trustor addresses the question of 'trust by whom?' Specification of the trustee addresses the question of 'trust in whom?' Clarity about trustors and trustees is an essential step towards reducing obfuscation of level issues that has occurred in the previous JV trust literature. In conceptualizing JV trust at the interpersonal level, the researcher may wish to study trust between, for example, the two senior JV

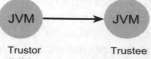

Fig. 15.1 JV trust at the interpersonal level

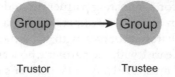

Fig. 15.2 JV trust at the inter-group level

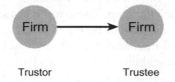

Fig. 15.3 JV trust at the inter-firm level

operations managers assigned to the JV from the two partner firms. Another way to conceptualize JV trust is to focus on inter-group trust between two groups of JV managers. Figure 15.2 refers to the situation where the researcher wishes to examine a group of JV managers as the trustor and a group of JV managers from a partner firm as the trustee. A possible research scenario would involve the trust between the two groups of board members assigned to the JV from the two partner firms. In the existing JV literature, most studies conceptualize JV trust in terms of trust between firms, that is, inter-firm trust. This conceptualization is represented in Figure 15.3.

Measurement and Analysis of JV Trust at the Interpersonal, Inter-Group and Inter-Firm Levels

Measuring JV Trust at the Interpersonal Level

To measure the amount of trust that a JV manager (trustor) has in another JV manager (trustee), as in Figure 15.1, the researcher would assess the trustor's trusting actions. With respect to specific measurement techniques to assess the amount of trust, the researcher has several options. One option is for the researcher to assume the role of outside observer and record behavioural incidents of a JV manager's trusting actions towards another JV manager. A detailed behavioural recording system could be developed to tally trusting behaviours. For example, the researcher could record the frequency that a JV manager reaches verbal agreements without the trustee's future obligations being explicitly stated, or the frequency of agreements done on a 'handshake' without written documentation. If a behavioural recording system is used, the researcher should provide inter-rater reliability results to demonstrate the internal consistency of the recording system.

A second measurement option is to collect individual-level interview or survey data from JV managers about the extent to which they have engaged in trusting behaviour towards the trustee. Survey or interview items could ask a JV manager to indicate the extent to which he or she has given the trustee information that could possibly jeopardize the JV or the parent firm. Survey or interview items could also assess a lack of trust. For example, the JV manager could be asked about the extent to which he or she had rejected the trustee's offers to enter unwritten agreements or the degree to which the JV manager checked with others about the activities of the trustee.

The amount of interpersonal (i.e. dyadic) trust between two JV managers may be examined using the above measurement techniques to collect data from JV managers as both trustor and trustee. The researcher would collect data from both JV managers about their trust in each other. For example, both JV managers would respond to survey items that assess the degree to which they have relied on each other to make key strategic or operational decisions, relied on each other to execute a task skilfully, or relied on each other for support in executing a job function.

Analysing JV Trust at the Interpersonal Level

The researcher may seek to test hypotheses about:

1. the amount of trust an individual JV manager has in another JV manager;
2. the amount of interpersonal (i.e. dyadic) trust between two JV managers; or
3. the mutuality of interpersonal (i.e. dyadic) trust between two JV managers.

A summary score of the amount of trust that an individual JV manager has in a trustee JV manager is simple: it would involve a sum or an index of central tendency (e.g. a mean, median, or mode) of the number of trusting behaviours. If, on the other hand, the researcher seeks to assess the amount of interpersonal trust between JV managers, individual-level data concerning both JV managers' trust in each other would be aggregated. In this case, the researcher would compute a central tendency index (e.g. a mean) based on both sets of individual-level data.

In addition to measuring the amount of trust, the researcher may assess the mutuality of interpersonal trust between two JV managers. Mutuality is defined by Smith (1992) and Smith and Barclay (1997) as capturing both the *amount* of trust between two individuals and the *congruence* (i.e. similarity) of trust scores between two individuals. As such, the congruence component of mutuality incorporates the dispersion of trust scores across both JV managers in a dyad. Using data from JV managers, mutuality would be calculated by taking the square root of the product of responses by JV managers:

$$\text{Trust mutuality} = \sqrt{(\text{JV Manager 1's trust} \times \text{JV Manager 2's trust})}$$

Using the square root of the product maintains the original metric of scales, which eases interpretation (Smith, 1992; Smith and Barclay, 1997). To illustrate the properties of the mutuality index, Smith (1992) showed the following dyadic trust scores, based on a hypothetical 1–7 response scale:

[1,1]= 1.00	[1,2]= 1.41	[1,3]= 1.73	[1,4]= 2.00	[2,2]= 2.00	[1,5]= 2.24
[1,6]= 2.45	[2,3]= 2.45	[1,7]= 2.65	[2,4]= 2.83	[3,3]= 3.00	[2,5]= 3.16
[2,6]= 3.46	[3,4]= 3.46	[3,5]= 3.87	[4,4]= 4.00	[3,6]= 4.24	[4,5]= 4.47
[3,7]= 4.58	[4,6]= 4.90	[5,5]= 5.00	[4,7]= 5.29	[5,6]= 5.48	[5,7]= 5.92
[6,6]= 6.00	[6,7]= 6.48	[7,7]= 7.00			

As indicated, two incongruent trust scores such as (5,7) ($\sqrt{5 \times 7} = 5.92$) produce a lower mutuality score than two congruent scores such as (6,6) ($\sqrt{6 \times 6} = 6.00$) (Smith, 1992: 9).[4] In sum, analysis of interpersonal trust between JV managers using only an index of central tendency (e.g. a mean) has the advantage of simplicity, whereas the advantage of the mutuality index is that it captures both the amount of trust and the congruence of trust.

Measuring JV Trust at the Inter-Group Level

To measure the amount of trust a group of JV managers (trustor) has in a counterpart group of JV managers (trustee), as in Figure 15.2, the researcher would assess the amount of the trustor group's trust in the trustee group. As stated previously, trust at the group level involves trusting action by the group based on some method of group decision-making, such as consensus or majority vote. Group-level manifestations of JV trust overlap to some degree with the individual-level manifestations of JV trust because groups involve concerted action by individuals.

The researcher has several measurement options. First, the researcher may assume the role of outside observer and record incidents of group trust. For example, it would be possible to record trusting actions by groups of business development executives, operations managers, or board members, such as when they provide their trustee group with strategic or competitive information. A second measurement option is to collect individual-level interview or

---

[4] There is one drawback of Smith's mutuality index, namely, that it treats as conceptually equivalent the following three pairs: [1,4] and [2,2]; [1,6] and [2,3]; [2,6] and [3,4].

survey data from members of a JV manager group concerning their trust towards members of a trustee group. As an example, survey items could query a group of operations managers about the degree to which they trusted their counterpart managers to carry out operational tasks. These individual-level responses would then be aggregated to the group level. The absence of trust could be measured in terms of the extent to which business development executives monitored their counterparts during the process of writing a JV contract. Additionally, it would be possible to measure trusting actions based on a content analysis of JV board meeting minutes. For example, the researcher could note incidents such as when a group of JV board members from one partner firm monitors the group of board members from the counterpart firm during deliberations about the JV's strategy.

Cummings and Bromiley (1996) have proposed a survey methodology that provides yet another option for measuring inter-group trust. They proposed administering a survey to trustee group members using wording such as 'We feel that——has been straight with us' and 'We think that——does not mislead us'. These individual-level survey responses from the members of a group of JV managers would be aggregated to develop a group-level index of trust.

Analysing Trust at the Inter-Group Level

Hypothesis testing about JV trust at the group level may focus on:

1. the amount of trust a JV manager group has in a trustee JV group;
2. the amount of inter-group trust between two groups of JV managers; and
3. the mutuality of inter-group trust between two groups of JV managers.

If the researcher wishes to analyse the amount of trust a group has in another group of managers, there are two alternatives. First, the researcher can compile a summary score (e.g. a mean) of trusting actions taken by a group of JV managers. Second, the researcher may construct an aggregate index of individual-level data regarding group members' trusting actions towards members of the trustee group. Smith's (1992) mutuality index could be applied to the inter-group case by using group-level trust scores from both groups of JV managers.

If aggregation of individual-level data is used, the researcher must justify aggregation by providing empirical evidence concerning the homogeneity of trust within groups. When data are available on multiple JV manager groups, two types of intra-class correlations (ICCs) can be computed to examine whether the degree of within-group homogeneity warrants within-group aggregation. ICC(1) and ICC(2) address different properties of aggregate (within-group) scores (James, 1982). ICC(1) indicates the agreement of individual respondents within a group of JV managers by comparing the between-group sum of squares to the total sum of squares from a one-way analysis of variance where the group is specified as the independent categorical variable. As indicated by Ostroff and Schmitt (1993), previous research has shown that ICC(1) values range from 0 to 0.5 with a median of 0.12. ICC(2) is a measure of the aggregate-level reliability of mean scores within a given group; it is the correlation between mean trust scores of two random samples of JV managers' scores drawn from the same group. ICC(2) values should be 0.6 or higher (Ostroff and Schmitt, 1993).

Measuring JV Trust at the Inter-Firm Level

In measuring the amount of trust a JV partner firm (trustor) has in the other partner firm (trustee), as in Figure 15.3, the researcher would examine the extent of the trustor firm's trusting actions. In measuring trust at the firm level, the sources of information and data collection techniques may differ compared with those at the person- or group-level. If the unit of theory is inter-firm trust, then the unit of measurement normally should be the firm. Consequently, the unit of analysis should be the firm as well. Although this logic seems straightforward, measurement of trust at the firm level is challenging because indirect measures of trusting action may be required. Measures of firm-level action are likely to be indirect (i.e. from archival sources).

The degree to which the partner firms adopt policies to openly share knowledge is a firm-level manifestation of trust. Knowledge-sharing could be measured by examining a firm's access to partner technology (Inkpen and Currall, 1997), the exchange of research and development personnel, or the exchange of executive personnel, of which the exemplar is allowing the partner firm to supply the chief executive of the new JV. Another measure would be the action by one firm to commit key technologies to the JV. This action could be measured by assessing the criticality of key JV technologies relative to parent-firm strategy. Also, researchers could study the allocation of responsibility for JV tasks. For example, trust would be signified by allowing critical JV managerial tasks to be controlled by the partner firm. By adopting approaches similar to those used in studies of JV control (e.g. Killing, 1983), researchers could identify the extent of partner decision-making responsibility for key JV decision areas.

Analysing JV Trust at the Inter-Firm Level

Analogous to trust at the interpersonal and inter-group levels, hypothesis testing about JV trust at the firm level may focus on:

1. the amount of trust a JV firm has in a trustee JV firm;
2. the amount of inter-firm trust between two partner firms; and
3. the mutuality of inter-firm trust between two firms.

To analyse the extent of a firm's trust in a trustee firm, a multi-component summary index could be based on counts of trusting actions, such as the number of times technology is shared, the number of personnel (research and development staff) exchanged, the number of key tasks given to the partner firm, the number of contract codicils required when JV objectives change (signifying the absence of trust), whether the JV partner firm is allowed to supply the chief executive of the new JV, the percentage of the partner's equity in the JV, or the presence of a contract clause giving the partner firm the option of future acquisition of the JV. An index of inter-firm trust could be compiled by aggregating the trusting actions of both partner firms. The trust mutuality index could also be applied to compute the mutuality of inter-firm trust.

Implications for Future Research

An important issue for future research is the extent of consistency across the three levels of trust. Indeed, Faulkner's (chap. 16, below) case-study evidence suggests that inconsistent trust across levels may be associated with poor JV performance. Specifically, Barney and Hansen (1994) posited that conflicts can arise between person and firm levels of trust, in that exchanges between JV managers from different firms may lead to strong interpersonal trust yet the extent of trust between the partner firms could be weak. Consider a situation of high competitive overlap between JV partner firms. The firms may be unwilling to establish firm-level policies to share knowledge because of the risk of its appropriation by the partner. As a result, the partner firms may be reluctant to create the conditions necessary for strong trust to emerge. However, within the JV itself, individual JV managers may have a different view of the risks associated with knowledge spillover. Strong trust could develop at the interpersonal level if JV managers are confident that opportunistic behaviour by their counterparts is unlikely. Therefore, one future research question concerns the degree to which strong interpersonal trust can neutralize, or compensate for, weak trust at the inter-firm level.

In conclusion, the objective of this chapter was to explicate conceptual, measurement, and analytical issues associated with studying JV trust at multiple levels. Further elaboration of the paper's framework will lead to greater clarity of level issues in research literature on JV trust. For example, future work might focus on the relationship between risk and trust at the interpersonal, inter-group, and inter-firm levels. As issues of level become clearer, future researchers should build developmental models of how trust emerges between JV managers, groups of JV managers, and JV partner firms. Additional quantitative analysis techniques might also be developed to capture other properties of relationships (e.g. reciprocity) among JV partners. The ideas we have proposed in this chapter serve as a starting point for greater alignment of theory, measurement, and analysis and, as a result, more systematic research findings in the area of JV trust.

338 CURRALL AND INKPEN

References

ALTER, C. and HAGE, J. (1993), *Organizations Working Together* (Newbury Park, Calif.: Sage).

AULAKH, P. S., KOTABE, M., and SAHAY, A. (1996), 'Trust and Performance in Cross-Border Marketing Partnerships: A Behavioral Approach', *Journal of International Business Studies*, 27: 1005–32.

BARNEY, J. and HANSEN, M. H. (1994), 'Trustworthiness as a Source of Competitive Advantage', *Strategic Management Journal*, 15: 175–90.

BEAMISH, P. W. and BANKS, J. C. (1987), 'Equity Joint Ventures and the Theory of the Multinational Enterprise', *Journal of International Business Studies*, 18 (summer): 1–16.

BORYS, B. and JEMISON, D. B. (1989), 'Hybrid Arrangements as Strategic Alliances: Theoretical Issues in Organizational Combinations', *Academy of Management Review*, 14: 234–49.

BROMILEY, P. and CUMMINGS, L. L. (1993), 'Organizations with Trust: Theory and Measurement', paper presented at the meeting of the Academy of Management Meetings, Atlanta, Ga.

BUCKLEY, P. J. and CASSON M. (1988), 'A Theory of Cooperation in International Business', in F. Contractor and P. Lorange (eds.), *Cooperative Strategies in International Business* (Lexington, Mass.: Lexington Books).

CUMMINGS, L. L. and BROMILEY, P. (1996), 'The Organizational Trust Inventory (OTI): Development and Validation', in R. M. Kramer and T. R. Tyler (eds.), *Trust in Organizations: Frontiers of Theory and Research* (Thousand Oaks, Calif.: Sage).

CURRALL, S. C. and JUDGE, T. A. (1995), 'Measuring Trust between Organizational Boundary Role Persons', *Organizational Behavior and Human Decision Processes*, 64: 151–70.

DEUTSCH, M. (1962), 'Cooperation and Trust: Some Theoretical Notes', in M. R. Jones (ed.), *Nebraska Symposium on Motivation* (Lincoln, Nbr.: University of Nebraska Press).

FICHMAN, M. and LEVINTHAL, D. A. (1991), 'Honeymoons and the Liability of Adolescence: A New Perspective on Duration Dependence in Social and Organizational Relationships', *Academy of Management Review*, 16: 442–68.

GAMBETTA, D. (1988), 'Can we Trust Trust?', in D. Gambetta (ed.), *Trust: Making and Breaking Cooperative Relations* (Oxford: Blackwell).

GIFFIN, K. (1967), 'The Contribution of Studies of Source Credibility to a Theory of Interpersonal Trust in the Communication Process', *Psychological Bulletin*, 68: 104–20.

GLICK, W. H. (1985), 'Conceptualizing and Measuring Organizational and Psychological Climate: Pitfalls in Multilevel Research', *Academy of Management Review*, 10: 601–16.

GRANOVETTER, M. (1992), 'Problems of Explanation in Economic Sociology', in N. Nohria and R. Eccles (eds.), *Networks and Organizations: Structure, Form, and Action* (Boston: Harvard Business School Press).

GULATI, R. (1995), 'Does Familiarity Breed Trust? The Implications of Repeated Ties for Contractual Choice in Alliances', *Academy of Management Journal*, 38: 85–112.

HAMEL, G. (1991), 'Competition for Competence and Inter-Partner Learning with International Strategic Alliances', *Strategic Management Journal*, 12: 83–104.

HARRIGAN, K. R. (1986), *Managing for Joint Venture Success* (Lexington, Mass.: Lexington Books).

HENNART, J. F. (1988), 'A Transactions Costs Theory of Equity JVs', *Strategic Management Journal*, 9: 361–74.

HOUSE, R., ROUSSEAU, D., and THOMAS-HUNT, T. (1995), 'The Meso Paradigm: A Framework for the Integration of Micro and Macro Organizational Behavior', in L. Cummings and B. Staw (eds.), *Research in Organizational Behavior* (Greenwich, Conn.: JAI Press).

INKPEN, A. C. (1995), *The Management of International Joint Ventures: An Organizational Learning Perspective* (London: Routledge).

——and CURRALL, S. C. (1997), 'International Joint Venture Trust: An Empirical Examination', in P. W. Beamish and J. P. Killing (eds.), *Cooperative Strategies: North American Perspectives* (San Francisco: The New Lexington Press).

——— (1998), 'The Nature, Antecedents, and Consequences of Joint Venture Trust', *Journal of International Management*, 4: 1–20.

ISEN, A., NYGREN, T., and ASHBY, G. (1988), 'Influence of Positive Affect on the Subjective Utility of Gains and Losses: It is Just not Worth the Risk', *Journal of Personality and Social Psychology*, 55: 710–17.

JAMES, L. R. (1982), 'Aggregation Bias in Estimates of Perceptual Agreement', *Journal of Applied Psychology*, 67: 219–29.

——JOYCE, W. F., and SLOCUM, J. W. (1988), 'Organizations do not Cognize', *Academy of Management Review*, 13: 129–32.

JARILLO, J. C. (1988), 'On Strategic Networks', *Strategic Management Journal*, 9: 31–41.

JOHNSON, J. L., CULLEN, J. B., SAKANO, T., and TAKENOUCHI, H. (1996), 'Setting the Stage for Trust and Strategic Integration in Japanese–U.S. Cooperative Alliances', *Journal of International Business Studies*, 27: 981–1004.

KEE, H. and KNOX, R. (1970), 'Conceptual and Methodological Considerations in the Study of Trust', *Journal of Conflict Resolution*, 14: 357–66.

KILLING, J. P. (1983), *Strategies for Joint Venture Success* (New York: Praeger).

KIMMEL, M. (1974), 'On Distinguishing Interpersonal Trust from Cooperative Responding in the Prisoner's Dilemma Game', PhD thesis (Wayne State University).

KLEIN, K. J., DANSEREAU, F., and HALL, R. J. (1994), 'Levels Issues in Theory Development, Data Collection, and Analysis', *Academy of Management Review*, 19: 195–229.

KOENIG, C. and VAN WIJK, G. (1991), 'Interfirm Alliances: The Role of Trust', in R. A. Thietart and J. Thepob (eds.), *Microeconomic Contribution to Strategic Management* (North-Holland: Elsevier).

KUMAR, N. (1996), 'The Power of Trust in Manufacturer–Retailer Relationships', *Harvard Business Review*, 74/6: 92–106.

——STERN, L. W., and ANDERSON, J. C. (1993), 'Conducting Interorganizational Research Using Key Informants', *Academy of Management Journal*, 36: 1633–51.

LORENZ, E. H. (1993), 'Flexible Production Systems and the Social Construction of Trust', *Politics and Society*, 21: 307–24.

MADHOK, A. (1995), 'Revisiting Multinational Firms' Tolerance for Joint Ventures: A Trust-Based Approach', *Journal of International Business Studies*, 26: 117–38.

MARCH, J. G. and SHAPIRA, Z. (1987), 'Managerial Perspectives on Risk and Risk Taking', *Management Science*, 33: 1404–18.

MAYER, R. C., DAVIS, J. H., and SCHOORMAN, F. D. (1995), 'An Integrative Model of Organizational Trust', *Academy of Management Review*, 20: 709–34.

MOHR, J. and SPEKMAN, R. (1994), 'Characteristics of Partnership Success, Partnership Attributes, Communication Behavior, and Conflict Resolution Techniques', *Strategic Management Journal*, 15: 135–52.

OSIGWEH, C. A. (1989), 'Concept Fallibility in Organizational Science', *Academy of Management Review*, 14: 579–94.

OSTROFF, C. and SCHMITT, N. (1993), 'Configurations of Organizational Effectiveness and Efficiency', *Academy of Management Journal*, 36: 1345–61.

PARKHE, A. (1993), 'Strategic Alliance Structuring: A Game Theoretic and Transaction Cost Examination of Interfirm Cooperation', *Academy of Management Journal*, 36: 794–829.

POWELL, W. W. (1996), 'Trust-Based Forms of Governance', in R. M. Kramer and T. R. Tyler (eds.), *Trust in Organizations: Frontiers of Theory and Research* (Thousand Oaks, Calif.: Sage).

REVE, T. (1990), 'The Firm as a Nexus of Internal and External Contracts', in M. Aoki, B. Gustafson, and O. Williamson (eds.), *The Firm as a Nexus of Treaties* (Newbury Park, Calif.: Sage).

ROTTER, J. (1980), 'Interpersonal Trust, Trustworthiness, and Gullibility', *American Psychologist*, 35: 1–7.

ROUSSEAU, D. M. (1985), 'Issues of Level in Organizational Research: Multi-Level and Cross-Level Perspectives', in L. Cummings and B. Staw (eds.), *Research in Organizational Behavior* (Greenwich, Conn.: JAI Press).

SHAPIRO, S. P. (1987), 'The Social Control of Impersonal Trust', *American Journal of Sociology*, 93: 623–58.

SITKIN, S. B. and PABLO, A. L. (1992), 'Reconceptualizing the Determinants of Risk Behavior', *Academy of Management Review*, 17: 9–38.

SMITH, J. B. (1992), 'Mutuality in Close Relationships: A Comparison of Approaches for Aggregating Individual-Level Data', paper presented at the annual meeting of the Academy of Management, Las Vegas, Nev.

—— and BARCLAY, D. W. (1997), 'The Effects of Organizational Differences and Trust on the Effectiveness of Selling Partner Relationships', *Journal of Marketing*, 61 (Jan.): 3–21.

TEECE, D. (1992), 'Competition, Cooperation, and Innovation: Organizational Arrangements for Regimes of Rapid Technological Progress', *Journal of Economic Behavior and Organization*, 18: 1–25.

YAN, A. and GRAY, B. (1994), 'Bargaining Power, Management Control, and Performance in United States–Chinese Joint Ventures: A Comparative Case Study', *Academy of Management Journal*, 37: 1478–1517.

ZAND, D. (1972), 'Trust and Managerial Problem Solving', *Administrative Science Quarterly*, 17: 229–39.

16

Trust and Control

Opposing or Complementary Functions?

DAVID O. FAULKNER

The concepts of trust and of control are frequently cited as central to the potential success of strategic alliances. Researchers are by no means united in their view of the definitions of either term, but all seem to agree that they are important. Indeed Chapter 15 of this book by Steve Currell and Andrew Inkpen discusses the issue of the different levels at which trust can be built, namely interpersonal, inter-group, and inter-firm. This chapter takes the view that to be effective at the latter two levels, trust-building must be grounded at an interpersonal level. It takes Child and Faulkner's (1998) concepts of three different forms of trust, and Geringer and Hebert's (1989) definition of control, and considers to what extent trust and control are antithetical or complementary forces in strategic alliances. Do good control systems foster increased trust, and poorly implemented control systems lead to feelings of corporate vulnerability, and hence the erosion of trust, or does the existence of trust make such control systems less necessary?

Trust is analysed into three forms:

1. Calculative trust, i.e. one partner calculates that the other can help them and trusts them in the hope that they will be as good as their word.
2. Predictive trust, i.e. one partner comes to believe that the other is competent to behave as they say they will and will actually do so, since they have done so in the past.
3. Affective trust, in which the partners get to like each other as people and trust takes on a more personal aspect.

Successful alliances do not necessarily need to reach the level of affective trust to be successful, but if they do so it is suggested that they are likely to be more robust and flexible when problems arise.

The scope of control follows Geringer and Hebert (1989) and covers the three dimensions of control that they identify i.e. (1) mechanisms (2) extent, and (3) focus. Thus control in alliances must be limited, if the alliance is to realize its creative aims, and the three identified dimensions provide a framework for determining the extent of control appropriate for optimizing an

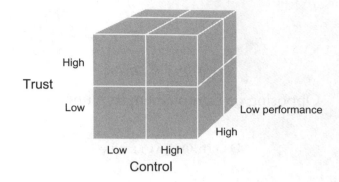

Fig. 16.1 Trust, Control, and Performance

alliance's opportunity realization without cramping the motivation of its executives.

The issues of trust and control are considered in relation to eight international alliance case studies with varying levels of performance success. The cases are Eurovynil Chloride, Imperial–Wintermans, ICI Pharma, the Cable and Wireless Japanese Consortium, IDC, Courtaulds–Nippon Paint, Dowty–Sema, Royal Bank of Scotland–Banco Santander, and Rover–Honda. A three-dimensional matrix (cf. Figure 16.1) is used, with trust, control, and success as its axes, to demonstrate how trust and control vary in their strength in relation to success in the case studies, and how they seem to be correlated. The discussion is based on qualitative interviews, and therefore cannot lead to necessarily generalizable conclusions. However, it offers insights into the way in which trust is important in international collaborations, and the role of control mechanisms in supplementing the growth of trust, or compensating for its relative absence, if high performance is to be achieved.

Trust and Control

'Trust'

Thorelli (1986) defines trust as follows: 'An assumption or reliance on the part of A that if either A or B encounters a problem in the fulfillment of his implicit or explicit transactional obligations, B may be counted on to do what A would do if B's resources were at A's disposal.' Trust in cooperative activity reduces the transaction cost of monitoring the activities of your partner, and thus is a route to competitive advantage through cost reduction. Lane (1998) identifies the role of calculation, understanding, and personal identification as key aspects of trust. Calculative trust is that form which 'involves expectations about another, based on a calculus which weighs the cost and benefits of certain courses of action to either the trustor or the trustee'. Lewicki and Bunker (1996) argue that this form of trust is based on the assurance that other people will do as they say, because the deterrent for violation is greater than the gains, and/or the rewards from preserving trust outweigh any from breaking it. 'In this view, trust is an on-going, market-oriented, economic calculation whose value is derived by determining the outcomes resulting from creating and sustaining the relationship relative to the costs of maintaining or severing it' (Lewicki and Bunker, 1996: 120).

Trust based upon calculation is likely to apply particularly to relationships which are new, and hence can only proceed on the basis of institutionalized protection or the reputation of the partner. It may also be the only form of trust which can apply to arm's-length and hence impersonal economic exchanges. However, if those exchanges become recurrent, such as with repeat mail-order business, then another form of trust may also emerge. This is based on increased mutual knowledge among the partners, which nurtures the realization that they share relevant expectations. Calculation-based trust is particularly important in the formation phase of strategic alliances.

A second and generally subsequent form of trust is based on a realistic prediction of the partner's behaviour in a given situation. This is cognitive trust. Such knowledge-based trust 'is grounded in the other's predictability—knowing the other sufficiently well so that the other's behaviour is anticipatable. Knowledge-based trust relies on information rather than deterrence' (Lewicki and Bunker, 1996: 121). The assumption of rationality contained in the calculative view of trust is relaxed somewhat in cognitive or predictive trust, because the trust here is founded upon both the security and comfort that the partner is well understood, and is known to share important assumptions with you.

A third view of trust is that it is based on people developing a personal affinity. This means they hold common values, including a common concept of moral obligation. As Lane (1998) points out, common values and norms of obligation can develop in a long-standing relationship, where trust was originally created in an incremental manner. This kind of trust is likely to find a parallel at the more interpersonal level, in what Lewicki and Bunker (1996) call 'identification-based trust'. Identification-based trust 'exists because the parties effectively understand and appreciate the other's wants; this mutual understanding is developed to the point that each can effectively act for the other' (cf. Royal Bank of Scotland and Banco Santander of Spain in case study 7). If friendship develops within a long-term relationship, the emotional bond thereby introduced is likely to provide a mainstay for identification-based trust, because it enables a person to 'feel' as well as to 'think' like the other. When people come to like each other, they are encouraged to place themselves voluntarily within the powers of another. This is what Brenkert (1998) calls 'the Voluntarist view' of trust. Trust which is based on people identifying with, and liking each other therefore derives from what we may call 'bonding' between them. This is similar to Sako's (1996) 'goodwill', trust in her tripartite analysis of the concept into contractual trust, competence trust, and goodwill trust. Goodwill trust is seen by Sako as the most important enhancer of a relationship. She recommends more concentration on 'enhancers' than 'safeguards'.

Similar to the threefold distinction between trust based on calculation, prediction, and bonding, is the broader distinction, made by McAllister (1995), between what he calls 'cognition-based' and 'affect-based' trust. Trust that is cognition-based rests upon the knowledge people have of others, and the evidence of their trustworthiness: 'available knowledge and "good reasons" serve as foundations for trust decisions'. McAllister points out that previous organizational researchers have assumed competence, responsibility, reliability, and dependability to be important sources of cognition-based trust.

Brenkert (1998) identifies a 'predictability view', which holds that trust denotes the extent to which one can predict that the person being trusted will act in good faith. While Brenkart argues that such prediction rests on 'a belief that one person has about another', this is consistent with the concept of cognition-based trust, because the belief almost certainly rests on a degree of knowledge about the other person, which is taken to constitute 'good reasons' for trust, however limited and imperfect that knowledge might be.

By contrast, affect-based trust, according to McAllister (1995: 26), is founded on the emotional bonds between people. These bonds express a genuine concern for the welfare of partners, a feeling that the relationships have intrinsic virtue, and a belief that these sentiments are reciprocated. In other words, they incorporate an identification with the other person's wishes and intentions. Affect-based trust is clearly a form which is most likely to develop and deepen through fairly intensive relating between people on a person-to-person basis over quite a long period of time. As such, it is facilitated by the ability to communicate well and to avoid misunderstandings or at least clear them up quickly. So mutual knowledge and the sharing of information between the people concerned remain essential conditions for such trust. Cultural and associated language differences tend to impede communication and easy understanding, and may therefore stand in the way of affect-based trust, e.g. the difficulty in developing it between the Japanese and Westerners. Perceived conflicts of interest will also make it hard to develop or maintain this kind of trust. In strategic alliances, affect-based trust is therefore difficult to achieve, and if it develops at all this is only likely to be the case after the alliance has been operating successfully, and up to the partners' expectations, over a period of some time. The distinction between cognition and affect in trust-based cooperative relationships suggests that such alliances are likely to form initially on the basis of essentially cognitive considerations, including calculation, but that, as the relationship matures, it may increasingly incorporate affect through the development of friendship ties.

Trust is, of course, socially constituted and strengthened by social interaction, cultural affinity between people, and the support of institutional norms and sanctions. Zucker (1986) argues that trust is socially produced through three main modes, of which the latter two have their bases in socially constituted entities. The first mode is one in which trust develops on the basis of the experience of past exchange or the expectations attached to future exchange. Production of trust in this mode arises through the mutual reinforcement of investments in trust, and the quality of the cooperation associated with it, and is consistent with the process of developing and deepening trust-based relations. The second mode is based on the sharing of common characteristics, such as ethnicity and culture. The third mode is one in which formal institutional mechanisms provide codes or guarantees that transactions will take place as promised. The possibility of the importance of control mechanisms to the development of trust makes an appearance here. Cooperation between organizations creates mutual dependence and requires trust in order to succeed. This comes down to trust between the individuals who are involved in the alliance. Uncertainty about partners' motives, and a lack of detailed knowledge about how they operate, requires that a basis for trust be found for cooperation to get under way in the first place.

Child and Faulkner (1998) have suggested that there are identifiable stages in the evolution of trust. Calculation is there in the first instance. The meeting of expectations leads to confident prediction, then bonding may progressively provide the foundations on which a deeper trust may develop. Trust is seen to develop gradually as the partners move from one stage to the next. This is consistent with the view that trust can be strengthened by the partners building up the number of positive exchanges between themselves. As the partners become increasingly aware of the mutual investment they have made in their relationship, the benefits they are deriving from it, and the costs of reneging on it, they have more incentive to carry it forward. The view of trust as an evolving process provides valuable clues about the way in which cooperative relationships can be developed both within and between organizations.

The conclusion that trust between partners can develop over time through continued interaction between them, from an initial basis that is purely calculative, is consistent with the experimental findings from iterated games: namely, that the probability of cooperation may be improved initially by providing mutual hostages, and then progressively reinforced by the benefits it is seen to provide.

Control

Control in strategic alliances refers to the process by which the partners influence, to varying degrees, the behaviour and output of the other partners and the managers of the alliance itself (Child and Faulkner, 1998). Killing (1983) saw control as depending primarily on equity holdings, and argued in favour of the dominant partner JV where one partner owned more than 50 per cent of the equity. This, he claimed, made control unambiguous, and led to better performance. A more recent discussion between the author and Killing, however, suggested that he was currently less certain of this view.

Others contend that the attempt to exercise more control than is necessary will not only incur additional direct costs, but could have negative consequences on performance and on the development of trust-based relationships. If one parent tries to exert too much control within an alliance, this may threaten the quality of its relations with its partners. As Schaan (1988: 5) puts it, 'in order to ensure the success of a joint venture, managers seek to strike a subtle balance between the desire and need to control the venture on the one hand, and the need to maintain harmonious relations with the partner(s) on the other hand'. Moreover, if parents either singly or together try to control their alliances too much, this may inhibit the flexibility which the latter need in order to develop within their own competitive environments (Bleeke and Ernst, 1993). So, as Ohmae (1993: 42) argues, 'managers must overcome the popular conception that total control increases chances of success'.

Geringer and Hebert (1989) identify three dimensions of control in international joint ventures, which in principle apply more generally to other types of alliance also. These are the *extent* of control exercised over a joint venture, the *focus* of that control, and the *mechanisms* by which control is exercised. 'Extent' is to be interpreted as a vertical force in that it measures the degree to which the partners exercise control over the alliance or grant it a degree of autonomy. 'Focus' is a horizontal force which identifies the functional areas in which a partner chooses to exercise control. The 'mechanisms' are the way in which the partner does so, and extend far beyond the traditionally identified mechanisms of equity ownership and board membership, although these mechanisms remain important.

Bjørn (1997), in a study of the interfaces in Danish companies between headquarters and foreign subsidiaries, advances a typology of control and coordination mechanisms which helps to identify the various mechanisms available to partners—e.g. transfer prices, information management, training and personnel development, policies, plans, targets, budgets, skills standardization, appointments, gatekeepers, project teams, boards of directors, and reporting systems. Given the existence of such a multiplicity of control mechanisms, Schaan (1988) contends that control can be exercised from a minority share position by careful selection and operation of specific mechanisms.

There is considerable dispute about the link between control and performance. Awadzi (1986) found no link between parental control and performance of JVs, and Bleeke and Ernst found 50:50 alliances to perform the best. Beamish (1988), reviewing studies on the control–performance link in developed and developing country alliances, concluded that when alliances are formed between developed and less-developed country partners, there tends to be an association between satisfactory performance and less-dominant control by the foreign partner. The argument is that a sharing of control with local partners will lead to a greater contribution from them, which can assist in coping with circumstances that are unfamiliar to the foreign partner, and therefore result in a higher return on investment. Beamish concludes that: 'What the literature seems to indicate is a different emphasis—in fact a weakening of the link—between dominant management control and good performance when study focus shifts from the developed countries to the less developed countries' (1988: 21).

Osland and Cavusgil (1996) report that they have found that the size of the joint venture measured in annual sales, equity, and expatriate personnel, affects the relationship between control and performance. They assessed performance in terms of partner satisfaction with goal attainment and with joint venture profitability. In each of the three small joint ventures they researched, split control was satisfactory to both sides. When the American partners had committed more money and personnel to the joint ventures, it became desirable in their eyes to control more of their management functions. They were not satisfied with their joint ventures' performance unless they had dominant control in them.

Child, Yan, and Lu (1997) found no consistent link between the relative level of control over the joint ventures held by the parent companies, and assessments of their performance. However, the joint ventures which their senior managers rated highly successful in profitability and growth tended to have a closer match between levels of control and partners' equity and resource provision, than did the more weakly performing joint ventures. This suggests that achieving a balance between the level of a partner's resourcing commitment to an alliance, and its management control of the alliance can impact upon the performance that is achieved. In the absence of such a balance, a parent company may well not have sufficient control to ensure an effective use of the resources it has provided.

Case studies

The case studies investigated are divided into joint ventures, collaborations (i.e. non-joint ventures) and a consortium. All present a similar problem in the development of trust. However the issue of control impacts the various alliance forms differentially. It is likely that control will be exercised most closely in the joint ventures, since there are more direct organizational mechanisms for this to take place in a hierarchical fashion. The consortium, with its large number of partners, presents a control problem for each one. The collaboration, without a joint venture company on which to focus, has of necessity to rely on subtler methods of control.

The Dowty–Sema Joint Venture

Dowty–Sema was set up as a joint venture in 1982 by the current partners' predecessor companies with the encouragement of the UK Ministry of Defence, in order to provide an alternative tenderer to Ferranti in the specialized market of command and control systems for ships. Until its integration into Bae–Sema in 1992 it was 50:50 owned by Dowty and Sema. The joint venture was a success in sales growth terms, being very good at obtaining work from the MOD. It grew in ten years from nothing to 110 staff and an annual turnover of £50 million. But as a company it suffered from its lack of independent assets with which to carry out the work: 90 per cent of the value of each contract was sub-contracted back to the owning partners Dowty and Sema in the form of work to be carried out. Only 10 per cent remained with the prime contractor Dowty–Sema. The venture was therefore little more than a 'shop window' for marketing and sales purposes.

All decisions of any importance only followed after lengthy committee meetings involving both the partners and the venture management. Due to these cumbersome organizational arrangements neither the partners nor the venture made much profit from the contracts landed by Dowty–Sema. Thus the flawed organizational arrangements made at set-up were compounded by inappropriate management behaviour, which impeded the genuine flourishing of the venture.

Trust never developed at many levels between the partners in Dowty–Sema. At board level relations were good on a personal basis, but the personnel from Dowty and from Sema, with their very different cultures, never trusted each other, even at the predictive level. There was grudging respect at best.

A Sema person's view of a Dowty man would be of an old and bold harbour engineer, a bit fuddy duddy, not that creative, always the one to raise artificial barriers to getting something done. The corresponding opinion by a Dowty person of a Sema person would be a 25-year-old fly-by-night, with wonderful ideas but without regard for their practicality, or the reality of engineering real systems that have to be put in ships and supported. This caused great difficulty from the outset, and it continues to cause great difficulty. (Davis, a D–S executive)

Control was retained very much in the parent companies, with Dowty–Sema as little more than a shell company at least in the first instance. At board level there was equal membership to reflect the 50:50 shareholding of the partners. Joint MDs were even appointed, but as this led to confusion in decision-making, they were replaced by a single MD who happened to come from Sema. He had little power, however, since when contracts were obtained the two partners divided them in half and took them into their parent companies. The joint venture only retained those activities that were neither obviously hardware (Dowty) nor software (Sema).

As we have become more successful we have become a threat to the sub-contractor operations. The actual sub-contractor organizations are divisions of the bigger entities, and report up the line to directors that sit on my Board. But every bit of work they have is sub-contracted from us, so they haven't been successful in diversifying out of that themselves, and this creates tension between us. (Warner, MD of Dowty–Sema)

An excessive concern for control by the shareholders led to long committee meetings, before any non-routine decision was taken, and as a result potentially profitable contracts were completed late and unprofitably.

It hasn't been wholly a success. We've been successful at expanding the business, but the sub-contractors haven't made the profit they hoped to. We took a big risk on the technology to win the submarine contract, and the implementation of that technology, especially on the software side, has cost a lot of money. You have to get three-way agreement to all decisions, so decision-making is too slow, and this has meant that they have lost money. (Warner)

The parents used a further mechanism to exercise control over the venture. They insisted that all staff belonged ultimately to the pay-roll of either one or the other parent company. This made it very difficult for the venture to develop into a real company with a clear identity. Although Guy Warner, the MD, reported to the Board of Dowty–Sema his performance appraisal was carried out in Sema.

There was considerable tension between the two partners in carrying out projects, and information flow between them was extremely guarded. Control extent by the partners was very high, even to the degree of stifling initiative outside the sales function. The focus of control was principally on the gaining and implementation of the contract. On a functional basis, however, Sema concentrated on setting up and controlling the financial systems, whilst Dowty focused on contract administration and monitoring. Overall, a high level of parent control was strongly correlated with a low level of trust between the partners on anything other than the very top level, and resulted in a company successful in sales terms but not in terms of profits.

The EVC Joint Venture

Eurovinyl Cloride Corporation is a joint venture set up in 1986 by ICI and Enichem of Italy to rationalize the production and sales of PVC in Europe. In order to do this it was judged necessary to retire up to 1 million tonnes of capacity from the joint capacity of the two partners. EVC is a 50:50 owned venture company based in Belgium, with the remit to sell PVC and allied products based largely on raw material provided by ICI and Enichem, and manufactured in plants still run by ICI and Enichem respectively.

This joint venture has to be regarded as relatively successful, since it achieved its primary objective of returning the area of activity for the partners to profit in normal non-recessionary times, largely through capacity rationalization and efficiency improvement. However, the fact that EVC was forced to buy 90 per cent of its raw materials at above market prices from the shareholders, and that production took place in factories owned by the partners, and not by EVC, has considerably constrained its developmental potential.

Basic culture differences between the partners have made life somewhat difficult for the EVC personnel. EVC cannot expect to be viable and indeed saleable until it has ownership of its manufacturing, and possibly raw-material-producing plants, so the joint venture cannot currently present itself as a self-standing business.

There has, according to senior executives of the joint venture, been a tendency for shareholders to be 'economical with the truth' on occasions when dealing with each other and with JV management, and therefore somewhat untrusting. John York, the retiring MD, suggested (though not in those terms) that trust was calculative, only moderately predictive, and not affective. Some acceptable trust was established within the JV, but not really between the shareholders or between the shareholders and the JV. The board of EVC reflected the 50 : 50 equity split between the partners, as did the most senior appointments. The first CEO was from ICI under a non-executive Enichem Chairman. However, it was agreed that after a period of time this would be reversed. The JV CEO was, however, given only limited autonomy as the shareholders constantly interfered.

They also had other powerful means of controlling the joint venture. The shareholders' agreement required that raw materials were bought from the shareholders at prices to be specified by them. Tripartite committees of ICI, Enichem, and EVC decided matters like the price of raw material transfers, but EVC had little power over these, if the parents agreed among themselves. Production was also carried out on parent company sites and in parent company factories. This significantly limited the JV's power of independent action. Furthermore, EVC personnel were largely seconded from the parent companies with a return ticket. They therefore frequently retained parent company loyalties, making it difficult for the JV to develop its own culture and identity.

Although major decisions influencing JV profitability were retained by the partners, the JV was allowed to keep most of its profits, and to make acquisitions when it could afford to do so. In this way it began to develop some independence over time. With regard to the focus of control, both partners concentrated on JV profitability, but functionally Enichem looked after production and ICI marketing. Overall a high level of partner control was correlated with limited trust between the partners, and in relation to the JV, and a feeling of only limited success. The feeling in the market was that the partners would sell EVC when the opportunity presented itself.

The ICI Pharma Joint Venture

ICI Pharma is a joint venture set up in 1972 by ICI Pharmaceuticals (60 per cent) and Sumitomo Chemicals (40 per cent) to produce and market certain ICI pharmaceutical products in Japan. ICI provides the product specification, whilst Sumitomo manufactures the product and physically distributes it. It also achieved Japanese clinical registration of the drugs. ICI Pharma markets and sells the products.

The joint venture has achieved an acceptably high share of the small part of the Japanese pharmaceutical market that is not dominated by Japanese national companies. In the eyes of the partners, the venture has met its measurable objectives, and achieved a good reputation in the industry in Japan. However, according to ICI, the lion's share of the profit has gone to Sumitomo. Cultures remain very separate. The ICI side believe that when the alliance was set up, Sumitomo got the best of the bargain, and have been insufficiently flexible to renegotiate the deal as this has become apparent. The existence of this opinion held by ICI is probably sufficient by itself to confine the alliance to the category of an alliances of only limited success.

Trust has never developed past the predictive stage on the ICI side, as they increasingly came to the view that they had been out-negotiated on the original deal. Also the people at ICI never really trusted or understood the Japanese, and in general have made little effort to do so. The joint venture therefore remains, despite its longevity, a company run by two quite separate companies, and with locally recruited staff uncertain of their identity.

Control, as in all JVs, depends ultimately on equity holdings and board membership. Sumitomo probably has most operational control, as the JV is sited in Japan and the ICI personnel are insufficiently motivated to get strongly involved in the operation of the company. ICI appoints the Chairman and President, and Sumitomo appoints the MD. Under him there is always a younger Japanese who runs the company on a day-to-day basis. The shareholders' agreement is also a control mechanism, but unfortunately the original agreement, with its pricing formulae, was supposed to last for ever! But ICI believe it is weighted towards giving Sumitomo most of the profit, so it is not a very useful control mechanism from ICI's viewpoint.

With regard to the extent of control, ICI has little day-to-day control, and is limited in its sanctions to preventing new ICI products going through the venture. It is currently embarking on manufacturing on its own account in Japan. As regards the focus of control, Sumitomo is responsible for pharmaceutical finishing and for distribution, and ICI is responsible for selling and overall company management, and also for providing the specifications of the products. Overall, from ICI's viewpoint, the level of trust is low and so is that of control. ICI's subsequent actions in setting up their own wholly owned subsidiaries in Japan indicates a negative attitude towards ICI Pharma.

The Cable and Wireless Japanese Consortium (IDC International)

Cable and Wireless are pursuing a strategy of becoming a global force in the telecommunications market. Given their existing limited size and financial power in global terms, this requires development through strategic alliances. The Japanese market is clearly important for this strategy, and C&W determined in 1986 to attempt to obtain the licence to become the second Japanese international carrier. In order to do this, they decided that a consortium company needed to be set up including some major Japanese corporations, in order to achieve credibility with the Japanese government. International Digital Corporation was therefore founded with C&W, Toyota, and C Itoh each holding 17 per cent of the equity and about 20 Japanese shareholders sharing the remainder. The consortium was successful, after a considerable battle with the Japanese government, in obtaining the international carrier licence.

The alliance has undoubtedly been a success in establishing itself and C&W in Japan. It has achieved a 16 per cent share of Japan's international telecommunications traffic. Japan has gone from having the highest prices in international telecommunications in the Asian region to some of the lowest, and from not being on the major networks of the world, it has in a few years become the major hub-centre for the whole area. Much of this is due to the stimulus provided by IDC.

Trust between the partners is generally high in IDC, since the consortium has been forged in adversity. Partners have won trust by their deeds not their words. They have gone through the calculative and predictive levels of trust, and generally reached the affective level. 'Attitudes are felt to be positive, and commitment and trust high. Despite the partners' differing long-term objectives, information is widely disseminated without mutual suspicion' (J. Soloman, C&W Director).

Control is exercised through cultural means in a very Japanese fashion i.e. through traditional forms of control like *nemawashi* and cultural Japanese protocols. *Nemawashi* is the Japanese term used to describe the heavy networking involved in achieving consensus decisions. High internal networking and consensus building is perhaps the Western equivalent of *nemawashi*. Decisions are taken consensually, so specific office holders have no great individual power. As regards specific mechanisms, there are no large legal documents; just a simple shareholder's agreement.

Main board membership is allocated according to shareholding. The three major shareholders have the key appointments: C&W provides the Managing Director, C Itoh the President, and Toyota the Chairman. Only a Japanese national may have a cheque-book, a factor that does not seem to concern C&W. Almost continuous meetings ensure no surprises and exercise control. There is no control on the level of information passage. Influence is achieved by C&W through their technology knowledge of the telecommunication business. The banks achieve influence through the provision of finance and the other shareholders through provision of customers.

Control by any one partner is also bound to be limited, as IDC is a consortium with around 20 partners. However the three partners with 51 per cent between them—C Itoh, Toyota, and C&W—naturally have the most control. Extent of control in a Japanese setting is difficult to gauge, since top-level decisions are not taken without consensus. The impression is that control is pretty centralized in the consortium, but that C&W have little control themselves, and have to depend on influence. The focus of control is strongly on technology and commercial relations, and most mechanisms are hidden from view in a typical Japanese fashion. Overall the venture comes out high on trust and low on control, but is quite successful in that IDC has achieved high market share, but is having more trouble achieving high profits in an increasingly competitive industrial arena.

The Courtaulds–Nippon Collaboration

Courtaulds set up a collaborative alliance with Nippon Paint of Japan in 1976, because it needed a reliable Japanese company to service its and its customers' needs in Japan. Nippon, for its part, wished to rise in the league table of Japanese marine paint companies, and regarded an alliance with Courtaulds, the acknowledged world leader in the area, as a significant step in helping it achieve this aim.

The alliance has a mixture of good and limiting characteristics, leading to considerable difficulty in predicting its future. On the good side, the partners have both benefited substantially from the relationship, and show character-istics of trust, commitment, and growing sensitivity to cultural differences. However, overall objectives increasingly cease to be congruent as Nippon becomes more successful, and develops global ambitions. Courtaulds, how-ever, insisted on a territorial non-compete condition, and this was incorpor-ated into the collaboration agreement. This was ultimately to cause Nippon problems.

The alliance has endured for a long time, and its prospects for the future probably depend crucially on the level of bonding achieved by the new generation of senior executives in both companies, and on the partners' ability to reconcile their objectives, and achieve greater organizational learn-ing. There is little doubt that both partners value the relationship greatly, although their respective objectives, and views of each other, differ to some degree. To Nippon, Courtaulds are a very strong global marketing company with whom they are happy to share joint global development. They see themselves as stronger technologically, however. Courtaulds see Nippon as greatly improved technologically, and as a strong partner to represent them in Japan, but probably not as an equal global partner in the worldwide marine paints market.

Trust between the partners has generally been good, although when the younger generation of executives of both companies became involved in the alliance it developed relationship problems, and Eryn Morris, the original Courtaulds main board champion for the alliance, had to become involved in the alliance once more in order to restore the rapidly disintegrating trust. It has always been good at a calculative level, and also at the predictive level. There is only patchy evidence to show a high level of trust at the affective level.

Control in a collaboration is always less direct than in a JV, since the ultimate mechanisms of main board membership and equity shareholding do not exist. The mechanism used by the partners was a legal agreement specifying territory, technology, and commercial limitations. In addition to this and more informally there was a main board champion in both partners, as well as 'gateway' executives on both sides. There were, however, other interfaces as well, as the alliance operated through projects and committees.

With regard to the extent of control, in this particular alliance, strategic decisions are made at board level, and implemented at 'gateway' level. The focus of control is on territory and on technology. Outside these areas the normal financial controls of royalty payments apply. Generally, there is a low level of control and a high level of trust. The collaboration has been very long-lived, and despite some problems has been viewed as quite successful by both partners.

The Imperial–Wintermans Collaboration

The collaboration between Imperial (Cigar Division) and Henri Wintermans in the marketing of Wintermans' cigars in the UK is an alliance that exchanges UK market access provided by Imperial for Wintermans, for technology transfer provided by Wintermans to update Imperial's cigar manufacturing technology. The alliance was formalized in 1989, and has been successful in that Imperial has met its target for sales of Wintermans' cigars, and Wintermans has transferred its technology.

There is a question that the limited possibilities for evolution of the alliance may place a limit on the alliance's capacity for growth. It may be that there is little more to go for in market share in the cigar market in the UK without Imperial and Wintermans attacking each other's share. On the technology side both companies are now 'state of the art'. Brand rationalization can probably go no further on the Imperial side, and not much further on Wintermans'.

Imperial talk speculatively of merging production units to achieve the greatest possible economies of scale, but this would be difficult to do without setting up a formal joint venture company, and with Wintermans operating worldwide and Imperial only in the UK this would present difficulties. Finally, the position of BAT as Wintermans' owners represents a major potential conflict of interest which may ultimately destroy the alliance.

At the beginning of the formal collaboration agreement, there was considerable distrust between the two companies. Wintermans felt that Imperial had not given priority to its interests when it operated the Wintermans UK sales agency, and Imperial salesmen resented having to sell Wintermans' products when they could sell their own with better margins. This distrust was overcome by Imperial being completely open in the areas of cooperation; also by their actions in deliberately pulling out of Imperial's competing brands, and by closing no longer required factories. Predictive trust followed from calculative trust, which itself had been difficult to establish with a disillusioned Wintermans. New Imperial management under Hanson ownership have tried the bonding approach as much as possible.

Control is carried out through the implemention of a collaboration agreement to be regularly reviewed every few years. The normal primary collaboration mechanisms of the single 'gatekeeper' for each partner is used less than in many alliances, although the Imperial Cigar MD and the Wintermans Marketing and Sales Director carry out this role to some extent. Other interfaces also exist however, e.g. in the areas of production, finance, and marketing. Information is shared widely, but strategy not so widely, as Wintermans is owned by BAT, a major competitor of Imperial.

The extent of control is seen in the fact that the relationship is concentrated at the head-of-cigars level, so that is where control is exercised. The focus of control is largely on sales for Wintermans, and on technology for Imperial. The level of trust is generally good now; control is not tight and within its limitations the alliance has been quite successful.

The RBS–Santander Collaboration

The alliance between Royal Bank of Scotland and Banco Santander of Spain, set up in 1988, is a partial union of two medium-sized national banks in the face of the expected Europeanization of the banking industry. The partners own a small minority of each other's shares. The alliance operates on many fronts, including joint ventures in Germany and Gibraltar, and a consortium for money transfer covering a number of European countries. This consortium, named IBOS, is to date the most successful part of the alliance, and was not foreseen as a significant project at the outset of the alliance, demonstrating the importance of allowing evolutionary forces to unfold in successful alliances. The alliance partners have learnt that they can achieve most of what they wish to achieve on the European scene through the extension of IBOS, without the added expenditure and risk of acquisition.

Over the years of the alliance's life, there has been considerable evolution of the relationship. Most of the activity areas set out at the beginning are now well under way cooperatively. The IBOS system is developing in a far wider fashion than had been envisaged, and staff are being exchanged on secondment between the partners. The alliance is a very successful venture from the cooperation viewpoint, representing a considerable increase in the Royal Bank's and Santander's European standing, and as a by-product has considerably strengthened RBS's ability to serve its customers in Central and South America, as Santander are traditionally strong in that region. However, customers flow only one way at present. The propensity of UK investors to go into Spain is not matched by those of Spanish investors to invest in the UK, so Santander tends to gain from increased sales more than does RBS.

Trust has almost deliberately gone through all three stages. The calculative stage was necessary to bring the alliance into existence in the first place. The predictive level was achieved through working together, some exchange of personnel, and both banks' willingness to buy into each other's shares to more than a nominal degree. RBS appreciated Santander's readiness to help them reduce the Kuwait Investment Office's large strategic holding in RBS. Affective trust developed through a number of anecdotally amusing incidents between the partners, and is evidenced by the fact that each will now allow the other partner to represent its interests with third parties.

A major control mechanism is the alliance agreement, put together by the partners at the outset. This has not, however, been allowed to constrain the scope of the alliance, and the IBOS system, perhaps the alliance's greatest claim to fame, was barely envisaged at the outset. A surveillance committee was established at top level to oversee the relationship, and gateway executives were appointed at Assistant Director level in Walter Stewart and Jose Saveedra, who have both been in post since the beginning. They effectively control the alliance at operational level. Both banks have invited each other to put representatives on their main boards and this has been carried out.

Increasingly, performance measures are being developed to assess the progress of the alliance. In addition accountants tot up costs once a year and compare the amounts spent on the alliance by both partners. The extent of control operates at several levels: strategic control is principally at top level, with the surveillance committee and board membership, with operational control at assistant director level with the gateway executives. The focus of control is wide-ranging, but does not extend to interference in the domestic banking activities of each partner by the other. Overall trust is high, direct control is low, and the alliance is regarded as very successful by both partners.

The Rover–Honda Collaboration

The alliance between Rover and Honda has been a very long-lasting one that led to the resurrection of Rover as a quality car-maker, and the effective entry of Honda into the European market. It started in 1979 as a simple arm's-length franchise for Rover to assemble a Honda car in the UK, badge it as a Triumph, and market it. It subsequently developed into a very wide-ranging alliance, including joint manufacturing, joint sourcing, design, and R&D. Only marketing and distribution have been handled separately in the UK.

The alliance was very fruitful from the viewpoint of both partners. Alone, neither was a world-class motor manufacturer. Honda were strong in the USA and a medium-sized player in Japan. Their European presence was negligible. Rover were strong in Europe but nowhere else. In fact 95 per cent of their production in 1980 was for Europe, including the UK. However, together Rover and Honda presented a powerful world force with a strong presence in Japan, the USA, and Europe.

Rover moved steadily into profit in the mid-1980s, largely as a result of its organizational learning from the alliance, and from 1990 as a subsidiary of British Aerospace, it contributed an annual profit to its parent, although the recession of the early 1990s inevitably damaged profits, and it is currently in difficulties once more. If quality, and a regenerated reputation, were prime objectives, however, these have certainly been established as a result of the alliance. The 800, the 200, and the 400 series are all generally acknowledged to be first-class cars from a quality viewpoint, and Rover's reputation is reflected in its return to people's high opinion.

Honda, for its part, has grown from a medium-sized player in global terms in 1978 with a turnover of around £4 billion to one with a worldwide sales level of more than £12 billion, of which 66 per cent is earned outside Japan, and a net profit after tax of more than £500 million in 1990. In Europe Honda's sales of cars have increased from a negligible amount in 1978 to £700 million or 191,000 units in 1990. Not only have Honda raised their European direct sales but they have also benefited from part of Rover's approximately 450,000 unit sales.

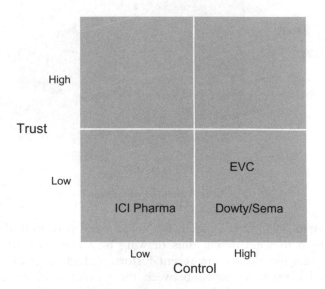

Fig. 16.2a Limited success alliances

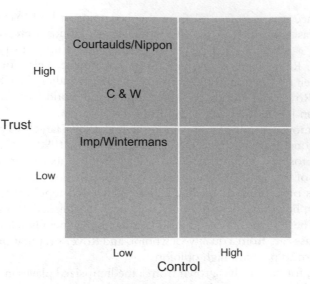

Fig. 16.2b Quite successful alliances

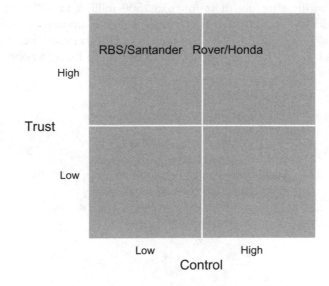

Fig. 16.2c Very successful alliances

However, in 1993 Rover's owners Bae sold the company to BMW, and the alliance began to wind down, thus drawing to a close one of the most successful strategic alliances in recent history. A high level of calculative and predictive trust developed between the partners without ever quite reaching the affective level. Unfortunately this did not extend to relations with British Aerospace, Rover's owners in the latter years of the alliance. For over a decade, however, relationships between Rover and Honda were very trusting.

With regard to control mechanisms, the relationship had strong Japanese characteristics in that legal agreements did not have a prominent place in the means of control. The Japanese approach is more that working together creates its own understanding, which is a form of control. Everything was done on a project basis. There was the appointment of respective Directors of Collaboration, Bacchus and Hayashi, to act as principal gateways. After the alliance had been operating some years a Statement of Understanding was drawn up, and in response to the perceived needs of the City, a 20 per cent cross shareholding was exchanged.

Project management methods of control were established, including separate agreements for each project, which were then policed by the project director, who transcended functional lines. There were many meetings— quarterly meetings between two top-level teams including the respective Presidents; *ad hoc* engineering and strategic meetings every 4 to 6 weeks, and a monthly meeting on quality and manufacturing issues; plus day-to-day *ad hoc* meetings and programming meetings. Then there were quarterly negotiations on prices. Overall, the alliance was characterized by moderate control mechanisms, high trust, and very high performance.

Conclusions

As can be seen in the unbundled three-dimensional matrix shown in (Figure 16.2) and in Table 16.1, the key factor in achieving high performance, at least in respect to the eight case studies reported, is a high level of trust. Both the very successful and the quite successful alliances exhibit high trust between the partners, which seems to have been accompanied with less concern for control. However, as the narrative shows, the trust does not always reach the level of affective trust. High predictive trust reduces transaction costs considerably, and hence increases competitive strength. It seems to be difficult to achieve affective trust across wide cultural boundaries, but this is not critical if the calculative and predictive levels are high.

The strength of control does not show such a clear pattern in relation to either trust or success. The two alliances judged to be the most successful were considered to have respectively low and moderate levels of control but high trust. The 'quite successful' alliance had high trust but low control. Of the limitedly successful alliances two exhibit high control and one low. The low control case is of ICI Pharma, where ICI seems to have ceased to regard the venture as its primary bridgehead in Japan, and may therefore have lost interest in it to some extent. It is of course also difficult to exercise control in Japan from the UK. There is some support, therefore, for Geringer and Hebert's view (1989) that too much control may stifle initiative and hence

TABLE 16.1

	Type	Trust	Control	Success
1 Dowty–Sema	jv	Low	High	Limited
2 EVC	jv	Moderate	High	Limited
3 ICI Pharma	jv	Low	Low	Limited
4 C&W	cons. jv	High	Low	Quite successful
5 Imperial–Wint	coll.	High	Low	Quite successful
6 Courtaulds–Nippon	coll.	High	Low	Quite successful
7 Royal Bank–Santander	coll.	High	Low	Very successful
8 Rover–Honda	coll.	High	Moderate	Very successful

lead to less successful ventures. Similarly, of course, lack of success may lead to a tightening of control in order to improve efficiency, and sometimes to compensate for a degree of lack of trust.

Part of the problem of regarding case studies in a static, analytic way is, of course, the difficulty in dealing with the process and time dimension. Different control mechanisms are developed at different times in the alliances, and the extent and nature of trust waxes and sometimes wanes in relation to internal and externally changing events. Performance also varies over time. To place an alliance in a particular position of a matrix is therefore necessarily over-simplistic, and a process approach to tracing the changes in control, trust, and performance in any one alliance may perhaps give greater insight into their relationship.

However, the cases recorded in this chapter have been investigated in some depth by the author, and the judgements made may therefore have some validity. To that extent there seems to be strong evidence linking trust with success, although it is not, of course, possible to assign directionality to the link. The question of control is more difficult, where the linkage seems to offer some evidence for the thesis that less control is necessary in situations where trust develops well. There is also some evidence to suggest that high control develops in situations where trust is low, and perhaps for both reasons performance may then be adversely affected due to a combination of low trust and low motivation ensuing from low autonomy.

References

AWADZI, W., KEDIA, B. L., and CHINTA, R. (1986), 'Performance Implications of Locus of Control and Complementary Resources in International Joint Ventures—An Empirical Study', paper presented at the Academy of International Business Conference, London.

BEAMISH, P. W. (1988), *Multinational Joint Ventures in Developing Countries* (London: Routledge).

BJØRN, L. B. (1997), 'Managing Uncertainty in Transnational Headquarters–Subsidiary Interfaces: Danish Companies in Japan and Germany', PhD thesis (Aarhus, Denmark).

BLEEKE, J. and ERNST, D. (1993), Collaborating to Compete: Using Strategic Alliances and Acquisitions in the Global Marketplace (New York: Wiley).

BRENKERT, G. G. (1998), 'Trust, Morality and International Business', in C. Lane and R. Backmann (eds.), *Trust Within and Between Organizations* (Oxford: Oxford University Press).

CHILD, J. and FAULKNER, D. O. (1998), *Strategies of Cooperation: Managing Alliances, Networks and Joint Ventures* (Oxford: Oxford University Press).

——— YAN, Y., and LU, Y. (1997), Ownership and Control in Sino-Foreign Joint Ventures, in P. W. Beamish and J. P. Killing (eds.), *Cooperative Strategies: Asian Pacific Perspectives* (San Francisco: The New Lexington Press), 181–225.

GERINGER, J. M. and HÉBERT, L. (1989), Control and Performance of International Joint Ventures', *Journal of International Business Studies*, 20: 235–54.

KILLING, J. P. (1983), *Strategies for Joint Venture Success* (New York: Praeger).

LANE, C. and BACKMANN, R. (eds.) (1997), *Trust Within and Between Organizations* (Oxford: Oxford University Press).

LEWICKI, R. J. and BENEDICT BUNKER, B. (1996), 'Developing and Maintaining Trust in Work Relationships', in R. M. Kramer and T. R. Tyler (eds.), *Trust in Organizations: Frontiers of Theory and Research* (Thousand Oaks, Calif.: Sage), 114–39.

McALLISTER, D. J. (1995), Affect- and Cognition-based Trust as Foundations for Interpersonal Cooperation in Organizations', *Academy of Management Journal*, 38/1: 24–59.

OHMAE, K. (1993), 'The Global Logic of Strategic Alliances', in J. Bleeke and D. Ernst (eds.), *Collaborating to Compete: Using Strategic Alliances and Acquisitions in the Global Marketplace* (New York: Wiley), 35–54.

OSLAND, G. E. and CAVUSGIL, T. S. (1996), 'Performance Issues in US–China Joint Ventures', *California Management Review*, 38:106–30.

SAKO, M. (1997), 'Trust Within and Between Organizations', in C. Lane and R. Backmann (eds.) *Trust Within and Between Organizations* (Oxford: Oxford University Press).

SCHAAN, J.-L. (1988) 'How to Control a Joint Venture even as a Minority Shareholder', *Journal of General Management*, 14: 4–16.

THORELLI, H. (1986), 'Networks: Between Markets and Hierarchies, *Strategic Management Journal*, 7: 37–51.

ZUCKER, L. G. (1986), 'Production of Trust: Institutional Sources of Economic Structure, 1840–1920', *Research in Organizational Behavior*, 8: 53–111.

Part V

Cooperative Strategy: The Future

We end with a section setting out some thoughts on the way in which research into cooperative activity between firms might develop in the future. It does not attempt to be a comprehensive crystal gaze into the issues that will interest researchers working after the publication of this book, but attempts merely to identify some important areas of interest that are currently discernible.

17

Reflections on the Study of Strategic Alliances

RANJAY GULATI AND EDWARD J. ZAJAC

It is hard to think of any issue that has been the subject of greater research in the last decade than that of strategic alliances. Scholars from a variety of backgrounds have chosen strategic alliances as an arena for scholarly inquiry, reflecting the fact that strategic alliances themselves have grown dramatically in number and in importance for many organizations. The significant scholarly attention paid to strategic alliances has resulted in valuable insights into the antecedents and consequences of strategic alliances that, in turn, have resulted in contributions to both theory and practice. Perhaps it is not so much the number of scholars pursuing this field of inquiry that make it interesting and exciting, as the heterogeneity of their backgrounds. The diverse theoretical orientations of alliance scholars has resulted in a rich stream of research that crosses disciplinary chasms to further our understanding of this important phenomenon. This book exemplifies very well this rich diversity of perspectives and the new insights emerging from such interdisciplinary approaches.

Given this abundance of research, is it possible that there may be diminishing returns to further alliance research? We think not. In fact, rather than recapitulating the major points of the previous chapters, we would like to use this opportunity to reflect on several issues within the study of alliances that could benefit from greater attention. We believe there are many fertile areas that still remain for those who are inspired by this important phenomenon, and we wish to address just a few of them. In this way, one can see that while this book should advance considerably our understanding of some fundamental issues about alliances, it should also provide a catalyst for future research, with most of the papers suggesting important avenues for future research on alliances.

In this chapter we will focus attention on two important and related issues that merit future attention: first, the role of the broader network context of firms for their alliances; and secondly, the factors that influence the performance of alliances and the benefits individual partners receive from alliances. Our focus on these two issues reflects our interests and is by no means intended to suggest that they are more important than some other topics. There are numerous other fertile arenas for research on alliances, some of which we will briefly refer to at the end of this chapter. Our intent is to take the 'depth over breadth' approach instead of trying to be comprehensive in presenting a laundry list of all or most possible potential topics for the study of alliances. We look at two particular topics in depth in order to illustrate the richness of opportunities that still remain within the study of alliances, and we would hope that a closer examination of other topics would reveal equally important research opportunities. As we read this important collection of papers on alliances we not only learned much that was new about this important phenomenon, but we also discovered numerous opportunities for future research. We hope that other readers will be equally inspired.

Alliances and Networks

For the sake of clarity, let us first define strategic alliances as voluntary arrangements between firms involving either a pooling or trading of resources. They can occur as a result of a wide range of motives and goals, take a variety of forms, and occur across vertical, horizontal, and other related boundaries. While this traditional definition is useful, it has tended to focus research attention on the alliance itself. However, we would like to suggest that a fruitful arena for future research would involve extending recent work that introduces a social network perspective to the study of strategic alliances (Gulati, 1998; Zajac, 1998). This perspective argues that alliance research needs to go beyond considering alliances as dyadic exchanges, and should also pay more attention to the fact that key precursors, processes, and outcomes associated with alliances can be defined and shaped in important ways by the social networks within which most firms are embedded. Network perspectives build on the general notion that economic actions are influenced by the social context in which actors are embedded and that actions can be influenced by the position of actors in social networks. Embeddedness refers to

'the fact that exchanges and discussions within a group typically have a history, and that this history results in the routinization and stabilization of linkages among members. As elements of ongoing social structures, actors do not respond solely to individualistically determined interests . . . a structure of relations affects the actions taken by the individual actors composing it. It does so by constraining the set of actions available to the individual actors and by changing the dispositions of those actors toward the actions they may take' (Marsden, 1981: 1210).

Underlying embeddedness is the quest for information to reduce uncertainty, a quest that has been identified as one of the main drivers of organizational action (Granovetter, 1985). Networks of contact between actors can be important sources of information for the participants, and what can matter is not only the identity of the members of a network but also the pattern of ties among them.

Scholars have only recently begun to explore the implications of the social structure resulting from inter-corporate networks on strategic alliances

(Gulati, 1998). The embeddedness of firms in social networks can both restrict and enable the alliances a firm enters. By influencing the extent to which firms have access to information about potential partners, social networks can alter the opportunity set firms perceive for viable alliances. Similarly, networks constrain the extent to which potential partners are aware of a focal firm and thus may constrain its set of choices for alliances.

Several recent studies have explored the importance of social embeddedness to the formation of alliances by firms. The first question examined has been at the firm level—which firms enter into alliances? Evidence suggests that the proclivity of firms to enter alliances is influenced not only by their financial and technological attributes (treated as proxies for strategic imperatives), but also by how they are embedded in social networks between firms (Kogut, Shan, and Walker, 1992; Gulati, 1999; Eisenhardt and Schoonhoven, 1996; Powell, Koput, and Smith-Doerr, 1996; Podolny and Stuart, 1995). Each network studied highlights a different underlying social process that enables central firms to enter alliances more frequently. The influence of social embeddedness on the formation of new alliances has also been observed at the dyad level, with a focus on who partners with whom. Results from some recent studies suggest that the cumulation of prior alliances between firms creates an important social structural context that influences which pairs of firms are likely to tie up with each other (Gulati, 1995*b*; Gulati and Gargiulo, 1999). The formation of dyadic ties between particular firms has also been studied in vertical alliances between buyers and suppliers and a recent study suggests that Japanese automotive assemblers tend to re-create their relationships in Japan in their North American operations (Martin, Mitchell, and Swaminathan, 1995).

The social explanation offered by the reported studies that highlight the role of embeddedness does not preclude the possibility of traditionally examining strategic imperatives or diminish their importance. These are indeed complementary elements, and a network perspective suggests that the conditions of mutual economic advantage are necessary but not sufficient conditions for the formation of an alliance between two firms. While considerations of an individual quest for resources and complementarity are relevant, it is a firm's social connections that help it identify new alliance opportunities and choose specific partners that possess such complementary assets.

Firms are embedded in multiple social networks and the implications of these manifold ties on alliance formation remains an open question. The evidence that exists thus far highlights the significance of one social network at a time on new alliances. The possible implications of the simultaneous and possibly conflicting influence of multiple social networks on alliance formation has yet to be systematically examined. For instance, one of the most widely studied inter-organizational networks has been board interlocks, and yet the implications of such ties and other inter-firm networks on alliances has largely been overlooked until recently (Gulati and Westphal, 1999). Further-more, the broader institutional context in which such networks are placed can also be influential (Dacin, Hitt, and Levitas, 1997).

The social networks in which firms are embedded can have far-reaching consequences beyond their influence on the creation of new alliances that have yet to be considered. For instance, the extent to which two partners are socially embedded can also influence their subsequent behaviour, and affect the likely future success of the alliance. Furthermore, a firm's portfolio of alliances and its network position in an industry can have a profound influence on its overall performance. Once two firms decide to enter an alliance, their relative proximity in the network may also influence the specific governance structure used to formalize the alliance (Gulati, 1995a; Gulati and Singh, 1998). These and many other questions that explore the connections between the social networks of firms and a whole host of issues associated with the dynamics of alliances remain important areas for future research.

A social network perspective on alliances can have both descriptive and normative outcomes that provide valuable insights for theories of strategic management, organizational theory, and sociology. Incorporating social net-work factors into our account of the alliance behaviour of firms not only provides us with a more accurate representation of the key influences on the strategic actions of firms, but has important implications for managerial practice as well, many of which have yet to be explored. For instance, an understanding of the network dynamics that influence the formation of new alliances can provide insights for managers on the path-dependent processes that may lock them into certain courses of action as a result of constraints from their current ties (Gulati and Gargiulo, 1999). They may choose to anticipate such concerns and proactively initiate selective network contacts that enhance their informational capabilities. Thus, by examining the specific way in which social networks may constrain firms' future actions and channel opportunities, firms themselves can begin to take a more forward-looking stance in the new ties they enter. They can be proactive in designing their networks and considering the ramifications on their future choices of each new tie they form. They may also selectively position themselves in networks to derive possible control benefits as well. Similarly, there are numerous insights that result from understanding the complexities associated with managing a portfolio of alliances and the relational capabilities required to do so successfully. Ultimately, managers want to know how to manage individual alliances, and a recognition of some of the dynamics at both the dyadic and network levels that influence the evolution and eventual perfor-mance of alliances can be extremely beneficial. An important challenge for scholars studying networks and alliances is to bridge the chasm between theory and practice and translate some of their important insights for man-agers of the alliances we study.

Performance of Alliances

An important issue for the study of alliances is their performance consequences, both in terms of the performance of the alliance relationship itself and the performance of firms entering alliances. This can be broken down into two related but distinct research questions:

1. What factors influence the success of alliances?
2. What is the effect of alliances on the performance of firms entering them?

The performance of alliances has received less attention than other areas because of some onerous research obstacles, which include the difficulty of measuring alliance performance and the logistical challenges of collecting the rich data necessary to assess these issues in greater detail. As a result, it remains one of the most exciting and under-explored areas. One of the vexatious obstacles to studying performance, and also one of the problems with the many studies that have reported high failure rates for alliances, is measuring performance itself (Anderson, 1990). Given the multifaceted objectives of many alliances, performance can be difficult to measure with financial outcomes. Furthermore, in most cases such measures simply do not exist. A further complication results from the dyadic nature of alliances. Sometimes performance is asymmetric: one firm achieves its objectives while the other fails to do so. For instance, several cases have been reported of alliances in which one partner had raced to learn the other's skills while the other did not have any such intentions (Doz, Hamel, and Prahalad, 1989; Hamel, 1991; Khanna, Gulati, and Nohria, 1998).

The primary approach to empirical studies of the performance of alliances has been to examine the termination of an alliance (Beamish, 1985; Levinthal and Fichman, 1988; Kogut, 1989). While these studies have provided valuable insights into the termination of alliances, their importance for understanding the performance of an alliance *per se* are limited by their failure to distinguish between natural and untimely terminations, and their implicit consideration of alliance performance as an either–or condition. Researchers have gone beyond the initial efforts that equated alliance termination with failure to try to uncover some of the factors associated with the success of alliances. These have entailed detailed surveys or careful fieldwork on alliances that uncovers the multiple facets of alliance performance and considers the perspectives of all the partners in the alliance (Harrigan, 1985; Heide and Miner, 1992; Parkhe, 1993; Gulati and Lawrence, 1999). Such approaches enable the collection of a host of measures, subjective and objective, on which performance can be assessed, as well as an examination of dyadic asymmetries in perceptions.

One potentially fruitful arena for future research would link our previous research question with this one and entail an examination of the impact of social networks in which firms are placed on the relative performance of their alliances, an area that has received limited attention. Once we acknowledge the importance of the multiplicity of social networks in which firms are placed, we can overcome such dyadic reductionism and examine whether alliances that are embedded to a greater or lesser degree in various networks perform better or worse than others and why. While there have been several efforts to explore differences in 'embedded' ties between firms and those that are less proximate they tend to make inference rather than directly assessing whether embedded ties themselves perform any better than other ties. The inference is based on an aggregate assessment of the survival properties of firms and its association with the extent of embedded ties those firms have entered, and not on a direct assessment of the relative success of individual alliances. Furthermore, such approaches generally treat embeddedness as an either–or proposition and have focused primarily on relational embeddedness resulting from proximate ties, while paying less attention to the importance of structural embeddedness. While such studies have advanced our understanding of the nature and importance of embedded ties, an important extension would be to focus directly on the performance of alliances and whether the extent of embeddedness in social networks is an important factor.

There is some evidence that alliances with embedded ties may perform better or last longer than others (Kogut, 1989; Levinthal and Fichman, 1988; Zaheer, McEvily, and Perrone, 1998; Gulati and Lawrence, 1997). However, this issue still remains to be fully explored. The extent to which an alliance is embedded is likely to influence its performance for several reasons. By being proximately situated in an alliance, the partnering firms are likely to have greater confidence and trust in each other, both because they have greater information and because the network creates a natural deterrent for bad behaviour that will damage reputation. Trust not only enables greater exchange of information, it also promotes ease of interaction and a flexible orientation on the part of each partner. All of these can create enabling conditions under which the success of an alliance is much more likely.

Do firms benefit from entering strategic alliances? This question is distinct from the previous one, which looked at the performance of alliances themselves, and instead it focuses on the performance consequences of alliances for the firms entering them. One approach to exploring this question is to consider the cooperative capabilities of firms. Evidence suggests that there may be systematic differences in the cooperative capabilities that firms build up as they have more experience with alliances and that the extent of this learning may affect the relative success of those firms with alliances (Lyles, 1988). This poses questions about what such capabilities are and what might be some systematic tactics firms use to internalize such capabilities. At least some of these capabilities include: identifying valuable alliance opportunities and good partners, using appropriate governance mechanisms, developing inter-firm knowledge-sharing routines, making requisite relationship-specific asset investments, and initiating necessary changes to the partnership as it evolves while also managing partner expectations (Doz, 1996; Dyer and Singh, 1998). The fact that a firm may have entered a wide array of alliances also suggests that it has to simultaneously manage this portfolio and address conflicting demands from different alliance partners. Furthermore, if the firm is at the centre of a network, it must pay particular attention to a series of strategic and organizational issues (Lorenzoni and Baden-Fuller, 1995). Developing such a portfolio perspective on alliances merits further consideration, especially since many firms are now situated in an array of alliances.

Since many other activities besides alliances can also influence the performance of firms, it can be difficult to empirically link the alliance activity of firms with their aggregate performance. As a result, scholars have looked for a variety of direct and indirect means to test this relationship. To estimate the effect of individual alliances on firm performance, several researchers have conducted event-study analyses on the stock market effects of alliance announcements (e.g. Koh and Venkatraman, 1991; Balakrishnan and Koza, 1993; Anand and Khanna, 1997). Inasmuch as the stock market reactions portend the likely future outcome from alliances, these results provide mixed evidence of the beneficial consequences of alliances for firms entering them.

Yet another approach to assess the aggregate influence of alliances on firm performance has been to examine the relationship between the extent to which firms are embedded in alliances and the likelihood of their survival. Thus, survival of firms is considered as a proxy for performance (e.g. Baum and Oliver, 1991, 1992). The alliances studied, on which firm survival may depend, have been those with vertical suppliers and with key institutions in the environment. The results of these studies suggest that such ties are generally beneficial in enhancing survival chances (Mitchell and Singh, 1996).

The approaches to studying alliances and firm performance discussed thus far have paid scant attention to the overarching networks in which firms may be embedded. This shifts the analytical focus away from simply the number of prior ties to membership in particular networks. Recent research highlights several industries in which networks, rather than firms, have become the organizing level at which firms compete with each other (Gomes-Casseres, 1996). As a result, the performance of a firm is influenced by the networks to which it belongs. Such approaches, which highlight the relative success of particular networks, can be further refined to identify the specific characteristics of the network that may enable it to provide positive benefits to its members (Gulati and Westphal, 1999). Two natural extensions of these studies would look not only at the network characteristics but also the position of individual organizations within the network in which they are placed. This could alert us both to possible informational benefits and to control benefits that may result from particular locations in specific networks. Furthermore, it would be fruitful to assess the performance effects across the multiplicity of networks in which firms are embedded. Other possible concerns include who controls the network and why and possible limits and constraints to the growth of networks.

Before concluding our chapter, we would like to mention briefly several additional areas that have not had the benefit of much research attention. For example, while our discussion to this point has emphasized macro perspectives on alliances (either at the network, alliance, or firm level), there are clearly more micro concerns that can have implications for alliance processes and outcomes. One example is the role of social psychological processes in strategic alliances. It is to be expected that researchers would take a more dispassionate and distanced view of alliances, and even research that addresses alliance processes has tended to treat alliances from a predominantly rational perspective (Zajac and Olsen, 1993; Ring and Van de Ven, 1994; Doz and Prahalad, 1998). Such a view, however, may obscure the fact that alliances involve complex human interactions and are likely to be affected significantly by conscious and even subconscious social psychological processes.

For example, the concept of trust, which is so often invoked in alliance research, is most interesting not as a rational, calculative concept, but as an emotional, affective concept. In particular, understanding the emotion of trust can help us understand why alliance partners don't see alliances as simply games with payoffs, but as an interpersonal exchange of emotions that can be highly positive (i.e. trust), but also highly negative (i.e. betrayal). Similarly, the concept of equity, also central in the study of cooperation, has its roots in human perceptions and emotions that diverge significantly from a dispassionate observer's perspective, or a game theorist's pay-off matrix. Taking a perspective that emphasizes the behavioural aspects, as well as the economic aspects, of organizational life could add significantly to our understanding of alliance formation, conflict, dissolution, and overall performance.

References

ANAND, B. N. and KHANNA, T. (1997), 'Do Firms Learn to Create Value?', *Working Paper* (Boston, Mass.: Harvard Business School).

ANDERSON, E. (1990), 'Two Firms, one Frontier: On Assessing Joint Venture Performance', *Sloan Management Review*, 31/2: 19–31.

BALAKRISHNAN, S. and KOZA, M. P. (1993), 'Information Asymmetry, Adverse Selection and Joint Ventures: Theory and Evidence', *Journal of Economic Behavior and Organization*, 20: 99–117.

BAUM, J. and OLIVER, C. (1991), 'Institutional Linkages and Organizational Mortality', *Administrative Science Quarterly*, 36: 187–218.

———— (1992), 'Institutional Embeddedness and the Dynamics of Organizational Behavior', *American Sociological Review*, 57: 540–59.

BEAMISH, P. (1985), 'The Characteristics of Joint Ventures in Developed and Developing Countries', *Columbia Journal of World Business*, 20: 13–19.

DACIN, M. T., HITT, M. A., and LEVITAS, E. (1997), 'Selecting Partners for Successful International Alliances: Examination of U.S. and Korean Firms', *Journal of World Business*, 32/1: 3–16.

DOZ, Y. (1996), 'The Evolution of Cooperation in Strategic Alliances: Initial Conditions or Learning Processes?', *Strategic Management Journal*, 17: 55–83.

——and PRAHALAD, C. K. (1998), *Alliance Advantage: The Art of Creating Value Through Partnering* (Boston: Havard Business School Press).

——HAMEL, G. and PRAHALAD, C. K. (1989) 'Collaborate with your Competitors and Win', *Harvard Business Review*, 67/1: 133–9.

DYER, J. H. and SINGH, H. (1998), 'The Relational View: Cooperative Strategy and Sources of Interorganizational Competitive Advantage', *Academy of Management Review*, 23/4: 660–79.

EISENHARDT, K. M. and SCHOONHOVEN, C. B. (1996), 'Resource-Based View of Strategic Alliance Formation: Strategic and Social Effects in Entrepreneurial Firms', *Organization Science*, 7/2: 136–50.

GRANOVETTER, M. (1985), 'Economic Action and Social Structure: A Theory of Embeddedness', *American Journal of Sociology*, 91/3: 481–510.

GULATI, R. (1995a), 'Familiarity Breeds Trust? The Implications of Repeated Ties on Contractual Choice in Alliances', *Academy of Management Journal*, 38: 85–112.

——(1995b), 'Social Structure and Alliance Formation Pattern: A Longitudinal Analysis', *Administrative Science Quarterly*, 40: 619–52.

——(1998), 'Alliances and Networks', *Strategic Management Journal*, 19: 293–317.

——(1999), 'Network Location and Learning: The Influence of Network Resources and their Capabilities on Alliance Formation', *Strategic Management Journal*, 20/5: 397–420.

——and SINGH, H. (1998), 'The Architecture of Cooperation: Managing Coordination Costs and Appropriation Concerns in Strategic Alliances', *Administrative Science Quarterly*, 43: 781–814.

——and GARGIULO, M. (1999), 'Where Do Interorganizational Networks Come From?', forthcoming in *American Journal of Sociology*.

——and LAWRENCE, P. (1999), 'The Diversity of Embedded Ties,' *Working Paper* (Evanston, Ill.: J. L. Kellogg Graduate School of Management, Northwestern University).

——and WESTPHAL, J. (1999), 'The Dark Side of Embeddedness: An Examination of the Influence of Direct and Indirect Board Interlocks and CEO/Board Relationships on Interfirm Alliances', forthcoming in *Administrative Science Quarterly*.

HAMEL, G. (1991), 'Competition for Competence and Inter-Partner Learning within International Strategic Alliances', *Strategic Management Journal*, 12: 83–103.

HARRIGAN, K. R. (1985), *Strategies for Joint Ventures* (Lexington, Mass.: Lexington Books).

HEIDE, J. and MINER, A. (1992), 'The Shadow of the Future: Effects of Anticipated Interaction and Frequency of Contact on Buyer–Seller Cooperation', *Academy of Management Journal*, 35: 265–91.

KHANNA, T., GULATI, R., and NOHRIA, N. (1998), 'The Dynamics of Learning Alliances: Competition, Cooperation, and Relative Scope', *Strategic Management Journal*, 19: 193–210.

KOGUT, B. (1989), 'The Stability of Joint Ventures: Reciprocity and Competitive Rivalry', *Journal of Industrial Economics*, 38: 183–98.

—— SHAN, W., and WALKER, G. (1992), 'The Make-or-Cooperate Decision in the Context of an Industry Network', in N. Nohria and R. Eccles (eds.), *Networks and Organizations: Structure, Form and Action* (Boston, Mass.: Harvard Business School Press), 348–65.

KOH, J. and VENKATRAMAN, N. (1991), 'Joint Venture Formations and Stock Market Reactions: An Assessment in the Information Technology Sector', *Academy of Management Journal*, 34/4: 869–92.

LEVINTHAL, D. A. and FICHMAN, M. (1988), 'Dynamics of Interorganizational Attachments: Auditor-Client Relationships', *Administrative Science Quarterly*, 33: 345–69.

LORENZONI, G. and BADEN-FULLER, C. (1995), 'Creating a Strategic Center to Manage a Web of Partners', *California Management Review*, 37/3: 146–63.

LYLES, M. A. (1988), 'Learning among Joint Venture-Sophisticated Firms', in F. K. Contractor and P. Lorange (eds.), *Cooperative Strategies in International Business* (Lexington, Mass.: Lexington Books), 301–16.

MARSDEN, P. V. (1981), 'Introducing Influence Processes into a System of Collective Decisions', *American Journal of Sociology*, 86: 1203–35.

MARTIN, X., MITCHELL, W., and SWAMINATHAN, A. (1995), 'Recreating and Extending Japanese Automobile Buyer–Supplier Links in North America', *Strategic Management Journal*, 16: 589–619.

MITCHELL, W. and SINGH, K. (1996), 'Precarious Collaboration: Business Survival after Partners Shut Down or Form New Partnerships', *Strategic Management Journal*, 17: 99–115.

PARKHE, A. (1993), 'Strategic Alliance Structuring: A Game Theoretic and Transaction Cost Examination of Interfirm Cooperation', *Academy of Management Journal*, 36: 794–829.

PODOLNY, J. M. and STUART, T. (1995), 'A Role-Based Ecology of Technological Change', *American Journal of Sociology*, 100: 1224–60.

POWELL, W. W., KOPUT, K., and SMITH-DOERR, L. (1996), 'Interorganizational Collaboration and the Locus of Innovation: Networks of Learning in Biotechnology', *Administrative Science Quarterly*, 41: 116–45.

RING, P. S. and VAN DE VEN, A. H. (1994), 'Developmental Processes of Cooperative Interorganizational Relationships', *Academy of Management Review*, 19/1: 90–118.

ZAHEER, A., McEVILY, B., and PERRONE, V. (1998), 'Does Trust Matter? Exploring the Effects of Interorganizational and Interpersonal Trust on Performance', *Organization Science*, Mar./April: 141–59.

ZAJAC, E. J. (1998), 'Commentary on "Alliances and Networks" by R. Gulati', *Strategic Management Journal*, 19: 319–21.

—— and OLSEN, C. P. (1993), 'From Transaction Cost to Transactional Value Analysis: Implications for the Study of Interorganizational Strategies', *Journal of Management Studies*, 30/1: 131–45.

18

Concluding Thoughts and Future Directions

DAVID O. FAULKNER AND MARK DE ROND

This volume has presented some of the significant research currently taking place in the field of cooperative strategy. The topic area may still not have reached the level of popularity in terms of books, journal articles, and academic teaching courses as has the area of competitive strategy, but it is rapidly catching up. Practising managers, politicians, legislators, and academics alike recognize that without cooperation the probability of survival in a globalizing, turbulent, and increasingly technologically sophisticated world is slim. Whilst competition must still weed out the inefficient, today's wealth creators and resource allocators can no longer afford to regard the rest of the world as enemies to be defeated in a battle for economic supremacy.

The contributors to the various chapters have attempted to develop further the various theories of cooperation and, in many cases, have tested them out in specific empirical scenarios. The most popular theories of cooperation—including transaction cost theory, resource-based theory, and resource dependency theory all get an airing and are applied to explain specific situations. Social network theory, an increasingly popular theme, is addressed by other contributors. The importance of learning is also emphasized as a critical factor in alliance success and frequently as a dominant rationale. The somewhat neglected area of the process by which alliances evolve is also tackled. Here we see the juxtaposition of authors who see a pattern in alliance evolution with those who conclude that the most predictable thing about alliances is the unpredictability of their evolution. It seems that few successful alliances develop in the way in which their creators initially imagined they would. Serendipity is, of course, fine so long as the partners are still able to claim success, even if it surfaces in ways they could not have anticipated.

Another area to receive prominent treatment from our contributors is that of the importance of particular types of behaviour by alliance partners if the alliance is to work successfully. Trust, commitment, and the importance of cultural congruity are singled out as areas that need particular attention in the development of close partner relationships. It is emphasized how important such relationships are if the alliances are to work well and the costs of mutual monitoring are to be minimized.

Gulati and Zajac (chap. 17) have already indicated some exciting avenues for future research into cooperative strategy, particularly concerning alliances and the networks in which these are embedded. Adding to their suggestions, we suggest some further avenues for future research below.

1. We live in an increasingly turbulent world made more so by the globalization of markets and by technological sophistication. A potential area of research concerns the role of cooperative strategy in providing one organizational means of coping with that turbulence. Strategy formulation has traditionally been taught by means of static analytical tools, of which the underlying assumptions are that the world changes only slowly, and that therefore a substantial element of stability can be assumed when formulating strategy. The theory of dynamic capabilities makes no such assumptions and places the opportunities for achieving sustainable competitive advantage with those firms able to develop dynamic capabilities. The role of cooperative strategy in developing such capabilities is one that researchers may wish to explore.

2. The organization of the MNC in a globalizing world, where the advantages of scale economies need to be balanced against the need for sensitive local responsiveness, is an issue likely to involve strategies of cooperation. To what extent, one might ask, will integrated multi-nationals transform into more flexible federated enterprises, able to be reconfigured to meet changing local demands and fashions?

3. Game theory has become increasingly used in economics, particularly to investigate the possibilities of tacit collusion in oligopoly conditions. It is becoming similarly popular in strategy for investigating cooperative behaviour. Currently such analyses tend to be limited to the two partner static analysis scenario. Game theory techniques could be applied to more complex situations, including those involving networks.

4. Few empirical works have tested the linkage between trust and alliance performance, using either financial measures or the attainment of specific objectives. Also, more theory development is needed on explicating relationships between trust and related constructs such as control systems, alliance structure, learning processes, and risk. Each of these types of research, however, needs a more rigorous operational measurement of the trust concept. Currall and Inkpen (chap. 15) have made some progress towards this objective in providing a framework for the conceptualization and measurement of trust at different levels.

5. Process-oriented research remains a neglected domain within the field of cooperative strategy, where the emphasis has traditionally been on formation issues and those related to performance. Yet, once the agreement is in place, how does an alliance evolve? And how much of this evolutionary process is within the control of management? Given a handful of process theories, many of which are sequential, predictive, and task-orientated, is it not about time to relax the managerial agenda and rhetoric that has dominated these earlier works?

6. To date, both theoretical and empirical studies appear to have generated an under-socialized account of alliances. Many practising managers, however, would readily agree on the importance of interpersonal relationships in cooperative ventures. Rather than continuing to treat alliances as 'faceless abstractions', one might study them as groups of cooperating individuals, with particular histories, loyalties, abilities, ambitions, agendas, and personalities. For instance, can one influence the continuity and performance of an alliance by changing its social make-up? Do some problematic alliances survive because of vested interests of certain individuals?

7. To what extent are alliances used as vehicles for gaining and retaining legitimacy within certain industries? Biotechnology companies, for instance, are uniquely keen to emphasize their alliances with large pharmaceuticals. How does the nature of alliances change once legitimacy has been established?

8. Within the out-sourcing literature, there is ample scope for both theory development and empirical work into relationship management. Selective out-sourcing, smart-sourcing (using various styles of out-sourcing), and back-sourcing (re-integration into the core business) are emerging topics in IT out-sourcing. As the Xerox Corporation case study (chap. 10) illustrated, a strategy of total out-sourcing can be complex, problematic, and difficult to sustain.

9. As there does not yet appear to be a unified and comprehensive theory of alliances, this remains a challenge waiting to be met. Will continued efforts result in a 'dominant design paradigm' for the field? Or will the research become increasingly eclectic, shaped by such disciplines as sociology, psychology, philosophy, anthropology, economics, physics, and mathematics, and specialist areas such as game theory, chaos theory, complexity theory, or even literary criticism? Will it seek traditional, positivist explanations of causality or yield to contingency, contextualist, or structuralist influences?

Within the province of contemplation, thought, and analysis the job is never finished. As soon as one writer logs out of his or her word processor, hoping to have contributed to the solution of a problem, another one starts and shows why this is but part of a more intricate story, and why a countervailing theory deserves attention. This book cannot do more than give some insights and an eclectic contribution in a growing and important field, but we hope it at least does that.

Index

Abbott, A., on networks 143
Abernathy, W. J., Clark, and Kantrow, on
    innovation styles 157
Abo, T., on control 289
absorbtion:
    acquisitions 286–7
    capacities 120, 121, 125–6
Achrol, R. S., Scheer, and Stern, on process 25
acquisitions:
    integration, national differences 283–304
    management practice characteristics 284–304
    and organizational culture 104–7
    and strategic assets 99
activities, IJV formation by 47–9, 50
adaptability, corporate 267
Adler, P. A., and Adler, on networks 144
affective trust 341, 343–4
agency theory 12–13
Ahern, R., on strategic hazards 119
Aiken, M., and Hage, on IOR theory 213
Airbus, and governance 142
Aldrich, H., and Sasaki:
    on cultural context 316–17
    on R&D collaboration 173, 174
Aldrich, H., and Whetten:
    on IOR theory 213
    on social network theory 20
alliance capitalism 140
alliances:
    differential learning 119–33
    formation rate 119
    international, interpersonal relationships
        307–19
    maintenance 141–2
    and networks 366–8
    performance 369–72
    preliminary considerations 109–10
    structures, and control 314–15
    termination, and performance measurement
        369
    trust 324–37
    and control 341–60
Alpha Jet Project 120, 122, 126–7, 131
Alter, C., and Hage, on trust 325
Alvesson, M., on knowledge
    professionalization 147
America, North, see North America
American firms:
    communication styles 290, 298–9
    control of acquisitions 288–9, 295–6
    integration levels 292, 293–4
    strategic philosophy 290–1, 300–1
Amit, R., and Schoemaker:
    on core competencies 136

    on strategic assets 98
analysis level, trust 326
Anand, B. N., and Khanna, on stock market
    effects 371
Anand, J., Anuddin, and Makino, on alliance
    structures 315
Anderson, E.:
    on payoffs 266
    on performance measurement 369
    on structures 263
Anderson, E., and Gatignon, on transaction cost
    theory 8
Angwin, D., on acquisitions 287
Anheiser, H., Gerhards, and Romo, on social
    capital 248
Applegate, L., and Monealegre, on out-sourcing
    211
appropriation, discourse as 145–7
appropriative learning 135–63
Argyris, C., and Schon, on organizational
    learning 19
Arino, A., and de la Torre, on process 24
Arrow, K. J., on agency theory 12
asset specificity 100–1
    and stability 270
asymmetric information, and learning
    alliances 132–3
asymmetric performance 369
Aulakh, P., Kotabe, and Sahay, on trust 315,
    326
Auster, E., on interpersonal exchanges 312
authority ranking, social resource exchange
    309–10
Awadzi, W., on control 346
Axelrod, R. M.:
    on cooperation 173, 216
    on game theory 16
    on opportunism 91

Bacharach, S., Bamberger, and Sonnenstuhl, on
    exchange perspectives 308
Badaracco, J. L., on NUMMI 129
Bae-Sema 348
Baghai, M., Coley, and White, on real options
    theory 17
Bain, J. S., on core competencies 137
Balakrishnan, S., and Koza:
    on learning 119
    on objectives 269
    on stock market effects 371
Banco Santander/Royal Bank of Scotland 18–19,
    342, 355–6, 360
BaR Skoda, IJVs 42–3
bargaining, transaction costs 103–4

379

Barkema, H. G., Bell, and Pennings:
  on governance 273
  on longevity 264
  on stability 261
Barley, S., on technology change effects 313
Barley, S. R., Freeman, and Hybels, on
      networks 267
Barnett, on RC theory 214
Barney, J., on resource-based view 10, 18, 103
Barney, J. B., and Hansen:
  on opportunism/competition 79, 87
  on trust 30–1, 337
Barney, J. B., and Ouchi, on agency theory 12
barriers, R&D cooperation 174
Barsoux, J.-L., and Lawrence, on strategic
      philosophy 290
Bartlett, C. A., and Goshal, on stability 261
Bass Ginsber Beer Co., IJVs 43
Bass plc, IJVs 43
BAT, and Imperial Wintermans 354–5
Baum, J., and Oliver, on survival 371
Beamish, P.:
  on alliance termination 369
  on control 346–7
  on IJVs 40
  on instability 243
  on longevity/stability 261
Beamish, P., and Banks:
  on longevity 264, 265
  on trust 325
Beamish, P., and Delios:
  on cultural context 316–17
  on IJVs 40
Becker, G., on knowledge resources 136
behaviour, cooperative 28–32, 324–37
behavioural dimension, out-sourcing 235–6
Bellcore 188–9
benefit, from strategic alliances 370–1
Berg, S. V., and Friedman, on stability 261
Berger, P. L., and Luckman, on shared meaning
      246
Berkowitz, S. D., on social network theory 20
Berle, A. A., and Means, on agency theory 12
Bertrand model, price competition 120, 122
Best, M. H.:
  on innovation styles 154
  on national innovation systems 148, 149
Biggart, N. W., and Hamilton, on networks 141,
      162
biotechnolgy industry, cooperative R&D 181, 182
Birkbys Plastics, supply chain partnering 196–201
Bjørn, L. B., on control 346
Blau, P. M.:
  on cooperation 173
  on social network theory 20
Bleeke, J., and Ernst:
  on alliances 3
  on commitment 31
  on control 346

on culture 29
on learning 119–20
on market power theory 5
Blodgett, L. L.:
  on governance 271, 273
  on stability 261
  and trust 249
Blois, K. J.:
  on out-sourcing 212
  on RC theory 214
board interlocks 367–8
Boddy, D., and Buchanan, on project management
      skills 193
Boddy, D. et al., on supply chain partnering 195
Boddy, D., and Gunson, on IT changes 193
Boddy, D., Macbeth, and Wagner:
  on exchange 211
  on process 26
Boisot, M., and Child, on transaction cost theory 8
Boje, D., and shared meaning 251
Borum, F., and Westenholz, on institutional
      context 318
Borys, B., and Jemison:
  on asset specificity 100–1
  on trust 324
Bosch, innovation styles 152, 155
Bouchikhi, H., de Rond, and Leroux:
  on process 25, 26
  on structures 23
Boudreaux, K. J., on divestment 273
Bougon, M. G., and Weick, on shared
      meaning 251
Bougon, M. G., Weick, and Binhorst, on shared
      meaning 246, 251
bounded rationality, and opportunism 77–8
Bouwen, R., and Steyaert, and shared meaning 252
Bower, J. L., and Murphy, on VLSI project 179,
      188
Bowman, C., and Faulkner, on strategic
      management 6
BP, IJVs 42
Bradach, J. L., and Eccles, on opportunism 79
Braverman, H., on operational control 145
Brenkert, G. G., on trust 343, 344
British American Tobacco, and Imperial
      Wintermans 354–5
British firms:
  communication styles 290
  control of acquisitions 288–9
  IJVs 40–54
  strategic philosophy 290–1
Bromiley, P., and Cummings, on trust 325
Bromwich, M., and Walker, on financial
      measurement 159
Brown, L. D., and Ashman:
  on collaborative efforts 243
  on power shifts 254
  on problem resolution 247, 250
Brown & Root, IJVs 42–3

Brown, L. T., Rugman, and Verbeke:
  on longevity/stability 261
  on opportunism 269
Browning, L., Beyer, and Shelter:
  on R&D 174, 188–9
  on trust 315
Bruce, M., and Morris, on innovation styles 157
Buchanan, D., and Boddy, on change 194–5, 207
Buckley, P., and Casson:
  on core competencies 137
  on forbearance 265
  on IJVs 48
  on internalization 57
  on knowledge markets 136
  on mutual forbearance 78
  on partners 331
  on transaction cost theory 7, 8
  on trust 30, 325
  on uncertainty 263
Buckley, P., and Chapman, on agency theory 13
bureaucratic costs 105
Burgelman, R. A., and Sayles, on structures 139
Burkhardt, M. E., and Brass, on technology change
    effects 313
Burnes, B., on organizational change failure 193
Burns, T., and Stalker, on structuralist approach to
    learning 139
Burrell, G., and Morgan, on research 255
Burt, R. S., on social network theory 20
business ecosystems 21–2
business networks, flagship firms 57–73
business process re-engineering (BPR)
    implementation 193
Butler, R., and Gill, on trust building 141
buyer–supplier relationships 87–8

Cable and Wireless:
  IJVs 42
  Japanese Consortium 342, 352–3, 360
calculative trust 341, 342–3
calculus-based trust 245, 248–9
Caledonian Gas, IJVs 42
Callon, M.:
  on knowledge transfer 143
  on pre-competitive R&D 140
Calori, R., and De Woot:
  on control 289
  on culture 285
  on strategic philosophy 290
Calori, R., Lubatkin, and Very, on control 288
Canada:
  alliance hazards study 119
  chemicals industry, flagship model 57, 70–1
  telecommunications industry, flagship model
    57
Cantwell, J., on resources 99
car industry, buyer–supplier relationships 87–8
Cartwright, S.,and Cooper:
  on organizational identity 106, 114

  on relationships 106
  on SOVs failure rate 96, 101
Casson, M., on trust building 141
Caves, E. E., on resource dependency 136
Chandler, A.:
  on alliance capitalism 140
  on control structures 150, 161
  on multiple actor assumption 63
  on national innovation systems 147, 148
change, models 194–5, 209
chemicals industry:
  cooperative R&D 180–1, 183
  flagship model 57, 70–1
Chess, K. et al., and shared meaning 252
Chi, T.:
  on acqusitions 99
  on governance 263, 265
  on resource-based view 11
  on TSIs 101
Chi, T., and Nystrom:
  on complementarity 113
  on SOV valuation 108
Child, J.:
  on control 288
  on culture 285
  on market power theory 5, 6
  on structures 23
  Yan, and Lu, on control 346–7
Child, J., and Faulkner:
  on agency theory 12
  on alliances 4
  on control 346
  on organizational learning 19, 20
  on out-sourcing 212
  on trust 30–1, 341, 345
Child, J., and Francis, on control structures 150
Child, J., and Loveridge:
  on appropriative learning 137
  on diffused innovation 156
Child, J., and Rodrigues, on organizational
    learning 19
China, IJVs 43, 44
  US joint ventures 317
Chrysler:
  buyer–supplier relationships 88
  collaborative relationships 61–2
Ciborra, C., on organizational learning 19
Clark, J.:
  on networks 143
  on production changes 193, 194
Clegg, S. R., on OD approach to learning 139
Coase, R. H., on resource-based view 11
Cohen, M. D., March, and Olsen, on process 26
Cohen, W., and Levinthal:
  on appropriative learning 138
  on learning capacity 121
  on networks 253
  on organizational learning 20
Coleman, J. S., on social capital 246, 248

Coleman, J. S., Katz, and Mendel, on diffused
     innovation 156
collaboration:
     alliances 347, 353–9
     assessment 243–56
     dissatisfaction with 74
     dynamics, IJVs 262
     flagship firms 61–2
     objectives 268–9
     organizational forms 74–95
     preconditions 175–80
     R&D cooperatives 173–91
     success/failure criteria 245–56
collective learning, and communities of
     interest 142–5
commitment 31–2, 180
communal sharing, social resource exchange
     309–10
communication styles, foreign acquisitions
     289–90, 298–300, 304
communities:
     of interest, and collective learning 142–5
     of practice 142–3
Compaq, and value 80
comparative statics approach, learning
     alliances 125
competitive advantage, five forces model
     (Porter) 57
competitive networks 371–2
competitors, key, five partners network 60
complementarity 150
     resources, SOVs 96–8, 105, 107, 108–13
concept stretching 327–9
concerted innovation 151–2, 155
Conner, K. R.:
     on opportunism 77
     on resource-based view 11
     on strategic assets 98
consortium alliances 347, 352–3
constraints, interpersonal 317–18
content agenda, supply chain partnering 202–3,
     203–5
contested innovation 151–2, 153–5
contextual factors, interpersonal exchanges 312
contracting, in Xerox 220–2, 228–30, 232–3
Contractor, F. J., and Lorange 40
     on strategic purposes 98
control:
     agenda, supply chain partnering 208
     alliance structures 314–15
     levels, foreign acquisitions 288–9, 295–8,
          303–4
     structures, and innovation 150
     and trust 341–60
     types 341, 345–7
Conway, S., on knowledge transfer 143
cooperation:
     behaviour 28–32, 328 n.
     capabilities 370–1

process 24–8
rationale 4
strategy 3–32
     implementation 193–210
     out-sourcing 211–39
cooperatives, R&D 173–91
Copeland, T. E., and Keenan, on real options
     theory 17
core competencies 98, 136–7
corporate opportunism 138
corporate performance, IJVs 267–72
corporate strategies, IJVs 267–8
cost sharing alliances 123
cost-effectiveness 74–6
cost-plus pricing, and integration 69
costs:
     governance 104–7
     rents, and SOV transactions 108
Courtaulds/Nippon paint, trust and control 342,
     353–4, 360
crony capitalism 148
Cropper, S., on sustainability 244
Cross, J., on out-sourcing 211
cross-cultural exchanges, strategic alliances
     307–19
cross-licensing 140
cross-sectoral collaborations, assessment 243–56
Crozier, M., on networks 143
Cullen, J. B., Johnson, and Sakano, on
     divestment 273
culture 28–30
     and acquisitions 285–7
     cross-cultural exchanges, strategic
          alliances 307–19
     cultural capital 136
     cultural context 316–18
     national 28–30
          acquisition integration 283–304
     organizational 104–7
Cummings, L. L., and Bromiley, on trust 335
Cunningham, M. T., on IOR theory 213
Currall, S. C., and Inkpen:
     on commitment 32
     on exchange expectations 312
     on trust 30–1, 315, 341
Currall, S. C., and Judge, on risk/reliance 329
customers, key, five partners network 60
Czech Republic, IJVs 42–3

d'Aspremont, C., and Jacquemin, on cooperative
     R&D 125
D'Aunno, T. A., and Zuckerman, on process 25
D'Aunno, T. A., Sutton, and Price, on institutional
     context 318
D'Cruz, J. R., and Rugman, on five partners
     model 57
D'Cruz, J. R., Gestrin, and Rugman, on five
     partners model 57
D&D, see design & development

Dacin, M. T., Hitt, and Levitas, on institutional context 368
Dassault Dornier Alpha Jet Project 120, 122, 126–7, 131
Datta, D. K., on integration 286
Datta, D. K., and Grant, on control 289
Davis, K. J., on Xerox/EDS 217
Davis, K. J., and Applegate, on Xerox/EDS 218
Dawson, P., on change 194
DeBondt, R., on cooperative R&D 125
De Bresson, C., and Amesso, on networks 141
de Rond, M., and Faulkner, on resource dependence theory 18–19
Defense Advanced Research Agency 188
Delhaise, F., on family networks 148
Denison, R. D., and Mishra, on culture 29
design & development (D&D), and innovation styles 157–60
design forms, cooperation 182, 184
Deutsch, M.:
    and Prisoner's Dilemma 328 n.
    on risk 329
    on trust 30
Devinney, T. M., on learning cost reduction function 123
DGXIII (EC), role in participant selection 177
Dickson, P., and Weaver:
    on exchange perspectives 308
    on interpersonal exchanges 307
    on technology change effects 313
Dierickx, I., and Cool, on resources 99
Dietrich, M., on RB collaboration 77
differential learning 119–33
differential payoffs, IJVs 266–7
diffused innovation 151, 155–7
DiRomualdo, A., and Gurbaxani, on TCT 214
discourse, as appropriation 145–7
divestment 136
    IJVs 273–4
divisional system, and integration 67–8
Dodgson, M.:
    on collaboration 88
    on structuralist approach to learning 139
Donaldson, L., on resource dependence theory 18
Donnellon, A., and Gray, on shared meaning 251
Donnellon, A., Gray, and Bougon, on shared meaning 246, 251
Dore, R.:
    on alliance capitalism 140
    on national innovation systems 149
Dornier Dassault Alpha Jet Project 120, 122, 126–7, 131
Dowty-Sema, trust and control 342, 348–9, 360
Doz, Y.:
    on alliance maintenance 141–2
    on complementarity 150
    on cooperation 173, 178
    on cooperative capabilities 370–1
    on culture 28
    on normalization 176
    on organizational learning 19
    on payoffs 266
    on performance assessment 27
    on process 24, 26
Doz, Y., and Baburoglu:
    on cooperative relationship 201
    on process 26
Doz, Y., and Hamel:
    on collaboration 179
    on exchange 211
Doz, Y., and Pralahad, on rationality 372
Doz, Y., and Shuen, on alliances 3
Doz, Y., Hamel, and Prahalad, on asymmetric performance 369
Drazin, R., and Van de Ven, on stability 261
Dunning, J. H.:
    on control 288–9
    on eclectic paradigm 57
    on realignments 271
DuPont Canada 70
Dwyer, F. R., Schurr, and Oh:
    on exchange 211
    on IOR theory 213
dyadic ties 367, 369
Dyer, J. H.:
    on mutual orientation 84, 85, 87–8
    on opportunism 79
Dyer, J. H., and Singh, on cooperative capabilities 370–1
Dymsza, W. A., on longevity/stability 261
dynamic capabilities 98
dynamics, IJVs 267–72

Earl, on out-sourcing 211, 212
Earley, P. C.:
    on exchange expectations 312
    on social market pricing 310
Eastern Europe, IJVs 42–3
Eastman Kodak, out-sourcing 211
EC, see European Community (EC)
eclectic paradigm (Dunning) 57
economic value added (Stewart) 159–60
economic viewpoint 4–17
Economist Intelligence Unit, on TQM implementation 193
ecosystems, business 21–2
Eden, C., and shared meaning 251, 252
EDS/Xerox Corporation, out-sourcing study 217–39
efficiency, in collaboration 74–95
efficiency-outcome dimension, out-sourcing 236–7
Egan, G., on change 194
Eisenhardt, K. M., on agency theory 12
Eisenhardt, K. M., and Schoonhoven:
    on exchange perspectives 308
    on interpersonal exchanges 307
    on social embeddedness 367

Eliasson, G., on value 80
embedded ties, and performance 370
embeddedness:
    IJVs 267
    networks 366–8
enablers, collaboration process 185
Engineering Employers Federation, and
    innovation 150
Enichem, Eurovinyl Chloride 342, 349–50, 360
environments, institutional 316–18
equality matching, social resource exchange
    309–10
equity alliances, trust 324–37
equity shareholding, in IJVs 49–52
Ericsson/Honeywell IJV 271
ESPRIT programme 174, 176, 188–9
EUREKA programme 175, 186–7, 188
Europe:
    telecommunications industry, flagship model 57
    see also Eastern Europe; Western Europe
European Community (EC):
    ESPRIT programme 174, 176, 188–9
    EUREKA programme 175, 186–7, 188
    funding rules 178
    JESSI programme 188–9
Eurovinyl Chloride, trust and control 342, 349–50,
    360
Evan, W. M., and Olk 174
Evans, P., on collaboration 243, 250
evolution:
    in collaboration process 180, 184
    process as 24–7
ex ante analysis, SOVs 109–10
ex ante selection, SOVs 110–11
ex post exchange conditions 269–72
ex post operation and maintenance 111–13
exchanges:
    conditions, ex post 269–72
    cross-cultural, strategic alliances 307–19
    interpersonal relationships 307–12
extent, control 341, 346

facticities (Granovetter) 142
Fagre, N., and Wells, on governance 271
failure:
    criteria 245–56
    organizational change 193
    and performance measurement 369
    shared organization ventures (SOVs) 96–116
family networks, role in Pacific Asia 148–9
Faulkner, D. O.:
    on alliances 3
    on commitment 32
    on control 288
    on cooperative behaviour 28
    on culture 29–30
    on exchange expectations 311
    on opportunism 79
    on out-sourcing 212

on performance assessment 27
on resource dependence theory 18
on strategic management 6
on trust 337
Faulkner, D. O., and de Rond:
    on alliances 324
    on commitment 32
    on trust 325
Fedor, K. J., and Werther, on alliances 3
Fichman, M., and Levinthal, on trust 325
finance, and strategic alliances 158–60
Financial Times, M&A database 41–2
Fiske, A., on social resource exchange 309–10
five forces model (Porter) 57
five partners model, MNEs 57–73
flagship firm theory 57–73
    NUMMI experience 130
flagship networks 101
flexibility, corporate 267
Fligstein, N., on institutional context 318
Florida, R., and Kenney, on OEMs 141
Florin, J., on trust 315
focal entities for collaboration 176–7
focus control 341, 346
Forbes, D., on NUMMI 129
Ford, D., on IOR theory 213
Ford Motor Company:
    buyer–supplier relationships 88
    and innovation 150
foreign acquisitions, national differences 283–304
Foresight programme (UK) 160
Forrest, J. E., and Martin:
    on alliances 3
    on process 25
Fortune, on buyer–supplier relationships 87–8
framework, R&D cooperation 174–83
France Telecom, collaborative relationships 62
Francis, A., Turk, and Willman, on transaction cost
    theory 8
Franko, L. G.:
    on flexibility 267
    on governance 273
    on longevity/stability 243, 261
Fransman, M. 174
Freeman, C., Sharp, and Walker:
    on networks 140
    on pre-competitive R&D 140
French firms:
    communication styles 290, 300
    control of acquisitions 288–9, 298
    integration levels 292, 293, 295
    strategic philosophy 290–1, 302–3
Froud, J. et al., on economic value added 159–60
Fruin, M., on Japanese business networks 62
FT M&A database 41–2
Fukijama, on social capital 248
Fulk, J., on technology change effects 313

Galaskiewicz, J., on IOR theory 213, 214

Galbraith, J. K., on open systems 203
Gambetta, D.:
    on risk 329
    on trust 325
game theory model 13–16
    differential learning 120, 122–33
Garud, R., on flexibility 267
Gemser, G., Leenders, and Wijnberg, on
        innovation styles 157
Genefke, J., on culture 29
General Motors (GM):
    and innovation 150
    Toyota NUMMI 16, 120, 122, 129–30
geographical distribution, IJVs 43–4
Geringer, J. M., and Hebert:
    on alliance structures 315
    on control 288, 341, 346
    on longevity 264
Geringer, J. M.:
    on alliance structures 315
    on complementarity 96
Gerlach, M. L., on Japanese business networks 62
German firms:
    communication styles 290, 299–300
    control of acquisitions 288–9, 297–8
    integration levels 292, 293, 294–5
    strategic philosophy 302
Germany:
    national innovation systems 147–8
    and networks 144
Ghemawat, P., Porter, and Rawlinson, on IJVs 41
Ghoshal, S., and Moran:
    on opportunism 77, 91
    on value 80
Gibson, D., and Rogers, on R&D 174
Giddens, A.:
    on social network theory 20
    on structures 23
Giffin, K., on reliance 329
Ginsber Beer Group, IJVs 43
Gioia, D., and Thomas, on organization
        structure 314
Glaister, K. W., on IJVs 40
Glaister, K. W., and Buckley, on IJVs 41
Glaister, K. W., Husan, and Buckley, on alliances 3
Glick, W. H., on level issues 326
Gluech, on management functions 63
GM, buyer–supplier relationships 88
goal achievement, and collaboration
        assessment 245, 248
Goetz, C. J., and Scott, on RC theory 213
Gomes-Casseras, B.:
    on alliances 307
    and business ecosystems 22
    on competitive networks 371–2
    on cooperatives failure 96
    on cultural context 317
    on governance 271
    on SOVs failure rate 101

Goold, M., and Campbell:
    on control structures 150, 151, 288
    on innovation styles 157
Gouldner, A., on innovation styles 153
governance:
    costs 104–7, 115
        analysis 269–72
        evolution 272–4
        structures 263, 265, 269–72
Grabher, G., on networks 142
Granovetter, M.:
    on information search 366
    on networks 142, 253
    on opportunism 79
    on social relations 81–2
    on trust 325
Grant, R. M., on resource dependence theory 10,
        18
Gray, B.:
    on collaboration 243, 244
    on cooperation 173, 180
    on cross-sector collaboration 243
    on exchange 211, 308
    on performance assessment 27–8
    on power shifts 254
    on research 255
    and shared meaning 250
Gray, B., and Hay, on collaborative efforts 243
Gray, B., and Purdy, on power shifts 255
Gray, B., and Wood, on collaborative efforts 243,
        244
Gray, B., and Yan:
    on bargaining 103–4
    on cultural context 317
    on process 25
Gray, B., Westley, and Brown:
    on networks 253
    on outcomes 244
    on power shifts 254
    on restructuring 244
    on social capital formation 246, 250
    on social impact 244
    on structure 246
Gray, B., Younglove-Webb, and Purdy, and shared
        meaning 252
Gricar, B., and Brown:
    on networks 253
    on power shifts 254
    on structure 246
Grindley, P., and Teece, on cross-licensing 140
Grindley, P., Mowery, and Silverman, on
        R&D 174
Groupe Accor, and value 80
Gulati, R.:
    on alliances 3, 24, 315, 325, 329 n.
    on cooperation 173, 178, 183
    on cultural context 317
    on game theory 14
    on networks 252, 253, 267

Gulati, R.: (cont.)
    on performance and network position 368
    on process 25
    on social network perspective 20, 21, 366, 367
    on strategic alliances 243
    on TC theory 90 n.
    on trust 250, 325
Gulati, R., and Gargiulio:
    on interdependencies 176
    on structural context 367, 368
Gulati, R., and Lawrence:
    on failure 369
    on performance and embedded ties 370
Gulati, R., and Nohria, on cooperatives failure
        96
Gulati, R., and Singh, on performance and network
        position 368
Gulati, R., and Westphal:
    on board interlocks 367–8
    on competitive networks 371–2
Gulati, R., and Zajac, on commitment 32
Gulati, R., Khanna, and Nohria:
    on commitment 31
    on game theory 14–15
Gupta, A. K., and Govindarajan:
    on core competencies 136
    on information flows 145, 161
    on SBUs 139
Gurbaxani, V., and Whang, on TCT 214

Hagedoorn, J.:
    on collaboration 74
    on cultural context 316–17
    on IJVs 40, 41
    on interpersonal exchanges 313
    on strategic alliances 243
Hagedoorn, J., and Narula, on interpersonal
        exchanges 313
Hagedoorn J., and Schakenraad, on IJVs 40, 41
Hagel, M., and Singer, on exchange 211
Hamel, G.:
    on alliance structures 315
    on asymmetric performance 369
    on financial measurement 159
    on IJVs 40
    on knowledge transfer 106, 110
    on learning 119, 132
    on longevity 264
    on objectives 269
    on organizational learning 19, 20
    on performance assessment 27, 248
    on structures 263
    and trust 249
Hamel, G., and Prahalad, on resource dependence
        theory 18
Hamel, G., Doz, and Prahalad:
    on alliances 3
    on learning 131
    on performance assessment 27

Hampden-Turner, C., and Trompenaars, on
        culture 285, 289
Hane, G. J., on R&D collaboration 173, 174
Hardy, C., on change 194
Hardy, C., and Phillips:
    on collaborative efforts 244
    on power shifts 244, 254
    on structure 246
harmony, and trust 328
Harrigan, K. R.:
    on alliances 3, 307
    on failure 369
    on flexibility 267
    on stability 261
    on strategic management 6
    on structures 263
    on trust 325
    on uncertainty 263
Haspeslagh, P., and Jemison, on integration 285,
        286–7
Hausler, J., Hans-Willy, and Lütz, on R&D 174,
        180, 183
Hax, A., and Majluf, on learning cost reduction
        function 123
hazards, strategic 119–33
Hearth, D., and Zaima, on divestment 273
Hebert, L.:
    on performance measurement 248
    and trust 250
Heide, J., and John, on trust 315
Heide, J., and Minor, on failure 369
Heifetz, R. A., on R&D 180
Heimer, C.:
    on restructuring 244
    and shared meaning 250
Helper, S., on supply chain relationships 145
Hennart, J. F.:
    on asset specificity 270
    on equity alliances 324
    on governance 263
    on SOVs 96
    on TC theory 79
    on transaction cost theory 8, 313
Hennart, J. F., Kim, and Zeng, on divestment 273
Hergert, M., and Morris, on IJVs 40, 41, 42, 48
Hickson, D. J., on culture 285
Hickson, D. J., and Pugh, on control 289
Hickson, D. J. et al., on knowledge transfer 143
Hilgarten, S., and shared meaning 251
Hill, C., on opportunism 82
Hill, C., and Hellriegel:
    on performance measurement 248
    on relationships 106, 110, 115
Hill, C., and Kim, on bureaucratic costs 105
Hill, C. et al., on cultural context 317
Hill, C., Hwang, and Kim, on TSIs 101
Himmelman, A. T., on power shifts 254
Hinings, C. R., Brown, and Greenwood, on
        change 194

Hirshman, A. O., and shared meaning 252
Hitt, M. A., and Ireland, on core competencies 136
Hladik, K. J.:
  on IJVs 40
  on payoffs 266
Hoechst, outsourcing R&D 158
Hofstede, G.:
  on control 289
  on culture 28, 29
holding acquisitions 286–7
Honda/Rover, trust and control 342, 356–9, 360
Honeywell/Ericsson IJV 271
Hong Zui Corp, IJVs 43
Hopwood, A. G., and Miller:
  on financial measurement 160
  on innovation styles 153
Horowitz, J., on control 289
House, R., Rousseau, and Thomas-Hunt, on level
    issues 326
Houston Oil, and Tenneco 106
Huber, G., on OD approach to learning 139
Huber, R. L., on out-sourcing 211
Huff, A., on innovation styles 157
human interactions, and networks 372
Hungarian/Western European collaborations 317
Hunt, S., and Nevin, on IOR theory 213
Huxham, C.:
  on collaboration 243
  and shared meaning 252
Huxham, C., and McDonald, on collaboration 243
Hymer, S. H., on market power theory 5

Ibarra, H., on social network theory 20
ICI:
  and divestment 136
  Eurovinyl Chloride 342, 349–50, 360
ICI Pharma, trust and control 342, 351, 360
identification-based trust 245, 248–9
IJVs, see international alliances, international joint
    ventures (IJVs)
Imperial Wintermans, trust and control 342,
    354–5, 360
India, IJVs 43, 44
Indonesia, IJVs 43
industrial organization (IO) theory 10–11
industries, IJV formation by 45–7, 50
inefficiency, in collaboration 74–95
information flows 145–6
information management, in Xerox 219–20, 225–8
information search, networks 366
information technology, out-sourcing 211–39
infrastructure, five partners network 60
Ingham, M., on alliances 3
Inkpen, A.:
  on organizational learning 19
  on trust 250, 327
Inkpen, A., and Beamish:
  on alliance maintenance 142
  on flexibility 267

Inkpen, A., and Crossan:
  on organizational learning 19
  on payoffs 266
Inkpen, A., and Currall:
  on partners 331, 336
  on risk/reliance 329
  on trust 315
innovation:
  styles 150–60
  systems, national 147–9
institutional context 316–18, 368
integration:
  agenda, supply chain partnering 208–9
  levels, national differences 292–5, 303
  skills 285–6
intent, and out-sourcing 232–3
inter-firm level, trust 324, 331, 332, 336–7
inter-group level, trust 324, 331, 332, 334–6
inter-organizational alliances, trust 324–37
inter-organizational relationship (IOR) theory
    213–15
interactions, and out-sourcing 234–5
interdependencies, R&D cooperation 175–6
internal governance costs 104–7, 115
internalization theory 57, 63, 64–5
International Digital Corporation (IDC), trust and
    control 342, 352–3, 360
international alliances:
  international joint ventures (IJVs) 40–54
    longevity/stability 261–76
  strategic, interpersonal relationships 307–19
  trust and control 341–60
interpersonal relationships:
  constraints 317–18
  exchange types 309–12
  international strategic alliances 307–19
  trust 324, 331, 332–4
investment/resources model, SOVs 107–13
invisible resources 98
irrationality, and networks 372
Isen, A., Nygren, and Ashby, on risk 330
ISO 2000, supply chain relationships 145
IT out-sourcing, in Xerox 220–2
Itaki, M., on transaction cost 270
Itami, H., on strategic assets 98
Itoh, Cable and Wireless Consortium 342, 352–3,
    360

Jackson, T., on core competencies 136
Jacobs, M. T., on strategic philosophy 290
Jain, P., on divestment 273
James, L. R., on ICCs 335
James, L. R., Joyce, and Slocum, on level
    issues 326
Jamous, H., and Peloille, on knowledge
    professionalization 146–7
Japan:
  car industry, TC reduction 87–8
  flagship networks 62

Japan: *(cont.)*
　IJVs 42, 44
　MITI:
　　role in participant selection 177
　　VLSI project 174, 179–80, 186–7
　national innovation systems 147–9
　and networks 144
　OEMs relation to west 141
　supply chain relationships 145
　vertical alliance practice 367
　see also Triad countries
Japanese firms:
　communication styles 290, 299
　control of acquisitions 289, 296–7
　integration levels 292, 293, 294, 303
　strategic philosophy 290–1, 301
Jarillo, J. C.:
　on collaborative structure 115
　on opportunism 79
　on RB collaboration 77
　on trust 325
Jemison, D. B., and Sitkin, on relationships 106
Jensen, M., and Meckling, on agency theory 12
Jepperson, R., and Meyer, on institutional
　　context 318
JESSI programme 188–9
Johanson, J., and Mattsson, on mutual
　　orientation 85
Johnson, M., on Xerox/EDS 226, 228
Johnson, J. L. *et al.*, on trust 325
Johnston, R., and Lawrence, on out-sourcing 212
Joint European Silicon Structures Initiative 188
joint venture alliances 347, 348–51
joint ventures, trust 324–37
Jones, C., Hesterly, and Borgatti, on social network
　　theory 20
journals, *see* press information
Jurgens, U., Naumann, and Rupp, on banking 159

Kamoche, K., on knowledge resources 136
Kanter, R. M.:
　on alliances 3
　on change 194
　on networks 143
　on performance assessment 27
　on stability 261
　on trust 30
Karpik, L., on networks 142, 161
Katz, R., and Allen, on networks 143
Kay, J. A., on game theory 15–16
Kearney, A. T., on TQM implementation 193
Kearns, D. T., and Nadler, on Xerox/EDS 218,
　　219
Kee, H., and Knox:
　on cooperative behaviour 328 n.
　on risk 329
　on trust 30
keiretsu, vertical 62
Keller, M., on NUMMI 129

Kennelly-McGinnis, S., on governance
　　mechanisms 244
Kern, T., on out-sourcing 211, 213, 214
Kern, T., and Willcocks:
　on instability 243
　on performance measurement 248
　on process 26
　and trust 249
Kerr, C., on national innovation systems 149
key informant dependence 326–7
Khanna, T., Gulati, and Nohria:
　on asymmetric performance 369
　on cooperation 173
　on objectives 269
　on private benefits 121
Killing, J. P.:
　on alliances 3
　on control 336, 346
　on governance 273
　on longevity/stability 261
　on performance measurement 248
　on trust 30
　Saxton & Serpa, on culture 29
Kim, D. J., and Kogut, on core competencies 137
Kim, L., on designer networks 160
Kim, W. C., and Mauborgne, on value 80
Kimberly, J. R., and Bouchikhi, on process 26
Kimmel, M.:
　on cooperative behavior 328 n.
　on trust 30
Klein, A, on divestment 273
Klein, B., Crawford, and Alchian, on
　　resourcing 265
Klein, K. J., Dansereau, and Hall:
　on alliance models 275
　on level issues 326
　on trust 326
Klepper, R., on out-sourcing 211
Klimoski, R., and Mohammed, on exchange
　　perspectives 308
knowledge:
　based trust 245, 248–9
　markets 136
　professionalization 146–7
　transfer 99, 105, 106
　　appropriative 135–63
Knudsen, C., on TC theory 90
Koenig, C., and van Wijk, on trust 325
Kogut, B.:
　on alliance termination 369
　on Ericsson/Honeywell IJV 271
　on instability 243
　on knowledge transfer 99
　on learning 119
　on performance and embedded ties 370
　on strategic purposes 98
　on transaction cost 8, 263, 273
Kogut, B., and Singh, on cultural context 317
Kogut, B., and Zander:

on appropriative learning 138, 161
on opportunism 77, 91
on resource-based theory of firm 58
Kogut, B., Shan, and Walker:
    on networks 267
    on social embeddedness 367
Koh, J., and Venkatraman, on stock market
        effects 371
Koontz, H., and O'Donnell, on management
        functions 63
Koza, M., and Lewin:
    on alliances 4
    on corporate strategies 267–8
    on learning 119
    on process 24
Koza, M., and Reuer, on performance
        measurement 248
Kramer, R. M., and Tyler, on exchange
        expectations 311
Kreiner, K., and Schultz, on
        interdependencies 176, 181
Kreps, D., on opportunism 84
Kumar, N., on trust 325
Kumar, N., Stern, and Anderson on
        consensus 327
Kumar, R., and Nti:
    on learning capacity 121, 128
    on opportunism 79

Lacity, M. C., and Hirschheim:
    on out-sourcing 211, 214
Lacity, M. C., and Willcocks:
    on out-sourcing 212
    on TCT 214
Lacity, M. C., Willcocks, and Feeny, on process 27
Lado, A. A., Boyd, and Hanlon, on opportunism/
        competition 79, 87
Lane, C.:
    on strategic philosophy 290
    on trust 342, 343
Lane, C., and Bachmann:
    on networks 139
    on trust building 141
Larson, A., on exchange perspectives 308, 309
Lawrence, P., on strategic philosophy 290
Lazonick, W.:
    on collaboration 88
    on financial measurement 159
    on national innovation systems 147
Lea, M., O'Shea, and Fung, on technology change
        effects 313
leadership, flagship firms 60–2
learning:
    agenda, supply chain partnering 206, 208
    appropriative 135–63
    collective, and communities of interest 142–5
    cost reduction function 123
    organizational 19–20
    in strategic alliances 119–33

Leavitt, H. J.:
    on change 194
    on open systems 203
    on process 26
Lei, D., on learning capacity 121
Leibenstein, H., on X-efficiency 81
Leung, K.:
    on interpersonal exchanges 311
    on social market pricing 310
level of trust issues 326, 331–7
Leveque, F. C., Bonazzi, and Quental, on
        cooperation 182
Levine, S., and White, on IOR theory 213
Levinthal, D. A., and Fichman:
    on alliance termination 369
    on performance and embedded ties 370
Lewicki, R. J., and Bunker:
    on trust 248–9, 342–3
Li, J.:
    on governance 273
    on stability 261
Li, J., and Guisinger, on longevity/stability 261
Li, J., and Shankar, on alliance structures 315
Lodge, G. C., and Vogel, on networks 144
Loh, L., and Ventakatram, on out-sourcing 211
longevity, international joint ventures 261–76
Lorange, P., and Roos:
    on alliances 3
    on culture 30
    on failure 141
    on payoffs 266
    on performance assessment 27
Lorange, P., Roos, and Bronn, on alliances 3
Lorenz, E. H., on risk 329
Lorenzoni, G., and Baden-Fuller, on cooperative
        capabilities 371
Lorsch, J., on change 194
Loveridge, R.:
    on appropriative learning 137, 162
    and business ecosystems 22
    on control structures 150
    on innovation styles 152
    on knowledge transfer 143, 145
    on network dyads 101
    on partner selection 109, 114
    on relationships 106
    on reputation 91
Loveridge, R., and Starkey, on diffused
        innovation 156
Lowndes, V., and Dkeleher, on trust building
        141
Lucas Industries:
    IJVs 43
    innovation styles 152, 153–5, 156
    Lucas-Varity merger 144
Lucas Pindad Aerospace Indonesia, IJVs 43
Lyles, M. A.:
    on alliance structures 315
    on cooperative capabilities 370

Lyles, M. A., and Reger, on culture 30
Lynch, R. P.:
  on alliances 3
  on performance assessment 27
  on trust 30

M-form, vertical integration 66–8
M&A database (FT) 41–2
McAllister, D. J., on trust 343–4
McAmmon, B. C., and Whittle, on IOR theory 213
Macaulay, S., on RC theory 214
Macbeth, D. K., on supply chain partnering 195
McCaffrey, D. P., Faerman, and Hart, on sustainability 244
McClelland, C. E., on national innovation systems 147
McFarlan, F. W., and Nolan:
  on out-sourcing 211, 212
  on process 27
McLoughlin, I., and Clark, on IT changes 193
Macneil, I. R., on RC theory 213, 214
Madhok, A.:
  on dissatisfaction 74
  and learning alliances 132
  on mutual forbearance 78
  on non-performance 104
  on RB collaboration 77, 88
  on relationships 99, 102, 106, 107, 111
  on resource-based view 11
  on social relations 81–2, 86, 92
  on trust 250, 325
  on value 75, 80
Madhok, A., and Tallman:
  on dissatisfaction 74
  on RB collaboration 77
  on social relations 82, 86, 92
  on SOV formation 99, 115
  on value 75
management:
  failure, vertical integration 66–8
  functions, flagship firm structure 63
  organizational culture 104–7
  practice characteristics 284–304
  see also trust
manufacturing, and IJVs 47–9, 50
March, J. G., and Shapira, on risk 330
March, J. G., Sproull, and Tamuz, on networks 142
market power theory 4–7
market pricing, social resource exchange 309–11
marketing, and IJVs 47–9, 50
Markus, M. L., on change 194
Marsden, P. V., on embeddedness 366
Marsh, D., on strategic philosophy 290
Martin, X., Mitchell, and Swaminathan, on dyadic ties 367
Marxian analysis, corporate opportunism 138
Mather, L., and Yngvesson, and shared meaning 251

Matsushita, vertical keiretsu 62
Maurice, M., Sorg, and Warner, on control 289
Mayer, C., on national innovation systems 148
Mayer, M., on networks 143
Mayer, R. C., Davis, and Schoorman, on risk 329, 330
MCC 174, 186–7, 188–9
measurement issues, IJV trust 324–37
mechanisms, control 341, 346
Mergers & Acquisitions database (FT) 41–2
Metinca Dirgantara, IJVs 43
Meyer, J., Boli, and Thomas, on institutional context 318
Microelectronics and Computer Corporation (MCC) 174, 186–7, 188–90
Microsoft, structure 139
Milgrom, P., and Roberts:
  on bargaining 103
  on governance costs 104
  on internal governance 106
  on mergers/acquisitions 97 n.
  on SOVs 96
Millington, A. I., and Bayliss, on stability 261
Mintzberg, H., on multiple actor assumption 63
misspecification, concept 328–9
Mitchell, W., and Singh:
  on flexibility 267
  on survival 371
MITI, role in participant selection 177
Mitsubishi Rayon, IJVs 42
MNEs, see multinational enterprises
models:
  change 194–5
  differential learning 120, 122–33
  IJV instability 261, 274–6
  process, R&D cooperation 183–90
  supply chain partnering 203–9
  transaction model, SOVs 107–13
Mody, A.:
  on learning 119
  on opportunism 88
Mohr, J., and Spekman:
  on alliances 3
  on trust 328
Monahan, G. E., on sharing rules 122
Montgomery, C. A., and Thomas, on divestment 273
Montgomery, C. A., Thomas, and Kamath, on divestment 273
Moore, J. F., on business ecosystems 21, 22
Morin, F., on shareholdings 159
Morishima, M., on family networks 148
Morosini, P., and Singh, on culture 285, 286
Mowery, D. C., on collaboration 74
Mueller, F., on knowledge resources 136
multi-divisional form, vertical integration 66–8
multinational enterprises (MNEs), flagship firm theory 57–73

multiple actor assumption 63
multiple method approach, collaboration
    assessment 243–56
Murray, F. A., and Mahon:
    on alliances 3
    on process 25
mutual forbearance, and value creation 78, 91
mutual orientation 78–85
mutuality 333–4

Nahapiet, J., and Ghoshal, on social capital
    formation 246, 248
Nalebuff, B., and Brandenburger, on game
    theory 15
NASA, and governance 142
Nash equilibrium, learning alliances 123, 125
Nathan, M. L., and Mitroff, and shared
    meaning 251
national cultures 28–30
national differences, acquisition integration
    283–304
national innovation systems 147–9
NEC:
    vertical *keiretsu* 62
    VLSI project 174, 179–80
Nelson, R. R.:
    on appropriative learning 138
    on national innovation systems 148
    on pre-competitive R&D 140
Nelson, R. R., and Winter, on managerial
    routine 114
networks:
    and alliances 366–8
    competitive 371–2
    dyads 101
    embeddedness, IJVs 267
    and the firm 135–63
    information search 366
    and innovation 139–42
    position, and performance 368
    relationships, MNEs 57–73
    social embeddedness 366–8
    social network theory 20–1
    structure changes, and collaboration 245, 246,
        252–3
new institutional economics (NIE) 137
New United Motor Manufacturing Inc
    (NUMMI) 120, 122, 129–30
Newall, S., and Clark, on occupational interest
    associations 160
newspapers, *see* press information
Newton Chemicals, IJVs 42
NIE, *see* new institutional economics (NIE)
Niederkofler, M., on trust 30
Niland, P., on NUMMI 129
Nippon paint/Courtaulds, trust and control 342,
    360
Nishigaki, Kouji, on financial measurement 159
Nissan, vertical *keiretsu* 62

Nixon, B., on financial measurement 160
Nohria, N., on social network theory 20
Nohria, N., and Eccles, on strategic alliances 243
non-business infrastructure, five partners
    network 60
non-Triad countries, IJVs 40–54
Nonaka, I., and Takeuchi:
    on appropriation 146, 155
    on organizational learning 20
Noorderhaven, N. G., on opportunism 77
Nooteboom, B., Berger, and Nooderhaven, on
    cultural context 317
Norburn, D., and Schoenberg, on culture 285
Nordberg, M., Campbell, and Verbeke, on cultural
    context 317
North America:
    IJVs 42, 44
    see also American firms; Triad countries; United
        States
North American Free Trade Area (NAFTA) 70–1
Nti, K. O.:
    on comparative statics approach 125
    on sharing rules 122
Nti, K. O., and Kumar:
    on complementarity 107–8, 110, 113
    on game theory 16
    on governance costs 105
    on knowledge transfer 105, 106
    on non-performance 104
    on partners 103
    on relationships 92
NUMMI 120, 122, 129–30

objectives, collaborative 268–9, 271
occupational interest associations 160
OD, *see* organization development (OD)
Ohmae, K.:
    on alliances 3
    on control 346
OIAs, *see* operational interest associations (OIAs)
Oliver, C., on IOR theory 213
Oliver, N. B., and Wilkinson, on emulation 284
Olk, P., on alliance structures 315
Olk, P., and Early:
    on commitment 32
    on exchange perspectives 308
    on interpersonal exchanges 307
    and trust 250
operational control, and managerial knowledge
    144–5
operational functions, flagship firm structure 64
operational interest associations (OIAs) 145
operational management, Xerox/EDS 223–6
opportunism:
    and stability 269–70
    in TC theory 77–9, 82, 84, 87–92
organization development (OD):
    approach to learning 138–9
    and innovation systems 147

organization structure, and strategy 314–16
organization theory viewpoint 17–24
organizational change failure 193
organizational culture 28–30, 104–7
organizational learning 19–20
organizational scripts 316
Orlikowski, W. J., on technology change
   effects 313
Osborn, R., and Hagedoorn:
   on interpersonal exchanges 313
   on networks 142
Osborn, R. N., and Baugh:
   on IJVs 41
   on resource sharing 99
Osigweh, C. A., on concept stretching 327
Osland, G. E., and Cavusgil, on control 346–7
Ostroff, C., and Schmidt, on ICCs 336
Ouchi, W. G.:
   on structures 263
   on transaction cost 112
out-sourcing:
   IT 211–39
   R&D 158
   Xerox Corporation/EDS study 217–39
Oviatt, B. M., and McDougall, on transaction cost
   theory 8
Owens-Corning alliance 107
Oxley, J. E.:
   on alliance research 275
   on collaboration 74

Pacific Asia, role of family networks 148
Pacific Rim, IJVs 43, 44
Pan, Y., and Tse, on cultural context 316–17
Papanastassiou, M., and Pearce, on interpersonal
   exchanges 313
parent firms, and IJV payoffs 265–7
Park, S. H., and Russo:
   on opportunism 269
   on stability 261
Park, S. H., and Ungson:
   on complementarity 150
   on cultural context 317
   on opportunism 269
   on stability 261
Parkhe, A.:
   on alliance structures 4, 315
   on complementarity 112, 113
   on cooperatives failure 96
   on cultural context 316–17
   on dissatisfaction 74
   on failure 369
   on game theory 15
   on IJVs 40
   on longevity 264
   on mutual orientation 84
   on opportunism 79
   on RB collaboration 77
   on relationships 100, 106

on resourcing 264
on transaction cost theory 8
on trust 325, 328
partners:
   ability to sustain R&D collaboration 178–9
   hazards of 119
   number in IJVs 49
   search for 109–10
   selection/negotiation 110–11, 177
   SOVs 103–4
   supply-chain 193, 195–210
   and trust 331
payoffs:
   IJVs 265–7
   learning alliances 124, 125–8
Pearce, J., and Branyiczki, on cultural context 317
Pearce, R. J.:
   on collaboration 82, 86
   on dissatisfaction 74
Pekar, P., and Allio, on alliances formation rate 119
Pennings, J. H., Barkema, and Douma, on
   stability 261
Penrose, E.:
   on resource dependency 11, 18, 136
   on strategic assets 98
Pentland, B., on interpersonal relationships 316
Pentland, B., and Reuter, on interpersonal
   relationships 316
performance:
   alliances 368–72
   assessment 27–8
   corporate, IJVs 267–72
   and embedded ties 370
   measurement 248, 369–72
   proxies, longevity/stability as 263–5
   trust and control 341–60
Peteraf, M.:
   on RB collaboration 77
   on rent-yielding assets 97
   on resource-based view 10
Peters, T., on innovation styles 152
Peters, T. J., and Waterman:
   on culture 28
   on open systems 203
Peterson, J. 174
Pettigrew, A.:
   on change 194, 195
   on knowledge transfer 143
   on OD approach to learning 139
   on process 26
Pettigrew, A. M., Ferlie, and McKee, on
   change 205
Pfeffer, J.:
   on change 194
   on resource dependence theory 18
Pfeffer, J., and Nowak, on stability 261
Pfeffer, J., and Salancik:
   on resource dependence theory 18
   on social network theory 20

Pindad, IJVs 43
Pisano, G. P., on transaction cost theory 313
Podolny, J. M., and Stuart, on social
     embeddedness 367
Polanyi, M., on appropriation 146
politics, internal 104–7
Porter, M. E.:
     on competitive strategy 3, 4–5, 6, 23
     on core competencies 136, 137
     on five forces model 57
     on out-sourcing 212
     on resource-based view 11
     on resource dependency 136
     on social capital 248
Porter, M. E., and Fuller, on competitive strategy 5
Porter, M. E., and Millar, on out-sourcing 212
post-contract management, Xerox/EDS 222–30
Potapchuk, W. R., and Polk:
     on cross-sector collaboration 243
     on problem resolution 247
Powell, W. W.:
     on governance 244
     on networks 140–1
     on opportunism 79
     on RB collaboration 77
     on restructuring 244
     on social network theory 20
     on social relations 81–2, 86
     on strategic alliances 243
     on trust 249, 325
Powell, W. W., and Brantley, on networks 267
Powell, W. W., Koput, and Smith-Doerr:
     on cooperation 182
     on restructuring 244
     on social embeddedness 367
     on technology change effects 313
power distribution shifts, and collaboration
     assessment 245, 254–5
power, inter-management, and integration 67–8
PPG 70
Prahalad, C. K., and Hamel:
     on core competencies 98 n., 136, 137
     on out-sourcing 211
     on SBUs 139
pre-competitive R&D 140
preconditions, collaboration 175–80
predictive trust 341, 343, 344
preservation acquisitions 286–7
press information, IJV databases 41–2
pricing, internal, and integration 68–70
Prisoner's Dilemma, Deutsch and 328 n.
private benefits, competitor alliances 121–2
problem resolution, and collaboration assessment
     245, 247–8
problem solving, normalization 176
process:
     agenda, supply chain partnering 202–3, 205–6
     as evolution 24–7
     forms, cooperation 182, 184

studies, cooperation 24–8
professionalization of knowledge 146–7
profit-centre concept 66–7
Provan, K., and Milward:
     on networks 252, 253
     on problem resolution 247
Putnam, L., on social capital 246, 248, 249, 250,
     252

R&D, see research & development
Radico Khaitan, IJVs 43
Rappa, M. A., on R&D 188
rationale, cooperation 4
RB collaboration, see resource-based theory,
     collaboration
RBT, see resource-based theory (RBT)
real options theory 17
Reason, P., on research 256
Reed, R., and DeFillippi, on resources 103, 114
relational contract (RC) theory 181, 213–15
relationships 92
     buyer–supplier 87–8
     interpersonal, international strategic alliances
          307–19
     social, and V-efficiency 81–2, 86, 92
     SOV formation, 102, 104–7, 111
     strategy, out-sourcing 211–39, 234–6
     see also social relations
relevance, interpersonal exchanges 312
reliance, and trust 329
renegotiation, Xerox/EDS 227–8
rents:
     assets 96–7
     capture, vertical integration 65–6
     costs, and SOV transactions 108
     decay over time 114
     earning capacity, and value 74–6
     realization theory 10
research:
     & development (R&D):
          cooperation 180–3
          cooperatives 173–90
          and innovation styles 157–60
          pre-competitive 140
     IJVs:
          interpretation 261, 274–6
          trust 324–37
          suggested 375–7
          trust misspecification 326–9
resource-based theory (RBT) 10–12, 58, 74–6, 97,
     98–100, 110, 112
     collaboration 76–83
     contributions, and IJV stability 264–5
     dependency theories 18–19, 136–7
     exchange, social 309–10
resources:
     investment model, SOVs 107–13
     invisible 98
     lack of 99

Reuer, J. J., and Koza:
    on objectives 269
    on performance assessment 28
Reuer, J. J., and Leiblen, on flexibility 267
Reve, T., on trust 325
reward systems, and integration 67
Ricardo, D., on resource-based view 11
Richardson, G. B.:
    on co-ordination 7
    on value 80
Ring, P. S.:
    on mutual orientation 84
    on opportunism 79
    on TC theory 90 n.
Ring, P. S., and Van de Ven:
    on cooperation 173, 182
    on exchange 211, 308, 309
    on interpersonal exchanges 307
    on mutual orientation 84
    on opportunism 79, 82
    on partners 103, 107, 111
    on performance assessment 27
    on process 24, 26
    on rationality 372
    on relationships 102, 114
    on resourcing 264
    on strategic alliances 243
    on trust 249, 315
risk, and trust 329, 330–1
rivalry, inter-management, and integration 66–7
Roberts, P., and Greenwood, on interpersonal
        constraints 317–18
Roberts, V. Z., on networks 253
Roehl, T. W., and Truitt:
    on alliances 3
    on performance assessment 27
Rosenfeld, J. D., on divestment 273
Rothwell, R. et al., on innovation styles 152
Rotter, J., on reliance 329
Rousseau, D.:
    on exchange expectations 311, 312
    on level issues 326
    on misspecification 328, 329
Rover/Honda, trust and control 342, 356–9, 360
Rowes, M. J., on national innovation systems
        149
Royal Bank of Scotland/Banco Santander 18–19,
        342, 355–6, 360
Royal Dutch Shell alliance 107
Rugman, A. M., on flagship model 71
Rugman, A. M., and D'Cruz:
    and business ecosystems 21
    on competitive strategy 6
    on flagship firms 130
    on flagship networks 101
    on governance costs 105
    on key partners 92
Rugman, A. M., and Verbecke, on asset exchange
        140

Rugman, A. M., D'Cruz, and Verbeke, on flagship
        model 58, 71
Rumelt, R. P.:
    on corporate performance 136
    on resource-based view 10
Rybczynski, R., on A&M 158

Sabel, C. F., on trust 30–1, 249
Sakakibara, N.:
    on R&D 174
    on VLSI project 179, 188
Sako, M.:
    on commitment 31
    on supply chain relationships 145
    on trust 30–1, 141, 343–4
Salk, J. E., on mergers/acquisitions 97 n., 115
Sanders, P., on Xerox/EDS 217
Saxton, T., on alliance structures 315
SBUs, see strategic business units (SBUs)
Schaan, J.-L., on control 346
Schank, R., and Abelson, on interpersonal
        relationships 316
Schein, E. H., on culture 28, 29
Scher, M. J., on networks 144
Schmitz, C.:
    on problem resolution 247
    and trust 249
Schon, D., on innovation styles 152
Schon, D., and Rein, on power shifts 244
Schumpeter, J.:
    on corporate opportunism 138
    on resource dependency 11, 136
Scott, J.:
    on cultural context 317
    on institutional context 318
    on networks 144
Scottish Power, IJVs 42
scripts, organizational 316
selection, transaction costs 103–4
Selsky, J. W., on problem resolution 247
Sematech, R&D cooperation 185–90
semiconductor industry, R&D cooperation
        185–90
services, IJV formation by 47–9, 50
Shama, A., on governance 271
Shapiro, D., Sheppard, and Cheraskin, and
        trust 249
Shapiro, S. P., on risk 330
shared meaning, and collaboration
        assessment 245, 246, 250–2
shared organization ventures (SOVs) 96–116
    failure rate 101
    TCE view 100–7
    transaction model 107–13
Shelanski, H. A., and Klein, on alliance models 275
Sherman, S., on alliance success rates 114
Shortell, S. M., and Zajac, on process 25
Shrivastava, P., on integration 286
Sievers, B., on research 255

Silverman, B. S., on collaboration 74
Silverman, B. S., Nickerson, and Freeman, on
    alliance models 275
Simard, P., on transaction cost theory 8
Simonin, B., and Helleloid, on alliance
    structures 315
Singh, K., and Mitchell, on alliances 3
Sinha, D. K., and Cusumano, on cost sharing
    alliances 123
Sink, D., on collaborative efforts 243
Sitkin, S. B., and Pablo, on risk 330
Skoda Koncern Plzen, IJVs 42–3
small to medium enterprises (SMEs), and flagship
    model 70–1
SMEs, organic structures 139
SMEs, see small to medium enterprises
Smircich, L., on shared meaning 246
Smith, A., invisible hand theory 14
Smith, J. B., on mutuality 333, 334, 335
Smith, J. B., and Barclay:
    on mutuality 333, 334
    on partners 331
Smith, K. G., Carroll, and Ashford, on
    collaboration 243
social capital generation 245–6, 248–50
social embeddedness, networks 366–8
social market pricing 309–11
social network theory 20–1
social relations, and V-efficiency 81–2, 86, 92
social resource exchange 309–10
social services, problem resolution 247
Sony, vertical *keiretsu* 62
Sorge, A., on communication styles 290
SOVs, see shared organization ventures
Spence, M., on learning cost reduction function
    123
Spender, J.-C., on innovation styles 157
stability, international joint ventures 261–76
Stern, R. N., and Barley, on social impact 244
Stewart, R. *et al.*:
    on communication styles 290
    on control 289
stock market effects, alliance announcements 371
Stopford, J. M., and Wells, on governance 271
strategic alliances 96
    assessment 243–56
    benefit from 370–1
    differential learning 119–33
    international, interpersonal relationships
        307–19
    and networks 366–8
    studying 365–72
    trust 324–37
strategic assets 98–100
strategic business units (SBUs) 139
strategic hazards 119–33
strategic leadership, flagship firms 60–2
strategic philosophy, foreign acquisitions 289–90,
    300–3, 304

strategic purposes 98
strategies, corporate, IJVs 267–8
strategy functions, flagship firm structure 63
Streek, W., on national innovation systems 147
structural analysis 23–4, 97
    approach to learning 139
    flagship firms 62–70
    and out-sourcing 233–4
success:
    alliances 369–72
    success/failure criteria 245–56
    trust and control 341, 357–8, 359–60
Sumitomo Chemicals, ICI Pharma 342, 351,
    360
Sun microsystems, supply chain partnering
    196–201
suppliers, key, five partners network 60
supply chain relationships 145, 193, 195–210
survival, and performance 371
sustainable competitive advantage (SCA) 11
Sydow, J., and Windeler:
    on social network theory 20
    on structures 23, 24
symbiosis acquisitions 286–7
synergy:
    promoting 115–16
    in SOVs 98–100

T-inefficiency, see transactional inefficiency
Tajfel, H.:
    on interpersonal exchanges 311
    on national innovation systems 149
takeovers, see acquisitions
Tallman, S. B.:
    on dissatisfaction 74
    on learning 120
    on resource-based view 11
    on social relations 92
Tallman & Shenkar:
    on divestment 273
    on partners 103, 109
    on relationships 106
    on strategic management 6
TC theory, see transaction cost, theory
TCE, see transaction cost, economics (TCE)
technology change effects, interpersonal
    exchanges 313–14
Teece, D.:
    on appropriative learning 137
    on collaboration 74
    on core competencies 137
    on networks 141
    on opportunism 269
Teece, D., and Pisano:
    on appropriative learning 137
    on value 80
Teece, D., Pisano, and Shuen, on strategic assets
    98
telecommunications industry, flagship model 57

Tenneco, and Houston Oil 106
Teubner, G., on networks 144
Texas Instruments, structure 139
theory level, trust 326
Thorelli, H. B.:
    on social network theory 20
    on trust 342
Tolstoy, L. 74, 75
Tomlinson, J. W. C., on partners 110
Toshiba, vertical *keiretsu* 62
total quality management (TQM)
        implementation 193
Toyota:
    Cable and Wireless Consortium 342, 352–3, 360
    General Motors (GM) NUMMI 16, 120, 122,
        129–30
    vertical *keiretsu* 62
transaction cost:
    analysis, and stability 269–70
    bargaining 103–4
    economics (TCE) 97, 100–7, 112–13
    and IJV stability 264–5
    theory (TCT) 7–9, 74–6, 78–9, 89–92, 214–16
        interpersonal exchanges 313
        vertical integration 63, 64–5
transaction model, SOVs 107–13
transaction-specific investments (TSI) 101–4
transactional inefficiency 76, 78–9, 85–92
transactional value analysis 107–13
transfer pricing, and integration 68–70
transition economies, IJVs 44
transition management, Xerox/EDS 222–3
Triad countries, IJVs 40–54
Triandis, H. C., and Bhawuk, on social
        exchange 310
Tripsas, M., Schrader, and Sobrero, on R&D
        collaboration 173
Trist, E.:
    on cooperation 173
    on cross-sector collaboration 243
    and shared meaning 250
    on social impact 244
trust 30–1
    alliance structures 315
    building 141
    and control 341–60
    joint ventures 324–37
    misspecification 326–9
    and social capital 248–9
    types 341, 342–5
TRW, and Lucas-Varity 144
TSI, *see* transaction-specific investments (TSI)
Tucker, J. B.:
    on Alpha Jet Project 127
    on learning 119
Turnbull, P., on Lucas 156
Turner, J. C., on interpersonal exchanges 311
Tyre, M. J., and Orlikowski, on technology change
        effects 313

uncertainty:
    networks 366
    and performance ambiguity 263–4
United Kingdom, *see* British firms
United States/China joint ventures 317
Utilicorp, IJVs 42
Uzzi, B., on interdependencies 176

value, in collaboration 74–6, 79–81
value inefficiency 76, 81–3, 85–92
Van de Ven, A. H.:
    on IOR theory 213
    on process 25
Van de Ven, A. H., and Ring:
    on IOR theory 213, 217
    on relational contracting 181
Van de Ven, A. H., and Walker:
    on cooperation 173
    on networks 252–3
Van Dyne, L., Graham, and Deinesch, on exchange
        expectations 311
Vancina, L., and Taillieu, and shared meaning 251,
        252
Vaughan, E., and Siefert, and shared meaning 251
Vebacom, IJVs 42
Vernon, R., on governance 271
vertical alliance practice, Japan 367
vertical integration:
    Japan 62
    MNEs 64–70
vertical *keiretsu* 62
Very, P., Lubatkin, and Calori, on culture 285
Very Large Scale Integration project 174, 179–80,
        186–7
Vickers, G., and shared meaning 250
VLSI project 174, 179–80, 186–7
Von Neumann, J., on game theory 13–14

Walsham, G., on Xerox/EDS 217
Wastell, D. G., White, and Kalawek, on BPR
        implementation 193
Webb, S., and Webb, on OIAs 145
Weick, K., on exchange perspectives 308
Weick, K., and Bougon, on shared meaning 246
Wellman, B., on social network theory 20
Wenger, E., and Kaserer, on Bosch 155
Wernerfelt, B., on resource dependence theory 10,
        18
Western Europe:
    IJVs 42, 44
    Hungary collaborations 317
    see also Triad countries
Westney, E., on Japanese business networks 62
Weston, J. F., Chung, and Hoag, on A&M 158
Whetten, D. A., on cooperation 173
White, H. C., on social network theory 20
Whitley, R.:
    on innovation styles 154
    on networks 141, 162

Whittington, R., on innovation styles 157
Whyte and Mackay (India), IJVs 43
Willcocks, L., and Choi, on out-sourcing 211, 216
Willcocks, L., and Kern, on out-sourcing 212
Willcocks, L., and Lacity, on out-sourcing 211, 212
Williamson, O. E.:
    on alliances 307
    on asset specificity 100–1, 102, 270
    on corporate opportunism 138
    on flexibility 267
    on innovation styles 157
    on M-form 66
    on networks 140–1
    on out-sourcing 212
    on resourcing 11, 264
    on social market pricing 310
    on TC theory 7–9, 75, 77, 79, 85, 89, 92, 214
Wilson, D. D., on IOR theory 213
Winter, S., on TC theory 90
Wintermans/Imperial, trust and control 342,
    354–5, 360
Wood, D., and Gray, on collaboration 243
Wood, S.:
    on core competencies 136
    on operational control 144
Woodward, J., on innovation styles 157, 158
World Bank, on national innovation systems 149

X-efficiency/X-inefficiency 81
Xerox Corporation/EDS, out-sourcing study
    217–39

Yan, A., and Gray:
    on cultural context 317
    on performance measurement 248
    on strategic objectives 245, 247
    on trust 250, 325

Zack, M., and McKenney, on technology change
    effects 313
Zagare, F. C., on game theory 13
Zaheer, A., and Venkatraman, on transaction
    cost 270
Zaheer, A., McEvily, and Perrone:
    on performance and embedded ties 370
    on trust 250, 315
Zajac, E. J., on social network perspective 366
Zajac, E. J., and Olsen:
    on mutual orientation 85
    on opportunism 79
    on partner search 109
    on rationality 372
    on RB collaboration 77
    on relationships 111, 114
    on structural analysis 97
    on transactional value analysis 107
Zand, D., on risk 329, 330
Ziller, R. C., on networks 253
Zucker, L.:
    on institutional context 318
    on trust 345